RESEARCH HANDBOOK ON LINE MANAGERS

T0314080

Research Handbook on Line Managers

Edited by

Keith Townsend

Professor of Human Resources and Employment Relations, Centre for Work, Organisation and Wellbeing, Griffith University, Australia

Anna Bos-Nehles

Assistant Professor in Human Resource Management, Faculty of Behavioural Management and Social Sciences, University of Twente, the Netherlands

Kaifeng Jiang

Professor of Management and Human Resources, Fisher College of Business, The Ohio State University, USA

Cheltenham, UK • Northampton, MA, USA

© Keith Townsend, Anna Bos-Nehles and Kaifeng Jiang 2022

Cover image: Max van den Oetelaar on Unsplash

All rights reserved. No part of this publication may be reproduced, stored in a retrieval system or transmitted in any form or by any means, electronic, mechanical or photocopying, recording, or otherwise without the prior permission of the publisher.

Published by
Edward Elgar Publishing Limited
The Lypiatts
15 Lansdown Road
Cheltenham
Glos GL50 2JA
UK

Edward Elgar Publishing, Inc.
William Pratt House
9 Dewey Court
Northampton
Massachusetts 01060
USA

Paperback edition 2024

A catalogue record for this book
is available from the British Library

Library of Congress Control Number: 2022944620

This book is available electronically in the **Elgar**online
Business subject collection
http://dx.doi.org/10.4337/9781839102745

ISBN 978 1 83910 273 8 (cased)
ISBN 978 1 83910 274 5 (eBook)
ISBN 978 1 0353 4054 5 (paperback)

Printed and bound by CPI Group (UK) Ltd, Croydon, CR0 4YY

Contents

v

Contributors

Carol Atkinson, Professor of HRM, Decent Work and Productivity (Research Centre), Manchester Metropolitan University Business School, UK.

Mieke Audenaert, Professor of People Management, Ghent University, Belgium.

Ina Aust, Professor of Human Resource Management with a specialization in CSR/sustainability, Louvain Research Institute in Management and Organizations, Université Catholique de Louvain, Belgium.

Hugh T.J. Bainbridge, Associate Professor, School of Management and Governance, Business School, University of New South Wales, Australia.

Anindita Roy Bannya, PhD candidate, School of Management and Governance, Business School, University of New South Wales, Australia.

Anna Bos-Nehles, Assistant Professor of Human Resource Management, Faculty of Behavioural, Management and Social Sciences, University of Twente, The Netherlands.

Julia Brandl, Full Professor of Human Resource Management and Employment Relations, University of Innsbruck, Austria.

Chris Brewster, Professor of International HRM, Henley Business School, University of Reading, UK.

Michael Brookes, Professor of HRM, Department of Business and Management, University of Southern Denmark, Slagelse, Denmark.

Edel Conway, Professor of Human Resource Management and Organisational Psychology, DCU Business School, Dublin City University, Ireland.

Charles Dahwa, Associate Fellow Decent Work and Productivity Research Centre, Manchester Metropolitan University Business School, UK.

Adelien Decramer, Professor of HRM, Ghent University, Belgium.

Sophie De Winne, Professor, KU Leuven, Faculty of Economics and Business, Belgium.

Ewold Drent, Researcher, School of Behavioural, Management and Social Sciences, University of Twente, The Netherlands.

Samantha Evans, Lecturer in Human Resource Management, Kent Business School, University of Kent, UK.

Virginia Fisher, Independent Researcher and Consultant.

Brian Harney, Professor of Strategy and HRM, Dublin City University Business School, Dublin City University, Ireland.

Rina Hastuti, RMIT University School of Management, Melbourne, Australia and Faculty of Islamic Business and Economics, UIN Raden Mas Said Surakarta, Central Java, Indonesia.

Rebecca Hewett, Associate Professor in HRM, Rotterdam School of Management, Erasmus University, The Netherlands.

Laura Innocenti, Lecturer in Human Resource Management and Organizational Behaviour, Department of Business and Management, LUISS Guido Carli University, Italy.

Kaifeng Jiang, Professor of Management and Human Resources, Fisher College of Business, The Ohio State University, USA.

Anne Keegan, Full Professor of Human Resource Management, College of Business, University College Dublin, Ireland.

Rebecca R. Kehoe, Associate Professor, ILR School, Cornell University, US.

Violetta Khoreva, Hanken School of Economics, Department of Management and Organization, Helsinki, Finland.

Joon Young Kim, PhD student, ILR School, Cornell University, US.

Karin A. King, Fellow and Lecturer, Department of Management, London School of Economics and Political Science, London, UK.

Sue Kinsey, Lecturer in Applied Management, University of Exeter, UK.

Eva Knies, Professor of Strategic HRM, Utrecht University School of Governance, The Netherlands.

Qian Yi Lee, Research Associate, Business School, Queensland University of Technology, Australia.

Rebecca Loudoun, Professor of Human Resource Management and Employment Relations Department of Employment Relations and Human Resources, Griffith University, Australia.

Ben Lupton, Professor of Employment, Decent Work and Productivity (Research Centre), Manchester Metropolitan University Business School, UK.

Elise Marescaux, Associate Professor, IESEG School of Management, Lille, France.

Leo McCann, Professor of Management, University of York, UK.

Jeroen Meijerink, Associate Professor of Human Resource Management, Faculty of Behavioural, Management and Social Sciences, University of Twente, The Netherlands.

Joanne Mildenhall, Paramedic and Doctoral Research Student, University of York, UK.

Atieh S. Mirfakhar, Integrated Researcher, Business Research Unit (BRU-IUL), Instituto Universitário de Lisboa (ISCTE-IUL), Portugal.

Kathy Monks, Emeritus Professor of Human Resource Management, DCU Business School, Dublin City University, Ireland.

Silvia Profili, Professor of Human Resource Management, Department of Human Sciences, European University of Rome, Italy.

Maarten Renkema, Assistant Professor, School of Behavioural, Management and Social Sciences, University of Twente, The Netherlands.

Adam Robertson, Sessional Lecturer and Research Fellow, Department of Employment Relations and Human Resources, Griffith University, Australia.

Philip Rogiers, Postdoctoral Researcher, Department of Work and Organisation Studies, KU Leuven, Belgium.

Sari Salojärvi, Hanken School of Economics, Department of Management and Organization, Helsinki, Finland.

Alessia Sammarra, Professor of Organization Theory and Human Resource Management, Department of Industrial Engineering, Information and Economics, University of L'Aquila, Italy.

Richard Saundry, Principal Research Fellow, University of Westminster, UK.

Amanda Shantz, Professor of Management, University of St Gallen, Switzerland.

David M. Sikora, Professor of Management, Department of Management, Parker College of Business, Georgia Southern University, US.

Andrew R. Timming, RMIT University School of Management, Melbourne, Australia.

Keith Townsend, Professor of Human Resource Management and Employment Relations Department of Employment Relations and Human Resources, Griffith University, Australia.

Ashlea Troth, Professor of Human Resource Management and Employment Relations Department of Employment Relations and Human Resources, Griffith University, Australia.

Jordi Trullen, Associate Professor, ESADE Business School, Ramon Llull University, Spain.

Mireia Valverde, Full Professor, Department of Business Management, Universitat Rovira i Virgili, Spain.

Anja Van den Broeck, Professor, KU Leuven, Faculty of Economics and Business, Belgium and North West University, Optentia, South Africa.

Jennifer Chelsea Veres, Teaching Associate and Research Assistant, Monash Business School, Monash University, Australia.

1. Line managers in human resource management: theory, analysis and new developments

Keith Townsend, Anna Bos-Nehles and Kaifeng Jiang

Line managers have played a role in organisations for as long as organisations have existed; in fact, it is commonly accepted that 'management' has been around for centuries prior to the 'industrialised era'. Davidson and Griffin (2000) argue that many ancient and medieval civilisations applied management functions in constructions such as, for example, the building of pyramids. While this may be the case, the largely slave-style labour used in the making of the pyramids holds limited transferability to the modern human resource management (HRM) driven organisations of the twenty-first century. According to Wren (1972: 36), the industrial revolution 'heralded a new age for man and society', and we would argue, along with many others, that the post-1980s era of HRM heralded a new age for all working people and society. Within this HRM era is an increasing level of importance for the line managers, with a growing body of academic research focusing on the significant role they play as implementers of human resources (HR) policy and practice.

In addition to the academic focus, throughout the world both practitioners and public policy are paying increasing attention to this body of managers with the publication of national reports and professional advice, highlighting the cruciality of their role in the workplace and need for support (ACAS, 2014; CIPD, 2015; ILM, 2009; Macleod and Clarke, 2009). Integrating HRM into the line, by devolvement and empowerment, was a central ambition of models of HRM (Storey, 2007: 33). If human resources were critical to business success, then line managers should both drive and deliver HR policies because they are responsible for 'co-ordinating and directing *all* resources in the business unit in the pursuit of bottom line results' (Legge, 1995: 113; see also Guest, 1991; Storey, 1992). With effective line managers, the HR professional is freed up to undertake more strategic roles within the organisation (Ulrich, 1997), resulting in an effective HR–line partnership (Bos-Nehles, 2010).

Throughout the late 1980s and early 1990s we began to see evidence that HRM was being returned to the line, where researchers noted a shift from production management to performance-focused activities that involved 'people responsibilities rather than purely technical responsibilities' (Lowe, 1992: 148). Throughout this time, a movement towards delayering, decentralisation of decision-making, new production processes, and pressure on costs and accountability (Hall and Torrington, 1998; Lowe, 1993) further intensified the focus on the role of the line manager. A recent review of the HR devolution literature presented a selection of 108 articles published between 1982 and 2020 that highlighted the increasingly important role of line managers in HRM research (Kurdi-Nakra et al., 2021). Based on this review the authors developed future research directions for research on line managers. In this book we respond to some of those suggestions for research directions, and present some more relevant line management roles in organisations.

Studies of line managers use a range of theoretical frameworks (although in some articles the theoretical underpinning was not obvious), which can be broadly categorised into two domains: theories of social exchange (Blau, 1964) and the HRM and strategic human resource management (SHRM) literature. Theories of social exchange, based on norms of reciprocity within social relationships, such as leader–member exchange (e.g. Farndale et al., 2011), perceived supervisor support (Kuvaas et al., 2014), the psychological contract (McDermott et al., 2013), signalling theory (e.g. Townsend et al., 2012) and attachment theory (Crawshaw and Game, 2015) provide a framework in studies conducted at the micro level exploring the line manager–employee relationship and its effect on employee attitudes and behaviours. Predominantly, however, studies draw on the HRM/SHRM literature, either to frame discussions on devolution trends and influences (e.g. Brewster et al., 2015; Budhwar and Sparrow, 2002; Cunningham and Hyman, 1999; Gennard and Kelly, 1997), or to theorise how HRM links to performance and the role of line managers in this process. In this category are articles drawing on the resource-based view of the firm (e.g. Bondarouk and Ruël, 2013), HR strength theory such as Bowen and Ostroff's (2004) concept of a 'strong' HR system (e.g. Björkman et al., 2011; De Winne et al., 2013; Ryu and Kim, 2013), models of the HR casual chain such as by Nishii and Wright (2008) (e.g. Purcell and Hutchinson, 2007; Vermeeren, 2014), and the ability–motivation–opportunity (AMO) theory of performance (e.g. Bos-Nehles et al., 2013). Other theories applied include role theory (e.g. Evans, 2015), utilised in studies examining the impact on line managers on HRM; stakeholder theory, which recognises that organisational units have multiple constituents and informs research exploring multiple HR agents (e.g. Kulik and Perry, 2008), agency theory (Caza, 2011); and social capital theory (Truss and Gill, 2009). There is clearly a vast array of theoretical frames that can be used which indicates the importance of the line manager role and the various perspectives that can be taken to understand the role.

Yet, while research on line managers has developed significantly throughout the last decades, there remain some problems with line manager research, certainly. For example, for a long time much of the research failed to engage in a detailed discussion on who or what exactly is a 'line manager', referring to an all-encompassing line manager, thus conflating many levels. A middle manager of a 60 000-strong organisation is not performing many, if indeed any, of the same tasks as a frontline manager of a team of ten employees in an organisation of only 120 employees. While there are many researchers aiming to disaggregate the line manager confusion, it remains persistent. Throughout this book we have encouraged authors to be explicit and to explain who their line managers are specifically, and only when the various different line manager roles are combined should the generic term be used.

LINE MANAGERS: WHO ARE THEY?

Inspired by the 81st meeting of the Academy of Management in 2021 and the paper by Steffensen et al. (2019), we aim to bring the manager back to management, specifically to human resource management through a focus on line managers. Line managers are situated 'between the strategic apex and operating core of the organisation' and thus they are the ones who 'mediate, negotiate, and interpret connections between the organisation's institutional (strategic) and technical (operational) levels' (Floyd and Wooldridge, 1997: 466). 'Line managers' is a container term for managers at different hierarchical positions ranging from first-line managers to senior managers. The expression 'first-line manager' or 'frontline manager' traditionally stands for the position representing the lowest level of management at the operational level, who manages a team of operational (non-managerial) employees on a day-to-day basis (Bos-Nehles, 2010; Hales, 2005). As Currie (2006: 6) points out, there is no 'well-defined homogenous group that can be differentiated easily from executive managers or from frontline managers'. Drawing on earlier work from Floyd and Wooldridge (1997) and Staehle and Schirmer (1992: 70), Currie continues that middle managers are 'employees who have at least two hierarchical levels under them'. Importantly, these levels of line managers, be they frontline managers or middle managers, remain employees of the organisations with the responsibility of managing other employees.

In their responsibility as managers of employees, line managers are responsible for management of the people in their teams (Evans, 2015; Purcell and Hutchinson, 2007). This role usually contains an HRM responsibility, which means that line managers are in the position to select, motivate, train, develop, appraise, commit, compensate and dismiss employees. Line managers thus clearly play an important role in operational HRM by managing the people in their team, department or unit.

LINE MANAGERS' ROLE IN HRM IMPLEMENTATION

Although scholars agree on the crucial HRM role that line managers play (Gilbert et al., 2015; Guest and Bos-Nehles, 2013; Op de Beeck et al., 2017; Purcell and Hutchinson, 2007; Townsend et al., 2012), HRM scholars do not agree about the details. According to many, line managers have a passive role in implementing HRM practices 'by the book' (Bos-Nehles et al., 2013: 873), which means that they follow guidelines and rules set by the HRM department. This linear implementation of HRM practices (Trullen et al., 2020; Van Mierlo et al., 2018) does not allow line managers any discretion from the intended HRM practices. Instead, they need to closely follow HRM directives to diminish an HRM variability (Bos-Nehles et al., 2020). The aim of this approach is to minimise the gaps between intended HRM practices (those HRM practices that are espoused by HRM based on strategic goals), actual HRM practices (those HRM practices that are implemented by line managers at the operational level) and perceived HRM practices (the experienced HRM practices by employees) (Makhecha et al., 2018; Nishii and Wright, 2008). According to Bos-Nehles et al. (2021), by deviating from intended courses line managers threaten the distinctiveness, consistency and consensus of HRM systems and thus prevent the HRM system from becoming strong (Bowen and Ostroff, 2004). Such a 'mechanistic view of organisations, where line managers should ideally act as both (neutral) receivers and senders of HRM messages decided elsewhere' (Bos-Nehles et al., 2021: 111), is imposed to help organisations reach strategic goals in the way designed and to develop a shared understanding of realised HRM experiences. To do so, line managers should enforce intended messages to employees and 'act as a deliverer and advocate of the espoused HR policies' to make sure that individual and organisational outcomes are reached (Pak and Kim, 2018: 2708). Although Bowen and Ostroff (2004) acknowledge that line managers play an active role as 'interpretive filters of HRM practices' (ibid.: 216), they need to act as messengers who translate strategic policies into their work units (Townsend et al., 2012) to affect employees' understanding of the quality of HRM systems in their organisations and thus introduce a common interpretation of among employees. The aim of this approach is to reach standardisation and consistency of implemented HRM practices in the organisation to shape a strong climate of shared employee behaviours.

There are many different ways presented in the literature for us to understand the role of line managers in the implementation of HRM. Most recently, Townsend et al. (2022) present the FLM specifically as an individual facing a conundrum: that they can be a master of their domain, and/or a victim of policies introduced by other departments, specifically the HR department. Proposing a more active and engaged role, Kehoe and Han (2020: 112) suggest that the line manager can be seen as a 'wilful and agentic human actor' who may proactively pursue autonomous initiatives at the operational level. Casting our gaze back further, Marchington and Grugulis (2000) remind us that line managers rarely act as 'robotic conformists', simply implementing policy without placing their own 'stamp' on the process. While these perspectives are presented differently, they all share a view that – to some extent – line managers would get the freedom to deviate from the intended course and 'adjust practices to reflect their needs' in a given situation with the aim of 'making HRM implementation more effective' (Bos-Nehles et al., 2017: 531). By locally modifying HRM practices, line managers can shape the horizontal and vertical fit of these practices to improve employee satisfaction, fulfilment and well-being (Kehoe and Han, 2020). As direct managers of operational employees, line managers are in a position to recognise employees' needs, and can give sense to HRM messages by translating them to the local situation and framing them as solutions in a way that employees are able to understand (Bondarouk et al., 2016). Such an approach may lead to within-organisation variability in the implementation of HRM (Pak and Kim, 2018), and to workforce differentiation (Kehoe and Han, 2020). Line managers may negotiate idiosyncratic deals (or 'i-deals') with employees in their teams, or engage in psychological contracts in which they employ a more customised approach to managing employees. As such, line managers may feel accountable for a fair implementation of HRM practices and agree on uncommon, non-standard applications of HRM practices that deviate from standard employment practices, such as extra developmental opportunities, extra salary beyond set pay levels, or on flexible work arrangements, such as telecommuting, virtual work or working from home, based on individual requests and needs (Kehoe and Han, 2020). Although local variability and differentiation may have positive consequences for employees, such as strategically segmenting the workforce (Lepak and Snell, 2002), meeting equity needs by appreciating individual efforts (Zhang et al., 2015), or fit with local requirements and needs (Bos-Nehles et al., 2017), it may also have negative consequences.

Kehoe and Han (2020) warn of legal issues because line managers may disregard labour and employment laws or apply biased practices, and of perceptions of unfairness of employees because of the customized approach and applying i-deals. Marescaux et al. (2013) also report perceptions of inequity among employees, and Nishii and Paluch (2018) indicate possible decreases or deterioration of HRM system strength. Recently, however, Bos-Nehles et al. (2021) have expressed opportunities to improve HRM system strength through line managers with discretion to locally modify HRM practices. HRM messages may also be perceived as distinctive, consistent and consensual in a less directive and mechanistic implementation model that grants line managers the freedom to take decision based on regional needs and fit.

Preferably HRM practices should be implemented in a more negotiated way in which organizational stakeholders have reached consensus on the best way to implement HRM practices for all involved agents and users. In such a solution espoused HRM practices fit the climate of the organisation and the values of the strategic and the operational business; that is, they are vertically and horizontally aligned, but operational goals and user needs are also considered from the beginning. To increase the chance of an effective implementation of HRM practices in which the HRM practices become routinised and institutionalised, we propose a more negotiated and consensus-driven adoption of HRM practices. In such a scenario, more organisational stakeholders would be involved in the design and development of HRM policies and practices. In fact, we suggest that line managers should also be consulted in this process, since they know what they need in order to develop employees at the operational level and secure a sustainable implementation of HRM practices. Once intended practices are developed, considering short- and long-term plans and the interests of a variety of stakeholders from various levels in the organisation, the chance of reducing the gap between intended and actual HRM practices becomes smaller. If this is the case, actual HRM practices have a higher chance of accomplishing the objectives for which the organisation adopted them (Trullen et al., 2020). This does not mean that line managers would not need to modify and shape HRM practices in the process of their implementation. However, once the intended practices are effective in content and process (Woodrow and Guest, 2014), and developed in cooperation and interaction, the chances are higher that adapting the practice during its implementation does not 'diminish the quality of implementation as long as the final practice can still fulfil its original purpose' (Trullen et al., 2020: 159).

In this book we present various ways in which line managers can implement HRM practices in the organisation. We consider the implementation of a variety of HRM policies and practices (content), a variety of implementation processes (process), and a variety of line management actors.

To do so, we have divided this book into three parts. Part I encompasses theories used in line management research. While we do not have a 'theory of line management' per se, we would argue that such an accomplishment is beyond reach, given the context-specific nature of what any line manager does, who a line manager might be, and how various different line manager roles are diverse both within organisations and between organisations. As such, we have contributions from a number of theoretical perspectives, including role theory, systems theory, social exchange theory, person–environment fit theory, attribution theory and paradox theory. Part I begins with Harney and Lee (Chapter 2), who consider the important role of agency of frontline managers through a systems theory lens to demonstrate the complex, yet interrelated aspects of frontline managers within organisations. Taking a more generic approach to line managers, Chapter 3 (Robertson and Veres) uses person–environment fit to explore the differences between the managed and the managers within the organisational context. Narrowing focus even further in Chapter 4, Evans considers the complexity of the various different line managers through using role theory, and the various tensions between role overload, role ambiguity and role conflict in the HRM system. We mentioned earlier in this introduction that the Blau influence over social exchange theory has influenced a great deal of line manager research. This history is reviewed by Bannya and Bainbridge in Chapter 5. Brandl, Keegan and Aust (Chapter 6) draw in a recognition that the requirement for line managers to be increasingly involved in HRM presents a situation of competing demands. Their chapter brings a relational approach to this paradox, to understand how individuals' responses to competing demands can either enable or hinder the dynamics before them. Finally in Part I, Hewett and Shantz take on attribution theory in Chapter 7, to discuss the role of line managers in the implementation of HRM practices.

Given the context-driven nature of both HRM and, more specifically, line managers in practice, it is no surprise that there is a diversity of research on the topic. This is explored and illustrated through Part II, the largest part of this book, titled 'Topics in Line Management Research'. This part begins with Kim and Kehoe (Chapter 8), who reconsider the traditional view of line managers as HRM implementors and place a focus on their individual agency. Equally, the authors continue, the HRM implementation role is usually only a relatively small part of the line manager's day-to-day workload. This leads neatly to the next chapter, by Sikora (Chapter 9), who considers the capabilities of line managers within the organisational system. Chapter 10 is our first chapter with empirical data, with Brookes and Brewster using the long-standing Cranet data to draw out the important role of national context in line manager experiences. Ironically, they find that the organisations with the most strategic HRM assign the least HRM responsibilities to line managers. Further demonstrating that context is very important, Knies, Decramer and Audenaert (Chapter 11) explore the experience of line managers within the public sector. The authors find that while there is an increasing likelihood that public sector organisations are looking more like those in the private sector, there remain differences, particularly for line managers.

Atkinson, Lupton and Dahwa provide an unusual contribution in Chapter 12, because they recognise that much of the line manager research relates to large firms. Their focus on small firms illuminates the complexity of HRM implementation by line managers when there is no internal HRM department in small firms. This chapter is followed by Townsend, Troth, and Loudoun (Chapter 13) who draw on a qualitative study of frontline managers (FLMs) to better understand how they see the leadership required in their role. This chapter demonstrates the context-specific nature of FLMs, while drawing patterns of expectations within the work of FLMs, and presents the 'pillars of frontline leadership'. Continuing the leadership theme in this part, in Chapter 14, Marescaux, Van den Broeck and De Winne argue that when line managers empower their employees this leads to a range of positive outcomes, including higher levels of autonomy, competence, satisfaction and negotiating i-deals.

By this stage, our authors have painted quite a picture of the line managers and their experiences within organisations. King (Chapter 15) progresses these ideas with a chapter on talent management, arguing that this is not a senior management responsibility: that in fact, all levels of managers within organisations play an important role in the policies and practices that shape and implement talent management. Surely all these pressures on line managers will lead to some negative outcomes? Saundry, Fisher and Kinsey consider this in Chapter 16 with their multimethod study of workplace conflict in the United Kingdom. These authors argue that the ability of managers to prevent, contain, manage and resolve conflict has important implications for organisations and the individuals within them. Our topic focus continues for the remaining four chapters of Part I, with Mirfakhar, Trullen and Valverde (Chapter 17) taking us to an area that is largely neglected in line manager research: senior managers. Certainly, senior managers are considered heavily in leadership research and general management research, but the specific area of human resource management is mostly silent on the topic of senior managers, the uppermost authority in organisations and the people who determine much of what HRM systems and their implementation will look like. Prolifi, Sammarra, Innocenti and Bos-Nehles (Chapter 18) examine the way in which line managers implement a very specific part of a HR system: that of work adjustment practices for chronically ill employees. This study demonstrates the complexity of line managers and their work to support not only healthy workers, but also those who have diseases that can be long in duration, and diverse in nature. Our final two chapters (Chapters 19 and 20) in this section are closely related. Hastuti and Timming (Chapter 19) consider line managers and the disclosure of mental illness in the workplace; a particularly timely contribution as we are – at the time of writing in 2021 – almost two years in to the COVID-19 pandemic. With a focus on a profession vital to the smooth operation of a modern society, Mildenhall and McCann (Chapter 20) consider the emergency services, specifically in relation to paramedics, and how important the support of line managers is for employees in a hierarchical, uniformed work culture.

Finally, we turn our attention to the future in Part III, which is driven by current practical and research trends, but as is all 'future-focused' research, contains some speculative musings of what may lie ahead for us. In Chapter 21, Monks and Conway focus on the influence of new technologies and COVID-19 on how future work is organized and experienced. They discuss frontline managers' role in managing the interaction between the technical, the social and the environmental consequences of these new changes. They also discuss how frontline management itself is changing as a result of technological advances. Their contribution is followed by Khoreva, Bos-Nehles and Salojärvi's Chapter 22 on the implementation of digitalisation. By identifying digitalisation as one of the major trends influencing future business, Khoreva and colleagues conducted an explorative inductive qualitative study to reveal the implementation process of digitalisation in organisations and to explore the role of line managers in digitalization implementation. They conclude their chapter by calling for more future research from different theoretical lenses to understand the implementation of digitalisation and the role of line managers in this.

Drent, Renkema and Bos-Nehles (Chapter 23) focus their attention on the role of line managers in the age of artificial intelligence. By conducting semi-structured interviews with HRM software vendors, they explore the new responsibilities of line managers due to the introduction of artificial intelligence in work processes, and discuss how organizations may pass over HRM responsibilities to artificial intelligence in the next phase of HRM devolution. In the final chapter (Chapter 24), Meijerink, Rogiers and Keegan discuss the implications of platform-enabled gig work for line managers. They first define the characteristics of platform-enabled gig work and introduce different types of online labor platforms. They then discuss the HRM-related paradoxes faced by line managers under different types of online labor platform models.

REFERENCES

ACAS (2014). *Front Line Managers Advisory Booklet*. June. Accessed 25 January 16 from: http://www .acas.org.uk/media/pdf/j/4/Front-line-managers-advisory-booklet.pdf.

Björkman, I., Ehrnrooth, M., Smale, A., and John, S. (2011). The determinants of line management internalisation of HRM practices in MNC subsidiaries. *International Journal of Human Resource Management, 22*(8), 1654–1671.

Blau, P. (1964). *Exchange and Power in Social Life*. New York: Wiley.

Bondarouk, T., Bos-Nehles, A., and Hesselink, X. (2016). Understanding the congruence of HRM frames in a healthcare organization. *Baltic Journal of Management, 11*(1), 2–20.

Bondarouk, T., and Ruël, H. (2013). The strategic value of e-HRM: results from an exploratory study in a governmental organization. *International Journal of Human Resource Management, 24*(2), 391–414.

Bos-Nehles, A. (2010). *The Line Makes the Difference: Line Managers as Effective HR Partners*. Zutphen, The Netherlands: CPI Wöhrmann Print Service.

Bos-Nehles, A., Bondarouk, T., and Labrenz, S. (2017). HRM implementation in multinational companies: the dynamics of multifaceted scenarios. *European Journal of International Management*, *11*(5), 515–536.

Bos-Nehles, A.C., Brees, J.R., De Winne, S.A., Hewett, R., Khoreva, V., et al. (2020). Beyond HRM implementation: new avenues for line managers through HRM differentiation. *Academy of Management Proceedings*, 1, 16519.

Bos-Nehles, A., Trullen, J., and Valverde, M. (2021). HRM system strength implementation: a multi-actor process perspective. In K. Sanders, H. Yang and C. Patel (eds), *Handbook on HR Process Research* (pp. 100–115). Cheltenham, UK and Northampton, MA, USA: Edward Elgar Publishing.

Bos-Nehles, A.C., Van Riemsdijk, M.J., and Looise, J.K. (2013). Employee perceptions of line management performance: applying the AMO theory to explain the effectiveness of line managers' HRM implementation. *Human Resource Management*, *52*(6), 861–877.

Bowen, D.E., and Ostroff, C. (2004). Understanding HRM–firm performance linkages: the role of the 'strength' of the HRM system. *Academy of Management Review*, *29*(2), 203–221.

Brewster, C., Brookes, M., and Gollan, P.J. (2015). The institutional antecedents of the assignment of HRM responsibilities to line managers. *Human Resource Management*, *54*(4), 577–597.

Budhwar, P.S., and Sparrow, P.R. (2002). Strategic HRM through the cultural looking glass: mapping the cognition of British and Indian managers. *Organization Studies*, *23*(4), 599–638.

Caza, A. (2011). Testing alternate predictions for the performance consequences of middle managers' discretion. *Human Resource Management*, *50*(1), 9–28.

CIPD (2015). *The Role of Line Managers in HR*. CIPD Factsheet. Accessed 25 January 2016 at http://www.cipd.co.uk/hr-resources/factsheets/role-line-managers-hr.aspx.

Crawshaw, J.R., and Game, A. (2015). The role of line managers in employee career management: an attachment theory perspective. *International Journal of Human Resource Management*, *26*(9), 1182–1203.

Cunningham, I., and Hyman, J. (1999). Devolving human resource responsibilities to the line: beginning of the end or a new beginning for personnel? *Personnel Review*, *28*(1–2), 9–27.

Currie, G. (2006). Reluctant but resourceful middle managers: the case of nurses in the NHS. *Journal of Nursing Management*, *14*, 5–12.

Davidson, P., and Griffin, R.W. (2000). *Management: Australia in a Global Context*. Sydney: John Wiley & Sons.

De Winne, S., Delmotte, J., Gilbert, C., and Sels, L. (2013). Comparing and explaining HR department effectiveness assessments: evidence from line managers and trade union representatives. *International Journal of Human Resource Management*, *24*(8), 1708–1735.

Evans, S. (2015). Juggling on the line: front line managers and their management of human resources in the retail industry. *Employee Relations*, *37*(4), 459–474.

Farndale, E., Van Ruiten, J., Kelliher, C., and Hope-Hailey, V. (2011). The influence of perceived employee voice on organizational commitment: an exchange perspective. *Human Resource Management*, *50*(1), 113–129.

Floyd, S.W., and Wooldridge, B. (1997). Middle management's strategic influence and organizational performance. *Journal of Management Studies*, *34*(3), 465–485.

Gennard, J., and Kelly, J. (1997). The unimportance of labels: the diffusion of the personnel/HRM function. *Industrial Relations Journal*, *28*(1), 27–42.

Gilbert, C., De Winne, S., and Sels, L. (2015). Strong HRM processes and line managers' effective HRM implementation: a balanced view. *Human Resource Management Journal*, *25*(4), 600–616.

Guest, E. (1991). Personnel management: the end of orthodoxy? *British Journal of Industrial Relations*, *29*, 149–175.

Guest, D., and Bos-Nehles, A. (2013). Human resource management and performance: the role of effective implementation. In J. Paauwe, D.E. Guest and P.M. Wright (eds), *Human Resource Management and Performance: Achievements and Challenges* (5th edn, pp. 79–96). Chichester: Wiley.

Hales, C. (2005). Rooted in supervision, branching into management: continuity and change in the role of first-line manager. *Journal of Management Studies*, *42*(3), 471–506.

Hall, L., and Torrington, D. (1998). Letting go or holding on-the devolution of operational personnel activities. *Human Resource Management Journal*, *8*(1), 41–55.

ILM (2009). *The Leadership and Management Talent Pipeline*. London: Institute of Leadership and Management.

Kehoe, R.R., and Han, J.H. (2020). An expanded conceptualization of line managers' involvement in human resource management. *Journal of Applied Psychology*, *105*(2), 111.

Kulik, C.T., and Perry, E.L. (2008). When less is more: the effect of devolution on HR's strategic role and construed image. *Human Resource Management*, *47*(3), 541–558.

Kurdi-Nakra, H., Kou, X., and Pak, J. (2021). The road taken and the path forward for HR devolution research: an evolutionary review. *Human Resource Management*. doi.org/10.1002/hrm.22091.

Kuvaas, B., Dysvik, A., and Buch, R. (2014). Antecedents and employee outcomes of line managers' perceptions of enabling HR practices. *Journal of Management Studies*, *51*(6), 845–868.

Legge, K. (1995). *Human Resource Management: Rhetoric and Realities*. Basingstoke: Palgrave Macmillan.

Lepak, D.P., and Snell, S.A. (2002). Examining the human resource architecture: the relationships among human capital, employment, and human resource configurations. *Journal of Management*, *28*(4), 517–543.

Lowe, J. (1992). Locating the line: the front-line supervisor and human resource management. In P. Blyton and P. Turnbull (eds), *Reassessing Human Resource Management* (pp. 148–167). London: SAGE.

Lowe, J. (1993). Manufacturing reform and the changing role of the production supervisor: the case of the automobile industry. *Journal of Management Studies*, *30*, 739–758.

MacLeod, D., and Clarke N. (2009). *Engaging for Success: Enhancing Performance Through Employee Engagement*. London: BIS

Makhecha, U.P., Srinivasan, V., Prabhu, G.N., and Mukherji, S. (2018). Multi-level gaps: a study of intended, actual and experienced human resource practices in a hypermarket chain in India. *International Journal of Human Resource Management*, *29*(2), 360–398.

Marchington, M., and Grugulis, I. (2000). 'Best practice' human resource management: perfect opportunity or dangerous illusion? *International Journal of Human Resource Management*, *11*(6), 1104–1124.

Marescaux, E., De Winne, S., and Sels, L. (2013). HR practices and HRM outcomes: the role of basic need satisfaction. *Personnel Review*, *42*(1), 4–27.

McDermott, A.M., Conway, E., Rousseau, D.M., and Flood, P.C. (2013). Promoting effective psychological contracts through leadership: the missing link between HR strategy and performance. *Human Resource Management*, *52*(2), 289–310.

Nishii, L.H., and Paluch, R.M. (2018). Leaders as HR sensegivers: four HR implementation behaviors that create strong HR systems. *Human Resource Management Review*, *28*(3), 319–323.

Nishii, L.H., and Wright, P.M. (2008). Variability within organizations: implications for strategic human resource management. In D.B. Smith (ed.), *The People Make the Place: Dynamic Linkages Between Individuals and Organizations* (pp. 225–248). New York: Taylor & Francis Group.

Op de Beeck, S., Wynen, J., and Hondeghem, A. (2017). Effective HRM implementation by line managers: relying on various sources of support. *International Journal of Public Administration*, *40*(2), 192–204.

Pak, J., and Kim, S. (2018). Team manager's implementation, high performance work systems intensity, and performance: a multilevel investigation. *Journal of Management*, *44*(7), 2690–2715.

Purcell, J., and Hutchinson, S. (2007). Front-line managers as agents in the HRM–performance causal chain: theory, analysis and evidence. *Human Resource Management Journal*, *17*(1), 3–20.

Ryu, S., and Kim, S. (2013). First-line managers' HR involvement and HR effectiveness: the case of South Korea. *Human Resource Management*, *52*(6), 947–966.

Staehle, W., and Schirmer, F. (1992). Lower level and middle level managers as the recipients and actors of human resource management. *International Studies of Management and Organisation*, *22*(1), 67–89

Steffensen Jr, D.S., Ellen III, B.P., Wang, G., and Ferris, G.R. (2019). Putting the 'management' back in human resource management: a review and agenda for future research. *Journal of Management*, *45*(6), 2387–2418.

Storey, J. (1992). *Developments in the Management of Human Resources*. Oxford: Blackwell

Storey, J. (2007). *Human Resource Management: A Critical Text*, 3rd edn. London: Thomson.

Townsend, K., Dundon, T., Cafferkey, K., and Kilroy, J. (2022). Victim or master of HRM implementation: the frontline manager conundrum. *Asia Pacific Journal of Human Resources*, 60(1), 79–96,

Townsend, K., Wilkinson, A., Allan, C., and Bamber, G. (2012). Mixed signals in HRM: the HRM role of hospital line managers 1. *Human Resource Management Journal*, 22(3), 267–282.

Trullen, J., Bos-Nehles, A., and Valverde, M. (2020). From intended to actual and beyond: a cross-disciplinary view of (human resource management) implementation. *International Journal of Management Reviews*, 22(2), 150–176.

Truss, C., and Gill, J. (2009). Managing the HR function: the role of social capital. *Personnel Review*, 38(6), 674–695.

Ulrich, D. (1997). Measuring human resources: an overview of practice and a prescription for results. *Human Resource Management*, 36(3), 303–320.

Van Mierlo, J., Bondarouk, T., and Sanders, K. (2018). The dynamic nature of HRM implementation: a structuration perspective. *International Journal of Human Resource Management*, 29(22), 3026–3045.

Vermeeren, B. (2014). Variability in HRM implementation among line managers and its effect on performance: a 2-1-2 mediational multilevel approach. *International Journal of Human Resource Management*, 25(22), 3039–3059.

Woodrow, C., and Guest, D.E. (2014). When good HR gets bad results: exploring the challenge of HR implementation in the case of workplace bullying. *Human Resource Management Journal*, 24(1), 38–56.

Wren, D.A. (1972). *The Evolution of Management Thought*. New York: Ronald Press.

Zhang, Y., Waldman, D.A., Han, Y.L., and Li, X.B. (2015). Paradoxical leader behaviors in people management: antecedents and consequences. *Academy of Management Journal*, 58, 538–566.

PART I

THEORIES IN LINE MANAGEMENT RESEARCH

2.   A systems theory perspective on the frontline manager role

Brian Harney and Qian Yi Lee

INTRODUCTION

The role of agency and the dynamics of systems are critical to understanding how people are managed. Ironically, while this is well understood in practice (e.g. Buckingham and Coffman, 1999), such understanding has not made a sufficient impact in human resource mangement (HRM) research. This chapter explores the critical role and agency of frontline managers through a systems lens. In so doing we note the limitations of existing understanding which tends to treat gaps between intended and experienced HRM as something to be avoided and mitigated versus acknowledged and embraced. By contrast, the classic lens of systems theory provides a rich intellectual heritage which captures the dynamics of frontline manager agency as grounded by contextually oriented concepts including emergence, informality, self-organizing and entropy. The second half of the chapter animates these principles in action, using the example of the frontline manager role in performance management. The chapter concludes by highlighting how the dynamics of system theory can help to advance understanding of frontline manager roles, including that which treats informal practice and deviance from established rules as a practical reality versus a detrimental fault line in HRM implementation.

THE ROLE OF FRONTLINE MANAGERS IN HRM: GRADUALLY, BUT POORLY, INCORPORATED

The role of both managerial and employee agency and the broader social systems in which they operated were critical to early scholarship in industrial relations and employment relations. Classic studies recognised the complexities and indeterminacies of the employment relationship and moved to explore organisations as adaptive social systems embedded in differing environmental contexts (Gouldner, 1954). In her classic study of manufacturing and technology, Joan Woodward (1965: 6) argued that 'industrial firms would have to be studied as complex social systems and line-staff relationships looked as part of the whole not in isolation'. While early work differentiating HRM from its predecessor, personnel management, did focus more on the dynamics of management and delegation of HRM to the line, in recent times this type of emphasis is much less evidenced. From the mid-1990s HRM's normative performance agenda and penchant for prescription left little room for agency or factors that might deviate from the predetermined productivity pathway to success. Consequently, there is widespread acknowledgement, not without some irony, that actual managers have appeared as a ghost-like figures in much HRM research (Harney and Collings, 2021; Nishii and Paluch, 2018; Steffensen et al., 2019). In part, this can be explained by the presumed alignment of managerial intent and agency central to achieving vertical and horizontal fit in strategic HRM and/or ensuring successful implementation of HRM in its high-performance work system variant (Harney et al., 2018). Early HRM–performance-oriented research retained a focus on 'intended' human resources (HR), founded on the assumption 'that simply having the appropriate HRM policies inevitably means that they will be effectively implemented and will produce the intended results in terms of individual behaviour and, at one remove, firm performance' (Truss, 2001: 1126).

In more recent times a steady stream of research exploring the so-called 'black box' of HRM–performance relationships has directed attention towards line managers. However, while recognising line managers as 'key intermediaries' in HRM, the focus of much of this research has been on minimising or (re)directing discretionary effort to enable a greater line of sight in the implementation of HRM (Harney and Cafferkey, 2014). This research is also characterised by a failure to draw upon a clear and consistent definition of line managers, including frontline managers. Line managers can be understood as those who work 'between the strategic apex and the operating core of the organisation' (Floyd and Wooldridge, 1996: 3), and typically consist of three distinct levels: senior line managers, middle line managers and frontline managers (Lewis et al., 2013: 9; Zhu et al., 2013: 72). Existing studies are limited by a tendency to take an aggregated view on the various levels of line managers (Evans, 2015: 460; Townsend, 2014: 164). As a distinct level of line manager, frontline managers play a critical role in organisations, but yet tend to be especially neglected (Hutchinson, 2008: 4; Hutchinson and Purcell, 2010: 357). Notably, frontline managers are the link between higher management and employees, with senior and middle line managers implementing policies and practices through them (Saville and Higgins, 1994: 25). Despite this significance, there is a tendency to reduce frontline managers to a weak link to be corrected or further aligned in a fixed system as part of a quest for optimal performance. Typically neglected is the context in which each and every frontline manager and their respective organisations operates (Farndale and Paauwe, 2018). In essence, the work of frontline managers is reduced to law-like patterns without significant powers of metamorphosis (Connolly, 2013). Yet these assumptions jar with what we already know about the role of frontline managers.

Research on HR in the leading consortium of companies identified a number of constraints impacting the delivery of HR by frontline managers, not least short-term pressures for performance, limited institutional support, and pragmatic limits on time and resources (McGovern et al., 1997). We know that line managers generally can have differing perspectives compared to HR executives as to the strategic contribution and value add of HR (Wright et al., 2001). In terms of impact, perceptions of frontline manager behaviour is linked to employee engagement (Alfes et al., 2013), while it is recognised that individual managers can have a differential performance impact, over and above organisational factors (Mollick, 2012). Harney and Jordan (2008) showed that frontline managers served as critical intermediaries in a call centre context, ameliorating the negative consequences of HRM practices. The focus here was less on creating and fostering organisational performance, but more on protecting against intended HRM. Frontline managers are often restricted in the amount of autonomy they have in decision-making, controlled in part by the expectations and instructions of their superiors. As a result, frontline managers (FLMs) frequently exercise discretion to prioritise their work when they are unable to achieve all their targets, thereby leading to inconsistencies in their approach to people management (Child and Partridge, 1982: 83). A study by Evans (2015) illuminates how FLMs actually have very limited autonomy in the tasks that are handed to them. However, what they do have is a lot of discretion in how to execute those tasks, as long as they keep within the preset boundaries and get the job done. All this highlights the significance of frontline managers in HRM, and the importance of providing a more contextual and holistic understanding of their role and impact, including as a strategic deviation from formal policy. As Boxall and Macky (2007: 267) observe:

> Line managers, including supervisors and team leaders, are responsible for converting much of management's intentions for HRM into actual HR practice, given the resources they have to work with, and their judgments [*sic*] about what will work and what serves their interests. It is useful therefore to think of HR practice as a wide range of actual managerial behaviour centred around a notional standard.

CAPTURING THE ROLE OF FRONTLINE MANAGERS: INSIGHTS FROM SYSTEMS THEORY

In this section we propose that systems theory is an appropriate lens to accommodate the wide range of actual frontline management behaviour, while also recognising the complexities of the context in which such behaviour is embedded. It is long acknowledged that the activities of HRM are embedded in open systems so that HRM 'should not be treated in isolation but in conjunction with the processes by which the policies, practices, and systems are implemented' (Steffensen et al., 2019: 2391). While the evolution of HRM has certainly been characterised by a reference to system-based logic – for example, the terminology and assumptions of high-performance work systems (HPWSs) or the logic of social exchange – there is a continued assumption that any gaps and or failures in implementation can be easily identified and remedied. As Harney (2019: 117) argues, 'absent are more broader considerations of context, emergence or a sense of the inherent tensions of the employment relationship'. It is informative that studies of managerial work depict a task characterised by fragmentation, variety and brevity, as opposed to a rational, linear and fixed contribution (Mintzberg, 1973). Indeed the frontline manager role has been highlighted as 'problematic' (Renwick, 2003) and underpinned by structural conflicts and contradictions (Hales, 2007). Unsurprising, that there have been calls to move beyond narrow conceptions of existing line manager roles to embrace their 'multifaceted influence' in the HR process (Kehoe and Han, 2020: 112), and management of competing demands as paradox navigators (Fu et al., 2020). We argue that a systems-informed understanding offers important contributions in this task.

Systems theory highlights the interdependence of organisational elements and the reality that all organisation functions and activities are conducted in the context of broader systems which can inform, shape and sometimes even determine behaviour (Von Bertalanffy, 1968). Despite the lack of explicit reference to the concept of systems theory, it has long influenced organisational research, including HR research (Boxall and Macky, 2009; Guest, 1997; Harney and Dundon, 2006; Townsend et al., 2013b). Organisations operate under both external and internal constraints, and there are multiple social systems within the organisation's internal environment (Heffernan et al., 2022). Systems theory is useful in examining the role of organisational HRM, as HR plays an integral role as 'the carriers of effort and motivation necessary to maintain the social system' while 'the social structures of human behaviour are largely responsible for the throughput transformation process' (Wright and Snell, 1991: 208). The logic of systems theory underpins the evolution of HR, including its recognition that HR systems rather than individual practices are more appropriate in explaining the contributions to organisational performance (Delaney and Huselid, 1996). Much HRM research has explored the link between HR systems or specific subsystems within the HR system and organisational performance (e.g. Boland and Fowler, 2000; Roh, 2018; Shin and Konrad, 2014). Just as the HR system is a subsystem of the organisation, so the HR system is also composed of multiple subsystems (Severance, 2001). Subsystems are also an important consideration because they can 'work together and use system processes to transform organisational inputs into performance outcomes' (Townsend et al., 2013b: 3064). Reflecting this appreciation for system and subsystem dynamics, a number of commonly articulated general systems theory conceptual components (see Cummings, 2015a; Garavan et al., 2021; Harney, 2019; Scott, 1995) have direct relevance for exploring the frontline manager role and experience, as follows.

Complexity

General systems theory was first used in organisational studies based on an open system understanding that organisations would try to create order through strategies and processes that were unique to them, based on the environment in which they operated (Clegg, 1990). A system has interrelated elements, and within open systems interactions with and feedback from the various elements affect the other elements within the system (Katz and Kahn, 1966). The simplicity or complexity of a system is dependent on the number of interactions between the elements. Organisations are continuously striving to reach a relatively stable equilibrium in open systems, because the context they operate in influences what their steady state is, which contrasts with the assumed definite equilibrium in closed systems (Koehler, 1969). While systems theory stresses the interdependence between an organisation's actions and the broader environment in which it is embedded, this does not imply smoothness and continuity in these relations. Central to open systems accounts is an emphasis on uncertainty, indeterminacy and, hence, an ability to capture complexity (Thompson and McHugh, 1995). Stated differently, an organisation and its environment compose a complex interactive system (Bedian, 1990). One consequence is that systems theorists caution against claiming determinate, law-like relationships of the kind found in mainstream HR–performance research, but instead speak of conditions of possibility and general tendencies (Harney, 2009). Even research of top-performing organisations has found an undercurrent of emergence, highlighting an entangled nature of formal policy and informal dynamics on the shop floor (Gratton et al., 1999). The pragmatic nature of everyday realities in the workplace highlights the flaw in relying on rational assumptions and predetermined action. In practice, frontline manager behaviour is more likely to reflect tactical optimums and 'muddling through' to secure ongoing, temporal commitment and the semblance of consensus (Lindblom, 1959).

Context

Systems-informed approaches are sensitive to local conditions and change (Dawkins and Barker, 2018). From the perspective of an open system, organisations are seen as one part of a series of social and economic networks (Edwards et al., 2002). Context is an important part of these networks, whereby the interdependence between an organisation's internal and external environment affects how it operates due to varying flows of people, resources and information (Harney and Dundon, 2006; Scott, 2003). In exploring the roles and activities of frontline managers, systems theory foregrounds contextual considerations. As Sikora and Ferris (2014) illuminate, the effective use of HR by line managers will be informed by a wide variety of contextual factors, including organisational culture, political considerations and broader social factors. For example, research has shown that the challenges confronted by frontline managers are likely to vary substantially based on based on different multinational business unit contexts within the same business (Nehles et al., 2006). Similarly, key events and changes are likely to be internalised by organisational members who imbue them with their own interpretation and meaning (Wilkinson et al., 2007). Just as frontline managers can facilitate effective HR, so they can equally fracture policy and intentions, especially if any prospective change challenges an established identity or social order of production (cf. Ezzamel et al., 2001).

Equifinality

Stemming from an emphasis on complexity and context, a further important open systems concept is that of equifinality. This holds that organisations can obtain the same end state from differing initial conditions and through different means. This concept might go some way in explaining the inconsistency in studies attempting to define the precise nature of desirable HRM practices (Harney, 2019). While some research has suggested the necessity to move beyond reductionist contingency theorising, few studies have explicitly embraced the logic that there are multiple, equally effective ways of meeting the same desired outcome. Exceptions include configurational theory, typologies and ideal types (Meyer et al., 1993), although these tend to abstract away the role of management or employees as agents explaining variance. Important in understanding frontline manager interventions is the role of immediate and proximal relationships, including local commitment with employees (Harney and Jordan, 2008). There is growing recognition of prospective variance in the frontline manager role (Bruno and Jordan, 2002; Kehoe and Han, 2020), with equifinality providing a means to avoid the assumption of 'omniscience of management and the uniformity of its approach to labour' (Marchington and Parker, 1990: 48).

Feedback Loops

Research which examines and seeks law-like relationships rarely allows for significant change. There is an implicit underlying assumption that organisations and their HR systems are something of an absorbent system that automatically reflects and returns the shocks and dissenting pressures applied to it. By contrast, the logic of open systems highlights that an organisation can only function because of ongoing engagement and adaptation to environmental forces (both external and internal). It follows that HR activities are not one-off, fixed and invariant structural interventions, but instead strive for a constant steady state (Koehler, 1969). From a systems logic, change is a function of feedback loops that operate at multiple levels, which can serve to reinforce the current dynamic or rupture its assumptions or operations. From a macro perspective, the relevance of such understanding is evidenced in an era of 'financialisation', where financial transactions and relationships external to the organisation (and independent of physical products or services) are deemed to continuously frame the employment relationship, frequently leaving frontline managers in inherently contradictory positions (Applebaum et al., 2013; Cushen and Harney, 2014). This broader political economy is itself 'a moving assemblage of interconnected sub-systems' (Connolly, 2013: 13). At a micro level, research has shown that the nature and dynamics of frontline manager voice and involvement in the HRM process shapes the critical relationships and opportunities to collaborate with senior management, ultimately determining the effectiveness of HRM (Alfes et al., 2013) . This aligns with a general understanding that HRM 'comes live in social interactions among organisational members, including those involved in formulating, communicating, and responding to elements of the HRM system' (Jackson et al., 2014: 4). Importantly, open systems theory promotes time-irreversibility, acknowledging that a system can never precisely return to a previous state. In systems terms, this is depicted by the term 'entropy'. The Covid-19 global pandemic and its dramatic consequences illuminate the fragility of organisations, and their underlying assumptions and ways of doing HR, in relation to the dynamics of change and challenge from the surrounding environment (Harney and Collings, 2021).

Sub-systems

Organisations operate under both external and internal constraints, and there are multiple social systems within the organisation's internal environment. According to Burns and Stalker (1961), subsystems can be grouped into either mechanistic (that is, formal) or organic (that is, informal) systems. The formal systems are structured based on the formalised rules and procedures in the organisation; the informal systems are implicit and fluid, based on informal practices and procedures that develop over time in the organisation (Nadler and Tushman, 1980). Research in the airline industry has shown how cross-functional accountability can be used to diffuse blame, highlighting the role of frontline managers in providing coaching and feedback (Gittel, 2000). Just as the HR system is a subsystem of the organisation, so the HR system is also composed of multiple subsystems which can operate in tandem or as deadly combinations (McClean and Collins, 2019). Frontline managers are therefore at the interface of practice and serve as conduits of multiple functional managers and agendas (for example, information technology, HR and customers) (Burgelman, 1983).

Dynamic Nature of Formality and Informality

A concern with systems also allows for the informality of practice that substitutes for, or fills, the silences of formal policy. This nexus between formal and informal organisation is something that cannot be captured within the high-performance work systems literature, with its exclusive focus on formal policy (Truss, 2001). Systems theory accommodates both formality and informality and does not privilege one over the other. Research shows how formal and informal systems can complement each other, working together to support individuals (Marchington and Suter, 2013; Townsend et al., 2013b). However, formal and informal systems can also compete with each other, working separately in the workplace. The presence of a formal system does not guarantee that all levels of the organisation will adhere to it, as agents such as frontline managers may have varying individual needs that are different from the organisation's (Selznick, 1981). Frontline managers who use discretion within their roles during the implementation of formal HR systems contribute to the development of informal systems. Nadler and Tushman's (1980) argument for formal and informal processes existing in an organisation concurrently was used in the development of their systems theory framework: formal processes are structured procedures developed explicitly for employees to perform for the achievement of organisational goals, and are usually recorded in writing; while informal processes are implicit, tending to develop and emerge over time. This distinction is frequently absent from traditional HR accounts, where informality is either ignored or stigmatised.

Overview

Overall it is clear that systems theory provides a means to move beyond the deficiencies of current understanding of the frontline manager role. Systems-informed concepts allow for a contextualised activity-level analysis of the dynamics of frontline manager discretion, competing priorities and expectations, the dynamics of relations and (in)formality, and an appreciation of the complex nature of tasks (Finkelstein and Peteraf, 2007). The outcomes emphasised are not purely financial or rationally determined, but include broader aspects of organisational survival, including table stakes, relative advantages and the maintenance of relationships. In order to further explicate the argument in the next section, we provide an application of systems-informed logic to the critical domain of performance management and frontline managers' role therein.

SYSTEMS THEORY APPLIED: FRONTLINE MANAGERS IN PERFORMANCE SYSTEMS

Systems theory is frequently conceptually invoked in HRM research or used as a conceptual architecture to structure reviews (e.g. Jackson et al., 2014). Exploring performance management (PM) research, Schleicher and colleagues argued that 'a systems approach is essential for distilling knowledge about the effectiveness of PM from the extant literature (as such questions ultimately rely on an examination of multiple components and how they interrelate)' (Schleicher et al., 2018: 2211). Indeed, a systems approach has been particularly influential in the development of performance management (Iwu et al., 2016). In this section we use performance management as an example to explore the application of systems theory to understand the dynamics of the frontline manager role. In so doing we argue that a systems lens provides a more contextual and holistic means to capture the 'wide range of actual management behaviour' (Boxall and Macky, 2007). Going back to the classic work of Thompson it is clear that frontline managers serve intermediary roles between the technical, managerial and institutional. Thompson argued that 'complex organization is a set of interdependent parts which together make up a whole in that each contributes something and receives something from the whole, which in turn is interdependent with some larger environment' (Thompson, 1967 [2005]: 6).

Using a specific HR practice helps to animate the role of the frontline managers and the value of systems-informed understanding of them. This focus also enables an exploration of open and closed systems dynamics. As per Thompson (1967 [2005]: 9): 'open systems theory holds that the processes going on within an organisation are significantly affected by the complexity of an organisation's environment. But this tradition also touches on matters important in the closed-system strategy: performance and deliberate decisions'. According to Brown and Lim (2019), line managers are involved in both formal and informal performance management activities, as they are in a position where they are responsible for evaluating performance and providing feedback. Exploration of frontline manager-enacted HR illuminates how organisational actors can approach workplace issues such as performance feedback though either a formal and/or an informal system. Notably, frontline managers are a critical link between higher levels of management and employees, as higher levels of management are more likely to design rather than implement performance systems and processes (Liang et al., 2007; Saville and Higgins, 1994). A frontline manager's authority originates from their position in the workplace (Leonard and Trusty, 2016). As such, frontline managers are involved in the implementation of HR practices such as performance management-related responsibilities as part of their supervisory responsibilities. The expansion of the frontline managers' role has led to them facing conflicting pressures in their job; while they lack the corresponding authority within the organisation, frontline managers are tasked with bridging the gap between the intended and actual performance management systems (Child and Partridge, 1982; Hales, 2005; Purcell and Hutchinson, 2007). Consistency within the implementation of the performance management systems affects how employees use innovation to reach their work goals (Audenaert et al., 2019); how frontline managers choose to implement performance management affects the consistency experiences by frontline employees. Just as organisations work toward reaching a steady state within the open systems where they operate (Koehler, 1981), so the frontline managers work within the performance management system to reach their idea of equilibrium based on the demands of their role and other organisational actors (Lee et al., 2021).

In order to further unpack the systems-informed dynamic of the frontline manager role, it is useful to draw on Floyd and Wooldridge (1997), who explored the multiple mechanisms by which middle management affect the strategy process. Their fourfold typology draws attention to the multiple roles that frontline managers must navigate (Fu et al., 2020). This enables us to capture the influence and agency of frontline managers as an intermediary between the institutional, the managerial and the technical (Thompson, 1967 [2005]). It also illuminates the complexities of frontline managers' role in realising the intended performance of the organisation, while sustaining the local commitment and social order to allow the organisation to function on a day-to-day basis. Specifically, for each role we draw out those aspects that are more official and formally designated, while also detailing those that are more unofficial and/or informal. It is clear that systems-based logic enables an in-depth analysis and dynamic understanding of how frontline managers continuously strive for homeostasis, or a 'steady state', rather than assuming a form of definitive equilibrium as per closed systems accounts (Cummings, 2015b; Koehler, 1969) of the kind found in much HRM research (Harley, 2015).

FLMs as Performance Management Implementers: Conduits and Translators

In the implementation role, frontline managers engage in an ongoing set of interventions to bring organisational action in line with deliberate or intended strategy. While allowing for some flexibility at the perimeters, in the main this emphasis reflects traditional understanding in HRM research whereby the frontline managers' role is to ensure that performance management strategy is realised exactly as intended. A key emphasis here is on uniformity and consistency, which are typically associated with enhanced organisational performance. Being consistent in the implementation of performance management is important in demonstrating to employees that it is a continuous process (Aguinis et al., 2012) that clarifies work goals for them, motivating them to display the ideal behaviours to achieve these work goals within their roles (DeNisi and Smith, 2014). Typically assumed is that there is initial clarity and consensus on strategy which is communicated and cascaded without change. From this textbook under-standing, failure to adhere to intended strategy is not sufficiently appreciated as a reality.

As per systems theory logic it is of course dangerous to imbue strategy as predetermined, as opposed to an empirical concept to be determined in particular circumstances (Harney and Collings, 2021; Wood, 1979). Frontline managers are not simple conduits: they are also translators. Frontline managers' action or inaction is often responsible for the difference between espoused HR policies and their enactment. Variance in this sense is not a reflection of an implementation gap which can be easily bridged, but instead reflects the political and social context in which frontline managers must exist on a day-to-day basis. In studying the application of performance-related pay schemes, Harris (2001) reported a lack of incentives, time and ownership framing the nature of frontline manager engagement with the performance management system. Notably, frontline managers were also conscious that the top-down per-formance management system included 'the potential for decisions that decreased rather than increased levels of employee trust', so that 'perceptions of fairness among the managers were frequently more closely related to those of the employees they supervised than the principles reflected in the systems they had to apply' (Harris, 2001: 1191). It is unsurprising, therefore, that even high-performing work organisations exhibit an ongoing gap between the espoused or intended theory of performance management and what is experienced in practice (Stiles et al., 1997). In this way the necessity of securing the local compliance of employees and balancing conflicting and emerging priorities are at the heart of the frontline manager role. Equally, however, frontline managers are agents of management so that, on paper at least, they need to be seen to be adhering to and implementing formal policy (see Gouldner, 1954). Research on the impact of financialisation or changes in production systems reveals that frontline man-agers frequently find themselves as the walking contradiction between formally articulated organisational policy and what everyone on the ground knows to be true (Bruno and Jordan, 2002; Cushen and Harney, 2014). The dynamic nature of these official and unofficial roles is captured in Table 2.1.

FLMs as Information Synthesisers: Aggregators and Satisficers

In their official role of implementing performance management systems, frontline managers are also tasked with collating and aggregating key performance data to be fed up to manage-ment. Relationships with management and HR can be critical in facilitating this process (Alfes et al., 2013), although in many instances frontline managers have little or no involvement in the design and development of the performance management system they are tasked with implementing. It follows that the official designated role as a performance management aggregator is often subtly reinterpreted or depoliticised. This is most obviously manifest in ranked performance ratings, where frontline managers have been found to group employees as average performers as opposed to providing distinctions which might risk fracturing their rela-tionship with frontline employees, thereby 'keeping their own trustworthiness intact' (Harris, 2001: 1188). Frontline managers play a key role in enacting and interpreting appraisal policy, reflecting the reality of an individual's experience of the company policy is that carried out by frontline management (Truss, 2001). Middle management and HR are one step removed from the reactions and sentiment of frontline employees, whereas frontline managers experience direct employee reactions: positive or negative. Appreciating the (in)action of frontline man-agers is best done with an appreciation of their role, not simply in an official capacity of max-

Table 2.1   *The dynamics of frontline manager roles*

Line manager role	Official role	Unofficial role
Implement intended PM strategy	**Conduit** Activities: ● monitor activities to support top management objectives ● translate goals into action plans ● translate goals into individual objectives ● sell top management initiatives to subordinates Objective: Implement HR-uniformity, compliance, consistency	**Translator** Activities: ● navigate the micro-dynamics of inclusion (Westley, 1990) ● maintenance of relations ● perceptions of fairness ● daily interaction, coaching, feedback (Gittell, 2000) Objective: Translate HR (Kehoe and Han, 2020)
Synthesise information	**Aggregator** Activities: ● formal metrics ● objective measurement of performance ● closed system Objective: Collect and collate – rational	**Satisficer** Activities: ● politicised measures ● secure cooperation ● protection of territory ● open system Objective: Interpret
Champion alternatives	**Strategic provision** Activities: ● upward communication ● knowledge of activities ● promote innovations Focus: Continuous improvement	**Strategic filtering** Activities: ● sustain relationships and leverage ● normative/peer pressure ● visibility and network Focus: Careerism and and power relations
Facilitate adaptability	**Leeway** Activities: ● sponsor experimentation ● capture learning ● relax regulation Focus: Proactive adaptability	**Custom and practice** Activities: ● emergent leadership ● political manoeuvring ● negotiated orders ● commission and omission Focus: Negotiated orders

imising rational information flows, but being mindful of pressure to secure future cooperation and in satisficing key stakeholders, both management and employees. Conway and Monks (2008) provide an interesting example from the healthcare context, where HR was devolving HR activities but retaining control of information systems. This led managers to create their own datasets as a means to circumvent control and retain autonomy.

FLMs' Role in Championing Alternatives: Strategic Provision and Strategic Filtering

A third role which Floyd and Wooldridge (1997) detail is that of championing alternatives. Here, in an official capacity, frontline managers can promote innovations and suggest changes which might improve company processes and performance. A likely undercurrent is a form of careerism and effort to get recognition and kudos from higher management. Again, critical here is the opportunity for, and maintenance of, a positive relationship with higher-level managers and HR (Alfes et al., 2013). This may also involve political reading of a situation to promote and push upwards those ideas which are in line with the broader zeitgeist of the time, versus those that are most objectively efficient. At the same time, frontline managers are likely to experience normative or peer pressure for conformity. As Pech (2001: 599) notes, 'normative influence is an instinctive survival mechanism serving to establish and maintain uniformity and stability'. Thus, while frontline managers may publically articulate the merits of innovation and change in how performance is managed, it is often the case that they will strive to reinforce predictable routines and maintain the status quo. Forms of subtle resistance can be linked to attempts to sustain workplace identities that have been built up over time, with employees who they supervise providing continuous reminders of same (see Ezzamel et al., 2001). Accompanying formal performance management systems and policy is also the reality that informal influence and visibility can be a critical factor informing subsequent evaluations and recommendations for advancement. Using the informal performance management system can help frontline managers to maintain the perception of performance of their employees and themselves by higher levels of management (Lee et al., 2021). In her detailed study of Hewlett-Packard, Truss (2001: 1144) found that 'although the formal policies turned strongly around the notion of measuring and rewarding individuals' work performance against targets that were closely related to the company's objectives, informally what counted was visibility and networking if people wanted to further their careers'. Frontline managers are inevitably at the core of shaping and being shaped by how informal practices and norms of behaviour interact with formal HR policies.

FLM and Adaptability: Leeway and Custom

Traditional HRM understanding of frontline managers' roles provides little sense of agency (Steffensen et al., 2019). Absent, therefore, is any appreciation that fruitful initiatives and understanding about managing people are likely to come from those with direct responsibility for this task. In exploring the role of adaptability, Floyd and Wooldridge (1997) stress the impact of downward influence, including relaxing regulation to get projects started and providing time, scope and a safe environment for experimentation and innovation. They also stress the significance of informal discussion and knowledge exchange. This emphasis aligns very much with what we know about frontline manager roles. Harney and Jordan's (2008) research in a call centre context finds frontline managers as key intermediaries, but not in the traditional linear sense of cascading strategy, as intended. Instead, frontline managers' efforts focused on ameliorating the negative consequences of the hard HR of the call centre environment. This was achieved via an 'emergent' leadership role which saw them introduce interventions akin to what might be subscribed to by best-practice HR, for example, improving morale and creating a sense of 'involvement' and 'a better atmosphere' among call centre employees. Interestingly this significant frontline manager role was implicitly recognised, with HR at the call centre only recruiting frontline managers with extensive experience in a similar role.

Kehoe and Han (2020) frame the downward autonomous line manager role as one of resisting, adapting or renewing intended or espoused strategic goals. As a result of their employee-facing role, frontline managers must frequently demonstrate leeway in interpreting and enacting intended HRM so as to achieve the consent and commitment of employees. This form of ongoing negotiation is long understood. In his classic in-depth study of a gypsum plant, Gouldner (1954: 173) observed that 'by a strange paradox, formal rules gave supervisors something with which they could "bargain" in order to secure informal cooperation from the workers'. Brown's classic study of piecework bargaining found that the patterns of 'indulgency' formed over time can morph into a form of customer and practice understood as 'a transactional rule of job regulation that arises from informal processes' (Brown, 1972: 48). Formed as a result of proactive initiative (commission) or low-level management error (omission), custom and practice can become accepted as a binding precedent by employees so that it does not simply augment formally negotiated rules, but moves to replace them (Brown, 1973). Assumptions of simplistic frontline manager compliance to intended performance management is therefore problematic. Moreover, it is not simply that frontline manager actions bends existing rules, but that the alternatives they operate by can become significant and imprinting. This adds an important employment relations understanding to Floyd and Wooldridge's argument. This is an area where frontline managers are rarely provided with organisational support or guidance (Teague and Roche, 2011).

Systems theory provides a framework which accommodates the diversity and ongoing tensions inherent to the frontline manager role. In HR terms, it allows for the lower-level system components and activities which interact with formal HR policy and shape how it is experienced and enacted. As our extension of Floyd and Wooldridge (1997) illustrates, this can encompass closed-system, top-down official intent, but equally open-system, bottom-up activities. In reality, managers in all organisations navigate between rationality, formality, personal preference and idiosyncrasy as the occasion demands. A long heritage of workplace studies provides a wealth of concepts related to the 'leeway function of rules' (Gouldner, 1954), or the role of custom and practice (Brown, 1972). A notable insight from this literature is that informal practices go much further than providing a lubricant to the formal system; rather, they are inevitable: 'the conclusion must be that informal practices are likely to be a permanent feature of industrial relations' (Terry, 1977: 88). A key consideration, therefore, becomes how frontline managers navigate a formal HR system that is bound by rules and expectations, but also operate within an informal system that allows them to get things done and work around the difficulties of the formal system. Our illustration of systems-informed understanding animates the various means by which this can occur in the context of frontline manager roles in performance management. At a minimum, this highlights the limits of narrow, formal and top-down understanding of the frontline manager role of the type assumed by many 'black box' studies which target bridging and resolving the intended–enacted HRM gap.

CONCLUSION

The exposition of systems theory presented in this chapter suggests a number of implications for future research. These include, firstly, the need for more in-depth and contextually embedded considerations of the frontline manager role. This line of research could draw from and extend research founded on HR process and signalling theory (Guest et al., 2021), and equally, from recent work which acknowledges the dynamic nature of HRM implementation (Trullen et al., 2020). Particularly rich insights are likely to come from studies that explore variance within similar industries or within specific organisations. Secondly, line manager research would benefit from more ethnographic studies and detailed observation of the practices, tensions and constraints that shape the day-to-day realities of the role. Finally, systems theory-informed understanding should not be reduced to a conceptual framing. There is much to learn from classic (Burns and Stalker, 1961; Katz and Kahn, 1966) and contemporary systems-informed research (Harney and Dundon, 2006; Townsend et al., 2013a). According to Stacey (1995), systems logic posits that simple functions can give rise to very intricate and unpredictable behavior that still exhibits underlying order. The application presented here also highlights how unofficial and informal frontline manager activities should not be reduced to 'second-class citizens' of analysis, surfaced merely to explain deficiencies or anomalies (Kehoe and Han, 2020). By stressing emergence and self-organised systems, and acknowledging agency, we gain a more comprehensive and realistic understanding of the frontline manager role than that of a narrow, deterministic implementer. Paying due attention to the nuances, agency and reinterpretation characteristics of the frontline manager role provides a platform for renewed understanding challenging conventional 'mind or close the gap' wisdom, and engaging with the complexities of formal and informal, deliberate and emergent dynamics. Ultimately, systems theory puts analysis in tune with the fragilities at the heart of every organisation and relationship. As Katz and Kahn (1966: 454) remind us, 'the fact organisation structure is created and maintained only as the members of the organisation interact in an ordered way suggests a high degree of openness, a persistent and inherent vulnerability to forces in the organisation's environment'.

REFERENCES

Aguinis, H., Joo, H., and Gottfredson, R.K. 2012. Performance management universals: think globally and act locally. *Business Horizons*, 55(4): 385–392.

Alfes, K., Truss, C., Soane, E.C., Rees, C., and Gatenby, M. 2013. The relationship between line manager behavior, perceived HRM practices, and individual performance: examining the mediating role of engagement. *Human Resource Management*, 52(6): 839–859.

Applebaum, E., Batt, R., and Clark, I. 2013. Implications of financial capitalism for employment relations research: evidence from breach of trust and implicit contracts in private equity buyouts. *British Journal of Industrial Relations*, 51(3): 498–518.

Audenaert, M., Decramer, A., George, B., Verschuere, B., and Van Waeyenberg, T. 2019. When employee performance management affects individual innovation in public organizations: the role of consistency and LMX. *International Journal of Human Resource Management*, 30(5): 815–834.

Bedian, A.G. 1990. Research notes and communications choice and determinism: a comment. *Strategic Management Journal*, 11: 571–573.

Boland, T., and Fowler, A. 2000. A systems perspective of performance management in public sector organisations. *International Journal of Public Sector Management*, 13(5): 417–446.

Boxall, P., and Macky, K. 2007. High-performance work systems and organisational performance: Bridging theory and practice. *Asia Pacific Journal of Human Resources*, 45(3): 261–270.

Boxall, P., and Macky, K. 2009. Research and theory on high-performance work systems: progressing the high involvement stream. *Human Resource Management Journal*, 19(1): 3–23.

Brown, M., and Lim, V.S. 2019. Understanding performance management and appraisal: supervisory and employee perspectives. In A. Wilkinson, N. Bacon, T. Redman and S. Snell (eds), *The SAGE Handbook of Human Resource Management* (pp. 191–209). London: SAGE Publications.

Brown, W. 1972. A consideration of custom and practice. *British Journal of Industrial Relations*, 10(1): 42–61.

Brown, W. 1973. *Piecework Bargaining*. London: Heinemann Educational Books.

Bruno, R., and Jordan, L. 2002. Lean production and the discourse of dissent: radicalizing the shop floor at Mitsubishi Motors? *WorkingUSA*, 6(1): 108–134.

Buckingham, M., and Coffman, C. 1999. *First, Break All the Rules: What the World's Greatest Managers do Differently*. Omaha, NE: Simon & Schuster.

Burgelman, R.A. 1983. A model of the interaction of strategic behaviour, corporate context and the concept of strategy. *Academy of Management Review*, 8(1): 61–70.

Burns, T., and Stalker, G. 1961. *The Management of Innovation*, 2nd edition. London: Tavistock Publications.

Child, J., and Partridge, B. 1982. *Lost Managers: Supervisors in Industry and Society*. Cambridge: Cambridge University Press.

Clegg, S.R. (1990), *Modern Organisations: Organisation Studies in the Postmodern World*. London: SAGE Publications.

Connolly, W.E. 2013. *The Fragility of Things: Self-Organizing Processes, Neo-Liberal Fantasies and Democratic Activism*. Durham, NC: Duke University Press.

Conway, E., and Monks, K. 2008. HR practices and commitment to change: an employee-level analysis. *Human Resource Management Journal*, 18(1): 72–89.

Cummings, T.G. 2015a. Open systems. In C. Cooper (ed.), *Wiley Encyclopedia of Management*, vol. 11, 3rd edition. Chichester: Wiley.

Cummings, T.G. 2015b. Systems theory. In C. Cooper (ed.), *Wiley Encyclopedia of Management*, vol. 11 3rd edition. Chichester: Wiley.

Cushen, J., and Harney, B. 2014. Broken promises: why SHRM does not always work. In B. Harney and K. Monks (eds), *Strategic HRM: Research and Practice in Ireland* (pp. 227–246). Dublin: Orpen.

Dawkins, C.E., and Barker, J.R. 2018. A complexity theory framework of issue movement. *Business and Society*, 59(6): 1110–1150.

Delaney, J.T., and Huselid, M.A. 1996. The impact of human resource management practices on perceptions of organizational performance. *Academy of Management Journal*, 39(4): 949–969.

DeNisi, A.S., and Smith, C.E. 2014. Performance appraisal, performance management, and firm-level performance: a review, a proposed model, and new directions for future research. *Academy of Management Annals*, 8(1): 127–179.

Edwards, P., Gilman, M., Ram, M., and Arrowsmith, J. 2002. Public policy, the performance of firms and the 'missing middle': the case of employment regulation and role for local business networks. *Policy Studies*, 32(1): 5–20.

Evans, S. 2015. Juggling on the line: front line managers and their management of human resources in the retail industry. *Employee Relations*, 37(4): 459–474.

Ezzamel, M., Wilmott, H., and Worthington, F. 2001. Power, control and resistance in the factory that time forgot. *Journal of Management Studies*, 28(8): 1053–1079.

Farndale, E., and Paauwe, J. 2018. SHRM and context: why firms want to be as different as legitimately possible. *Journal of Organizational Effectiveness: People and Performance*, 5: 202–210.

Finkelstein, S., and Peteraf, M. 2007. Managerial activities: a missing link in management discretion theory. *Strategic Organization*, 5(3): 237–248.

Floyd, S.W., and Wooldridge, B. 1996. *The Strategic Middle Manager: How to Create and Sustain Competitive Advantage*. San Francisco, CA: Jossey-Bass.

Floyd, S.W., and Wooldridge, B. 1997. Middle management's strategic influence and organizational performance. *Journal of Management Studies*, 34(3): 465–485.

Fu, N., Flood, P.C., Rousseau, D.M., and Morris, T. 2020. Line managers as paradox navigators in HRM implementation: balancing consistency and individual responsiveness. *Journal of Management*, 46(2): 203–233.

Garavan, T.N., McCarthy, A., Lai, Y., Clarke, N., Carbery, R., et al. 2021. Putting the system back into training and firm performance research: a review and research agenda. *Human Resource Management Journal*, 31(4): 870–903.

Gittel, J. 2000. The paradox of coordination and control. *California Management Review*, 42(3): 101–117.

Gouldner, A.W. 1954. *Patterns of Industrial Bureaucracy*. New York: Free Press.

Gratton, L., Hope-Hailey, V., Stiles, P., and Truss, C. 1999. *Strategic Human Resource Management: Corporate Rhetoric and Human Reality*. Oxford: Oxford University Press.

Guest, D. 1997. Human resource management and performance: a review and research agenda. *International Journal of Human Resource Management*, 8(3): 263–276.

Guest, D.E., Sanders, K., Rodrigues, R., and Oliveira, T. 2021. Signalling theory as a framework for analysing human resource management processes and integrating human resource attribution theories: a conceptual analysis and empirical exploration. *Human Resource Management Journal*, 31(3): 796–818.

Hales, C. 2005. Rooted in supervision, branching into management: continuity and change in the role of first-line manager. *Journal of Management Studies*, 42(3): 471–506.

Hales, C. 2007. Structural contradiction and sense-making in the first-line manager role. *Irish Journal of Management*, 28(1): 147–179.

Harley, B. 2015. 'The one best way?' 'Scientific' research on HRM and the threat to critical scholarship. *Human Resource Management*, 25(4): 399–407.

Harney, B. 2009. Exploring the road less travelled in HRM–performance research: a critical realist alternative to big science. *Proceedings of the Labor and Employment Relations Association 61st Annual Meeting*, LERA.

Harney, B. 2019. Systems theory: forgotten legacy and future prospects. In K. Townsend, K. Cafferkey, A. McDermott and T. Dundon (eds), *Elgar Introduction to Theories of Human Resources and Employment Relations* (pp. 112–127). Cheltenham, UK and Northampton, MA, USA: Edward Elgar Publishing.

Harney, B., and Cafferkey, K. 2014. The role of the line manager in HRM–performance research. In P. Davim and C. Machado (eds), *Work Organization and Human Resource Management*. London: Springer, pp.43–53.

Harney, B., and Collings, D.G. 2021. Navigating the shifting landscapes of HRM. *Human Resource Management Review*, https://doi.org/10.1016/j.hrmr.2021.100824.

Harney, B., and Dundon, T. 2006. Capturing complexity: Developing an integrated approach to analysing HRM in SMEs. *Human Resource Management Journal*, 16(1): 48–73.

Harney, B., and Jordan, C. 2008. Unlocking the black box: line managers and HRM performance in a call centre context. *International Journal of Productivity and Performance Management*, 57(4): 275–296.

Harney, B., Dundon, T., and Wilkinson, A. 2018. Employment relations and human resource management. In A. Wilkinson, T. Dundon, J. Donaghey and A. Covin (eds), *Routledge Companion of Employment Relations* (pp. 122–138). London: Routledge.

Harris, L. 2001. Rewarding employee performance: line manager's values, beliefs and perspectives. *International Journal of Human Resource Management*, 12(7): 1182–1192.

Heffernan, M., Cafferkey, K., Harney, B., Townsend, K., and Dundon, T. 2022. HRM system strength and employee well-being: the role of internal process and open systems. *Asia Pacific Journal of Human Resources*, 60(1): 171–193.

Hutchinson, S. 2008. The role of front line managers in bringing policies to life. CESR Review, April. Bristol: UWE Bristol.

Hutchinson, S., and Purcell, J. 2010. Managing ward managers for roles in HRM in the NHS: overworked and under-resourced. *Human Resource Management Journal*, 20(4): 357–374.

Iwu, C.G., Kapondoro, L., Twum-Darko, M., and Lose, T. 2016. Strategic human resource metrics: a perspective of the general systems theory. *Acta Universitatis Danubius: Oeconomica*, 12(2): 5–24.

Jackson, S.E., Schuler, R.S., and Jiang, K. 2014. An aspirational framework for strategic HRM. *Academy of Management Annals*, 8(1): 1–56.

Katz, D., and Kahn, R.L. 1966. *The Social Psychology of Organizations*. New York: John Wiley & Sons.

Kehoe, R.R., and Han, J.H. 2020. An expanded conceptualization of line managers' involvement in human resource management. *Journal of Applied Psychology*, 105(2): 111–129.

Koehler, W. 1969. Closed and open systems. In F.E. Emery (ed.), *Systems Thinking* (pp. 59–59). Harmondsworth: Penguin.

Koehler, W. 1981. Closed and open systems. In F.E. Emery (ed.), *Systems Thinking* (2nd edition, pp. 59–69). Harmondsworth: Penguin Books.

Lee, Q.Y., Townsend, K., and Wilkinson, A. 2021. Frontline managers' implementation of the formal and informal performance management systems. *Personnel Review*, 50(1): 379–398.

Leonard, E., and Trusty, K. 2016. *Supervision: Concepts and Practices of Management* (13th edition). Boston, MA: Cengage Learning.

Lewis, P.S., Goodman, S.H., Fandt, P.M., and Michlitsch, J.F. 2013. *Management: Challenges for Tomorrow's Leaders* (5th edition). Mason, OH: Thomson South-Western.

Liang, H., Saraf, N., Hu, Q., and Xue, Y. 2007. Assimilation of enterprise systems: the effect of institutional pressures and the mediating role of top management. *MIS Quarterly*, 31(1): 59–87.

Lindblom, C.E. 1959. The science of 'muddling through'. *Public Administration Review*, 19: 79–88.

Marchington, M., and Parker, P. 1990. *Changing Patterns of Employee Relations*. Brighton: Harvester Wheatsheaf.

Marchington, M., and Suter, J. 2013. Where informality really matters: patterns of employee involvement and participation (EIP) in a non-union firm. *Industrial Relations: A Journal of Economy and Society*, 52(1): 284–313.

McClean, E., and Collins, C.J. 2019. Expanding the concept of fit in strategic human resource management: an examination of the relationship between human resource practices and charismatic leadership on organizational outcomes. *Human Resource Management*, 58(2): 187–202.

McGovern, P., Gratton, L., Hope Hailey, V., Stiles, P., and Truss, C. 1997. Human resource management on the line? *Human Resource Management Journal*, 7(4): 12–29.

Meyer, A., Tsui, A., and Hinings, C.R. 1993. Configurational approaches to organisational analysis. *Academy of Management Journal*, 36(6): 1175–1195.

Mintzberg, H. 1973. *The Nature of Managerial Work*. New York: Harper Row.

Mollick, E. 2012. People and process, suits and innovators: the role of individuals in firm performance *Strategic Management Journal*, 33(1): 1001–1015.

Nadler, D.A., and Tushman, M.L. 1980. A model for diagnosing organizational behavior. *Organizational Dynamics*, 9(2): 35–51.

Nehles, A., van Riemsdijk, M., Kok, I., and Looise, J. 2006. Implementing human resource management successfully: a first-line management challenge. *Management Revue*, 17(3): 256–273.

Nishii, L., and Paluch, R. 2018. Leaders as HR sensegivers: four HR implementation behaviors that create stron HR systems. *Human Resource Management Review*, 28(3): 319–323.

Pech, R. 2001. Reflections: Termites, group behaviour, and the loss of innovation: conformity rules! *Journal of Managerial Psychology*, 16(7): 559–574.

Purcell, J., and Hutchinson, S. 2007. Frontline managers as agents in the HRM–performance causal chain: theory, analysis and evidence. *Human Resource Management Journal*, 17(1): 3–20.

Renwick, D. 2003. Line manager involvement in HRM: an inside view. *Employee Relations*, 25(3): 262–280.

Roh, J. 2018. Improving the government performance management system in South Korea. *Asian Education and Development Studies*, 7(3): 266–278.

Saville, J., and Higgins, M. 1994. *Australian Management: A First-Line Perspective*. South Melbourne: Macmillan Education Australia.

Schleicher, D., Baumann, H., Sullivan, D., Levy, P.E., Hargrove, D., and Barros-Rivera, B. 2018. Putting the system into performance management systems: a review and agenda for performance management research. *Journal of Management*, 44(6): 2209–2245.

Scott, R.W. 1995. *Institutions and Organizations*. Thousand Oaks, CA: Sage.

Scott, R.W. 2003. *Organizations: Rational, Natural and Open Systems* (5th edition). London: Pearson International.

Selznick, P. 1981. Foundations of the theory of organizations. In F.E. Emery (ed.), *Systems Thinking* (2nd edition, pp. 301–321). Harmondsworth: Penguin Books.

Severance, F.L. 2001. *Systems Modelling and Simulation: An Introduction*. Chichester: John Wiley & Sons.

Shin, D., and Konrad, A.M. 2014. Causality between high-performance work systems and organizational performance. *Journal of Management*, 43(4): 973–997.

Sikora, D., and Ferris, G.R. 2014. Strategic human resource practice implementation: the critical role of line management. *Human Resource Management Review*, 14(3): 271–281

Stacey, R.D. 1995. The science of complexity: an alternative perspective for strategic change process. *Strategic Management Journal*, 12: 477--495.

Steffensen, D.S., Ellen, B.P., Wang, G., and Ferris, G.R. 2019. Putting the 'management' back in human resource management: a review and agenda for future research. *Journal of Management*, 45(6): 2387–2418.

Stiles, P., Gratton, L., Truss, C., Hope Hailey, V., and McGovern, P. 1997. Performance management and the psychological contract. *Human Resource Management Journal*, 7: 57–66.

Teague, P., and Roche, B. 2011. Line managers and the management of workplace conflict: evidence from Ireland. *Human Resource Management Journal*, 22(3): 235–251.

Terry, M. 1977. The inevitable growth of informality. *British Journal of Industrial Relations*, 15(1): 76–90.

Thompson, J.D. 1967 [2005]. *Organizations in Action: Social Science Bases of Administrative Theory*. New Brunswick, NJ: Transaction Publications.

Thompson, P., and McHugh, D. 1995. *Work Organisations: A Critical Introduction* (2nd edition). London: Macmillan Press.

Townsend, K. 2014. The role of line managers in employee voice systems. In A. Wilkinson, J. Donaghey, T. Dundon and R.B. Freeman (eds), *Handbook of Research on Employee Voice* (pp. 155–169). Cheltenham, UK and Northampton, MA, USA: Edward Elgar Publishing.

Townsend, K., Lawrence, S., and Wilkinson, A. 2013a. The role of hospitals' HRM in shaping clinical performance: a holistic approach. *International Journal of Human Resource Management*, 24(16): 3062–3085.

Townsend, K., Lawrence, S.A., and Wilkinson, A. 2013b. The role of hospitals' HRM in shaping clinical performance: a holistic approach. *International Journal of Human Resource Management*, 24(16): 3062–3085.

Trullen, J., Bos-Nehles, A., and Valverde, M. 2020. From intended to actual and beyond: a cross-disciplinary view of (human resource management) implementation. *International Journal of Management Reviews*. https://doi.org/10.1111/ijmr.12220(n/a).

Truss, C. 2001. Complexities and controversies in linking HRM with organizational outcomes. *Journal of Management Studies*, 38(8): 1121–1149.

Von Bertalanffy, L. 1968. *General Systems Theory: Foundations, Developments and Applications*. New York: George Braziller.

Westley, F. 1990. Middle managers and strategy: the microdynamics of inclusion. *Strategic Management Journal*, 11(1), 337–351.

Wilkinson, A., Dundon, T., and Grugulis, I. 2007. Information but not consultation: exploring employee involvement in SMEs. *International Journal of Human Resource Management*, 18(7): 1279–1297.

Wood, S. 1979. A reappraisal of the contingency approach to organisation. *Journal of Management Studies*, 16(3): 334–354.

Woodward, J. 1965. *Industrial Organisation: Theory and Practice*. Oxford: Oxford University Press.

Wright, P.M., McMahan, G., Snell, S., and Gerhart, B. 2001. Comparing line and HR executives' perceptions of HR effectiveness: services, roles and contributions. *Human Resource Management*, 40(2): 111–123.

Wright, P.M., and Snell, S.A. 1991. Toward an integrative view of strategic human resource management. *Human Resource Management Review*, 1(3): 203–225.

Zhu, C.J., Cooper, B., De Cieri, H., and Thomson, S.B. 2013. Devolvement of HR practices in transitional economies: evidence from China. In M. Warner (ed.), *Human Resource Management 'With Chinese Characteristics': Facing the Challenges of Globalization* (pp. 70–85). Oxford: Routledge.

3. Fitting the line: a review of person–environment fit theory in line manager research

Adam Robertson and Jennifer Chelsea Veres

Over the last few decades, an increasing body of literature has focused on understanding the unique role line managers play in the modern organisation (e.g., Bos-Nehles et al., 2013; Hales, 2005, 2006/2007; Townsend, 2013; Townsend and Hutchinson, 2017). Line managers are responsible for directly managing individual employees or teams, and in turn, report to a higher level of management on the performance and well-being of the employees or teams they manage (CIPD, 2019). Irrespective of this integral role, research remains limited in understanding how line managers navigate the unique context of their work environment and take part in organisational human resource (HR) practices (Townsend and Hutchinson, 2017; Tyskbo, 2020). Without a clear understanding of the 'how', we are limited in our ability to differentiate between the pressures line managers face as both 'the managers' and 'the managed' (Townsend and Hutchinson, 2017). Person–environment (P-E) fit theory provides a unique lens to understand this missing area of line manager research.

As a process-oriented theory, P-E fit generally considers the degree to which an individual's characteristics are compatible with their environment (Harrison, 1985). In an organisational context, this reflects the degree to which a line manager's characteristics, such as their attitudes, behaviours or individual-level outcomes, result from the interaction with the organisational environment in which they work (Edwards, 1996). Although P-E fit theory has its roots in over 100 years of management literature (Kristof-Brown et al., 2005), a renewed focus on theoretical development in the last two decades has led to a surge of new research (e.g. Edwards, 2008; Edwards and Cable, 2009; Shipp and Jansen, 2011; Van Vianen, 2018; Vleugels et al., 2018a, 2018b). Given this renewed interest and development, our chapter seeks to understand the applicability of P-E fit theory in line manager research.

Our chapter makes three key contributions to the evolving literature on line managers. First, our chapter provides a helpful guide for researchers applying P-E fit theory to line manager research. By outlining the history, current conceptualisations, methodological considerations and recent advancements in P-E fit theory, we provide researchers with a practical starting point to expand their understanding of the theory and apply it to investigate new and exciting research questions. Second, this chapter provides a detailed summary of P-E fit theory and line manager research at different levels of management. Line manager researchers have continually called for a better understanding of how managers at the frontline, middle and senior levels of management are managed, supervised and negotiate the demands of their daily work life (McCarthy et al., 2010; Townsend, 2013; Townsend and Hutchinson, 2017). By reviewing the P-E fit and line manager literature, we can better understand how the individual characteristics of line managers at different levels of the organisation are influenced by the competing demands and requirements of their working environment.

Finally, while the P-E fit literature has no shortage of reviews (e.g. Arthur et al., 2006; Edwards, 1991; Kristof-Brown et al., 2005; Van Vianen, 2018), the focus has been on individuals and not the specific experiences of line managers. This concern is compounded by the fact that previous reviews have not differentiated between managers at frontline, middle or senior levels of management. By providing an illustrative review of the P-E fit and line manager literature, we provide helpful insight into the areas that have been investigated and those which are ripe for future research.

We begin by providing line manager researchers with a detailed overview of the history, current conceptualisations, methodological considerations and recent advancements of P-E fit theory. We then review the literature and provide an overview of the existing P-E fit and line manager research, identifying a number of methodological and theoretical shortcomings. Finally, we provide researchers with several suggestions for future research that can advance our understanding of line managers.

HISTORY AND CURRENT CONCEPTUALISATIONS OF PERSON–ENVIRONMENT FIT THEORY

P-E fit theory is grounded in Lewin's (1951) behavioural research, suggesting that an individual's behaviour is a function of the person (P) and their environment (E) rather than the person and the environment separately. P-E fit theory operates on the assumption that individuals desire to fit with their environment, as this allows for general consistency, reduced uncertainty and, ultimately, an increase in satisfaction (Yu, 2013). The theory gained popularity in the 1970s and 1980s as an effective lens to study the psychological processes underpinning stress (Edwards and Cooper, 1990; Pervin, 1967). The field of psychology had often debated whether stress was a function of the 'person' or the 'situation' (Mischel, 2009). By utilising a P-E fit perspective, scholars understood individual stress as the misfit between the characteristics of an individual and their environment (French et al., 1982). As stated by Rauthmann et al. (2015, p. 363), 'the person and the situation at any given moment are inextricably interwoven'.

P-E fit theory is operationalised around three basic principles (Van Vianen, 2018). First, the combination of the person and the environment is a more powerful predictor of individual attitudes, behaviours and outcomes than either component in isolation (Schneider, 1987). Second, individuals will experience more significant outcomes when personal and environmental attributes are congruent (Harrison, 1978). Third, in the absence of congruence, known as misfit, individuals may experience negative psychological, physiological and behavioural outcomes, known as 'strains' (Edwards and Cooper, 1990). Misfit can be experienced as both deficiency and excess (Edwards et al., 1998). Deficiency occurs when the environment offers less than the individual needs, whereas excess occurs when the environment offers more than the individual needs (Van Vianen, 2018).

P-E fit theory has often been conceptualised as a process theory because it articulates the mechanisms by which person and environment constructs influence strain, without specifying the particular content dimensions on which the person and the environment should be examined (Harrison, 1985). This conceptualisation has led scholars to break down the theory into five key types of P-E fit: person–vocation, person–job, person–organisation, person–group and person–supervisor fit (Kristof-Brown et al., 2005). These five types of fit are categorised as either complementary or supplementary fit.

Complementary fit occurs when an individual's characteristics fill a gap in the current environment, or vice versa (Kristof-Brown et al., 2005). This is accomplished through a fit between environmental supplies and personal motives, goals and values (that is, supplies–values or S-V fit), or a fit between environmental demands and personal skills and abilities (that is, demands–ability or D-A fit) (French et al., 1982). The two key types of complementary fit are person–vocation and person–job fit. Alternatively, supplementary fit 'exists when the individual and environment are similar' (Kristof-Brown et al., 2005: 288). The three key types of supplementary fit are person–organisation, person–group and person–supervisor fit.

Complementary Types of Fit

Person–vocation fit (P-V fit), arguably one of the broader types of fit, refers to matching individuals with careers that meet their interests (Kristof-Brown et al., 2005). P-V fit draws from Holland's (1985) model of vocational personality types, which argues that individuals are drawn to work environments in which they are able to express their interests. Personality profiles in Holland's model are categorised as realistic, investigative, artistic, social, enterprising and conventional (Van Vianen, 2018). It is suggested that individuals predominantly possess one of these personality profiles, and will experience the best fit or congruence with careers that match their profile.

Person–job fit (P-J fit) refers to the relationship between an individual's characteristics and those of the job or task required (Kristof-Brown et al., 2005). There are two key conceptualisations of P-J fit. The first refers back to the aforementioned demands–abilities fit (D-A fit). Here, employee knowledge, skills and abilities align with the requirements of the task or the job. The second conceptualisation refers to the aforementioned supply–values fit (S-V fit), which is the degree to which an employee's needs, desires or preferences are being met by the jobs they perform (Kristof-Brown et al., 2005).

Supplementary Types of Fit

Person–organisation fit (P-O fit) addresses the degree of compatibility or fit between an employee and their entire organisation. P-O fit was first conceptualised by Tom (1971), who proposed that individuals are most successful in organisations that share their same personalities. In the beginning, P-O fit tended to be operationalised through the lens of personality–climate congruence (Christiansen et al., 1997). However, the subsequent validation of the 'organisation culture profile' (O'Reilly et al., 1991) solidified value congruence as the defining operationalisation of P-O fit (Kristof-Brown et al., 2005).

Person–group fit (P-G fit) focuses on the interpersonal compatibility between individuals and their workgroups (Judge and Ferris, 1992; Werbel and Gilliland, 1999). This area of fit research has received limited attention, with the majority of research focusing on examining P-G fit on personality traits (Barsade et al., 2000; Hobman et al., 2003; Strauss et al., 2001).

Person–supervisor fit (P-S fit) looks at the dyadic relationships between individuals and their work environments, specifically the match between supervisors and subordinates (Van Vianen, 2000). This type of P-E fit is highlighted by investigations into leader–follower value congruence (Krishnan, 2002), supervisor–subordinate personality similarity (Schaubroeck and Simon, 2002) and manager–employee goal congruence (Witt, 1998).

PERSON–ENVIRONMENT FIT MEASUREMENT

The relationship between a person and their environment can be assessed using a direct or an indirect approach (Kristof-Brown et al., 2005). A direct approach, also known as 'perceived fit', asks an individual to make a direct assessment of their compatibility with the environment (Van Vianen, 2018). For example, 'to what extent do your knowledge, skills, and abilities match the requirements of the job?' (Saks and Ashforth, 1997: 406). Edwards et al. (2006) further break down this approach into 'molecular' and 'molar'. A molecular approach focuses on an individual's perceived misfit; whereas a molar approach involves directly measuring the perceived fit, match or similarity between the person and the environment.

Perceived fit is often considered the most proximal and robust predictor of individual decisions and behaviours (Kristof-Brown and Billsberry, 2013). However, scholars have often criticised this approach as a weak conceptualisation of fit theory (Van Vianen, 2018). Specifically, perceptions of direct fit are believed to be influenced by cognitive manipulation, making them less reliable and subject to consistency biases (Kristof-Brown et al., 2005). Assessments of direct fit also tend to have high correlations with job attitudes, suggesting that individual behaviour may result from an affective reaction to job satisfaction rather than the perceived fit between personal and environmental attributes (Edwards et al., 2006). Finally, because direct approaches to fit conflate the person and the environment, they are unable to provide an understanding of how different levels of personal and environmental attributes interact to influence individual behaviour (Edwards et al., 2006). For this reason, direct approaches to fit cannot investigate all three basic principles of P–E fit theory (Van Vianen, 2018).

In contrast to the above, an indirect approach assesses P–E fit by comparing separately measured person and environment variables (Edwards et al., 2006). For example, 'what level of formal education do you feel is needed by a person in a job such as yours? … How much schooling have you had?' (French et al., 1982: 20). Indirect assessments of person and environment variables can be obtained directly from the individual, known as subjective fit; or from other sources, known as objective fit (Van Vianen, 2018). Utilising this approach, fit is determined by the level of discrepancy between the variables, with lower levels of discrepancies representing higher levels of fit (Van Vianen, 2018).

Early applications of fit theory calculated the level of discrepancy using the algebraic, absolute or quadratic difference between a single personal and environmental attribute, or using the correlation between a set of personal and environmental attributes (Van Vianen, 2018). While popular in the 1980s to early 2000s, the use of difference scores has grown out of favour for several reasons, such as poor reliability, reduced interpretation, untested constraints, and reducing an inherently three-dimensional relationship between the two component measures and an outcome variable to two dimensions (Edwards, 2002).

The disadvantages associated with difference scores have led to the use of polynomial regression response surface analysis (PRRSA) to investigate the level of discrepancy between personal and environmental attributes (Kristof-Brown et al., 2005). The benefit of PRRSA is that it avoids collapsing person and environment measures onto a single score and instead includes both measures and their higher-ordered terms (P^2, PxE, E^2) as predictors of an outcome (Edwards and Parry, 1993). This approach allows for the creation of a three-dimensional surface plot that provides a more detailed understanding of the relationship (Kristof-Brown et al., 2005).

Overall, indirect assessments of fit are often more reliable, less prone to consistency biases, and allow for the complete testing of the three basic principles of P-E fit theory (Van Vianen, 2018). However, this approach is not without shortcomings. Indirect approaches to fit rest on the assumption that combining separate measures of personal or environmental attributes is a proxy for an individual's cognitive comparison process (Edwards et al., 2006). However, little is known about how individuals combine beliefs about themselves and their environment into perceptions of P-E fit (Edwards et al., 2006). Therefore, these linkages may not be so straightforward. Furthermore, while PRRSA offers several methodological advantages over direct or difference score approaches, many scholars have failed to properly understand and apply the methodology (Cohen et al., 2010; Shanock et al., 2010). Therefore, we recommend that line manager researchers use caution when selecting a direct or indirect approach to P-E fit measurement.

RENEWED INTEREST IN PERSON–ENVIRONMENT FIT

Over the last decade, there has been increasing interest in applying P-E fit theory to unique organisational research questions. A search of the Web of Science database for the term *person* fit* identifies 193 articles published on P-E fit theory prior to 2010, and 382 articles published in the last decade. This renewed interest can likely be traced back to a call for theoretical advancement by Edwards (2008). Reviewing over 100 years of P-E fit research, Edwards (2008) suggested that the theory is being held back due to a failure to evaluate the status and development of the theory, promote the integration of different theoretical understandings of P-E fit, confront the actual meaning of fit, define the content of person and environment dimensions, and complete the cycle that runs from theory to empiricism and back to theory. By bringing attention to the stagnation and opportunity in P-E fit theory, scholars have begun focusing on two exciting theoretical opportunities: a move towards dynamic assessments of fit (Shipp and Jansen, 2011; Vleugels et al., 2018a) and fit profiles (Vleugels et al., 2018b).

The idea of dynamic fit is not new and can be traced back to Lewin (1943), who suggested that behaviour is a function of both the person and their psychological environment at a given time only. Unfortunately, although this approach accounts for the likelihood that changes in the environment may combine with changes in the person to influence fit (Edwards et al., 1998), the majority of fit research has become overly static and ignores the potential for temporal variability (Vleugels et al., 2018a). This is concerning, as a temporal context can provide a greater understanding of how individuals define and experience fit (Shipp and Jansen, 2011).

Thankfully, recent advancements in dynamic methodologies such as the experience sampling method (ESM) (e.g. Beal, 2015) have made it easier for scholars to investigate dynamic perceptions of P-E fit. The goal of dynamic fit research is to understand how individuals craft and make sense of their fit experiences, using recollections of past fit, perceptions of current fit, and anticipations of future fit (Shipp and Jansen, 2011). For example, perspectives of P-E fit may be momentarily intertwined with affect and performance, suggesting that line managers may alter their fit judgements based on their immediate experiences in the workplace (Vleugels et al., 2018a). Research into this area is still underdeveloped, but a few studies have reported that fit perceptions can vary daily (Kivlighan et al., 2015; Tepper et al., 2018; Vleugels et al., 2018a).

A dynamic fit perspective has also been used to advance research into P-E fit profiles (Vleugels et al., 2018b). This research challenges the idea that individuals will either fit or misfit their environment, suggesting that individuals may vary their perceived fit within predefined fit profiles. Whereas static perceptions of P-E fit suggest that high levels of fit result in more favourable outcomes, a profile approach suggests that these static fit perceptions are only baselines and may be subject to increasing levels of variability (Vleugels et al., 2018b). Those individuals who have large fluctuations around their average level of fit may experience different thoughts, feelings and behaviours in the workplace compared to those with more stable fit profiles. While research into this area is still evolving, initial results suggest that individuals can be classified into five different categories depending on their average level and variability of fit perceptions: stable fits, dynamic fits, mavericks, weak fits and misfits (Vleugels et al., 2018b). This research also suggests that fit and misfit are not dichotomous constructs, as individuals can experience both congruence and incongruence at different times within a predefined fit profile. Thus, it may be advantageous for an organisation to hire a line manager who displays the correct composition of fit and misfit instead of hiring a line manager who fits perfectly. Overall, by applying a dynamic fit or fit profile approach, researchers can advance their understanding of line manager experiences at work.

A REVIEW OF PERSON–ENVIRONMENT FIT AND LINE MANAGERS RESEARCH

In light of these increasing trends, it is appropriate to review the literature emerging on P-E fit and line managers to create a clearer understanding of the different lines of enquiry. Specifically, we aim to examine the role that P-E fit has played in research investigating the work experiences of line managers. To achieve this, we have performed an illustrative review of the literature between 1980 and 2020 on the topic of P-E fit and line managers at all levels of management.

We adopted an approach utilised by Tse et al. (2018) to conduct our review. First, we ran a search for *person* fit, congruence* and *manager* in the Web of Science database.[1] We aimed to provide an overview of P-E fit theory's current conceptualisations and applications in line manager research. Thus, we limited our search to empirical articles published since 1980. To ensure that we captured only those articles that conjointly discussed P-E fit and line managers, we rejected any article dealing with *person* fit, congruence*, or *managers* alone. Our initial search resulted in 581 relevant articles. These results were further filtered to include only those journals that had an 'A' or better ranking by the Australian Business Deans Council (ABDC, 2019), or a Clarivate Analytics Web of Science two-year impact factor greater than 1.50 in the category of 'Business', 'Management', 'Applied Psychology', 'Social Psychology', 'Healthcare', 'Public Administration' and 'Hospitality/Tourism'. This filter reduced our results to 143 relevant articles.

Two additional filtering steps were implemented to ensure that the articles were relevant to both P-E fit theory and line manager research alike. First, we reviewed the title, abstract and keywords of all articles to ensure that each one met our search criteria. This review reduced

---

[1]   '*' is a wildcard term allowing us to capture all types of P-E fit.

Table 3.1   *P-E fit and line manager research in peer-reviewed journals, 1980–2020*

Journal	2-year impact factor	Number of articles published
Asia Pacific Journal of Management	3.064	1
Australian Journal of Management	1.065	1
Frontiers in Psychology	2.067	1
Health Care Management Review	2.667	1
International Journal of Manpower	0.953	1
Journal of Applied Psychology	5.851	1
Journal of Business Ethics	4.141	5
Journal of Business and Psychology	3.289	2
Journal of Business Research	4.874	1
Journal of Occupational and Organizational Psychology	2.652	1
Journal of Organizational Behavior	5.026	1
Journal of Public Administration Research and Theory	3.289	1
Leadership Quarterly	6.642	1
Organizational Behavior and Human Decision Processes	2.304	1
Personality and Individual Differences	2.311	1
Public Administration Review	4.063	2
		N = 22

our results to 54 relevant articles. Next, we downloaded the remaining articles and performed an in-depth review of the literature review, methodology and discussion sections to ensure that each article contributed to the P-E fit and line manager literature. Our in-depth review established that while some of the articles discussed both P-E fit and line managers, their focus was on employees rather than line managers specifically. We also found several articles that focused on self–other and perceptual agreement rather than fit. As these studies typically do not assess how well the line manager 'fits' with the organisational context, we removed them in line with previous reviews into P-E fit theory (e.g. Kristof-Brown et al., 2005; Van Vianen, 2018). Following this in-depth process, 22 peer-reviewed articles examining P-E fit and line managers remained for analysis. These articles were published in top-tier journals between 1980 and 2020. Table 3.1 contains a summary of journal titles, highlighting the number of articles published in each journal.

Our review indicates that four P-E fit types have been used to understand line managers across the frontline, middle, senior and aggregated levels of management: (1) person–vocation (P-V fit); (2) person–job (P-J fit); (3) person–organisation (P-O fit); and (4) person–supervisor (P-S fit). We also found one qualitative article that focused on P-E fit theory instead of a specific type of fit. As each fit type has its focus, accompanying mechanisms and assumptions that guided the development of hypotheses, we have summarised our findings according to the fit type. Table 3.2 summarises the articles in our review, organised by fit type and line manager hierarchical level.

Person–Environment Fit (P-E Fit)

Although most P-E fit research focuses on a specific type of fit (Kristof-Brown et al., 2005; Van Vianen, 2018), our review uncovered a qualitative article that focused on P-E fit theory and line managers more comprehensively. In contrast to the remaining articles in our review, Ashforth et al. (2017) investigated a relatively nascent area of research that explores the impact

Table 3.2   *P-E fit type, line manager level and topic areas*

Person–environment fit type	Level of line manager	Topic areas in P-E fit and line manager research	Number of articles	Example studies
Person–environment fit (non-specific)	Line managers (aggregate)	Congruence work: behaviours, sensemaking and sensegiving that help individuals to adjust and develop a stronger sense of person–environment fit	1	Ashforth et al., 2017
Person–vocation fit	Line managers (aggregate)	Vocational personality and work environment congruence	2	Furnham et al., 1995; Donohue, 2014
Person–job fit	Line managers (aggregate)	Demands–ability fit; manager–environment social/cultural skill congruence	2	Devloo et al., 2011; Wang et al., 2017
Person–organisation fit	Senior	Employee–organisation value congruence; manager–organisation corporate identity meaning congruence; manager–organisation value congruence	3	Huang et al., 2005; Flint et al., 2018; Macinati et al., 2018
	Middle	Employee–organisation value congruence	1	Jensen, 2017
	Frontline	Manager–organisation goal congruence	1	Zhang et al., 2018
	Line managers (aggregate)	Manager–organisation value congruence; manager–organisation ethical congruence	5	Posner and Schmidt, 1993; Elango et al., 2010; Posner, 2010; Suar and Khuntia, 2010; Coursey et al., 2012
Person–supervisor fit	Senior	Leader–employee moral development congruence; supervisor–subordinate emotional intelligence similarity	2	Schminke et al., 2005; Sears and Holmvall, 2010
	Middle	Managers–employee gender congruence	1	Grissom et al., 2012
	Frontline	Leader–member demographic similarity; supervisor–subordinate goal congruence; manager–subordinate value congruence	3	Pelled and Xin, 1997; Witt, 1998; Isaac et al., 2004
	Line managers (aggregate)	Managers–subordinates cognitive style congruence	1	Allinson et al., 2001

of line managers on employee fit. Specifically, the authors investigated the role of 'congruence work', which they define as 'behaviors, sensemaking, and sense giving that [line managers] engage in to increase perceptions of fit between aspects of the environment and others and/or themselves' (ibid.: 1264). The authors found that across multiple hierarchical levels, line managers engage in three practices that help new employees to increase their perceptions of fit when performing 'dirty work', which they define as occupations that are physically, socially or morally tainted.

First, managers can help overcome an employees' aversion to dirty work by actively engaging in the recruitment/selection process. Specifically, managers should select individuals with an affinity for the work and provide them with a realistic job preview to help foreshadow the job requirements and demands. Second, managers can help new employees to adjust to their role by engaging in a socialisation process that helps employees to develop perspective-taking skills, manage external relationships, and immerse themselves into the role. Finally, managers can help to strengthen an employees' fit by fostering their social validation, mitigating their exposure or harm from the salient hazards of dirty work, and helping them to distinguish between the public and private spaces where stigmatised tasks are undertaken. Specifically, managers should select individuals with an affinity for the work and provide them with a realistic job preview to help foreshadow the job requirements and demands. This exciting and relatively underdeveloped area of research will be discussed further within the future research directions of this chapter.

Person–Vocation Fit (P-V Fit)

Our review identified two articles that investigate person–vocation fit and line managers at the aggregated level of management. Both articles focused on the congruence between a line manager's vocational personality and their corresponding work environment. Furnham et al. (1995) identified that the congruence between personality and work environment led to increased job satisfaction amongst line managers. Subsequent research by Donohue (2014) further explored this relationship and found that congruence was also a strong predictor of whether line managers would persist in or change their careers. Donohue's research suggests that those managers who persisted in their careers had greater congruence and stronger vocational identity than managers who changed careers. To this point, managers who had changed careers were more likely to move into new positions that were more congruent with their vocational personality. These results suggest that organisations should provide a working environment that aligns with a line manager's vocational personality.

Person–Job Fit (P-J Fit)

Our review uncovered two articles that investigated person–job fit and line managers at the aggregated level of management. The first study investigated line managers' home and host value congruence, using interviews from 25 Chinese expatriate managers (Wang et al., 2017). The results suggest that expatriate line managers may need to exert more effort into developing interpersonal, perceptual and communication skills while working in developed countries, to cope with incongruent home and host values. In contrast, while working in less-developed countries, line managers should focus on self-maintenance skills, such as stress reduction and self-confidence, which are required due to the more demanding host-country circumstances. Overall, the researchers found that line managers can achieve greater cross-cultural adjustment by displaying greater home and host cultural congruence.

The second study investigated the role of line managers' beliefs and ideas about the malleability of their personality traits in understanding how demands–ability (D-A) misfit influences feedback-seeking behaviour (Devloo et al., 2011). In a study of 303 line managers, researchers found that when a line manager believes their personal attributes are malleable, as opposed to fixed, they are more likely to seek feedback from supervisors or peers when managerial tasks demands are incongruent with their abilities. However, this effect was only significant when demand and ability scores were low to average. When demand and ability scores were both high and congruent, feedback-seeking was highest. Interestingly, the positive effect of incongruence at low to average levels was found to be significant regardless of whether demands or abilities exceeded one another. This research suggests that line managers will seek to improve their skills through feedback-seeking regardless of whether organisational demands are high or low.

Person–Organisation Fit (P-O Fit)

Our review found ten articles investigating person–organisation fit at the frontline, middle, senior and aggregated levels of management. At the frontline level, we found one article investigating the influence of manager–organisation goal congruence on important employee work outcomes (Zhang et al., 2018). Specifically, the researchers found that line manager goal congruence strengthens the relationship between organisational-level high-performance work systems (HPWS) and employee-experienced HPWS. Furthermore, the interaction effect of goal congruence on organisation-level HPWS indirectly influenced employee job performance and satisfaction sequentially through employee-experienced HPWS and organisation-based self-esteem. At the middle manager level, we found one article suggesting that line manager transformational leadership training was positively related to employee–organisational value congruence (Jensen, 2017). However, these results were at a marginal significance level (0.076) and should be interpreted with caution.

Three of the ten articles from our review examined different types of congruence at the senior manager level. The first article investigated the influence of chief executive officer (CEO) leadership behaviours on employee–organisation value congruence (Huang et al., 2005). The researchers found that when CEOs displayed higher levels of charismatic leadership, employees were more likely to report value congruence with their organisation. Furthermore, when value congruence was higher, employees were more likely to put in extra effort, be satisfied with their leader, and become more committed to the organisation. Next, Macinati et al. (2018) found that higher involvement in managerial duties, such as budgetary participation, was positively related to senior manager–organisation value congruence. This value congruence was found to lead to greater levels of managerial job engagement and performance. The final article at the senior manager level was a qualitative analysis of 153 managers, which identified that managers might hold multiple meanings of organisational identity that they contextualise and apply as the situation requires (Flint et al., 2018). This ambidexterity of corporate identity meanings may prevent identity congruence between the manager and the organisation, but also allows the senior manager to create, alter or extend what their organisation is known for.

The remaining five P-O fit articles identified in our review investigated person–organisation fit at the aggregated management level. The first four of these articles investigated manager–organisation value congruence. One study suggested that managers who felt their personal values were more congruent with the organisations were more likely to report positive attitudes about their work and the ethical practices of their colleagues (Posner and Schmidt, 1993). In a follow-up study two decades later, value congruence was also found to result in stronger managerial bonds with their organisations and more positive affective feelings about their work and impact (Posner, 2010). Two further studies on manager–organisation value congruence suggested that congruence is positively related to public sector motivation, organisational commitment and job performance; and negatively related to unethical workplace practices (Coursey et al., 2012; Suar and Khuntia, 2010). The final article investigating person–organisation fit found that higher levels of ethical congruence between line managers and their organisation increase the likelihood that line managers will make positive ethical choices (Elango et al., 2010). Interestingly, the researchers also found that younger managers were more likely to be influenced by the organisation's ethics, whereas older managers were more likely to make ethical choices.

Person–Supervisor Fit (P-S Fit)

Concerning person–supervisor fit, our review identified seven articles that investigated line manager fit at the frontline, middle, senior and aggregated levels of management. At the frontline level, one study identified that supervisor–subordinate goal congruence effectively mitigated the negative impact of organisational politics on employee job commitment and performance (Witt, 1998). A second study looked at frontline supervisor–subordinate value congruence and found that supervisors can accurately estimate congruence of terminal values, which are values associated with desirable end-states of existence (Isaac et al., 2004). Unfortunately, frontline supervisors could not display awareness or estimate real value congruence for employee work and instrumental values, which are most relevant to achieving organisational goals. On the other hand, employees were only aware and able to estimate value congruence for frontline supervisor work values. The final study at the frontline level investigated gender congruence between frontline leader and member (Pelled and Xin, 1997). The researchers found that gender similarity negatively correlated with employee absence, which was stronger in dyads with female leaders. That is, female employees were less likely to be absent when their frontline manager was also a female.

At the middle manager level, we found one study investigating gender congruence of principals and teachers in elementary and secondary schools (Grissom et al., 2012). The results suggest that gender congruence has a significant effect, with lower satisfaction and higher turnover among male teachers with female principals. In contrast, female teachers reported similar ratings on outcomes irrespective of principal gender.

At the senior manager level, two studies investigated manager–employee moral development and emotional intelligence congruence. Results suggest that the highest levels of employee satisfaction and commitment, and the lowest levels of turnover, are associated with manager–employee congruence on ratings of moral development (Schminke et al., 2005). When employee moral development ratings were incongruent with their leader, these outcomes were found to be more harmful. However, the positive effects of congruence were most significant at moderate levels of moral development, with less pronounced effects reported at lower and higher levels of congruence. Another study investigated the similarity between manager–employee emotional intelligence (EI) and found a positive association between congruence and leader–member exchange (LMX) (Sears and Holmvall, 2010). These results suggest that higher levels of LMX are found in dyads with high levels of EI congruence between managers and employees. The final article, by Allinson et al. (2001), investigated person–supervisor fit at the aggregated management level. In a study of 142 manager–subordinate dyads at multiple levels in the organisation, the researchers identified that cognitive similarity between leaders and followers resulted in greater levels of employee-reported LMX.

Limitations of Findings

Our review of the literature provides an illustrative overview of P-E fit theory in line manager research. While it is encouraging to identify 22 articles published at the frontline, middle, senior and aggregated levels of management, a review of Figure 3.1 shows that the majority of fit theory research has been at the aggregated level of management. These articles look at two or more levels, or do not specify the level of management. This approach to line manager research is concerning, as line managers' roles, responsibilities and work experiences are

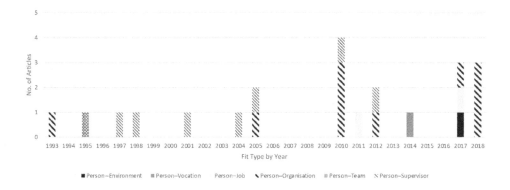

Figure 3.1　　*P-E fit and line manager research: line manager level by year*

unique to the level of management (Hales, 2005, 2006/2007; Townsend, 2013; Townsend and Hutchinson, 2017). Many important research questions investigating the work experiences of frontline, middle and senior managers remain unanswered. For example, given the increasing devolution of role responsibilities to frontline managers (FLMs) from higher levels of management (Hales, 2005, 2006/2007), how do FLMs manage the fit between their role demands and abilities (for example, D-A fit), and how does this influence their leadership behaviours?

Another limitation of the existing research is a focus on specific types of fit to the exclusion of others. A review of Figure 3.2 shows that most P-E fit line manager research, although limited, has primarily focused on person–organisation and person–supervisor fit. While these fit perspectives are important, additional questions concerning line manager person–vocation and person–job fit remain unanswered. Furthermore, our review uncovered no articles investigating line manager person–team fit, leaving substantial gaps in our understanding of line manager experiences within work teams.

Our review also uncovered several methodological limitations that raise concerns about the reliability of conclusions drawn from the literature. First, the majority of the articles utilised a cross-sectional research design. We did not find any articles that utilised a dynamic fit or temporal profiles approach to study line managers. A static approach to P-E fit research may provide an incomplete understanding of how line managers define and experience fit in the

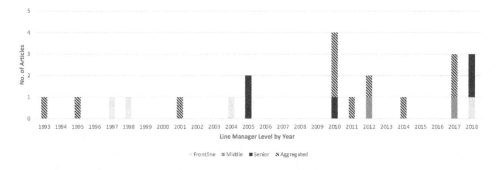

Figure 3.2　　*P-E fit and line manager research: P-E fit type by year*

workplace (Shipp and Jansen, 2011). Second, we identified eight articles that utilised difference scores to investigate P-E fit and line managers. As stated previously, the use of difference scores is highly problematic and raises questions about the reliability of the results (Edwards, 2002; Edwards and Parry, 1993).

Third, while it is encouraging to see the use of PRRSA in P-E fit line manager research, scholars appear to be having difficulty understanding the methodology. One of the critical features of response surface analysis is the first principal axis, which describes the overall orientation of the response surface (Edwards, 2002). This axis is used to determine where the response surface peaks or troughs (Edwards and Cable, 2009). Studies of congruence often hypothesise that the outcome (that is, job satisfaction) is maximised along the line of perfect congruence (Edwards and Parry, 1993). For this hypothesis to be confirmed, the first principal axis must have a slope of 1 and an intercept of 0 (Edwards and Cable, 2009). Otherwise, the response surface is rotated, and the outcome of interest is not maximised at congruence. In our review, both articles that utilised PRRSA did not investigate the first principal axis, or showed heavily rotated surfaces, thus raising doubts about the congruence effects reported.

Finally, we found ten articles that ignored the independence assumption of ordinary least squares (OLS) regression (Hofmann, 1997; Klein et al., 1994). For example, several studies utilised samples where subordinates were nested in dyads or workgroups with the same line manager, or multiple line managers nested in different organisations. This approach is concerning, as nesting reduces the independence of the sample and may influence the reliability of the results (Bliese, 2000; Klein et al., 1994). Opportunities to address these limitations in future research are discussed in the next section.

FUTURE RESEARCH OPPORTUNITIES

As outlined in our review, the use of P-E fit theory to explore and understand line managers has been relatively underutilised. This section seeks to make recommendations for future research. Our review of P-E fit and line manager research found that the literature has primarily focused on investigating person–organisation (P-O) and person–supervisor (P-S) fit in areas such as goal or value congruence. Understanding line managers' motivations through goal congruence and how line managers align with organisational values provides a helpful foundation for understanding job satisfaction (Locke, 1976), work design (Kulik et al., 1987), organisational culture (Schneider, 1987) and the quality of work-life (Rice et al., 1985). However, future research should go beyond understanding congruence in isolation and instead seek to understand the circumstances and outcomes surrounding line manager misfit. As optimal fit or congruence may not always be possible, and constantly striving to achieve optimal fit can inhibit individual capacity to learn, develop and adapt, focusing on instances of misfit can illuminate problematic attributes or outcomes that can ultimately reduce satisfaction (Van Vianen, 2018).

Further to this point, line manager researchers should also focus on other types of fit, in particular, person–vocation (P-V) fit and person–job (P-J) fit. Additional research investigating line manager P-V fit would allow for a more detailed examination of Holland's (1985) model of vocational personality in relation to all levels of line managers. Future research may also explore different personality models, such as the five-factor model (also known as the 'Big Five'). The Big Five is a commonly used framework to assess and evaluate social behaviour

(Costa and McCrae, 1992; Judge et al., 2002; Lievens et al., 2006), and has been used to examine outcomes such as job performance (Mount et al., 1998), leadership (Campbell et al., 2003; Judge et al., 2002) and team cohesion (Barrick et al., 1998). The Big Five personality model may provide a more comprehensive understanding of line managers' P-V fit than can be achieved using Holland's (1985) model.

Concerning P-J fit, future research could explore line manager fit perceptions in different parts of their role. The literature suggests that line managers are responsible for various organisational roles and responsibilities, such as planning/scheduling work, giving praise and coaching employees, and carrying out operational work tasks (Hales, 2005). Given the variety of work tasks, it may be possible for a line manager to experience fit in one part of their role and misfit in others. By applying a supplies–value (S-V) or demands–abilities (D-A) fit perspective, organisations can investigate the areas where line managers are succeeding and where they may require further training and development. By understanding how a line manager experiences P-J fit throughout the whole of their role, we can more clearly understand how line managers navigate their daily working lives.

It follows from these suggestions that future research should also examine P-E fit at the various levels of line managers. As highlighted throughout our review, much of P-E fit and line manager research has predominantly focused on the aggregated management level. However, Townsend and Kellner (2015) highlight the importance of delineating the different levels of line managers. In particular, the authors distinguish between frontline managers, middle managers and senior managers. As frontline managers are typically required to possess specific operational skills and knowledge (Townsend and Kellner, 2015), the use of P-V or P-J fit theory could provide a deeper understanding of how frontline managers fit with their role. In particular, examining Holland's (1985) model of vocational personality types in frontline managers could provide insight into the types of work environments in which they can express their interests. Further to this point, Kilroy and Dundon (2015) also explored different types of frontline managers, which they distinguish as policy enactors, organisational leaders and employee coaches. Future research could draw on these types of frontline managers and P-E fit theory to better understand each type of frontline manager.

Line manager researchers could also focus their investigations into the recruitment and selection processes of line managers. Townsend and Kellner (2015) suggest that future research should include models of recruitment and promotions based on the skills required for the new role. P-E fit theory allows for the examination of fit between environmental demands and personal skills and abilities – that is, demands–ability (D-A) fit (French et al., 1982) – indicating that P-E fit would be particularly useful to develop a more nuanced understanding of the recruitment and selection process. Townsend and Kellner (2015) also highlight the importance of understanding the relationships between frontline managers and the middle managers they report to. P-S fit is beneficial for understanding this relationship, and could be used to explore fit or misfit between frontline manager skills and abilities and the desired expectations driven by middle managers. To this point, line managers are likely to have several employees who report to them. For example, Townsend et al. (2016) indicate that line managers may be responsible for up to 200 subcontractors in a construction context. This organisational reality highlights the importance of considering context and sample, but also suggests that P-S fit may be helpful when examining the fit or misfit between line managers' expectations and the skills and abilities of subcontractors.

The valuable relationships that line managers establish with employees and supervisors high-light their unique challenges as 'the managers' and 'the managed'. A line manager occupies a unique 'person-in-the-middle' position that receives valuable resources and direction from above (Tangirala et al., 2007; Wilson et al., 2010) and distributes them to employees below (Eisenberger et al., 2020). In other words, a line manager occupies the role of the 'person' in their fit perceptions with the supervisor, and the role of the 'environment' in an employee's fit perceptions with the line manager. This organisational reality suggests an exciting future research avenue that explores how fit perceptions in one context can influence fit perceptions in another. For example, a line manager may experience poor value-congruence with their supervisor, which negatively influences their ability to acquire resources from above and meet the needs of employees below. In a similar light, only one study in our review investigated the impact of line managers on employee perceptions of fit. This relatively underdeveloped area of research highlights the crucial role that line managers play in creating a working environment which allows employees to experience fit and succeed in their roles. A better understanding of how line managers can influence the fit perceptions of employees will help scholars and practitioners to develop training and development programs that equip line managers with the most effective tools to help them succeed in their roles.

Our review also identified several methodological shortcomings in the literature. These shortcomings included articles that utilised difference scores instead of PRRSA, a failure to account for multilevel effects properly, and reliance on cross-sectional research designs that ignore the dynamic nature of line manager fit. While it is discouraging to see these limitations in the literature, it is also an opportunity for future research. Over the last two decades, several methodological advances in P-E fit theory have reduced the burden of entry for researchers wishing to study fit effects (e.g. Nestler et al., 2019; Su et al., 2019; Zyphur et al., 2016). We will discuss several of these opportunities below.

First, as previously mentioned, the literature generally agrees that PRRSA is required to avoid the methodological shortcomings of difference scores (Edwards, 2002; Edwards and Parry, 1993). However, researchers have tended to shy away from PRRSA due to a lack of understanding on how to properly apply the methodology. Several scholars have recognised this reluctance and have created detailed guides to help researchers understand and apply PRRSA to their research (e.g. Cohen et al., 2010; Edwards, 2002; Shanock et al., 2010). These helpful guides have led to a gradual increase in the use of PRRSA within the literature (Van Vianen, 2018).

Making PRRSA more readily available for line manager researchers removes a substantial barrier to entry that may have been limiting the number of studies investigating line manager fit experiences within organisations. It also provides an opportunity for line manager research-ers to revisit some of the previous findings within the literature. Given the methodological shortcomings of difference scores (Edwards, 2002; Edwards and Parry, 1993), a PRRSA approach may challenge, contradict or even provide additional confirmation to previous findings. Overall, we encourage line manager researchers to learn and apply PRRSA when investigating P-E fit relationships within organisations.

Second, researchers should address multilevel analysis issues within the P-E fit–line manager literature. As previously noted, almost 50 per cent of the articles found in our review may have ignored the independence assumption of OLS regression. This approach is particularly concerning as line manager research assumes that there are different levels of management within an organisation (Townsend and Dundon, 2015). For example, a group of employees may report to a frontline manager (FLM), who subsequently reports to the same middle or senior manager as other FLMs. This scenario is inherently multilevel (Klein et al., 1994). Therefore, it is crucial to account for the degree to which the responses of employees and line managers in the same reporting group are influenced by, and depend on, their group membership (Bliese, 2000). The absence of multilevel analysis in P-E fit–line manager research is likely due to the limited examples of the approach being applied to PRRSA (Nestler et al., 2019). In recent years several scholars have started to address this shortcoming. There are now several leading examples of how to use multilevel modelling to investigate P-E fit in line manager research (e.g. Nestler et al., 2019; Zyphur et al., 2016).

A multilevel approach to P-E fit–line manager research opens up the door for several exciting research questions. For example, scholars have been calling for additional research investigating how line manager perceptions of human resource management (HRM) practices influence employee perceptions of HRM practices (Alfes et al., 2013; Brewster et al., 2013). It might be that FLMs who experience positive value congruence with senior managers on HRM shape their subordinates' perceptions and attitudes towards HRM. Other scholars have suggested that additional research is required to better understand how line managers are managed by their superiors (Townsend and Hutchinson, 2017). A multilevel approach would allow us to look at how a senior managers' leadership style can influence the relationship between FLM demands–ability fit and important outcomes such as FLM job satisfaction and engagement. Taken together, a multilevel P-E fit approach could allow for a clearer understanding of how the organisational context influences the experiences of line managers.

Third, our review did not identify any studies that utilised a dynamic or temporal profiles approach to investigate line managers' P-E fit. This finding is concerning, as stable perceptions of fit will not provide a clear understanding of how line managers alter their fit judgements based on their immediate work experiences (Vleugels et al., 2018a). However, the absence of existing research creates an opportunity for the advancement of the theory. According to Shipp and Jensen (2011), opportunities for further research include understanding the unique boundary conditions that lead to changes in line manager fit perceptions over time; whether certain types of fit remain more stable than others; investigating feedback loops between fit perceptions and outcomes; and investigating the influence of past fit perceptions on current and future fit perceptions. A dynamic fit approach also allows researchers to answer calls in the literature to evaluate changes in the effect of line manager behaviour and HRM practices over time (Alfes et al., 2013). This approach will provide a clearer understanding of the specific complexities that line managers face on a daily basis (Tyskbo, 2020).

A dynamic fit approach can also be used to understand how FLMs react and respond to the increasing role responsibilities delegated from higher levels of management over time. The FLM literature is full of examples of unexpected responsibilities bestowed upon FLMs over the last few decades (Hales, 2005, 2006/2007; Townsend and Russell, 2013). According to Hutchinson and Purcell (2010), although these responsibilities have been delegated to FLMs from above, there is often a perceptual difference amongst senior managers on the role responsibilities and time constraints experienced by FLMs. By utilising a dynamic fit approach, researchers can investigate the daily variation in demand–abilities fit experienced by FLMs and explore how it influences daily outcomes important to senior managers. Concerning line manager fit profiles, opportunities exist for researchers to investigate how these profiles are established and what environmental factors may influence their development (Vleugels et al., 2018b). Furthermore, researchers could investigate whether line managers change their fit profile over time, such as experiencing different fit profiles within the same organisation (Vleugels et al., 2018b).

Finally, in addition to the opportunities discussed above, recent advances in statistical software have provided opportunities for researchers seeking to investigate line managers' fit relationships. An important aspect of understanding line manager behaviour is breaking down the psychological processes that explain the phenomenon of interest (MacKinnon et al., 2012). Important questions such as 'How are line managers managed?' and 'How does the organisational context influence line manager experiences?' (Townsend and Hutchinson, 2017) are incomplete without an understanding of what aspects, if any, mediate the relationship between line manager fit and outcomes of interest. A mediation analysis specifies a causal chain of relations where an antecedent variable influences a mediating variable, which in turn influences a dependent variable (MacKinnon et al., 2012). For example, the relationship between a line manager's value congruence and their intention to stay in the current job may be mediated by their senior manager's level of open communication and predictability (Edwards and Cable, 2009).

Unfortunately, the use of mediation analysis in P-E fit research has been held back by methodological difficulties. Whereas a typical mediation analysis has one independent variable (that is, line manager values), fit investigations using PRRSA will have five polynomial terms (that is, line manager values, organisational values, two nonlinear terms and an interaction term). Until recently, the established method of investigating mediation in fit research has been the block variable approach (Cable and Edwards, 2004; Edwards and Cable, 2009; Heise, 1972). However, by using block variables we lose vital information about the response surface, which prevents a comparison of direct, indirect and total effect responses surfaces. This added complexity has often resulted in fit research being performed independently of other meaningful predictors of work outcomes (Kristof-Brown et al., 2005). However, statistical programs such as Mplus (Muthén and Muthén, 1998–2019) allow researchers to keep sight of the five polynomial terms and design models that fully investigate mediated relationships. A recent example is Beus et al. (2020), who investigated the effect of regulatory focus climate misfit on organisational productivity through organisational commitment. By utilising new statistical software to perform mediation analyses, we can better understand how line managers experience P-E fit within their organisation.

CONCLUSION

This chapter aimed to present P-E fit theory as a unique lens to understand how line managers navigate and contribute to the work environment. Our detailed overview of the history, current conceptualisations, methodological considerations and renewed interest in P-E fit theory provides scholars with a practical starting point to expand their understanding of the theory and apply it to investigate new and exciting research questions. We also provided scholars with an illustrative review of the literature investigating line managers from a P-E fit perspective. Our review demonstrated that although the field has continued to take steps forward in theorising and measurement, many fundamental challenges and questions remain unanswered. In particular, future research would benefit from an investigation into the circumstances and outcomes associated with misfit, a greater understanding of line manager person–vocation and person–job fit, how fit perceptions as the 'the manager' and 'the managed' influence one another, and a focus on individual levels of management instead of the aggregate. Further to this point, scholars should apply a multilevel perspective and recent methodological advancements to improve our understanding of the psychological processes underpinning line manager P-E fit. Rectifying these challenges has the potential to advance our understanding of how line managers navigate and experience their day-to-day working life. We are hopeful that this chapter will provide a strong foundation and a set of research ideas for developing our understanding of the integral role that P-E fit theory can play in understanding line managers in the workplace.

REFERENCES

The 22 top-tier articles which form the basis of this review are denoted by an asterisk.

Alfes, K., Truss, C., Soane, E.C., Rees, C., and Gatenby, M. (2013). The relationship between line manager behavior, perceived HRM practices, and individual performance: Examining the mediating role of engagement. *Human Resource Management*, *52*(6), 839–859. doi:10.1002/hrm.21512.

*Allinson, C.W., Armstrong, S.J., and Hayes, J. (2001). The evects of cognitive style on leader–member exchange: A study of manager–subordinate dyads. *Journal of Occupational and Organizational Psychology*, *74*(2), 201–220. doi:10.1348/096317901167316.

Arthur, W., Bell, S.T., Villado, A.J., and Doverspike, D. (2006). The use of person–organization fit in employment decision making: An assessment of its criterion-related validity. *Journal of Applied Psychology*, *91*(4), 786–801. doi:10.1037/0021-9010.91.4.786.

*Ashforth, B.E., Kreiner, G.E., Clark, M.A., and Fugate, M. (2017). Congruence work in stigmatized occupations: A managerial lens on employee fit with dirty work. *Journal of Organizational Behavior*, *38*(8), 1260–1279. doi:10.1002/job.2201.

Australian Business Deans Council (ABDC) (2019). ABDC Journal Quality List. https://abdc.edu.au/research/abdc-journal-quality-list/.

Barrick, M.R., Stewart, G.L., Neubert, M.J., and Mount, M.K. (1998). Relating member ability and personality to work-team processes and team effectiveness. *Journal of Applied Psychology*, *83*(3), 377–391. doi:10.1037/0021-9010.83.3.377.

Barsade, S.G., Ward, A.J., Jean, D.F.T., and Sonnenfeld, J.A. (2000). To your heart's content: A model of affective diversity in top management teams. *Administrative Science Quarterly*, *45*(4), 802–836. doi:10.2307/2667020.

Beal, D.J. (2015). Esm 2.0: State of the art and future potential of experience sampling methods in organizational research. *Annual Review of Organizational Psychology and Organizational Behavior*, *2*, 383–407. doi:10.1146/annurev-orgpsych-032414-111335.

Beus, J.M., Lucianetti, L., and Arthur, W.J. (2020). Clash of the climates: Examining the paradoxical effects of climates for promotion and prevention. *Personnel Psychology*, *73*(2), 241–269. doi:10.1111/peps.12338.

Bliese, P.D. (2000). Within-group agreement, non-independence, and reliability: Implications for data aggregation and analysis. In K.J. Klein and S.W. Kozlowski (eds), *Multilevel Theory, Research, and Methods in Organizations: Foundations, Extensions, and New Directions* (pp. 349–381). San Francisco, CA: Jossey-Bass.

Bos-Nehles, A.C., Van Riemsdijk, M.J., and Looise, J.K. (2013). Employee perceptions of line management performance: Applying the AMO theory to explain the effectiveness of line managers' HRM implementation. *Human Resource Management*, *52*(6), 861–877. doi:10.1002/hrm.21578.

Brewster, C., Gollan, P.J., and Wright, P.M. (2013). Guest editors' note: Human resource management and the line. *Human Resource Management*, *52*(6), 829–838. doi:10.1002/hrm.21594.

Cable, D.M., and Edwards, J.R. (2004). Complementary and supplementary fit: A theoretical and empirical integration. *Journal of Applied Psychology*, *89*(5), 822–834. doi:10.1037/0021-9010.89.5.822.

Campbell, L., Simpson, J.A., Stewart, M., and Manning, J. (2003). Putting personality in social context: Extraversion, emergent leadership, and the availability of rewards. *Personality and Social Psychology Bulletin*, *29*(12), 1547–1559. doi:10.1177/0146167203256920.

Christiansen, N., Villanova, P., and Mikulay, S. (1997). Political influence compatibility: Fitting the person to the climate. *Journal of Organizational Behavior*, *18*(6), 709–730. doi:10.1002/(sici)1099 -1379(199711)18:6<709::aid-job811>3.0.co;2-4.

CIPD (2019). Line managers' role in supporting the people profession. Retrieved from https://www.cipd .co.uk/knowledge/fundamentals/people/hr/line-managers-factsheet.

Cohen, A., Nahum-Shani, I., and Doveh, E. (2010). Further insight and additional inference methods for polynomial regression applied to the analysis of congruence. *Multivariate Behavioral Research*, *45*(5), 828–852. doi:10.1080/00273171.2010.519272.

Costa, P.T.J., and McCrae, R.R. (1992). Four ways five factors are basic. *Personality and Individual Differences*, *13*(6), 653–665. doi:10.1016/0191-8869(92)90236-i.

*Coursey, D., Yang, K., and Pandey, S.K. (2012). Public service motivation (PSM) and support for citizen participation: A test of Perry and Vandenabeele's reformulation of PSM theory. *Public Administration Review*, *72*(4), 572–582. doi:10.111/j.1540-6210.2012.02581.x.

*Devloo, T., Anseel, F., and Beuckelaer, A.D. (2011). Do managers use feedback seeking as a strategy to regulate demands–abilities misfit? The moderating role of implicit person theory. *Journal of Business and Psychology*, *26*(4), 453–465. doi:10.1007/s10869-010-9200-7.

*Donohue, R. (2014). Holland's constructs in relation to career persistence and career change: A study of Australian managerial and professional workers. *Australian Journal of Management*, *39*(2), 167–189. doi:10.1177/0312896213501179.

Edwards, J.R. (1991). Person–job fit: A conceptual integration, literature review, and methodological critique. In C.L. Cooper and I.T. Robertson (eds), *International Review of Industrial and Organizational Psychology* (Vol. 6, pp. 283–357). New York: Wiley.

Edwards, J.R. (1996). An examination of competing versions of the person–environment fit approach to stress. *Academy of Management Journal*, *39*(2), 292–339. doi:10.2307/256782.

Edwards, J.R. (2002). Alternatives to difference scores: Polynominal regression analysis and response surface methodology. In F. Drasgow and N. Schmitt (eds), *Measuring and Analyzing Behavior in Organizations: Advances in Measurement and Data Analysis* (pp. 350–400). San Francisco, CA: Jossey-Bass.

Edwards, J.R. (2008). Person–environment fit in organizations: An assessment of theoretical progress. *Academy of Management Annals*, *2*(1), 167–230. doi:10.1080/19416520802211503.

Edwards, J.R., and Cable, D.M. (2009). The value of value congruence. *Journal of Applied Psychology*, *94*(3), 654–677. doi:10.1037/a0014891.

Edwards, J.R., and Cooper, C.L. (1990). The person–environment fit approach to stress: Recurring problems and some suggested solutions. *Journal of Organizational Behavior*, *11*(4), 293–307. doi:10 .1002/job.4030110405.

Edwards, J.R., and Parry, M.E. (1993). The use of polynominal regression equations as an alternative to difference scores in organizational research. *Academy of Management Journal*, *36*(6), 1577–1613. doi:10.5465/256822.

Edwards, J.R., Cable, D.M., Williamson, I.O., Lambert, L.S., and Shipp, A.J. (2006). The phenomenology of fit: Linking the person and environment to the subjective experience of person–environment fit. *Journal of Applied Psychology*, *91*(4), 802–827. doi:10.1037/0021-9010.91.4.802.

Edwards, J.R., Caplan, R.D., and Van Harrison, R. (1998). Person–environment fit theory: Conceptual foundations, empirical evidence, and directions for future research. In C.L. Cooper (ed.), *Theories of Organizational Stress* (pp. 28–67). Oxford: Oxford University Press.

Eisenberger, R., Rhoades, L., and Wen, X. (2020). Perceived organizational support: Why caring about employees counts. *Annual Review of Organizational Psychology and Organizational Behavior*, *7*(1), 101–124. doi:10.1146/annurev-orgpsych-012119-044917.

*Elango, B., Paul, K., Kundu, S.K., and Paudel, S.K. (2010). Organizational ethics, individual ethics, and ethical intentions in international decision-making. *Journal of Business Ethics*, *97*(4), 543–561. doi: 10.1007/s10551-010-0524-z.

*Flint, D.J., Signori, P., and Golicic, S.L. (2018). Corporate identity congruence: A meanings-based analysis. *Journal of Business Research*, *86*(1), 68–82. doi:10.1016/j.jbusres.2018.01.052.

French, J.R.P., Caplan, R.D., and Harrison, V.R. (1982). *The Mechanisms of Job Stress and Strain*. Chichester, UK and New York, USA: Wiley.

*Furnham, A., Toop, A., Lewis, C., and Fisher, A. (1995). P-E fit and job satisfaction: A failure to support Holland's theory in three British samples. *Personality and Individual Differences, 19*(5), 677–690. doi:10.1016/0191-8869(95)00091-j.

*Grissom, J.A., Nicholson-Crotty, J., and Keiser, L. (2012). Does my boss's gender matter? Explaining job satisfaction and employee turnover in the public sector. *Journal of Public Administration Research and Theory, 22*(4), 649–673. doi:10.1093/jopart/mus004.

Hales, C. (2005). Rooted in supervision, branching into management: Continuity and change in the role of first-line manager. *Journal of Management Studies, 42*(3), 471–506. doi:10.1111/j.1467-6486.2005 .00506.x.

Hales, C. (2006/2007). Moving down the line? The shifting boundary between middle and first-line management. *Journal of General Management, 32*(2), 31–55. doi:10.2495/fsi070311.

Harrison, R.V. (1978). Person–environment fit and job stress. In C.L. Cooper and R. Payne (eds), *Stress at Work* (pp. 175–205). New York: Wiley.

Harrison, R.V. (1985). The person–environment fit model and the study of job stress. In T.A. Beehr and R.S. Bhagat (eds), *Human Stress and Cognition in Organizations* (pp. 23–35). New York: Wiley.

Heise, D.R. (1972). Employing nominal variables, induced variables, and block variables in path analyses. *Sociological Methods and Research, 1*(2), 147–173. doi:10.1177/004912417200100201.

Hobman, E.V., Bordia, P., and Gallois, C. (2003). Consequences of feeling dissimilar from others in a work team. *Journal of Business and Psychology, 17*(3), 301–325. doi:10.1023/A:1022837207241.

Hofmann, D.A. (1997). An overview of the logic and rationale of hierarchical linear models. *Journal of Management, 23*(6), 723–744. doi:10.1177/014920639702300602.

Holland, J.L. (1985). *Making Vocational Choices: A Theory of Vocational Personalities and Work Environments* (2nd edn). Englewood Cliffs, NJ: Prentice-Hall.

*Huang, M.-P., Cheng, B.-S., and Chou, L.-F. (2005). Fitting in organizational values: The mediating role of person–organization fit between ceo charismatic leadership and employee outcomes. *International Journal of Manpower, 26*(1), 35–49. doi:10.1108/01437720510587262.

Hutchinson, S., and Purcell, J. (2010). Managing ward managers for roles in HRM in the NHS: Overworked and under-resourced. *Human Resource Management Journal, 20*(4), 357–374. doi:10 .1111/j.1748-8583.2010.00141.x.

*Isaac, R.G., Wilson, K.L., and Pitt, D.C. (2004). Value congruence awareness: Part 1. DNA testing sheds light on functionalism. *Journal of Business Ethics, 54*(2), 191–201. doi:10.1007/s10551-004 -1168-7.

*Jensen, U.T. (2017). Does perceived societal impact moderate the effect of transformational leadership on value congruence? Evidence from a field experiment. *Public Administration Review, 78*(1), 48–57. doi:10.1111/puar.12852.

Judge, T.A., and Ferris, G.R. (1992). The elusive criterion of fit in human resources staffing decisions. *Human Resource Planning, 15*(4), 47–67.

Judge, T.A., Bono, J.E., Ilies, R., and Gerhardt, M.W. (2002). Personality and leadership: A qualitative and quantitative review. *Journal of Applied Psychology, 87*(4), 765–780. doi:10.1037/0021-9010.87 .4.765.

Kilroy, J., and Dundon, T. (2015). The multiple faces of front line managers. *Employee Relations, 37*(4), 410–427. doi:10.1108/ER-06-2014-0071.

Kivlighan, D.M.J., Li, X., and Gillis, L. (2015). Do I fit with my group? Within-member and within-group fit with the group in engaged group climate and group members feeling involved and valued. *Group Dynamics: Theory, Research, and Practice, 19*(2), 106–121. doi:10.1037/gdn0000025.

Klein, K.J., Dansereau, F., and Hall, R.J. (1994). Levels issues in theory development, data collection, and analysis. *Academy of Management Review, 19*(2), 195–229. doi:10.2307/258703.

Krishnan, V.R. (2002). Transformational leadership and value system congruence. *International Journal of Value-Based Management, 15*(1), 19–33. doi:10.1023/A:1013029427977.

Kristof-Brown, A.L., and Billsberry, J. (2013). *Organizational Fit: Key Issues and New Directions.* Chichester: Wiley.

Kristof-Brown, A.L., Zimmerman, R.D., and Johnson, E.C. (2005). Consequences of individuals' fit at work: A meta-analysis of person–job, person–organization, person–group, and person–supervisor fit. *Personnel Psychology, 58*(2), 281–342. doi:10.1111/j.1744-6570.2005.00672.x.

Kulik, C.T., Oldham, G.R., and Hackman, J.R. (1987). Work design as an approach to person–environment fit. *Journal of Vocational Behavior*, *31*(3), 278–296. doi:10.1016/0001-8791(87)90044-3.

Lewin, K. (1943). Defining the 'field at a given time'. *Psychological Review*, *50*(3), 292–310. doi:10.1037/h0062738.

Lewin, K. (1951). *Field Theory in Social Science*. New York: Harper.

Lievens, F., Chasteen, C.S., Day, E.A., and Christiansen, N.D. (2006). Large-scale investigation of the role of trait activation theory for understanding assessment center convergent and discriminant validity. *Journal of Applied Psychology*, *91*(2), 247–258. doi:10.1037/0021-9010.91.2.247.

Locke, E.A. (1976). The nature and causes of job satisfaction. In M. Dunnette (ed.), *Handbook of Industrial and Organizational Psychology* (pp. 1297–1350). Chicago, IL: Rand McNally.

*Macinati, M.S., Nieddu, L., and Rizzo, M.G. (2018). Examining the role of value congruence, professional identity, and managerial job engagement in the budgetary participation–performance link. *Health Care Management Review*, *45*(4), 290–301. doi:10.1097/hmr.0000000000000231.

MacKinnon, D.P., Cheong, J., and Pirlott, A.G. (2012). Statistical mediation analysis. In H. Cooper, P.M. Camic, D.L. Long, A.T. Panter, D. Rindskopf and K.J. Sher (eds), *APA Handbook of Research Methods in Psychology, Volume 2: Research Designs: Quantitative, Qualitative, Neuropsychological, and Biological* (pp. 313–331). Washington, DC: American Psychological Association.

McCarthy, A., Darcy, C., and Grady, G. (2010). Work–life balance policy and practice: Understanding line manager attitudes and behaviors. *Human Resource Management Review*, *20*(2), 158–167. doi:10.1016/j.hrmr.2009.12.001.

Mischel, W. (2009). From personality and assessment (1968) to personality science, 2009. *Journal of Research in Personality*, *43*(2), 282–290. doi:10.1016/j.jrp.2008.12.037.

Mount, M.K., Barrick, M.R., and Stewart, G.L. (1998). Five-factor model of personality and performance in jobs involving interpersonal interactions. *Human Performance*, *11*(2–3), 145–165. doi:10.1080/08959285.1998.9668029.

Muthén, L.K., and Muthén, B.O. (1998–2019). *Mplus User's Guide. Eighth Edition*. Los Angeles, CA: Muthén and Muthén.

Nestler, S., Humberg, S., and Schönbrodt, F.D. (2019). Response surface analysis with multilevel data: Illustration for the case of congruence hypotheses. *Psychological Methods*, *24*(3), 291–308. doi:10.1037/met0000199.

O'Reilly, C.A., Chatman, J., and Caldwell, D.F. (1991). People and organizational culture: A profile comparison approach to assessing person–organization fit. *Academy of Management Journal*, *34*(3), 487–516. doi:10.2307/256404.

*Pelled, L.H., and Xin, K.R. (1997). Birds of a feather: Leader–member demographic similarity and organizational attachment in Mexico. *Leadership Quarterly*, *8*(4), 433–450. doi:10.1016/s1048-9843(97)90023-0.

Pervin, L.A. (1967). Satisfaction and perceived self-environment similarity: A semantic differential study of student–college interaction. *Journal of Personality*, *35*(4), 623–634. doi:10.1111/j.1467-6494.1967.tb01452.x.

*Posner, B.Z. (2010). Another look at the impact of personal and organizational values congruency. *Journal of Business Ethics*, *97*(4), 535–541. doi:10.1007/s10551-010-0530-1.

*Posner, B.Z., and Schmidt, W.H. (1993). Values congruence and differences between the interplay of personal and organizational value systems. *Journal of Business Ethics*, *12*(5), 341–347. doi:10.1007/bf00882023.

Rauthmann, J.F., Sherman, R.A., and Funder, D.C. (2015). Principles of situation research: Towards a better understanding of psychological situations. *European Journal of Personality*, *29*(3), 363–381. doi:10.1002/per.1994.

Rice, R.W., McFarlin, D.B., Hunt, R.G., and Near, J.P. (1985). Organizational work and the perceived quality of life: Toward a conceptual model. *Academy of Management Review*, *10*(2), 296–310. doi:10.2307/257971.

Saks, A.M., and Ashforth, B.E. (1997). A longitudinal investigation of the relationships between job information sources, applicant perceptions of fit, and work outcomes. *Personnel Psychology*, *50*(2), 395–426. doi:10.1111/j.1744-6570.1997.tb00913.x.

Schaubroeck, J., and Simon, S.K.L. (2002). How similarity to peers and supervisor influences organizational advancement in different cultures. *Academy of Management Journal*, *45*(6), 1120–1136. doi: 10.2307/3069428.

*Schminke, M., Ambrose, M.L., and Neubaum, D.O. (2005). The effect of leader moral development on ethical climate and employee attitudes. *Organizational Behavior and Human Decision Processes*, *97*(2), 135–151. doi:10.1016/j.obhdp.2005.03.006.

Schneider, B. (1987). The people make the place. *Personnel Psychology*, *40*(3), 437–453. doi:10.1111/j .1744-6570.1987.tb00609.x.

*Sears, G.J., and Holmvall, C.M. (2010). The joint influence of supervisor and subordinate emotional intelligence on leader–member exchange. *Journal of Business and Psychology*, *25*(4), 593–605. doi: 10.1007/s10869-009-9152-y.

Shanock, L.R., Baran, B.E., Gentry, W.A., Pattison, S.C., and Heggestad, E.D. (2010). Polynominal regression with response surface analysis: A powerful approach for examining moderation and overcoming limitations of difference scores. *Journal of Business and Psychology*, *25*(4), 543–554. doi:10 .1007/s10869-010-9183-4.

Shipp, A.J., and Jansen, K.J. (2011). Reinterpreting thime in fit theory: Crafting and recrafting narratives of fit in medias res. *Academy of Management Review*, *36*(1), 76–101. doi:10.5465/amr.2011 .55662565.

Strauss, J.P., Barrick, M.R., and Connerley, M.L. (2001). An investigation of personality similarity effects (relational and perceived) on peer and supervisor ratings and the role of familiarity and liking. *Journal of Occupational and Organizational Psychology*, *74*(5), 637–657. doi:10.1348/ 096317901167569.

Su, R., Zhang, Q., Liu, Y., and Tay, L. (2019). Modeling congruence in organizational research with latent moderated structural equations. *Journal of Applied Psychology*, *104*(11), 1404–1433. doi:10 .1037/apl0000411.

*Suar, D., and Khuntia, R. (2010). Influence of personal values and value congruence on unethical practices and work behavior. *Journal of Business Ethics*, *97*(3), 443–460. doi:10.1007/s10551-010 -0517-y.

Tangirala, S., Green, S.G., and Ramanujam, R. (2007). In the shadow of the boss's boss: Effects of supervisors' upward exchange relationships on employees. *Journal of Applied Psychology*, *92*(2), 309–320. doi:10.1037/0021-9010.92.2.309.

Tepper, B.J., Dimotakis, N., Lambert, L.S., Koopman, J., Matta, F.K., et al. (2018). Examining follower responses to transformational leadership from a dynamic, person–environment fit perspective. *Academy of Management Journal*, *61*(4), 1–61. doi:10.5465/amj.2014.0163.

Tom, V.R. (1971). The role of personality and organizational images in the recruiting process. *Organizational Behavior and Human Performance*, *6*(5), 573–592. doi:10.1016/S0030-5073(71)80008 -9.

Townsend, K. (2013). To what extent do line managers play a role in modern industrial relations? *Asia Pacific Journal of Human Resources*, *51*(4), 421–436. doi:10.1111/1744-7941.12015.

Townsend, K., and Dundon, T. (2015). Understanding the role of line managers in employment relations in the modern organisation. *Employee Relations*, *37*(4), 1–10. doi:10.1108/ER-01-2015-0018.

Townsend, K., and Hutchinson, S. (2017). Line managers in industrial relations: Where are we now and where are we next? *Journal of Industrial Relations*, *59*(2), 139–152. doi:10.1177/0022185616671163.

Townsend, K., and Kellner, A. (2015). Managing the front-line manager. In A. Wilkinson, K. Townsend and G. Suder (eds), *Handbook of Research on Managing Managers*. Cheltenham, UK and Northampton, MA, USA: Edward Elgar Publishing.

Townsend, K., and Russell, B. (2013). Investigating the nuances of change in front-line managers' work. *Labour and Industry*, *23*(2), 168–181. doi:10.1080/10301763.2013.820683.

Townsend, K., Loudoun, R., and Markwell, K. (2016). The role of line managers in creating and maintaining healthy work environments on project construction sites. *Construction Management and Economics*, *34*(9), 611–621. doi:10.1080/01446193.2016.1195911.

Tse, H.H.M., Troth, A.C., Ashkanasy, N.M., and Collins, A.L. (2018). Affect and leader–member exchange in the new millennium: A state-of-art review and guiding framework. *Leadership Quarterly*, *29*(1), 135–149. doi:10.1016/j.leaqua.2017.10.002.

Tyskbo, D. (2020). Line management involvement in performance appraisal work: Toward a practice-based understanding. *Employee Relations*, *42*(3), 818–844. doi:10.1108/ER-06-2019-0236.

Van Vianen, A.E.M. (2000). Person–organization fit: The match between newcomers' and recruiters' preferences for organizational cultures. *Personnel Psychology*, *53*(1), 113–149. doi:10.1111/j.1744-6570.2000.tb00196.x.

Van Vianen, A.E.M. (2018). Person–environment fit: A review of its basic tenets. *Annual Review of Organizational Psychology and Organizational Behavior*, *5*(1), 75–101. doi:10.1146/annurev-orgpsych-032117-104702.

Vleugels, W., Cooman, R.D., Verbruggen, M., and Solinger, O. (2018a). Understanding dynamic change in perceptions of person–environment fit: An exploration of competing theoretical perspectives. *Journal of Organizational Behavior*, *39*(9), 1066–1080. doi:10.1002/job.2294.

Vleugels, W., Tierens, H., Billsberry, J., Verbruggen, M., and Cooman, R.D. (2018b). Profiles of fit and misfit: A repeated weekly measures study of perceived value congruence. *European Journal of Work and Organizational Psychology*, *28*(5), 616–630. doi:10.1080/1359432x.2019.1583279.

*Wang, D., Fan, D., Freeman, S., and Zhu, C.J. (2017). Exploring cross-cultural skills for expatriate managers from Chinese multinationals: Congruence and contextualization. *Asia Pacific Journal of Management*, *34*(1), 123–146. doi:10.1007/s10490-016-9474-z.

Werbel, J.D., and Gilliland, S.W. (1999). Person–environment fit in the selection process. In G.R. Ferris (ed.), *Research in Personnel and Human Resource Management* (Vol. 17, pp. 209–243). Stamford, CT: JAI Press.

Wilson, K.S., Sin, H.-P., and Conlon, D.E. (2010). What about the leader in leader–member exchange? The impact of resource exchange and substitutability on the leader. *Academy of Management Review*, *35*(3), 358–372. doi:10.5465/amr.2010.51141654.

*Witt, L.A. (1998). Enhancing organizational goal congruence: A solution to organizational politics. *Journal of Applied Psychology*, *83*(4), 666–674. doi:10.1037/0021-9010.83.4.666.

Yu, K.Y.T. (2013). A motivational model of person–environment fit: Psychological motives as drivers of change. In A.L. Kristof-Brown and J. Billsberry (eds), *Organizational Fit: Key Issues and New Directions* (pp. 19–49). Chichester: Wiley-Blackwell.

*Zhang, J., Akhtar, M.N., Bal, P.M., Zhang, Y., and Talat, U. (2018). How do high-performance work systems affect individual outcomes: A multilevel perspective. *Frontiers in Psychology*, *9*(1), 1–13. doi:10.3389/fpsyg.2018.00586.

Zyphur, M.J., Zammuto, R.F., and Zhang, Z. (2016). Multilevel latent polynomial regression for modeling (in)congruence across organizational groups: The case of organizational culture research. *Organizational Research Methods*, *19*(1), 53–79. doi:10.1177/1094428115588570.

4. Line managers, role theory and HRM

Samantha Evans

INTRODUCTION

Within the human resources management (HRM) literature there is both theoretical and empirical agreement that line managers are critical actors in the delivery of HRM. They act as key agents in the delivery of HRM and are highly influential in employee performance outcomes (Purcell and Hutchinson, 2007; Hutchinson and Purcell, 2010; Alfes et al., 2013). The focus of much research has been on the human resources (HR) responsibilities of line managers and problems associated with devolution. The evidence suggests that while line managers have considerable responsibility for HRM, they are a source of poor HR implementation (McGovern et al., 1997; Evans, 2015). Recent studies have begun to move beyond examining which HRM responsibilities line managers hold, to exploring what influences their HRM decision-making processes, and any links between line managers, HRM and performance. However, despite considerable research, the literature remains inconclusive about how HRM has an impact on performance, including the role of line managers in this process (Guest, 2011).

With line managers being such key actors in the implementation of HRM, it is critical that they consistently and skilfully execute their HRM responsibilities in ways that are congruent with original strategy and policy (Trullen et al., 2020). However, research has found that line managers are often the source of gaps between intended and actual HRM as they adapt, or even replace, an organization's intended HR practices (Kehoe and Hun Han, 2020). In doing so, they become a source of variance not only in the HRM process, but also in the content of HR practices within and across organizations. This is compounded by their multiple roles and responsibilities and organizational position, which brings a range of tensions to the job (Child and Partridge, 1982; Hales, 2005). There is also evidence that line managers are experiencing an overall increase in work responsibilities and tasks, with an associated decline in the quality of their work (Townsend and Russell, 2013). This context suggests that line managers may be exposed to multiple sources of role stress, which is known to weaken the performance of role holders (Showail et al., 2013; Kauppila, 2014). Research has found that the role stress of line managers can affect their efficacy of HRM implementation (Gilbert et al., 2011; Evans, 2017), so this chapter will use role theory to explore the relationship between line managers and HR implementation.

ROLE THEORY AND ROLE STRESS

Organizational role theory views businesses as systems of roles, whereby a role comprises a set of normative expectations corresponding to the incumbent's position within the organization (Katz and Kahn, 1966). A role is associated with expectations that generate behaviour to induce conformity, and involves interactions with individuals occupying other related positions, referred to as role partners (Biddle, 1986). Role dynamics recognizes that a range of factors influence an individual's role behaviour, including organizational, individual and interpersonal factors (Kahn et al., 1964). This framework states that role behaviour is determined by: (1) the role tasks of the incumbent; (2) the patterns of interaction between a person and their role partners; (3) a person's individual factors and (4) the broader organizational context. These act as conditioning variables in relation to a person's role behaviour and have the ability to exert significant influence on the tasks and responsibilities of role holders (Kahn et al., 1964).

Role theory depicts how various features of an organizational role can expose an individual to stress, such that when the expectations of the role holder are 'conflicting, ambiguous, or overloading, the focal person will experience role stress' (Ortqvist and Wincent, 2006: 399). The theory distinguishes between different sources of role stress, comprising role conflict, role overload and role ambiguity. Role conflict relates to inconsistencies in the expectations of role incumbents, such that compliance with one expectation would make it difficult or impossible to fulfil other requirements of the role. Role overload occurs when there is an incompatibility between the volume of work and the resources available to complete the work. Role ambiguity follows when there is little or no information about role expectations, or the role expectations lack clarity (Rizzo et al., 1970; Turner, 1978).

Role stress is often associated with lower performance levels in the role holder (Tubré and Collins, 2000; Showail et al., 2013), and related to several specific negative performance outcomes. These include: reduced levels of organizational and work commitment (Slattery et al., 2008); increased labour turnover and intention to quit (Hang-Yue et al., 2005); stress and frustration in the role (Deery et al., 2002); reduced levels of organizational citizenship behaviour (Eatough et al., 2011); lower job satisfaction (Showail et al., 2013); and less confidence in decision-making (Rizzo et al., 1970). In addition, the three sources of role stress have different relationships with job performance; for example, research shows that role ambiguity has stronger negative associations with task performance than role conflict and role overload (Tubré and Collins, 2000; Gilboa et al., 2008).

The extent to which role holders accept sources of role stress is disputed in the literature. Structural role theory asserts that individuals accept role stressors (Biddle, 1979, 1986). Conversely, process role theory contends that role holders engage in behaviour that defies the expectations placed upon them in response to role stress (Turner, 1962). Such behaviour has been termed role-making, role renegotiation or job-crafting. The ability to role-make has a strong correlation with the degree of discretion the incumbent has over how to accomplish work tasks. For example, a higher level of job autonomy 'enables workers to role-make, to negotiate the expectations that role partners attempt to impose' (Troyer et al., 2000: 414). As such, role holders may engage in role-making to enact physical or cognitive changes that alter the content and meaning of their job, as well as the quality of their relationship with others in the workplace (Wrzesniewski and Dutton, 2001). This is often in response to role stressors, such that role-making is deployed in an attempt to secure more support from role partners, increase levels of autonomy, take on more challenging job demands, or decrease hindering job demands (Tims et al., 2012). Related to HRM, studies show that line managers have a significant degree of discretion in their HRM responsibilities (Purcell and Hutchinson, 2007), which presents opportunities to renegotiate their HR role. This suggests that when line managers experience role stress they may be more likely to role-make in their HRM responsibilities, which will in turn influence the extent to which they implement HRM as intended.

SOURCES OF ROLE STRESS FOR LINE MANAGERS

A wide range of responsibilities and increasing workloads makes line managers predisposed to multiple sources of role stress. It is therefore important to consider sources, of role stress to identify their influence on line managers' implementation of HRM. Factors known to contribute to line managers' role stress include the multiplicity of their job tasks and role partners; their position in the organizational hierarchy; their knowledge, skills and abilities; and their individual personality and motivation.

The Multiple Roles and Responsibilities of Line Managers

Line managers occupy an often indispensable position between the corporate organization, operations, employees and customers, with associated expectations to undertake multiple tasks. In essence, their job involves concurrently engaging in the role of manager, colleague, team member and employee, often fulfilling the roles of technical expert, coordinator, leader, innovator and change facilitator (Gilbert et al., 2015). The literature reflects this in its use of numerous titles for line managers, underlining their distribution through the organizational hierarchy, for example, senior/top, middle or lower management; first-line manager, team leader or supervisor; and the diversity of roles they enact, for example, organizational leader, coach, policy enactor, budget holder or performance manager (Kilroy and Dundon, 2015). In addition, line managers are assuming increased responsibility for their team or business unit, with accompanying accountability for results, which have added to the pressures associated with their role (Brewster and Larsen, 2000).

The multiple roles and responsibilities of line managers are a key factor in shaping expected role behaviours. With line managers at all levels of the organizational hierarchy having a degree of HR responsibility within their role remit, the multiple demands made of line managers impact upon the execution of their HRM responsibilities (Stanton et al., 2010). Research suggests that tensions between different role expectations for line managers, manifested through role overload, role ambiguity and role conflict, does undermine successful HR implementation (Hutchinson and Purcell, 2010; Gilbert et al., 2011; Evans, 2017).

With ever-increasing demands on line managers and HR devolution adding to an already extensive workload, a lack of time to perform all their duties well, including their HRM responsibilities, contributes to poor HR implementation. Role overload, through organizational delayering, increased general workloads, and time pressures, are reasons cited by line managers for not implementing HRM as intended (McGovern et al., 1997; Townsend and Russell, 2013). Increasing responsibilities also contribute to role conflict where contradictory demands create tensions around what tasks take priority. Many line managers find themselves working in organizations that demand high levels of quality while striving for greater efficiencies. Such a context consigns line managers to juggling performance expectations of high quality against a backdrop of operational efficiency. This is compounded when performance targets focus on budgets and tangible measures rather than HR outcomes (Evans, 2017). As a result, line managers pay less attention to the intended implementation of HRM, with a tendency to prioritize operational tasks over HR issues (Woodrow and Guest, 2014). The multiplicity of roles undertaken by line managers also makes it unclear what is required for expected performance in their role, which exposes them to role ambiguity (McConville, 2006).

This compromises their ability to implement HRM as intended, and can lead to inconsistencies in HRM process due to a lack of clarity and guidance in the expectations of their HR role.

In summary, research shows us that the wide-ranging nature of line managers' roles and responsibilities creates a challenging framework for HRM implementation. These ever-increasing responsibilities mean that line managers are subject to significant pressures associated with role expectations of managing human, financial and physical resources (Brewster and Larsen, 2000; Trullen et al., 2020). The increase in responsibilities, combined with the multiplicity of roles inherent to being a line manager, exposes incumbents to a variety of role stressors, which in turn becomes a factor in HRM not being implemented as intended.

Role Partners

The various organizational actors with whom line managers interact shape the expectations of behaviour and influence their role behaviours. Greater consideration to potential intragroup and intergroup differences is needed to improve our understanding of HR implementation and to challenge the assumption that line managers routinely implement HRM as intended (López-Cotarelo, 2018). Line managers' multidirectional involvement in HRM requires them to work with other key HR actors such as chief executive officers, senior management and HR specialists (McDermott et al., 2015; Trullen et al., 2016). In addition, line managers work closely with their staff in executing their HR responsibilities, while some also deal directly with customers and other organizational stakeholders. Using a role-theoretic lens facilitates consideration of the contribution of role partners to line managers' role stress, and any implications of this for HR implementation.

A critical role partner for line managers is the organization's HR department, with HR professionals often being the role senders and line managers the role receivers (Yuliza et al., 2019). Effective internal communication between role sender and role receiver facilitates role clarity, with ambiguity arising from poor communication between the two partners (Malhotra and Ackfeldt, 2016). A lack of support and training from HR professionals can lead to role ambiguity, whereby line managers lack a clear definition of their HR role or advice from HR professionals on managing the different expectations of their role partners (McConville, 2006; Hutchinson and Purcell, 2010). Perceptual divergence between line managers and HR professionals can have a negative impact on HR implementation (Maxwell and Watson, 2006). Correspondingly, employees' satisfaction with HR implementation is stronger when HR professionals are supportive of line managers (Bos-Nehles et al., 2013). The evidence strongly supports the notion that HR departments have a significant influence on line managers' implementation performance (Guest and Bos-Nehles, 2013; Trullen et al., 2016).

Line managers' relationship with senior managers and organizational leaders also influences their levels and sources of role stress. Leader–member exchange and transformational leadership improves role clarity by increasing the availability of knowledge and other resources (Whitaker et al., 2007), whereas laissez-faire leadership aggravates role ambiguity (Skogstad et al., 2007). Moreover, senior leaders' HR background and credibility, employee-centred value beliefs and support for the HR department improves line managers' HR implementation by mediating both ambiguity and conflict in their role (Arthur et al., 2016). Thus, senior management and leadership can ease role ambiguity and conflict for line managers around their HRM responsibilities, but only when leaders are considered to be credible in their support of HRM policy and practice. Yet, research studies find that while line managers are taking increasing responsibility for HRM, they do not receive adequate support from senior management, which exacerbates their experience of role stress and negatively affects HR implementation (Hutchinson and Purcell, 2010; Evans, 2015, 2017). Without support from effective organizational leaders, the role stress of line managers is likely to impede their ability to successfully implement HRM.

Line managers are heavily involved in engaging with their staff, which renders employees key role partners. While line managers are essential to HR implementation, employees have been described as playing a more supplementary role (Meijerink et al., 2016). Nevertheless, the interaction between these two role partners remains important, with line managers being a source of critical influence on employees' perceptions of HRM (Sikora and Ferris, 2014), employee outcomes (Nishii et al., 2008), attitudes and behaviours (Alfes et al., 2013), and their affective commitment to the organization (Bos-Nehles and Meijerink, 2018). The number of subordinates for which a line manager has responsibility also influences employee perceptions of their HR effectiveness. The greater the number of subordinates, the more likely a line manager will be perceived as ineffective in their HR role (Gilbert et al., 2015). Therefore, the quantity of role partners is an important consideration when evaluating the effectiveness of line managers' implementation of HRM. Also, while line managers have been found to alter HR policy for their own self-interest (Evans, 2015), some adapt HRM to benefit their employees (Tyskbo, 2020). Therefore, the relationship between line manager and employees and any associated role stress can influence both the implementation of HRM and the outcomes for employees.

Some line managers, particularly those working in the service sector, also act as intermediaries between the corporate organization, frontline employees and customers, making customers one of their role partners. Such a boundary-spanning role can increase an incumbent's susceptibility to role stress, with a considerable impact on their performance (Churchill et al., 1985; Troyer et al., 2000). Added pressure emanates from corporate strategies of productivity and quality that are often characteristic of the service sector (Korczynski, 2002). Juggling the demands of different role partners, both internal and external to the organization, is likely to exacerbate work role stress and have a detrimental impact on HR implementation.

In engaging with multiple organizational actors, line managers occupy a complex role with diverse behavioural expectations demanded of them, which exposes them to a range of role stressors. Research has shown that where role partners are supportive, line managers are prone to rate themselves as more effective in their HR implementation, while employees are more likely to positively perceive HRM (Bos-Nehles et al., 2013; Op de Beeck et al., 2016). Where role partners have their own specific interests and different interpretations of HR practices, line managers are more likely to experience role conflict and ambiguity in their HR role (Makhecha et al., 2018). Such role stress is likely to reduce consistency in HR implementation and increase the likelihood of poor HR implementation by line managers.

Hierarchical Levels of Line Management

The literature and research has tended to classify line managers as a generic homogenous group, with little delineation between the hierarchal structures of management within organizations. Yet, a manager's position in the organizational structure is a factor in their implementation of HRM (Kehoe and Hun Han, 2020). Therefore, it is important to consider how the demarcations between management hierarchies may influence role stress for line managers and their implementation of HRM.

Line managers tend to occupy boundary-spanning roles that operate across a number of interfaces with a multitude of role partners. This increases their exposure to role stress, particularly in the form of ambiguity and conflict (Rigopoulou et al., 2012). For example, frontline managers tend to be the 'final frontier' in an organization's managerial structure (Hales, 2005: 473), often acting as broker between frontline employees, customers and the organization. Such boundary-spanning roles increase the likelihood of role stress (Floyd and Wooldridge, 1997), which has a negative effect on line managers' HR implementation (Evans, 2017). In a similar way, middle managers also serve in an intermediate position, with their role associated with managing the demands of upper management alongside junior managers and employees, which increases their propensity for role conflict (McConville, 2006). For both frontline and middle managers, the interactions with multiple role senders and role partners makes their role expectations less clearly defined, increasing the prospect of role ambiguity. As such, a line manager's position in the organizational structure and their associated propensity for role stress can influence their implementation of HRM.

Individual Factors

It is clear from the literature that line managers are agentic actors with a range of knowledge, skills, competencies, values and motivation to perform their HR role (Woodhams and Lupton, 2006; Vermeeren, 2014; Kehoe and Hun Han, 2020). Their ability to carry out their HR responsibilities is vital to the effective implementation of HRM (Bos-Nehles et al., 2013; Trullen et al., 2016, 2020) and employees' perceptions of HRM (Gilbert et al., 2015). This is augmented by the motivation of line managers (Kulik and Bainbridge, 2006), who when lacking motivation in their HR role can deem HR practices as extraneous and therefore ignore them (Guest and Bos-Nehles, 2013). This is exacerbated when line managers experience role stress which increases the likelihood of role-making and HR policies being disregarded, or not implemented as intended (McConville, 2006; Evans, 2015, 2017).

THE INFLUENCE OF CONTEXT

Line managers' role and their implementation of HRM is contextually embedded at the organizational, sector and national levels. Organizational factors such as culture, size, structure, systems and processes, together with the wider environment such as the industry and country of operation, all impact on the nature of line managers' roles and their experience of role stress. These are thus important in shaping line managers' interpretation and implementation of HRM.

Organizational cultures that are supportive of HRM have been proven to encourage line managers to implement policy as intended (Sikora and Ferris, 2014). Deviation from corporate HR practices by line managers is more likely when contextual factors, such as informal organizational structures, greater managerial discretion, and cultures that favour adaptability, are present (Kehoe and Hun Han, 2020). The boundary conditions in which line managers operate can also encourage, or discourage, more consistent HR implementation. For example, in certain organization structures, such as geographically dispersed units and subsidiaries of MNCs, managerial discretion and ambiguity for line managers may be higher, whereas in bureaucratic hierarchies with strong HRM processes, role clarity and the pressure for consistent HR practice implementation may be greater (Gilbert et al., 2015; Kehoe and Hun Han, 2020). Correspondingly, line managers are more likely to resist their HR role in informal and flexible environments, such as those found in organic, matrix structures and smaller organizations (Woodhams and Lupton, 2006). Organizational restructuring, particularly delayering exercises, also plays a role in line managers' role overload by reducing their available resources, such as time available to fully implement HR policies (McGovern et al., 1997; Bos-Nehles, 2010; Hutchinson and Purcell, 2010)

Organizational systems and processes, including HR systems, are another potential source of role stress for line managers. While a strong HRM climate does not necessarily equate to consistent and effective HR implementation by line managers, it may limit their ability to role-make in response to role stressors. The rationale being that strong HRM processes improve role clarity and afford line managers less discretionary power in deciding how to execute their HR role (Gilbert et al., 2015). An emphasis on accountability in their HRM responsibilities improves role clarity for line managers, and increases the likelihood of more extensive, consistent HR implementation (Kehoe and Hun Han, 2020). However, an outcome-based control style, where role holders are informed of their objectives without an accompanying explanation of how to behave, can cause role ambiguity and a gap between intended and actual HRM because line managers are less likely to understand, or value, their HR role (Kauppila, 2014).

The content and nature of strategy, both corporate and HR, is another organizational factor that can either mitigate, or exacerbate, role stress for line managers. Mutually reinforcing corporate strategies, which are reflective of culture and climate, will enhance role clarity and reduce the potential for role conflict. Yet, organizations often have concurrent strategies of productivity and quality, which can escalate role stress amongst employees (Luria et al., 2014). HR strategy also needs to be consistent in content and aligned to the organization's context if it is to support line managers in carrying out their HR role. However, HRM itself can be both complex and contradictory (Boxall et al., 2011), with line managers having to manage the competing challenges of treating people fairly and equitably when implementing HRM (Fu et al., 2020). When HR strategy and policy is lacking in sufficient content, or does not align with the environment in which the line manager is operating, there is an increased propensity for line managers to deviate from intended HRM (Kehoe and Hun Han, 2020). This can be attributed to a lack of clarity caused by sparse policies, and experiences of role conflict that poorly aligned strategy will bring to role holders.

The industry sector in which a line manager works is another important environmental factor to consider when exploring why line managers behave as they do. For example, the role of line managers in the service sector has been argued to require significant HRM skills and expertise (Grugulis et al., 2011). Managers working in the service sector have a high propensity for role stress because of the interplay between the service context in which they work and their organizational position (Troyer et al., 2000). Role stress associated with working in such a context has a greater influence on employee performance than skill, motivation, personal aptitude or organizational factors (Churchill et al., 1985). Research on line managers working in the health sector has drawn similar conclusions, with evidence of role conflict, ambiguity and overload influencing frontline managers' implementation of HRM (Hutchinson and Purcell, 2010; Townsend et al., 2011; Woodrow and Guest, 2014). Thus, industry context is a factor in line managers' experiences of role stress and their execution of HRM. This seems particularly prevalent for line managers working in a service environment, who are often juggling a myriad of role partners with paradoxical corporate and HR strategies and associated role behaviours that are both demanding and inconsistent.

Furthermore, the international context and national culture within which a line manager operates can influence levels and sources of role stress. In hierarchical cultures where leadership is directive, the scope for role ambiguity reduces, and vice versa in more egalitarian national cultures (Showail et al., 2013). Problems also occur when managers work overseas as part of a multinational organization. Role ambiguity is more likely when there is a disconnection between the parent company and an overseas subsidiary (Gong et al., 2001), or when working in a country whose culture is very different (Showail et al., 2013). For example, managers accustomed to working in a hierarchical national culture bring expectations of a directive leadership style and suffer role ambiguity in more egalitarian cultures (Newman and Nollen, 1996; Trompenaars and Hampden-Turner, 1998). The complexity of working across national boundaries adds to the propensity for such managers suffering role stress, with implications for HR implementation.

CONSEQUENCES AND OUTCOMES OF ROLE THEORY FOR LINE MANAGERS AND HRM

Line managers play a key role in their organization's HR systems and often have a high level of responsibility with a related degree of discretion in their HR role. Critically, line managers' HR implementation has an impact on employees, teams and organizational effectiveness (Townsend et al., 2012; Bos Nehles et al., 2013; López-Cotarelo, 2018). While a large proportion of research studies have focused on the question what HRM is implemented, and more recently how managers implement HRM, little work has considered why line managers implement HRM in the way that they do.

In applying role theory to line managers' HR implementation, research has identified work role stress to be a contributing factor in variability and inconsistency between intended and implemented HRM in organizations (Hutchinson and Purcell, 2010; Gilbert et al., 2011; Evans, 2017). This can be attributed to line managers informally renegotiating their HR role and responsibilities by adapting HR policies. It is apparent that line managers do not willingly accept the role stressors associated with their organizational position, but instead renegotiate the expectations imposed upon them, as theorized by process role theory. As line managers juggle a range of responsibilities and a myriad of role partners, tasks that afford them less discretion and more accountability, such as those related to financial and other tangible performance outcomes, are prioritized (Troyer et al., 2000). HRM responsibilities offer line managers greater opportunity for discretionary behaviour and role-making, with empirical research confirming that their role-making tends to be undertaken in their HR responsibilities (Evans, 2017). Their ability to renegotiate their HR role is facilitated by a high level of responsibility for HRM alongside a lack of institutional support, monitoring, or incentives to implement practice according to central policy, providing the opportunity to modify or resist intended policy (Teague and Roche, 2012).

The organizational reality is that line managers often interpret and adapt HRM policies in response to their working environment and any accompanying role stress. Line managers implement HRM in quite distinct ways to adapt HRM to suit the local context (López-Cotarelo, 2018). They fashion adaptions to HR practices to make the system work in a local context, including acting in favour of other interests (Tyskbo, 2020) as well as serving self-interest (Evans, 2015). In doing so, the critical influence of line managers' role partners is evident, supporting the notion that HR implementation is relational and social in nature (Bos-Nehles and Meijerink, 2018).

Furthermore, the source of role stress has different outcomes for HR implementation, with research studies identifying how line managers' execution of HR practices differ according to the type of role stress they experience. Role overload compels line managers to enact their role set according to the resources available to them, with a lack of time commonly cited as a reason to neglect some HR tasks. Role conflict occurs where conflicting and contradictory demands are made of line managers, such as the paradoxical strategies of quality enhancement and cost reduction, or the inherently conflicting behavioural demands of HRM. When experiencing role conflict, line managers tend to prioritise the more tangible and immediate demands of their role. Subsequently, intangible responsibilities such as longer-term, high-road HRM practises, which are hard to measure using tangible performance targets, are less likely to be implemented as intended, or may even be totally disregarded. Finally, role ambiguity evolves from a lack of clear corporate direction and limited support from associated role partners, particularly HRM professionals. This leaves line managers unsure as to how the organization wants HRM to be implemented, or what to prioritize, while undermining their HRM skills and confidence, compromising their ability to implement HRM as intended.

CONCLUSIONS

In conclusion, the adoption of a role-theoretic framework highlights the complex nature of line managers' roles and their experiences of role stress. These managers are subject to a wide range of normative expectations corresponding to their organizational position and exposure to varied sources of role stress. In response to these role stressors, line managers have been found to engage in role-making, role renegotiation and job-crafting behaviours to challenge the expectations placed upon them. In doing so, they make physical or cognitive changes that alter the content and meaning of their job, as well as their relationship with role partners. In terms of their HR role, line managers have been found to make adaptions in HR implementation, often in response to their sources of role stress. This challenges any notion that line managers routinely implement HRM as intended. It shows line managers are agentic actors in the HRM process by renegotiating their HR role, which in turn shapes the consistency and quality of HR implementation. However, the relationship between role stress and HR implementation is a nuanced picture, with different role stressors affecting HR implementation in different ways. Role overload and conflict seem to bring about a renegotiation, or even total neglect, of more intangible or costly HR policies; whereas role ambiguity seems to challenge line managers' ability to confidently, and consistently, implement HRM. In adopting a role-theoretic lens, we can surmise that role stress is a key factor in line managers' HR implementation, with them being more likely to adapt HRM practice when subjected to role stress related to the demands of their job, their role partners and the context in which they execute their role.

REFERENCES

Alfes, K., Truss, C., Soane, E.C., Rees, C., and Gatenby, M. (2013). The relationship between line manager behaviour, perceived HRM practices and individual performance: examining the mediating role of engagement. *Human Resource Management*, 52, 839–859.

Arthur, J.B., Herdman, A.O., and Yang, J. (2016). How top management HR beliefs and values affect high-performance work system adoption and implementation effectiveness. *Human Resource Management*, 55(3), 413–435.

Biddle, B.J. (1979). *Role Theory: Expectations, Identities and Behaviors*. New York: Wiley.

Biddle, B.J. (1986). Recent development in role theory. *Annual Review of Sociology*, 12, 67–92.

Bos-Nehles, A. (2010). The line makes the difference: line managers as effective HR partners. Doctoral thesis, Universiteit Twente.

Bos-Nehles, A.C., and Meijerink, J.G. (2018). HRM implementation by multiple HRM actors: a social exchange perspective. *International Journal of Human Resource Management*, 29(22), 3068–3092.

Bos-Nehles, A.C., Van Riemsdijk, M.J., and Looise J.K. (2013). Employee perceptions of line management performance: applying the AMO theory to explain the effectiveness of line managers' HRM implementation. Human Resource Management, 52, 861–877.

Boxall, P., Ang, S.H., and Bartram, T. (2011). Analysing the 'Black Box' of HRM: uncovering HR goals, mediators, and outcomes in a standardized service environment. *Journal of Management Studies*, 48, 1504–1532.

Brewster, C., and Larsen H.H. (2000). Responsibility in human resource management: the role of the line. In C. Brewster and H.H. Larsen (eds), *Human Resource Management in Northern Europe: Dilemmas and Strategy*. Oxford: Blackwell, pp. 195–218.

Child, J., and Partridge, B. (1982). *Lost Managers: Supervisors in Industry and Society*. Cambridge: Cambridge University Press.

Churchill, G.A., Ford, N.A., Hartley, S.W., and Walker, O.C. (1985). The determinants of salesperson performance: a meta-analysis. *Journal of Marketing Research*, 22, 103–118.

Deery, S., Iverson, R., and Walsh, J. (2002). Work relationships in telephone call centres: understanding emotional exhaustion and employee withdrawal. *Journal of Management Studies*, 39, 471–496.

Evans, S. (2015). Juggling on the line: front line managers and their management of human resources in the retail industry. *Employee Relations*, 37, 459–474.

Evans, S. (2017). HRM and front line managers: the influence of role stress. *International Journal of Human Resource Management*, 28, 3128–3148.

Eatough, E.M., Chang, C.H, Miloslavic, S.A., and Johnson, R.E. (2011). Relationships of role stressors with organizational citizenship behavior: a meta-analysis. *Journal of Applied Psychology*, 96, 619–632.

Floyd, S.W., and Wooldridge, B. (1997). Middle management's strategic influence and organizational performance. *Journal of Management Studies*, 34, 465–485.

Fu, N., Flood, P.C., Rousseau, D.M., and Morris, T. (2020). Line managers as paradox navigators in hrm implementation: balancing consistency and individual responsiveness. Journal of Management, 46, 203–233.

Gilbert, C., De Winne, S., and Sels, L. (2011). Antecedents of front-line managers' perceptions of HR role stressors. *Personnel Review*, 40, 549–569.

Gilbert, C., De Winne, S., and Sels, L., (2015). Strong HRM processes and line managers' effective HRM implementation: a balanced view. *Human Resource Management Journal*, 25, 600–616.

Gilboa, S., Shirom, A., Fried, Y., and Cooper, C. (2008). A meta-analysis of work demand stressors and job performance: examining main and moderating effects. *Personnel Psychology*, 61, 227–271.

Gong, Y., Shenker, O., Luo, Y., and Nyaw, M. (2001). Role conflict and ambiguity of CEOs in international joint ventures: a transaction cost perspective. *Journal of Applied Psychology*, 86, 764–773.

Grugulis, I., Bozhurt, O., and Clegg, J. (2011). No place to hide? The realities of leadership in UK supermarkets. In Grugulis I. and Bozhurt O. (eds), *Retail Work*. Basingstoke: Palgrave Macmillan, pp. 193–212.

Guest, D. (2011). Human resource management and performance: still searching for some answers. *Human Resource Management Journal*, 21, 3–13.

Guest, D.E., and Bos-Nehles, A. (2013). HRM and performance: the role of effective implementation. In J. Paauwe, D. Guest and P. Wright (eds), *HRM and Performance: Achievements and Challenges* Chichester: Wiley, pp. 79–96.

Hales, C. (2005). Rooted in supervision, branching into management: continuity and change in the role of first line manager. *Journal of Management Studies*, 4, 471–506.

Hang-Yue, N., Foley, S., and Loi, R. (2005). Work role stressors and turnover intentions: a study of professional clergy in Hong Kong. *International Journal of Human Resource Management*, 16, 2133–2146.

Hutchinson, S., and Purcell, J. (2010). Managing ward managers for roles in HRM in the NHS: overworked and under-resourced. *Human Resource Management Journal*, 20, 357–374.

Kahn, R.L., Wolfe, D.M., Quinn, R.P., Snoek, J.D., and Rosenthal, R.A. (1964). *Organizational Stress: Studies in Role Conflict and Ambiguity*. New York: Wiley.

Katz, D., and Kahn, R.L. (1966). *The Social Psychology of Organizations*, 2nd edn. New York: Wiley.

Kauppila, O.P. (2014). So, what am I supposed to do? A multilevel examination of role clarity. *Journal of Management Studies*, 51, 737–763.

Kehoe, R.R., and Hun Han, J. (2020). An expanded conceptualization of line managers' involvement in human resource management. *Journal of Applied Psychology*, 105, 111–129.

Kilroy, J., and Dundon, T. (2015). The multiple faces of front line managers. *Employee Relations*, 37, 410–427.

Korczynski, M. (2002). *HRM in Service Work*. Basingstoke: Palgrave.

Kulik, C.T., and Bainbridge, H.T. (2006). HR and the line: the distribution of HR activities in Australian organisations. *Asia Pacific Journal of Human Resources*, 44, 240–256.

López-Cotarelo, J. (2018) Line managers and HRM: a managerial discretion perspective. *Human Resource Management Journal*, 28, 255–271.

Luria, G., Yagil, D., and Gal, I. (2014). Quality and productivity: role conflict in the service context. *Service Industries Journal*, 34, 955–973.

Makhecha, U.P., Vasanthi S., Prabhu, G.N., and Mukherji, S. (2018). Multi-level gaps: a study of intended, actual and experienced human resource practices in a hypermarket chain in India. *International Journal of Human Resource Management*, 29, 360–398.

Malhotra, N., and Ackfeldt, A.L. (2016). Internal communication and prosocial service behaviors of front-line employees: investigating mediating mechanisms. *Journal of Business Research*, 69, 4132–4139.

Maxwell, G.A., and Watson, S. (2006). Perspectives in line managers in HRM: Hilton International's UK hotels. *International Journal of Human Resource Management*, 17, 1152–1170.

McConville, T. (2006). Devolved HRM responsibilities, middle-managers and role dissonance. *Personnel Review*, 35, 637–653.

McDermott, A.M., Fitzgerald, L., Van Gestel, N.M., and Keating, M.A. (2015). From bipartite to tripartite devolved HRM in professional service contexts: evidence from hospitals in three countries. *Human Resource Management*, 54, 813–831.

McGovern, P., Gratton, L., Hope-Hailey, V., Stiles, P., and Truss, C. (1997). Human resource management on the line? *Human Resource Management Journal*, 7, 12–29.

Meijerink, J.G., Bondarouk, T., and Lepak, D.P. (2016). Employees as active consumers of HRM: linking employees' HRM competences with their perceptions of HRM service value. *Human Resource Management*, 55, 219–240.

Newman, K., and Nollen, S. (1996). Culture and congruence: the fit between management practices and national culture. *Journal of International Business Studies*, 27, 753–779.

Nishii, L.H., Lepak, D.P., and Schneider, B. (2008). Employee attributions of the 'why' of HR practices: their effects on employee attitudes and behaviors, and customer satisfaction. *Personnel Psychology*, 61, 503–545.

Op de Beeck, S., Wynen, J., and Hondeghem, A. (2016). HRM implementation by line managers: explaining the discrepancy in HR–line perceptions of HR devolution. *International Journal of Human Resource Management*, 27, 1901–1919.

Ortqvist, D., and Wincent, J. (2006). Prominent consequences of role stress: a meta-analytic review. *International Journal of Stress Management*, 13, 399–422.

Purcell, J., and Hutchinson, S. (2007). Front-line managers as agents in the HRM–performance causal chain: theory, analysis and evidence. *Human Resource Management Journal*, 17, 3–20.

Rigopoulou, I., Theodosiou, M., Katsilea, E., and Perdikis, N. (2012). Information control, role perceptions, and work outcomes of boundary-spanning frontline managers. *Journal of Business Research*, 65, 626–633.

Rizzo, J.R., House, R.J., and Lirtzman, S.I. (1970). Role conflict and ambiguity in complex organizations. *Administrative Science Quarterly*, 15, 150–162.

Showail, S.J., McLean Parks, J., and Smith, F.I. (2013). Foreign workers in Saudi Arabia: a field study of role ambiguity, identification, information-seeking, organizational support and performance. *International Journal of Human Resource Management*, 24, 3957–3979.

Sikora, D.M., and Ferris, G.R. (2014). Strategic human resource practice implementation: the critical role of line management. *Human Resource Management Review*, 24, 271–281.

Skogstad, A., Einarsen, S., Torsheim, T., Aasland, M.S., and Hetland, H. (2007). The destructiveness of laissez-faire leadership behavior. *Journal of Occupational Health Psychology*, 12, 80–92.

Slattery, J., Selvarajan, T.T., and Anderson, J.E. (2008). The influences of new employee development practices upon role stressors and work-related attitudes of temporary employees. *International Journal of Human Resource Management*, 19, 2268–2293.

Stanton, P., Young, S. Bartram, T., and Leggat, S.G. (2010). Singing the same song: translating HRM messages across management hierarchies in Australian hospitals. *International Journal of Human Resource Management*, 21, 567–581

Teague, P., and Roche, W.K. (2012). Line managers and the management of workplace conflict: evidence from Ireland. *Human Resource Management Journal*, 22, 235–251.

Tims, M., Bakker, A.B., and Derks, D. (2012). Development and validation of the job-crafting scale. *Journal of Vocational Behaviour*, 80, 173–186

Townsend, K., and Russell B. (2013). Investigating the nuances of front-line managers' work. *Labour and Industry: A Journal of the Social and Economic Relations of Work*, 23, 168–181.

Townsend, K., Wilkinson, A., and Allan, C. (2012). Mixed signals in HRM: the HRM role of hospital line managers. *Human Resource Management Journal*, 22, 267–282.

Townsend, K., Wilkinson, C., Allan, C., and Bamber, G. (2011). Accidental, unprepared and unsupported: the ward managers' journey. *International Journal of Human Resource Management*, 23, 204–220.

Trompenaars, A., and Hampden-Turner, C. (1998). *Riding the Waves of Culture: Understanding Cultural Diversity in Global Business* (2nd edn), New York: McGraw Hill.

Troyer, L., Mueller, C.W., and Osinsky, P.I. (2000). Who's the boss? A role theoretic analysis of customer work. *Work and Occupations*, 27, 406–427.

Trullen, J., Bos-Nehles, A., and Valverde, M. (2020). From intended to actual and beyond: a cross-disciplinary view of (human resource management) implementation. *International Journal of Management Reviews*, 22, 150–176.

Trullen J., Sytirpe, L., Bonache, J., and Valverde, M. (2016). The HR department's contribution to line managers' effective implementation of HR practices. *Human Resource Management Journal*, 26, 449–470.

Tubré, T.C., and Collins, J.M. (2000). Jackson and Schuler (1985) revisited: a meta-analysis of the relationships between role ambiguity, role conflict, and job performance. *Journal of Management*, 26, 155–169.

Turner, R.H. (1962). Role-taking: process versus conformity. In Arnold M. Rose (ed.), *Human Behavior and Social Processes: An Interactionist Approach*. Boston, MA: Houghton Mifflin, pp. 20–40.

Turner, R.H. (1978). The role and the person. *American Journal of Sociology*, 81, 1–23.

Tyskbo, D. (2020), Line management involvement in performance appraisal work. *Employee Relations*, 42, 818–844.

Vermeeren, B. (2014). Variability in HRM implementation among line managers and its effect on performance: a 2-1-2 mediational multilevel approach. *International Journal of Human Resource Management*, 25, 3039–3059.

Whitaker, B.G., Dahling, J.J., and Levy, P. (2007). The development of a feedback environment and role clarity model of job performance. *Journal of Management*, 33, 570–591.

Woodhams, C., and Lupton, B. (2006). Gender-based equal opportunities policy and practice in small firms: the impact of HR professionals. *Human Resource Management Journal, 16*, 74–97.

Woodrow, C., and Guest, D. (2014). When good HR gets bad results: exploring the challenge of HR implementation in the case of workplace bullying. *Human Resource Management Journal*, 24, 38–56.

Wrzesniewski, A., and Dutton, J.E. (2001). Crafting a job: re-visioning employees as active crafters of their work. *Academy of Management Review*, 26, 179–201.

Yuliza, M.Y., Poh Wai Choo, K., Jayaraman, N., Newaz, R., and Muhammad, Z. (2019). HR line managers' reflections on HR effectiveness through HR roles and role stressors, *South East European Journal of Economics and Business*, 14, 34–48.

5. Frontline managers and human resource management: a social exchange theory perspective

Anindita Roy Bannya and Hugh T.J. Bainbridge

THE FRONTLINE MANAGER: THE IMPORTANCE OF PERSONAL RELATIONSHIPS

Frontline managers (FLMs) (also known as first-line managers) are the first level of management. They supervise employees with non-managerial duties and have reporting responsibilities to more senior managers (Hales, 2005). FLMs usually comprise the majority of an organisation's managers. FLMs have broad people management responsibilities for day-to-day activities relating to the oversight of their team. Beyond this, FLMs are central to the implementation of formal human resources (HR) policies and practices (Kehoe and Han, 2020; Trullen et al., 2020). While the specific activities of FLMs vary widely, they regularly implement HR policy guidance via selecting new employees, delivering training and conducting performance appraisals.

Fundamental to FLM HR responsibilities is that they are undertaken via interpersonal relationships that connect the FLM to subordinates, HR representatives, and senior managers. The FLM–employee relationship is the context in which FLMs draw upon HR policies to direct, develop and motivate employees (Trullen et al., 2020). FLMs thus shape employee perceptions of, attitudes towards, and behaviours in response to, HR practices (Bos-Nehles and Meijerink, 2018). The FLM–HR representative relationship involves an exchange in which HR representatives support FLMs who enact HR policies (Larsen and Brewster, 2003). HR representatives typically lead the design of HR policies and practices. These are communicated to FLMs, with the quality of this interaction affecting understanding and acceptance (Gilbert et al., 2011b). This support enhances FLMs' ability to successfully implement HR (Bos-Nehles and Meijerink, 2018). In the other direction of the exchange, FLMs share operationally relevant matters that inform decision-making in HR departments. The FLM–senior manager relationship consists of interactions that shape FLM views about the people-related implications of organisational strategy (Gilbert et al., 2011b; Guest, 1987). It is also the channel by which senior managers identify whether HR-related performance goals have been achieved at the operational level.

HR research underlines the centrality of relationships to the FLM role and that performance is enhanced when these intraorganisational relationships are of high quality (Buhusayen et al., 2021; Hales, 2005). Espoused HR practices are more successfully implemented when FLMs have strong relationships with employees, HR managers, and senior managers (Bos-Nehles and Meijerink, 2018; Martinson and Deleon, 2016). FLMs with better employee relationships enhance employee perceptions of, and satisfaction with, HR practices (Martinson and Deleon, 2016; Purcell and Hutchinson, 2007). FLM motivation to implement HR practices is also enhanced by support from HR representatives (for example, advice or consultation) and senior managers (for example, providing FLMs time to understand and implement HR practices) (Bos-Nehles and Meijerink, 2018).

This introduction sets the context for our focus on interpersonal relationships in the undertaking of the HR-related roles of FLMs. We now turn to exploring how social exchange theory (SET) provides a framework for examining FLM relationships with employees, HR representatives and senior managers, across the remainder of this chapter.

SOCIAL EXCHANGE THEORY

A range of theories are applied to studying interpersonal relationships in organisations. For example, attachment theory (Yip et al., 2018), relational coordination (Gittell et al., 2010), social network and social capital theory (Collins and Clark, 2003; Jiang and Liu, 2015) and SET (Cropanzano and Mitchell, 2005) provide perspectives for examining the constellation of relationships that make up the organisational environment. Among these, one of the most influential in HR field is SET. The interest of HRM researchers in SET is consistent with the broader organisational literature, where SET has gained major prominence. SET is widely applied in fields as diverse as governance, leadership, networks, organisational justice, psychological contracts and power (Cropanzano and Mitchell, 2005). The utility of SET arises from its provision of a broadly applicable framework for considering how individuals form relationships through exchanges of resources. The resources in these social exchanges can be material (for example, money, gifts) or intangible resources (for example, respect, information, love).

There exists a plurality of views about the specific conceptualisation of social exchange due to the breadth of contributors to SET. Nevertheless, there is broad agreement that social exchange denotes the pattern of repeated interactions that generate obligations for the individuals involved (Emerson, 1976). These interactions are viewed as interdependent, as they are informed by the behaviour of the exchange partner. According to SET, a relationship between actors influences the success of the exchange, and a fruitful exchange can elicit increasing commitment to the relationship. The outcome of these exchanges may be a high-quality relationship that benefits the exchange partners.

Reviews of SET (e.g., Cropanzano and Mitchell, 2005) outline several elements that are shared across the different articulations of SET. These pertain to the rules and norms that govern the exchange relationship, the resources of exchange, and social exchange relationships. In terms of rules and norms, SET theorists hold that if exchanges are to develop into mutually trusting relationships, rules or frameworks need to develop in order to guide the exchange process (Gouldner, 1960). Most applications of SET in organisational research have concentrated on reciprocity as a rule of exchange; and within this, interdependent exchanges as a type of reciprocity (Cropanzano and Mitchell, 2005). The idea of reciprocal interdependence arises from an understanding that interpersonal exchanges are contingent. That is, the action of one exchange partner informs the partner's response. Thus, if one provides a resource, the partner receiving this benefit is likely to reciprocate. An employee who receives a resource (for example, a pay rise) should feel an obligation to exhibit attitudes and behaviours desired by the organisation to repay it (for example, greater attitudinal and behavioural commitment). This reciprocity behaviour is voluntary, and the obligations and expectations are often implicit and unvoiced (Blau, 1964; Cross and Dundon, 2019). Provision of a resource and reciprocation by the partner generates an ongoing, self-reinforcing cycle. However, continuation of the exchange relationship is dependent on whether the partner who received a benefit responds in kind. Repeated instances of non-reciprocation lead to a breakdown of the exchange relationship. In sum, this interdependency means that exchange relationships are best considered as continually evolving rather than static in nature (Cropanzano and Mitchell, 2005; Cross and Dundon, 2019). By providing a framework for conceptualising this process, SET provides a useful tool for considering the obligations, trust, and expectations central to reciprocating exchange relationships in organisations, and especially those related to the exchange of HR-related resources. The types of resources that are exchanged are also a focus for SET researchers. In broad terms, resources (love, status, information, money, goods, services) can be usefully described as being either economic or socio-economic (Foa and Foa, 1974, 1980). Economic resources are tangible resources that allow for fulfillment of financial needs. Socio-economic resources are intangible resources that address social and esteem needs. Alternatively, resources in an exchange relationship can be classified in terms of whether they originate from employers or employees (Tsui et al., 1997). Finally, a key feature of SET is a recognition that social exchange relationships involve a sequence of resource exchanges between interacting partners, with obligations that are governed by rules of exchange. This relationship can occur between employees and their supervisors, co-workers, organisations, customers and suppliers (Cropanzano and Mitchell, 2005). Employees tend to contribute to the relationship with different actors based on the value they assign to the benefits they receive from each actor.

SOCIAL EXCHANGE, LEADER–MEMBER EXCHANGE AND PERCEIVED SUPPORT

SET is a broad framework that is widely applied to examining exchange relationships across actors and contexts. However, HR researchers also have at their disposal several targeted theoretical elaborations for considering exchange relationships in organisations, in the form of leader–member exchange (LMX) theory, perceived organisational support (POS) and perceived supervisor support (PSS).

Leader–Member Exchange

Drawing on a social exchange perspective, leader–member exchange (LMX) theory focuses on the supervisor–subordinate dyad. While LMX is applicable to considering this dyad at any level of the organisational hierarchy, researchers have focused on the FLM–employee relationship (Rockstuhl et al., 2012). As befits its consideration of this dyad in an organisational context, these exchanges are viewed from the standpoint of task-based rather than liking-based (that is, friendship) relationships (Graen and Uhl-Bien, 1995). LMX theory characterises influences on supervisor–subordinate relationship quality and provides a perspective on the development of this dyadic relationship.

LMX holds that mutual respect, trust and esteem contribute to shaping exchange quality (Anand et al., 2016; Dansereau et al., 1975). In practice, though, FLMs face limitations in their available social capital and time. This means that they typically develop relationships of varying quality with subordinates (Graen and Uhl-Bien, 1995). These different quality FLM–employee relationships have FLM, subordinate and organisational consequences. A large literature has considered how LMX quality affects the exchange of resources between employees and FLMs (Cropanzano and Mitchell, 2005). It indicates that lower LMX has unfavourable HR-related consequences. To illustrate, employees with lower LMX report less trust, favours and respect from their FLMs, and hold more negative perceptions of the organisational context (for example, perceptions of work politics) (Erdogan and Bauer, 2016; Rosen et al., 2011).

Perceived Organisational Support and Perceived Supervisor Support

Perceived organisational support (POS) is widely applied to study the connection between employees and their employing organisation (Farndale et al., 2011). POS is the employees' perception of what senior managers, as an embodiment or representative of the organisation, do to ensure employee success and well-being. Thus, POS provides a framework for examining the relationships that employees have with senior managers (Albrecht and Travaglione, 2003; Farndale and Kelliher, 2013). Indeed, since supervisors are the 'face' of the organisation, POS is often understood as perceived supervisor support (PSS), as it is the FLM who implements organisational HR policies and practices while making idiosyncratic work arrangements (i-deals) with individuals. POS and PSS are an antecedent to trust; a critical element of relationships between employees and senior managers (Albrecht and Travaglione, 2003). Trust is generated when the receipt of support signals to employees that they are valued by the senior managers who have authority to influence employment conditions (Albrecht and Travaglione, 2003; Eisenberger et al., 1990). Perceptions of support are based on an employee's inference of whether the decisions of managers are beneficial or detrimental to the individual (Farndale and Kelliher, 2013). Consistent with principles of reciprocity, POS and PSS increase employees' felt obligation to exhibit in-role and extra-role behaviours to facilitate organisational goal attainment. In the following, to be parsimonious, we use the SET terminology when discussing broader issues, while noting specific elaborations of the social exchange perspective (for example, LMX) where this detail is relevant to the issues being discussed.

SOCIAL EXCHANGE THEORY AND THE HRM LITERATURE

Recent reviews of theories in the HRM literature note the wide application of SET (e.g., Cooke et al., 2019; Cross and Dundon, 2019; Harney and Alkhalaf, 2021). This interest is reflected in several articles that focus on the intersection of SET and HRM (e.g., Cross and Dundon, 2019; Min et al., 2017). In the preparation of this chapter, we conducted an independent assessment of the prevalence of SET in the 2001–20 HRM literature. We reviewed journals by searching for the subject terms 'Human Resource Management', 'HR practices' or 'HRM' in combination with 'Social Exchange Theory', anywhere within the abstract, title, and keywords. While our review was more representative than exhaustive in nature, our search still identified 433 articles that addressed SET in relation to HRM issues. As a basis of comparison, similar searches on alternative theoretical frameworks in the HRM literature identified 126 (ability, motivation and opportunity theory) and 299 (resource-based view) articles. This disparity highlights the strong interest of HRM researchers in SET. We represent this data in Figure 5.1

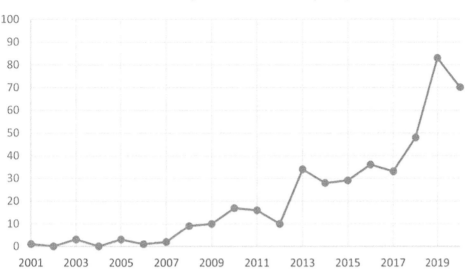

Number of journal articles per year

Note: Data obtained from Web of Science Core Collection.

Figure 5.1   *Social exchange theory in HRM research, 2001–20*

to illustrate the rapid growth of literature at the intersection of HRM and SET across the last two decades.

Social Exchange Theory and Frontline Managers

A major contributor to the popularity of SET is its utility as an explanatory mechanism in the HRM–outcome relationship. Researchers have thus drawn upon SET as a broad framework as well as its specific features to conceptualise how HR practices affect exchange relationships, and how relationship features affect outcomes. As the FLM is a key player in these HR-based interactions, we now turn to examining the FLM in connection with SET, and specifically, the FLM's intraorganisational relationships with employees, HR representatives, and senior managers.

HR responsibilities are a major component of an FLM's role (Bos-Nehles and Meijerink, 2018; Kulik and Bainbridge, 2006). FLMs bridge the gap between employees and HR representatives, and between employees and senior managers (Steffensen et al., 2019). This position involves the FLM in ongoing social exchanges with these groups. Social exchange processes are central to employee training, development and performance management activities that FLMs undertake. Exchange processes also apply to the FLM's relationship with HR representatives. HR managers seek to have policies implemented by FLMs, while FLMs seek support from HR to address challenging personnel issues. The FLM's relationship with senior managers is also an unfolding process where each actor exchanges valued resources. SET provides a framework for examining these FLM relationships and their consequences. In the following sections, we consider how SET is used to explore the FLM's HR role in connection with: (1) employees; (2) HR managers; and (3) senior managers.

FRONTLINE MANAGERS AND EMPLOYEES

A supervisor and subordinate are connected by an official reporting line. This reporting relationship develops further via the ongoing interactions as job tasks are assigned to a subordinate, progress is communicated back to the supervisor, and resources are exchanged between them. This FLM–employee relationship involves the exchange of HR-related resources via the FLM's implementation of HR practices (Kehoe and Han, 2020; Trullen et al., 2020). HR practices such as training and access to flexible working arrangements provide resources (human capital acquisition, opportunities to better manage competing demands) that are valued by employees. In turn, these resources generate an obligation to reciprocate.

Reciprocation occurs when employees provide something that is organisationally valued. Indeed, it is well established that high-quality relationships enhance a range of job-relevant attitudes. For example, employees reciprocate with greater satisfaction, engagement and commitment when FLMs are supportive (Brunetto et al., 2014; Dewettinck and Vroonen, 2017; Fletcher, 2019; Gilbert et al., 2011b; Shuck et al., 2014). Affective organisational commitment increases when FLMs are developmental (Marescaux et al., 2019). SET-based research also reveals that supporting, developing, recognising, consulting and empowering subordinates elicits employee commitment (Gilbert et al., 2011b). Reciprocation can manifest via behaviours such as enhanced performance, organisational citizenship behaviour, innovative outcomes and behavioural commitment. Furthermore, developmental FLM activities lead to employee task performance (Marescaux et al., 2019) and deteriorating FLM–employee relationships that are characterised by employee perceptions of psychological contract breach reduce performance (Chen et al., 2008). A perception that FLMs are interested in an employee's well-being reduces turnover intentions (Newman et al., 2012). Another study by Bos-Nehles and Veenendaal (2019) considered the exchange relationship as an explanation for the connection between HR practices and innovative work behaviour. They argued that the organisational climate can help employees to understand what to reciprocate, with an innovation climate conveying to employees the value that the organisation places on innovative behaviours (Bos-Nehles and Veenendaal, 2019).

HR Antecedents to Social Exchange

The HR literature provides support for a view that HR practices (in bundles or individually) strengthen FLM–employee relationships. When FLMs implement valued HR practices, it signals to employees that FLMs care for their well-being and are willing to invest in them. This enhances employee perceptions and prompts reciprocation via positive attitudes and behaviour (Bos-Nehles and Meijerink, 2018; Gould-Williams, 2007; Guzzo and Noonan, 1994). FLMs who exhibit concern for employees by offering these HR practices initiate high-quality exchange relationships with employees (Allen et al., 2003). In contrast, adversarial FLM behaviour can instigate a situation of ongoing negative FLM–employee interactions (Uhl-Bien and Maslyn, 2003), and employees who fail to appreciate the benefits of HR practices report worse relational outcomes (Godard, 2004; Ramsay et al., 2000).

HR practice bundles

Overall, the evidence suggests that an FLM's implementation of HR practices has a strong influence on the FLM–employee relationship. FLMs are often responsible for the implementation of HR practices, and employees assess whether the FLM has invested in a subordinate through these practices. This investment generates a felt obligation in employees to reciprocate with something of value to the FLM. Effective management processes in relation to HR practices can thus allow FLMs and employees to develop and maintain high-quality social exchange relationships. Indeed, research suggests that FLM enactment of HR practices enhances relationships with subordinates and creates a supportive work environment (Macky and Boxall, 2007; Meyer and Smith, 2000; Wu and Chaturvedi, 2009). For example, Marescaux et al. (2019) identified that developmental FLM behaviours enhance the benefit of other HR practices such as career counselling. Chen et al. (2021), report that the effect of collectivism-oriented HRM on team creativity is partially mediated by interpersonal harmony. High-performance work practices (HPWPs) implemented by FLMs influence relational coordination among team members via team affective commitment (Raineri and Valenzuela-Ibarra, forthcoming). HPWPs create employee obligations to reciprocate via greater increased organisational identification (Liu et al., 2020). Additionally, high-commitment HRM creates a sequence where FLMs are supported by senior managers, and FLMs then support their subordinates (Latorre et al., 2020). SET and reciprocity beliefs have also been used to explain why work–life programme bundles implemented by FLMs enhance employee dedication, responsible behaviour and perceived organisational performance (Akter et al., 2020a, 2020b).

Individual HR practices

In terms of recruitment and selection, SET has been used to understand the role of reciprocity in recruitment when offering bonuses for referrals. Pieper et al. (2018) found that a referral bonus and its amount increased the likelihood of a referral, and explained that the bonus motivates employees to reciprocate by offering a referral. However, perceived risk in the social exchange process reduced referring likelihood. A fear that a 'bad hire' will affect the employee's relationship with the organisation and FLM reduces reciprocity beliefs that otherwise might be generated by offering a referral bonus. SET has also been applied to consider the implications of changes in job design. One recent example is that of Farid et al. (2019), who identified how enhancing job autonomy increases employee trust in FLMs and leads to employee reciprocation via extra-role behaviour.

Formal performance management aims to provide clear goals, expectations and outcomes of appraisals, while informal performance management activities help employees to meet performance criteria by providing more timely feedback. The FLM's efforts to help a subordinate meet performance criteria convey the FLM's interest in an employee's success. Supported employees reciprocate with increased job satisfaction, engagement and innovative work behaviour (Bak, 2020; Dewettinck and Vroonen, 2017). High-quality feedback creates a supportive environment (Eisenberger et al., 1986), and Dewettinck and Vroonen (2017) showed that the way FLMs enact performance management (for example, frequency, duration) affects the exchange relationship and, in turn, employee job satisfaction. An FLM's commitment to helpful performance management activities generates reciprocity beliefs that manifest as increased job satisfaction and engagement (Dewettinck and Vroonen, 2017). Other research identifies that useful feedback on employee performance indicates that their development and well-being matters to the FLM. Employees then reciprocate via more innovative behaviours

(Bak, 2020). Employees who do not receive fair and timely feedback perceive a psychological contract breach and reciprocate by reducing innovative behaviours (Eva et al., 2019). SET has also been invoked to consider training and mentoring opportunities. Marescaux et al. (2019) investigated the effects of FLM developmental behaviours. Actions such as mentoring strengthen the FLM–employee relationship as it signals that the FLM wishes to promote employee growth and development. In contrast, low development signals an imbalance between an employee's contribution and what is received in return.

Social Exchange Outcomes

FLM–employee exchange relationship quality has a range of important work consequences, and we address these via our consideration of employee awareness of and access to HR practices, and their effectiveness.

Employee awareness of HR practices

A high-quality FLM–employee relationship improves employee awareness of HR practices (Bos-Nehles and Meijerink, 2018). This is important, as greater knowledge of HR investments improves employee commitment (Bos-Nehles and Meijerink, 2018). Employee awareness of HR practices develops due to the mutual trust and obligations within a strong relationship that motivate FLMs to provide greater information and support to subordinates. Employees who report greater LMX thus have more favourable perceptions relating to available HR practices (Martinson and Deleon, 2016). Further, high-quality FLM–employee supportive relationships are associated with the FLM sharing job and organisational knowledge and opportunities to pursue such as challenging assignments that allow employee growth (Seibert et al., 2001). These resources enhance the likelihood that employees will reciprocate by forming positive views of developmental HR policies and opportunities (Kraimer et al., 2011).

Access to HR practices

In high-quality relationships, FLMs offer increased access to beneficial HR practices (Liao et al., 2009; Liden and Graen, 1980). When employees have low-quality relationships with their FLMs, they are less successful at negotiating desired task-related i-deals (Morf et al., 2019). FLMs with low LMX perceive that subordinates, when granted i-deals, will not reciprocate in ways that are consistent with the FLM's interest, but will instead aim to serve their own needs. The extent of trust in an FLM influences the likelihood of obtaining mentoring (Richard et al., 2009). LMX also influences opportunities for employee development (Newman et al., 2011; Richard et al., 2009). The higher the LMX quality, the more the subordinates receive developmental opportunities from their FLMs. In turn, this positively affects subordinates' perceptions of their organisation's support for their development (Kraimer et al., 2011). In contrast, employee perceptions of psychological contract breach are negatively correlated with LMX quality and responses from the supervisor, in terms of the mentoring provided to the employee (Chen et al., 2008).

Effectiveness of HR practices

FLMs allocate different levels of resources to their subordinates depending on the quality of their relationship. Subordinates with high LMX receive more tangible and intangible resources from their FLMs. Due to this unequal distribution of resources, high LMX enhances subordinates' satisfaction with HR practices, and views of HR practice quality and effectiveness (Lapierre et al., 2006; Sanders et al., 2010; Yousaf et al., 2011). Employees with high LMX have greater trust in, and respect for, their FLMs and reciprocate by forming positive perceptions of HR (Bos-Nehles and Meijerink, 2018; Martinson and Deleon, 2016). A recent illustration of SET-related HR research in this area is by Audenaert et al. (2019), who identified that employees were more likely to view a performance management system as supportive rather than controlling when they had high-quality LMX with their FLMs.

FRONTLINE MANAGERS AND HR MANAGERS

An FLM's relationship with HR representatives can be mutually beneficial. For the FLM, access to HR knowledge and resources helps to address both routine and complex employee issues. For HR representatives, the relationship is an opportunity to leverage influence if FLMs can successfully implement HR policies. However, despite the importance of this relationship, SET-based HRM research has emphasised the FLM–employee relationship. FLM relationships with other actors have attracted relatively little attention. Still, the available research clearly conveys the utility of SET to an examination of the FLM–HR relationship.

The FLM–HR relationship is increasingly seen as an important influence on espoused and enacted HRM practices (Bos-Nehles and Meijerink, 2018). Espoused HRM practices are the intentions of organisational decision-makers. Enacted HR practices are those experienced by employees (Nishii and Rich, 2014; Nishii et al., 2018). FLMs often fail to enact espoused practices as intended. This may be due to a lack of support for FLMs, who then lack the motivation and competencies to enact HR practices effectively (Bos-Nehles and Meijerink, 2018). When HR representatives provide support and training to FLMs on how to implement HR, FLMs exhibit greater desire, skills and ability to enact these practices (Renwick, 2003).

A review of the way that SET has been applied in connection to the FLM–HR relationship reveals an emphasis on the role of FLMs and of HR managers in HR implementation. Bos-Nehles and Meijerink (2018) drew upon SET to explore how the HR department affects FLM enactment of HR. They found that FLMs' perceptions of HR support and provided capacity improved their motivation to implement HR practices. This finding suggests a need for HR departments to provide advice, consultation and support services to encourage FLMs in the HR implementation process. HR departments can also help FLMs to overcome implementation barriers by increasing FLM capacity to manage their time across HR and non-HR activities (Bos-Nehles and Meijerink, 2018). The support provided by HR representatives to FLMs enhances the perceived value of HR practices and clarifies how FLMs can contribute to organisational goals by enacting them. FLMs gain higher confidence in their ability to implement HR practices and perceive HR responsibilities as less burdensome when they receive support from the HR representatives (Gilbert et al., 2011a, 2015). Reciprocity beliefs arising from HR department support are also associated with FLM motivation to implement HR (Bos-Nehles and Meijerink, 2018). FLMs who are motivated to implement HR practices engage in frequent conversations with employees about HR practices and the role of the practices in helping employees achieve their own and organisational goals. Motivated FLMs align employee aspirations with an organisation's objectives, and this can flow translate into greater employee affective commitment (Bos-Nehles and Meijerink, 2018).

FRONTLINE MANAGERS AND SENIOR MANAGERS

For the FLM, high-quality relationships with senior managers provide access to the necessary support and guidance to be effective in their HR responsibilities. For senior managers, good relationships with FLMs ensure that strategic imperatives are translated into effective people-related activity at the lower level of the organisational hierarchy. High-quality relationships provide for an effective coordination of resources and achievement of organisational goals (Bos-Nehles et al., 2017; Op de Beeck et al., 2016; Trullen et al., 2016; Vermeeren, 2014). Relationship quality is thus a central theme in research on the FLM–senior manager relationship and its effects on FLM implementation of HR practices.

Senior managers play a pivotal role in shaping FLM understanding of HRM practices and how HR practices are linked with organisational performance (Bowen and Ostroff, 2004; Stanton et al., 2010). Senior managers' attitudes towards HR practices signal to FLMs the importance of HR, and affect how FLMs implement the practices (John and Björkman, 2015; Stanton et al., 2010). Senior managers benefit from trusted FLMs when pursuing HR initiatives (Korsgaard et al., 1995). When senior managers trust FLMs, they allocate resources to FLMs to achieve HR goals (Hasson et al., 2014). Senior manager understanding of FLM training and development needs influences FLM HR implementation (de Jong et al., 1999; Maxwell and Watson, 2006). This is because FLMs who do not receive adequate opportunities for development, in turn, acknowledge fewer subordinate training and development needs (Storey, 1992). Additionally, feedback from senior managers on plans to implement HR practices influences FLM perceptions of HR priorities (Hasson et al., 2014). Thus, senior managers enhance FLMs' capacity to implement HR, and FLMs reciprocate via improved HR effectiveness (Bos-Nehles and Meijerink, 2018; Hasson et al., 2014). FLMs often develop informal working arrangements with subordinates that require approval and support from senior managers. Receipt of this support and advice increases FLM confidence in senior managers and improves the implementation of HR (Williams, 2019). Senior managers can improve their relationships with FLMs by providing opportunities to participate in the decision-making process (Holland et al., 2017; Huang et al., 2016). Consistent with SET, these actions enhance relationship quality by providing a forum for building trust in senior managers (Farndale et al., 2011). Thus, senior managers who provide an opportunity to engage on HR issues strengthen relationships and improve FLM implementation of HR. In contrast, a lack of senior manager support reduces FLM commitment to implementing HR practices (Hasson et al., 2014). FLMs develop cynical reactions when they believe that senior managers are selfish and dishonest when communicating changes in organisational practices and circumstances (Prouska and Psychogios, 2019). These reactions, and a lack of FLM trust in senior managers, motivate FLMs to withhold information from them due to a fear of consequences (Prouska and Psychogios, 2019).

FUTURE RESEARCH DIRECTIONS

Our review of SET in connection to FLMs is suggestive of several gaps in this literature.

Construct Clarity

Although SET has received extensive attention in the HR literature, there is often a lack of clarity in the conceptualisation and a lack of refinement in the measurement of the processes that are central to SET. One problem is that SET is often invoked as a broad explanation for an unmeasured process connecting a predictor and outcome. A typical example would be a study that invokes SET to explain an association between HR practices implemented in an organisation and firm performance, but does not examine a SET-related mediating variable. Another problematic area of the literature is the prevalence of studies that examine variables that are conceivably related to SET, but that are operationalised in very general terms (for example, generalised perceptions of support). Future research that utilises more precise measures that are fundamental to core SET features would allow significant advances. It should also be noted that how researchers operationalise key SET concepts such as 'resources' varies widely. This variation imposes some challenges on efforts to synthesise findings in the field.

Operationalisation of HRM

An important distinction in the HRM literature is between espoused and enacted HRM practices (Khilji and Wang, 2006; Nishii et al., 2018). As noted, espoused practices are HR practices formulated by HR and senior managers (Khilji and Wang, 2006). Enacted practices are actual practices that are experienced by employees. Perceived practices are what employees think about the practices (Khilji and Wang, 2006). It is well recognised that gaps arise between HR practices intended by HR representatives and senior managers, those enacted by FLMs, and those perceived by employees (Nishii and Wright, 2008). As FLMs can affect the size of the gap between the enacted and perceived HR practices (Kehoe and Wright, 2013), there is an opportunity to draw upon SET to understand how different FLM–employee relationships (positive, negative, ambivalent, indifferent) (Petriglieri, 2015) influence employee perceptions of HR. For instance, adversarial FLM behaviours could prompt employees to reciprocate in damaging ways that distort their perception of HR practices. Additionally, research is needed to better understand how senior managers affect the people management activities of FLMs. Studies of senior manager behaviours that create an obligation from the FLM to prioritise effective HR practice implementation would be instructive.

Considering Contested HR Practices

From a social exchange perspective, when an organisation invests in HRM, it motivates employees to reciprocate. However, an important but largely untested assumption guiding the HR literature is that the FLM's resource investment in implementing an HR practice will be viewed positively by an employee. This is intriguing, as there seem to be good grounds to anticipate that HR resource investments may in some circumstances be viewed negatively, and thus detrimentally affect relationship quality. To illustrate, employees sometimes react negatively to the implementation of diversity and inclusion initiatives (Harrison et al., 2006; Hideg et al., 2011). Little consideration has been given to these negative reactions in the context of SET. Researchers are thus encouraged to consider the reactions of employees and FLMs (both positive and negative) to diversity and inclusion practices such as affirmative action (AA) and equal employment opportunity (EEO) initiatives. A further issue arises when one considers that FLMs are often held responsible for implementing these practices, but do so in ways that diverge from those intended by the organisation (Castilla and Benard, 2010; Noon and Ogbonna, 2021). One potential cause of this divergence may be an FLM's belief that implementing a practice as originally intended would harm important subordinate relationships. This can prompt the FLM to adapt the practice to remove or adjust elements that are problematic. Little research, however, considers these challenges and how FLMs, HR representatives, senior managers and employees navigate them. For researchers, this divergence between espoused and implemented HR is an area worthy of greater attention.

Methodological Issues

Our chapter concludes with a reflection on several methodological issues. We note that research on HR and SET is hindered by ambiguity on the referent or actors under consideration. Both theory and empirical measures take diverse approaches about who an employee has an exchange relationship with (for example, FLM, HR, the organisation). Furthermore, we note that the literature is limited by its emphasis on research designs that focus on a specific interpersonal interaction, which neglects the unfolding nature of the relationship and its history. At the start of this chapter we drew attention to the dynamic nature of exchange relationships. However, researchers very rarely go beyond the examination of a single time period, or a single exchange (for example, to examine the effect of increased training investments at time 1 on LMX quality measured at time 2). Future research that takes a more nuanced approach to examining a longer period of interactions, and particularly that which focuses on the beginning and end of a working relationship, would provide an important advance to the HRM literature.

REFERENCES

Akter, K., Ali, M., and Chang, A. (2020a). Work–life programs and performance in Australian organisations: the role of organisation size and industry type. *Asia Pacific Journal of Human Resources, 49*, 516–536. doi:10.1111/1744-7941.12235.

Akter, K., Ali, M., and Chang, A. (2020b). Work–life programmes and organisational outcomes: the role of the human resource system. *Personnel Review, 49*, 516–536. doi:10.1108/PR-10-2018-0408.

Albrecht, S., and Travaglione, A. (2003). Trust in public-sector senior management. *International Journal of Human Resource Management, 14*, 76–92. doi:10.1080/09585190210158529.

Allen, D.G., Shore, L.M., and Griffeth, R.W. (2003). The role of perceived organizational support and supportive human resource practices in the turnover process. *Journal of Management, 29*, 99–118. doi:10.1177/014920630302900107.

Anand, S., Vidyarthi, P.R., and Park, H.S. (2016). LMX differentiation: Understanding relational leadership at individual and group levels. In T.N. Bauer and B. Erdogan (eds), *The Oxford Handbook of Leader–Member Exchange* (pp. 263–291). Oxford University Press.

Audenaert, M., Decramer, A., George, B., Verschuere, B., and Van Waeyenberg, T. (2019). When employee performance management affects individual innovation in public organizations: the role of consistency and LMX. *International Journal of Human Resource Management, 30*, 815–834. doi:10.1080/09585192.2016.1239220.

Bak, H. (2020). Supervisor feedback and innovative work behavior: the mediating roles of trust in supervisor and affective commitment. *Frontiers in Psychology, 11*, 1–12. doi:10.3389/fpsyg.2020.559160.

Blau, P. (1964). *Exchange and Power in Social Life*. Wiley.

Bos-Nehles, A.C., and Meijerink, J.G. (2018). HRM implementation by multiple HRM actors: a social exchange perspective. *International Journal of Human Resource Management, 29*, 3068–3092. doi: 10.1080/09585192.2018.1443958.

Bos-Nehles, A.C., and Veenendaal, A.A.R. (2019). Perceptions of HR practices and innovative work behavior: the moderating effect of an innovative climate. *International Journal of Human Resource Management, 30*, 2661–2683. doi:10.1080/09585192.2017.1380680.

Bos-Nehles, A., Bondarouk, T., and Nijenhuis, K. (2017). Innovative work behaviour in knowledge-intensive public sector organizations: the case of supervisors in the Netherlands fire services. *International Journal of Human Resource Management, 28*, 379–398. doi:10.1080/09585192.2016.1244894.

Bowen, D.E., and Ostroff, C. (2004). Understanding HRM–firm performance linkages: the role of the 'strength' of the HRM system. *Academy of Management Review, 29*, 203–221.

Brunetto, Y., Shacklock, K., Teo, S., and Farr-Wharton, R. (2014). The impact of management on the engagement and well-being of high emotional labour employees. *International Journal of Human Resource Management, 25*, 2345–2363. doi:10.1080/09585192.2013.877056.

Buhusayen, B., Seet, P.S., and Coetzer, A. (2021). Front-line management during radical organisational change: social exchange and paradox interpretations. *Sustainability, 13*, 893. doi:10.3390/su13020893.

Castilla, E.J., and Benard, S. (2010). The paradox of meritocracy in organizations. *Administrative Science Quarterly, 55*, 543–576.

Chen, S., Fan, Y., Zhang, G., and Zhang, Y. (2021). Collectivism-oriented human resource management on team creativity: effects of interpersonal harmony and human resource management strength. *International Journal of Human Resource Management, 32*, 3805–3832. doi:10.1080/09585192.2019.1640765.

Chen, Z.X., Tsui, A.S., and Zhong, L. (2008). Reactions to psychological contract breach: a dual perspective. *Journal of Organizational Behavior, 29*, 527–548.

Collins, C.J., and Clark, K.D. (2003). Strategic human resource practices, top management team social networks, and firm performance: the role of human resource practices in creating organizational competitive advantage. *Academy of Management Journal, 46*, 740–751. doi:10.2307/30040665.

Cooke, F.L., Wood, G., Wang, M., and Veen, A. (2019). How far has international HRM travelled? A systematic review of literature on multinational corporations (2000–2014). *Human Resource Management Review, 29*, 59–75. doi:10.1016/j.hrmr.2018.05.001.

Cropanzano, R., and Mitchell, M.S. (2005). Social exchange theory: an interdisciplinary review. *Journal of Management, 31*, 874–900. doi:10.1177/0149206305279602.

Cross, C., and Dundon, T. (2019). Social exchange theory, employment relations and human resource management. In K. Townsend, K. Cafferkey, A.M. McDermott and T. Dundon (eds), *Elgar Introduction to Theories of Human Resources and Employment Relations* (pp. 264–279). Edward Elgar Publishing.

Dansereau, F., Graen, G., and Haga, W.J. (1975). A vertical dyad linkage approach to leadership within formal organizations: a longitudinal investigation of the role making process. *Organizational Behavior and Human Performance, 13*, 46–78. doi:10.1016/0030-5073(75)90005.

de Jong, J.A., Leenders, F.J., and Thijssen, J.G. (1999). HRD tasks of first-level managers. *Journal of Workplace Learning, 11*, 176–183.

Dewettinck, K., and Vroonen, W. (2017). Antecedents and consequences of performance management enactment by front-line managers: evidence from Belgium. *International Journal of Human Resource Management, 28*, 2473–2502. doi:10.1080/09585192.2015.1137608.

Eisenberger, R., Fasolo, P., and Davis-LaMastro, V. (1990). Perceived organizational support and employee diligence, commitment, and innovation. *Journal of Applied Psychology, 75*, 51–59.

Eisenberger, R., Huntington, R., Hutchinson, S., and Sowa, D. (1986). Perceived organizational support. *Journal of Applied Psychology, 71*, 500–507.

Emerson, R.M. (1976). Social exchange theory. *Annual Review of Sociology, 2*, 335–362.

Erdogan, B., and Bauer, T.N. (2016). LMX theory: a glimpse into the future. In T.N. Bauer and B. Erdogan (eds), *The Oxford Handbook of Leader–Member Exchange* (pp. 413–421). Oxford University Press.

Eva, N., Meacham, H., Newman, A., Schwarz, G., and Tham, T.L. (2019). Is coworker feedback more important than supervisor feedback for increasing innovative behavior? *Human Resource Management*, *58*, 383–396. doi:10.1002/hrm.21960.

Farid, T., Iqbal, S., Ma, J., Castro-González, S., Khattak, A., and Khan, M.K. (2019). Employees' perceptions of CSR, work engagement, and organizational citizenship behavior: the mediating effects of organizational justice. *International Journal of Environmental Research and Public Health*, *16*, 1731. doi:10.3390/ijerph16101731.

Farndale, E., and Kelliher, C. (2013). Implementing performance appraisal: exploring the employee experience. *Human Resource Management*, *52*, 879–897. doi:10.1002/hrm.21575.

Farndale, E., Van Ruiten, J., Kelliher, C., and Hope-Hailey, V. (2011). The influence of perceived employee voice on organizational commitment: an exchange perspective. *Human Resource Management*, *50*, 113–129. doi:10.1002/hrm.20404.

Fletcher, L. (2019). How can personal development lead to increased engagement? The roles of meaningfulness and perceived line manager relations. *International Journal of Human Resource Management*, *30*, 1203–1226. doi:10.1080/09585192.2016.1184177.

Foa, U.G., and Foa, E.B. (1974). *Societal Structures of the Mind*. Charles C. Thomas.

Foa, U.G., and Foa, E.B. (1980). Resource theory: interpersonal behavior as exchange. In K.J. Gergen, M.S. Greenberg and R.H. Willis (eds), *Social Exchange: Advances in Theory and Research* (pp. 77–94). Plenum.

Gilbert, C., De Winne, S., and Sels, L. (2011a). Antecedents of front-line managers' perceptions of HR role stressors. *Personnel Review*, *40*, 549–569.

Gilbert, C., De Winne, S., and Sels, L. (2011b). The influence of line managers and HR department on employees' affective commitment. *International Journal of Human Resource Management*, *22*, 1618–1637. doi:10.1080/09585192.2011.565646.

Gilbert, C., De Winne, S., and Sels, L. (2015). Strong HRM processes and line managers' effective HRM implementation: a balanced view. *Human Resource Management Journal*, *25*, 600–616.

Gittell, J.H., Seidner, R., and Wimbush, J. (2010). A relational model of how high-performance work systems work. *Organization Science*, *21*, 490-506. doi:10.1287/orsc.1090.0446.

Godard, J. (2004). A critical assessment of the high-performing paradigm. *British Journal of Industrial Relations*, *42*, 349–378.

Gould-Williams, J. (2007). HR practices, organizational climate and employee outcomes: evaluating social exchange relationships in local government. *International Journal of Human Resource Management*, *18*, 1627–1647. doi:10.1080/09585190701570700.

Gouldner, A.W. (1960). The norm of reciprocity: a preliminary statement. *American Sociological Review*, *25*, 161–178. doi:10.2307/2092623.

Graen, G.B., and Uhl-Bien, M. (1995). The relationship-based approach to leadership: Development of LMX theory of leadership over 25 years: applying a multi-level, multi-domain perspective. *Leadership Quarterly*, *6*, 219–247. doi:10.1016/1048-9843(95)90036-5.

Guest, D. (1987). Human resource management and industrial relations. *Journal of Management Studies*, *24*, 503–521.

Guzzo, R.A., and Noonan, K.A. (1994). Human resource practices as communications and the psychological contract. *Human Resource Management*, *33*, 447–462.

Hales, C. (2005). Rooted in supervision, branching into management: continuity and change in the role of first-line manager. *Journal of Management Studies*, *42*, 471–506.

Harney, B., and Alkhalaf, H. (2021). A quarter-century review of HRM in small and medium-sized enterprises: capturing what we know, exploring where we need to go. *Human Resource Management*, *60*, 5–29. doi:10.1002/hrm.22010.

Harrison, D.A., Kravitz, D.A., Mayer, D.M., Leslie, L.M., and Lev-Arey, D. (2006). Understanding attitudes toward affirmative action programs in employment: summary and meta-analysis of 35 years of research. *Journal of Applied Psychology*, *91*, 1013–1036. doi:10.1037/0021-9010.91.5.1013.

Hasson, H., Villaume, K., Schwarz, U., and Palm, K. (2014). Managing implementation: roles of line managers, senior managers, and human resource professionals in an occupational health intervention. *Journal of Occupational and Environmental Medicine*, *56*, 58–65.

Hideg, I., Michela, J.L., and Ferris, D.L. (2011). Overcoming negative reactions of nonbeneficiaries to employment equity: the effect of participation in policy formulation. *Journal of Applied Psychology, 96*, 363–376. doi:10.1037/a0020969.

Holland, P., Cooper, B., and Sheehan, C. (2017). Employee voice, supervisor support, and engagement: the mediating role of trust. *Human Resource Management, 56*, 915–929. doi:10.1002/hrm.21809.

Huang, J.L., Bramble, R.J., Liu, M.Q., Aqwa, J.J., Ott-Holland, C.J., et al. (2016). Rethinking the association between extraversion and job satisfaction: the role of interpersonal job context. *Journal of Occupational and Organizational Psychology, 89*, 683–691. doi:10.1111/joop.12138.

Jiang, J.Y., and Liu, C.W. (2015). High performance work systems and organizational effectiveness: the mediating role of social capital. *Human Resource Management Review, 25*, 126–137. doi:10.1016/j.hrmr.2014.09.001.

John, S., and Björkman, I. (2015). In the eyes of the beholder: the HRM capabilities of the HR function as perceived by managers and professionals. *Human Resource Management Journal, 25*, 424–442.

Kehoe, R.R., and Han, J.H. (2020). An expanded conceptualization of line managers' involvement in human resource management. *Journal of Applied Psychology, 105*, 111–129. doi:10.1037/apl0000426.

Kehoe, R.R., and Wright, P.M. (2013). The impact of high-performance human resource practices on employees' attitudes and behaviors. *Journal of Management, 39*, 366–391. doi:10.1177/0149206310365901.

Khilji, S.E., and Wang, X.Y. (2006). 'Intended' and 'implemented' HRM: the missing linchpin in strategic human resource management research. *International Journal of Human Resource Management, 17*, 1171–1189. doi:10.1080/09585190600756384.

Korsgaard, M.A., Schweiger, D.M., and Sapienza, H.J. (1995). Building commitment, attachment, and trust in strategic decision-making teams: the role of procedural justice. *Academy of Management Journal, 38*, 60–84.

Kraimer, M.L., Seibert, S.E., Wayne, S.J., Liden, R.C., and Bravo, J. (2011). Antecedents and outcomes of organizational support for development: the critical role of career opportunities. *Journal of Applied Psychology, 96*, 485–500. doi:10.1037/a0021452.

Kulik, C.T., and Bainbridge, H.T.J. (2006). HR and the line: The distribution of HR activities in Australian organisations. *Asia Pacific Journal of Human Resources, 44*, 240–256.

Lapierre, L.M., Hackett, R.D., and Taggar, S. (2006). A test of the links between family interference with work, job enrichment and leader–member exchange. *Applied Psychology – an International Review / Psychologie Appliquee – Revue Internationale, 55*, 489–511. doi:10.1111/j.1464-0597.2006.00234.x.

Larsen, H.H., and Brewster, C. (2003). Line management responsibility for HRM: what is happening in Europe? *Employee Relations, 25*, 228–244. doi:10.1108/01425450310475838.

Latorre, F., Ramos, J., Gracia, F.J., and Tomás, I. (2020). How high-commitment HRM relates to PC violation and outcomes: the mediating role of supervisor support and PC fulfilment at individual and organizational levels. *European Management Journal, 38*, 462–476.

Liao, H., Toya, K., Lepak, D.P., and Hong, Y. (2009). Do they see eye to eye? Management and employee perspectives of high-performance work systems and influence processes on service quality. *Journal of Applied Psychology, 94*, 371–391. doi:10.1037/a0013504.

Liden, R.C., and Graen, G. (1980). Generalizability of the vertical dyad linkage model of leadership. *Academy of Management Journal, 23*, 451–465.

Liu, F., Chow, I.H.-S., and Huang, M. (2020). High-performance work systems and organizational identification: the mediating role of organizational justice and the moderating role of supervisor support. *Personnel Review, 49*. 939–955. doi:10.1108/PR-10-2018-0382.

Macky, K., and Boxall, P. (2007). The relationship between 'high-performance work practices' and employee attitudes: an investigation of additive and interaction effects. *International Journal of Human Resource Management, 18*, 537–567. doi:10.1080/09585190601178745.

Marescaux, E., De Winne, S., and Forrier, A. (2019). Developmental HRM, employee well-being and performance: the moderating role of developing leadership. *European Management Review, 16*, 317–331.

Martinson, B., and Deleon, J. (2016). Testing the effect of LMX and HR system strength on employee and work unit outcomes. *Advances in Business Research, 7*, 91–103.

Maxwell, G.A., and Watson, S. (2006). Perspectives on line managers in human resource management: Hilton International's UK hotels. *International Journal of Human Resource Management*, *17*, 1152–1170. doi:10.1080/09585190600697638.

Meyer, J.P., and Smith, C.A. (2000). HRM practices and organizational commitment: test of a mediation model. *Canadian Journal of Administrative Sciences*, *17*, 319–331.

Min, M., Bambacas, M., and Zhu, Y. (2017). Evolution of SHRM/HPWS and social exchange theory. In M. Min, M. Bambacas and Y. Zhu (eds), *Strategic Human Resource Management in China: A Multiple Perspective* (pp. 10–42). Routledge.

Morf, M., Bakker, A.B., and Feierabend, A. (2019). Bankers closing idiosyncratic deals: implications for organisational cynicism. *Human Resource Management Journal*, *29*, 585–599. doi:10.1111/1748-8583.12245 .

Newman, A., Thanacoody, R., and Hui, W. (2011). The impact of employee perceptions of training on organizational commitment and turnover intentions: a study of multinationals in the Chinese service sector. *International Journal of Human Resource Management*, *22*, 1765–1787. doi:10.1080/09585192.2011.565667.

Newman, A., Thanacoody, R., and Hui, W. (2012). The effects of perceived organizational support, perceived supervisor support and intra-organizational network resources on turnover intentions: a study of Chinese employees in multinational enterprises. *Personnel Review*, *41*, 56–72. doi:10.1108/00483481211189947.

Nishii, L.H., and Rich, R.E. (2014). Creating inclusive climates in diverse organizations. In B.M. Ferdman and B.R. Deane (eds), *Diversity at Work: The Practice of Inclusion* (pp. 330–363). John Wiley & Sons.

Nishii, L.H., and Wright, P.M. (2008). Variability within organizations: implications for strategic human resource management. In D.B. Smith (ed.), *The People Make the Place: Dynamic Linkages Between Individuals and Organizations* (pp. 225–248). Lawrence Erlbaum.

Nishii, L.H., Khattab, J., Shemla, M., and Paluch, R.M. (2018). A multi-level process model for understanding diversity practice effectiveness. *Academy of Management Annals*, *12*, 37–82. doi:10.5465/annals.2016.0044.

Noon, M., and Ogbonna, E. (2021). Controlling management to deliver diversity and inclusion: prospects and limits. *Human Resource Management Journal*, *31*, 619–638. doi:10.1111/1748-8583.12332.

Op de Beeck, S., Wynen, J., and Hondeghem, A. (2016). HRM implementation by line managers: explaining the discrepancy in HR–line perceptions of HR devolution. *International Journal of Human Resource Management*, *27*, 1901–1919. doi:10.1080/09585192.2015.1088562.

Petriglieri, J.L. (2015). Co-creating relationship repair: pathways to reconstructing destabilized organizational identification. *Administrative Science Quarterly*, *60*, 518–557. doi:10.1177/0001839215579234.

Pieper, J.R., Greenwald, J.M., and Schlachter, S.D. (2018). Motivating employee referrals: the interactive effects of the referral bonus, perceived risk in referring, and affective commitment. *Human Resource Management*, *57*, 1159–1174. doi:10.1002/hrm.21895.

Prouska, R., and Psychogios, A. (2019). Should I say something? A framework for understanding silence from a line manager's perspective during an economic crisis. *Economic and Industrial Democracy*, *40*, 611–635.

Purcell, J., and Hutchinson, S. (2007). Front-line managers as agents in the HRM–performance causal chain: theory, analysis and evidence. *Human Resource Management Journal*, *17*, 3–20.

Raineri, A., and Valenzuela-Ibarra, S. (forthcoming). The role of inter-team relational coordination in the high-performance work systems–team performance linkage. *International Journal of Human Resource Management*. doi:10.1080/09585192.2021.1928729.

Ramsay, H., Scholarios, D., and Harley, B. (2000). Employee and high-performance work systems: testing inside the black box. *British Journal of Industrial Relations*, *38*, 501–531.

Renwick, D. (2003). Line manager involvement in HRM: an inside view. *Employee Relations*, *25*, 262–280. doi:10.1108/01425450310475856.

Richard, O.C., Ismail, K.M., Bhuian, S.N., and Taylor, E.C. (2009). Mentoring in supervisor–subordinate dyads: antecedents, consequences, and test of a mediation model of mentorship. *Journal of Business Research*, *62*, 1110–1118.

Rockstuhl, T., Dulebohn, J.H., Ang, S., and Shore, L.M. (2012). Leader–member exchange (LMX) and culture: a meta-analysis of correlates of LMX across 23 countries. *Journal of Applied Psychology, 97,* 1097–1130. doi:10.1037/a0029978.

Rosen, C.C., Harris, K.J., and Kacmar, K.M. (2011). LMX, context perceptions, and performance: an uncertainty management perspective. *Journal of Management, 37,* 819–838. doi:10.1177/0149206310365727.

Sanders, K., Moorkamp, M., Torka, N., Groeneveld, S., and Groeneveld, C. (2010). How to support innovative behaviour? The role of LMX and satisfaction with HR practices. *Technology and Investment, 1,* 59–68. doi:10.4236/ti.2010.11007.

Seibert, S.E., Kraimer, M.L., and Liden, R.C. (2001). A social capital theory of career success. *Academy of Management Journal, 44,* 219–237. doi:10.2307/3069452.

Shuck, B., Twyford, D., Reio Jr, T.G., and Shuck, A. (2014). Human resource development practices and employee engagement: examining the connection with employee turnover intentions. *Human Resource Development Quarterly, 25,* 239–270.

Stanton, P., Young, S., Bartram, T., and Leggat, S.G. (2010). Singing the same song: translating HRM messages across management hierarchies in Australian hospitals. *International Journal of Human Resource Management, 21,* 567–581. doi:10.1080/09585191003612075.

Steffensen, D.S., Ellen, B.P., Wang, G., and Ferris, G.R. (2019). Putting the 'management' back in human resource management: a review and agenda for future research. *Journal of Management, 45,* 2387–2418. doi:10.1177/0149206318816179.

Storey, J. (1992). *Developments in the Management of Human Resources: An Analytical Review.* Blackwell.

Trullen, J., Bos-Nehles, A., and Valverde, M. (2020). From intended to actual and beyond: a cross-disciplinary view of (human resource management) implementation. *International Journal of Management Reviews, 22,* 150–176. doi:10.1111/ijmr.12220.

Trullen, J., Stirpe, L., Bonache, J., and Valverde, M. (2016). The HR department's contribution to line managers' effective implementation of HR practices. *Human Resource Management Journal, 26,* 449–470. doi:10.1111/1748-8583.12116.

Tsui, A.S., Pearce, J.L., Porter, L.W., and Tripoli, A.M. (1997). Alternative approaches to the employee–organization relationship: does investment in employees pay off? *Academy of Management Journal, 40,* 1089–1121.

Uhl-Bien, M., and Maslyn, J.M. (2003). Reciprocity in manager–subordinate relationships: components, configurations, and outcomes. *Journal of Management, 29,* 511–532. doi:10.1016/s0149-2063(03)00023-0.

Vermeeren, B. (2014). Variability in HRM implementation among line managers and its effect on performance: a 2-1-2 mediational multilevel approach. *International Journal of Human Resource Management, 25,* 3039–3059. doi:10.1080/09585192.2014.934891.

Williams, P. (2019). Support for supervisors: HR enabling flexible work. *Employee Relations, 41,* 914–930.

Wu, P.C., and Chaturvedi, S. (2009). The role of procedural justice and power distance in the relationship between high performance work systems and employee attitudes: a multilevel perspective. *Journal of Management, 35,* 1228–1247. doi:10.1177/0149206308331097.

Yip, J., Ehrhardt, K., Black, H., and Walker, D.O. (2018). Attachment theory at work: a review and directions for future research. *Journal of Organizational Behavior, 39,* 185–198. doi:10.1002/job.2204.

Yousaf, A., Sanders, K., Torka, N., and Ardts, J. (2011). Having two bosses: considering the relationships between LMX, satisfaction with HR practices, and organizational commitment. *International Journal of Human Resource Management, 22,* 3109–3126.

6. Line managers and HRM: a relational approach to paradox

Julia Brandl, Anne Keegan and Ina Aust

INTRODUCTION

Line managers' involvement in human resource management (HRM) activities is by now an established field in the HRM literature (for recent overviews, see Kehoe and Han, 2020; Kurdi-Nakra et al., 2021). While early research asked whether or not responsibility for HRM activities could be devolved from human resources (HR) specialists to line managers, HRM scholars today widely agree that managing employees is a genuine task of all managers in work organizations. Many contributions on line managers' HRM involvement explicitly recognize competing demands, focusing on tensions (e.g., Hutchinson and Purcell, 2010) and stress (e.g., Evans, 2017; Gilbert et al., 2011). While this literature offers valuable insights into the experience of competing demands, theoretical perspectives (for example, role theory) overlook individual responses when faced with tensions, the dynamics these responses trigger, and HRM outcomes including the impact on organizational viability (Boxall and Purcell, 2016).

One way that research on line manager HRM involvement can develop, in terms of drawing connections between responses to competing demands on the one hand, and organizational outcomes on the other, is through theory borrowing, that is, the transfer of theoretical concepts and perspectives from related disciplines. In this chapter, we engage in theory borrowing by mobilizing insights from paradox research (Fairhurst et al., 2016; Smith and Lewis, 2011; Smith et al., 2017) to provide an analytical perspective on line managers' responses to competing demands and their implications for organizational outcomes. Paradox research has emerged in organization and management studies over the last 20 years and points to enduring competing demands in organizational settings. This perspective proposes that recognition of and active engagement with competing demands fosters beneficial learning dynamics in organizations.

Using a relational approach to paradox, this chapter discusses how line managers co-produce learning dynamics through both their responses to competing demands and their relationships with other HRM actors, that is, other line managers, HR specialists, and employees. As we will show, organizational learning dynamics depend on the nature of the relationship, specifically how much the response from one HRM actor affects the other actor's response to paradox. To ground our arguments, we first outline key tenets of the paradox perspective. We then use these concepts to develop a framework for studying responses to paradox and learning dynamics. Finally, we identify levers for line managers' active engagement with competing demands and discuss how training and supportive practices may contribute to this engagement.

KEY TENETS OF THE PARADOX PERSPECTIVE

The paradox perspective has its origins in debates on organizational viability, which commends a focus on the ongoing nature of tensions and a dynamic view of coping with and responding to them. Paradox research is a rapidly growing field in management studies (Schad et al., 2019). In the field of HRM and employment relations, the relevance of such research is increasingly recognized (Keegan et al., 2019). Recently, we proposed a paradox framework on HRM tensions (Aust et al., 2017: 419ff.). Here, we summarize the key elements of this framework—the nature of tensions (paradox), responses, and unfolding dynamics—and then present applications in the HRM field.

Paradox

A widely agreed definition of paradox refers to competing demands that are contradictory and interrelated, exist simultaneously, and persist over time (Smith and Lewis, 2011: 382). This definition highlights that contradictory demands are "tied in a web of mutual interactions and cannot be disentangled" (Smith et al., 2017: 1).

In their authoritative literature review, Smith and Lewis (2011) suggest that competing demands can be latent or salient. In the latter case, tensions come to the surface and are experienced as conflict regarding how competing demands can be handled. Smith and Lewis (2011) propose three conditions under which competing demands are likely to become salient: plurality, change, and scarcity. Plurality "derives from diversification of types of employees/groups in the workplace with different interests, preferences, terms and conditions of employment, formal employment relationships, etc." (Aust et al., 2017: 420). Change:

> is endemic to HRM systems and is related to dynamism in institutional/legal arrangements regarding employees' rights and employers' responsibilities; product market competition; introduction of new organizational strategies for competing; new models for the HRM function; new technologies and how these order and shape employment relationships and possibilities for employees to interact with the HRM function, etc. (Aust et al., 2017: 421)

And scarcity "is linked with contextual or internal developments including loose/tight product and labour markets; increasing/decreasing firm financial resources; fluctuations in labour supply/demand; changing societal norms regarding training and development of school-leavers; etc." (Aust et al., 2017: 421).

In the field of HRM, studies have documented that change and plurality foster salience. For example, Kozica and Brandl (2015) show that tensions between decisiveness and doubt for first-line managers become salient after HRM policies have changed. Brandl and Bullinger (2017) show how competing demands became salient when senior managers explain their evaluation of HRM policies in front of a heterogeneous audience.

Responses to Paradox

When competing demands become salient, actors are prompted to respond to tensions. In paradox research, responses can be clustered as proactive and defensive in nature (for an overview, see Keegan et al., 2019). Proactive responses refer to ways of managing that are based on accepting paradoxical tensions and taking contradictory demands into account. By contrast, defensive responses involve behavior that ignores the paradoxical nature of competing demands and treats them (mistakenly) as alternatives. A central claim of the paradox perspective is that management should use proactive responses, which pay attention to multiple demands simultaneously (both/and) and navigate the tensions between them (Smith and Lewis, 2011). Contingency approaches, in comparison, advise managers to choose between competing demands (either/or), and develop one-sided solutions based on priorities.

Dynamics

The paradox perspective assumes that responses to paradox create dynamics that are constitutive for organizational viability. Putnam et al. (2016: 81) define these dynamics as "iterative spirals or self-reinforcing sequences of events that grow out of the ways that actors process contradictions." Smith and Lewis (2011) distinguish vicious and virtuous cycles based on how actors frame and respond to tensions. Vicious cycles lower organizational viability and result from defensive responses. They "undermine individual self-efficacy and well-being, as well as deteriorate organizational capabilities" (Berti and Simpson, 2021: 253). In contrast, virtuous cycles enable viability and are based on "both/and" management approaches. Organizational viability is characterized by actors engaging with tensions actively and working through them in constructive and self-reinforcing ways premised on accepting both/and elements (Smith and Lewis, 2011). With its emphasis on adaptation of organizations for organizational survival, the paradox perspective postulates that those who wish to retain an organization's basic features need to focus on organizational learning and change, rather than on developing solutions to complexity (as, for instance, a configurational perspective would suggest).

In the search for understanding about how dynamics unfold and how vicious cycles can be enabled, recent paradox literature has proposed a relational approach to managing paradox where the nature of dynamics depends on how managers translate paradox to other actors who they supervise (Nielsen and Hansen, 2020; Pradies et al., 2021a). Recognizing that cooperation with other HRM actors is crucial for line managers, this chapter develops this relational approach for modeling how translations of paradoxes to others influences outcomes of learning and organizational viability.

HRM INVOLVEMENT OF LINE MANAGERS

We will briefly discuss what we mean by line manager involvement in HRM before analyzing how relationships with other HRM actors shape virtuous cycles. Following Boxall and Purcell, we define HRM as "the process through which management builds the workforce and tries to create the human performances that the organization needs" (Boxall and Purcell, 2016: 28). This process has been characterized as entailing the design of HRM policies, transformation of these policies into daily practices, and perceptions of HRM practices by employees (Wright and Nishii, 2013). Line managers are involved in this process through cooperation with other HRM actors when implementing HRM practices, and by influencing employees' perceptions of which behaviors are expected and valued by the organization (Bos-Nehles et al., 2013; Townsend et al., 2012).

Based on this conceptualization, we view line managers as key players in the "HR Triad" (Jackson et al., 2009), which includes HR professionals and target employees. In line with the

HR triad, we assume that line managers cooperate with several other HRM actors and thus probably encounter a range of competing demands in these relationships. While much of the literature on line managers' HRM involvement refers to the hierarchical level or positions of individuals, we draw attention to their interdependencies with other HRM actors.

Following Nielsen and Hansen (2020), we distinguish dependencies of participants within a relationship and use the terms paradox "navigators" and "co-navigators" to discuss how managers translate paradox. We adopt the following terminology in the rest of the discussion. First, we use "navigator" for those actors in an HRM-related relationship who translate paradox, and the term "co-navigator" for actors who they supervise. The navigators' views constitute the foundation for virtuous cycles, as their framing of competing demands affects co-navigators' experiences of paradox and development of responses. We go beyond categorizing HRM actors as first-line managers, senior managers, or HR professionals, as is commonly done in HRM literature, since these labels focus on structural positions and say little about the influence actors have in translating paradox and influencing dynamics. A relational approach is also helpful for highlighting the different dependencies in which specific HRM actors engage in as they cooperate with others; in some interactions acting as navigators, in others as co-navigators. For example, how a first-line manager translates competing demands can be expected to matter for how employees experience tensions, but the scope of this first-line manager for translating tensions may be influenced by another supervising manager. In the next section, we draw on the concepts of the paradox approach to develop an analytical perspective for examining how the translation of competing demands affects receiving HRM actors' experiences of tensions and dynamics.

RESPONSES TO PARADOX: CONSTELLATIONS AND OUTCOMES

A relational paradox approach assumes that "individual actors' paradox response strategies influence and are influenced by other actors' coping space and available coping strategy repertoire" (Nielsen and Hansen, 2020: 3). This implies that for understanding the dynamics from paradox, we need to analyze how managers respond to paradox jointly with an analysis of targeted employees' responses. Here, we employ the relational approach to propose four possible constellations of paradox responses and resulting dynamics for individual HRM actors and/or their relationships (Table 6.1). We suggest that the specific dynamics depend on whether navigator, co-navigator, or both respond proactively or defensively to paradox. Furthermore, we propose that collective dynamics are conditional on the responses from all HRM actors involved in the relationship. In constellations where only one HRM actor (navigator or co-navigator) responds proactively and the other responds defensively, this may lead to vicious cycles for the HRM actor with the proactive response.

The framework presumes that relationships between navigators and co-navigators can be either loosely or tightly coupled (Orton and Weick, 1990), and that the degree of coupling affects whether learning dynamics occur for the relationship or for the individual actors only.

When their relationship with others is tightly coupled, line managers' responses produce effects not only for their own range of activities, but also for how other actors in the HR triad co-produce tensions. For example, first-line managers' responses to paradox and their coping strategies can empower or disempower targeted employees' proactive responses. In this

Table 6.1   *Paradox response constellations in dyadic relationships*

Paradox navigator / Paradox co-navigator	Defensive response	Proactive response
Defensive response	(1) vicious dynamics for relationship ("collective downward spiral") (e.g., McCracken et al., 2017)	(2) vicious dynamics for co-navigator (e.g., Ali and Brandl, 2018; Tracy, 2004)
Proactive response	(3) vicious dynamics for navigator (e.g., Brandl et al., 2019)	(4) virtuous dynamics for relationship ("collective learning") (e.g., Francis and Keegan, 2020; Fu et al., 2020)

case, HRM actors' influence on each other's response is high and may be more likely to spur dynamics in their relationship (for example, collective learning, collective downward spiral).

We identify two constellations as relevant here. In constellation 1, defensive responses from navigators lower chances for proactive responses from co-navigators. In the context of the employment relationship, the interpretation of situations by line managers in upper hierarchical levels defines the (legitimate) activities and responses for other HRM actors or at least sets boundaries for such interpretations. Response options to tensions are fewer for those who are addressed by and subject to HRM policies than for those transforming such policies into practice. This implies that defensive responses from line managers lower the chances for proactive responses from employees. McCracken et al. (2017) illustrate constellation 1 with the maladaptation phase in relationships between line managers and HR business partners.

In constellation 4, proactive responses from line managers increase the chances for proactive responses from other HRM actors. Classic workplace admonitions to "do more with less," for example, can force workers into uncomfortable situations where excessive workloads and absurd workplace performance pressures are justified by paradoxical framing of demands without resources to support to achieve them. For example, Francis and Keegan (2020) identified supportive dialogue with line managers, premised on acceptance of the existence of such tensions, as fundamental to learning and creative responses, and without which double-binds were felt to be persistent and debilitating. A study by Fu et al. (2020: 205) emphasizes processes of line manager interactions with employees as valuable resources for navigating paradoxes of treating people consistently and differentially:

> the nature of daily interactions with direct reports, individually and in combination, providing opportunities for allocating feedback, development, interpersonal problem solving, and so forth across team members. It manifests in decisions regarding how to apply HRM practices both consistently across diverse subordinates and in response to specific individual circumstances, including differential contributions.

In contrast, when the relationship is loosely coupled, involved HRM actors may handle and experience paradox in different ways. Their possibilities to influence each other's responses are low, so that outcomes are more likely experienced by the individual HRM actors than affecting the collective relationship. This assumes that HRM actors have a degree of autonomy, that may sometimes lead them to implement and use HRM policies selectively when managers encounter complex situations with contradictory demands. According to Jackson et al. (2014: 4), line managers interpret HRM policies "as they strive to respond to specific and rapidly changing situations." Similarly, employees as knowledgeable individuals are able to interpret and react to line managers' directives and improvizations in different ways (Trullen et al., 2020).

In constellation 2, co-navigators deal proactively with tensions despite defensive responses from navigators. For instance, employees may reflect on paradoxical aspects in managing employees, while line managers ignore these aspects, prioritizing some demands over others. In their empirical study, Ali and Brandl (2018) observe how employees recognized that line managers violated meritocratic performance standards in hiring processes, for hiring candidates with a favorable political background, and how they problematized this behavior in private conversation, but nevertheless confirmed the selection decisions based on these performance standards. Since they felt discouraged from articulating their concerns in the workplace, recognizing these tensions was associated with difficult emotions and discomfort. Tracy (2004) shows that a climate of silence can lead to withdrawal from involvement.

Finally, constellation 3 depicts situations where navigators deal proactively with HRM tensions, while co-navigators remain defensive, which may spur vicious cycles for navigators. For example, Brandl et al. (2019) report that HR managers can experience fundamental doubts about the influence of HRM policies on organizational performance, and wish to paint a more realistic approach about HRM, but are unable to challenge the aspirational demands aimed towards HRM from other HRM actors. Since competing demands typically affect the manager's identity and challenge their sense of coherence, it is extremely difficult for individuals to navigate tensions, especially when opportunities for making sense with others about these tensions are lacking.

The framework presented in Table 6.1 highlights outcomes related to the nature of dyadic relationships between two or more HRM actors. While relationships constitute important elements for examining paradox, the analytical focus of a relational paradox approach is not limited to addressing dynamics in interactions. Considerable writing in paradox literature takes the position that paradox is nested in work organizations and co-evolving with the responses of organizational actors (e.g., Jarzabkowski et al., 2013; Lewis, 2000). Responses to competing demands in one interaction have implications for responses in subsequent interactions in the same relation, and for interactions of other HRM actors.

In the HRM domain, research by Keegan et al. (2018) investigates how tensions arise from the distribution of HRM responsibilities over different actors and according to different organizing structures. Any attempts to resolve such tensions by enacting particular structures (for example, Ulrich-style three-legged stools) often sow the seeds of future tensions (for example, between complexity and simplicity) and the very solutions trigger dynamically co-evolving tensions and responses over time. Given this conceptual foundation, each relationship needs to be recognized as an element of a process in which several HRM actors cooperate in defining performance outcomes for the organization, transforming HRM policies into daily practices and seeking to shape others' perceptions of HRM.

In the next section, we review the conditions that encourage active engagement with competing demands, with a focus on immediate factors as well as enabling conditions.

CONDITIONS FOR VIRTUOUS CYCLES

When competing demands are contradictory and interrelated, exist simultaneously, and persist over time (Smith and Lewis, 2011: 382), line managers' "both/and" responses are preferable over choices which prioritize one demand over others. Whether paradox spurs virtuous or vicious cycles, and how vicious cycles may be mitigated, is influenced by several factors. This section outlines key levers for fostering active engagement with tensions that have received attention in previous paradox research. We group these levers into two broad areas: (1) paradox mindsets that are enabled by training and education; and (2) practical accomplishments that are enabled by supportive organizational practices (Figure 6.1).

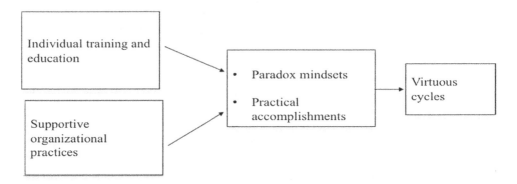

Figure 6.1   Conditions for virtuous cycles

Paradox Mindsets

One factor which paradox scholars pay attention to is the line manager's conceptual approach to tensions; in other words, their paradox mindset. A paradox mindset refers to embracing competing demands through being open to solutions, accepting ambiguity, employing creativity, and using opposites to confront conflict and engage in continuous learning. A paradox mindset can be defined as "a tendency to value, accept and feel comfortable with tensions" (Miron-Spektor et al., 2018) or to make sense of paradox.

Based on prior paradox research we assume here that having a paradox mindset, or not, influences the outcome of whether individuals suffer emotionally when tensions arise, or whether they are able to respond to tensions creatively and thrive at work. Acceptance and sensemaking of multiple, contradictory perspectives and requirements have been identified as important skills for leaders (including line managers) to support their followers (Pradies et al., 2021b). Several studies on leadership have shown the importance of acceptance and cognitive aspects of dealing with paradoxical tensions such as sensemaking (Keller, 2015), holistic thinking, integrative complexity (Zhang et al., 2015), reflexivity (Lüscher and Lewis, 2008), and critical thinking (Mink et al., 1989) (based on Pradies et al., 2021b). To translate acceptance into concrete action, extant research also highlights the importance of actors dealing with uncertainty and ambiguity in ways that provide guidance to others. The capacity to convey the meaning of ambiguous cues, and therefore to engage in sensegiving to followers (Gioia and

Chittipeddi, 1991) even in the midst of uncertainty, is important in dealing with paradoxical tensions. Research has identified skills including confidence, defined as "inner strength to take risks, to act on uncertainty and ambiguity rather than become anxious and defensive" (Smith and Lewis, 2011: 229), communication and conflict management skills (Smith and Lewis, 2011), and finally, team management skills (Pradies et al., 2021a).

Paradox mindsets go beyond cognition and behavior and refer also to the emotional aspects of coping with paradox. Researchers highlight the importance of a combination of both "cognitive and behavioral complexity and emotional equanimity" (Smith and Lewis, 2011: 389). Keegan et al. (2019) have argued that HRM tensions will never go away and that accepting them as a normal part of organizational life can lead to an emotional relief for those confronted with such tensions on a regular basis. Research on turbulent change processes by Sanchez-Burks and Huy (2009) underpins the importance of emotion management during paradoxical and ambiguous situations. The authors offer the concept of "emotional aperture" to convey the need for change leaders to scan and detect varying collective emotional responses to the turbulence of change. They "show how emotional aperture can help leaders recognize and deal with diverse collective emotions that arise during strategic renewal and other emotionally turbulent processes" (Sanchez-Burks and Huy, 2009: 22). The value of nurturing a paradoxical mindset, and modeling it, has also been demonstrated. A study by Liu et al. (2020) shows that employees with a paradox mindset are more innovative and thrive at work, and the study also shows that the leaders' (line managers') paradox mindsets have a positive influence on employees' innovative work behavior.

Practical Accomplishments

Paradox research suggests that dealing with paradoxes is an eminently practical accomplishment (Smets et al., 2019). This requires attention to how HRM actors handle paradoxical tensions during interactions, and not only to cognitive operations.

Schneider et al. (2021) identify three practices which frontline managers use to create resources for handling paradoxical tensions in everyday work with customers: situational reframing, organizational preframing, and institutional deframing. In situational reframing, frontline managers restore customer orientation after unpleasant experiences; this means both to make the situation look as if the customer is king, and to stick to predefined (formal) procedures. In organizational preframing, they anticipate tensions and provisionally alter organizational procedures and meaning to maintain customer orientation (for example, they create a new price category for services to meet customer requests and generate revenues, when existing price categories appear inadequate to customers). Finally, in institutional deframing, frontline managers "draw on powerful institutionalized beliefs to de-emphasize customer orientation to justify the existing and potentially conflicting organizational procedures" (Schneider et al., 2021: 1292).

While the research focused empirically on manager–customer relations, the concepts developed in this study can be used as analytical tools for examining how HRM actors translate HRM policies and practices to others. The findings by Schneider et al. (2021) imply that, in principle, all line managers can use proactive responses for navigating paradoxical demands, since actors are able to activate local resources or create resources during interactions. These insights are especially useful for examining how managers who possess relatively few resources practically accomplish managing paradoxes proactively.

While some scholarship associates active engagement with competing demands with individual traits (e.g., Keller et al., 2017; Miron-Spektor et al., 2018), most paradox literature assumes that individuals' readiness for managing paradox proactively can be developed and is contextually enabled or hindered (e.g., Liu et al., 2020). Education/training and organizational support are enabling factors frequently addressed in scholarly debates. We now review how they may influence line managers' paradoxical thinking and their practical accomplishments in proactively handling paradox.

Education and Training

Lüscher and Lewis (2008) suggest that organizational actors can be trained to approach tensions as "both/and" paradoxes. They can be enabled to accept and accommodate the absurdity of paradoxes in the form of mixed messages and contradictions (Putnam, 1986) in order to be able to work through them. Fu et al. (2020) also show that line managers can be made aware of how their interactions with employees can enable open and accepting approaches to paradoxes (for example, consistent versus differential treatment) providing that paradoxes are framed appropriately and interactions are managed thoughtfully to engage (and not deny) the paradox.

There is a growing literature regarding training and guidance specifically for line managers to avoid vicious cycles and enable proactive responses to tensions (e.g., Lewis and Dehler, 2000; Link and Müller, 2015). Lewis and Dehler (2000) describe elements of a pedagogical strategy for management education which encourages students to explore contradictions and complexity. The authors view paradox training in terms of three principles: (1) constructing complexity from simplicity; (2) discovering inner paradoxes (critical self-reflection); and (3) learning to "read" complexity (that is, recognize the value and limitations of isolated perceptions). While these strategy elements are discussed for raising the awareness of paradox with students, the questions that these trainings address (for example, "How can students become comfortable with tensions? How can they find rationality in the seemingly absurd?") are also potentially relevant for line manager training in the workplace. Lewis and Dehler (2000) present a number of practical exercises that serve to develop the capacity for paradoxical thinking, building on action research and methods for advancing complexity thinking.

Supportive Organizational Practices

Paradox literature points to the importance of paying attention to the organizational context and whether it enables, or constrains, switching from vicious to virtuous cycles. The organizational context provides cues for interpretation of events that over time become shared and come to shape "taken-for-granted social prescriptions" (Battilana and Dorado, 2010: 1419, in Berti and Simpson, 2021: 8). This "interpretative context" (Pradies et al., 2020) can both strengthen, and undermine, whether "recipients" of paradoxical messages feel empowered to voice concerns, seek support, and question the nature of the tensions they confront (Francis and Keegan, 2020). HRM actors' responses to paradoxical tensions may be affected and constrained by power constellations in organizational settings (Aust et al., 2017: 414) due to power imbalances (Putnam, 1986; Putnam et al., 2016) who underline the importance of power. Recent paradox research (Berti and Simpson, 2021) has more specifically examined paradoxes in managerial (authority) relationships and vicious cycles associated with the lack of agency on the part of (less powerful) employees. Berti and Simpson (2021) assert that "power relations can also influence mindsets" (ibid.: 254). "Actors lacking agency are unable to harness the generative potential of organizational tensions due to their incapability towards choosing a legitimate response" (ibid.: 255). However, the cultivation of supportive conversational practices in organizations can enable line managers and employees to work through tensions, as Francis and Keegan (2020) found in their research: "those targeted by paradoxical (engagement) strategies need explicit workplace *resources* including supportive conversational practices to cope with and work though tensions." Resources, including those embedded in the organization's interpretative context, are an important aspect of context and enable actors to approach tensions proactively. However, "to enact proactive responses, individuals require not only appropriate interpretive contexts (Knight and Paroutis, 2017), but also need resources empowering their ability to choose (for example, decisional autonomy, psychological safety, material assets, and cognitive capabilities" (Berti and Simpson, 2021: 256). Such resources can also be highly practical and material in nature, including ensuring that employees have the right equipment to combine competing priorities efficiently (Francis and Keegan, 2020), scheduling time for meetings and conferences (including travel budget), and permission to compensate employees with additional days off (Kozica and Brandl, 2015).

CONCLUSIONS AND SUGGESTIONS FOR FUTURE RESEARCH

The goal of this chapter was to introduce an analytical perspective on line managers' responses to competing demands and their implications for organizational outcomes. We use concepts from paradox research (Fairhurst et al., 2016; Smith and Lewis, 2011; Smith et al., 2017) to show that HRM actors can respond to competing demands in different ways and organizational learning dynamics depend on the nature of the relationship; specifically, how much the response from one HRM actor affects the other actor's response to paradox. While HRM actors inevitably engage with competing demands, active engagement with tensions arising from these is required from all participants in the relationship in order to foster organizational learning and viability, and to avoid vicious cycles of defensive and emotionally damaging reactions.

Paradox literature provides rich insights on the conditions that support line managers' and other HRM actors' active engagement with competing demands. Conditions were reviewed in terms of both factors immediately involved in interactions (mindset, accomplishment) as well as enabling conditions (supportive organizational practices, education and training). The message emerging is that line managers' readiness for managing paradox proactively can be developed, rather than being seen as a relatively immutable personal trait. This implies that HRM scholars need to examine how activities and structures foster a paradox mindset among line managers (for example, through training or coaching activities) in order to increase the cognitive flexibility and emotional resilience of individuals and to support them to thrive at work. Irrespective of whether the development of paradox readiness occurs as a hands-on seminar for experienced practitioners, or is part of management education in universities, a pedagogical strategy for addressing challenges in line manager HRM involvement (effectively) needs to recognize two requirements. First, it is necessary to start from the idea that making competing demands in managing employees salient to employees can be useful and productive for organizational dynamics. Since much contemporary line management education builds on a unitarist HRM paradigm, where conflict tends to be negatively connotated and competing demands are suggested to require either/or choices, realizing this idea requires HRM scholars (and practitioners) to make a shift to a pluralist paradigm. Second, the content of education needs to include basic paradoxes inherent in the employment relationship in the context of contemporary society. In this context, it may be worthwhile for HRM scholars to reconsider that (future) line managers may be better served for solving problems in work organizations by a realistic portrayal of HRM, not an idealized one.

For HRM scholars interested in analytical perspectives on line manager research, the relational paradox approach offers a valuable perspective on the role of line managers in influencing organizational learning and viability through responses to paradox and translating these to other HRM actors. Beyond perspectives that focus on role tensions and stress in the context of HRM involvement, the framework that we introduce in this chapter suggests how organizational outcomes can be linked to patterns of interactions and relationships, and is open for further developments and enrichments from a relational view of HRM (e.g., Soltis et al., 2018).

Finally, adopting paradox as a theoretical perspective implies a change in framing of desirable HRM outcomes. If competing demands persist and organizations require virtuous cycles for viability, single targets such as performance or well-being cannot be viewed as targets for managing, but rather as temporary and disputable possible outcomes. Line manager work may be better analysed for its contribution to facilitating organizational learning by working through tensions between competing and simultaneous priorities. Favereau (1989) argued that salaries de facto reflect not only competencies or hierarchy levels, but also employers' expectations of a manager's contributions to organizational learning. Using a paradox mindset for practically handling competing demands is the answer that a relational paradox approach commends for meeting these expectations.

ACKNOWLEDGEMENTS

The authors thank Dr Anna Bos-Nehles for her helpful comments on an earlier version of this chapter.

REFERENCES

Ali, Q., and Brandl, J. (2018). How complex domination enables selection: Academic hiring conventions in a Pakistani university. *European Journal of Cultural and Political Sociology*, 5(1–2), 140–164.
Aust, I., Brandl, J., Keegan, A., and Lensges, M. (2017). Tensions in managing human resources. In W.K. Smith, M.W. Lewis, P. Jarzabkowski, and A. Langley (eds), *The Oxford Handbook of Organizational Paradox* (pp. 413–433). Oxford: Oxford University Press.
Berti, M., and Simpson, A. (2021). The dark side of organizational paradoxes: The dynamics of disempowerment. *Academy of Management Review*, 46(2). doi:https://doi.org/10.5465/amr.2017.0208.
Bos-Nehles, A.C., Van Riemsdijk, M.J., and Kees Looise, J. (2013). Employee perceptions of line management performance: Applying the AMO theory to explain the effectiveness of line managers' HRM implementation. *Human Resource Management*, 52(6), 861–877.
Boxall, P., and Purcell, J. (2016). *Strategy and Human Resource Management* (4th edn). Basingstoke: Palgrave Macmillan.
Brandl, J., and Bullinger, B. (2017). Individuals' considerations when responding to competing logics. *Journal of Management Inquiry*, 26(2), 181–192.

Brandl, J., Dreher, J., and Schneider, A. (2019). "The HR generalist is dead": A phenomenological perspective on decoupling. *Research in the Sociology of Organizations. Microfoundations of Institutions, 65A,* 85–97. https://doi.org/10.1108/S0733-558X2019000065A010.

Evans, S. (2017). HRM and front line managers: The influence of role stress. *International Journal of Human Resource Management, 28*(22), 3128–3148.

Fairhurst, G.T., Smith, W.K., Banghart, S.G., Lewis, M.W., Putnam, L.L., et al. (2016). Diverging and converging: Integrative insights on a paradox meta-perspective. *Academy of Management Annals, 10*(1), 173–182.

Favereau, Olivier (1989). Marchés internes, marchés externes. *Revue économique, 40*(2), 273–328.

Francis, H., and Keegan, A. (2020). The ethics of engagement in an age of austerity: A paradox perspective. *Journal of Business Ethics, 162*(3), 593–607.

Fu, N., Flood, P.C., Rousseau, D.M., and Morris, T. (2020). Line managers as paradox navigators in HRM implementation: Balancing consistency and individual responsiveness. *Journal of Management, 46*(2), 203–233.

Gilbert, C., De Winne, S., and Sels, L. (2011). Antecedents of front-line managers' perceptions of HR role stressors. *Personnel Review, 40,* 549–569.

Gioia, D.A., and Chittipeddi, K. (1991). Sensemaking and sensegiving in strategic change initiation. *Strategic Management Journal, 12*(6), 433–448.

Hutchinson, S. and Purcell, J. (2010). Managing ward managers for roles in HRM in the NHS: Overworked and under-resourced. *Human Resource Management Journal,* 20, 357–374. https://doi.org/10.1111/j.1748-8583.2010.00141.x.

Jackson, S.E., Schuler, R.S., and Jiang, K. (2014). An aspirational framework for strategic human resource management. *Academy of Management Annals, 8*(1), 1–56.

Jackson, S.E., Schuler, R.S., and Werner, S. (2009). *Managing Human Resources* (10th edn). Mason, OH: Southwestern Cengage Publishing Company.

Jarzabkowski, P., Lê, J.K., and Van de Ven, A.H. (2013). Responding to competing strategic demands: How organizing, belonging, and performing paradoxes coevolve. *Strategic Organization, 11*(3), 1476–1270.

Keegan, A., Bitterling, I., Sylva, H., and Hoeksema, L. (2018). Organizing the HRM function: Responses to paradoxes, variety, and dynamism. *Human Resource Management, 57*(5), 1111–1126.

Keegan, A., Brandl, J., and Aust, I. (2019). Human resource management and paradox theory. In K. Townsend, K. Cafferkey, A.M. McDermott, and T. Dundon (eds), *Elgar Introduction to Theories of Human Resources and Employment Relations* (pp. 199–216). Cheltenham, UK and Northampton, MA, USA: Edward Elgar Publishing.

Kehoe, R.R., and Han, J.H. (2020). An expanded conceptualization of line managers' involvement in human resource management. *Journal of Applied Psychology, 105*(2), 111.

Keller, D. (2015). Leadership of international schools: Understanding and managing dualities. *Educational Management Administration and Leadership, 43*(6), 900–917.

Keller, J., Loewenstein, J., and Yan, J. (2017). Culture, conditions and paradoxical frames. *Organization Studies, 38*(3–4), 539–560.

Knight, E., and Paroutis, S. (2017). Becoming salient: The TMT leader's role in shaping the interpretive context of paradoxical tensions. *Organization Studies, 38*(3–4), 403–432.

Kozica, A., and Brandl, J. (2015). Handling paradoxical tensions through conventions: The case of performance appraisal. *German Journal of Human Resource Management, 29*(1), 49–68.

Kurdi-Nakra, H., Kou, X., and Pak, J. (2021). The road taken and the path forward for HR devolution research: An evolutionary review. *Human Resource Management,* 1–20. https://doi.org/10.1002/hrm.22091.

Lewis, M.W. (2000). Exploring paradox: Toward a more comprehensive guide. *Academy of Management Review, 25*(4), 760–776.

Lewis, M.W., and Dehler, G.E. (2000). Learning through paradox: A pedagogical strategy for exploring contradictions and complexity. *Journal of Management Education,* 24, 708–725.

Link, K., and Müller, B. (2015). Delegating HR work to the line: Emerging tensions and insights from a paradox perspective. *German Journal of Human Resource Management, 29*(3–4), 280–293.

Liu, Y., Xu, S., and Zhang, B. (2020). Thriving at work: how a paradox mindset influences innovative work behavior. *Journal of Applied Behavioral Science, 56*(3), 347–366.

Lüscher, L.S., and Lewis, M.W. (2008). Organizational change and managerial sensemaking: Working through paradox. *Academy of Management Journal, 51*(2), 221–240.

McCracken, M., O'Kane, P., Brown, T.C., and McCrory, M. (2017). Human resource business partner lifecycle model: Exploring how the relationship between HRBPs and their line manager partners evolves. *Human Resource Management Journal, 27*(1), 58–74.

Mink, O., Rogers, R., and Watkins, K., 1989. Creative leadership: Discovering paradoxes of innovation and risk. *Contemporary Educational Psychology, 14*(3), 228–240.

Miron-Spektor, E., Ingram, A., Keller, J., Smith, W.K., and Lewis, M.W. (2018). Microfoundations of organizational paradox: The problem is how we think about the problem. *Academy of Management Journal, 61*(1), 26–45.

Nielsen, R.K., and Hansen, P. (2020). Exploring the unintended consequences of managerial 'paradox sharing' with subordinates and superiors: The case of the Royal Danish Defence. Paper presented at the European Group of Organization Studies Colloquium, Hamburg.

Orton, J.D., and Weick, K.E. (1990). Loosely coupled systems: A reconceptualization. *Academy of Management Review, 15*(2), 203–223.

Pradies, C., Aust, I., Bednarek, R., Brandl, J., Carmine, S., et al. (2021a). The lived experience of paradox: How individuals navigate tensions during the pandemic crisis. *Journal of Management Inquiry,* 30(2), 154–167. doi:10.1177/1056492620986874.

Pradies, C., Delanghe, M., and Lewis, M.W. (2021b). Paradox, leadership, and the connecting leader. In J. Zahira (ed.), *The Connecting Leader: Serving Concurrently as a Leader and a Follower* (pp. 99–130). Charlotte, NC: IAP.

Pradies, C., Tunarosa, A., Lewis, M.W., and Courtois, J. (2020). From vicious to virtuous paradox dynamics: The social-symbolic work of supporting actors. *Organization Studies,* 42(8), 1241–1263, DOI: 10.1177/0170840620907200.

Putnam, L.L. (1986). Contradictions and paradoxes in organizations. In L. Thayer (ed.), *Organization-Communication: Emerging Perspectives* (Vol. 1, pp. 151–167). Norwood, NJ: Ablex Norwood.

Putnam, L.L., Fairhurst, G.T., and Banghart, S. (2016). Contradictions, dialectics, and paradoxes in organizations: A constitutive approach. *Academy of Management Annals, 10*(1), 65–171.

Sanchez-Burks, J., and Huy, Q.N. (2009). Emotional aperture and strategic change: The accurate recognition of collective emotions. *Organization Science, 20*(1), 22–34.

Schad, J., Lewis, M.W., and Smith, W.K. (2019). Quo vadis, paradox? Centripetal and centrifugal forces in theory development. *Strategic Organization, 17*(1), 107–119.

Schneider, A., Bullinger, B., and Brandl, J. (2021). Resourcing under tensions: How frontline employees create resources to balance paradoxical tensions. *Organization Studies, 42*(8), 1291–1317. doi:10.1177/0170840620926825.

Smets, M., Cowan, A.M., Athanasopoulou, A., Moos, C., and Morris, T.J. (2019). From taking to making paradox: A multi-level perspective on how CEOs balance nested paradoxes. *Academy of Management Proceedings.* doi:10.5465/ambpp.2019.112.

Smith, W.K., and Lewis, M.W. (2011). Toward a theory of paradox: A dynamic equilibrium model of organizing. *Academy of Management Review, 36*(2), 381–403.

Smith, W.K., Lewis, M.W., Jarzabkowski, P., and Langley, A. (eds) (2017). *The Oxford Handbook of Organizational Paradox.* Oxford: Oxford University Press.

Soltis, S.M., Brass, D.J., and Lepak, D.P. (2018). Social resource management: Integrating social network theory and human resource management. *Academy of Management Annals,* 12(2), 537–573.

Townsend, K., Wilkinson, A., Allan, C., and Bamber, G. (2012). Mixed signals in HRM: The HRM role of hospital line managers. *Human Resource Management Journal, 22*(3), 267–282.

Tracy, S.J. (2004). Dialectic, contradiction, or double bind? Analyzing and theorizing employee reactions to organizational tension. *Journal of Applied Communication Research, 32*(2), 119–146.

Trullen, J., Bos-Nehles, A., and Valverde, M. (2020). From intended to actual and beyond: A cross-disciplinary view of (human resource management) implementation. *International Journal of Management Reviews, 22*(2), 150–176.

Wright, P.M., and Nishii, L.H. (2013). Strategic HRM and organizational behavior: integrating multiple levels of analysis. In J. Paauwe, D.E. Guest, and P.M. Wright (eds), *HRM and Performance. Achievements and Challenges* (pp. 1–24). Chichester: Wiley.

7. The role of line managers in the formation of employees' HR attributions

Rebecca Hewett and Amanda Shantz

INTRODUCTION

A body of research spanning over a decade has established that employees' responses to human resources (HR) practices are informed by the attributions that they make about the intention of the practices. Do HR practices exist to support them to be happier and more productive, to enforce compliance and control, or because of legislative requirements? HR attributions are important for our understanding of managers' implementation of HR practices because attributions help us to understand the relational context of HR practices. Although some research suggests that managers' own HR attributions are associated with the attributions made by employees, this process is likely highly complex. In this chapter, we draw on theory and research from social psychology about social processes involved in attribution formation to propose three potential pathways through which line managers inform employees' HR attributions: (1) a direct path through communication processes; (2) a complex trickle-down process that is moderated by multiple factors; and (3) that managers themselves are the focus of the attribution, rather than the organization. With this chapter, we hope to inspire new research that examines the role of line managers in employee HR attribution formation.

The last 30 years has seen an increasing devolution of responsibility for implementing HR practices to line managers (Nishii and Wright, 2008; Steffensen et al., 2019), placing additional importance on line managers to "bring HR policies to life" (Purcell and Hutchinson, 2007: 17). This means that line managers can shape the way that employees experience, and therefore form perceptions about, HR practices (Den Hartog et al., 2013; Liao et al., 2009), which ultimately informs individual and organizational performance (Perry and Kulik, 2008; Steffensen et al., 2019). But how do employees perceive HR practices, and how do line managers' own perceptions inform this?

One of the most influential theories of HR perceptions to emerge over the last decade is the theory of HR attributions (Nishii et al., 2008). Attribution theory has its roots in social psychology, and its central tenet is that attributions are causal explanations that individuals make about events, actions, or behaviors to make sense of their experiences, and these attributions inform their response (Heider, 1958; Kelley, 1973; Weiner, 1985). Applying this to the HR domain, Nishii et al. (2008) proposed that employees form attributional explanations for their organization's systems of HR practices, and employees' responses to HR practices depend on why they believe the practices exist in the first place. The bulk of initial research on HR attributions demonstrated that they have important implications for employees' attitudinal and behavioral responses at work (see Hewett et al., 2018 for a review), and an emerging stream of HR attributions research has examined their antecedents (e.g. Beijer et al., 2019; Hewett et al., 2019; Van De Voorde and Beijer, 2015). Although theory and research on the antecedents of HR attributions has brought the field some way, the role of the line manager has been relatively neglected (Hewett, 2021) despite their important role in shaping employees' experiences of HR practices.

Prior research suggests that line managers are important conduits of the organization's strategy (McGovern et al., 1997), they embody the values of the organization (Eisenberger et al., 1986), and they act as "interpretive filters of HRM [human resource management] practices" (Bowen and Ostroff, 2004: 216). Line managers are therefore involved in the attribution process because they "draw the attention of followers to particular aspects of the broader HR and organizational structure and transform cues that are ambiguous, implicit, loosely coupled, and complex into a concrete pattern of meaning for followers" (Nishii and Paluch, 2018: 320). It is therefore reasonable to assume that line managers' own attributions of HR practices influence employees' attributions of the same. This is supported by research that has shown that managers and employees are more likely to share the same understanding of HR practices if managers communicate job- and organization-specific information in a straightforward way that is applicable to employees (Den Hartog et al., 2013), and that line manager HR attributions are sometimes positively associated with those of their employees (Beijer et al., 2019).

However, this perfect match between line managers' and employees' attributions is by no means a foregone conclusion. Research suggests that the relationship between manager and employee perceptions of HR is inconsistent and complex (Liao et al., 2009; Steffensen et al., 2019), and this is likely the case for attributions of HR practices too. In fact, Mitchell (1982: 66) noted that "attributions seem to be only moderately related to action," suggesting that line managers' attributions are not the only factor that influence their HR implementation behavior and employees' corresponding responses. Hence, there is little reason to believe that manager and employee HR attributions always coincide.

In this chapter, we take a step back to consider three ways to position line managers in influencing employees' HR attributions. We do not necessarily subscribe to one approach or another, but instead evaluate these alternative possibilities in light of existing research and theory, with the anticipation that it will provoke future research in this important area. The first way to conceptualize the role of the line manager is that there is a direct process from manager attributions to employee attributions through communication of the organization's intentions (Beijer et al., 2019). Second, we consider the complexity of a trickle-down effect (Wo et al., 2019) whereby the organizations' intentions are transmitted to employees through not only line managers' attributions but also their implementation behavior (Katou et al., 2021; Yang and Arthur, 2019), both of which are moderated by multiple factors (Russell et al., 2018). Finally, we draw on Kelley's (1973) attribution theory to suggest that the target of employees' HR attributions may not always be "the organization" (Nishii et al., 2008), but could also be line managers themselves, depending on the nature of the information on which attributions are based. These three alternative models are depicted in Figure 7.1.

Through our review, we explain variability in HR attributional processes by recognizing that line managers may not always buy into the strategic orientation of the HR practices. For instance, just because a line manager believes that the organization intends HR practices to increase employees' well-being does not necessarily mean that they agree with this intent. Instead, line managers interpret intent in light of their own motivations, goals, and beliefs, and act accordingly. It is their actions, as well as their attributions, that directly influence employees' attributions. Overall, we suggest that the HR attributions framework offers multiple insights into how line manager implementation shapes employees' responses to HR practices through their attributions. We begin by providing an introduction to HR attributions, and then turn to the three possible configurations of line manager involvement in the formation of employees' HR attributions.

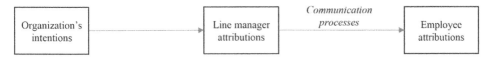

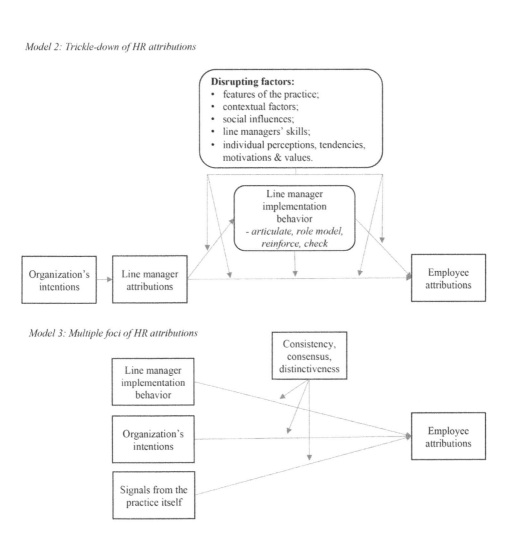

Figure 7.1   Alternative models of how line managers inform employees' HR attributions

HR ATTRIBUTIONS THEORY

Although early HR research leveraged attribution theory to explore employee perceptions of HR practices (e.g. Bacon and Blyton, 2005; Koys, 1991), theory on HR attributions came into its own with the publication of Nishii et al.'s (2008) empirically grounded framework. The gist of the theory is that employees respond to HR practices (such as training, reward, selection processes, performance evaluation, and attendance policies) depending on why they believe the HR practice exists in the first place. Nishii et al. categorized HR attributions along three dimensions: (1) reasons that are internal versus external to the organization; and internal attributions are further categorized as: (2) having either a commitment versus control orientation; and (3) being focused on the individual versus the organization. The product of these overlapping dimensions is five attributional explanations that employees may make for why HR practices exist: (1) to enhance quality (performance); (2) to improve employee well-being; (3) to exploit employees; (4) to reduce costs; and (5) to comply with trade unions.

Empirical research has primarily focused on internal attributions, and specifically on the distinction between commitment and control, with most research concluding that quality/performance and well-being attributions are one factor, representing the mutual benefits of HR practices (see Hewett et al., 2018). External attributions have received less empirical attention, particularly given that empirical research indicates that external attributions do not significantly predict individual or group-level attitudinal or behavioral outcomes (Beijer et al., 2019; Montag-Smit and Smit, 2021; Nishii et al., 2008). However, Hewett et al. (2019) found that external attributions could be further differentiated according to whether they focus on more employee-centric outcomes (for example, trade union compliance) or organization-centric outcomes (for example, external reporting compliance), and other research indicates that the intent of practices may be attributed to other external factors (for example, a tick-box exercise; McGivern and Ferlie, 2007).

The importance of HR attributions in explaining the relationship between HR practices and valuable outcomes has been supported by empirical research (see Hewett et al., 2018 for a review), which has found that HR attributions relate to outcomes including organizational commitment (Fontinha et al., 2012; Nishii et al., 2008; Van De Voorde and Beijer, 2015), job satisfaction (Nishii et al., 2008; Tandung, 2016; Valizade et al., 2016), well-being (Shantz et al., 2016), citizenship behaviors (Nishii et al., 2008; Yang and Arthur, 2019), and individual (Chen and Wang, 2014) and team performance (Fan et al., 2020; Nishii et al., 2008). In broad terms, commitment-focused attributions (for example, well-being or performance) are generally related to more positive outcomes; whereas control-focused attributions (for example, cost-saving or exploitation) are typically related to negative outcomes; external attributions (for example, trade union compliance) tend not to be significantly related to negative or positive employee outcomes (Hewett et al., 2018).

A smaller body of research has examined antecedents to employees' HR attributions. Several studies have examined the relationship between HR practices themselves and HR attributions. Katou et al. (2021) focused on HR practices in general, while Sanders et al. (2019) and Van De Voorde and Beijer (2015) examined high-performance work practices (HPWPs); each study found that practices themselves related positively to commitment-focused attributions, and were negatively related to control-focused attributions. Montag-Smit and Smit (2021) focused on a more complex relationship between different approaches to pay secrecy and HR attributions. Research has also found that individuals' underlying beliefs inform their

HR attributions. Montag-Smit and Smit found that the above relationship was moderated by individuals' preferences for pay secrecy; and Hewett et al. (2019) found that individuals' evaluation of the fairness of workload allocation practices informed HR attributions, and this was moderated by their underlying cynicism towards the organization (which is a stable belief). Finally, in the only study to date that has examined social antecedents to HR attributions, Beijer et al. (2019) examined the relationship between line employees' own attributions and those of their co-workers and line manager.

Overall, there is now a substantial body of work which supports the theory that HR attributions represent an important step in the process (Nishii and Wright, 2008) between practices themselves and the attitudinal and behavioral outcomes that are important for organizational functioning (Hewett et al., 2018). Although the HR literature has recognized the important role of line managers in forming HR perceptions more generally (Kehoe and Han, 2019; Steffensen et al., 2019), researchers are only beginning to consider the role of line managers in HR attributional processes (Beijer et al., 2019; Katou et al., 2021; Yang and Arthur, 2019). Given the nascent stage of theorizing on how line managers are involved in employee HR attribution formation, we offer three suggestions that we hope will encourage future research in this important area.

DIRECT TRANSFERENCE OF ATTRIBUTIONS

One way to conceptualize the role of line managers in HR attribution formation is that line managers' own HR attributions directly influence the attributions made by employees. The only study to date that has examined line managers' role in forming HR attributions is based on this assumption: Beijer et al. (2019) found that line managers' commitment-focused HR attributions were positively associated with employees' attributions of the same. Beijer and colleagues drew on social information processing theory (Salancik and Pfeffer, 1978) to suggest that line managers' HR attributions shape the messages that they send to employees about the intention behind the practice, which then informs employees' attributions. This is an intriguing proposition, because scholars in other areas of organizational scholarship have considered the relational processes involved in attribution formation and the implications of convergent or divergent manager–employee attributions (Eberly et al., 2011; Gardner et al., 2019; Martinko and Gardner, 1987), but there is no precedent within attributions theory to suggest that there is a strong causal link between one actor's attributions and another's. This is particularly important given that the attributional process is informed by multiple factors, including underlying beliefs, information from the environment, and motivation to make certain attributions (Kelley and Michela, 1980).

Interestingly, Beijer et al. (2019) only found a positive relationship between line manager and employee attributions of commitment, not control-focused attributions. One potential reason is that people are motivated to be liked by others, and endeavor to be seen as rational, attractive, and benevolent (e.g. Bolino et al., 2016). Line managers are therefore more likely to translate the intention of HR practices when their perceptions of the practice are positive or uncontroversial, as this reflects more positively on them, as implementers of the practice (e.g. Beijer et al., 2019; Gjerde and Alvesson, 2020). When line managers attribute the practices to motives that are more negative (for example, exploitation of employees), they may hide this knowledge by behaving in ways that are inconsistent with the attribution.

Beijer and colleagues' study is consistent with research in the organizational sciences more broadly which recognizes that line manager perceptions of their organization (or manager) are related to the perceptions, attitudes, and behaviors of their subordinates (Wo et al., 2015); and a growing body of research has examined these so-called "trickle-down" effects (see Wo et al., 2019 for a review). The trickle-down effect is important here because it explains how the intentions of one party (for example, senior managers, the organization) are filtered to another (for example, the employee) through a transmitter (for example, the line manager; Wo et al., 2015). However, trickle-down processes are more complex than a simple one-to-one transfer of attitudes, behavior, or perceptions (Wo et al., 2019).

TRICKLE-DOWN EFFECT OF ATTRIBUTIONS

When we consider the complexity with which one person's beliefs about HR practices transfer to another's beliefs about the same, the processes through which this transfer occurs seem highly relevant. Nishii and Paluch (2018) highlighted that line managers' attitudes and actions are particularly influential in employees' sensemaking of HR practices, through the way that managers articulate, role-model, reinforce, and check followers' understanding about the intention of HR practices; these same actions are key for trickle-down effects to occur (Wo et al., 2015, 2019). This suggests that line managers' implementation behaviors are an important mechanism to explain when and how this trickle-down occurs (Russell et al., 2018).

A first way to position line managers' implementation behaviors in a trickle-down process is as a mediator between their own and their employees' attributions. This is represented in a study by Yang and Arthur (2019), who found that line managers' commitment-focused HR attributions were positively related to their implementation of commitment-focused HR practices, which in turn related to employees' perceptions of these practices. Although employee HR attributions were not the focal outcome, this supports the basic premise that line manager attributions inform their actions, which inform employees' evaluation of practices. Two assumptions underpin this model. The first is that individuals' attributions shape their behavior. This is supported by research on attributions in the context of performance evaluation, which have been found to inform evaluations and subsequent actions (e.g. Green and Liden, 1980; Knowlton and Mitchell, 1980). The second assumption is that line managers' actions inform employees' HR attributions. Research on perceptions of HR practices shows quite clearly that line manager behaviors can significantly alter employee perceptions of them (López-Cotarelo, 2018; Piening et al., 2014; Trullen et al., 2016). More specifically, Katou et al. (2021) found that, at the team level, line managers' implementation behavior informed team-level HR attributions (positively with commitment-focused attributions, and negatively with control-focused attributions). Likewise, evidence suggests that employees' attributions are informed by their perception of the fairness of procedures (Hewett et al., 2018), and the evaluation of fairness of HR practices is heavily influenced by manager behaviors (e.g. Brockner et al., 2009).

However, trickle-down is not always so straightforward. From an attributional perspective, Heider's (1958) original thinking about attributions would place line managers as just one feature of the environment to which employees attend in order to make causal inferences about HR practices. Heider suggested that attributions depend on the attributes of the object, the context in which it is perceived, and the manner in which it is perceived, along with the characteristics of the perceiver. The attributions of line managers are therefore merely one piece of the puzzle. For instance, research shows that features of the HR practices themselves (Katou et al., 2021; Sanders et al., 2019; Van De Voorde and Beijer, 2015), employees' evaluation of both practices and the organizational environment (Hewett et al., 2019), and the attributions of co-workers (Beijer et al., 2019), influence employees' HR attributions.

It is therefore unlikely that there is a linear transfer of HR attributions from the line manager to the employee, via line manager implementation. For example, research on perceptions of HR suggests that managers' and employees' perceptions may not always coincide, because they pay attention to different aspects of the practices: managers' perceptions of HR practices are informed by the extent to which the practice helps to make their job easier (Kuvaas et al., 2014) and is suitably adaptable to their needs (Conway and Monks, 2010); while employee perceptions of HR practices are filtered through their managers' implementation (Den Hartog et al., 2013; Purcell and Hutchinson, 2007) and their own values and beliefs (Piening et al., 2014). As such, there are likely moderators that relate to features of the HR practice, the line manager, and employees, that may disrupt the processes by which line managers influence employee HR attribution formation.

DISRUPTION OF THE TRICKLE-DOWN EFFECT

While there is reason to expect that individuals working closely together—for example, line managers and their employees, or groups of co-workers—might share the same understanding of the intention of HR practices (Beijer et al., 2019; Fan et al., 2020), the process of this transmission is likely to be complex (Wo et al., 2019). Although, as we previously established, line manager implementation can shape employee HR attribution formation, the implementation may be moderated by factors related to the manager. For example, line managers are more likely to implement practices as they are intended if they have the relevant skills or experience to do so (Sikora et al., 2015), or if they feel that the HR practice enables their effectiveness as people managers (Kuvaas et al., 2014). Likewise, Mitchell (1982) suggested that the relationship between attribution and action is far from clear, and there are likely to be more factors that influence actions aside from attributions themselves. This idea is reflected in Russell et al.'s (2018) theoretical proposition that the relationship between line manager implementation and employees' HR attributions is moderated by line managers' implementation style (as well as by followers' affective and attributional tendencies). One additional set of factors that may be particularly important from the perspective of attributional processes are managers' motives (Kelley and Michela, 1980).

Motives may disrupt the trickle-down of the organizations' intentions to employees via line managers in several ways. First, there may be a misalignment between a manager's motives and the organization's intentions; in such cases, managers may actively try to present a different image of HR practices to employees. For example, managers who hold a "bottom-line mentality" focus on achieving business goals at the expense of commitment-focused outcomes such as employee well-being (Quade et al., 2020), and research suggests that this mentality informs employees' own mentality and behavior (Greenbaum et al., 2012). This indicates that, even if managers believe that HR practices are intended to engender commitment, their control-focused beliefs may be more salient from the perspective of employees. In their study of the implementation of reduced working hours, Kossek et al. (2016) found that some managers were suspicious "by nature" and failed to understand why employees would want a reduced workload if it was not to shirk their responsibilities (thereby representing a control-focused mindset). Likewise, McGivern and Ferlie (2007) found that while employees welcomed aspects of the performance appraisal process focused on engendering commitment, the managers' reframing of the appraisal as a "tick-box" exercise (which could constitute an external attribution) led to overall disappointment with the process.

The opposite may also be true. Managers may block or reframe the purpose of HR practices that they attribute to exploitation motives to protect their employees from, for instance, work intensification, company surveillance, or excessive red tape (López-Cotarelo, 2018). For example, Gjerde and Alvesson (2020) found that middle managers in universities act as "umbrella carriers" to protect employees from negative issues and crises, and organizational practices that managers see as unnecessary or unhelpful, in order to reduce employee anxiety and maintain a positive working environment. A mismatch between the attributions that line managers make, and their own beliefs about how to manage others, may therefore lead line managers to intentionally block the organization's motives or repackage the intention behind HR practices.

In their review of research on the trickle-down effect in other areas of organizational science, Wo et al. (2019) highlighted other factors that might disrupt the trickle-down of signals from the organization to employees via line managers, including individuals' ability to process information (aligned to research that demonstrates that managers' HR-related ability informs implementation; Sikora et al., 2015) and the salience of information (which is addressed in Bowen and Ostroff's, 2004, theory of HR system strength). Russell et al. (2018) also suggested that employees' attributional tendencies may moderate the relationship: entertaining the possibility that employees with an internal attributional tendency are more likely to attribute the implementation of an HR practice to internal characteristics of the manager; whereas employees with an external attributional tendency are more likely to attribute the HR practice to the organization. This raises an interesting question, which we specifically address next, regarding to whom employees make HR attributions.

MANAGERS AS THE FOCUS OF HR ATTRIBUTIONS

An assumption that underpins the explanations that we have so far provided for how line managers inform employees' HR attributions is that line managers are somehow involved in the attributional process, and that employees' HR attributions focus on the organization's intentions (Nishii et al., 2008). Rather than anthropomorphizing the organization, attributions could actually be a representation of an evaluation of line manager behavior itself, or the actions of specific individuals in HR. In other words, when researchers ask employees about their attributions of HR practices, are these attributions based on the organization's intentions, or on the intentions of their line manager?

Returning to some of the fundamental principles of attribution formation from social psychology, Kelley (1967, 1973) was the first to suggest that, given the complexity of information about an event or action, causal attributions can be focused toward another person, but also to factors from the environment (an "entity"). This means that, for example, an employee might consider their ability to work flexibly as due to their manager's desire to engender commitment, the HR department's efforts, or organizational goals. Kelley (1973) introduced

Table 7.1   *Kelley's (1973) covariation model applied to HR attributions*

My ability to work flexibly is to support my well-being and effectiveness because ...	Consistency	Consensus	Distinctiveness
Entity: my organization has supportive practices in general	High	High	High
Person: my manager is a supportive person in general	High	Low	Low
Circumstance: the practice itself is inherently about supporting employees when they need it	Low	Low	High

his "covariation model" to explain that the attributed cause of an action depends on the extent to which information about that cause is distinct, consistent, and whether there is consensus. Distinctiveness occurs when information stands out from the environment (for example, my organization is generally strict about working hours, but my manager has allowed me flexibility). Information is consistent when it is aligned to how a person normally behaves in a given situation (for example, my manager has allowed me some time off work in the past). Finally, consensus reflects the extent to which individuals behave in the same way towards other people (for example, my manager allows everyone in the team to be flexible with our working hours).

The configuration of these characteristics defines the source of individuals' attributions, as represented in Table 7.1. This implies that line managers' behavior has more influence over employees' attributions when they behave in the same way over time (high consistency), but this stands in contrast to the organization's strategy or HR practices (low consensus and distinctiveness). Likewise, when the intention of the practice itself is clear (high distinctiveness), there is high consistency in how practices are applied between teams, and the practice is universally applied (high consensus), individuals are more likely to focus their HR attribution on the intentions of the organization. Finally, when the purpose of a specific practice clearly delivers one message that is different from the general behavior of the manager and the way in which people are treated within the organization (high distinctiveness, low consensus, low consistency), individuals are likely to base their HR attribution on the practice(s) itself. This is supported by evidence that demonstrates that HR decisions—whether fair or unfair—are attributed to practices rather than managers when the practice is particularly salient (Greenberg, 2003; Korsgaard et al., 2002). Likewise, Katou et al. (2021) found that the strength of the HR system (consistency, consensus, and distinctiveness combined) predicted individual employees' HR attributions; yet at the group level, line manager implementation and the simple presence of practices predicted employees' HR attributions. Although the use of consistency, consensus, and distinctiveness is different in this model (drawing from the work of Bowen and Ostroff, 2004), the principle that individuals can focus their attributions on different sources seems to be supported.

This highlights that HR attributions could vary both in their content (for example, commitment or control) but also that the focus of this is more complex than simply internal versus external. This also underscores a question posed by Hewett (2021) about the defining features of internal/external attributions in the context of HR. In social psychology the focus of internal/external is often clear (normally, a focal person or event), but in HR attributions, internal/external could vary depending on the type of practice and who implements the practice. In Nishii et al.'s (2008) original work, "external" refers to factors outside of the organization's control, but if line managers are seen to embody HR practices, "external" could actually be the central HR department, senior decision-makers, or other more distal factors within the organization. Current measures of HR attributions (e.g., Nishii et al., 2008; Shantz et al., 2016) only specify the "organization's intentions" and not how those intentions are formed. Overall, this highlights that the relationship between line managers' implementation behavior and employees' HR attributions is shaped by the context of this behavior, and points to the need to better understand the basis of employees' HR attributions.

AVENUES FOR FUTURE RESEARCH

Our discussion of the role of line managers in shaping employees' HR attributions raises a number of areas for potential research. Overall, it is clear that questions remain about the positioning of line managers in explaining how intended HR practices relate to employee-level outcomes (the so-called "HR process chain"; Sanders and Yang, 2016). We can only truly answer some of these questions with robust empirical research that moves beyond cross-sectional relationships (which has dominated research to date; Hewett, 2021; Hewett et al., 2018), to examine causal links and the complexity of social relations. We therefore implore researchers to consider research design carefully before tackling these, and other, questions.

We described three ways to conceptualize the role of line managers in employee HR attribution formation. The most straightforward configuration is that line managers' attributions directly influence employees' attributions through communication processes (Beijer et al., 2019). This line of research could be extended in several ways. First, while we know that communication is important in shaping the transfer of HR-related perceptions from managers to employees (Den Hartog et al., 2013), the nature of these communication processes in attribution formation could be elaborated. There is no clear precedent within the attribution theories, upon which HR attributions theory is based, to suggest that individuals' attributions—which are formed as a result of a complex interplay of personal and environmental factors (Kelley and Michela, 1980) —should directly transfer to others. Communication plays an important part in the relational processes involved in attribution formation (Barry and Crant, 2000). A greater number of actors involved in the process (which is certainly true within HR; Bredin and Söderlund, 2011) creates more complexity in communication processes (Shumate and Fulk, 2004) that may inhibit a clear understanding of the intentions of practices. Future research is therefore needed to explicitly dig into the communication processes that operate between individuals in the process of attribution formation, whether those are one way (manager to employee) or multi-actor.

This also provides opportunities to examine how line managers can inform collective attributional processes. Although Nishii et al. (2008) originally operationalized employees' HR attributions at the group level, and research suggests that line manager implementation predicts HR attributions at the group level (Katou et al., 2021), the majority of research to date has focused only on individual-level attributional processes. Future research could examine, for example, line manager behaviors and attitudes as antecedents to group-level agreement and factors that predict the strength of shared attributions, as opposed to those that predict only variance at the group level (see research on climate strength that distinguishes between the two; Schneider et al., 2002). Further theoretical elaboration of these collective processes could come from research on relational attributions. Eberly et al. (2011) were the first to position attributions as a relational construct, such that individuals' responses to phenomena are shaped not only by their own attributions but by also the extent to which attributions are (in)congruent with those of others (for example, between employees and line managers). This recognizes that attributions do not exist in a relational vacuum but, rather, that individuals compare their own attributions to significant others (Eberly et al., 2011; Gardner et al., 2019; Martinko and Gardner, 1987) to make sense of a situation. While we have focused primarily on employees and line managers, there are clearly multiple stakeholders involved in HR processes, even beyond organizational boundaries (for example, customers, family members, and the community; Hewett and Shantz, 2021). Future research could make use of social network analysis (which has been relatively underutilized in HR research to date; Hollenbeck and Jamieson, 2015) to examine the complex interplay of social interactions in the formation of HR attributions.

We highlighted that the trickle-down process of the organization's intentions to employees via line managers is complex. Although there is increasing recognition of this complexity in general terms (Kehoe and Han, 2019; Russell et al., 2018), the theoretical and methodological insights from the trickle-down literature (Wo et al., 2019) could be leveraged in HR attribution research to better explain how trickle-down occurs. The trickle-down literature is particularly germane to line managers' role in employee HR attribution formation, because it explains the indirect influence of the organization's intentions with respect to HR practices on employee attributions, via line managers. For instance, one of the most common mechanisms used to explain trickle-down is role-modelling (Bandura, 1986): line managers imitate and model the behavior of their managers, and this modeled behavior influences how they treat employees, thereby informing employee perceptions (Wo et al., 2015). The importance of this in the HR domain has been highlighted (Nishii and Paluch, 2018), but not empirically examined. Likewise, in their review of the trickle-down literature, Wo et al. (2019) argued that although there are likely to be multiple mechanisms that explain trickle-down effects (specific feelings, behaviors, or attitudes), few studies actually test competing mechanisms. Future research should therefore examine multiple pathways to develop theoretically parsimonious explanations for how line manager HR attributions trickle down to employees. Building on the research that we have reviewed here, there may be alternative communication pathways (Beijer et al., 2019) or behavioral pathways (Katou et al., 2021; Nishii and Paluch, 2018) between line managers' HR attributions and those of employees. In other words, is it managers' "talk" or "walk," or a combination of the two, that most influences employees' attributions? Building on some ideas set out in research on relational attributions (e.g., Eberly et al., 2011; Gardner et al., 2019), it may also be that cues in the organizational environment indirectly influence the formation of the same attribution in both line managers and employees, thereby weakening the direct relationship.

We also discussed reasons why the organization's intentions might not directly trickle down to employees via their line manager. We focused specifically on managers' motives as a potential boundary condition, and further research could explore the implications of this incongruence more. For example, Nishii et al. (2018) suggested that individuals' responses to diversity management practices are informed by their evaluation of whether their manager's reasons for implementing the practices are authentic (for example, whether they are being true to themselves, and whether words and deeds are consistent). This suggests that even though line managers may be motivated to present a specific attribution to their employees for benevolent reasons (for example, to protect them; Gjerde and Alvesson, 2020), employees may respond unfavorably if they believe this to be inconsistent with their managers' own beliefs, or if the manager is unconvincing in reframing the purpose of the practice (so that signals of intent are inconsistent). Research could explore the implications of incongruence between managers' actual attributions of intent and those that they present to others: if this incongruence is visible, it might inform employees' perceptions of HR practices through perceptions of inauthenticity (Avolio and Walumbwa, 2006: 201; Nishii et al., 2018); but even when successful, this kind of impression management could be detrimental to managers' own well-being or performance (Klotz et al., 2018).

Future research may also go beyond line manager characteristics and examine the quality of the relationship between line managers and employees as moderators. Martinko and Gardner (1987) theorized that the congruence between line manager and employee attributions about employees' underperformance is strengthened when their relationship is characterized as close and is free from conflict. This is supported by empirical research by Sue-Chan et al. (2011), who found that leader–member exchange (LMX) was positively associated with subordinates' attributions that their manager's intentions with respect to coaching behavior were in others' interest (associated with positive outcomes) and negatively with attributions of self-interest (associated with negative outcomes). Sue-Chan et al. argued that LMX informed the experience of coaching from the perspective of both parties, which shaped the attributional sense-making process (Weiner, 1985). This would suggest that manager–employee relations are not only an antecedent to attributions, but also may provide a lens through which behaviors are appraised to inform attributions.

Related to this, several of our discussion points could inspire future research drawing from the field of leadership, to examine how specific leader-related behaviors or leadership styles inform the processes we have examined here. Building on Nishii et al.'s (2018) suggestion that the perception of managers' authenticity shapes how employees respond to HR practices, scholarship on authentic leadership (Avolio and Walumbwa, 2006) could be harnessed. When leaders are perceived as "walking the talk" they may strengthen the signals of the HR practice (as suggested by Gill et al., 2018), indicating that authentic leadership could strengthen the trickle-down of HR attributions. Specific leadership styles also provide signals in themselves (Steffensen et al., 2019), which could shape the messages sent about the intention behind HR practices. For example, leaders adopting a transformational (Ng and Sears, 2012; Vermeeren, 2014) or servant leadership style (van Dierendonck, 2011) are more likely to implement commitment-focused HR practices; whereas those adopting transactional leadership (Lopez-Cabrales et al., 2017) or engaging in abusive supervision (Tepper, 2000) focus on practices that aim to control behavior. These leadership styles may serve to disrupt or enhance the signal of the HR practice. A practice which the organization intends to enhance commitment may be perceived as controlling if implemented by an abusive manager. Likewise, a transformational leader may make the commitment-focused goals of the practice more salient, even if organizational leaders or HR practitioners see the practice as a tool for control. This is supported by research that shows that specific leadership behaviors can strengthen the messages sent by strong HR practices (for example, ethical leadership; Neves et al., 2018) and can compensate for weaker HR practices in informing employee behaviors (for example, empowering leadership; Hong et al., 2016).

Our suggestion that employees' attributions could be targeted at their manager, the organization, or the practice itself, depending on the characteristics of the attributional context, also raises an interesting avenue for future research. If employees' attributions are focused on these different sources, it begs the question of whether employees are able to differentiate between the different foci. Current approaches to measurement do not allow us to differentiate between the focus of the attribution, but future research could begin to explore this, taking inspiration from other areas of organizational scholarship. For example, research on bullying has examined the attributed source of bullying—whether the organization, the work environment, or specific individuals are to blame—and Samnani (2013) drew on Kelley's covariation principle, as we do here, to explain why these may differ. Given the exploratory nature of the questions we raise about attributional focus, qualitative methods would be valuable, as in the study by Liefooghe and MacKenzie Davey (2001), where they uncovered differences in how individuals attribute the source of bullying. More deductive research could draw on Weiner's (1985) concept of the locus of causality to examine the source of HR attributions. For example, Russell (1982) developed a scale based on Weiner's dimensions in which respondents are asked to indicate the extent to which the cause of an event "reflects you" versus "reflects your situation" (ibid.: 1140) on a semantic difference scale. The same approach could be used to examine, for example, the extent to which individuals' HR attributions are based on "the intentions of the organization" versus "the intentions of your manager."

In this chapter we have focused specifically on line managers, but it is also clear that managers at different levels of the organization inform employees' responses to HR practices (Steffensen et al., 2019), and there may be additional factors associated with this that shape the influence of managers on employees' HR attributions. For example, Gjerde and Alvesson (2020) found that managers were more able to "protect" their employees from control-focused practices if they had more agency. This agency may often come from seniority, but could also be a function of organizational structures and control mechanisms; senior and middle managers are also often line managers, and are likely able to exert more influence than line managers in more junior supervisory positions (Steffensen et al., 2019). Sanders et al. (2019) found that the relationship between HPWPs and HR attributions was stronger for individuals with low power distance, which may also imply that when hierarchical seniority is less important, individuals base their attributions more on the explicit goals of practices themselves, rather than the way their manager implements them.

Likewise, in a growing number of organizations, traditional line management structures do not apply. For example, in project-based organizing, multiple actors are often involved in the implementation of HR practices (Bredin and Söderlund, 2011), with additional emphasis on employees themselves (Keegan and Den Hartog, 2019); and in the gig economy, many traditional line management tasks have been replaced by algorithms and apps (Duggan et al., 2020). These factors are likely to influence the extent to which the line manager is instrumental in shaping employees' HR attributions. Further research could dig further into how factors such as the relative position of the manager, the closeness of manager–employee relationships (Martinko and Gardner, 1987; Sue-Chan et al., 2011), and alternative forms of organizing inform the role of managers in attributional processes.

In summary, some of the questions that future research on the role of line managers in HR attributional processes include:

- To what extent do communication or behavioral processes (or both) explain the relationship between manager and employee HR attributions? What are the implications of these different mechanisms?

- What are the implications of incongruence between managers' beliefs and their espoused HR attributions from the perspective of both employees and managers?
- How do factors such as agency, power, and the strength and quality of the manager–employee relationship moderate the "trickle-down" of manager attributions to employee HR attributions?
- How do social networks beyond manager–employee dyads inform HR attributions, and which characteristics inform the relative influence of different social actors on HR attribution formation?
- Are the observed relationships between HR attributions made by employees and those of their line manager (and co-workers) explained by causal mechanisms, or are they representative of a relational process of attribution formation?
- How do characteristics of the informational environment (in terms of consistency, consensus, and distinctiveness) inform the extent to which employees' attributions are based on line manager, organizational, or more temporal factors? What are the implications of these different attributional foci?

CONCLUDING REMARKS

Over the past decade or so, HR attributions theory has become highly influential in explaining variability in employees' responses to HR practices. Given the now extensive body of research on the role of line managers in informing employees' reactions to HR practices, it is clear that line managers must play a key role in shaping these attributions, but the nature of this role is so far unclear. In this chapter we have suggested three possible avenues for elaborating this: (1) line managers' own HR attributions may influence their employees via communication processes; (2) there may be a more complex process of trickle-down which recognizes that individuals' attributions are informed by multiple factors, including managers own motives, which could influence the extent to which the organization's intentions transfer successfully to employees' attributions; and (3) we finally point out that line managers' behavior may be the focus of HR attributions rather than the organizations' intentions, which then raises questions about their role within this process. We hope that this chapter sparks new research ideas to elaborate this important and interesting body of work.

REFERENCES

Avolio, B.J., and Walumbwa, F.O. (2006). Authentic leadership: Moving HR leaders to a higher level. In J.J. Martocchio (ed.), *Research in Personnel and Human Resources Management* (Vol. 25, pp. 273–304). Emerald Group Publishing. https://doi.org/10.1016/S0742-7301(06)25007-2.
Bacon, N., and Blyton, P. (2005). Worker responses to teamworking: Exploring employee attributions of managerial motives. *International Journal of Human Resource Management*, 16(2), 238–255.
Bandura, A. (1986). *Social Foundations of Thought and Action: A Social Cognitive Theory*. Prentice-Hall.
Barry, B., and Crant, J.M. (2000). Dyadic communication relationships in organizations: An attribution/expectancy approach. *Organization Science*, 11(6), 648–664. https://doi.org/10.1287/orsc.11.6.648.12537.
Beijer, S., Van De Voorde, K., and Tims, M. (2019). An interpersonal perspective on HR attributions: Examining the role of line managers, coworkers, and similarity in work-related motivations. *Frontiers in Psychology*, 10(July), 1–10. https://doi.org/10.3389/fpsyg.2019.01509.

Bolino, M., Long, D., and Turnley, W. (2016). Impression management in organizations: Critical questions, answers, and areas for future research. *Annual Review of Organizational Psychology and Organizational Behavior*, *3*, 377–406.

Bowen, D.E., and Ostroff, C. (2004). Understanding HRM–firm performance linkages: The role of the "strength" of the HRM system. *Academy of Management Review*, *29*(2), 203–221. https://doi.org/10.5465/AMR.2004.12736076.

Bredin, K., and Söderlund, J. (2011). The HR quadriad: A framework for the analysis of HRM in project-based organizations. *International Journal of Human Resource Management*, *22*(10), 2202–2221.

Brockner, J., Wiesenfeld, B., and Diekmann, K. (2009). Towards a "fairer" conception of process fairness: Why, when and how more may not always be better than less. *Academy of Management Annals*, *3*, 183–216. https://doi.org/10.1080/19416520903047228.

Chen, D., and Wang, Z. (2014). The effects of human resource attributions on employee outcomes during organizational change. *Social Behavior and Personality: An International Journal*, *42*. https://doi.org/10.2224/sbp.2014.42.9.1431.

Conway, E., and Monks, K. (2010). The devolution of HRM to middle managers in the Irish health service. *Personnel Review*, *39*(3), 361–374. https://doi.org/10.1108/00483481011030548.

Den Hartog, D.N., Boon, C., Verburg, R.M., and Croon, M.A. (2013). HRM, communication, satisfaction, and perceived performance: A cross-level test. *Journal of Management*, *39*(6), 1637–1665. https://doi.org/10.1177/0149206312440118.

Duggan, J., Sherman, U., Carbery, R., and McDonnell, A. (2020). Algorithmic management and app-work in the gig economy: A research agenda for employment relations and HRM. *Human Resource Management Journal*, *30*(1), 114–132. https://doi.org/10.1111/1748-8583.12258.

Eberly, M.B., Holley, E.C., Johnson, M.D., and Mitchell, T.R. (2011). Beyond internal and external: A dyadic theory of relational attributions. *Academy of Management Review*, *36*(4), 731–753. https://doi.org/10.5465/amr.2009.0371.

Eisenberger, R., Huntington, R., Hutchison, S., and Sowa, D. (1986). Perceived organizational support. *Journal of Applied Psychology*, *71*(3), 500–507. https://doi.org/10.1037/0021-9010.71.3.500.

Fan, D., Huang, Y., and Timming, A.R. (2020). Team-level human resource attributions and performance. *Human Resource Management Journal*. https://doi.org/10.1111/1748-8583.12330.

Fontinha, R., José Chambel, M., and De Cuyper, N. (2012). HR attributions and the dual commitment of outsourced IT workers. *Personnel Review*, *41*(6), 832–848.

Gardner, W.L., Karam, E.P., Tribble, L.L., and Cogliser, C.C. (2019). The missing link? Implications of internal, external, and relational attribution combinations for leader–member exchange, relationship work, self-work, and conflict. *Journal of Organizational Behavior*, *40*(5), 554–569. https://doi.org/10.1002/job.2349.

Gill, C., Gardner, W., Claeys, J., and Vangronsvelt, K. (2018). Using theory on authentic leadership to build a strong human resource management system. *Human Resource Management Review* 28, 304–318.

Gjerde, S., and Alvesson, M. (2020). Sandwiched: Exploring role and identity of middle managers in the genuine middle. *Human Relations*, *73*(1), 124–151. https://doi.org/10.1177/0018726718823243.

Green, S.G., and Liden, R.C. (1980). Contextual and attributional influences on control decisions. *Journal of Applied Psychology*, *65*(4), 453.

Greenbaum, R.L., Mawritz, M.B., and Eissa, G. (2012). Bottom-line mentality as an antecedent of social undermining and the moderating roles of core self-evaluations and conscientiousness. *Journal of Applied Psychology*, *97*(2), 343.

Greenberg, J. (2003). Creating unfairness by mandating fair procedures: The hidden hazards of a pay-for-performance plan. *Human Resource Management Review*, *13*(1), 41–57. https://doi.org/10.1016/S1053-4822(02)00098-0.

Heider, F. (1958). *The Psychology of Interpersonal Relations*. Martino Publishing.

Hewett, R. (2021). HR Attributions: A critical review and research agenda. In K. Sanders, H. Yang, and C. Patel (eds), *HR Process Research: Taking Stock and Exploring New Avenues* (pp. 7–26). Edward Elgar Publishing.

Hewett, R., and Shantz, A. (2021). A theory of HR co-creation. *Human Resource Management Review*, 100823. https://doi.org/10.1016/j.hrmr.2021.100823.

Hewett, R., Shantz, A., and Mundy, J. (2019). Information, beliefs, and motivation: The antecedents to human resource attributions. *Journal of Organizational Behavior*, *40*(5), 570–586. https://doi.org/10.1002/job.2353.

Hewett, R., Shantz, A., Mundy, J., and Alfes, K. (2018). Attribution theories in human resource management research: A review and research agenda. *International Journal of Human Resource Management*, *29*(1), 87–126. https://doi.org/10.1080/09585192.2017.1380062.

Hollenbeck, J.R., and Jamieson, B.B. (2015). Human capital, social capital, and social network analysis: Implications for strategic human resource management. *Academy of Management Perspectives*, 29(3), 370–385.

Hong, Y., Liao, H., Raub, S., and Han, J.H. (2016). What it takes to get proactive: An integrative multilevel model of the antecedents of personal initiative. *Journal of Applied Psychology*, 101, 687–701.

Katou, A.A., Budhwar, P.S., and Patel, C. (2021). Line manager implementation and employee HR attributions mediating mechanisms in the HRM system—Organizational performance relationship: A multilevel and multipath study. *Human Resource Management Journal*, 31(3), 775–795.

Keegan, A., and Den Hartog, D. (2019). Doing it for themselves? Performance appraisal in project-based organisations, the role of employees, and challenges to theory. *Human Resource Management Journal*, 29(2), 217–237.

Kehoe, R.R., and Han, J.H. (2019). An expanded conceptualization of line managers' involvement in human resource management. *Journal of Applied Psychology*. https://doi.org/10.1037/apl0000426.

Kelley, H.H. (1967). Attribution theory in social psychology. *Nebraska Symposium on Motivation*. http://psycnet.apa.org/psycinfo/1968-13540-001.

Kelley, H.H. (1973). The processes of causal attribution. *American Psychologist*, *28*(2), 107–128. https://doi.org/10.1037/h0034225.

Kelley, H.H., and Michela, J.L. (1980). Attribution theory and research. *Annual Review of Psychology*, *31*(1), 457–501.

Klotz, A.C., He, W., Yam, K.C., Bolino, M.C., Wei, W., and Houston III, L. (2018). Good actors but bad apples: Deviant consequences of daily impression management at work. *Journal of Applied Psychology*, *103*(10), 1145–1154. https://doi.org/10.1037/apl0000335.

Knowlton, W.A., and Mitchell, T.R. (1980). Effects of causal attributions on supervisor's evaluation of subordinate performance. *Journal of Applied Psychology*, *65*(4), 459.

Korsgaard, M.A., Brodt, S.E., and Whitener, E.M. (2002). Trust in the face of conflict: The role of managerial trustworthy behavior and organizational context. *Journal of Applied Psychology*, *87*(2), 312.

Kossek, E.E., Ollier-Malaterre, A., Lee, M.D., Pichler, S., and Hall, D.T. (2016). Line managers' rationales for professionals' reduced-load work in embracing and ambivalent organizations. *Human Resource Management*, *55*(1), 143–171. https://doi.org/10.1002/hrm.21722.

Koys, D.J. (1991). Fairness, legal compliance, and organizational commitment. *Employee Responsibilities and Rights Journal*, *4*(4), 283–291. https://doi.org/10.1007/BF01385033.

Kuvaas, B., Dysvik, A., and Buch, R. (2014). Antecedents and employee outcomes of line managers' perceptions of enabling HR practices. *Journal of Management Studies*, *51*(6), 845–868.

Liao, H., Toya, K., Lepak, D.P., and Hong, Y. (2009). Do they see eye to eye? Management and employee perspectives of high-performance work systems and influence processes on service quality. *Journal of Applied Psychology*, 94(2), 371.

Liefooghe, A.P.D., and Mackenzie Davey, K. (2001). Accounts of workplace bullying: The role of the organization. *European Journal of Work and Organizational Psychology*, 10, 375–392.

Lopez-Cabrales, A., Bornay-Barrachina, M., and Diaz-Fernandez, M. (2017). Leadership and dynamic capabilities: The role of HR systems. *Personnel Review*, *46*, 255–276.

López-Cotarelo, J. (2018). Line managers and HRM: A managerial discretion perspective. *Human Resource Management Journal*, *28*(2), 255–271.

Martinko, M.J., and Gardner, W.L. (1987). The leader/member attribution process. *Academy of Management Review*, *12*(2), 235–249.

McGivern, G., and Ferlie, E. (2007). Playing tick-box games: Interrelating defences in professional appraisal. *Human Relations*, *60*(9), 1361–1385.

McGovern, P., Gratton, L., Hope-Hailey, V., Stiles, P., and Truss, C. (1997). Human resource management on the line? *Human Resource Management Journal*, *7*(4), 12–29.

Mitchell, T.R. (1982). Attributions and actions: A note of caution. *Journal of Management*, 8(1), 65–74. https://doi.org/10.1177/014920638200800104.

Montag-Smit, T.A., and Smit, B.W. (2021). What are you hiding? Employee attributions for pay secrecy policies. *Human Resource Management Journal*, 31(3), 704–728.

Neves, P., Almeida, P., and Velez, M.J. (2018). Reducing intentions to resist future change: Combined effects of commitment-based HR practices and ethical leadership. *Human Resource Management*, 57, 249–261.

Ng, E.S., and Sears, G.J. (2012). CEO leadership styles and the implementation of organizational diversity practices: Moderating effects of social values and age. *Journal of Business Ethics*, 105, 41–52.

Nishii, L.H., and Paluch, R.M. (2018). Leaders as HR sensegivers: Four HR implementation behaviors that create strong HR systems. *Human Resource Management Review*, 28(3), 319–323. https://doi .org/10.1016/j.hrmr.2018.02.007.

Nishii, L.H., and Wright, P.M. (2008). Variability within organizations: Implications for strategic human resource management. In D.B. Smith (ed.), *The People Make the Place: Dynamic Linkages between Individuals and Organizations* (pp. 225–248). Lawrence Erlbaum Associates.

Nishii, L.H., Khattab, J., Shemla, M., and Paluch, R.M. (2018). A multi-level process model for understanding diversity practice effectiveness. *Academy of Management Annals*, 12(1), 37–82.

Nishii, L.H., Lepak, D.P., and Schneider, B. (2008). Employee attributions of the "why" of HR practices: Their effects on employee attitudes and behaviors, and customer satisfaction. *Personnel Psychology*, 61(3), 503–545.

Perry, E.L., and Kulik, C.T. (2008). The devolution of HR to the line: Implications for perceptions of people management effectiveness. *International Journal of Human Resource Management*, 19(2), 262–273.

Piening, E.P., Baluch, A.M., and Ridder, H.-G. (2014). Mind the intended–implemented gap: Understanding employees' perceptions of HRM. *Human Resource Management*, 53(4), 545–567.

Purcell, J., and Hutchinson, S. (2007). Front-line managers as agents in the HRM–performance causal chain: Theory, analysis and evidence. *Human Resource Management Journal*, 17(1), 3–20.

Quade, M.J., McLarty, B.D., and Bonner, J.M. (2020). The influence of supervisor bottom-line mentality and employee bottom-line mentality on leader–member exchange and subsequent employee performance. *Human Relations*, 73(8), 1157–1181.

Russell, D. (1982). The causal dimension scale: A measure of how individuals perceive causes. *Journal of Personality and Social Psychology*, 42, 1137.

Russell, Z.A., Steffensen, D.S., Ellen, B.P., Zhang, L., Bishoff, J.D., and Ferris, G.R. (2018). High performance work practice implementation and employee impressions of line manager leadership. *Human Resource Management Review*, 28(3), 258–270. https://doi.org/10.1016/j.hrmr.2018.02.003.

Salancik, G.R., and Pfeffer, J. (1978). A social information processing approach to job attitudes and task design. *Administrative Science Quarterly*, 23(2), 224–253.

Samnani, A.-K. (2013). Embracing new directions in workplace bullying research: A paradigmatic approach. *Journal of Management Inquiry*, 22(1), 26–36.

Sanders, K., and Yang, H. (2016). The HRM process approach: The influence of employees' attribution to explain the HRM–performance relationship. *Human Resource Management*, 55(2), 201–217.

Sanders, K., Yang, H., and Li, X. (2019). Quality enhancement or cost reduction? The influence of high-performance work systems and power distance orientation on employee human resource attributions. *International Journal of Human Resource Management*, 1–28. https://doi.org/10.1080/ 09585192.2019.1675740.

Schneider, B., Salvaggio, A.N., and Subirats, M. (2002). Climate strength: A new direction for climate research. *Journal of Applied Psychology*, 87(2), 220–229.

Shantz, A., Arevshatian, L., Alfes, K., and Bailey, C. (2016). The effect of HRM attributions on emotional exhaustion and the mediating roles of job involvement and work overload. *Human Resource Management Journal*, 26(2), 172–191.

Shumate, M., and Fulk, J. (2004). Boundaries and role conflict when work and family are colocated: A communication network and symbolic interaction approach. *Human Relations*, 57(1), 55–74. https://doi.org/10.1177/0018726704042714.

Sikora, D., Ferris, G.R., and Van Iddekinge, C.H. (2015). Line manager implementation perceptions as a mediator of relations between high-performance work practices and employee outcomes. *Journal of Applied Psychology, 100*(6), 1908.

Steffensen, D.S., Ellen, B.P., Wang, G., and Ferris, G.R. (2019). Putting the "management" back in human resource management: A review and agenda for future research. *Journal of Management, 45*(6), 2387–2418. https://doi.org/10.1177/0149206318816179.

Sue-Chan, C., Chen, Z., and Lam, W. (2011). LMX, coaching attributions, and employee performance. *Group and Organization Management, 36*(4), 466–498. https://doi.org/10.1177/1059601111408896.

Tandung, J.C. (2016). The link between HR attributions and employees' turnover intentions. *Gadjah Mada International Journal of Business, 18*(1), 55.

Tepper, B.J. (2000). Consequences of abusive supervision. *Academy of Management Journal, 43*(2), 178-190.

Trullen, J., Stirpe, L., Bonache, J., and Valverde, M. (2016). The HR department's contribution to line managers' effective implementation of HR practices. *Human Resource Management Journal, 26*(4), 449–470. https://doi.org/10.1111/1748-8583.12116.

Valizade, D., Ogbonnaya, C., Tregaskis, O., and Forde, C. (2016). A mutual gains perspective on workplace partnership: Employee outcomes and the mediating role of the employment relations climate. *Human Resource Management Journal, 26*(3), 351–368.

Van De Voorde, K., and Beijer, S. (2015). The role of employee HR attributions in the relationship between high-performance work systems and employee outcomes. *Human Resource Management Journal, 25*(1), 62–78.

Van Dierendonck, D. (2011). Servant leadership: A review and synthesis. *Journal of Management, 37*, 1228–1261.

Vermeeren, B. (2014). Variability in HRM implementation among line managers and its effect on performance: A 2-1-2 mediational multilevel approach. *International Journal of Human Resource Management, 25*, 3039–3059.

Weiner, B. (1985). An attributional theory of achievement motivation and emotion. *Psychological Review, 92*(4), 548.

Wo, D.X., Ambrose, M.L., and Schminke, M. (2015). What drives trickle-down effects? A test of multiple mediation processes. *Academy of Management Journal, 58*(6), 1848–1868.

Wo, D.X., Schminke, M., and Ambrose, M.L. (2019). Trickle-down, trickle-out, trickle-up, trickle-in, and trickle-around effects: An integrative perspective on indirect social influence phenomena. *Journal of Management, 45*(6), 2263–2292.

Yang, J., and Arthur, J.B. (2019). Implementing commitment HR practices: Line manager attributions and employee reactions. *International Journal of Human Resource Management, 1–31.* https://doi.org/10.1080/09585192.2019.1629986.

PART II

TOPICS IN LINE MANAGEMENT RESEARCH

8. The underappreciated role of line managers in human resource management

Joon Young Kim and Rebecca R. Kehoe

Over the course of roughly three decades of scholarship in the strategic human resource management (SHRM) literature, researchers have amassed substantial evidence of the many benefits of organizations' investments in their human resources. Most often, this research has focused on the positive effect of organizations' use of high-performance or high-commitment human resources (HR) systems—that is, systems of HR practices aimed to improve the abilities, motivation, and opportunities of employees to make desired contributions in their work—on a variety of employee, operational, and financial outcomes. Importantly, this research has demonstrated that organizations' increased use of such HR systems is associated with greater organizational commitment (Gong et al., 2009) and job satisfaction (Takeuchi et al., 2009) as well as higher levels of job performance and organizational citizenship behavior (Kehoe and Wright, 2013; Sun et al., 2007) among employees; higher levels of workforce productivity (Chadwick et al., 2015; MacDuffie, 1995) and innovation capabilities (Collins and Smith, 2006; Kehoe and Collins, 2017); and stronger financial performance (see Combs et al., 2006 for a meta-analytic review).

While the majority of extant research in the SHRM literature has focused on the consequences of HR content—that is, on how particular systems of HR practices influence key employee and operational outcomes—in recent years, SHRM scholars have devoted increasing attention to examining the critical roles of line managers in the delivery (or, most frequently, the implementation) of these HR practices (Kehoe and Han, 2020). In this chapter, we characterize the current state of SHRM scholarship on line managers' influence in the HR context across various levels of the organization. In so doing, we make several observations which lay the foundation for recommendations for future research in this realm.

First, research on the involvement of line managers in human resource management (HRM) has been characterized by a disproportionate focus on line managers as implementers of HR practices. This work has centered on the idea that line managers' varied abilities, motivation, and opportunities to implement an organization's espoused HR practices lead to variance in the extent to which employees perceive and respond to these practices in intended ways. Implementation has largely been characterized as a top-down process, with line managers acting as conveyers or messengers responsible for delivering organizations' espoused HR practices to employees. Missing from much of this research is the acknowledgment that line managers may not only implement HR practices, but may alternatively, or also, approach their roles in HR practice delivery in qualitatively different ways (Bos-Nehles et al., 2017; Trullen et al., 2020), such as by playing more agentic roles in meaningfully changing an organization's espoused HR practices, or by introducing new HR practices altogether (Kehoe and Han, 2020).

Second, SHRM research in this vein has most often focused on the implications of line managers' HR practice delivery behaviors for observed variance in HR practice implementation at the unit level. There is indeed evidence that line managers may play important roles in shaping differentiated HR practice experiences at the individual level, such as through the negotiation of idiosyncratic deals with specific employees (e.g., Rousseau et al., 2006), and through the effects of leader–member exchange (LMX) on the HR practice experiences of their subordinates more generally (e.g., Martinson and Deleon, 2016). There is also research documenting the implications of line managers' involvement in the development of HR policy at the organization level (e.g., Currie and Procter, 2001). However, this area of study has been disproportionately characterized by research favoring the unit level. Further, there has been little integration of insights across research streams examining line managers' roles at different levels; for instance, examining how line managers' input into organization-level HR policy influences their abilities, motivation, and opportunities to implement and/or adapt HR practices in their leadership roles at the unit level, or in their dyadic encounters and negotiations with individual employees.

Third, research examining the involvement of line managers in HRM tends to make little or no acknowledgment that HRM represents only a limited portion of a line manager's role in an organization. This is important, as line managers' jobs are centered around significant strategic and operational commitments which are likely to shape the lenses through which they view and enact their roles in HR practice implementation. This acknowledgment is important, in that understanding line managers' roles in HRM in the broader context of their roles as organizational actors sheds light on the factors that are likely to be most impactful in shaping line managers' propensities to engage in various ways with an organization's HR practices (for example, depending on the consistency and/or conflict of the implementation of these practices with the other facets of line managers' responsibilities).

We structure the chapter as a review of extant research within the three key levels at which line managers have meaningful HR practice involvement in organizations: namely, the unit level, the employee level, and the organization level. The unit-level section elaborates on research examining the effect of line managers' relevant abilities, motivation, and opportunities to implement an organizations' espoused HR practices, and on the consequences of such variance in HR practice implementation across units within an organization. Additionally, this section touches on other ways (that is, outside of the actual implementation of HR practices) that line managers may influence the experience of HR practices within their units, such as through their leadership behaviors and/or through their influences on the unit climate. The employee-level section focuses on line managers' roles in generating meaningful within-unit variance in employees' perceptions of and responses to HR practices. In particular, in this section, we review research considering how characteristics of line managers' dyadic relationships with their employees shape employees' experiences with HR practices, as well as research focusing on line managers' roles in negotiating idiosyncratic deals (i-deals)—or individualized arrangements surrounding work practices—with individual employees. In the organization-level section, we discuss two streams of research examining line managers' influences on HRM at the organization level: namely, research examining formal organizational mechanisms for line managers to provide input into organizations' HR practices, and research examining the roles of line managers in the planning and enactment of organizations' workforce differentiation strategies. Finally, following our review of extant scholarship, we offer integrative insights developed through our consideration of work spanning these three organizational levels, setting the stage for three key directions that we believe represent fruitful avenues for future inquiry.

It is important to note that there is inconsistent use of the term "line managers" within the SHRM literature. Throughout this chapter, we use the term "line managers" as a common label to refer to individuals who are responsible for the management of employees but who may vary in the organizational level at which they work. When discussing specific studies, we use the terminology used by the study's authors.

UNIT LEVEL

Although organizations' formal HR practices are most often designed within the HR function, the delivery of these practices often falls to line managers with responsibility for managing employees throughout the organization. Indeed, it is often line managers who make critical hiring decisions, conduct performance appraisals, and make recommendations related to training, rewards, and promotions within the units they manage. As a result, line managers are frequently the sources of employees' most direct experiences with an organization's HR practices, as well as the sources of meaningful variance in HR practice delivery within organizations.

While line managers' roles as critical HR actors were highlighted in early SHRM theory (e.g., Wright and Snell, 1998), with few exceptions, it has been only relatively recently that scholars have devoted focused attention to examining line managers as important sources of variance in HR practice delivery observed at the unit level. Research considering line managers' influence on between-unit variance in HRM has fallen into two broad research streams which differ with respect to their treatment of line managers' roles in the HR practice delivery process. The first research stream characterizes line managers' roles in HRM solely in terms of their responsibilities for HR practice implementation. This work focuses on the antecedents and consequences of line managers' HR practice implementation behaviors that result in between-unit variance in employees' HR practice perceptions and outcomes. The second research stream extends the conceptualization of line managers' roles in HRM beyond HR practice implementation, exploring the idea that line managers' other behaviors and interactions with employees may influence employees' perceptions of HR practices less directly by shaping the broader context in which HR practices are delivered and experienced.

Traditional Work on Implementation

Research on HR practice implementation has focused on the within-organization variance resulting from differences in line managers' implementation of HR practices at the unit level (Pak and Kim, 2018). This work has generally taken the view that inconsistency in implementation undermines organizations' HR practice investments, and has sought to identify both contributing factors and consequences associated with unplanned variation in line managers' HR practice implementation behaviors (Khilji and Wang, 2006; Woodrow and Guest, 2014). Most often, scholars have applied the ability–motivation–opportunity (AMO) framework (Appelbaum et al., 2000) from the broader SHRM literature in this area of inquiry, reasoning that line managers' relevant abilities, motivation, and opportunities will determine their effectiveness in implementing an organization's HR practices (Bos-Nehles et al., 2013; Gilbert et al., 2015).

Ability

Scholars examining the abilities underlying effective HR practice implementation (see Sikora, Chapter 9 in this book) have considered both narrow HRM-related competencies such as familiarity with relevant legal requirements or an understanding of focal HR practices (Hall and Torrington, 1998; Lowe, 1992), and broader skill sets such as people management skills (McGovern et al., 1997) and political skill (Sikora et al., 2015). Drawing explicitly on the AMO model, Bos-Nehles et al. (2013) and Kellner et al. (2016) studied how line managers' motivation and opportunities interact with their relevant abilities in determining HR practice implementation effectiveness. In particular, Bos-Nehles et al. (2013) demonstrated in their study of a naval defense company and a construction company that line managers' competencies—which they measured as occupational self-efficacy and HR training—were the strongest predictor of HR practice implementation effectiveness. Further, the positive effect of these competencies was enhanced by line managers' opportunity, or the extent to which they reported having the relevant capacity, support, policy, and procedures required to perform HRM tasks and responsibilities; but was not enhanced by line managers' implementation motivation. In comparison, Kellner et al.'s (2016) qualitative study of frontline managers in hospitals suggested that both motivation and opportunity may enhance the positive effects of line managers' abilities in shaping HRM performance. Sikora et al. (2015) also demonstrated the importance of line managers' relevant abilities, finding that line managers' HRM competency and political skill were positively related to their implementation of high-performance work systems, which in turn were positively related to employees' perceptions of the use of participative decision-making processes and job performance, and negatively related to employees' turnover intentions.

Motivation

Scholars have conceptualized motivation in the context of HR practice implementation as line managers' desire and willingness to implement an organization's espoused HR practices (Bos-Nehles et al., 2013). This work suggests that line managers will be more motivated to implement HR practices when they have a personal appreciation for the value of HRM (McGovern, 1999), and when they understand the rationale for their own HRM involvement (Maxwell and Watson, 2006). Indeed, Trullen et al. (2016) found that line managers demonstrate greater motivation for HR practice implementation when they are personally involved in the development of HR practices. Importantly, scholars have also demonstrated the value of organizations' efforts aimed explicitly at fostering line managers' interest in HR practice implementation, such as through the use of rewards and performance appraisals connected to line managers' HR practice implementation behaviors (McGovern, 1999; Swart and Kinnie, 2013), and through efforts to make line managers feel greater support from the HR department (Dewettinck and Vroonen, 2017).

Scholars have also demonstrated the importance of contextual factors such as culture, climate, and political support for HRM in shaping line managers' HRM-oriented motivation (Sikora and Ferris, 2014). Whereas certain organizational cultures and politics may hinder the introduction of effective HR practices by fostering line managers' resistance to change (Pfeffer, 1996), organizational values that emphasize the importance of HRM may increase line managers' openness and commitment to HR practices and foster their acceptance of HRM responsibilities (Heraty and Morley, 1995; Hutchinson and Purcell, 2003; Watson et al., 2007). Consistent with this logic, Sikora and Ferris (2011) found that an organizational culture that is supportive of HRM activities favorably influences line managers' HR practice implementation decisions and behaviors. The authors also demonstrated that line managers' perceptions of the appropriateness and effectiveness of their firm's HR practices are critical antecedents to extensive HR practice implementation (as rated by line managers).

In an interesting contrast to these findings, Bos-Nehles et al. (2013) found that line managers' motivation to implement an organization's HR practices were rated as less effective in their implementation by employees. In reflecting on these findings, the authors speculated that highly motivated line managers may be more likely to stick to the guidelines and rules set by the HR department, and less likely to demonstrate flexibility when it comes to employees' idiosyncratic needs. Indeed, this difference in rater perspective (that is, employees versus line managers) highlights an important consideration in our interpretation of findings on line managers' implementation motivation in particular (that is: motivation toward what end, specifically?) as well as findings on HR practice implementation outcomes more generally (that is: effective from whose point of view?).

Opportunity

Line managers' opportunities to engage in HR practice implementation have been conceptualized in terms of having the requisite support, authority, and time to effectively engage in implementation. Research examining the role of support (Bos-Nehles et al., 2013; Hall and Torrington, 1998; Kuvaas et al., 2014) suggests that line managers will be more effective in implementing HR practices when they receive advice and coaching from HRM specialists. Other research emphasizes the finite nature of line managers' time, acknowledging that HR practice implementation is just one portion of line managers' sometimes competing roles in organizations. This work has demonstrated that situational and operational constraints, such as role conflicts (Evans, 2017; Hailey et al., 2005; Hutchinson and Purcell, 2010; Whittaker and Marchington, 2003) or work overload (Cunningham and Hyman, 1999; Evans, 2017; Hutchinson and Purcell, 2010; Maxwell and Watson, 2006; Whittaker and Marchington, 2003), may exert pressures on the time and attention of line managers, which may limit their opportunity to implement HR practices. For instance, in a study of senior and board-level line managers, Whitaker and Marchington (2003) determined that managers often perceive conflicting demands and competing priorities between HRM (that is, developing their staff) and operational tasks (that is, meeting business targets), leading to work overload that compromises their performance of HRM responsibilities; insights also reported in studies of line managers in hotels (Maxwell and Watson, 2006) and hospitals (Kellner et al., 2016).

Finally, research on HR devolution, which is defined as the delegation of responsibility for implementing HR practices to line managers, has emphasized the provision of opportunity associated with the empowerment of line managers in the implementation of HR practices. HR devolution has been linked to positive employee and organizational outcomes (Perry and Kulik, 2008; Ryu and Kim, 2013), a finding which scholars have explained in a few ways. First, HR devolution may enable the HR function to take on a more strategic role within the organization (Mitchell et al., 2013). In particular, when administrative HRM activities are shifted to line managers, Mitchell et al. (2013) argue, HRM professionals can take on the role of organizational change agents (for example, in more effectively supporting the organization's adoption of high-performance HR practices). Second, HR devolution may contribute to the strength of an organization's HR system (Bowen and Ostroff, 2004), as frontline managers who are engaged with employees on a daily basis may have greater opportunity to deliver distinctive, consistent, and consensus-enhancing messages related to the organization's HR practices to their employees relative to members of the HR function who may otherwise be responsible for implementation (Ryu and Kim, 2013). Finally, it is important to highlight that situational constraints can interfere with HR devolution efforts by negatively shaping line managers' perceptions of their actual opportunities to engage with HR practices. For instance, Op de Beeck et al. (2016) demonstrated that when line managers perceive higher levels of "red tape" and more limited flexibility in the rules governing their HRM responsibilities, they report reduced perceptions of HR devolution.

Broader Roles of Line Managers in the HR Delivery Process

Whereas research on HR practice implementation focuses exclusively on line managers' actual enactment of HR practices, scholars have also demonstrated that line managers may shape employees' HRM perceptions and responses through their broader influences on the context in which HR practices are delivered and experienced (Alfes et al., 2013; Bredin and Söderlund, 2007; Dysvik and Kuvaas, 2012; Purcell and Hutchinson, 2007; Vermeeren, 2014). For instance, scholars have demonstrated that line managers' personal characteristics, leadership styles, and communications may indirectly influence employees' perceptions and interpretations of HR practices through their effects on the unit climate and HRM environment. Scholars in this vein have drawn on theories of social influence, such as attribution theory (Heider, 1958) and social exchange theory (Blau, 1964), to understand how line managers' influences on the unit context may contribute to intraorganizational variability in HR practice delivery and outcomes.

Attribution theory suggests that individuals attach different meanings to social stimuli as a function of the broader context in which stimuli are embedded, and that these meanings influence individuals' subsequent attitudinal and behavioral responses. Because line managers play central roles in the communication of an organization's HRM strategy and associated HR practices within their units, they exert considerable influence on the HRM-related attributions formed by their employees. In this regard, Bowen and Ostroff (2004) highlighted the importance of line managers in conveying consistent messaging about HR practices to ensure the formation of consistent interpretations of what behaviors are likely to be valued and rewarded, thereby fostering the development of a strong climate in which employees share a common understanding of desired contributions. For instance, Fu et al. (2020) demonstrated that line managers' consistent HR practice implementation, applying HR practices across team members uniformly, is positively related to employees' job performance. Additionally, scholars have pointed to the importance of line managers in communicating the reason, or purpose, for HR practices in an organization, as employees' attributions related to why an organization uses a set of HR practices influence their attitudinal and behavioral responses (Nishii et al., 2008).

Social exchange theory suggests that the quality of individuals' exchange relationships determines the level of mutual trust, support, and reciprocity that the exchange partners will share. From this perspective, beyond line managers' influence on employees' HRM attributions through their HRM-related communications, research has highlighted that line managers' leadership styles, personalities, and behaviors may exert meaningful influences on employees' HR practice perceptions and responses (Nishii and Wright, 2007). For instance, Gilbert et al. (2011) noted that line managers could enhance employees' affective commitment by engaging in effective relations-oriented leadership behaviors, thereby fostering a more favorable HRM environment. Other scholars have focused on the interactive and reciprocal relationship between HR practices and line managers' leadership styles. For instance, drawing on the theory of impression formation (Kunda and Thagard, 1996), Russell et al. (2018) theorized that line managers with greater political skill are better able to implement HR practices in a way that signals concern for employees, which is likely to favorably influence employees' attributions about managers' intentions behind their HR practice implementation and their perception of the manager as a leader. Parallel to this idea is Purcell and Hutchison's (2007) speculation that inadequately designed HR practices can be "rescued" by favorable leadership by line managers.

Taking a different perspective in an empirical study of line managers in Chinese shoe stores, Jiang et al. (2015) found that line managers' service leadership substituted for high-performance work systems in supporting favorable unit-level outcomes, including collective customer knowledge and service climate. Other scholars have found that the HRM-related actions taken by line managers may influence the HRM environment at the unit level. For instance, line managers may affect employees' job experiences by determining the level of job autonomy given to the employees through work designs, or by providing them with valuable resources such as training and rewards (Tierney and Farmer, 2002).

In sum, research focusing on line managers' roles in HR practice delivery at the unit level suggests that line managers may exert both direct and indirect effects on how employees experience, make sense of, and respond to an organization's HR practices.

EMPLOYEE LEVEL

Importantly, researchers have also demonstrated the important role of line managers and supervisors in generating meaningful "within-unit" variance in HRM. That is, in addition to line managers' responsibilities for differences in the HRM experiences and outcomes of employees in different units, line managers' unique relationships and interactions with individual employees have been shown to result in heterogeneity in employees' individual HRM experiences and outcomes, within the same unit and under the same manager. Importantly, these heterogeneous experiences have important implications for employees' attitudinal and behavioral outcomes.

Two distinct streams of research shed light on the influences of frontline managers and supervisors on the unique and differentiated HRM experiences and outcomes of individual employees within their units. The first research stream in this vein, which focuses on variability in the extent or degree to which employees perceive, are satisfied with, and/or respond as intended to a set of HR practices, is rooted more squarely in the SHRM literature. This research emerged from scholars' recognition of the multilevel nature of the key relationships within the "black box" of SHRM, or the process through which HR systems affect firm performance (Nishii and Wright, 2007; Van Beurden et al., 2021). The second stream of research in this vein focuses on idiosyncratic deals (i-deals), or individualized arrangements negotiated between individual employees and their supervisors (Rousseau et al., 2006). This research sheds light on the antecedents and outcomes associated with individual employees' experiences, with qualitatively different HR practices that result from their personal negotiations with their supervisor.

Line Managers as Sources of Within-Unit Variability in HRM Delivery and Outcomes

Scholars have primarily drawn on social information processing theory and social exchange theory in their consideration of line managers' influences on employees' unique experiences with, and reactions to, the same set of HR practices. While both of these theories have also been used in explaining managers' roles in HR practice communication and interpretation more generally (that is, at the unit level), research in this vein has drawn on these perspectives in theorizing about the roles of leaders in the context of their dyadic interactions and relationships with their subordinates. Social information processing theory (Salancik and Pfeffer, 1978) suggests that individuals use information and signals from other actors in their social environment to help interpret new situations or experiences. From this perspective, within a unit, employees' unique perceptions of and reactions to HR practices may be shaped by the direct messaging conveyed through line managers' communication of the practices, as well as by the sensemaking in which they engage with their peers as they seek to interpret and understand HR practices in the broader context of their employment relationship (on which the line manager is also likely to have exerted significant influence over time) (Kehoe and Wright, 2013; Renkema et al., 2017). To the extent that a line manager's communication patterns and exchange relationships vary across employees, within-unit variance in HRM experiences and outcomes is likely to result.

Consistent with the social information processing perspective, Jiang et al. (2017) demonstrated that both line managers' and co-workers' perceptions of HR practices positively relate to focal employees' HR practice perceptions, while Beijer et al. (2019) found that employees' HR practice attributions were heavily influenced by the HR practice attributions made by their managers, providing support for line managers' roles in both communicating and interpreting HR practice information for their employees. In an interesting contrast to these findings, Liao et al. (2009) found that manager-rated high-performance work practices were not significantly related to employee-rated high-performance work practices, though these authors did find that the within-unit variance was much greater than the between-unit variance in employee-rated HR practices, raising the possibility that some of the disconnect may have been driven by within-unit heterogeneity in managers' communication with employees about HR practices.

Drawing on social exchange theory (Blau, 1964), scholars have suggested that the quality of employees' unique exchange relationships with the organization as an employer, as well as the quality of leader–member exchange (LMX) characterizing their dyadic relationships with their line manager, are likely to shape their interpretations of and responses to HR practices. Consistent with this view, research has demonstrated that line managers' and employees' dyadic relationships influence employees' perceptions of HR practice implementation (Bos-Nehles and Meijerink, 2018), and strengthen the positive effect of HR practices on employee helping and voice behaviors (Wang et al., 2019). Others examining the role of the employee–leader relationship have found that employees' perceptions of effective enactment of HR practices and effective relations-oriented leadership behavior by their line manager are positively related to employees' affective commitment (Gilbert et al., 2011), and that employees' attachment styles with their leader interact with HR practices to predict employee innovative behavior (Černe et al., 2018). Finally, scholars specifically examining the role of LMX in this vein have obtained consistent findings demonstrating that LMX is a significant predictor of employees' HR practices perceptions (Martinson and Deleon, 2016) and satisfaction with HR practices (Sanders et al., 2010; Yousaf et al., 2011), with these employee-rated

HRM experiences mediating the effect of LMX on key attitudinal and behavioral outcomes such as job satisfaction, affective organizational commitment, and innovative behavior.

Line Managers as Negotiators of Idiosyncratic Deals

Research on i-deals suggests that another important way that leaders contribute to differentiated HRM experiences and outcomes among employees is in their negotiation of customized arrangements with individual employees which deviate from an organization's standard HR practices (Rousseau et al., 2006). While the content of i-deals varies, research suggests that common domains across which i-deals are negotiated include pay, flexibility (in the scheduling and/or location of work), and the nature and scope of work responsibilities (Gajendran et al., 2015; Kossek et al., 2016; Rosen et al., 2013).

By definition, i-deals are expected to be mutually beneficial for the employee and the organization, though they may be viewed quite differently across actors and under different circumstances. For example, organizations may view i-deals as a way to reward high performers, as a point of differentiation in a competitive labor market, or as a low-stakes, experimental approach to adapting to a changing environment (Rousseau et al., 2006). In addition to these aims, supervisors may use i-deals in an attempt to overcome suboptimal HR practices adopted by the organization, or to mitigate a psychological contract breach (Guerrero et al., 2014). Of note, while Hornung and colleagues demonstrated that LMX quality is positively related to the negotiation of i-deals between a supervisor and employees (Hornung et al., 2010, 2014), Anand et al. (2010) found that i-deals may substitute for high-quality LMX in supporting employees' organizational citizenship behaviors.

Indeed, i-deals tend to have positive outcomes for the employees who negotiate them, with such employees displaying more positive work attitudes, that is, increased satisfaction (Rosen et al., 2013) and commitment (Liu et al., 2013), reduced turnover intentions (Ho and Tekleab, 2016); and more positive work behaviors, that is, constructive voice (Ng and Feldman, 2015), organizational citizenship behaviors (Anand et al., 2010), and job performance (Gajendran et al., 2015). Meanwhile, it is also important to note that the effects of i-deals on a focal employee's co-workers may be positive or negative, ranging from increased collective commitment at the unit level (Bal and Boehm, 2019) to feelings of envy, ostracism, and the development of a competitive climate (Ng, 2017), with these effects varying depending on the content, transparency, and perceived fairness of the i-deals in question (Bal and Boehm, 2019; Greenberg et al., 2004; Rousseau et al., 2006).

While most of the research on i-deals has been focused on these arrangements from the employee perspective, the demonstrated prevalence and impact of these agreements in organizations highlight that i-deals indeed represent a significant mechanism through which managers shape the unique HRM experiences of their employees. Thus, developing a more comprehensive understanding of the antecedents and consequences of i-deals from the managerial perspective represents an important need for future scholarship (Liao et al., 2016).

ORGANIZATION LEVEL

Although scholars have traditionally focused on the roles of line managers in HR practice delivery within their units, a few streams of research have highlighted that line managers may also shape HRM policy at the organization level. By implication, this work suggests that, in addition to line managers' responsibility for variance in employees' HRM experiences at the unit and employee levels, line managers may contribute to additional variance in HR practice both within and across organizations.

Two streams of research shed light on the influences of line managers through systematic input on HRM policy. The first research stream focuses on the adoption of formal mechanisms within organizations to facilitate line managers' involvement in the design of HRM policies and practices. This research has examined factors that may increase the extensiveness and quality of line manager input when such mechanisms are in place. The second stream of research focuses on workforce differentiation, which is rooted in the notion that organizations may take varied approaches in managing different segments of their workforce based on differences in the value and/or strategic importance of different jobs or employees (Huselid and Becker, 2011). Because a key underpinning of workforce differentiation is the assumption of shared responsibility for strategic workforce performance between line managers and HRM professionals (Becker and Huselid, 2006), scholars in this area have emphasized the importance of line managers' involvement in the design and execution of workforce differentiation initiatives in organizations.

Mechanisms for Line Managers' Input into HRM Policy

A small portion of research on HR practice implementation and HR devolution has focused on the involvement of line managers in providing input into HR policy. For instance, drawing on Floyd and Wooldridge's framework of middle manager influence from the strategic management literature (Floyd and Wooldridge, 1992, 1994, 1997), Currie and Procter (2001) demonstrated that line managers who were involved in the formulation of a new pay scheme were more motivated when it came to its implementation. This involvement, the authors suggested, is likely to be most effective when line managers are given opportunities to contribute their operational expertise during the HR practice design phase in order to ensure the relevance and feasibility of HRM policies within their local contexts. In such circumstances, line managers may take on roles within which they initiate, influence, and drive strategic change associated with new HRM policy. Similarly, Trullen et al. (2016) demonstrated that line managers' involvement in HR practice design is associated with greater motivation for HR practice implementation. The authors suggested that including line managers early in the development of HR practices encouraged them to feel that the initiative was their own.

Scholars have reasoned that an important factor that shapes the nature of line managers' involvement in HR practice design may be the quality of line managers' relationships, or partnerships, with the HR function. Indeed, Currie and Procter (2001) proposed that one way to foster this relationship would be to structure the HR function to encourage HR managers to work more closely with line managers. Consistent with this notion, scholars have suggested that the partnership between line managers and HR managers is critical, because it facilitates a clear division of tasks between HR and line managers as well as the communication between both parties (e.g., Bos-Nehles and Van Riemsdijk, 2014; Whittaker and Marchington, 2003). Similarly, Kim et al. (2018) found that HR practices oriented toward developing HR managers' social networks with line managers help to facilitate the formation of a shared language between them, with one visible benefit of the relationship being a reduction in employee turnover. Lastly, both scholarly research and HRM practitioners reports (Garavan et al., 2012;

Heinen and O'Neill, 2004; Martin and Schmidt, 2010; Ready and Conger, 2007; Stadler, 2011) have reported on the involvement of line managers in organizations' talent review sessions (that is, GE's Session C; P&G's Talent Review), where HR leaders gather insights from line managers in making decisions related to the identification of strategic jobs and the development of key employees. Such sessions serve the dual purpose of developing line managers' buy-in to critical HRM decisions, as well as improving the effectiveness of these decisions through the incorporation of line managers' operational knowledge and awareness of the environment and talent needs at the local level.

Workforce Differentiation

Workforce differentiation refers to the disproportionate investment into particular segments of an organization's workforce based on the distinct characteristics of employee skill sets and their relative contribution to the organization's value-creating activities. Scholars have advanced multiple approaches to workforce differentiation. For instance, while Lepak and Snell's (1999) "HR architecture" proposed the utilization of different employment modes based on the differential uniqueness and value of employees' skill sets, Becker, Huselid, and colleagues (Becker and Huselid, 2006; Becker et al., 2009; Huselid and Becker, 2011) argued for the segmentation of jobs and positions, based on their strategic value within an organization. Within either approach, to be successful, workforce differentiation requires both effective workforce segmentation based on the value and uniqueness of individual employees and/or employee groups; and effective implementation of differentiated HR practices and investments. Because the success of these combined activities relies on line managers' endorsement of the underlying segmentation decisions and accountability for results (Huselid and Becker, 2011), scholars have made a case for line managers' involvement throughout the planning and execution process (Kehoe and Han, 2020).

In sum, research on mechanisms for line managers' input into organizations' HRM policy and workforce differentiation sheds light on the ways in which line managers may contribute to organization-level differences in HR policy and practice. While relatively limited, this work highlights the potential value in offering line managers opportunities for providing such input, in part due to their vantage points at important intersections between employees and higher-level leadership in the organization (Currie and Procter, 2001).

DISCUSSION

Our review of extant research in this chapter demonstrates that the SHRM literature has made reasonable progress in understanding the role of line managers in HRM. Indeed, emerging research in this vein reflects scholars' recognition that line managers, at a minimum, play an important role in the implementation of an organization's HR practices (Sikora et al., 2015), and that line managers' individual characteristics (McGovern et al., 1997; Mitchell et al., 2013) and situational factors (Op de Beeck et al., 2016; Sikora and Ferris, 2014) significantly influence their effectiveness in this capacity. Perhaps not surprisingly, most of this research has been focused on line managers' influences in implementing HR practices at the unit level, which is both intuitive and important for at least two reasons. First, a focus on line managers' HR practice implementation behaviors and outcomes at the unit level is reflective of line managers' span of influence and responsibility for managing a group of employees, and is the level at which line managers' accountability for performance is likely to occur. Second, and relatedly, this focus is consistent with, and sheds light on, evidence of meaningful variance in HR practice utilization and perceptions reported by scholars in the broader SHRM literature (Gardner et al., 2011; Kehoe and Collins, 2017). In particular, integrating insights from the research reviewed here with prior studies demonstrating variance in the employment of particular HR systems across units within an organization highlights the centrality of line managers in employees' HRM experiences: variability in employees' experiences with a single system of HR practices within the same organization may be driven in part by differences in the abilities, motivation, and opportunities of their respective line managers. At the same time, line managers' varied leadership styles and behaviors may interact in meaningful ways with the formal HR practices available for their use within an organization.

We also gain valuable insights from research focusing on the roles of line managers in HRM at other levels. Research examining line managers' unique influences on individual employees' HRM perceptions and responses, and in the negotiation of i-deals, offers additional evidence that line managers are not simply messengers consistently delivering the practices set forth by the HR function. Rather, this research suggests that beyond the factors that lead to differences in typical HR practice implementation behaviors across line managers and units, characteristics of line managers' dyadic relationships with their employees can generate additional variance in employees' HRM experiences and outcomes within the same unit and under the same manager.

Finally, research examining the presence and effectiveness of mechanisms through which line managers may offer input into HRM policy and decision-making at the organization level shows great promise, yet this may be the smallest and least-developed stream of research in this realm. In particular, this research offers meaningful insights into the multiple gains that may be achieved in organizations by investing in structural and relational approaches to support line managers' participation in HR practice design. First, with formal opportunities for line managers to provide input into the development of HR practices, organizations can improve the relevance of their HR practices by leveraging the specialized expertise and knowledge of line managers, and thereby accounting for the unique requirements of the multiple local contexts across which line managers are employed. Second, the opportunity to provide such input may strengthen line managers' motivation to implement the organization's HR practices due to the increased support and buy-in that line managers develop through their involvement in this capacity with the HR function.

Moving Forward with an Agenda for Future Research

A reflection on the extant research on line managers' roles in HRM leads to a few observations. First, perhaps given its situation within the broader SHRM literature, this research, with a few exceptions (e.g., Evans, 2017; Hutchinson and Purcell, 2010; Whittaker and Marchington, 2003), tends to prioritize line managers' roles as implementers of HR practices over—and often to the exclusion of—line managers' core responsibilities for the operations of their units or functions. This is problematic, as line managers are likely to view their strategic and operational responsibilities within their units as central to their role and identity in an organization. As a result, line managers' perspectives on their responsibilities for implementing HR practices are likely to heavily depend on the extent to which they view HR practices, and the time and resources required to implement them, as supporting versus interfering with their strategic and operational goals. Thus, further inquiry into how line managers perceive and manage the intersection of these multiple responsibilities is needed.

Second, with the exception of work on i-deals (which, to date, has focused much more on the employees receiving i-deals than on the managers negotiating them), research has tended to assume that line manager-generated variance in HR practice delivery is effectively captured by examining the extent to which line managers implement a particular set of HR practices. Until recently (Kehoe and Han, 2020), there has been limited consideration of line managers' modification of HR practices (for exceptions, see Bos-Nehles et al., 2017; Trullen et al., 2020; and Van Mierlo et al., 2018) and even less consideration of line managers' roles in introducing new HR practices. However, returning to the point that line managers are likely to prioritize their broader strategic or operational responsibilities over their roles in HR practice implementation, it is reasonable to expect some level of qualitative variability in the practices that line managers ultimately use in managing their employees, particularly among line managers who lack confidence in the alignment of an organization's HR practices in supporting their units' needs, and who have expertise or experience related to other HR practices that they believe will better suit their unit contexts.

Third, extant work in this realm has offered little in the way of integrative insights from research on line managers' involvement and influence in HRM at different levels. Beyond the missed theoretical opportunities which this leaves unexplored, we believe that this is a significant practical oversight, as line managers who are actively engaged in HRM are likely to be motivated to maximize the impact of their investments, which may take the form of leveraging their efforts to increase their impact across levels, spanning individual employees, units, and the broader organization. Understanding the conditions under which cross-level influences associated with line managers' HRM-related efforts are most likely to occur and to be effective is thus an important area of inquiry.

These observations point to a broad array of potential directions for future research. In the sections that follow, we discuss what we believe are three particularly promising avenues of inquiry in this area.

Line managers' autonomous (strategic) HR behavior
One approach to exploring how line managers' HRM responsibilities might fit within their multiple other roles in an organization is to consider how and when line managers proactively leverage their positions as HR practice implementers to support the attainment of their operational and strategic goals. While this idea lacks precedence in the SHRM literature, Kehoe and Han (2020) drew on insights from research on autonomous strategic behavior within the strategic management literature in their consideration of what forms such efforts might take. Research on autonomous strategic behavior focuses on deliberate activities through which line managers deviate from the organization's intended strategic plans or practices (Mirabeau and Maguire, 2014). Such activities may be contained to the local level or may serve as the foundational components of emergent (or bottom-up) strategy, as opposed to induced (or top-down) strategy (Burgelman, 1983; Mintzberg, 1978). Line managers engage in autonomous strategic behavior for a variety of reasons, including to fulfill expectations of their role in the organization (Minztberg and Waters, 1985), to cope with the incompleteness of extant practices (Inkpen and Choudhury, 1995), and/or to facilitate adaptability to ensure the alignment of practices with their local environments (Mirabeau and Maguire, 2014).

Kehoe and Han (2020) suggest that within the context of line managers' autonomous strategic behaviors, they may adapt and introduce unsanctioned HR practices to support the workforce requirements of achieving their local goals. Such autonomous HR behavior may take a variety of forms. For instance, Mirabeau and Maguire (2014) found that a line manager planned and delivered customized training sessions to facilitate call center operators' abilities to adopt a multilingual call flow procedure. In this case, the line manager engaged in an autonomous HR behavior by explicitly modifying an organization's espoused HR practices (that is, training) to support the requests of regional clients for increased accessibility of the call center's services.

Alternatively, autonomous HR behavior may take the form of line managers applying previously individual-level i-deals to expanded groups of strategically valuable employees. This idea is consistent with Rousseau et al.'s (2006) speculation that the strategic value of employee groups might increase the likelihood of i-deals occurring within a unit, as focused efforts to meet the unique needs of key employees may increase their commitment to the organization. In a similar vein, line managers may target individualized work arrangements specifically to star performers (Ford and Newstrom, 1999; Frank, 1985; Rousseau, 2005), as their contributions are likely to be particularly valuable in planning and enacting effective responses to the requirements of a unit's local environment. Importantly, the strategic utilization of i-deals as an approach to supporting unit-level needs is a reflection of how line managers may leverage their efforts at one level (that is, individual) to reap benefits at other levels in an organization.

Moving forward, research in pursuit of this line of inquiry would benefit from the development of more systematic characterization of when and how line managers are most likely to engage in autonomous strategic HR behaviors, as well as the implications of these behaviors across various levels of the organization. For instance, it would be informative to examine the consequences of modifications to HR practices that are functional and well aligned at the local unit level for broader HRM policy at the organization level. Additionally, further research is needed to understand the competencies required by line managers to engage in effective and adaptive HR practice modification, as well as the organizational structures and policies that are most likely to support or—when consistency is critical—inhibit such behaviors.

Line managers' ad hoc upward influences on HRM policy

An important extension of the idea that line managers may adapt or introduce HR practices within their units is the possibility that some line managers may be further motivated to shape, or change, formal HRM policy at the organization level. Such motivation may be rooted in the desire to elevate the status of a line manager's unit, to increase the standing of the line manager in the organization, and/or in a line manager's genuine, inherent interest in shaping the organization's approach to managing people. In some cases, the formal mechanisms instituted to invite structured input from line managers into particular facets of HRM policy (that is, workforce differentiation) may not suit these objectives. And while there is limited consideration within the SHRM literature of line managers' potential ad hoc influences on HRM policy, two streams of research outside the HR literature offer insights into how we may begin to understand when, how, and to what end line managers may exert ad hoc upward influence within the realm of HRM policy.

The first research stream in this vein investigates "issue-selling" behaviors of line managers. Although the extant issue-selling literature mainly focuses on issues outside of the HRM context, Kehoe and Han (2020) highlighted that line managers may engage in issue-selling efforts as they seek organizational resources, legitimacy, and/or social support for their adaptation and introduction of HR practices at local levels. From this perspective, the authors suggested that line managers may instigate transformative change in the formal HR system at the organization level.

Issue-selling has been defined as the "voluntary behaviors which organizational members use to influence the organizational agenda by getting those above them to pay attention to an issue" (Dutton and Ashford, 1993). This literature has primarily focused on the contextual and individual factors that shape both the likelihood and the effectiveness of line managers' issue-selling efforts directed toward top management. For instance, research has demonstrated that factors such as the openness of top management and the supportiveness of an organiza-tion's culture influence the likelihood that lower-level managers will engage in issue-selling efforts. Meanwhile, line managers' issue-selling strategies have an important effect on the outcome of these efforts. For example, in their study of an international oil company, Ashford and Detert (2015) noted that a regional sales manager was responsible for persuading the organization to adopt the industry's best practices for managing sales employees by intention-ally connecting them to the top management team's goals for the sales division.

The second research stream in this vein focuses on "emergent strategy": a topic within the strategic management literature which, in contrast to adopting the traditional view of strate-gic planning as a purely deliberate, top-down process, focuses on the formation of strategy through bottom-up initiatives in which actors at various levels of the organization initiate and champion strategic change (Mintzberg, 1978). Research on emergent strategy has found that once the emergent strategy appears and gains legitimation by top management, it leads to changes in the organization's intended strategy (Mirabeau and Maguire, 2014). Mintzberg (1987) describes this phenomenon with the idea that "patterns from the past" become "plans for the future."

While research in these two research streams has thus far received limited attention in the HRM context, an application of insights from these two literatures may lead to inquiry and new insights related to when line managers are mostly likely to engage in upward-directed influence efforts, as well as when these efforts are likely to have intended effects in shaping an organization's HRM policy. While this phenomenon is more readily apparent in case studies and anecdotal observations of HR practice in organizations than in scholarly research, Mirabeau and Maguire (2014) documented its occurrence in a study of telecommunications firms in an examination of the process through which a line manager orchestrated changes in regional training practices to meet the idiosyncratic needs of customers in the local environ-ment. Such research undertakings in this vein have the potential to shed light on the intentional and agentic roles of line managers as potential sources of HRM transformation. This notion offers an important complement to the prevailing top-down model of HRM that has dominated SHRM scholarship to date (Kehoe and Han, 2020).

Line managers' roles in vertical HR alignment
The above considerations of line managers' autonomous HR behaviors and ad hoc upward influences on HRM policy invite an additional consideration of line managers' influences on the vertical alignment of their organizations' HR systems. The concept of vertical alignment—the fit of an organization's HR system with the requirements of its environment—has been foundational in SHRM research (Baird and Meshoulam, 1988; Schuler and Jackson, 1987). Often, research in this vein has focused on an organization's strategy as the relevant target of

alignment for its HR system, with scholars arguing that particular HR systems are better suited to supporting the needs of organizations pursuing specific strategies, that is: cost leadership, innovation, or quality enhancement (Schuler and Jackson, 1987); exploration or exploitation (Collins and Kehoe, 2017); first-mover, fast follower, or fence-sitter market entry (Han et al., 2019). In other cases, scholars have considered vertical alignment in terms of the fit of organizations' HR systems with relevant industry characteristics, including industry dynamism (Chadwick et al., 2013), capital intensity (Datta et al., 2005), and growth (Chadwick et al., 2013; Datta et al., 2005), as well as other attributes of the general environment, such as labor market conditions (Sun et al., 2007).

Line managers' various forms of involvement in HRM have the potential to exert several influences on the vertical alignment of HR practices at different levels of an organization. Perhaps most intuitive, weak implementation (or any implementation less than the fullest extent intended) of an organization's espoused HR practices by a line manager may compromise the vertical alignment of these practices at the unit level. That is, to the extent that an organization has designed HR practices that are well aligned with the requirements of its strategy and broader environment, and to the extent that line managers are operating in units that face similar environments to the organization as a whole, weak HR practice implementation may undermine a unit's abilities to cope with environmental requirements.

In other cases, line managers find themselves facing demands in their local unit environments that differ from the demands characterizing an organization's broader environment. In these cases, line managers may introduce HR practices that deviate from those espoused by the organization, thereby engaging in the aforementioned activity of autonomous strategic HR behavior. For example, if line managers fail to see the value of the HR practices that are espoused by the organization, they may ignore or deviate from the delegated HR practices (Bos-Nehles et al., 2017). In doing so, such line managers proactively leverage their roles in HR practice delivery to strategically and intentionally modify or stray from the organization's espoused HR practices in order to support the workforce requirements associated with meeting their operational and strategic goals in their local context. To the extent that these efforts are effective, line managers' autonomous strategic HR behaviors may increase the vertical alignment of HR practices at the local level, albeit by deviating from the HR practices that are supported at the organization level.

Importantly, the situations described above at the unit level are also likely to have important implications for vertical alignment at the organization level. For instance, to the extent that an organization faces uniform and consistent environments across all units, line managers' strong implementation of an organization's espoused HR practices across units is likely to support the vertical alignment achieved by the organization as a whole. Further, within organizations comprised of units that face distinct or dynamic environments, line managers' modification or introduction of HR practices to meet the distinct needs of their units' local environments improves the vertical alignment of HR practices throughout the organization with respect to the organizations' many and varied environments.

Line managers may also contribute to vertical alignment at the organization level by propelling an organization to make formal changes in its centralized HR system to meet the changing requirements in the broader organizational environment. Particularly when an organization is operating in a dynamic environment, it is likely to be extremely difficult for the top management team and/or the HR function to keep abreast of environmental changes. Since line managers are "on the ground," interacting with external stakeholders (Dutton et al., 1997) and frontline employees (Huy, 2002), they serve as critical touchpoints for information about environmental changes. As line managers identify and share information about changes in the environment, and propose the centralized modification or introduction of HR practices to address such changes (that is, through the issue-selling efforts mentioned earlier), they may be the instigators of formal change in organization-level HR systems that provide for improved alignment with the rapidly changing environment. We envision a range of promising research directions in this vein. For instance, how do different organizational environments shape an organization's patterns of HR-related decision-making and communication among organizational actors? To what extent do such patterns influence line managers' roles in HR?

CONCLUSION

In this chapter, we have reviewed the extant research examining line managers' involvement in human resource management at different levels of the organization. Our review underscored the need for SHRM scholars to more carefully consider the broader contexts surrounding line managers' HRM involvement in research, including the varied non-HRM roles that line managers play in their organizations, the implications of line managers' HRM-related behaviors at one organizational level for HR practice and outcomes at other organizational levels, and the intersection of line managers' HRM-related behaviors with the requirements of the organization's external environment with which many line managers are likely to often engage. We have sought to lay the foundation, and offer specific suggestions, for future research to address open questions along these lines.

REFERENCES

Alfes, K., Truss, C., Soane, E.C., Rees, C., and Gatenby, M. (2013). The relationship between line manager behavior, perceived HRM practices, and individual performance: Examining the mediating role of engagement. *Human Resource Management*, 52(6), 839–859.

Anand, S., Vidyarthi, P.R., Liden, R.C., and Rousseau, D.M. (2010). Good citizens in poor-quality relationships: Idiosyncratic deals as a substitute for relationship quality. *Academy of Management Journal*, 53(5), 970–988.

Appelbaum, E., Bailey, T., Berg, P., and Kalleberg, A. (2000). *Manufacturing Advantage: Why High-Performance Work Systems Pay Off*. Ithaca, NY: Cornell University Press.

Ashford, S.J., and Detert, J.R. (2015). Get the boss to buy in. *Harvard Business Review*, 93, 72–79.

Baird, L., and Meshoulam, I. (1988). Managing two fits of strategic human resource management. *Academy of Management Review*, 13(1), 116–128.

Bal, P.M., and Boehm, S.A. (2019). How do i-deals influence client satisfaction? The role of exhaustion, collective commitment, and age diversity. *Journal of Management*, 45(4), 1461–1487.

Becker, B.E., and Huselid, M.A. (2006). Strategic human resources management: Where do we go from here? *Journal of Management*, 32(6), 898–925.

Becker, B.E., Huselid, M.A., and Beatty, R.W. (2009). *The Differentiated Workforce: Transforming Talent into Strategic Impact*. Boston, MA: Harvard Business Press.

Beijer, S., Van De Voorde, K., and Tims, M. (2019). An interpersonal perspective on HR attributions: Examining the role of line managers, coworkers, and similarity in work-related motivations. *Frontiers in Psychology*, 10, 1–10.

Blau, P.M. (1964), *Exchange and Power in Social Life*. New York: Wiley.

Bos-Nehles, A.C., and Meijerink, J.G. (2018). HRM implementation by multiple HRM actors: A social exchange perspective. *International Journal of Human Resource Management*, 29(22), 3068–3092.

Bos-Nehles, A., and Van Riemsdijk, M. (2014). Innovating HRM implementation: The influence of organisational contingencies on the HRM role of line managers. *Advanced Series in Management*, 14, 101–133.

Bos-Nehles, A.C., Bondarouk, T., and Labrenz, S. (2017). HRM implementation in multinational companies: The dynamics of multifaceted scenarios. *European Journal of International Management*, 11(5), 515–536.

Bos-Nehles, A.C., Van Riemsdijk, M.J., and Looise, J.K. (2013). Employee perceptions of line management performance: Applying the AMO theory to explain the effectiveness of line managers' HRM implementation. *Human Resource Management*, 52(6), 861–877.

Bowen, D.E., and Ostroff, C. (2004). Understanding HRM–firm performance linkages: The role of the "strength" of the HRM system. *Academy of Management Review*, 29(2), 203–221.

Bredin, K., and Söderlund, J. (2007). Reconceptualising line management in project-based organisations: The case of competence coaches at Tetra Pak. *Personnel Review*, 36(5), 815–833.

Burgelman, R.A. (1983). A model of the interaction of strategic behavior, corporate context, and the concept of strategy. *Academy of Management Review*, 8(1), 61–70.

Černe, M., Batistič, S., and Kenda, R. (2018). HR systems, attachment styles with leaders, and the creativity–innovation nexus. *Human Resource Management Review*, 28(3), 271–288.

Chadwick, C., Super, J.F., and Kwon, K. (2015). Resource orchestration in practice: CEO emphasis on SHRM, commitment-based HR systems, and firm performance. *Strategic Management Journal*, 36, 360–376.

Chadwick, C., Way, S.A., Kerr, G., and Thacker, J.W. (2013). Boundary conditions of the high-investment human resource systems–small-firm labor productivity relationship. *Personnel Psychology*, 66, 311–343.

Collins, C., and Kehoe, R.R. (2017). Examining strategic fit and misfit in the management of knowledge workers. *ILR Review*, 70(2), 308–335.

Collins, C., and Smith, K.G. (2006). Knowledge exchange and combination: The role of human resource practices in the performance of high-technology firms. *Academy of Management Journal*, 49(3), 544–560.

Combs, J., Liu, Y., Hall, A., and Ketchen, D. (2006). How much do high-performance work practices matter? A meta-analysis of their effects on organizational performance. *Personnel Psychology*, 59, 501–528.

Cunningham, I., and Hyman, J. (1999). Devolving human resource responsibilities to the line: Beginning of the end or a new beginning for personnel. *Personnel Review*, 28(1–2), 9–27.

Currie, G., and Procter, S. (2001). Exploring the relationship between HR and middle managers. *Human Resource Management Journal*, 11(3), 53–69.

Datta, D.K., Guthrie, J.P., and Wright, P.M. (2005). Human resource management and labor productivity: Does industry matter? *Academy of Management Journal*, 48(1), 135–145.

Dewettinck, K., and Vroonen, W. (2017). Antecedents and consequences of performance management enactment by front-line managers: Evidence from Belgium. *International Journal of Human Resource Management*, 28(17), 2473–2502.

Dutton, J.E., and Ashford, S.J. (1993). Selling issues to top management. *Academy of Management Review*, 18(3), 397–428.

Dutton, J.E., Ashford, S.J., O'Neill, R.M., Hayes, E., and Wierba, E.E. (1997). Reading the wind: How middle managers assess the context for selling issues to top managers. *Strategic Management Journal*, 18(5), 407–425.

Dysvik, A., and Kuvaas, B. (2012). Perceived supervisor support climate, perceived investment in employee development climate, and business-unit performance. *Human Resource Management*, 51(5), 651–664.

Evans, S. (2017). HRM and front line managers: The influence of role stress. *International Journal of Human Resource Management*, 28(22), 3128–3148.

Floyd, S.W., and Wooldridge, B. (1992). Middle management involvement in strategy and its association with strategic type: A research note. *Strategic Management Journal*, 13, 153–167.

Floyd, S.W., and Wooldridge, B. (1994). Dinosaurs or dynamos? Recognizing middle management's strategic role. *Academy of Management Executive*, 8(4), 47–57.

Floyd, S.W, and Wooldridge, B. (1997). Middle management's strategic influence and organizational performance. *Journal of Managemmt Studies*, 34(3), 465–485.

Ford, R., and Newstrom, J. (1999). Dues-paying: Managing the costs of recognition. *Business Horizons*, 42(4), 14–20.

Frank, R.H. (1985). *Choosing the Right Pond: Human Behavior and the Quest for Status*. New York: Oxford University Press.

Fu, N., Flood, P.C., Rousseau, D.M., and Morris, T. (2020). Line managers as paradox navigators in HRM implementation: Balancing consistency and individual responsiveness. *Journal of Management*, 46(2), 203–233.

Gajendran, R.S., Harrison, D.A., and Delaney-Klinger, K. (2015). Are telecommuters remotely good citizens? Unpacking telecommuting's effects on performance via i-deals and job resources. *Personnel Psychology*, 68, 353–393.

Garavan, T.N., Carbery, R., and Rock, A. (2012). Mapping talent development: Definition, scope and architecture. *European Journal of Training and Development*, 36(1), 5–24.

Gardner, T.M., Wright, P.M., and Moynihan, L.M. (2011). The impact of motivation, empowerment, and skill-enhancing practices on aggregate voluntary turnover: The mediating effect of collective affective commitment. *Personnel Psychology*, 64, 315–350.

Gilbert, C., De Winne, S., and Sels, L. (2011). The influence of line managers and HR department on employees' affective commitment. *International Journal of Human Resource Management*, 22(8), 1618–1637.

Gilbert, C., De Winne, S., and Sels, L. (2015). Strong HRM processes and line managers' effective HRM implementation: A balanced view. *Human Resource Management Journal*, 25(4), 600–616.

Gong, Y., Law, K.S., Chang, S., and Xin, K.R. (2009). Human resources management and firm performance: The differential role of managerial affective and continuance commitment. *Journal of Applied Psychology*, 94(1), 263–275.

Greenberg, J., Roberge, M.É., Ho, V.T., and Rousseau, D.M. (2004). Fairness and idiosyncratic work arrangements: Justice as an i-deal. *Research in Personnel and Human Resources Management*, 23, 1–34.

Guerrero, S., Bentein, K., and Lapalme, M.È. (2014). Idiosyncratic deals and high performers' organizational commitment. *Journal of Business and Psychology*, 29, 323–334.

Hailey, V.H., Farndale, E., and Truss, C. (2005). The HR department's role in organisational performance. *Human Resource Management Journal*, 15(3), 49–66.

Hall, L., and Torrington, D. (1998). Letting go or holding on – The devolution of operational personnel activities. *Human Resource Management Journal*, 8(1), 41–55.

Han, J.H., Kang, S., Oh, I.-S., Kehoe, R.R., and Lepak, D.P. (2019). The Goldilocks effect of strategic human resource management? Optimizing the benefits of a high-performance work system through the dual alignment of vertical and horizontal fit. *Academy of Management Journal*, 62(5), 1388–1412.

Heider, F. (1958). *The Psychology of Interpersonal Relations*. New York: Wiley.

Heinen, J.S., and O'Neill, C. (2004). Managing talent to maximize performance. *Employment Relations Today*, 31(2), 67–82.

Heraty, N., and Morley, M. (1995). Line managers and human resource development. *Journal of European Industrial Training*, 19(10), 31–37.

Ho, V.T., and Tekleab, A.G. (2016). A model of idiosyncratic deal-making and attitudinal outcomes. *Journal of Managerial Psychology*, 31, 642–656.

Hornung, S., Rousseau, D.M., Glaser, J., Angerer, P., and Weigl, M. (2010). Beyond top-down and bottom-up work redesign: Customizing job content through idiosyncratic deals. *Journal of Organizational Behavior*, 31, 187–215.

Hornung, S., Rousseau, D.M., Weigl, M., Müller, A., and Glaser, J. (2014). Redesigning work through idiosyncratic deals. *European Journal of Work and Organizational Psychology*, 23(4), 608–626.

Huselid, M.A., and Becker, B.E. (2011). Bridging micro and macro domains: Workforce differentiation and strategic human resource management. *Journal of Management*, 37(2), 421–428.

Hutchinson, S., and Purcell, J. (2003). *Bringing Policies to Life: The Vital Role of Front Line Managers in People Management*. Research report. London: CIPD.

Hutchinson, S., and Purcell, J. (2010). Managing ward managers for roles in HRM in the NHS: Overworked and under-resourced. *Human Resource Management Journal*, 20(4), 357–374.

Huy, Q.N. (2002). Emotional balancing of organizational continuity and radical change: The contribution of middle managers. *Administrative Science Quarterly*, 47, 31–69.

Inkpen, A., and Choudhury, N. (1995). The seeking of strategy where it is not: Towards a theory of strategy absence. *Strategic Management Journal*, 16(4), 313–323.

Jiang, K., Chuang, C.-H., and Chiao, Y.-C. (2015). Developing collective customer knowledge and service climate: The interaction between service-oriented high-performance work systems and service leadership. *Journal of Applied Psychology*, 100(4), 1089–1106.

Jiang, K., Hu, J., Liu, S., and Lepak, D.P. (2017). Understanding employees' perceptions of human resource practices: Effects of demographic dissimilarity to managers and coworkers. *Human Resource Management*, 56(1), 69–91.

Kehoe, R.R., and Collins, C. (2017). Human resource management and unit performance in knowledge-intensive work. *Journal of Applied Psychology*, 102(8), 1222–1236.

Kehoe, R.R., and Han, J.H. (2020). An expanded conceptualization of line managers' involvement in human resource management. *Journal of Applied Psychology*, 105(2), 111–129.

Kehoe, R.R., and Wright, P.M. (2013). The impact of high-performance human resource practices on employees' attitudes and behaviors. *Journal of Management*, 39(2), 366–391.

Kellner, A., Townsend, K., Wilkinson, A., Lawrence, S.A., and Greenfield, D. (2016). Learning to manage: development experiences of hospital frontline managers. *Human Resource Management Journal*, 26(4), 505–522.

Khilji, S.E., and Wang, X. (2006). "Intended" and "implemented" HRM: The missing linchpin in strategic human resource management research. *International Journal of Human Resource Management*, 17(7), 1171–1189.

Kim, S., Su, Z.-X., and Wright, P.M. (2018). The "HR–line-connecting HRM system" and its effects on employee turnover. *Human Resource Management*, 57(5), 1219–1231.

Kossek, E.E., Ollier-Malaterre, A., Lee, M.D., Pichler, S., and Hall, D.T. (2016). Line managers' rationales for professionals' reduced-load work in embracing and ambivalent organizations. *Human Resource Management*, 55(1), 143–171.

Kunda, Z., and Thagard, P. (1996). Forming impressions from stereotypes, traits, and behaviors: A parallel-constraint-satisfaction theory. *Psychological Review*, 103(2), 284–308.

Kuvaas, B., Dysvik, A., and Buch, R. (2014). Antecedents and employee outcomes of line managers' perceptions of enabling HR practices. *Journal of Management Studies*, 51(6), 845–868.

Lepak, D.P., and Snell, S.A. (1999). The human resource architecture: Toward a theory of human capital allocation and development. *Academy of Management Review*, 24(1), 31–48.

Liao, C., Wayne, S.J., and Rousseau, D.M. (2016). Idiosyncratic deals in contemporary organizations: A qualitative and meta-analytical review. *Journal of Organizational Behavior*, 37, S9–S29.

Liao, H., Toya, K., Lepak, D.P., and Hong, Y. (2009). Do they see eye to eye? Management and employee perspectives of high-performance work systems and influence processes on service quality. *Journal of Applied Psychology*, 94(2), 371–391.

Liu, J., Lee, C., Hui, C., Kwan, H.K., and Wu, L.Z. (2013). Idiosyncratic deals and employee outcomes: The mediating roles of social exchange and self-enhancement and the moderating role of individualism. *Journal of Applied Psychology*, 98(5), 832–840.

Lowe, J. (1992). Locating the line: The front-line supervisor and human resource management. In P. Blyton and P. Turnbull (eds), *Reassessing Human Resource Management* (pp. 148–168). London: SAGE.

MacDuffie, J.P. (1995). Human resource bundles and manufacturing performance: Organizational logic and flexible production systems in the world auto industry. *Industrial and Labor Relations Review*, 48(2), 197–221.

Martin, J., and Schmidt, C. (2010). How to keep your top talent. *Harvard Business Review*, 88(5), 54–61.

Martinson, B., and Deleon, J. (2016). Testing the effect of LMX and HR system strength on employee and work unit outcomes. *Advances in Business Research*, 7, 91–103.

Maxwell, G.A., and Watson, S. (2006). Perspectives on line managers in human resource management: Hilton International's UK hotels. *International Journal of Human Resource Management*, 17(6), 1152–1170.

McGovern, P. (1999). HRM policies and management practices. In L. Gratton, V. Hope-Hailey, P. Stiles, and C. Truss (eds), *Strategic Human Resource Management* (pp. 133–152). Oxford: Oxford University Press.

McGovern, P., Gratton, L., Hope-Hailey, V., Stiles, P., and Truss, C. (1997). Human resource management on the line? *Human Resource Management Journal*, 7(4), 12–29.

Mintzberg, H. (1978). Patterns in strategy formation. *Management Science*, 24(9), 934–948.

Mintzberg, H. (1987). The strategy concept I: Five Ps for strategy. *California Management Review*, 30(1), 11–32.

Mintzberg, H., and Waters, J.A. (1985). Of strategies, deliberate and emergent. *Strategic Management Journal*, 6, 257–272.

Mirabeau, L., and Maguire, S. (2014). From autonomous strategic behavior to emergent strategy. *Strategic Management Journal*, 35, 1202–1229.

Mitchell, R., Obeidat, S., and Bray, M. (2013). The effect of strategic human resource management on organizational performance: The mediating role of high-performance human resource practices. *Human Resource Management*, 52(6), 899–921.

Ng, T.W.H. (2017). Can idiosyncratic deals promote perceptions of competitive climate, felt ostracism, and turnover? *Journal of Vocational Behavior*, 99, 118–131.

Ng, T.W.H., and Feldman, D.C. (2015). Idiosyncratic deals and voice behavior. *Journal of Management*, 41(3), 893–928.

Nishii, L.H., and Wright, P.M. (2007). Variability within organizations: Implications for strategic human resource management. CAHRS Working Paper.

Nishii, L.H., Lepak, D.P., and Schneider, B. (2008). Employee attributions of the "why" of HR practices: Their effects on employee attitudes and behaviors, and customer satisfaction. *Personnel Psychology*, 61, 503–545.

Op de Beeck, S., Wynen, J., and Hondeghem, A. (2016). HRM implementation by line managers: Explaining the discrepancy in HR–line perceptions of HR devolution. *International Journal of Human Resource Management*, 27(17), 1901–1919.

Pak, J., and Kim, S. (2018). Team manager's implementation, high performance work systems intensity, and performance: A multilevel investigation. *Journal of Management*, 44(7), 2690–2715.

Perry, E.L., and Kulik, C.T. (2008). The devolution of HR to the line: Implications for perceptions of people management effectiveness. *International Journal of Human Resource Management*, 19(2), 262–273.

Pfeffer, J. (1996). When it comes to "best practises" – Why do organizations do dumb things? *Organizational Dynamics*, 25(1), 33–44.

Purcell, J., and Hutchinson, S. (2007). Front-line managers as agents in the HRM–performance causal chain: Theory, analysis and evidence. *Human Resource Management Journal*, 17(1), 3–20.

Ready, D.A., and Conger, J.A. (2007). Make your company a talent factory. *Harvard Business Review*, 85(6), 68–77.

Renkema, M., Meijerink, J., and Bondarouk, T. (2017). Advancing multilevel thinking in human resource management research: Applications and guidelines. *Human Resource Management Review*, 27, 397–415.

Rosen, C.C., Slater, D.J., Chang, C.-H.D., and Johnson, R.E. (2013). Let's make a deal: Development and validation of the ex post i-deals scale. *Journal of Management*, 39(3), 709–742.

Rousseau, D.M. (2005). *I-deals: Idiosyncratic Deals Employees Bargain for Themselves*. New York: Sharpe.

Rousseau, D.M., Ho, V.T., and Greenberg, J. (2006). I-deals: Idiosyncratic terms in employment relationships. *Academy of Management Review*, 31(4), 977–994.

Russell, Z.A., Steffensen, D.S., Ellen, B.P., Zhang, L., Bishoff, J.D., and Ferris, G.R. (2018). High performance work practice implementation and employee impressions of line manager leadership. *Human Resource Management Review*, 28, 258–270.

Ryu, S., and Kim, S. (2013). First-line managers' HR involvement and HR effectiveness: The case of South Korea. *Human Resource Management*, 52(6), 947–966.

Salancik, G.R., and Pfeffer, J. (1978). A social information processing approach to job attitudes and task design. *Administrative Science Quarterly*, 23(2), 224–253.

Sanders, K., Moorkamp, M., Torka, N., Groeneveld, S., and Groeneveld, C. (2010). How to support innovative behaviour? The role of LMX and satisfaction with HR practices. *Technology and Investment*, 1, 59–68.

Schuler, R.S., and Jackson, S.E. (1987). Linking competitive strategies with human resource management practices. *Academy of Management Executive*, 1(3), 207–219.

Sikora, D., and Ferris, G.R. (2011). Critical factors in human resource practice implementation: Implications of cross-cultural contextual issues. *International Journal of Human Resources Development and Management*, 11, 112–140.

Sikora, D., and Ferris, G.R. (2014). Strategic human resource practice implementation: The critical role of line management. *Human Resource Management Review*, 24, 271–281.

Sikora, D., Ferris, G.R., and Van Iddekinge, C.H. (2015). Line manager implementation perceptions as a mediator of relations between high-performance work practices and employee outcomes. *Journal of Applied Psychology*, 100(6), 1908–1918.

Stadler, K. (2011). Talent reviews: The key to effective succession management. *Business Strategy Series*, 12(5), 264–271.

Sun, L.-Y., Aryee, S., and Law, K.S. (2007). High-performance human resource practices, citizenship behavior, and organizational performance: A relational perspective. *Academy of Management Journal*, 50(3), 558–577.

Swart, J., and Kinnie, N. (2013). Managing multidimensional knowledge assets: HR configurations in professional service firms. *Human Resource Management Journal*, 23(2), 160–179.

Takeuchi, R., Chen, G., and Lepak, D.P. (2009). Through the looking glass of a social system: Cross-level effects of high-performance work systems on employees' attitudes. *Personnel Psychology*, 62, 1–29.

Tierney, P., and Farmer, S.M. (2002). Creative self-efficacy: Potential antecedents and relationship to creative performance. *Academy of Management Journal*, 45, 1137–1148.

Trullen, J., Bos-Nehles, A.C., and Valverde, M. (2020). From intended to actual and beyond: A cross-disciplinary view of (human resource management) implementation. *International Journal of Management Reviews*, 22, 150–176.

Trullen, J., Stirpe, L., Bonache, J., and Valverde, M. (2016). The HR department's contribution to line managers' effective implementation of HR practices. *Human Resource Management Journal*, 26(4), 449–470.

Van Beurden, J., Van De Voorde, K., and Van Veldhoven, M. (2021). The employee perspective on HR practices: A systematic literature review, integration and outlook. *International Journal of Human Resource Management*, 32(2), 359–393.

Van Mierlo, J., Bondarouk, T., and Sanders, K. (2018). The dynamic nature of HRM implementation: A structuration perspective. *International Journal of Human Resource Management*, 29(22), 3026–3045.

Vermeeren, B. (2014). Variability in HRM implementation among line managers and its effect on performance: A 2-1-2 mediational multilevel approach. *International Journal of Human Resource Management*, 25(22), 3039–3059.

Wang, C.H., Baba, V.V., Hackett, R.D., and Hong, Y. (2019). Employee-experienced high-performance work systems in facilitating employee helping and voice: The role of employees' proximal perceptions and trust in the supervisor. *Human Performance*, 32(2), 69–91.

Watson, S., Maxwell, G.A., and Farquharson, L. (2007). Line managers' views on adopting human resource roles: The case of Hilton (UK) hotels. *Employee Relations*, 29(1), 30–49.

Whittaker, S., and Marchington, M. (2003). Devolving HR responsibility to the line: Threat, opportunity or partnership? *Employee Relations*, 25(3), 245–261.

Woodrow, C., and Guest, D.E. (2014). When good HR gets bad results: Exploring the challenge of HR implementation in the case of workplace bullying. *Human Resource Management Journal*, 24(1), 38–56.

Wright, P.M., and Snell, S.A. (1998). Toward a unifying framework for exploring fit and flexibility in strategic human resource management. *Academy of Management Review*, 23, 756–772.

Yousaf, A., Sanders, K., Torka, N., and Ardts, J. (2011). Having two bosses: Considering the relationships between LMX, satisfaction with HR practices, and organizational commitment. *International Journal of Human Resource Management*, 22(15), 3109–3126.

9. Line manager capabilities and human resource practice implementation

David M. Sikora

INTRODUCTION

In most organizations, the human resources (HR) department is responsible for the development of HR practices designed to help the firm reach its strategic and business objectives. Due to their positive impact on firm performance, HR practices such as formal performance appraisal programs, compensation linked to performance, employee participation and feedback programs, and the use of structured employee selection programs, are often labeled "high-performance HR practices." The business advantages of using these practices include improvements in firm performance, including lower employee turnover, higher productivity, and greater sales and profit growth (Combs et al., 2006; Gratton and Truss, 2003; Kehoe and Collins, 2017; Wright et al., 2005; Wright and Nishii, 2013).

While HR and senior management typically develop their firm's HR practices, line managers generally are responsible for implementing those practices throughout the organization (Harris, 2001; Nishii et al., 2008; Su and Wright, 2012; Wright and Nishii, 2013). However, while many companies attempt to promote their use of high-performance HR practices, their line managers usually vary in their implementation levels and efforts (Nishii et al., 2018; Van Iddekinge et al., 2009). Consequently, because of this implementation variance, HR practices described in detail by the HR function may only exist on paper (Guest et al., 2013; Khilji and Wang, 2006; Lengnick-Hall et al., 2009). In fact, many firms fail to meet desired performance levels not because their HR practices are poorly designed, but because line managers often fail to effectively implement those practices (Gilbert et al., 2015; Woodrow and Guest, 2014; Wright et al., 2001). For instance, researchers note that low line manager involvement is often a weak link in otherwise well-designed performance management systems (Den Hartog et al., 2013; Harris, 2001; Nishii et al., 2018). Because they frequently consider it unnecessary, line managers often fail to take on HR responsibilities (Nishii et al., 2018; Woodrow and Guest, 2014). Similarly, Evans (2015) notes that employee involvement levels are lower when companies face middle management resistance to HR implementation.

Despite some managers' resistance to using their organizations' HR practices, HR implementation appears to play a significant role in organizational success. Gratton and Truss (2003) describe HR implementation as the degree to which HR practices are put into effect by line managers, and note that HR implementation is central to successful employee management and, in turn, to improved firm performance. More recently, Trullen et al. (2020) expand on this HR implementation definition by noting two key points. First, they define HR implementation as a dynamic process which involves multiple individuals (that is, line managers, HR managers, and user employees), starting with the adoption of a new HR practice and ending with the routine use of that practice. Bos-Nehles et al. (2013) and Gratton and Truss (2003) both address the importance of HR implementation and its impact on firm performance.

Additionally, Trullen et al. (2020) distinguish HR implementation from HR implementation effectiveness, which they see as the outcome of the implementation process.

This research highlights the key role that line managers play in making each organization's HR practices real to the firm's employees and, ultimately, in attaining performance improvements (Bowen and Ostroff, 2004; Nishii and Paluch, 2018). Given this critical role, this chapter explores the vital capabilities (that is, the factors enhancing or limiting a manager's ability to accomplish something) shaping line managers' implementation decisions and efforts. This is important because those implementation decisions and efforts ultimately impact the effectiveness of an organization's HR practices as seen in employees' workplace attitudes, motivation, and/or behaviors. In doing this, the chapter makes three contributions. First, it identifies line manager capabilities needed for HR implementation success. Next, it identifies how those capabilities contribute to improved firm performance. Finally, it identifies future directions for line manager capability and HR implementation research.

THEORETICAL FOUNDATIONS

Prior to examining the line manager capabilities which help to drive effective HR implementation, it is important to understand the theoretical foundation used to categorize these capabilities. These theories include social context theory, human resources system strength, and the theory of planned behavior. Social context theory provides a social setting for understanding line managers' implementation activities. Because managers work within their organization's social setting, it is vital to understand the impact that these social interactions have in shaping managers' decisions on whether, and how, to implement their organizations' HR practices. Next, human resources systems strength theory further clarifies the social factors impacting managers' HR implementation decisions and efforts. In this view, social factors help to shape managers' implementation activities. Subsequently, this plays a key role in determining their employees' HR practice understanding and acceptance. Finally, the theory of planned behavior provides a foundation for understanding line managers' individual capabilities that also shape their implementation efforts. Beyond the social factors impacting implementation efforts, each manager's individual attitudes, behaviors, and skills also play a key role in the implementation of their organization's HR practices. Together, these three theories were selected because they provide the needed framework for understanding both the social and the individual factors that are key to effective HR implementation.

Social Context Theory

Social context theory (Ferris et al., 1998) as related to human resource systems states that a variety of social factors, including an organization's culture, climate, political atmosphere, and social interactions, impact the development and implementation of HR practices, and ultimately, organizational effectiveness level. This model asserts that these important social considerations affect the types of HR practices that are implemented by an organization's line managers.

In social context theory, organizational culture represents an organization's deeply shared attitudes, assumptions, and core values. As these characteristics are consistently shared across the organization, they influence the organization's governance and employee behavior (Hatch,

1993). For example, if holding job candidates to elevated hiring standards is a deeply held organizational belief, a firm's line managers also are more likely to consistently implement this practice.

While similar to organizational culture, organizational climate is employees' more short-term or temporary understanding of their workplace (Denison, 1996). Climate can impact HR implementation by influencing line managers' views about the importance of various HR practices. Consequently, if line managers view some HR practices as short-lived management whims, social context theory suggests that they would be less likely to implement those practices.

Finally, an organization's political considerations and social interactions also are important elements of social context theory. Mintzberg (1985) suggested that organizations are "political arenas" where social interactions such as positioning, power use, alliance building, and conflicting interests not only determine what gets done, but also describe its culture. Political considerations also help to explain the disconnect between culture and HR practice implementation. For example, Johns (1993) argued that HR practices can be adopted because of organizational politics, federal regulation, or environmental demands, and less so for their business impact. Consequently, when this occurs, line managers might be skeptical of certain HR practices and resist their implementation.

Overall, the social context model highlights how an organization's beliefs, values, and political issues drive HR practice development and line manager implementation (Ferris et al., 1998). This theory provides important context for line managers' HR practice implementation decisions. For example, when line managers believe that their organization's culture does not value effective employee management, they may be less likely to implement their firm's HR practices. Likewise, if line manager attitudes concentrate highly on production goals at the expense of other management objectives, they may choose not to employ some of their firm's HR practices which they feel may hinder production objectives.

Human Resource System Strength

The second theory impacting line managers' HR implementation efforts is Bowen and Ostroff's (2004) view of HR system strength. In this view, and reinforced in Ostroff and Bowen (2016), strong HR systems are comprised of three interrelated features: consistency, consensus, and distinctiveness. Consistency is defined as the degree to which different HR practices within the HR system match and reinforce each other. Beyond complementary HR practices, consistency also refers to the regularity of HR implementation over time, along with the perceived validity and instrumentality of managers' implementation efforts. For instance, regarding complementary practices, consistency is high when a firm's performance management standards are directly linked to its compensation practices. In this example, when an employee receives a high-level performance rating, a consistent HR system ensures that the employee also receives a similarly high salary raise and/or bonus payment.

Consensus in HR systems reflects the level of agreement between the major stakeholders of the HR practices (that is, the line managers, HR managers, employees, and/or senior management). In this view, a strong HR system has a high level of agreement across line managers, employees, and senior management. For instance, when executives hold job candidates to high, clearly defined hiring standards, line managers and other employees throughout the organization should likewise hold those candidates to similar hiring standards. In other words, there should be little HR practice deviation across the organization.

Finally, distinctiveness is the degree to which the HR system is visible, understandable, legitimate, and relevant to the firm. To benefit the firm, line managers must make the organization's HR practices visible to their employees. Managers also must ensure that employees comprehend those practices, why the practices are important, and how the practices contribute to business success. In this view, line mangers assume the important role of shaping employees' understanding of HR practices and implementing those practices by making them clear, real, and significant to their employees.

Together, social context theory and HR system strength theory share much common ground. In both views, a variety of higher-level social context factors shape line managers' individual HR implementation decisions. The success of those decisions is impacted by social factors including top management HR support, line managers' beliefs about the importance of people, and the involvement of both HR professionals and line managers in the business planning process (Bowen and Ostroff, 2004). Both theories also support the view that line managers' attitudes and behaviors help to shape employees' HR practice views. For example, social context theory suggests that line manager HR implementation behaviors are impacted by situational cues such as their organization's culture, climate, political considerations, and social interactions. Similarly, HR system strength states that line managers' HR implementation behaviors influence their employees' HR understanding and acceptance. Together, both theories provide a strong foundation for understanding and anticipating line managers' HR practice implementation decisions and behaviors.

Theory of Planned Behavior

While these socially based theories account for much of line managers' approach to HR implementation, each manager's individual capabilities must also be considered. Ajzen's (1991) theory of planned behavior proposes that the best predictors of someone's behaviors are their individual attitudes, norms, and perceived behavioral control level. In Ajzen's view, attitudes are defined as individuals' attitudes towards specific behaviors (not their general attitudes). Norms are defined as one's subjective beliefs about how others will view their behaviors. Lastly, perceived behavioral control level is defined as perceptions of how easily one can perform a given behavior.

Ajzen's (1991) theory further proposes that individuals' overall behavior-focused attitudes are based on beliefs about the likelihood of certain outcomes, and their evaluations of those outcomes. For example, beliefs about the loss of autonomy (that is, an outcome) may influence a line manager's attitude toward the implementation of HR practices. Similarly, line managers' attitude toward using HR practices represents a possible workplace norm. In this example, if most line managers believe that HR practices are ineffective, then an organizational norm about not using certain HR practices likely develops. Conversely, if managers believe that it is important to comply with senior management directives to fully implement HR practices, then these norms likely will positively affect their HR implementation intentions and behaviors. Finally, line managers' perceived behavioral control beliefs may be related to factors such as their HR capacity, skill level, and/or motivation level. For example, when managers believe their HR skills and motivation are high, they likely also believe that it is relatively simple to implement HR practices. In these circumstances, the theory of planned behavior predicts that their HR practice implementation levels will be higher.

LINE MANAGER CAPABILITIES

Line manager HR capabilities and competencies (that is, the skills and abilities needed for successfully accomplishing a line manager's job objectives) are common themes within the HR literature. In research designed to empirically test various HR manager competencies, researchers identify three critical competencies. These include business knowledge, customer expertise, and change management capabilities (Becker et al., 2001; Ulrich et al., 1995). Han et al. (2006) also explored HR competencies, and defined them as an individual's foundational attributes, including their business knowledge, skills, and abilities.

Obviously, while HR competencies are key for HR managers, they also directly impact line managers' effective job performance (Bos-Nehles et al., 2013; Trullen et al., 2016). When managing their teams, managers need many HR competencies, including training and development, staffing, performance management, compensation, and employee relations capabilities. These skills play a critical role in successful HR implementation.

If line managers lack the capabilities needed to solve challenging employee issues, successful HR implementation is difficult. When this occurs, many managers are likely just to do whatever they believe is right. Unfortunately, this might not be the proper way to implement the organization's preferred HR practices (Nehles et al., 2006).

Early studies exploring line managers' HR capabilities note that managers often lack HR knowledge and abilities (Lo et al., 2015; Op de Beeck et al., 2016). For instance, line managers often lack full knowledge of HR legal obligations (Hall and Torrington, 1998). They may also have limited employee relations abilities (Woodrow and Guest, 2014). Finally, Gollan et al. (2015) note that line managers frequently implement HR practices based only on their common sense opinion of what should be done, or fail to deal with HR issues early enough to effectively resolve problems (Harris et al., 2002).

For many first-time or recently promoted line managers, implementing their organization's HR practices and effectively managing their employees are new activities. Consequently, many line managers express concerns about the level of HR skills needed to implement their organization's HR practices (Harris et al., 2002; Keegan et al., 2012; Whittaker and Marchington, 2003). In many cases, they say that their HR skills are lacking, and this hurts their job performance (Hope-Hailey et al., 2005; Trullen et al., 2016).

Addressing these line manager capability gaps is key to helping managers confidently and effectively implement their firm's HR practices. In turn, better line manager implementation leads to improved business performance (Nehles et al., 2006). Specifically, Sikora et al. (2015) note direct relationships between HR implementation levels and lower employee turnover intentions, higher job performance, and greater employee participation.

A MODEL OF LINE MANAGER IMPLEMENTATION CAPABILITIES

Based on social context, HR system strength, and planned behavior theories, line manager HR implementation behaviors clearly are influenced by strong social and individual components. First, managers constantly work within social environments when dealing with their customers, superiors, peers, and/or subordinates. Effective managers understand and then adapt to these social forces. Next, a manager's individual capabilities help to determine their organizational and job effectiveness. Highly effective managers use their individual skills and abilities to produce better job results. Together, these social and individual factors provide a solid grounding for a model of line manager HR implementation capabilities.

In this model, individual and social factors shape the effectiveness of line managers' HR implementation efforts. In turn, the effectiveness of those implementation activities directly impacts organizational performance. The social factors impacting line managers' implementation efforts include political skill level, organizational culture and climate understanding, the quality of managers' interactions with their employees, and the effectiveness of their working relationship with their firm's HR department. As each of those elements improve, managers' implementation efforts should lead to more effective HR implementation levels.

This model's individual factors include many elements. These include each manager's work capacity, HR competency level, motivation level, accountability level, ability to make HR real to employees, and perceptions about HR practice appropriateness and effectiveness. Like the social factors, as these individual factors improve, they should also lead to more effective HR implementation levels.

In turn, when HR implementation levels improve, both individual and organizational-level performance should also improve (Sikora and Ferris, 2014). Sikora et al. (2015) empirically provided support for this by demonstrating a significant positive relationship between HR implementation level and individual-level turnover intentions, job performance, and participative decision-making. While the relationship between line managers' HR implementation levels and individual performance is generally significant, the relationship between HR implementation and organizational performance is still unclear. Currently, the relationship between line managers' HR implementation levels and organizational-level outcomes such as employee productivity, annual employee turnover, sales growth, and/or profit growth, remain to be tested. Figure 9.1 illustrates line manager capabilities, HR implementation, and improved performance.

Line Manager Social Capabilities

Political skill

The social factors influencing line managers' HR implementation efforts start with political skill. Pfeffer and Pfeffer (1981) and Mintzberg (1985) both describe organizations as political entities. Mintzberg (1985) further argues that organizations are fundamentally political. As a result, both Pfeffer and Mintzberg suggest that individual political skill is vital to personal effectiveness in these political environments.

Ferris et al. (2005, p. 127) define political skill as "the ability to effectively understand others at work, and to use such knowledge to influence others to act in ways that enhance one's personal and/or organizational objectives." Ferris et al. (2007) further state that political

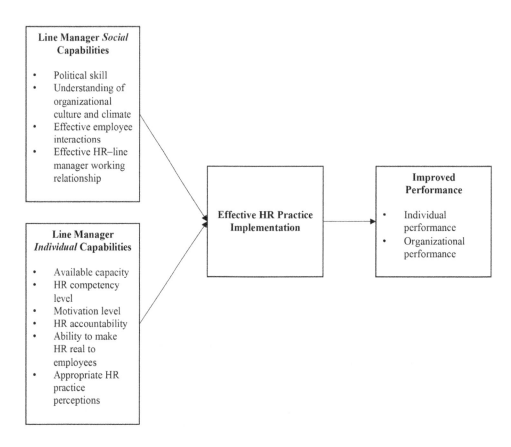

Figure 9.1   Line manager capabilities, HR implementation, and improved performance

skill encompasses four key dimensions: social astuteness, interpersonal influence, networking ability, and apparent sincerity. Politically skilled individuals are also very adaptable. Their political skill provides them with a sense of self-confidence that inspires others' trust and confidence, and promotes their individual credibility (Ferris et al., 2007). As a result, political skill appears to have a positive impact on individual, group, and/or organizational performance.

Line manager political skill levels also appear likely to influence their HR implementation efforts. Ferris et al. (1998) propose that an organization's social and political environment influences and shapes the linkages between HR systems, HR implementation, and ultimately, organizational effectiveness. When these social and political traits are strongly shared throughout the firm, they greatly influence the organization's governance and employee behavior (Hatch, 1993).

Pfeffer (1996) proposes that organizational power and politics create pressures that influence a firm's use of HR practices. In Pfeffer's view, these political pressures can either promote or hinder line managers' use of important HR practices associated with improved performance. Similarly, Johns (1993) states that HR practices are often implemented because of organizational politics, and less so because of their business contribution.

Researchers offer support for the influence of political issues in line managers' HR implementation efforts. Van der Zee et al. (2002) show that an organization's social and political demands shape the use of effective employee selection practices. In a similar study, Cassell et al. (2002) show that organizational political concerns influence line managers' HR implementation choices and actions. Heraty and Morley (1995) find that political support is essential to foster line manager HR implementation acceptance. Next, Watson et al. (2007) observe that a major influence on managers' HR attitudes is their belief about whether they feel HR is considered important by their organization. Finally, Sikora et al. (2015) demonstrate a significant and positive relationship between line manager political skill and HR implementation levels.

These results support the view that political skill plays a key role in line manager HR implementation activities. To put themselves in a more favorable political position, managers may decide to implement more of their organization's HR practices. When successful HR implementation is a significant organizational belief, especially at senior organizational levels, politically skilled managers are more apt to consistently use those practices. Conversely, if line managers recognize that organizational HR support is low, then politically astute managers may be less likely to implement their company's HR practices.

Understanding of organizational culture and climate
Organizational culture is defined as an organization's long-term, deeply shared attitudes, norms, and values (Denison, 1996; Ferris et al., 1998). These norms and values help to determine employee and line manager behaviors. Ajzen (1991) proposes that organizational culture is a crucial factor shaping management behavior. For example, cultures encouraging HR practice use will likely increase managers' implementation behaviors. Conversely, norms devaluing HR practices should decrease implementation activity. Pfeffer (1996) suggests that organizational culture and politics create cultures that may encourage (or discourage) managers' use of effective employee management practices. In a similar study, Cassell et al. (2002) found that organizational culture regarding HR greatly impacts line managers' HR implementation behaviors.

Alternatively, organizational climate is individuals' more short-term and variable organizational interpretation (Denison, 1996; Ferris et al., 1998; Kopelman et al., 1990). Kopelman et al. (1990) argue that organizational climate encompasses an organization's key goals, work methods, employee support, and the type of rewards provided for good job performance. Similarly, Schneider et al. (1980) describe climate as employees' perceptions of the practices, procedures, and behaviors that are rewarded, supported, and expected in an organization.

Gaining line managers' HR commitment requires two things. First, there should be a strong organizational culture emphasizing effective HR management and leadership (Hutchinson and Purcell, 2003). Next, line managers must understand that the organization values HR, and expects all managers to fully implement the organization's HR practices (Bowen and Ostroff, 2004). Heraty and Morley (1995) similarly state that organizational support, and line manager understanding of that support, is essential for improving manager acceptance of HR responsibilities. Finally, Watson et al. (2007) argue that one of the key factors shaping line managers' HR attitudes is the degree to which they believe HR is considered vital by the firm.

These studies show that culture and climate play an important role in shaping line manager behaviors. They clearly highlight the link between culture and managers' implementation efforts. When the organization deeply values HR implementation, and line managers fully understand and support that commitment, managers are much more likely to effectively implement the firm's HR practices.

Effective employee interactions

Ajzen's (1991) theory of planned behavior proposes that individuals' behavioral attitudes are based on their beliefs about the likely outcomes of that behavior, and their evaluations of those outcomes. Beliefs about potential employee reactions to the use of a new HR practice (an outcome) may shape a line manager's attitudes toward the implementation of that practice. For example, if a manager believes that employees will positively view a new performance management practice, they are more likely to implement that practice. Similarly, if most managers believe that it is important to conform with their employees' views, then these norms likely will also affect their HR implementation behaviors. Conversely, if managers believe that employee reactions to certain HR practices will be negative, they may choose not to implement those practices.

Bowen and Ostroff (2004) argue that "strong" HR climates are those where employees reflect a shared perception and interpretation of HR practices and their expected outcomes. They further state that employees' attitudinal and behavioral responses to HR practices are a function of only the practices they perceive to exist in their workplace. Consequently, these HR practices need to be made salient and shared with employees for those practices to attract employee attention and demonstrate intended employee effects. Bowen and Ostroff further contend that supervisors serve as interpretive filters of HR practices. Therefore, when they visibly implement HR practices, along with building high-quality employee relationships, the result is more effective employee HR interpretations.

In carrying out this key role, line managers' credibility with their employees is vital. This credibility typically arises from the quality of their employee relationships. When manager–subordinate relationships are strong and credible, managers likely feel that their employees trust them when implementing new HR practices. This trust "earns" managers the benefit of the doubt that is sometimes needed to ensure employee understanding and acceptance of an organization's HR practices. Ultimately, effective HR practices, coupled with a visible supervisor, and quality supervisor–employee relationships, foster stronger connections among HR, climate, and workplace performance than each individually would.

Effective HR–line manager working relationship

The quality of social interactions between the HR department and line managers also appear to play an important role in HR implementation (Sikora and Ferris, 2014). When the HR–line management relationship is positive, managers likely have greater trust in the HR function. As a result, supervisors are apt to place more value on HR's guidance, and work with HR to effectively implement their employee management duties. Conversely, when supervisor attitudes towards the HR department are poor, then working together is doubtful. When this happens, HR implementation likely declines.

For example, Trullen et al. (2016) found that HR policy is principally accomplished through HR–line management collaborations. Likewise, Whitaker and Marchington's (2003) study on managers' HR views described how line managers see HR support as vital to their job performance. Most of the managers they interviewed believed that a high-quality HR relationship improved their employee management effectiveness. As a result, trust between HR and supervisors is a key HR practice enabler (Garavan et al., 1993).

Renwick's (2003) research explored HR–line management relationship quality regarding the transfer of traditional HR duties to the line. This inquiry shows that when supervisors assume greater HR responsibilities, they expect some level of HR department reciprocity. However, when this does not occur, the result is lower HR–supervisor relationship quality. Renwick also remarks that many managers believe that while they are increasingly responsible for HR activities, there is often little HR department flexibility or gratitude for their work. In this circumstance, managers' negative attitudes toward the organization's HR department, and about using their company's HR practices, represents a possible organizational norm. If the generally accepted belief of most managers is that HR practices are time-consuming and have little business impact, then an organizational norm about not using HR practices is likely to develop.

Clearly, social interactions that influence HR–line management relationship quality also are likely to significantly impact line manager HR implementation efforts. When social relationships between the HR department and line management are effective, supervisor HR implementation actions should increase. When these interactions and the ongoing HR–line relationship are weak, then supervisor HR implementation efforts will likely decrease.

Line Manager Individual Capabilities

Beyond the social factors shaping line manager HR implementation decisions and efforts, numerous individual factors also need to be considered. These include managers' workload capacity, HR competencies, motivation, accountability, ability to make HR real to employees, and perceptions about HR practice appropriateness and effectiveness.

Available capacity

Line managers face many work and time demands. Typically, line managers are required to meet production or service goals, stay within various operating procedures, solve unforeseen work problems, and manage their employees in a productive way. Due to these occasionally conflicting pressures, managers may face difficult decisions regarding the allocation of their limited time resources.

When carrying out their job duties, each manager balances a wide variety of competing obligations, tasks, and time demands. Together, the volume of these requirements determines the manager's ability or willingness to take on more responsibilities. Thus, HR duties compete with many other job responsibilities for a share of the line managers' available capacity. When line managers' capacity is limited, their ability to fully execute their organization's HR practices may also be limited. Conversely, when their job capacity is greater, their ability to implement HR practices likewise should be greater.

Managers need time to effectively implement their organization's HR practices. This capacity issue is highlighted in numerous studies. For example, in many cases, HR tasks are delegated to line managers without reducing their other job duties. This creates capacity issues which curtail the amount of time available for effective employee management (Brewster and Larsen, 2000). Next, the short-term nature of much supervisor activity leads managers to place a greater priority on the achievement of operating numbers and goals (McGovern et al., 1997). Likewise, researchers note that when short-term operational pressures dominate, line managers typically are unable to devote adequate time to HR responsibilities (Gratton et al., 1999;

Renwick, 2000). In these instances, when faced with possibly conflicting demands, many line managers are more likely to focus on operating concerns over HR implementation.

In addition to short-term managerial demands, Harris et al. (2002) observe that while some supervisors support taking on HR responsibilities, many feel that those HR responsibilities are forced on them, and therefore are reluctant to get more fully involved. In these cases, line managers' capacity attitudes can be impacted by how HR responsibilities are assigned. When HR duties are forced on managers without their prior knowledge or involvement, some managers are more likely to believe that they cannot handle this additional work.

This research indicates that managers' job capacity is an important element in HR implementation. In a study assessing staffing practice implementation, van der Zee et al. (2002) note that time constraints often prevent the adoption of high-quality employee selection practices. Likewise, Watson et al. (2007) note that heavy workloads and short-term job pressures are key obstacles to line management HR implementation.

Although capacity issues likely limit line management HR implementation activities, the opposite also seems to be true. Renwick's (2003) research finds that when supervisors feel fewer job demands, their HR implementation attention is higher. Clearly, when line managers' perceived task capacity is higher, their HR implementation behaviors also should be greater.

HR competency level

"Competency" is a widespread term used in many research studies. Hoffmann (1999) cited three definitions for this concept. The first meaning was visible performance (Bowden and Masters, 1993), the second was an individual's performance quality (Rutherford, 1995), and the third, one's fundamental attributes (Sternberg and Kolligian, 1990).

"Competency" is also a frequent term in the HR literature. HR researchers use a similar description when classifying HR competencies. In research intended to develop and empirically test HR manager competencies, scholars find data supporting three competency spheres. These include business knowledge, field expertise, and change management skills (Becker et al., 2001; Ulrich et al., 1995). Han et al. (2006) also examined the subject of HR competencies, and identified them as an individual's core attributes, such as their HR knowledge, skills, or abilities.

Obviously, HR competencies are critical for HR managers; however, they also play an important role in line managers' effective job performance. When managing their subordinates, line managers need many HR competencies, including workforce planning, employee selection, compensation, training, performance appraisal, and employee relations skills. Clearly, these attributes play a key part in successful HR implementation.

When line managers lack the HR competencies required to solve difficult employee issues, effective HR implementation likely is difficult. In these situations, some managers may just fall back on their business instincts and do whatever they believe is right. However, this might not be the appropriate way to carry out the organization's intended HR practices (Nehles et al., 2006).

Line managers' HR competencies play a key role in their ability to effectively implement their organization's HR practices. With any difficult or unfamiliar work practice, when managers lack necessary competencies, their inclination and capability to implement those practices likely is reduced. Conversely, a deeper skill level and better understanding of the practice's goals and connections to job and company objectives should increase a manager's confidence in using the practices. Ajzen's (1991) theory of planned behavior helps to explain this issue. When line managers lack HR skills, their perceived behavioral control level is also likely to be low. Accordingly, Ajzen's theory predicts that managers' subsequent potential to perform that behavior (that is, HR implementation) will be low.

Van der Zee et al. (2002) suggests that because many line managers lack robust HR competencies and training, they likely lack the proficiency needed to effectively implement their firm's HR practices. Similarly, researchers note that in most situations managers do not know of the research promoting the use of effective HR practices. Cassell et al. (2002) observe that line managers frequently lack HR competencies, which often present an HR implementation barrier. Finally, Kulik and Bainbridge (2006) find that a key reason for line managers not expanding their HR practice involvement is their lack of HR skills.

Beyond formal HR competency levels, many line managers simply do not see themselves as HR authorities, and believe that this issue is a major hindrance to effectively conducting their employee management responsibilities (Renwick, 2003). Kulik (2004) similarly observes that because many line managers have little or no HR training, they do not see HR as a central element of their job duties. Finally, Watson et al. (2007) also note that low HR skill levels among managers results in lower confidence levels, which hinder the completion of their HR tasks.

Clearly, if organizations wish to increase the effectiveness of their line managers' HR implementation, they must invest in building those manager's HR competency levels. Line managers need to believe that they have the HR knowledge and competence to address challenging and complicated employee management issues. When managers believe that they possess these critical competencies, then their HR implementation efforts also should grow.

Motivation level

Pinder (1998) described motivation as internal and external influences that initiate behavior, and determine its direction, intensity, and duration. Accordingly, for line managers, internal and external motivation levels also impact their willingness and intent to implement their firm's HR practices. Nehles et al. (2006) suggest that while managers may have the time needed to perform HR responsibilities, they may not want to spend time on these tasks. The authors suggest that line managers' motivation to perform HR duties is a critical condition for successful HR implementation. In their view, varying line manager motivation levels result in differing HR implementation efforts.

Personal incentives (Harris et al., 2002) and/or organizational incentives (Whittaker and Marchington, 2003) impact managers' motivation and their resulting HR implementation efforts. For example, Brewster and Larsen (2000) and Renwick (2003) show that without personal incentives, line managers show little interest in HR duties. The findings regarding organizational incentives are similar. The lack of these incentives negatively impacts managers' motivation to perform HR practices, and results in their regularly focusing on operational issues over HR issues (Harris et al., 2002; McGovern et al., 1997).

When managers are highly motivated, they are more apt to accept their sometimes difficult and/or time-consuming HR implementation activities. While managers may possess many HR abilities, they might lack the motivation needed to transform that expertise into HR implementation performance (Nehles et al., 2006). Gilbert et al. (2015) support this view by finding positive links between line managers' HR implementation efforts and their ability and motivation levels. Trullen et al. (2016) similarly note that managers' implementation actions are positively related to their motivation levels. Overall, this research indicates that line managers' desire and motivation levels directly impact their HR implementation behaviors. When their HR motivation is high, their resulting HR implementation efforts are also higher.

HR accountability

Line manager accountability is a political behavior that directly impacts HR implementation (Sikora and Ferris, 2014). Across different organizations, and different departments within a single firm, some line managers are held more accountable than others. When politically astute managers believe that accountability is an important norm within their company, they likely welcome being answerable for carrying out their job responsibilities. In these cases, they also are more likely to implement their HR duties. In this way, higher HR accountability likely increases managers' focus on HR implementation. Conversely, due to their many job demands, managers not directly accountable for HR implementation are more apt to let those responsibilities slip.

Numerous studies support this view. For instance, Renwick (2000) observes that while many managers accept their HR responsibilities, this responsibility also needs to be accompanied by greater accountability. Renwick suggests that accountability is a key factor shaping the performance of managers' HR responsibilities. Similarly, Cassell et al.'s (2002) study of small business line managers notes that accountability is a key HR implementation concern. These small business managers believe that while they are accountable for implementing their organization's HR practices, there is little formal evaluation of HR practice success. Renwick (2003) also finds that line managers believe that they are assuming more HR responsibilities and accountability, yet often they are given little authority in carrying out those tasks. Finally, Watson et al. (2007) state that clear HR practice accountability is key for effective line manager HR implementation.

These studies demonstrate how line manager accountability is important in shaping subsequent HR implementation efforts. When senior managers value HR accountability, then politically astute managers are more likely to implement HR in their departments. However, due to heavy line manager workloads, when organizations do not hold managers accountable for implementing HR practices it appears likely that managers' HR implementation actions will decline.

Ability to make HR real to employees

Nishii and Paluch (2018) propose that line managers play a critical role in making their organization's HR practices real to their employees. They call this concept HR "sensegiving." In this view, managers fulfill the role of "giving sense" to their firm's HR practices. This is done in four ways. First, managers articulate their firm's intended HR messages to their employees. Next, managers role model HR practice expectations. Through giving employee feedback and rewards, managers also reinforce their firm's HR system behavior expectations. Finally, managers play a key role in assessing their subordinates' understanding of the firm's HR practices. Together, as managers carry out these roles, they make their organization's HR practices salient to their employees.

Other HR researchers discuss how line managers act as interpretive filters of HR practices within their organizations. When managers implement HR practices, they build shared employee understanding and improve organizational culture (Bowen and Ostroff, 2004; Ostroff and Bowen, 2016). Bowen and Ostroff (2004) state that when managers implement HR practices in a reliable and organized way, those practices will have a synergistic impact on firm performance. Conversely, Ferris et al. (1998) note the potential downside to managers' ineffective HR implementation efforts. They note that managers' poor HR implementation efforts result in unfavorable employee attitudes, and ultimately harm organizational outcomes.

Clearly, line managers play a critical role in shaping employee attitudes and job behaviors. Managers who effectively implement their firm's HR practices, make HR real to their employees. When HR is made real, it has a positive impact on employee attitudes and workplace behaviors. Subsequently, these successes encourage managers to further implement HR practices. Together this creates a mutually reinforcing cycle of HR implementation and improved workplace performance.

The final individual factors impacting line manager HR implementation are those associated with the organization's HR practices. In most organizations, line managers are ultimately responsible for HR implementation. Consequently, their perceptions of those practices are crucial. When managers do not feel that the practices are appropriate or effective, they are less likely to implement them (Sikora and Ferris, 2011). When doing their job, managers evaluate the appropriateness of their organization's HR practices. This evaluation includes making decisions about whether specific HR practices are pertinent, realistic, and/or effective in helping to meet their job goals. When managers believe that the practices are helpful and appropriate in carrying out their job responsibilities, they are more likely to implement them.

Appropriate HR practice perceptions

Ajzen (1991) states that attitudes impact behavior. Consequently, line managers' attitudes about the appropriateness of their firm's HR practices should influence their implementation behaviors. When managers' attitudes about HR practice appropriateness are positive, the theory of planned behavior (Ajzen, 1991) suggests that implementation will also be higher.

This view is supported in numerous research studies. In a Dutch study examining the use of effective staffing practices, line managers had apprehensions about the perceived appropriateness of certain HR practices (van Der Zee et al., 2002). This included doubts about the practices' relevance and/or usefulness. Wright et al. (2001) illustrate how manager acceptance of HR practice appropriateness increased their HR implementation efforts. Whittaker and Marchington (2003) similarly observe that because line managers are directly involved in the workplace, they are best positioned to decide on HR practice appropriateness. Consequently, their decisions result in certain practices being implemented, while others are ignored.

Line manager perceptions of HR practice appropriateness seem to be directly linked to HR implementation. When managers believe that their organization's HR practices are not beneficial to themselves or their department, they likely have negative perceptions of HR appropriateness. Subsequently, their HR implementation efforts will likely decline. Conversely, when HR practice perceptions are positive, their HR implementation actions will likely increase.

Perceived HR effectiveness

Perceived HR effectiveness reflects line managers' perceptions of the benefit and/or business value of their organization's HR practices in helping them to meet their job goals. This can incorporate improving productivity, increasing workplace efficiency, meeting production objectives, and/or improving employee relations. A high level of perceived value should result in a higher level of line manager HR implementation (Sikora and Ferris, 2011). Like HR practice appropriateness, Ajzen's (1991) theory of planned behavior similarly impacts this issue. When line managers' perceptions about the value of their organization's HR practice are positive, they should increase their implementation efforts. If these attitudes are negative, HR implementation will likely decrease or become less effective.

Renwick (2000) notes how line managers' failure to benefit from HR practices limits their subsequent HR implementation efforts. Likewise, Terpstra and Rozell (1997) explain that when managers are unaware of, or do not trust in, their organization's HR practices, they are less likely to implement them. Conversely, Cassell et al. (2002) state that when managers do see HR benefits, they increase their use of those practices. These studies clearly highlight that line managers' perceptions of the effectiveness of their firm's HR practices are directly linked to HR implementation. When managers believe that HR practices improve their job effectiveness, they are more apt to fully implement those practices.

DISCUSSION

Future Research Directions

While some studies discussed above note uneven or inconsistent line manager capabilities and/or HR implementation levels, few of those studies explore the reasons behind these inconsistencies. Woodrow and Guest (2014) stress the importance of understanding how line managers' capabilities help to shape HR system strength and HR implementation efforts. As a result, numerous important HR implementation themes remain understudied. These include the effects of manager–employee relationship quality, manager personality differences, and organizational differences.

Manager–employee relationship quality

Evans and Davis (2015) suggest that future research efforts should focus on the tensions and challenges facing line managers as they implement HR practices. An example of this type of tension is the quality of manager–employee relationships. High- or low-quality manager–employee relationships seem likely to impact HR implementation efforts. For instance, building on the work of Bos-Nehles and Meijerink (2018), researchers could continue examining how the quality of the leader–member exchange (LMX) relationship between managers and subordinates shapes line managers' implementation efforts. Alternatively, from the employee's viewpoint, does LMX quality impact subordinates' perceptions of their manager's implementation actions? Because many managers experience poor-quality employee relationships, HR scholars should explore how HR implementation differs between good versus poor employee relationship quality. Additionally, while manager–employee relationship quality likely shapes implementation efforts, researchers should also explore how relationship quality impacts the effectiveness of those implementation activities.

Personality differences

Other line manager issues deserving further study include the impact of line manager personality differences on HR implementation efforts. For example, do certain line manager personality types impact manager capabilities and their subsequent implementation actions more than others? Perhaps driven, Theory X managers approach their HR implementation activities differently than those with a Theory Y personality. Other personality differences impacting implementation efforts likely include the managers' extroversion preferences. Conceivably, more extroverted managers might communicate their organization's HR practices differently than more introverted managers. If so, how does this difference affect the effectiveness of those HR implementation actions (Sikora et al., 2015)? Conscientiousness also might impact implementation efforts. Highly conscientious mangers likely approach HR implementation in a more organized and systematic way than other managers. Finally, how do line manager personality differences impact decisions not to implement an organization's HR practices (Woodrow and Guest, 2014)? Perhaps there are certain manager personality preferences such as discretion and/or independence which are negatively related to HR implementation.

Organizational differences
Bos-Nehles et al. (2013) suggest including the effect of organizational structure differences on the effectiveness of line managers' HR implementation capabilities. For example, does a manager's organizational level impact their HR implementation capabilities? If so, how? It seems likely that first-level supervisors approach HR implementation differently than those in executive positions. Next, job function differences seem likely to impact implementation efforts. Perhaps marketing managers implement HR practices differently than manufacturing managers? Line management responsibilities (as opposed to staff responsibilities) also might influence HR implementation. Finally, other organizational factors impacting HR implementation likely include business strategy differences. For example, do organizations using a best price strategy implement their HR practices differently than those with a best customer service or best product business strategy?

Practical Implications

This chapter highlights several key practitioner insights. For example, rather than HR departments developing additional HR practices for use throughout their organizations, this chapter suggests that focusing on improving line manager implementation capabilities may provide greater performance benefits. If HR managers aim to improve employee outcomes, then focusing on improving manager capabilities and their implementation of existing HR practices should be their priority. Once the existing manager capabilities are more fully developed across the organization, then introducing new HR practices makes more sense.

Next, organizations should systematically assess their line managers' implementation capabilities. The identification of desired manager capabilities, and the assessment of each manager's proficiency levels, helps organizations to identify skill gaps and target limited training resources. As organizations repeat this process over time, manager capabilities will increase, and their resulting implementation efforts will also likely improve. This assessment process also could reveal the need for other interventions. For example, managers need to be held accountable for developing and using the capabilities described in this chapter. Similarly, to further support skill development, organizations should explore the use of training and implementation incentives.

Finally, organizations should examine the reasons why certain managers are not implementing their firm's high-performance work practices (Sikora et al., 2015; Woodrow and Guest, 2014). Perhaps this is due to a lack of manager skills and abilities. However, it also could be attributable to other factors such as poorly developed HR practices, an organizational culture lacking HR support, and/or low manager HR motivation. Clearly, to improve future performance, organizations should understand both sides of their managers' HR implementation efforts: why manager use, or chose not to use, the firm's HR practices.

CONCLUSION

This chapter highlights the critical role of line managers' social and individual capabilities in shaping HR implementation and in subsequent performance improvements. Because most line managers are technical experts in their areas of responsibility, many lack the knowledge and capabilities needed for effective HR implementation. As shown, line manager capabilities are key to better HR implementation. Therefore, organizations wanting to improve individual and organizational performance must invest in the development of their line managers' skills, abilities, and capabilities.

REFERENCES

Ajzen, I. (1991). The theory of planned behavior. *Organizational Behavior and Human Decision Processes, 50*, 179–211.

Becker, B.E., Huselid, M.A., and Ulrich, D. (2001). *The HR Scorecard: Linking People, Strategy and Performance*. Boston, MA: Harvard Business School Press.

Bos-Nehles, AC., and Meijerink, J.G. (2018). HRM implementation by multiple HRM actors: A social exchange perspective. *International Journal of Human Resource Management, 29*(22), 3068–3092.

Bos-Nehles, A.C., Van Riemsdijk, M.J., and Looise, J.K. (2013). Employee perceptions of line management performance: Applying the AMO theory to explain the effectiveness of line managers' HRM implementation. *Human Resource Management, 52*(6), 861–877.

Bowden, J., and Masters, G. (1993). *Implications for Higher Education of a Competency-Based Approach to Education and Training*. Canberra: AGPS.

Bowen, D.E., and Ostroff, C. (2004). Understanding HRM–firm performance linkages: The role of the "strength" of the HRM system. *Academy of Management Review, 29*, 203–221.

Brewster, C., and Larsen, H.H. (2000). Responsibility in human resource management: The role of the line. In Chris Brewster and Henrik Holt Larsen (eds), *Human Resource Management in Northern Europe: Trends, Dilemmas and Strategy* (pp. 1–23). Oxford: Blackwell Publishing.

Cassell, C., Nadin, S., Gray, M., and Clegg, C. (2002). Exploring human resource management practices in small and medium sized enterprises. *Personnel Review, 31*(5–6), 671–695.

Combs, J., Liu, Y., Hall, A., and Ketchen, D. (2006). How much do high-performance work practices matter? A meta-analysis of their effects on organizational performance. *Personnel Psychology, 59*(3), 501–528.

Den Hartog, D.N., Boon, C., Verburg, R.M., and Croon, M.A. (2013). HRM, communication, satisfaction, and perceived performance: A cross-level test. *Journal of Management, 39*(6), 1637–1665.

Denison, D.R. (1996). What is the difference between organizational culture and organizational climate? A native's point of view on a decade of paradigm wars. *Academy of Management Review, 21*, 619–654.

Evans, S. (2015). Juggling on the line: Front line managers and their management of human resources in the retail industry. *Employee Relations, 37*(4), 459–474.

Evans, W.R., and Davis, W.D. (2015). High-performance work systems as an initiator of employee proactivity and flexible work processes. *Organization Management Journal, 12*(2), 64–74.

Ferris, G.R., Arthur, M., Berkson, H., Kaplan, D., Harrell-Cook, G., and Frink, D. (1998). Toward a social context theory of the human resource management–organization effectiveness relationship. *Human Resource Management Review, 8*(3), 235–264.

Ferris, G.R., Treadway, D.C., Kolodinsky, R.W., Hochwarter, W.A., Kacmar, C.J., et al. (2005). Development and validation of the political skill inventory. *Journal of Management, 31*, 126–152.

Ferris, G.R., Treadway, D.C., Perrewé, P.L., Brouer, R.L., Douglas, C., and Lux, S. (2007). Political skill in organizations. *Journal of Management*, *33*, 290.

Garavan, T.N., Barnicle, B. and Heraty, N. (1993). The training and development function: Its search for power and influence in organizations. *Journal of European Industrial Training*, *17*(7), 22–32.

Gilbert, C., De Winne, S., and Sels, L. (2015). The influence of line managers and HR department on employees' affective commitment. *International Journal of Human Resource Management*, *22*(8), 1618–1637.

Gollan, P.J., Kalfa, S., and Xu, Y. (2015). Strategic HRM and devolving HR to the line: Cochlear during the shift to lean manufacturing. *Asia Pacific Journal of Human Resources*, *53*(2), 144–162.

Gratton, L., and Truss, C. (2003). The three-dimensional people strategy: Putting human resources policies into action. *Academy of Management Executive*, *17*(3), 74–86.

Gratton, L., Hope-Hailey, V., Stiles, P., and Truss, C. (1999). Linking individual performance to business strategy: The people process model. *Human Resource Management*, *38*(1), 17–31.

Guest, D.E., Wright, P., and Paauwe, J. (2013). Progress and prospects. In D.E. Guest, J. Paauwe, and P. Wright (eds), *HRM and Performance: Achievements and Challenges* (pp. 197–205). Chichester: John Wiley & Sons.

Hall, L., and Torrington, D. (1998). Letting go or holding on: The devolution of operational personnel activities. *Human Resource Management Journal*, *8*(1), 41–55.

Han, J., Chou, P., Chao, M., and Wright, P.M. (2006). The HR competencies–HR effectiveness link: A study in Taiwanese high-tech companies. *Human Resource Management*, *45*(3), 391–406.

Harris, L. (2001). Rewarding employee performance: Line managers' values, beliefs and perspectives. *International Journal of Human Resource Management*, *12*(7), 1182–1192.

Harris, L., Doughty, D., and Kirk, S. (2002). The devolution of HR responsibilities: Perspectives from the UK's public sector. *Journal of European Industrial Training*, *26*(5), 218–229.

Hatch, M.J. (1993). The dynamics of organizational culture. *Academy of Management Review*, *18*, 657–693.

Heraty, N., and Morley, M. (1995). Line managers and human resource development. *Journal of European Industrial Training*, *19*(10), 31–37.

Hoffmann, T. (1999). The meanings of competency. *Journal of European Industrial Training*, *23*(6), 275–285.

Hope-Hailey, V., Farndale, E., and Truss, C. (2005). The HR department's role in organizational performance. *Human Resource Management Journal*, *15*(3), 49–66.

Hutchinson, S., and Purcell, J. (2003). *Bringing Policies to Life: The Vital Role of Front Line Managers in People Management*. London: CIPD.

Johns, G. (1993). Constraints on the adoption of psychology-based personnel practices: Lessons from organizational innovation. *Personnel Psychology*, *46*, 569–592.

Keegan, A., Huemann, M., and Turner, J.R. (2012). Beyond the line: Exploring the HRM responsibilities of line managers, project managers and the HRM department in four project-oriented companies in the Netherlands, Austria, the UK and the USA. *International Journal of Human Resource Management*, *23*(15), 3085–3104.

Kehoe, R.R., and Collins, C.J. (2017). Human resource management and unit performance in knowledge-intensive work. *Journal of Applied Psychology*, *102*(8), 1222.

Khilji, S.E., and Wang, X. (2006). Intended and implemented HRM: The missing lynchpin in strategic human resource management. *International Journal of Human Resource Management*, *17*(7), 1171–1189.

Kopelman, R.E., Brief, A.P., and Guzzo, R.A. (1990). The role of climate and culture in productivity. *Organizational Climate and Culture*, *282*, 318.

Kulik, C.T. (2004). *Human Resources for the Non-HR Manager*. Mahwah, NJ: Lawrence Erlbaum Associates.

Kulik, C.T., and Bainbridge, H.T. (2006). HR and the line: The distribution of HR activities in Australian organizations. *Asia Pacific Journal of Human Resources*, *44*(2), 240–256.

Lengnick-Hall, M.L., Lengnick-Hall, C.A., Andrade, L.S., and Drake, B. (2009). Strategic human resource management: The evolution of the field. *Human Resource Management Review*, *19*, 64–85.

Lo, K., Macky, K., and Pio, E. (2015). The HR competency requirements for strategic and functional HR practitioners. *International Journal of Human Resource Management*, *26*(18), 2308–2328.

McGovern, P., Gratton, L., Hope-Hailey, V., Stiles, P., and Truss, C. (1997). Human resource management on the line? *Human Resource Management Journal*, 7(4), 12–29.

Mintzberg, H. (1985). The organization as political arena. *Journal of Management Studies*, 22, 133–154.

Nehles, A.C., Van Riemsdijk, M., Kok, I., and Looise, J.K. (2006). Implementing human resource management successfully: A first-line management challenge. *Management Revue*, 17(3), 256–273.

Nishii, L.H., and Paluch, R.M. (2018). Leaders as HR sensegivers: Four HR implementation behaviors that create strong HR systems. *Human Resource Management Review*, 28(3), 319–323.

Nishii, L.H., Khattab, J., Shemla, M., and Paluch, R.M. (2018). A multi-level process model for understanding diversity practice effectiveness. *Academy of Management Annals*, 12(1), 37–82.

Nishii, L.H., Lepak, D.P., and Schneider, B. (2008). Employee attributions of the "why" of HR practices: Their effects on employee attitudes and behaviors, and customer satisfaction. *Personnel Psychology*, 61(3), 503–545.

Op de Beeck, S., Wynen, J., and Hondeghem, A. (2016). HRM implementation by line managers: Explaining the discrepancy in HR–line perceptions of HR devolution. *International Journal of Human Resource Management*, 27(17), 1901–1919.

Ostroff, C., and Bowen, D.E. (2016). Reflections on the 2014 decade award: Is there strength in the construct of HR system strength? *Academy of Management Review*, 41(2), 196–214.

Pfeffer, J. (1996). When it comes to "best practices," why do smart organizations occasionally do dumb things? *Organizational Dynamics*, 25(1), 33–44.

Pfeffer, J., and Pfeffer, J. (1981). *Power in Organizations* (Vol. 33). Marshfield, MA: Pitman.

Pinder, C.C. (1998). *Work Motivation in Organizational Behavior*. Upper Saddle River, NJ: Prentice-Hall.

Renwick, D. (2000). HR–line work relations: A review, pilot case and research agenda. *Employee Relations*, 22(2), 179–205.

Renwick, D. (2003). Line manager involvement in HRM: An inside view. *Employee Relations*, 25(3), 262–280.

Rutherford, P. (1995). *Competency Based Assessment.* Melbourne: Pitman.

Schneider, B., Parkington, J.J., and Buxton, V.M. (1980). Employee and customer perceptions of service in banks. *Administrative Science Quarterly*, 25(2), 252–267.

Sikora, D., and Ferris, G.R. (2011). Critical factors in human resource practice implementation: Implications of cross-cultural contextual issues. *International Journal of Human Resources Development and Management*, 11, 112–140.

Sikora, D.M., and Ferris, G.R. (2014). Strategic human resources practice implementation: The critical role of line management. *Human Resource Management Review*, 24(3), 271–281.

Sikora, D.M., Ferris, G.R., and Van Iddekinge, C.H. (2015). Line manager implementation perceptions as a mediator of relations between high-performance work practices and employee outcomes. *Journal of Applied Psychology*, 100(6), 1908.

Sternberg, R., and Kolligian Jr, J. (1990). *Competence Considered.* New Haven, CT: Yale University Press.

Su, Z.X., and Wright, P.M. (2012). The effective human resource management system in transitional China: A hybrid of commitment and control practices. *International Journal of Human Resource Management*, 23(10), 2065–2086.

Terpstra, D.E., and Rozell, E.J. (1997). Why some potentially effective staffing practices are seldom used. *Public Personnel Management*, 26(4), 483–495.

Trullen, J., Bos-Nehles, A., and Valverde, M. (2020). From intended to actual and beyond: A cross-disciplinary view of (human resource management) implementation. *International Journal of Management Reviews*, 22(2), 150–176.

Trullen, J., Stirpe, L., Bonache, J., and Valverde, M. (2016). The HR department's contribution to line managers' effective implementation of HR practices. *Human Resource Management Journal*, 26(4), 449–470.

Ulrich, D., Brockbank, W., Yeung, A.K., and Lake, D.G. (1995). Human resource competencies: An empirical assessment. *Human Resource Management*, 34, 473–495.

van der Zee, K.I., Bakker, A.B., and Bakker, P. (2002). Why are structured interviews so rarely used in personnel selection? *Journal of Applied Psychology*, 87(1), 176–184.

Van Iddekinge, C.H., Ferris, G.R., Perrewé, P.L., Perryman, A.A., Blass, F.R., and Heetderks, T.D. (2009). Effects of selection and training on unit-level performance over time: A latent growth modeling approach. *Journal of Applied Psychology*, *94*(4), 829–843.

Watson, S., Maxwell, G.A., and Farquharson, L. (2007). Line managers' views on adopting human resource roles: The case of Hilton (UK) hotels. *Employee Relations*, *29*(1), 30–49.

Whittaker, S., and Marchington, M. (2003). Devolving HR responsibility to the line: Threat opportunity or partnership? *Employee Relations*, *25*(3), 245–261.

Woodrow, C., and Guest, D.E. (2014). When good HR gets bad results: Exploring the challenge of HR implementation in the case of workplace bullying. *Human Resource Management Journal*, *24*(1), 38–56.

Wright, P.M., Gardner, T.M., Moynihan, L.M., and Allen, M.R. (2005). The relationship between HR practices and firm performance: Examining causal order. *Personnel Psychology*, *58*, 406–446.

Wright, P.M., McMahan, G.C., Snell, S.A., and Gerhart, G. (2001). Comparing line and HR executives' perceptions of HR effectiveness: Services, roles and contributions. *Human Resource Management*, *40*(2), 111–123.

Wright, P.M., and Nishii, L.H. (2013). Strategic HRM and organizational behavior: Integrating multiple levels of analysis. In D. Guest, J. Paauwe, and P. Wright (eds), *Human Resource Management and Performance: Building the Evidence Base* (pp. 97–110). Hoboken, NJ: Blackwell Publishing.

10. The allocation of HRM responsibilities to line managers: where is it most likely to happen?

Michael Brookes and Chris Brewster

This chapter uses large-scale international data to examine the extent to which human resource management (HRM) responsibilities are assigned to line managers, and how far this varies with geography. Much of the debate about line management's responsibility for HRM focuses upon how strongly the line management role is accepted, but we ask whether and why it is more widely accepted in some national contexts than in others. We explore the impact of a variety of internal organisational characteristics, and of the kind of economy in which organisations operate. What proportion of organisations assign HRM responsibilities to the line, and how far is this dependent on country or market economy? We will discuss the implications of our findings for future research and for practice.

We know that HRM varies substantially by country (Brewster et al., 2018), but much of the debate about the role of line managers in HRM (Bondarouk et al., 2018; Nehles et al., 2006; Trullen and Valverde, 2017) is rather generalised, perhaps partly because it is based on case studies or limited numbers of cases (Townsend et al., 2012). Teasing out the differences between countries allows us to understand better how HRM responsibilities may vary with cultural and institutional setting, and challenges any assumptions of universalism or 'one size fits all'. This chapter, therefore, focuses on the differences between national economies in the way human resource management responsibilities are allocated.

It is by now widely accepted that the link from HRM policies to HRM outcomes is hard to establish (Guest et al., 2013; Paauwe and Farndale, 2018). There are issues concerning which stakeholders we are addressing (Beer et al., 2015), meaning that there are debates about what kinds of outcomes we look for. For example, owners or shareholders may only be interested in the most financially cost-effective HRM possible, ignoring the effect of certain HRM practices on employees or on the local community. National or local governments may look at a firm's HRM in terms of whether it provides steady employment, contributes taxes, and leads to improvements in the environment. Pressure groups may be concerned to ensure (to take just one of many possible examples) that a firm's HRM policies and practices encourages the integration of migrants or refugees. A key role for senior HRM specialists is in balancing these interests appropriately (Beer et al., 2015).

Even if a business is able to achieve the required balance between stakeholders interests, however, there are serious problems involved in measuring these differing outcomes, and in connecting them back to specific HRM policies (Guest, 2011). As noted elsewhere in this book, organisations may determine their HRM policies, usually a function carried out by HRM specialists, but a key intervening variable is that employee responses and reactions are determined less by those policies than by the day-to-day actions of line managers; there is a potential disconnect between the specialists' HRM policies, the line managers' HRM practices, and the employees' perceptions of the business's HRM (Bos-Nehles et al., 2020; Nishii et al., 2008; Wright and Nishii, 2013). People react to how their immediate bosses treat them, rather than to the policies set out by remote specialists in human resource management. HRM policies may be supported or challenged by line management behaviours, and those behaviours in turn may alleviate or exacerbate employee reactions; this is a two-way relationship (Trullen et al., 2016). And this will be dependent upon context. Thus, for example, if a firm in a Western country has an equal opportunities policy, the fact that a particular manager may treat women or people with darker-coloured skin differently may make those employees react even more negatively. However, in the same circumstances in an Arab country, the employees may feel that the firm's policy is inappropriate, and that there are certain things that women should not be asked to compete with men for, and that black employees are not appropriate for, and believe that the manager is reflecting reality and treating them properly. The interplay between people's line management and the HRM policies (Currie and Proctor, 2001) is discussed in detail elsewhere in this book.

So, this interplay, and the role and responsibility of line managers in human resource management, is not uniform across countries. We eschew discussion of the advantages and problems of allocating HRM responsibilities to the line; these have already been comprehensively covered in Chapter 1 and are examined in detail in other chapters in this book. Rather, we ask (continuing debates and research started in, for example, Brewster et al., 2013, 2015; Gooderham et al., 2015; Holt Larson and Brewster, 2003): how does this differ between countries? Which countries are more, and which less, likely to allocate HRM responsibilities to the line? And how is this changing over time? In particular, we show that there is a strong, clear ranking of the assignment of HRM responsibilities to line managers, and that it is consistent over time, with the Nordic countries assigning them the most responsibility, then the 'Rhineland' economies and, finally, with the Anglo-Saxon liberal market economies assigning least authority to their line managers. We also show that those organisations with powerful strategic HRM departments are considerably less likely to assign HRM responsibilities to line managers. Important changes in the world economy (our evidence covers before and after the Global Financial Crisis of 2008 onwards, but not the 2020–21 COVID-19 pandemic) make little difference, except for a reduced influence of firm size and trade union membership. We show and explain our evidence and draw some conclusions for the wider debate on the assignment of HRM responsibilities to line managers.

COMPARATIVE CAPITALISMS

If we assume that HRM policies are translated into HRM practice by line managers in their treatment of and day-to-day interactions with employees, and the psychological processes through which employees attach meanings to HRM practices (Li et al., 2011; Nishii et al., 2008; Sanders et al., 2008), then both cultural theories (Hofstede and Minkov, 2010; House et al., 2004) and institutional theories (Amable, 2003; Hall and Soskice, 2001; Whitley, 1999, 2007) would imply that the extent of delegation to line managers and of employee reactions to those interactions are likely to vary from country to country. We believe that institutional effects may have more impact on HRM practices than cultural differences – it is easier to avoid employing people with a stereotypical cultural mindset in a particular country than it is to bypass that country's legislation (Vaiman and Brewster, 2015) – and that institutional theory provides a useful means of categorising national differences. The theories of comparative capitalisms (Amable, 2003; Hall and Soskice, 2001; Jackson and Deeg, 2008; Whitley, 1999,

2007; and for the link to HRM, see Wood et al., 2014) provide us with a means of comparing at least some of the developed countries. The research evidence, as with most management and most human resource management research generally, tends to be heavily concentrated in the Western, educated, industrialised, rich, democratic (WEIRD) countries (Henrich et al., 2010), and although there are beginning to be wider studies, our theory and our evidence comes from these advanced states. There is very little evidence on the allocation of HRM responsibilities to line managers in the rest of the world, and we will have to leave conclusions there until more research has been conducted.

Abstracting from these various theories, we can see different categories of market economies in the advanced countries. The comparative capitalisms specialists have as one category the liberal market economies (LMEs), the native English-speaking countries of North America, Ireland and the United Kingdom (UK), and Australia and New Zealand; the archetypical example is the United States of America (USA). In these countries, competition is king and is encouraged by constitutions and laws; collaborating businesses must be careful not to fall foul of antitrust or anti-monopoly legislation. The role of government is to set a baseline and then keep out of the way; government should be 'small', the public sector is small, and therefore taxes can be low. Trade unions, which aim to 'interfere' in business, are discouraged and tend to have limited roles. There are as few laws as possible governing business, and employment relationships, and limited resources are devoted to enforcement of those laws.

By contrast, the coordinated market economies (CMEs) of the 'Rhineland' states of Western and Central Europe can be typified by Germany. Japan is sometimes included amongst these countries. Here, competition is secondary to long-term stability, and there are powerful institutions such as employers' associations encouraging mutual activities, not just between businesses but also between businesses and government; local and national governments often have shareholdings in major businesses in their area. Trade unions are powerful and employment standards are rigorous and sustained by an extensive network of regulations. Education levels are high and more evenly spread than in the LMEs. Employees tend to stay with their employer for long periods, and changing employer is not common.

A third group of countries consists of the Nordic states, the social democratic economies (SDEs), typified by Sweden. Businesses are more constrained by legislation than are businesses in the LMEs, but less so than in the CMEs. However, norms of how firms should behave are clear and widely supported, and legitimacy depends on following those norms. Governments are involved in and support and constrain human resource management practice (several of these states have laws on the equal representation of women on boards of directors, for example). Trade union membership is noticeably higher than in the other two types of economy, and includes managerial-level staff. Taxes are high and social services are of markedly good quality. Education levels are amongst the highest in the world and quality education is even more broadly distributed than in the CMEs.

How might we expect these three different sets of economies to differ in respect of the assignment of HRM responsibilities to line managers? We know that they do. Previous research (Brewster et al., 2015) used the same institutional characterisations of countries, and although a number of other factors such as size and trade union membership were significant, even when these were controlled for the kind of capitalism was significantly correlated with the extent of assignment of HRM responsibilities to line managers. In other words, in some countries HRM is less centralised than it is in others; it is much more widely accepted that line managers' responsibilities include significant elements of responsibility for HRM including, *inter alia*, how their people are treated and how much they cost, meaning that the specialist HRM department has less control of HRM. We are interested here to ask: was this a factor of the economic circumstances of the time? Was it significantly changed by the Global Financial Crisis that occurred from 2008 onwards? Or are these differences continuing as before, in how much responsibility for human resource management is given by different countries to line managers?

METHODS

To explore these questions, we make use of the repeating Cranet survey of HRM. This covers a cross-section of establishments in samples that in each country are structured by industry employment and are representative at the national level. The survey is repeated every five years or so, and now includes over 40 countries. The research is based on a postal questionnaire, covering issues relating to HRM, and the questionnaire is completed by the most senior person with responsibility for HRM in each organisation. It is targeted at organisations with at least 100 employees, since it is assumed likely that smaller organisations may not have a distinct and professional HRM function. Of course, the vast majority of businesses are small and medium-sized enterprises, and most employment is in them; and only a small proportion of them employ formal human resource management specialists, and even fewer have formal HRM departments. In such cases, responsibility for HRM is automatically with the line managers (see Chapter 12 in this book). By collecting data only from firms with human resource management departments we ensure that the allocation of responsibilities between the specialists and the line managers is always a live issue. For the purposes of this chapter, we utilise the most recent wave of the data available at the time of writing in 2022, for 2015–16, and include countries that clearly fit into the Amable (2003) categorisation of economy types. These countries are Austria, Belgium, Germany and the Netherlands as the CMEs; Denmark, Finland, Sweden and Norway as the SDEs; and, finally, the UK, the USA, Australia and South Africa as the LMEs. This gave us a total of 1690 establishments across these 12 countries for the purposes of the empirical analysis.

The analysis for this chapter is based upon an ordinary least squares (OLS) regression model estimating the extent to which each organisation assigns responsibility for key HRM decisions to line managers. The dependent variable for this regression model is constructed from the responses to questions asking where primary responsibility lies for major policy decisions. This covers five areas: pay and benefits; recruitment and selection; training and development; industrial relations; and workforce expansion/reduction. We use the words 'assignment of HRM responsibilities to line managers' to avoid discussing 'devolution of HRM responsibilities to line managers'; a commonly used expression, but one that erroneously implies that responsibilities were at some stage the responsibility of the HRM department and have been 'sent out' to line managers. Logically, as organisations grew and developed HRM departments, responsibility was ceded from the line managers to the HRM department; but in fact, as research (Brewster et al., 2015) shows, in most areas of HRM responsibility is shared and changes little over time.

Questionnaire responses in each of the five areas of HRM policy are coded 1 if the primary responsibility is assigned to the line manager or 0 if it is retained by the HRM function. The standard reliability test is applied to these five variables, and with a Cronbach's alpha of

0.766, it is a statistically valid and robust step to combine the five responses into a single scale. This assignment scale is constructed using Mokken scaling (Sijtsma and Molenaar, 2002), a non-parametric, probabilistic approach that weights the responses based on the likelihood of a zero response to each question. Therefore, in this instance, the areas where responsibility for HRM is least likely to be assigned to line managers are of relatively greater importance to the overall scale. The outcome being that the assignment scale creates a value for each establishment between 0 and 100 reflecting the extent of that organisation's commitment to assigning responsibilities to line managers. Those organisations assigning responsibility in all five key areas will have a value of 100; those assigning none of those will have a value of 0. The vast majority of organisations will lie somewhere in between, with their value reflecting both the number of areas that they assign to line managers as well as the relative scarcity of assignment in each case.

For the explanatory variables within the OLS regression model, the extent of assignment of HRM responsibilities to line managers indicated by this scale is estimated as a function of size, sector, strategic HRM, trade union density and economy type. Size is measured by the total number of employees within the organisation, and sector is a dummy variable separating public and private sector organisations. Strategic HRM reflects the role that the HRM department plays in corporate strategic business (that is, other than HRM) decisions, and is another dummy variable taking on the value 1 if specialists from the HRM department are involved in the decision-making process prior to implementation, and 0 if HRM is only consulted after implementation or not consulted at all. Trade union density is the proportion of employees who are trade union members; and economy type is a final set of dummy variables separating the CMEs, SDEs and LMEs. The reference category for the OLS model is a private sector organisation in an LME country with no strategic role for HRM.

FINDINGS

Table 10.1 reports the results from running the OLS regression model on extent of assignment: they replicate the empirical analysis undertaken by Brewster et al. (2015), but utilising a more recent wave of the Cranet data. These results are very largely consistent with the previous findings (Brewster et al., 2015): although there may be differences between the private and public sector (see Chapter 11 in this book), and it may vary by country, overall there continues to be no statistically significant difference between private and public sector organisations in relation to their approaches to the assignment of HRM responsibilities to line managers. In other words, location is a better determinant of assignment of HRM responsibilities to the line than is sector: the public and private sectors in any one country are likely to allocate HRM responsibilities broadly equally, and differently from other countries; and the public sector in any one country is not likely to allocate responsibilities the same way as the public sector in another capitalist economy type.

Organisations with a more strategic role for HRM remain considerably less likely to assign responsibilities to line managers. It seems that the more the HRM departmental specialists work closely with the senior executives in their organisation, the less willing they are to concede a role in HRM to line managers. The survey data does not enable us to explain why this is, but we might speculate that as the senior HRM specialists work increasingly closely with the board (line managers at their level, as discussed in Boada-Cuerva et al., 2019; Larsen

Table 10.1   Assignment scale OLS regression results

Variable	Coefficient	t ratio	Significance	Mean
Constant	39.033***	18.48	0.000	
Total employees (000s)	−0.085*	−1.66	0.097	3.161
Public sector	2.568	1.324	0.186	0.286
Strategic HRM	−11.97***	−5.86	0.000	0.815
Union density	0.022	0.72	0.469	39.36
Rhineland	14.641***	6.44	0.000	0.195
Nordic	21.417***	9.72	0.000	0.393
Dependent variable	Assignment scale			
Mean	41.89			
Observations	1690			
R-squared	0.11			

Note: *, ** and *** indicates significance at 10%, 5% and 1% levels, respectively.

and Brewster, 2003), their fear of 'maverick' lower-level line managers taking unexpected action creates a pressure for control, so that they can ensure that they can 'deliver' to these board members. Ironically, it seems that the calls in the literature for HRM to take up positions and to be influential at the top level conflict with other calls in the literature for HRM to share responsibilities for the management of employees with line managers; and whichever call is prioritised, our evidence is clear that in reality it is the desire for influence at the top level (and therefore the desire to ensure control over line managers) that predominates. Strategic HRM is correlated with less HRM responsibility for line managers.

The most important finding is that there is again a clear ranking, with Nordic countries by far the most likely to assign HRM responsibilities to line managers, LMEs the least, and the Rhineland countries lying somewhere in between. Although the organisations based in the Rhineland economies lie between the other two economy types, there is still a significantly greater tendency towards assignment within Rhineland economies than there is within the LMEs. Not only does the extent of assignment of HRM responsibilities to the line differ significantly between types of market economy, but also the ranking of the various market economies on this issue stays stable over time. We note that in the social democratic economies shop- and office-floor workers tend to be better educated, that line managers tend to undertake degrees that include social sciences, that managers are often members of trade unions – which take the view that their role is to ensure the success of the firm so that their members have secure work into the future – and that society has clear expectations of the ways that businesses should behave towards their workers and, indeed, all their stakeholders. Line managers, therefore, may be in a better position to undertake HRM activities, and the specialist department finds it easier to trust that they will do things correctly. Some of the same factors apply in the coordinated market countries, though managers are not usually trade union members, and stakeholder rights are ensured by legislation rather than by common consent. In these circumstances, firms may be more likely to trust their line managers to handle employee issues. Such factors apply much less commonly in the more competitive liberal market economies.

When compared to the findings of Brewster et al. (2015), there are some changes over the years, however, particularly in relation to organisational size and union density. First, larger firms are still less likely to assign responsibilities to line managers, though now this only just achieves significance at the 10 per cent level. Thus, although the size of the organization does affect the extent of allocation of HRM responsibilities to line managers, with larger organizations less likely to do so than smaller ones, it does not have the same impact that it used to have. This indicates that either smaller organisations (above our threshold of 100 employees) are reducing the extent to which they assign responsibilities to line managers, or larger organisations are increasing it. Closer inspection of the data from the last two waves of the Cranet data – that is, 2008/09 and 2015/16 – indicates that there has actually been a reduction in the extent of assignment across the board, with the mean of the assignment scale falling by 4 percentage points between 2008/09 and 2015/16. To express this finding in simple language, despite numerous texts calling for an increase in the assignment of human resource management responsibilities to line managers, in fact, in the latest years for which data is available, allocation of such responsibilities has reduced; and reduced across the board. Why this has occurred and whether it correlates with what have been suggested to be 'waves' of assignment of HRM responsibilities to the line (see Chapter 1 in this book) we cannot tell from our data, though we suspect that part of the change may be a result of centralisation required by the increasing use of technology in HRM (Bondarouk and Brewster, 2016). The reduction has been marginally more pronounced amongst the smaller organisations, leading to the reduction in the level of significance for firm size, meaning that size is less of an explanatory factor than it was for the extent of allocation of responsibilities to the line.

The second key finding in the comparison over time is that, in relation to union density, having more union members no longer reduces the likelihood of assignment. Previously, we had supposed that the more union density there was in the organisation, the more likely it was that HRM specialists would want to control HRM decision-making, controlling key HRM decisions so that the unions would have less room to identify differences between departments (an almost inevitable corollary of more line management control) and would be able to argue for 'levelling up'. Indeed, in previous rounds of the survey, higher trade union membership was associated with a greater centralisation of HRM decisions away from line managers. The new findings are at odds with the previous findings, showing no significant difference between more or less unionised organisations. It seems likely that the continuing, and arguably increasing, weakness of the trade unions means that organisations that do recognise the unions no longer have to strive for central control: there is less that the unions can do about departmental or individual differences.

Once again, and in line with our previous analysis (Brewster et al., 2015), there is a relatively low predictive power of the empirical model, with an R^2 of only 11 per cent. This probably indicates the presence of two factors. First, there are likely to be factors influencing the decision to assign responsibilities that are not present within this dataset. We cannot, for example, test for management philosophy, management history or different leaderships within the businesses. Human resource management departments can take action to improve the capability and performance of line managers in HRM; even if it appears that they rarely do. Each of these internal influences, and important external influences we have been unable to pick up, may well have had a significant influence on assignment of HRM responsibilities to the line, but we have no way of assessing it. Second, the findings indicate a good deal of agency at the firm level in terms of assigning responsibilities or not assigning HRM responsibilities to line managers. Although economy type and strategic HRM, in particular, are strong influencers upon the decision, they are far from being deterministic, and in any country, in any size of firm, it is still ultimately an individual and local decision with no obvious penalties for pursuing a path at odds with the majority of organizations.

WHAT DO THE FINDINGS MEAN?

A new round of data is being collected in 2022, but comparing the latest available data to the previous rounds, we find some consistency and some areas of change. The main finding is that every time the data is collected, a key contributor to the assignment of HRM responsibilities to line managers is country, or, at least, market economy (Brewster et al., 2015). The Anglo-Saxon LMEs have the most centralised HRM, with little room being allowed, formally at least, for line managers to exercise any substantive autonomy. We note that much of the debate about the role of line managers in human resource management has taken place in these economies. In the Anglo-Saxon countries managers who do not follow policy to the letter or go against HRM policies are seen as mavericks and are subject to penalties. There is a whole literature, mainly from the LMEs, about HRM strength (Bowen and Ostroff, 2004; Dello Russo et al., 2018; Hauff et al., 2017; Li et al., 2011), much of it based on the (undeclared) assumption that line managers following HRM policy as written must be a 'good thing'. In the LMEs, management training is specialised, so that only those with a specific interest in social aspects of management study human resource management (Witt and Jackson, 2016) and the subject is not well understood and is, indeed, unwelcome to many line managers. There is an irony here, because it is in the English-speaking countries that the notion of HRM involving a significant role for line managers has been most discussed (Purcell and Hutchinson, 2007; Whittaker and Marchington, 2003; Wright, 2008; and for the latest summary of the discussion, albeit written by Dutch colleagues, see Bos-Nehles et al., 2020. See also Chapter 3 in this book). Perhaps it is because it is so rare in those nations that it has become such a subject of interest and debate.

The CME countries continue to assign significantly more responsibility to line managers than do the LMEs. These are countries where management training is often subsumed into other programmes (engineering or economics), and the management of staff is generally included in management training (Brewster et al., 2105). The extensive legislation and the constant pressure of trade unions and works councils, allied to supportive regulation, ensures that managers are constantly aware of the importance of HRM (Cristiani and Peiró, 2018; Pedrini, 2016).

The greatest extent of assignment of HRM responsibilities to line managers occurs in the Nordic SDEs. In countries such as Finland, Sweden and Norway, trade unionism is widespread, even amongst managers, and there is a widely accepted moral imperative that certain behaviours in the drive for profits are unacceptable, and likely to trigger consumer and even possible government reaction. Managers are part of the most educated populations in the world, and most of them understand the situation and their role in the organisation and see the value of trying to manage while bearing the interests of their staff in mind.

Despite arguments from people such as Streeck (2009, 2014) and Wilkinson and Wood (2017), and the more triumphalist American-centric view (see e.g., Iseke and Schneider, 2012) that economic pressures are causing other economies to become ever more like the USA, and by implication the LMEs, and despite the pressures created by the 2008 Global Financial Crisis, in terms of assignment of HRM responsibilities to line managers, at least, these distinctive national patterns continue. Of course, we accept that these are overall averages. Even within these broad categories, in each country there will be some organisations allocating more or less responsibility to line managers (Walker et al., 2014).

We also find, and largely against all definitions of strategic HRM (Witcher and Chau, 2012), that within any economic type it is the organisations that have the most strategic HRM, as we have defined it here, that assign the least HRM responsibilities to line managers. This is ironic, given that the definitions of strategic HRM (Hendry and Pettigrew, 1986; Lengnick-Hall et al., 2019; Lepak and Shaw, 2008) have always involved a demand, not always thought through, not just for HRM specialists to be operating at and close to senior line managers who are board members, who will generally seek consistency of action across their organisation, but also close to lower-level line managers in each department, who will generally seek differentiation. The notion of business partnering (Heizmann and Fox, 2019; Wright, 2008) obscures but does not resolve this paradox (Fu et al., 2020). In practice, as our evidence makes clear, HRM departments that operate close to the board and are involved from the outset in major corporate decisions beyond HRM tend to hold responsibility for HRM to themselves. This too is a trend that has continued consistently before and after the Global Financial Crisis.

In one way, this makes sense: as HRM specialists and departments become more strategic, more closely aligned to what they see as the key stakeholders – the senior executives and the owners of the businesses – the more likely they may be to cohere authority to themselves. Having reached these positions of influence, why give their power away to ill-trained line managers, who are already busy and who may have little interest in managing people (see Blyton and Turnbull, 1992; Chapter 1 in this book)? Such managers will probably only want to bend to fit their own circumstances the policies that the HRM department has agreed with senior executives. In larger firms the problem will be exacerbated by a greater use of technology for managing the staff, and a lack of willingness to allow others access. Overall, it seems that the definitions of strategic HRM (SHRM) (Witcher and Chau, 2012) that have stressed line management responsibilities, even arguing for increasing line management responsibilities, as a key element of SHRM – without any evidence, other than some idiosyncratic case studies – are poorly thought through and confused.

Some things have changed since the Global Financial Crisis. Till then, larger firms and those with more union members were less likely to assign responsibility for HRM to line managers. There was an obvious logic to this: larger firms and those with a greater trade union presence were more likely to be visible to the general public. If line managers went off, as the lawyers say, on a frolic of their own and acted against company policy and treated employees differently from the way other managers treated them, the consequences would soon be known about and could be severe. Whether the line manager behaved in ways that gave some employees less than others (acting, for example, in contravention of a paid overtime commitment), or whether they were more generous (giving extra days off, for example) unions and other pressure groups would be quickly involved, demanding an equalling up for all staff (Townsend and Dundon, 2015). These larger businesses, and those with more trade union involvement, could not risk it, so held HRM under tight centralised control.

After the crisis, however, the influence of company size has reduced, and trade union membership no longer has any statistically significant impact upon line management responsibility for HRM. Why might this be? Clearly, we need further research, but one reading might be that the crisis led to a reduction in average company size, and certainly led to yet further reductions in trade union power (Drahokoupil and Jepsen, 2017; Lenaerts et al., 2018).

In addition, the increase in precarity, encompassing greater prevalence of self-employment, fixed-term and zero hours contracts, as well as casual employment, may have led to greater agency for line managers even within larger organisations. It became more apparent that, apart from a few internet giants, very few businesses were unaffected by the requirement to 'tighten their belts'. Individual line managers offering more or less to their employees, or treating them better or worse, could be excused by claiming that the firm could no longer afford one-size-fits-all HRM policies, or that such actions were perhaps the harbingers of what might follow if people reacted badly. There is evidence that, in some European countries at least, the continued, even unlawful, downgrading of employees' terms and conditions have become 'institutionalised' (Psychogios et al., 2020). All of this has been taking place within an environment in which, at least as evidenced by the Cranet data, there has been noticeable but a not sizeable reduction in the extent of assignment of HRM responsibilities to line managers across all firms. Therefore, establishing the key drivers of this, as well as highlighting the role played by post-financial crisis adjustments, is a further imperative for future research.

The next round of the Cranet surveys will take place after the impact of the 2020/21 COVID-19 pandemic. Clearly, the pandemic is having and is going to have enormous effects on the ways people work and are managed. At this stage we have no evidence of how that will affect the relationship between HRM departments and line managers and the HRM responsibilities of the line. It does seem likely, however, that these will continue to vary from country to country.

If HRM policies are defined by HRM specialists, HRM practice is almost always defined by the actions of line managers. HRM policies are of course important (and, we note, are much easier to research), but it is HRM practice that will determine employee reactions and hence the success (however one defines that) of the organisation: all else being equal, well-managed workforces will outperform poorly managed workforces. However, this does not take place in a vacuum: HRM always operates within a context, and country is one of the key elements of that context.

We need further research to examine these effects over time. We also need further research in a wider range of countries beyond the WEIRD states. It may well be that in less-developed countries, in state capitalist or in communist capitalist countries, the whole notion of the responsibility for HRM of line managers assumes a different perspective. The requirement for emic research becomes important. Examining the impact of geographical distinctiveness on the assignment of HRM responsibilities to line managers is not common, but we look forward to further research in this area.

REFERENCES

Amable, B. 2003. *The Diversity of Modern Capitalism*. Oxford: Oxford University Press.
Beer, M., Boselie, P. and Brewster, C. 2015. Back to the future: Implications for the field of HRM of the multi-stakeholder perspective proposed 30 years ago. *Human Resource Management*, 54(3), 427–438
Blyton, P. and Turnbull, P. 1992. *Reassessing Human Resource Management*. London: SAGE Publications.
Boada-Cuerva, M., Trullen, J. and Valverde, M. 2019. Top management: The missing stakeholder in the HRM literature. *International Journal of Human Resource Management*, 30(1), 63–95.
Bondarouk, T. and Brewster, C. 2016. Conceptualising the future of HRM and technology research. *International Journal of Human Resource Management*, 27(21), 2579–2671

Bondaruk, T., Trullen, J. and Valverde, M. 2018. It's never a straight line: Advancing knowledge on HRM implementation. *International Journal of Human Resource Management*, 29, 2995–3000.

Bos-Nehles, A., Van der Heijden, B., Van Riemsdijk, M. and Looise, J.K. 2020. Line management attributions for effective HRM implementation. *Employee Relations: The International Journal*, 42(3), 735–760.

Bowen, D.E. and Ostroff, C. 2004. Understanding HRM–firm performance linkages: The role of the 'strength' of the HRM system. *Academy of Management Review*, 29(2), 203–221.

Brewster, C., Brookes, M. and Gollan, P.J. 2015. The institutional antecedents of the assignment of HRM responsibilities to line managers. *Human Resource Management*, 54(4), 577–597

Brewster, C., Gollan, P. and Wright, P.M. 2013. Guest editors' note: Human resource management and the line. *Human Resource Management*, 52(6), 829–838.

Brewster, C., Mayrhofer, W. and Farndale, E. 2018. *A Handbook of Comparative Human Resource Management* (2nd edition). Cheltenham, UK and Northampton, MA, USA: Edward Elgar Publishing.

Cristiani, A. and Peiró, J.M. 2018. Human resource function, unions and varieties of capitalism: Exploring their impact on human resource management practices based on CRANET data. *Employee Relations*, 40(6), 1072–1098.

Currie, G. and Procter, S. 2001. Exploring the relationship between HR and middle managers. *Human Resource Management Journal*, 11(3), 53–69.

Dello Russo, S., Mascia, D. and Morandi, F. 2018. Individual perceptions of HR practices, HRM strength and appropriateness of care: A meso, multilevel approach. *International Journal of Human Resource Management*, 29(2), 286–310.

Drahokoupil, J. and Jepsen, M. 2017. The digital economy and its implications for labour: The platform economy. *Transfer*, 23(2), 103–119.

Fu, N., Flood, P.C., Rousseau, D.M. and Morris, T. 2020. Line managers as paradox navigators in HRM implementation: Balancing consistency and individual responsiveness. *Journal of Management*, 46(2), 203–233.

Guest, D.E. 2011. Human resource management and performance: Still searching for some answers. *Human Resource Management Journal*, 21(1), 3–13.

Guest, D.E., Paauwe, J. and Wright, P.M. 2013. *HRM and Performance: Building the Evidence Base*. San Francisco, CA: John Wiley & Sons.

Gooderham, P.N., Morley, M.J., Parry, E. and Stavrou, E. 2015. National and firm-level drivers of the devolution of HRM decision making to line managers. *Journal of International Business Studies*, 46(6), 715–723.

Hall, P.A. and Soskice, D. (eds). 2001. *Varieties of Capitalism: The Institutional Foundations of Comparative Advantage*. Oxford: Oxford University Press.

Hauff, S., Alewell, D. and Katrin Hansen, N. 2017. HRM system strength and HRM target achievement – toward a broader understanding of HRM processes. *Human Resource Management*, 56(5), 715–729.

Heizmann, H. and Fox, S. 2019. O partner, where art thou? A critical discursive analysis of HR managers' struggle for legitimacy. *International Journal of Human Resource Management*, 30(13), 2026–2048.

Hendry, C. and Pettigrew, A. 1986. The practice of strategic human resource management. *Personnel Review*, 15(5), 3–8.

Henrich, J., Heine, S.J. and Norenzayan, A. 2010. The weirdest people in the world? *Behavioral and Brain Sciences*, 33(2–3), 1–75.

Hofstede, G. and Minkov, M. 2010. *Cultures and Organizations: Software of the Mind* (Revised and expanded 3rd edition). New York: McGraw-Hill.

House, R.J., Hanges, P.J., Javidan, M., Dorfman, P.W. and Gupta, V. (eds). 2004. *Culture, Leadership, and Organizations: The GLOBE Study of 62 Societies*. Thousand Oaks, CA: SAGE.

Iseke, A. and Schneider, M. 2012. Transfer of employment practices, varieties of capitalism and national employment systems: A review. *Industrielle Beziehungen / German Journal of Industrial Relations*, 19(2), 236–252.

Jackson, G. and Deeg, R. 2008. Comparing capitalisms: Understanding institutional diversity and its implications for international business. *Journal of International Business Studies*, 39(4), 540–561.

Larsen, H.H. and Brewster, C. 2003. Line management responsibility for HRM: What's happening in Europe? *Employee Relations*, 25(3), 228–244.

Lenaerts, K., Kilhoffer, Z. and Akgüç, M. 2018. Traditional and new forms of organisation and representation in the platform economy. *Work Organisation, Labour and Globalisation*, 12(2), 60–78.

Lengnick-Hall, C.A., Lengnick-Hall, M.L., Neely, A. and Bonner, R.L. 2019. Something old, something new: Reframing the integration of social capital into strategic HRM research. *Academy of Management Perspectives*, 7 March. https://doi.org/10.5465/amp.2018.0028.

Lepak, D.P. and Shaw, J.D. 2008. Strategic HRM in North America: Looking to the future. *International Journal of Human Resource Management*, 19(8), 1486–1499.

Li, X., Frenkel, S. and Sanders, K. 2011. Strategic HRM as process: How HR systems and organizational climate strength influence Chinese employee attitudes. *International Journal of Human Resource Management*, 22(9), 1825–1840.

Nehles, A.C., Van Riemsdijk, M., Kok, I. and Looise, J.K. 2006. Implementing human resource management successfully: A first-line management challenge. *Management Revue*, 17(3), 256–273.

Nishii, L.H., Lepak, D.P. and Schneider, B. 2008. Employee attributions of the 'why' of HR practices: Their effects on employee attitudes and behaviors, and customer satisfaction. *Personnel Psychology*, 61(3), 503–545.

Paauwe, J. and Farndale, E. 2018. *Strategy, HRM, and Performance. A Contextual Approach* (2nd edition). Oxford: Oxford University Press.

Pedrini, G. 2016. Varieties of capitalism in Europe: An inter-temporal comparison of HR policies. *Personnel Review*, 45(3), 480–504.

Psychogios, A.G., Szamosi, L.T., Prouska, R. and Brewster, C. 2020. Varieties of crisis and working conditions: A comparative study between Greece and Serbia. *European Journal of Industrial Relations*, 26(1), 91–106.

Purcell, J. and Hutchinson, S. 2007. Front-line managers as agents in the HRM–performance causal chain: Theory, analysis and evidence. *Human Resource Management Journal*, 17(1), 3–20.

Sanders, K., Dorenbosch, L. and de Reuver, R. 2008. The impact of individual and shared employee perceptions of HRM on affective commitment. *Personnel Review*, 37(4), 412–425.

Sijtsma, K. and Molenaar, I.W. (2002). *Introduction to Nonparametric Item Response Theory*. London: SAGE.

Streeck, W. 2009. *Reforming Capitalism*. Oxford: Oxford University Press.

Streeck, W. 2014. How will capitalism end? *New Left Review*, 87, 35–64.

Townsend, K. and Dundon, T. 2015. Understanding the role of line managers in employment relations in the modern organisation. *Employee Relations*, 37(4), 1–10.

Townsend, K., Wilkinson, A., Allan, C. and Bamber, G. 2012. Mixed signals in HRM: The HRM role of hospital line managers. *Human Resource Management Journal*, 22(3), 267–282.

Trullen, J. and Valverde, M. 2017. HR professionals' use of influence in the effective implementation of HR practices. *European Journal of International Management*, 11(5), 537–556.

Trullen, J., Stirpe, L., Bonache, J. and Valverde, M. 2016. The HR department's contribution to line managers' effective implementation of HR practices. *Human Resource Management Journal*, 26(4), 449–470.

Vaiman, V. and Brewster, C. 2015. How far do cultural differences explain the differences between nations? Implications for HRM. *International Journal of Human Resource Management*, 26(2), 151–164.

Walker, J.T., Brewster, C. and Wood, G. 2014. Diversity between and within varieties of capitalism: Transnational survey evidence. *Industrial and Corporate Change*, 23(2), 493–533.

Whitley, R.D. 1999. *Divergent Capitalisms: The Social Structuring and Change of Business Systems*. Oxford: Oxford University Press.

Whitley, R.D. 2007. *Business Systems and Organizational Capabilities*. Oxford: Oxford University Press.

Whittaker, S., and Marchington, M. 2003. Devolving HR responsibility to the line – Threat, opportunity or partnership? *Employee Relations*, 25(3), 245–261.

Wilkinson, A. and Wood, G. 2017 Global trends and crises, comparative capitalism and HRM. *International Journal of Human Resource Management*, 28(18), 2503–2518

Witcher, B.J. and Chau, V.S. 2012. Varieties of capitalism and strategic management: Managing performance in multinationals after the global financial crisis. *British Journal of Management*, 23, S58–S73 DOI: 10.1111/j.1467-8551.2012.00816.x.

Witt, M.A. and Jackson, G. 2016. Varieties of capitalism and institutional comparative advantage: A test and reinterpretation. *Journal of International Business Studies*, 47, 778–806.

Wood, G., Brewster, C. and Brookes, M. 2014. *Human Resource Management and the Institutional Perspective*. London: Routledge.

Wright, C. 2008. Reinventing human resource management: Business partners, internal consultants and the limits to professionalization. *Human Relations*, 61(8), 1063–1086.

Wright, P.M. and Nishii, L. 2013. Strategic HRM and organizational behaviour: Integrating multiple levels of analysis. In J. Paauwe, D. Guest and P.M. Wright (eds), *HRM and Performance: Achievements and Challenges*. Chichester: Wiley, pp. 97–110.

11. Line managers in the public sector

Eva Knies, Adelien Decramer and Mieke Audenaert

INTRODUCTION

Over the past decade, there has been a growing recognition that line managers play an important role in human resource management (HRM) (HRM) (Purcell and Hutchinson, 2007). On the one hand, line managers are responsible for HRM implementation (Brewster et al., 2014), and on the other hand their leadership behaviour (Gilbert et al., 2011) impacts upon the attitudes and behaviours, and ultimately the performance, of the employees they supervise. These two components are together labelled as people management (Purcell and Hutchinson, 2007; Knies et al., 2020). Scholarly interest has mainly been focused on people management in a private sector context. As people management in the public sector is not 'business as usual' (Knies et al., 2018a), because of various sector-specific characteristics, this chapter focuses on line managers' role in HRM in a public sector context.

First, we discuss the role that public sector managers play in HRM. It is often argued that, traditionally, line managers play a more modest role in HRM in the public sector compared to private organizations. In 1997, Poole and Jenkins found that in the public sector the main responsibility for HRM is more likely to be vested in the HR department rather than in line management. In 2008, McGuire et al. argued that a devolution of HR responsibilities to line managers was taking place in public organizations. Indeed, a recent empirical study by Brewster et al. (2014: 591) indicated that 'that there is no real difference in the likelihood of assigning responsibility to line managers across the public and private sectors'.

Second, we discuss two public sector characteristics that have an impact on the role of line managers in HRM. The first one is the room for discretion that line managers have to manage work and people. Traditionally, public organizations are characterized by detailed personnel systems and regulations (Boyne et al., 1999; Kessler et al., 2000; Truss, 2008, 2009), which are strongly focused on standardisation. This limits the decision-making authority of line managers in general and for HRM-related issues in particular. This raises the question of what impact line managers' people management activities have on various outcomes. The other public characteristic we discuss is that line managers are typically selected and promoted based on their professional, not their people management, expertise. This is, among other factors, the result of the closed career system in many public organizations (Brewer, 2005). It is often the best doctor or teacher who is selected for a management position, or the one who has the longest tenure (Hutchinson and Wood, 1995). This raises all kind of questions related to the abilities of these line managers (Op de Beeck, 2016), their motivation to perform managerial tasks (Bainbridge, 2015), and their loyalty towards the profession versus their loyalty towards the organization (De Wit, 2012).

Third, we discuss the impact of public managers' people management activities on various types of outcomes. We do so by focusing on the effects of public sector people management activities in general. We take the paper by Leroy et al. (2018) and their seven ways in which people management can be studied as the framework for our analysis.

Finally, we focus on the effects of one important HRM practice – performance management – and discuss this in more depth. We selected this particular HRM practice as Borst and Blom (2021) have concluded that performance management is one of the most studied HRM practices in public sector studies on HRM and well-being.

In this chapter we make a distinction between top managers on the one hand, and middle and frontline managers on the other. Managers on all these hierarchical levels have people management responsibilities, although the nature of their responsibilities varies. Top or senior managers mainly have a responsibility for designing the organization's HRM policies and creating the conditions for effective implementation. Middle and frontline managers are primarily responsible for implementing people management (Wright and Nishii, 2013).

In this chapter, we draw on several bodies of knowledge: the general HRM and leadership literature on the one hand, and the public administration/public management literature on the other hand. Including theoretical and empirical insights from the latter body of knowledge allows us to contextualize insights from the general HRM and leadership literature for public sector organizations (Knies et al., 2018a).

To define what constitutes the public sector, we use two sets of criteria. The first set are formal in nature, stating that organizations are public when they are government-owned, government-funded, and where political authorities are the primary stakeholder (Rainey, 2014). The second set of criteria defines organizations as public when they produce public value, that is, when they improve 'the quality of individual and collective life for citizens' (Moore, 2013: 8). We consider organizations that meet (one of) these sets of criteria as public.

LINE MANAGERS' ROLE IN PUBLIC SECTOR HRM

Before discussing the role of line managers in public sector HRM, we will first elaborate on the distinctiveness of public sector HRM, as this has implications for the way HRM practices are designed and implemented (e.g. Knies et al., 2021). We take the framework of Farnham and Horton (1996) as our starting point, as this provides a comprehensive overview of traditional public/private differences in HRM.

According to Farnham and Horton (1996), public sector HRM is traditionally characterized by: (1) a paternalistic style of management; (2) standardized employment practices; (3) collectivist industrial relations; and (4) the aspiration to be a 'model employer'. The second and third elements are particularly relevant for our argument. Standardized employment practices are based on the principal of equal treatment, meaning that employees performing the same jobs are paid the same wage and have similar employment conditions. This leaves little room for tailor-made arrangements. A related characteristic is that industrial relations are traditionally collectivist in nature, meaning that trade unions and works councils have a strong voice when it comes to bargaining employment conditions. These traditional public sector characteristics have implications for the involvement of line managers in the implementation of HRM. According to Brewster et al. (2014: 582):

> The safest way to ensure consistency is to ensure that one group (the HRM specialists) has responsibility for the terms and conditions of employment of those workers. In such organizations ... the need to establish consistency of behavior on the part of management toward employees may discourage allocation of people management responsibilities to line managers.

Indeed, research by Poole and Jenkins (1997) in the late 1990s shows that line managers in the public sector play a less prominent role in HRM implementation compared to line managers in the private sector. The responsibility for various HRM practices, such as job design, was vested more often in the HRM department, and less so in line management than in private sector organizations. Poole and Jenkins (1997) explain these differences by pointing at bureaucratization and union involvement. They also point towards organizational size as an explanation, as larger organizations tend to be more centralized compared to smaller organizations.

In the 2000s, several papers were published that discussed the devolution of HRM responsibilities to line managers in a public sector context (e.g. Harris et al., 2002; McGuire et al., 2008; Conway and Monks, 2010). These studies all describe a reconsideration of the role of line managers in HRM. A main driver for this shift is the introduction of a new public management (NPM)-inspired way of working. NPM is characterized by a stress on private sector styles of management, a shift to greater competition, the use of explicit standards and measures of performance, and a greater emphasis on output controls (Hood, 1991). In order to be able to respond to stakeholders' demands for high-quality public services, public organizations reviewed their internal structures. Many public organizations devolved HRM responsibilities so that 'line managers are provided with an opportunity to engage with day-to-day people management decision-making, while HR [human resources] specialists can work on achieving closer alignment of an organization's systems and processes with corporate objectives, while remaining sensitive to external environmental changes' (McGuire et al., 2008: 74).

The most recent paper addressing public/private sector differences in HRM responsibilities is by Brewster et al. (2014). They studied the assignment of HRM responsibilities to the line and the institutional characteristics that act as antecedents. Based on a large international dataset surveying senior HRM managers from larger organizations, Brewster et al. show that approximately half of the organizations assign HRM responsibilities to line managers. They also show that there is no significant difference in the extent to which HRM responsibilities are assigned to line managers across the public and private sectors. However, we must note that this finding may also result from the fact that only HRM managers were surveyed, as Op de Beeck et al. (2016) showed that HRM managers and line managers can have different perceptions of HRM devolution.

Overall, over the past decades we have witnessed two related trends in the assignment of HRM responsibilities to the line. First, there is a trend of devolution of HRM responsibilities from the HR department to line managers (e.g. McGuire et al., 2008). Second, there is a trend of decreasing differences between the public and private sectors regarding the assignment of HRM responsibilities to the line (e.g. Poole and Jenkins, 1997; Brewster et al., 2014). Although the latter might suggest that people management in the public sector is no longer distinct from the private sector, we argue that there are still significant sectoral differences (e.g. Knies et al., 2018a), which we will elaborate upon in the next section.

SECTOR-SPECIFIC CHALLENGES FOR LINE MANAGERS IN THE PUBLIC SECTOR

In this section we discuss two public sector-specific challenges that impact upon people management by public managers. The first is the limited room for discretion that public managers have compared to their private sector counterparts (Boyne et al., 1999; Rainey, 2014). The second is the closed career system in the public sector (Brewer, 2005), and the fact that many public managers are promoted based on their skills as a professional and not as a manager (e.g. Blumenthal et al., 2012). We will elaborate on both issues below.

First, one of the questions intriguing leadership and public management scholars is whether and to what extent public managers can make a difference for performance. It is often argued that public managers are constrained by government oversight, detailed rules and regulations and red tape. This holds for both management in general (Rainey, 2014), and for HRM in particular (Boyne et al., 1999; Kessler et al., 2000; Truss, 2008, 2009). This leads to the fundamental question of whether managers can make a difference.

There are two schools of thought. The first is a 'constraints school', advocating that managers only have limited impact on performance of employees and the organization as a whole. The other is a 'leadership school', that argues that despite constraints, public managers still have sufficient discretion to make a difference. Overall, the balance between the constraints school and the leadership school has now shifted in favour of the latter (Bass, 1985).

Although it is now acknowledged that public managers can make a difference despite contextual constraints, the question remains to what extent and how the limited room for discretion impacts upon public people management. Knies and Leisink (2014) studied the room for discretion experienced by public managers in the police and healthcare sectors. They found that the level of room for discretion that public managers experience is relatively low. Even more salient is their finding that room for discretion is significantly related to people management performance. That is, public managers who experience less room for discretion are less motivated to support employees, and as a result show less people management support. This indicates that contextual constraints have an impact on public people management.

Nonetheless, it would be too easy to just recommend decreasing the number of rules and regulations, as these serve an important function in the public sector. On the one hand, this goes back to the issue of equal treatment (Farnham and Horton, 1996). On the other hand, these rules serve the purpose of accountability. As public organizations are held accountable by politicians and the wider public, strong internal control mechanisms often serve a purpose. This implies that determining the optimal level of discretion of public managers is a balancing act (Knies and Leisink, 2014: 123).

Second, because of the closed career system in many public organizations (Brewer, 2005), managers are often promoted based on their professional track record and/or on their tenure (Hutchinson and Wood, 1995), and less so on their managerial expertise and experience (e.g. Blumenthal et al., 2012; Op de Beeck, 2016). We must note, however, that also in the private sector there is a shortage of good leaders. As a result, people are promoted or selected for managerial positions not for their people management skills, but based on their professional expertise. Or, even worse, their promotion is based on their overconfidence, which is misinterpreted as a signal of leadership potential (Chamorro-Premuzic, 2019).

The advantage of the approach of appointing professionals as manager is that these public managers are familiar with the services provided by the organization and know what it takes to work with service users. This may increase their credibility. However, there are also potential downsides to this approach, of which we highlight three.

First, quite often public managers lack the required knowledge and skills to perform their people management tasks. This may be the case because their people management skills and potential are not assessed before they are appointed as managers. This holds for both knowledge of formal policies and procedures, and for soft skills such as coaching employees

(Knies et al., 2021). As we know from research that people management abilities are positively related to people management effectiveness (Bos-Nehles et al., 2013), this approach to appointing managers might not be very effective. Indeed, research conducted in a public sector context shows that a lack of people management abilities decreases people management performance. Van Waeyenberg and Decramer (2018) showed that school managers' ability to implement performance management systems is positively related to employees' performance management system satisfaction. This relationship is mediated by employees' perceptions of the strength of the system. Similarly, Knies and Leisink (2014) conducted research in police and healthcare sectors and showed that line managers' ability to support employees positively affects the level of supervisory support.

A second drawback is that some public managers lack the motivation to perform people management tasks, as they are primarily driven by professional values. If managers are forced to perform people management tasks without the autonomous motivation to do so, they will likely fail to deliver (Harris et al., 2002). Studies conducted in a private sector context have shown that managers are often reluctant to take up a people management role (Bos-Nehles, 2010), for example because they do not recognize the added value of people management (Thornhill and Saunders, 1998). Research conducted in a public sector context shows that intrinsic motivation of managers is indeed significantly related to the delivery of people management (e.g. Knies and Leisink, 2014; Van Waeyenberg and Decramer, 2018). Additionally, Knies and Leisink (2014) showed that public managers' willingness to conduct people management is partly dependent on the level of room for discretion they experience in their role. That is, if public managers experience little room for discretion to implement HRM so that it fits the local context of their team, this will limit their motivation for people management.

Finally, given their professional background, public managers often experience a sense of loyalty towards the professionals working in their team while at the same time feeling loyalty towards the organization and its mission (De Wit, 2012). This can be beneficial in balancing the interests of different stakeholders, but on the other hand it can lead to loyalty conflicts if stakeholders' interests are not aligned. Loyalty conflicts especially take place when managers are promoted within the same organization, meaning that they now manage their former colleagues. This is frequently the case in the public sector (De Wit, 2012).

The sector-specific challenges described here shape people management in the public sector but may also impact on its effectiveness. In the next section we therefore turn to research on the effects of public sector people management.

IMPACT OF PEOPLE MANAGEMENT ON OUTCOMES IN THE PUBLIC SECTOR

In this section, we seek to answer the question of what we can conclude from research on people management (the interrelationship between HRM and leadership behaviour) and its effects in a public sector context. According to Leroy et al. (2018) there are seven ways in which people management can be studied, depending on how HRM and leadership are integrated, namely: independent, enactment, supplementary fit, synergistic fit, complementary fit, perceptual filter and dynamic fit. Below we discuss the effects of people management in the public sector based on past research, using the Leroy et al. (2018) typology as our framework.

First, HRM and leadership can operate in independence from each other, which implies that 'HRM and leadership have independent main effects on followers' (Leroy et al., 2018: 253). As discussed above, managers in the public sector might have less leeway in whether and how to conduct HRM, because of detailed rules and stringent procedures which determine how several HRM practices should be executed. There is often little or no leeway regarding HRM practices such as recruitment and selection, appraisal, and compensation and benefits. Often, the salary system is fixed and managers have little or no say in their team members' salary levels. Especially in large public organizations, managers might not have very much leeway in how to organize the hiring and selection process.

However, the level of leeway varies for different HRM practices. Bauwens et al. (2019b) found that material rewards are more constrained and formalized and less individualized than developmental rewards (such as training and opportunities for participation, and expected contributions such as personal goals, targets and expectations in the workplace). The latter are job resources in which public managers can have more impact at the team level. Although public managers may face certain restrictions pertaining to their managerial autonomy to implement HRM, Knies et al. (2018b) found that supportive HRM practices and the implementation of tailor-made employment arrangements fostered mission achievement by enhancing thoughtful care in elderly care organizations.

Second, managers can enact the practices that are developed by the HRM department. This implies that managers bring HRM practices alive. The HRM implementation model by Guest and Bos-Nehles (2013) shows that managers are considered the primary implementers of HRM practices. Whereas the HRM department can delineate the espoused HRM practices, managers are responsible for implementing these and thus they ultimately affect employee perceptions of HRM (Nishii and Paluch, 2018).

Building on a multiple-case study of health and social services organizations, Piening et al. (2014: 561) developed propositions to predict when the espoused HRM practices would be congruent with the implemented HRM practices by the managers. They propose that 'when there is agreement among HR decision makers about the intended HR practices, organizations that leverage their resources effectively are more likely to achieve congruency between intended and implemented HRM'. Moreover, their case studies suggest that when the intended HRM plays a more strategic role in the organization, line managers are more inclined to implement HR practices as they were originally intended.

Furthermore, according to the perspective of enactment, leadership functions as a mediator between HRM and employee outcomes. According to Leroy et al. (2018: 253) this ignores 'some of the power and politics in the reality of many organizations where the HRM department seldom has the power to motivate or force leaders in the desired direction'. Public managers may be more restricted in their approaches to HRM, and enactment of HRM practices may be stronger than in the private sector. Indeed, there is empirical support for the enactment perspective in a public sector context. Schopman et al. (2017) found that transformational leadership explains the linkage between perceptions of high-commitment HRM and healthcare workers' motivation to continue to work in healthcare.

In addition to the possibility that enactment is shown by leadership that functions as a mediator between HRM and employee outcomes, Bos-Nehles and Audenaert (2019) suggest that HRM perceptions can mediate leadership and employee outcomes. Specifically, they propose that positive perceptions of the leader–member exchange (LMX) relationship based on perceptions of trust, respect and obligations to the manager can foster satisfaction with HRM, which in turn has a positive impact on employee outcomes. In support of this proposition, Vermeeren et al. (2014) have found that a stimulating leadership style fosters the implementation of HRM practices, whereas a correcting leadership style has no effect on the number of implemented HRM practices. In another study, Vermeeren's (2014) findings again supported that the supervisor's leadership style is a prerequisite for the successful implementation of HRM. The latter study explains differences in the extent to which HRM is implemented in different work units of a Dutch municipality. Interestingly, the enacted HRM practices explain why some work units perform better than others. In addition, this study found that individual employees' perceptions explain why team-level HRM implementation translates into perceived united performance, as suggested in the model of Nishii and Wright (2008).

Taken together, the discussed studies support that leaders' enactment of HRM can depend on their leadership style, and vice versa, implemented HRM practices can foster positive employee perceptions of the leadership style. Although red tape and bureaucratic structures may lower the room for discretion that managers have to implement HRM practices in the public sector, leadership and HRM enactment both seem to have a crucial impact on outcomes in public organizations. The enactment of HRM by the manager is important as it affects crucial employee outcomes pertaining to well-being and performance, as well as organizational performance.

Third and fourth, according to the 'supplementary fit' and the 'synergistic fit' reasoning, HRM and leadership function independently, but they depend on each other for being effective. In analytical terms this implies that HRM and leadership interact. The effects of this interaction would be optimal when leadership behaviours and signals from HRM are aligned (Leroy et al., 2018). The synergistic fit perspective goes a step further than the supplementary fit perspective by suggesting that when operating from the same value set, HRM and leadership can mutually reinforce each other. According to this perspective, the outcome is greater than the sum of the individual parts.

Empirical studies show support for supplementary rather than for synergistic fit. Bos-Nehles et al. (2017) build on qualitative research among fire service workers and conclude that HRM practices and leadership behaviours can supplement each other for generating and implementing innovating ideas. Whereas the managers may be particularly able to foster idea generation, HRM practices such as appraisals can foster innovation realization, and HR managers could bring 'people together that could realize the potential of innovative ideas between different units of the organization' (Bos-Nehles et al., 2017: 395). Also, other studies support the relevance of aligned signals from leadership behaviours. For instance, the study by Audenaert et al. (2017) in a large public organization found that consistency among social exchange signals of HRM practices and LMX quality leads to the most optimal employee reactions in terms of psychological empowerment. The HRM practices signal the espoused social exchange orientation, and LMX entails the inferred social exchange orientation. Consistency on these signals fosters clarity on the level of investments and the degree of socio-emotional support employees can rely on in the longer term.

Fifth, in contrast with the supplementary and synergistic fit perspectives, the 'complementary fit' model argues that it may be useful for HRM and leadership to combine oppositional value perspectives. In that way, HRM and leadership can complement each other to achieve improved results (Leroy et al., 2018).

In the public sector, due to budget constraints and austerity measures, certain jobs evolve away from mutual investment jobs with a high degree of material and developmental investments in the employee and high expected contributions in terms of the quality and quantity of the work. Instead, there is an increase of overdemanding jobs in which the expected contributions are high relative to the investments in the employee (Audenaert et al., 2019b). Research has considered to what extent leadership can complement the job's HRM resources and demands.

On the one hand, research by Audenaert et al. (2017) shows that a high-quality LMX relationship can compensate for overdemanding jobs with fewer investments in the employee. On the other hand, when employees are on the receiving end of HRM practices that signal that the organization cares for them and values their contributions, low-quality LMX may lead to less meaningful assignments and impact through participation. Apparently 'the compensation of resources from the leader for resources from HRM systems does not work in both directions' (Audenaert et al., 2017: 15).

Studies confirm that managers' behaviours appear to substitute for HRM practices to some extent: LMX can compensate for an economic orientation of HRM, but the opposite may not be possible, as HRM may not be able to compensate for an economic orientation of LMX (Audenaert et al., 2017, 2019a).

Sixth, the 'perceptual filter' perspective suggests that the effectiveness of HRM and leadership depends on how employees perceive both. Furthermore, perceptions of HRM and leadership can also function as a perception filter towards each other (Leroy et al., 2018).

Research suggests that LMX and the involved trust in the manager functions as an interpretative scheme through which employees interpret HRM (Audenaert et al., 2017, 2019a). This idea builds on the assumption that LMX may operate as an interpretation framework (Gerstner and Day, 1997) through which employees respond to HRM practices. In this regard, employees may also compare the expectations that are signalled from the HRM practices applied to them with those from their leader.

Seventh, the 'dynamic fit' perspective regards fit as a dynamic concept that changes over time. This idea would require panel studies with repeated measures to look at repeated interactions between HRM practices and leadership in order to create alignment according to any of the above-mentioned perspectives (Leroy et al., 2018). We know of no studies that have applied this perspective in a public sector context.

In sum, studies on people management in the public sector have taken different perspectives, and can continue to do so, linked to the specific research question and to the context of the study. It may be relevant though for future studies to consider which of the perspectives are most appropriate to the study. It is important to do so in the theorization phase of the study (prior to designing the study), as it impacts upon levels of analyses of the studied HRM and leadership variables, and analysis approaches (for example, direct effects, interaction effects, polynomial effects).

LINE MANAGERS' ROLE IN PUBLIC SECTOR PERFORMANCE MANAGEMENT

This section deals with a specific application of people management, namely the role of line management in the effectiveness of performance management in the public sector. Considering that performance management is under scrutiny in many public sector organizations (Gerrish, 2016), we deem it relevant to focus in depth on this specific application of people management.

Line managers have an immense impact on the effectiveness of performance management (Den Hartog et al., 2004). Performance management is a critical HRM practice as it facilitates performance and development in organizations (Tseng and Levy, 2019). Performance management is described as a cyclical and continuous HRM process with different phases such as planning, monitoring, evaluation and (eventually) reward of individual and team performance, and aligning performance with the strategic goal of the organization (Aguinis, 2009). It is used more and more in public sector organizations (Gruman and Saks, 2011; Van Thielen, 2019). According to the literature, the adoption of these systems should lead to higher employee engagement, development and individual performance, and higher organizational performance (e.g. Fletcher and Williams, 1996; Schleicher et al., 2018).

Performance management is a significant feature of public sector organizations that adopted this HRM practice initiated by the NPM paradigm. There is, however, a paradox between the popularity of performance management in public organizations (George et al., 2020) and the critical voices against performance management that emphasize the negative side-effects associated with the implementation of performance management systems in a public sector context.

Indeed, in the literature and in practice, there is a heated debate regarding the negative side-effects associated with the implementation of performance management systems (Latham and Locke, 2007; Ordóñez et al., 2009). This is in line with the conflicting outcomes approach of HRM (e.g. Van De Voorde et al., 2012) that considers employees' and employers' interests to be conflicting. Applied to performance management, it is suggested that there may be trade-offs between employee and organizational outcomes. More specifically, the impact of performance management on the physical indicators of well-being are often described to be incongruent with performance outcomes (Van De Voorde et al., 2012; Van Waeyenberg et al., 2022).

Many authors suggest that the effectiveness of performance management may depend on several boundary conditions, and that an ideal performance management system compromises several features such as: 'strategic congruence, context congruence, thoroughness, practicality, meaningfulness, specificity, reliability, validity, fairness inclusiveness, openness, standardisation, ethicality etc' (Aguinis, 2009: 22). In this chapter, we specifically focus on the role of leadership in the effectiveness of performance management in the public sector.

There are several reasons why we analyse the role of the line manager in the process of performance management. Within the (public) management and HRM literature, there is a strong emphasis on the pivotal role of the line manager in the process of performance management. Line managers serve as interpretive filters of performance management practices in organizations (Tseng and Levy, 2019; Van Thielen, 2019), affecting how performance management is implemented within the organization. The perception that employees have of the performance management system in use is determined, on the one hand, by the manner in which the leaders/ line managers implement the performance management system, and on the other hand, by the leadership/management behaviour the leader/line manager displays (Knies et al., 2020).

A distinction can be made between the adoption at the organizational level and the implementation – by the line manager – at the team level. More specifically, public sector organizations can adopt (sometimes coerced by law and legislation) a 'formal' performance management system at the organizational level, but it is the line manager/supervisor who has to implement and use these formal performance management practices in their team (Schleicher et al., 2018; Bauwens, 2019; Tseng and Levy, 2019). As a result, there can be variation in the implementation within the organization.

Moreover, there is sometimes a huge divide between 'formal' and 'informal' processes of performance management in the organization, due to the enactment of the line manager.

Finally, we observe that many scholars point at the importance of the manager–employee interactions embedded in the performance management process (Tseng and Levy, 2019). The empirical studies in HRM and public management that have sought to identify the impact of performance management in the public sector have a strong emphasis on how the performance management system is implemented by the line manager. We assess this empirical evidence and focus on the following prevalent elements of the performance management process and the implementation by the line manager: fairness; the ability, motivation and opportunity of the line manager; communication of a strong performance management system by the line manager; and manager–employee interactions.

Fairness

According to Aguinis (2009), a good performance management system is acceptable and is perceived as fair by all participants. We can apply the three different perceptions of fairness (or justice; Colquitt et al., 2001) to performance management: distributive, procedural and interactional justice.

Bauwens et al. (2019a) examined how the implementation of performance management has an impact on burnout and organizational citizenship behaviour (OCB) among academics in (Flemish) higher education institutions. In their study, there was a large emphasis on the role of heads of department and team leaders of research groups: they had to implement the system in the unit. Bauwens et al. (2019a) examined the performance management fairness dimensions as a mechanism to understand burnout and OCB-related behaviours among academics. The study shows that performance management fairness, more specifically distributive and interactional fairness of performance management, do not impact upon OCB directly but rather indirectly through the disengagement dimension of burnout. Bauwens et al. (2019a) formulate very specific recommendations for the line manager: they should focus on maintaining fair outcomes, treating academic employees fairly, and providing them with adequate information.

Ability, Motivation and Opportunity of the Line Manager

A crucial question is: to what extent does the leader/line manager have the ability, motivation and opportunity (AMO) to implement the performance management system effectively? The effectiveness of performance management implementation is expected to be a function of three factors (Van Waeyenberg, 2018): (1) line managers should have the ability to enact the activities that are involved in performance management; (2) they should be motivated to perform these activities; and (3) line managers should have sufficient opportunity to fulfil these activities.

Van Waeyenberg (2018) found that the implementation of performance management in education will be more effective when the line manager has the ability and the motivation to enact performance management processes. Moreover, he found that the implementation of these systems will be more effective when line managers do not experience role conflict.

Role conflict could interfere with the opportunity to implement these performance management (Van Waeyenberg and Decramer, 2018). The author found that line managers' AMO to implement performance management systems in education was positively related to teachers' satisfaction with the performance management system. These relationships were mediated by employees' perceptions that the performance management system is 'strong'. This brings us to our next feature: communication of a strong system.

Communication of a Strong Performance Management System

Communication by the line manager is put forward in the literature as a crucial antecedent for the effective implementation of performance management (Biron et al., 2011). Performance management has been described as a communication process that signals the organization's expectations of employees. Moreover, the so-called strong performance management system is effective, according to scholars (see e.g. Decramer, 2020), by conveying information in a distinctive, consistent and consensual way (Bowen and Ostroff, 2004).

This process approach is linked to the theoretical foundation within the field of HRM which has made the strategic HRM research field more aware of 'the complex, multilevel, multisource mechanisms, turning HR activities into valuable employee and organizational outcomes' (Van Thielen, 2019). Performance management has the purpose to provide signals – via the line manager – to employees about the behavior, attitudes and skills that are desired in the organization (Aguinis et al., 2013) by setting goals that are monitored and evaluated, in line with the overall strategic objectives. A strong performance management signals that its features are salient across employees, and that the system is clear and understood. Indeed, performance management systems are described as instruments of communication between organizations, management and employees (Biron et al., 2011).

Manager–Employee Interactions

A last crucial factor is the way in which the employees perceive their relationship with the leader. Leader–member exchange (LMX) seems to have an impact on the relationship between performance management and innovation. In a study by Audenaert et al. (2019a), we see that the manager is a driver for employee behaviour in the public sector. Employees' perceptions of the relationship with the manager function as a lens through which the employees perceive performance management. This lens thus affects the effectiveness of performance management (Audenaert et al., 2019a).

In sum, studies on the role of the line manager in the process of performance management in the public sector show that the role of the line manager in the performance management process is crucial. The effectiveness of the performance management system will depend on the role played by the line managers. Future research on the people management issues of performance management should consider the particular importance of multilevel issues in the public sector, considering the multilayer context in which performance management in the public sector is embedded.

CONCLUSION

In this chapter we have examined line managers' people management in a public sector context. We have focused particularly on distinctive sectoral characteristics that impact upon the way people management takes shape in public organizations. Also, we have studied the effects of public managers' people management on several outcomes, both generally and for the HRM practice of performance management. In doing so, we have shown that although public organizations are increasingly starting to look like private organizations, it is still important to take context into account, as people management in the public sector is not business as usual. We call on researchers to conduct more research on line managers' people management in a public sector context, and to systematically compare the public and private sectors. This will provide an even better understanding of this important topic.

REFERENCES

Aguinis, H. (2009). *Performance Management* (2nd edn). Upper Saddle River, NJ: Pearson Prentice Hall.

Aguinis, H., Joo, H., and Gottfredson, R.K. (2013). What monetary rewards can and cannot do: How to show employees the money. *Business Horizons, 56*, 241–249.

Audenaert, M., Decramer, A., George, B., Verschuere, B., and Van Waeyenberg, T. (2019a). When employee performance management affects individual innovation in public organizations: The role of consistency and LMX. *International Journal of Human Resource Management, 30*(5), 815–834.

Audenaert, M., George, B., and Decramer, A. (2019b). How a demanding employment relationship relates to affective commitment in public organizations: A multilevel analysis. *Public Administration, 97*(1), 11–27.

Audenaert, M., Vanderstraeten, A., and Buyens, D. (2017). When affective well-being is empowered: The joint role of leader–member exchange and the employment relationship. *International Journal of Human Resource Management, 28*(15), 2208–2227.

Bainbridge, H. (2015). Devolving people management to the line: How different rationales for devolution influence people management effectiveness. *Personnel Review, 44*(6), 847–865.

Bass, B. (1985). *Leadership and Performance Beyond Expectations*. New York: Free Press / Collier Macmillan.

Bauwens, R. (2019). Performance management implementation in higher education: Leaders, success conditions and implications for well-being and performance. Doctoral dissertation, Ghent University.

Bauwens, R., Audenaert, M., Huisman, J., and Decramer, A. (2019a). Performance management fairness and burnout: implications for organizational citizenship behaviors. *Studies in Higher Education, 44*(3), 584–598.

Bauwens, R., Decramer, A., and Audenaert, M. (2019b). Challenged by great expectations? Examining cross-level moderations and curvilinearity in the public sector job demands–resources model. *Review of Public Personnel Administration*, 0734371X19884102.

Biron, M., Farndale, E., and Paauwe, J. (2011). Performance management effectiveness: Lessons from world-leading firms. *International Journal of Human Resource Management, 22*(6), 1294–1311.

Blumenthal, D.M., Bernard, K., Bohnen, J., and Bohmer, R. (2012). Addressing the leadership gap in medicine: Residents' need for systematic leadership development training. *Academic Medicine, 87*(4), 513–522.

Borst, R., and Blom, R. (2021). HRM and Well-being in the public sector: A systematic literature review. In B. Steijn and E. Knies (eds), *Research Handbook on HRM in the Public Sector* (pp. 172–188). Cheltenham, UK and Northampton, MA, USA: Edward Elgar Publishing.

Bos-Nehles, A. (2010). The line makes the difference: Line managers as effective HR partners. Doctoral dissertation, Universiteit Twente.

Bos-Nehles, A., and Audenaert, M. (2019). LMX and HRM: A multi-level review of how LMX is used to explain the employment relationship. In Keith Townsend, Kenneth Cafferkey, Aoife M. McDermott and Tony Dundon (eds), *Elgar Introduction to Theories of Human Resources and Employment Relations* (pp. 336–351). Cheltenham, UK and Northampton, MA, USA: Edward Elgar Publishing.

Bos-Nehles, A., Bondarouk, T., and Nijenhuis, K. (2017). Innovative work behaviour in knowledge-intensive public sector organizations: The case of supervisors in the Netherlands fire services. *International Journal of Human Resource Management*, 28(2), 379–398.

Bos-Nehles, A.C., Van Riemsdijk, M.J., and Looise, J.K. (2013). Employee perceptions of line management performance: Applying the AMO theory to explain the effectiveness of line managers' HRM implementation. *Human Resource Management*, 52(6), 861–877.

Bowen, D.E., and Ostroff, C. (2004). Understanding HRM–firm performance linkages: The role of the "strength" of the HRM system. *Academy of Management Review*, 29(2), 203–221.

Boyne, G., Poole, M., and Jenkins, G. (1999). Human resource management in the public and private sectors: An empirical comparison. *Public Administration*, 77(2), 407–420.

Brewer, G.A. (2005). In the eye of the storm: Frontline supervisors and federal agency performance. *Journal of Public Administration Research and Theory*, 15, 505–527.

Brewster, C., Brookes, M., and Gollan, P. (2014). The institutional antecedents of the assignment of HRM responsibilities to line managers. *Human Resource Management*, 54, 577–597.

Chamorro-Premuzic, T. (2019). *Why Do So Many Incompetent Men Become Leaders? (And How to Fix It)*. Boston, MA: Harvard Business Press.

Colquitt, J. A., Conlon, D.E., Wesson, M.J., Porter, C.O., and Ng, K.Y. (2001). Justice at the millennium: A meta-analytic review of 25 years of organizational justice research. *Journal of Applied Psychology*, 86(3), 425–455

Conway, E., and Monks, K. (2010). The devolution of HRM to middle managers in the Irish health service. *Personnel Review*, 39(3), 361–374.

Decramer, A. (2020). *Making Organisations Work*. Gent: Owl Press.

De Wit, B.C. (2012). Loyale leiders. Een onderzoek naar de loyaliteit van leidinggevenden aan docenten in het voortgezet onderwijs. Doctoral dissertation, Utrecht University.

Den Hartog, D.N., Boselie, P., and Paauwe, J. (2004). Performance management: A model and research agenda. *Applied Psychology: An International Review*, 53(4), 556–569.

Farnham, D., and Horton, S. (1996). *Managing People in the Public Services*. London: Macmillan.

Fletcher, C., and Williams, R. (1996). Performance management, job satisfaction and organizational commitment. *British Journal of Management*, 7(2), 169–179.

George, B., Baekgaard, M., Decramer, A., Audenaert, M., and Goeminne, S. (2020). Institutional isomorphism, negativity bias and performance information use by politicians: A survey experiment. *Public Administration*, 98, 14–28.

Gerrish, E. (2016). The impact of performance management on performance in public organizations: A meta-analysis. *Public Administration Review*, 76(1), 48–66.

Gerstner, C., and Day, D. (1997). Meta-analytic review of leader–member exchange theory: Correlates and construct issues. *Journal of Applied Psychology*, 82(6), 827–844.

Gilbert, C., De Winne, S., and Sels, L. (2011). The influence of line managers and HR department on employees' affective commitment. *International Journal of Human Resource Management*, 22, 1618–1637.

Gruman, J.A., and Saks, A.M. (2011). Performance management and employee engagement. *Human Resource Management Review*, 21(2), 123–136.

Guest, D.E., and Bos-Nehles, A. (2013). HRM and performance: The role of effective implementation. In J. Paauwe, D. Guest and P. Wright (eds), *HRM and Performance: Achievements and Challenges* (pp. 79–96). Chichester: Wiley.

Harris, L., Doughty, D., and Kirk, S. (2002). The devolution of HR responsibilities: Perspectives from the UK's public sector. *Journal of European Industrial Training*, 26(5), 218–229.

Hood, C. (1991). A public management for all seasons? *Public Administration*, 69, 3–19.

Hutchinson, S., and Wood, S. (1995). The UK experience. In S. Hutchinson and C. Brewster (eds), *Personnel and the Line: Developing the New Relationship*. Wimbledon: IPM.

Kessler, I., Purcell, J., and Coyle Shapiro, J. (2000). New forms of employment relations in the public services: the limits of strategic choice. *Industrial Relations Journal*, 31(1), 17–34.

Knies, E., Boselie, P., Gould-Williams, J., and Vandenabeele, W. (2018a). Strategic human resource management and public sector performance: Context matters. *International Journal of Human Resource Management*, 1–13. DOI: 10.1080/09585192.2017.1407088.

Knies, E., and Leisink, P. (2014). Leadership behavior in public organizations: A study of supervisory support by police and medical center middle managers. *Review of Public Personnel Administration*, *34*(2), 108–127.

Knies, E., Leisink, P., and Kraus-Hoogeveen, S. (2018b). Frontline managers' contribution to mission achievement: A study of how people management affects thoughtful care. *Human Service Organizations: Management, Leadership and Governance*, *42*(2), 166–184.

Knies, E., Leisink, P., and Van de Schoot, R. (2020). People management: Developing and testing a measurement scale. *International Journal of Human Resource Management*, *31*(6), 705–737.

Knies, E., Op de Beeck, S., and Hondeghem, A. (2021). Antecedents of managers' people management: Using the AMO model to explain differences in HRM implementation and leadership. In P. Leisink, L.B. Andersen, G.A. Brewer, C.B. Jacobsen, E. Knies and W. Vandenabeele (eds), *Managing for Public Service Performance: How People and Values Make a Difference* (pp. 123–141), Oxford: Oxford University Press.

Latham, G.P., and Locke, E.A. (2007). New developments in and directions for goal-setting research. *European Psychologist*, *12*(4), 290–300.

Leroy, H., Segers, J., Van Dierendonck, D., and Den Hartog, D. (2018). Managing people in organizations: Integrating the study of HRM and leadership. *Human Resource Management Review*, *28*(3), 249–257.

McGuire, D., Stoner, L., and Mylona, S. (2008). The role of line managers as human resource agents in fostering organizational change in public services. *Journal of Change Management*, *8*(1), 73–84.

Moore, M. (2013). *Recognizing Public Value*. Cambridge, MA: Harvard University Press.

Nishii, L.H., and Paluch, R.M. (2018). Leaders as HR sensegivers: Four HR implementation behaviors that create strong HR systems. *Human Resource Management Review*, *28*(3), 319–323.

Nishii, L.H., and Wright, P.M. (2008). Variability within organizations: Implications for strategic human resource management. In D.B. Smith (ed.), *The People Make the Place: Dynamic Linkages Between Individuals and Organizations* (pp. 225–248). New York: Taylor & Francis Group.

Op de Beeck, S. (2016). HRM responsibilities in the public sector: The role of line managers. Doctoral thesis, Faculty of Social Sciences, KU Leuven, Belgium.

Op de Beeck, S., Wynen, J., and Hondeghem, A. (2016). HRM implementation by line managers: Explaining the discrepancy in HR–line perceptions of HR devolution. *International Journal of Human Resource Management*, *27*(17), 1901–1919.

Ordóñez, L.L.D., Schweitzer, M.M.E., Galinsky, A.D., and Bazerman, M.H. (2009). Goals gone wild: The systematic side effects of over-prescribing goal setting. *Academy of Management Perspectives*, *23*(1), 6–16.

Piening, E.P., Baluch, A.M., and Ridder, H.G. (2014). Mind the intended–implemented gap: Understanding employees' perceptions of HRM. *Human Resource Management*, *53*(4), 545–567.

Poole, M., and Jenkins, G. (1997), Responsibilities for human resource management practices in the modern enterprise. *Personnel Review*, *26*, 333–356.

Purcell, J., and Hutchinson, S. (2007). Front-line managers as agents in the HRM–performance causal chain: Theory, analysis and evidence. *Human Resource Management Journal*, *17*, 3–20.

Rainey, H. (2014), *Understanding and Managing Public Organizations*. San Francisco, CA: Jossey-Bass.

Schleicher, D.J., Baumann, H.M., Sullivan, D.W., Levy, P.E., Hargrove, D.C., and Barros-Rivera, B.A. (2018). Putting the system into performance management systems: A review and agenda for performance management research. *Journal of Management*, *44*(6), 2209–2245.

Schopman, L.M., Kalshoven, K., and Boon, C. (2017). When health care workers perceive high-commitment HRM will they be motivated to continue working in health care? It may depend on their supervisor and intrinsic motivation. *International Journal of Human Resource Management*, *28*(4), 657–677.

Thornhill, A., and Saunders, M.N. (1998). What if line managers don't realize they're responsible for HR? *Personnel Review*, *27*(6), 460–476.

Truss, C. (2008). Continuity and change: The role of the HR function in the modern public sector. *Public Administration*, *86*(4), 1071–1088.

Truss, C. (2009). Changing HR functional forms in the UK public sector. *International Journal of Human Resource Management*, *20*(4), 717–737.

Tseng, S.T., and Levy, P.E. (2019). A multilevel leadership process framework of performance management. *Human Resource Management Review*, (May), 0–1. https://doi.org/10.1016/j.hrmr.2018.10.001.

Van De Voorde, K., Paauwe, J., and Van Veldhoven, M. (2012). Employee well-being and the HRM–organizational performance relationship: A review of quantitative studies. *International Journal of Management Reviews*, *14*(4), 391–407.

Van Thielen, T. (2019). Performance management in policing: Context, process and outcomes. PhD dissertation, Ghent University, 5 November.

Van Waeyenberg, T. (2018). Performance management systems, employee well-being and performance. Doctoral dissertation, Ghent University.

Van Waeyenberg, T., and Decramer, A. (2018). Line managers' AMO to manage employees' performance: The route to effective and satisfying performance management. *International Journal of Human Resource Management*, *29*(22), 3093–3114.

Van Waeyenberg, T., Peccei, R., and Decramer, A. (2022). Performance management and teacher performance: The role of affective organizational commitment and exhaustion. *International Journal of Human Resource Management*, *33*(4), 623–646.

Vermeeren, B. (2014). Variability in HRM implementation among line managers and its effect on performance: A 2-1-2 mediational multilevel approach. *International Journal of Human Resource Management*, *25*(22), 3039–3059.

Vermeeren, B., Kuipers, B., and Steijn, B. (2014). Does leadership style make a difference? Linking HRM, job satisfaction, and organizational performance. *Review of Public Personnel Administration*, *34*(2), 174–195.

Wright, P., and Nishii, L.H. (2013), Strategic HRM and organizational behaviour: Integrating multiple levels of analysis. In J. Paauwe, D. Guest and P. Wright (eds), *HRM and Performance: Achievements and Challenges* (pp. 97–110). Chichester: Wiley.

12. HRM in small firms: owner-managers as line managers

Carol Atkinson, Ben Lupton and Charles Dahwa

INTRODUCTION

This book takes as its topic line managers and human resource management (HRM), which is important and deserving of detailed exploration. In this chapter, however, we argue that much discussion of this topic assumes, often implicitly, a large firm model. By this, we mean that there is a presumption, based on strategic HRM models, of specialist human resources (HR) practitioners/departments based within an organisation that design and deliver HR policy and practice that a professional line management structure is then tasked with implementing (see, e.g., Purcell and Hutchinson, 2007). Again, in line with strategic HRM models, these HR practices are typically sophisticated, applied in bundles or sets, and are intended to enhance organisational performance (Harney and Dundon, 2006). As we explain throughout this chapter, these assumptions are not necessarily well founded in small firms that are run by their owner-managers, often with no specialist HR support, and the theorised top-down approach to implementation is absent. Yet there is limited research around how and why small firm owner-managers implement HR practice, where implementation is the process of uptake of HR practices as opposed to their outcomes (Trullen et al., 2020).

This is an important knowledge gap. Harney and Alkhalaf's (2020) recent paper makes an important contribution in reviewing research on strategic HRM in small and medium-sized enterprises (SMEs) over the past 25 years and notes that much ground has been covered. Yet it too notes that there is little on HR implementation in SMEs, and that the small firm sector is vital in both developed and developing economies. An Organisation for Economic Co-operation and Development (OECD, 2017) report, for example, suggests that, in the OECD area, SMEs account for around 99 per cent of all firms and 70 per cent of employment. The same report evidences their importance in emerging economies, where they contribute around 45 per cent of employment and a third of gross domestic product (GDP), and that they contribute around half of employment and GDP in most countries regardless of income levels. In this chapter, we have a particular focus on small firms (those employing fewer than 50 people; EU, 2011), in the United Kingdom (UK), which similarly make a substantial contribution to both the country's economic activity and its employment levels.

The chapter begins with consideration of why owner-managers might differ from line managers in relation to HRM implementation and the implications of this. In small firms, owner-managers are key actors and yet are neglected in the implementation debate which has focused on, for example, HR professionals, senior and line managers, and employees (Trullen et al., 2020). It then turns to consider in some detail, drawing on two projects that we have carried out, enactment of HR in small firms; in particular, the perspectives of owner-managers on people management, and the use of business support services to design and implement HR practice. The chapter concludes with discussion of the implications of our work for policy, practice and theory.

OWNER-MANAGERS NOT LINE MANAGERS: WHY DOES THIS MATTER?

As we note above, most research on line managers and HRM presumes a large firm site of operation. Purcell and Hutchinson's (2007) work on frontline managers is an excellent example of this and proposes a widely recognised and well-respected model of HR implementation predicated on a divide between intended and actual HR practices. In this, intended HR practices are designed by HR practitioners, based in specialist HR departments, and then devolved to line managers for implementation within their teams. There has been much debate as to how successful this implementation then is (Townsend et al., 2012), and the extent to which misalignment between intended and actual HR practices creates negative employee outcomes and ultimately undermines the improved performance that HR practices are intended to deliver (see, e.g., Nishii et al., 2008). Purcell and Hutchinson's (2007) model, and much of the wider debate on line managers and HRM, does however overlook two key points about HR practice in small firms. First, it presumes that there is a formal HR department working in conjunction with line managers. In small firms, however, this is rarely so. Second, it presumes that HR practice is formal, and as we explore in what follows, this is again often not the case in small firms. Both points raise questions as to the extent to which current models of HR implementation are appropriate to the small firm context. We seek to address these questions throughout the chapter.

Influence of the Owner-Manager

Research on HRM in small firms has consistently drawn attention to the influence of the owner-manager on HR practice (Harney and Alkhalaf, 2020; Steijvers et al., 2017). As we have noted above, many small firms lack an HR department or specialist, and engagement (or not) with HR practice will then be owner-manager driven, rather than cascaded from the HR department as in larger firms (Klaas et al., 2012; Kroon et al., 2013). The tipping point in employing an HR specialist is generally around 80–100 employees (CIPD, 2014), meaning that the vast majority of small firms do not have access to an internal HR specialist. Owner-manager perspectives on HR are thus central to its operation in their firm. Harney and Alkhalaf (2020: 8) refer to the 'owner-manager imprint' on HR policy and practice, and there has been a good deal of attention paid in the literature to the form that this 'imprint' can take. A broad range of factors has been identified as having an influence, for example, the management philosophy and values of the owner-manager (e.g. Jones et al., 2007), their experience and understanding of HRM (e.g. Klaas et al., 2012), and their identity and background (e.g. Steijvers et al., 2017). Below, we explore what is known about how owner-manager characteristics and perspectives influence the approach of small firms to managing their human resources.

Owner-managers in a small firm can necessarily – as result of being much closer to the firm's day-to-day activities and having personal relationships with many if not all of the staff – have much more direct impact on employment practices than their counterparts in a large organisation (Garavan et al., 2016; Nolan and Garavan, 2016). This is likely in large part to underlie the diverse and often idiosyncratic approaches to HR in small firms (Cassell et al., 2001). However, as many commentators have suggested, this is shaped not only by the proximity of the owner-manager, but also by their desire for autonomy (Jones et al., 2007). In many cases, the firm is the owner-manager's main project in life, and in a sense an extension of their personality and values (Wilkinson, 1999). A desire to run the firm 'my way' naturally follows from this, and restrictions on this may be resisted. Employment regulations, for example, may be resisted as bureaucratic infringements on owner-manager autonomy, though recent research suggests a more nuanced picture (Atkinson et al., 2016; Kitching, 2016). Similar arguments underpin the distinctive preference for informality in management in SMEs that is recorded widely in the literature (Bacon and Hoque, 2005; Cardon and Stevens, 2004; Garavan et al., 2016; Harney and Dundon, 2006). Formal HR policies and practices, despite evidence for their effectiveness (Razouk, 2011; Sheehan, 2014; Steijvers et al., 2017), may be unattractive to small firm owner-managers who want to 'run their own show', or where they are incongruent with the preference for management through the strength and closeness of personal relationships (Atkinson et al., 2016; Woodhams and Lupton, 2006). They may also allow for a level of communication, flexibility and responsiveness that larger firms may struggle to replicate, and be strategically effective (Marchington et al., 2003). Accordingly, the adoption of formal 'good' HR practice may be resisted, though it is important to note that formal HR practice is present in many small firms, and often co-exists alongside more informal approaches (Atkinson et al., 2016; Verryenne et al., 2013).

Owner-Managers and HR Practice

It is not only the owner-manager's approach and preferences that will affect how they manage people, but also their knowledge and expertise. In many cases, and for reasons we explore below, this may be limited. Timming (2011) identified in his study a striking lack of knowledge of HR amongst many small firm owner-managers, even as to what the term meant, and Mayson and Barrett (2006) drew attention to the lack of understanding of the strategic potential of HR interventions. As Kroon et al. (2013) note, the implementation of HR practice in small firms depends on the owner-manager recognising the business benefits of addressing HR issues and challenges, and allocating resources to deal with them (Tocher and Rutherford, 2009). Whereas in larger firms this task falls to specialist HR managers with professional training and experience, or is delegated to line managers who are supported by formal HR systems and advice (López-Cotarelo, 2018; Trullen et al., 2016), in smaller firms the nature and form of HR activity will be dependent on the experience and understanding of the owner-manager. As Klaas et al. (2012) suggest, the level of exposure to HR practices among small firm owner-managers will vary considerably and will often depend on whether they have had management experience in larger organisations. As these authors note, much knowledge of HR issues and practices, and their implementation, is tacit and difficult to gather through non-experiential learning. Knowing where to go for expert HR knowledge is also a valuable resource, as we will explore later in the chapter; and as Klaas et al. (2012) point out, small firm owner managers will vary greatly in this regard, in ways which are likely to impact on their approach to HR matters.

The general point is that experience of HR practice is likely to colour owner-managers' approach to people management challenges when they run their own businesses (Cope and Watts, 2000; Mayson and Barrett, 2017), and the nature of this experience is likely to impact on whether or not this leads to the sophisticated and progressive practice, that is, well designed to deliver mutual gains and enhanced performance, advocated by strategic HRM (Atkinson and Lucas, 2013). More specifically, there is a developing body of evidence that the presence of HR expertise and experience amongst owner-managers is associated with the adoption of HR practices and effective HR systems (Georgiadis and Pitelis, 2012; Klaas et al., 2012). Mazzarol (2003), in his case study analysis of the role of HR practices in small firm growth, identified management experience and education level as two of the key influences in developing HR policy and practice to support growth, though recognising that the nature of their influence can be indirect, working through impact on the company structure and the nature of the work environment. Likewise, Newman and Sheikh (2014: 424) found that 'managerial experience and educational background [of the chief executive officer] has some influence over the adoption of good HR practices in small firms'. On the other side of the coin, Nankervis et al. (2002) discovered a lack of awareness and understanding among small firm owner-managers of a potential strategic and transformational role for HR, focusing instead on its administrative support function.

Owner-Manager Ideologies

A further factor that has been identified as influencing small firm owner-managers' approaches to HR is their ideology towards managing people, and the values that underpin that (Combs et al., 2018; Jaouen and Lasch, 2015; Marlow et al., 2010; Mayson and Barrett, 2017; Tocher and Rutherford, 2009). While in a larger firm, organisational values are likely to shape HR practice, in smaller organisations these shaping values are likely to be those of the owner-manager (Jaouen and Lasch, 2015; Lai et al., 2017; Marlow et al., 2010). These values may be influenced by previous management or organisational experience, or management education (see above), but are more likely to be influenced by the wider life experiences and value systems of the owner-manager and are thus likely to be highly idiosyncratic. Disparate perceptual frameworks serve as a lens through which small firm owner-managers configure and operationalise employment systems.

A number of writers have explored how owner-managers' attitudes and values impact on the approach to HR within the firm. Both Messersmith and Wales (2013), and Mazzarol (2003), point to the importance of an owner-manager orientation towards, or commitment to, regarding employees as partners in the business in shaping HR systems that support growth. Doherty and Norton (2013) show, in their case study of a UK bakery, how the values and ideology of the managing director were key drivers to the development of good HR practice. They speak of the 'dynamism and values of the owner' (ibid.: 143) and of the 'particular form of "tough love" that he has created in the business' (ibid.: 140), which finds its expression in a suite of HR policies and practices. Ho et al. (2010) showed how the influence and role of the chief executive officer (CEO) had an impact on the range of HR practice in the biotech sector in New Zealand, and Garavan et al. (2016) reported that the nature of development programmes was strongly shaped by owner-manager attitudes.

A further factor that is likely to impact on the approach of an owner-manager to managing people is the nature of the enterprise and their rationale for being in business. Owner-manager motivations for establishing their businesses have significant impact on their approaches to people management. Owner-managers predominantly influenced by opportunity entrepreneurial motivation mostly harbour aspirations beyond just survival when they venture into business (Dahwa, 2019; Farmer, 2011; Kautonen, 2015). Consequently, notwithstanding their preference for control and independence, because of their more growth- and wealth-oriented strategic aspirations, they are often favourably disposed to adopt formal or progressive HR practices. Such owner-managers of small firms tend to consider employees as a strategic resource critical for business growth, and invest resources and expertise in them. For example, Kroon et al. (2013) found a relationship between the entrepreneurial orientation of the owner-manager (associated with risk-taking, proactivity and an orientation towards growth) and the adoption of HR practices. However, not all owner-managers start their enterprises with an intention to grow. Those who enter business involuntarily (for example, as a result of redundancy), or who have a 'lifestyle' business, may be driven by different imperatives, for example survival or sustainability (Harney and Alkhalaf, 2020), and may be less inclined to invest in the development of the human resource, or inclined to invest in it in different ways.

Family-Owned Small Firms

Finally, many small firms are family owned. A study by the Office for National Statistics in the UK (ONS, 2017) found that family-owned and family-run SMEs were less likely than other firms to have formal management practices, and were on average less productive. The relative lack of investment in formal HR practices may result in part from the focus on meeting family legacy concerns as opposed to following a growth agenda. It may also be that the formalisation is perceived to cut across the family relationships and hierarchies within the firm, and in some cases impinge on the freedom to follow through a pro-family agenda in, for example, recruitment and progression (Aparicio et al., 2017; Basco, 2014; Combs et al., 2018; Dahwa, 2019; Fang et al., 2016; Firfiray et al., 2018). Family discourses may also foster paternalistic management styles and exacerbate the impact of owner-manager autonomy (Holliday, 1995). That said, recent research indicates that some family firms are more likely to adopt formal HR practices than others (Steijvers et al., 2017). Unsurprisingly, given the foregoing discussion, the identity and background of the owner-manager was key. Firms with a CEO who was a family member, and those with a more highly educated CEO, were found to be more likely to have adopted formal HR practices.

In summary, we have so far outlined why current models of HR implementation that rely on an HR manager/line manager division might not apply in small firms, and the key influence of the owner-manager on HR in small firms. In the remainder of the chapter, we illustrate these issues in more detail using data from two recent research studies that we have conducted.

IMPLEMENTATION OF HR PRACTICE IN SMALL FIRMS

First, in this section, we use the third author's, Dahwa (2019) PhD study to offer insight into owner-manager perspectives on people management in small firms; second, we draw on the first and second authors', Atkinson and Lupton, evaluation of a project that offered HR support services to small firms to illustrate how design and implementation of HR practices operate in this context (Atkinson et al., 2017).

Owner-Manager Perspectives on People Management in Small Firms

Dahwa's (2019) study confirms the above discussion on how owner-manager background and perspectives influence HR practice in small firms and contribute to its diversity (e.g. also Basco, 2014; Combs et al., 2018; Jaouen and Lasch, 2015; Lai et al., 2017; Mallett and Wapshott, 2016; Marlow et al., 2010; Mayson and Barrett, 2017; Nolan and Garavan, 2016). Dahwa conducted in-depth interviews with 29 SME owner-managers in the north-west of England between 2016 and 2018, exploring their attitudes and approaches to managing people, and the experiences and circumstances that influenced them. Firms in a range of sectors were represented in the study, and the owner-managers were diverse in gender and ethnicity and had varying levels of experience in business. Drawing on this data, we illustrate four key factors identified in the preceding discussion – knowledge and expertise, ideology and values, business entrance and aspirations, and family involvement – and support these with quotes that use pseudonyms to ensure confidentiality and anonymity.

Owner-manager knowledge and expertise

Dahwa's study showed that perceptions about people management tended to flow from the level of knowledge and understanding of the small firm owner-managers. One respondent, Anna, acknowledged difficulties with performance appraisal and employment law. Another, Hendricks, expressed his limited knowledge about managing people and his uncertainty about how to use recruitment criteria. Pedro was open about his lack of understanding of people management and the employment law: 'I don't know anything about it' (see Timming, 2011). In contrast, there were several small firm owner-managers in the study who were clear about what people management entailed. For example, Gilbert described listening to and understanding employees, training them, motivating them and rewarding them. What also emerged in these owner-managers' discourses was the need for a 'vision' (Clayton), 'management structure' (Enock), 'policy and procedures' (David) and 'treating them [employees] with respect' (Lloyd), suggesting that at least certain aspects of formal HR were to be found in these small firms.

Small firms' owner-managers drew their knowledge and general understanding about people management from two main sources: their education and experience (Klaas et al., 2012; Newman and Sheikh, 2014). Through education, they acquired foundational knowledge and understanding about people issues, and those that undertook higher education built on that with more academic knowledge. Further, their experience as employees offered practical experience of the work environment and of larger firm approaches. Some owner-managers had run multiple businesses and gained people management experience in these. Dahwa concluded from his analysis that small firm owner-managers with limited experience in managing people and/or limited educational knowledge of HRM tended to avoid formal HR practices. Hendricks, for example, had few educational qualifications, having no management experience during his career, and relied mostly on informal people management approaches. This changed when he recruited a degree-level educated operations director with industrial experience who introduced formal HR practices: 'Our Ops Director helped us to put up all those things [formal HR practices] ... He likes structure' (Hendricks). Here particularly, recruitment processes had been improved and even psychometric tests introduced.

Another important influence was the nature of previous people management experiences. For example, if these had been unpleasant, owner-managers tended to be reluctant to take on employees and the challenges of managing them. Ken, for example, had been frustrated, when working for his friend, by the employment relations and working conditions that he experienced. He started his own business and was adamant that he would not recruit employees, but just work alone. In summary, higher education and positive people management experience tended to encourage owner-managers of small firms to embrace (some) formal HRM practices (Dahwa, 2019).

People management ideology and values
Dahwa (2019) also found evidence that owner-managers' approach to people management drew on their idiosyncratic, subjective perceptions and interpretations about employment matters. Those owner-managers who were predominantly positively disposed towards employing people and confident in managing them tended to work towards engaging employees through 'good' management:

> I like them [employees], I don't want them to leave because I like them … then the month end meetings is our way of reminding people on what we do where we are … we try and make sure our people are listened to … nearly everybody in the office earns above us. So the more work they do the more bonus. Before the Financial Conduct Authority came into being, we had already decided that we are going to train … investing in people. (Gilbert)

Gilbert was an example of a small firm owner-manager who did not just perceive employees positively, but strongly believed that without employees the firm could not achieve its aspirations. Such owner-managers tended to be more receptive to formal HR practices such as monthly team briefings, involving their employees, motivating and rewarding them. In contrast, small firm owner-managers who held more negative perceptions about employees and the challenges of managing them often preferred either not to recruit employees, or to outsource to contractors when the need arose for particular critical skills. Here, Anna lists a number of concerns around managing people that underlay her reluctance to take on employees: 'finding the right person … having people working for you, it takes that control away … having to do the review … the employment contract. You never know … ever changing … you just don't know … its difficult … the expenses keep on' (Anna).

Dahwa (2019) further evidenced how personal values were pivotal during both shaping the approach to managing people and the enactment of HRM practices. Many small firm owner-managers stressed that they were in business to 'do it for themselves and by themselves' and taking on employees was not within their scheme of things: '[why getting into business, how to operate it and with whom] was a question of doing it for myself … so that my life could go and move forward' (Joe).

Upon further probing, Joe revealed a desire for 'flexibility and freedom' and to live the 'lifestyle' he wished for. Most owner-managers with similar views avoided adopting formal HR practices. In contrast, numerous small firm owner-managers, such as Gilbert (above), valued employees as crucial in achieving their aspirations and sought to effectively recruit and retain employees. Values again influenced day-to-day relations with employees; Gilbert, for example, allowed employees to share their views through staff meetings and rewarded them with bonuses. Gilbert explained how he still wanted to support employees even where they engaged in inappropriate behaviours: 'because people [employees] have got mortgages to pay and you don't want to do that [fire employees] to somebody if you can help it' (Gilbert).

Similarly, Riccardo acknowledged having a set of 'Christian values' that shaped his approach to people management and went on to mention how because of his Christian faith he strove to build very strong close relationships with his employees: 'I have always had a reputation for not only getting to know the member of staff, but I often know about their family about their kids' (Riccardo).

Similarly to Gilbert, Riccardo indicated that, due to the 'loyalties' he had with his employees and the underlying Christian values, he found it very difficult to institute disciplinary action. Most small firm owner-managers who recruited employees valued closer interpersonal relationships, which they considered crucial in building trust and loyalty. Their rationale was that trust and loyalty was a more cost-effective strategy for employee motivation, empowerment and involvement than most prescriptions of formal HRM practices, which required money and expertise.

Business entrance and aspirations

Owner-manager motivations for establishing their businesses had significant impact on their approaches to people management (Harney and Alkhalaf, 2020). Both 'opportunity' and 'necessity' entrepreneurial motivations (Williams and Williams, 2012) – that is, reflecting the contrast between owner manager who 'choose' to go into business and those who drawn into it by circumstance – were evidenced. Those influenced by opportunity entrepreneurial motivation harboured aspirations beyond just survival when they ventured into business: 'there was an element of money, financial motivation in there as well thinking of making money, becoming a millionaire' (Calvin).

Notably, those who came voluntarily into business tended to feel this desire quite early during their upbringing or while in college or high school: 'so, I was always of the mind of doing my own thing [growing up and further impressed this desire during university studies] … I just knew I was going to work for myself' (Ashok).

What was also important about this opportunity entrepreneurial motivation was that owner-managers drew on their prior acceptance of risk associated with operating a business, including the risks associated with managing people. Even where they lacked competency in people management, where the costs seemed high or employment law not favourable, or where they experienced difficulties with employees, they were not deterred. Their voluntary entrance into business, and pursuit of aspirations beyond survival, meant that they were willing to acquire knowledge and adapt their approach to employment to fit the context: 'So, I went back [to university on an SME development programme] as well after that course. I implemented more policies, implemented you know different procedures' (Derrick).

Dahwa found that those small firm owner-managers who went voluntarily into business and were driven by beyond-survival aspirations tended to embrace some formal HR practices, alongside the informal approach more typical of small firms. This contrasted sharply with how small firm owner-managers who were entered into business through necessity rather than choice tended to approach people management. These 'necessity' owner-managers emphasised survival as their major aspiration, and this tended not to be associated with the adoption of more formal HR practices. Redundancy was often a key driver for business establishment, as was the case with, Anna, who was made redundant from her role in a major bank: 'Because I have been out of work for a long time nobody wanted to employ me … I needed some money from somewhere … so I started my own business' (Anna).

Anna's motivation was to do what was necessary to support her family. Growing the business was not a key driver for her, and in this context taking on employees, and the management tasks associated with that, was an unnecessary burden. Indeed, many small firm owner-managers in Dahwa's study who adopted a survival aspiration also adopted the 'it just has to be only me' mantra, which then precluded adoption of formal HR practices. Survival motives, however, were often incompatible with recruiting employees at all, as Ken opined: '[I] decided I didn't want any employees any more, it just had to be only me' (Ken).

However, Ken was also driven in this view by his negative experiences of managing under-performing employees in a previous information technology business. Managing employees was a 'hassle' for Ken, and he took the decision not to do it in his second business.

The influences of both opportunity and necessity entrepreneurial motivation on owner managers' choices are well documented in research (Farmer, 2011; Kautonen, 2015). While voluntary entrance into business tended to lead to greater propensity to take on employees and adopt some formal HRM practices, the reverse was the case for involuntary business operators who mostly preferred working alone.

Family involvement

The role of family was a very important factor that influenced people management in the small firms in Dahwa's study. In narrating their business life stories, most owner-managers reflected on the implications of their business journeys for their families. Apart from seeking to look after their families (see Anna above), several small firm owner-managers also brought in family members in management roles or as employees. This had a significant impact on people management. Shelton recounted how he was employed as a managing director by his father-in-law. His father-in-law later brought his youngest son, Hendricks, into the business, and Shelton found himself by-passed: 'but I must point out that Hendricks was a golden boy; so, this is what I said; blood is thicker than water' (Shelton).

Robert was driven by a desire to keep his business in the family in the next generation. 'This particular business, here, I would like to hold on to it, I would love it to stay in the family … especially my son, it would be better.' Robert recruited his son as chief finance officer, rather than a fully qualified 'outsider', and even though he reported that he had adopted some formal HR practices in the firm, his narrative was coloured by reminders that the business is a family business, and that his son must and will ultimately take over from him.

As Shelton's and Robert's cases illustrate, the work environment of family-owned small firms can often afford preferential treatment to family employees, cutting across formal management structures. Dominant family interests and loyalties of owner-managers in small family firms tended to work against formal HR practices, whose execution implied neutral treatment and went against the cherished 'blood is thicker than water' family and work ethos.

In summary, Dahwa (2019) argues that HR practice in small firms is diverse and heavily influenced by the owner-manager's values about people relations, perceptions about employees and managing them. He evidences a constellation of key drivers for HRM in small firms, including business motivation, people management perception, people management knowledge/understanding, values and family involvement. He argues that these lead to three broad people management approaches by owner-managers. First, those who prefer to work alone, avoiding people management issues and especially the need for compliance with employment law, and who outsource work to contractors when necessary. Second, those owner-managers who have a largely informal approach to managing people, but embrace some formal HRM practice where necessary. This is most often adopted by small firm owner-managers who enter voluntarily into business and hold positive perceptions about employees and managing them. Third, those owner-managers who emphasise the 'family' nature of their business, whose dictum of 'blood is thicker than water' tends to work against the adoption of formal HR practices. Of these three people management approaches, Dahwa (2019) argues that adopting formal HR practices while allowing for some informality in people management presents most opportunities for business growth, employment creation with job security, and enhanced socio-economic development. Dahwa goes on to argue that supporting owner-managers to adopt strategies to further buttress employee productivity within this approach is important, and requires innovative and effective people management capacity-building interventions that allow for the idiosyncratic differences of the owner-managers concerned. He suggests that policy-makers, academia and industry need to foster effective ways to stimulate a people management mindset for survivalist owner-managers of small firms. The rationale is to strive to ensure a growing population of owner-managers who shift from being largely negative about employees and managing them to holding more positive perceptions and desiring more to grow through the creation of permanent jobs. Similarly, there is need to find novel solutions to support owner-managers of small family firms to engage more non-family employees and upscale their businesses while still retaining their shareholding and being true to their family legacies (Dahwa, 2019).

Dahwa's (2019) study thus identifies the need for HR support for small firm owner-managers, but stops at that point. We now continue to report a second study that we conducted (Atkinson et al., 2017), which considers in detail what and how such support could be offered, and to what effect.

HR SUPPORT FOR SMALL FIRM OWNER-MANAGERS

As we noted at the outset of the chapter, the absence of an HR department or specialist is a particular concern in that it compromises the ability of small firms to design and implement effective HR practice. Dahwa's study presented further evidence of how HR practice can then often be lacking or absent in small firms. Both raise the question of how to support owner-managers in their people management endeavours. Given the previously discussed importance of small firms to national economies, this has become a focus of substantial interest to policy-makers. Indeed, as Webber et al. (2010) note, the provision of effective advice has become a cornerstone of government policy across the world (OECD, 2017). It is important to note, however, that policy will vary by country, and we report here on support for small firms in the UK context.

The UK has a mixed economy of government and independently provided business support services. The latter include consultancy and professional service firms, but concern over market failure in this provision (Johnson et al., 2007) has led to increasing levels of state-funded support services (Mole et al., 2017). This comes mainly through Local Enterprise Partnerships (LEPs), which are partnerships between local authorities and business to promote local economic growth and job creation, and the associated Growth Hubs, which are particularly focused on supporting SMEs and helping them to grow and create new employment.[1] Brown and Mawson (2016) note, however, that much of this support is aimed at providing start-up businesses with access to support in relation to finance, investment and exports, to address deficits in their resources in these areas. Take-up of these services is often limited, however, with Mole et al. (2017) suggesting that less than half of SMEs in their study accessed them across a three-year period. A further concern is that these support services rarely have a specific focus on people management/HR matters. This would appear to be a missed opportunity, given the well-established relationships between HR and performance (Jiang et al., 2012), with growing evidence that these relationships hold good in SMEs (Harney and Alkhalaf, 2020). This begs the question of the extent to which a shift in policy focus is needed to support effective HR practice in small firms.

We discuss here findings from our evaluation of a Chartered Institute of Personnel and Development (CIPD) project, People Skills, designed to tackle this issue by delivering free advice on people management to small firm owner-managers (Atkinson et al., 2017). Data in this section is taken from that report. Through the project, independent HR consultants worked on a one-to-one basis with owner-managers to design HR interventions that identified and addressed people issues in the firm. Consultants essentially operated as an external HR department, providing more effective advice than the solicitors or accountants that SMEs often rely on for HR advice (Kitching, 2016). Wu et al. (2015) also argue that external advisors are more likely to create uptake of HR practice than internal ones in small firms, so again the project offered great potential to change practice.

HR consultants worked with firms to develop deeper understanding of their needs over a period of time, to support the design and implementation of bespoke HR interventions. These interventions were wide-ranging in nature. Many worked on basic matters such as employment contracts and handbooks, but found these really beneficial. Participants suggested that prior to getting support their HR practice had been 'knee jerk and chaotic' and that they had not known what they were doing. The support put them 'on a secure footing' gave them a 'suit of armour' and was 'an absolute life saver'. Getting the basics right also helped to develop more sophisticated HR practice. One small firm that began working with the project to address its employment contracts, for example, eventually went on to develop and introduce a new performance management system; and another similarly moved from basic HR work to focus on line manager training and development. One even set up a learning academy to train its own apprentices, and attached pay and performance structures to this, which was considered a 'massive achievement'. Vignettes of the case study firms and the HR practices they introduced can be found in Atkinson et al. (2017). The conclusion drawn was that HR practice is possible and beneficial in small firms, but that it might look different to larger firms.

The important role of HR support in promoting uptake of HR practice in these small firms was clear. In a survey comparison between small firms that had taken part in the project and those that had not, participants were more likely to have invested in training and development in the past year, to feel that this was money well spent, and that this had improved key business metrics. While a small sample, the support seemed to have developed positive attitudes to HR matters, which are often lacking in small firms. One owner-manager, for example, suggested: [The People Skills consultant] taught me so much about HR that I never knew, and I'm sure

---

[1]   https://www.gov.uk/government/news/full-network-of-39-growth-hubs-boost-business-support -across-the-country.

that there are hundreds and thousands of businesses around England that are just the same.' The project team were also proud of the impact of the project, despite 'ups and downs'. The project manager argued: 'Those engaged with the programme have had a positive experience and got lots of value from it. They've had their eyes opened from this which is great. Providing this support to SMEs makes a big difference, adds value, helps them grow and be better.'

Uptake of support was, however, relatively low and we consider in what follows some of the reasons for this, the implications and how this might inform a future research agenda.

FUTURE RESEARCH AGENDA AND POLICY IMPLICATIONS

As we noted at the outset, a typical large firm model of HR implementation presumes a specialist HR department that delivers effective HR practices appropriate to that environment, and works with line managers to convince them of the benefit of their implementation. Indeed, line managers are generally required by their employing organisations to implement these policies (albeit evidence shows that they can do this more or less effectively). No such imperative exists in small firms. Our research suggests a need for better understanding of why owner-managers engage (or do not) with HR support, in relation to awareness levels and readiness to engage in order to promote more effective, sector-appropriate HR practice.

Awareness of HR and HR support services

Awareness of the benefits of HR is often lacking, as our findings demonstrate: owner-managers were typically time-poor and could readily see the need for finance and marketing, but not HR. People matters did not come high up the 'to do' list, as noted by the project manager: 'Some owner managers absolutely get it and do it effortlessly but for others, they rumble on with endless challenges and headaches because of the lack of support and understanding that you can improve how you manage people and it becomes easier and better.'

Many thought that HR was only formal policies and procedures, and did not appreciate the wider value of good people management and its strategic contribution. Many owner-managers also had a focus simply on survival, and that precluded consideration of anything more strategic. Lack of a strategic approach meant many owner managers engaged with support for a particular issue, often operational; for example, contracts of employment or maternity leave. Often once the issue was resolved, engagement ended. Some disengaged once a solution had been suggested as they perceived it to be too big a job; for example, one firm that was advised to harmonise terms and conditions and simply felt unable to address this, given wider pressures.

Lack of engagement also related in large part to lack of awareness of the HR support itself, given the fragmented nature of small firms' support services, and owner-managers who often did not know where to turn (Mallet and Wapshott, 2016 found similar). Attracting their attention was also very difficult. Traditional means (for example, leaflets, emails, social media) had limited success, and more innovative methods, such as seminars on topics of interest (for example, employment law, employee engagement) were more successfully used as a means to promote the project, with information being provided during the seminar. Partner networks were also vital in generating engagement; the locations where partners were deeply embedded and offered existing services with strong small firm relationships being much more successful in generating engagement than where this was not the case. This, however, did mean that hard-to-reach small firms remained elusive. Word of mouth was also important, from both HR consultant and owner-manager networks, as the more formal channels could be off-putting to small firms, but took time to build. While the project could operate as an external HR department, creating awareness of this and understanding of its benefit was a substantial challenge, particularly for hard-to-reach firms.

More research is needed into both how to create owner-manager awareness of the benefits of HR practice and how to generate their engagement with what support exists. Traditional leadership and management programmes, often offered to small firm owner-managers through Growth Hubs, are an obvious way to do this. In other research (Atkinson and Lupton, 2019), however, we have noted that such programmes over a number of decades seem to have had limited effect in creating this understanding. In that research, we have argued that creating communities of practice in which small firm owner-managers build networks with those who can communicate and reinforce the value of good HR practice (often from larger firms) are an important additional mechanism through which to generate a perceived need for support. Further research will be important for policy-makers seeking to design support services that offer maximum benefit.

Readiness to Engage

There has been very little research into why small firm owner-managers introduce HR. In their recent paper on strategic HRM in SMEs, Harney and Alkhalaf (2020) suggest that it is often introduced in small firms as a result of what they refer to as 'presenting issues'. These include: changes of ownership, succession, introduction of professional managers, declining performance, corporate shocks, intensified competition, venture capital influence, and the perception of HR as a problem or challenge. This has resonance with our work, in relation to why small firms engaged with the HR support service and then went on to introduce HR interventions. We identified five main 'cues' (Atkinson et al., 2022).

First was a perceived need for HR (discussed above) and second was the capacity to work with HR advisors. To an extent this relates to time pressures noted earlier, but an important factor that we identified was understanding and confidence. For example, one owner-manager suggested that he had not learnt anything about HR in his architecture training and that the project support had given him the confidence to work with the consultants to address HR matters. Second, the confidence that the planned interventions were feasible was also a strong influence as to whether owner-managers moved from taking advice to implementing it.

Third, small firm owner-managers often preferred to work in a relatively informal manner, but the uptake of HR practice generally requires a more formalised approach. As small firms grow, many owner-managers recognise the need for more formality and this was so in our evaluation: 'When we were small, we perhaps let things lapse. Now we've got bigger [HR consultant] has helped us set it up for the future ... Handbooks and things like that. It's really helpful.' Despite this, there was an ongoing preference for informality and a desire to balance the two so that, as one owner-manager said, they could 'keep the fun'. As Harney and Dundon (2006) assert, the enactment of HR practice is as important as its form, and we argue that too little is known about the dynamics of formality in small firms.

A fourth factor was previous large firm experience, where it was notable that many of the small firm owner-managers who engaged with HR support did so based on their experience in larger firms where they were used to having policy and practice to guide them. Without this, they felt vulnerable and exposed to people management risks. This plays into our earlier suggestion about the benefit of communities of practice in which those from large firms can share experience and knowledge with those from smaller firms.

Finally, change in ownership impacted upon willingness to take up HR support. In several family firms, new family members had joined and, with a fresh pair of eyes, had seen a need for change and sought to disrupt the status quo. In some cases, these family members had come from larger firms and brought that experience with them. This often created tensions in the leadership team, with one using the project to attempt to challenge a mentality that 'we don't have to do that [good employment practice], we're only a wee business'. Similarly, in one firm that had been bought out and had a new owner-manager, project support was used to leverage change and increased formalisation.

Again, understanding of small firm owner-managers' readiness to engage with HR practice and support is at its very early stages. More research is needed into these presenting issues or cues, and these insights will be important in informing effective policy responses.

CONCLUSIONS

We began the chapter by arguing that current models of HR implementation assume a large firm model predicated on an internal HR department and a professional line management structure. In what followed, we have demonstrated that this is a model that is unlikely to hold good for many small firms. These are typically run by owner-managers whose perspectives on people management are influential, wide-ranging and varied, and not dictated by a centralised department. They often lack expertise, are unsure where to find support and, even where support is identified, are unable or unwilling to access it, work with it and implement its recommendations. Yet we have demonstrated that in certain circumstances HR can be implemented to good effect in small firms, even if on different terms to larger firms. Our discussion is confined to small firm owner-managers, who are, of course, a very specific form of line manager. Some of our findings, however, may have wider resonance. For example, many frontline managers face heavy workloads in delivery of their remits, are usually not HR specialists, and often lack confidence in, and awareness and understanding of, HR practice and where to obtain support. While they may differ to those in small firms, mechanisms to generate awareness, understanding and confidence, and to ensure ready access to internal HR support, will be important in delivering effective HR practice even in larger firms.

The research reported in this chapter is important, given the contribution of small firms to national economies, and has implications for policy, practice and theory. For policy-makers, dedicated HR support services have the potential to make a valuable contribution to small firm operations, operating as an external HR department, but attention is needed to the design and communication of these services. Novel approaches to awareness-raising are needed to complement existing leadership and management training programmes. Creating an owner-manager readiness to engage with services and implement HR practices is vital if HR is to make its potential contribution to the performance of this sector. In terms of practice, we have shown that investment in HR practice in small firms is valuable and can reap dividends, even if only a single or a few practices are used and these are 'light touch' in formality. Different approaches can be effective in the small firm sector. Finally, we have evidenced that more nuanced theories of HR implementation are needed to capture the complexities of the small firm context, and call on researchers to pay attention to developing appropriate models.

REFERENCES

Aparicio, G., Basco, R., Iturralde, T. and Maseda, A. (2017) 'An exploratory study of firm goals in the context of family firms: An institutional logics perspective'. *Journal of Family Business Strategy*, 8 pp. 157–169.

Atkinson, C. and Lucas, R. (2013) Worker responses to HR practice in adult social care in England. *Human Resource Management Journal,* 23 pp. 296–312.

Atkinson, C. and Lupton, B. (2019) *Productivity and Place: The Role of LEPs.* London: CIPD.

Atkinson, C., Lupton, B., Kynighou, A. and Antcliff, V. (2022) 'Small firms, owner managers and (strategic?) human resource management'. *Human Resource Management Journal*, 32 pp. 449–469.

Atkinson, C., Lupton, B., Kynighou, A., Antcliff, V. and Carter, J. (2017) *People Skills: Building Ambition and HR Capability in Small UK Firms.* London: CIPD.

Atkinson, C., Wapshott, R. and Mallett, O. (2016) 'You try to be a fair employer: Regulation and employment relationships in medium-sized firms'. *International Small Business Journal*, 34(1) pp. 16–33.

Bacon, N. and Hoque, K. (2005) 'HRM in the SME sector'. *International Journal of Human Resource Management*, 16(11) pp. 1796–1999.

Basco, R. (2014) 'Exploring the influence of the family upon firm performance: Does strategic behaviour matter?' *International Small Business Journal*, 32 pp. 967–995.

Brown, R. and Mawson, S. (2016) 'Targeted support for high growth firms: Theoretical constraints, unintended consequences and future policy challenges'. *Environment and Planning C: Government and Policy*, 34 pp. 816–836.

Cardon, M. and Stevens, C. (2004) 'Managing human resources in small organizations: What do we know?' *Human Resource Management Review*, 14(3) pp. 295–323.

Cassell, C., Nadin, S. and Gray, M. (2001) The use and effectiveness of benchmarking in SMEs. *Benchmarking: An International Journal,* 8 pp. 212–222.

CIPD (2014) *Recruiting and Developing Talented People for SME Growth.* London: CIPD.

Combs, J., Jaskiewicz, P., Shanine, K. and Balkin, D. (2018) 'Making sense of HR in family firms: Antecedents, moderators, and outcomes'. *Human Resource Management Review*, 28 pp. 1–4.

Cope, J. and Watts, G. (2000) 'Learning by doing: An exploration of experience, critical incident and reflection in entrepreneurial learning'. *International Journal of Entrepreneurial Behaviour*, 6(3) pp. 104–124.

Dahwa, C. (2019) Understanding people management in small and medium enterprises: An entrepreneurial learning perspective. PhD, Manchester Metropolitan University.

Doherty, L. and Norton, A. (2013) 'Making and measuring "good" HR practice in an SME: The case of a Yorkshire bakery'. *Employee Relations*, 36(2) pp. 128–147.

EU (2011) SME definition. https://ec.europa.eu/growth/smes/sme-definition_en.

Fang, H.C., Randolph, R.V.D.G., Memili, E. and Chrisman, J.J. (2016) 'Does size matter? The moderating effects of firm size on the employment of nonfamily managers in privately held family SMEs'. *Entrepreneurship: Theory and Practice*, 40(5) pp. 1017–1039.

Farmer, S. (2011) 'The behavioral impact of entrepreneur identity aspiration and prior entrepreneurial experience'. *Entrepreneurship Theory and Practice*, March pp. 245–273.

Firfiray, S., Cruz, C., Neacsu, I. and Gomez-Mejia, L.R. (2018) 'Is nepotism so bad for family firms? A socioemotional wealth approach'. *Human Resource Management Review*, 28(1) pp. 83–97.

Garavan, T., Watson, S., Carbery, R. and O'Brien, F. (2016) 'The antecedents of leadership development practices in SMEs: The influence of HRM strategy and practice'. *International Small Business Journal*, 34(6) pp. 870–890.

Georgiadis, A. and Pitelis, C. (2012) 'Human resources and SME performance in services: Empirical evidence from the UK'. *International Journal of Human Resource Management*, 23(4) pp. 808–818.

Harney, B. and Alkhalaf, H. (2020) 'A quarter-century review of HRM in small and medium-sized enterprises: Capturing what we know, exploring where we need to go'. *Human Resource Management.* DOI: 10.1002/hrm.22010.

Harney, B. and Dundon, T. (2006) 'Capturing complexity: Developing an integrated approach to analysing HRM in SMEs'. *Human Resource Management Journal*, 16(1) pp. 48–73.

Ho, M., Wilson, M. and Chen, S. (2010) 'HRM in New Zealand biotechnology SMEs: Emergence of employment systems through entrepreneurship'. *International Journal of Human Resource Management*, 21(3) pp. 313–336.

Holliday, R. (1995) *Investigation Small Firms: Nice Work?* London: Routledge.

Jaouen, A. and Lasch, F. (2015) 'A new typology of micro-firm owner-managers'. *International Small Business Journal*, 33 pp. 397–421.

Jiang, K., Lepak, D., Hu, J. and Baer, J. (2012) 'How does human resource management influence organizational outcomes? A meta-analytic investigation of mediating mechanisms'. *Academy of Management Journal*, 55(6) pp. 1264–1294.

Johnson, S., Webber, D. and Thomas, W. (2007) 'Which SMEs use external business advice? A multivariate subregional study'. *Environment and Planning A*, 39 pp. 1981–1997.

Jones, O., McPherson, A., Thorpe, R. and Ghecham, A. (2007) 'The evolution of business knowledge in SMEs: conceptualizing strategic space'. *Strategic Choice*, 16 pp. 281–294.

Kautonen, T. (2015) 'Robustness of the theory of planned behavior in predicting entrepreneurial intentions and actions'. *Entrepreneurship Theory and Practice*, 39(3) pp. 655–674.

Kitching, J. (2016) 'Between vulnerable compliance and confident ignorance: Small employers, regulatory discovery practices and external support networks'. *International Small Business Journal*, 34(5) pp. 601–617.

Klaas, B., Semadeni, M., Klimchak, M. and Ward, A. (2012) 'High-performance work system implementation in small and medium enterprises: A knowledge-creation perspective'. *Human Resource Management*, 51(4) pp. 487–510.

Kroon, B., Van De Voorde, K. and Timmers, J. (2013) 'High performance work practices in small firms: a resource-poverty and strategic decision-making perspective'. *Small Business Economics.* 10.1007/s11187-012-9425-0.

Lai, Y., Saridakis, G. and Johnstone, S. (2017) 'Human resource practices, employee attitudes and small firm performance'. *International Small Business Journal*, 35(4) pp. 470–494.

Lopez-Cotarelo, J. (2018) 'Line managers and HRM: A managerial discretion perspective'. *Human Resource Management Journal*, 28 pp. 255–271.

Mallett, O. and Wapshott, R. (2016) Making sense of support for small businesses. Discussion paper.

Marchington, M., Carroll, M. and Boxall, P. (2003) 'Labour scarcity and the survival of small firms'. *Human Resource Management Journal*, 13(4) pp. 5–22.

Marlow, S., Taylor, S. and Thompson, A. (2010) 'Informality and formality in medium-sized companies: Contestation and synchronization'. *British Journal of Management*, 21 pp. 954–966.

Mayson, S. and Barrett, R. (2006) 'The "science" and "practice" of HRM in small firms'. *Human Resource Management Review*, 16(4) pp. 447–455.

Mayson, S. and Barrett, R. (2017) 'A new argument using embeddedness and sensemaking to explain small firms' responses to employment regulation'. *Human Resource Management Journal*, 27(1) pp. 189–202.

Mazzarol, T. (2003) 'A model of small business HR growth management'. *International Journal of Entrepreneurial Behaviour and Research*, 9(1) pp. 27–49.

Messersmith, J. and Wales, W. (2013) 'Entrepreneurial orientation and performance in young firms: The role of human resource management'. *International Small Business Journal*, 31(2) pp. 115–136.

Mole, K., North, D. and Baldock, R. (2017) 'Which SMEs seek external support? Business characteristics, management behaviour and external influences in a contingency approach'. *Environment and Planning C*, 35(3) pp. 476–499.

Nankervis, A., Compton, R. and Savery, L. (2002) 'Strategic HRM in small and medium enterprises: A CEO's perspective?' *Asia Pacific Journal of Human Resources*, 40(2) pp. 260–273.

Newman, A. and Sheikh, A. (2014) 'Determinants of best HR practices in Chinese SMEs'. *Journal of Small Business and Enterprise Development*, 21(3) pp. 414–430.

Nishii, L., Lepak, D. and Scheider, B. (2008) 'Employee attributions about the "why" of HR practices: Their effects on employee attitudes and behaviours and customer satisfaction'. *Personnel Psychology*, 61(3) pp. 503–545.

Nolan, C. and Garavan, T. (2016) 'Human resource development in SMEs: A systematic review of the literature'. *International Journal of Management Reviews*, 18(1) pp. 85–107.

OECD (2017) *Enhancing the Contributions of SMEs in a Global and Digitalised Economy*. https://www.oecd.org/industry/C-MIN-2017-8-EN.pdf: OECD.

ONS (2017) 'Management practices and productivity among manufacturing businesses in Great Britain: Experimental estimates for 2015'. https://www.ons.gov.uk/employmentandlabourmarket/peopleinwork/labourproductivity/articles/experimentaldataonthemanagementpracticesofmanufacturingbusinessesingreatbritain/experimentalestimatesfor2015.

Purcell, J. and Hutchinson, S. (2007) 'Front line managers as agents in the HRM–performance causal chain: Theory, analysis and evidence'. *Human Resource Management Journal*, 17(1) pp. 3–20.

Razouk, A. (2011) 'High-performance work systems and performance of French small- and medium-sized enterprises: examining causal order'. *International Journal of Human Resource Management*, 22(2) pp. 311–330.

Sheehan, M. (2014) 'Human resource management and performance: Evidence from small and medium-sized firms'. *International Small Business Journal*, 32(5) pp. 545–570.

Steijvers, T., Lybaert, N. and Dekker, J. (2017) 'Formal human resource practices in family firms'. *Journal of Family Business Management*, 7(2) pp. 151–165.

Timming, A. (2011) 'What do tattoo artists know about HRM? Recruitment and selection in the body art sector'. *Employee Relations*, 33(5) pp. 570–584.

Tocher, M. and Rutherford, N. (2009) 'Perceived acute HRM problems in SMEs: An empirical examination'. *Entrepreneurship: Theory and Practice*, 33 pp. 455–479.

Townsend, K., Wilkinson, A., Allan, C. and Bamber, G. (2012) Mixed signals in HRM: The HRM role of hospital line managers. *Human Resource Management Journal*, 22, 267–282.

Trullen, J., Bos-Nehles, A. and Valverde, M. (2020) 'From intended to actual and beyond: A cross-disciplinary view of (human resource management) implementation'. *International Journal of Management Reviews*, 22 pp. 150–176.

Trullen, J., Stirpe, L., Bonache, J. and Valverde, M. (2016) 'The HR department's contribution to line managers' effective implementation of HR practices'. *Human Resource Management Journal*, 26 pp. 449–470.

Verreynne, M.-L., Parker, P. and Wilson, M. (2013) 'Employment systems in small firms: A multilevel analysis'. *International Small Business Journal*, 31(4) pp. 405–431.

Webber, D., Johnson, S. and Fargher, S. (2010) 'Sector variations in SMEs' use of business advice'. *Local Economy*, 25(4) pp. 339–355.

Wilkinson, A. (1999) 'Employment relations in SMEs'. *Employee Relations*, 21(3) pp. 206–217.

Williams, N. and Williams, C. (2012) 'Evaluating the socio-spatial contingency of entrepreneurial motivations: A case study of English deprived urban neighbourhoods'. *Entrepreneurship and Regional Development*, 24 pp. 661–684.

Woodhams, C. and Lupton, B. (2006) 'Does size matter? Gender based equal opportunity in UK small and medium enterprises'. *Women in Management Review*, 21(2) pp. 143–169.

Wu, N., Hoque, K., Bacon, N. and Bou Llusar, J. (2015) 'High-performance work systems and workplace performance in small, medium-sized and large firms'. *Human Resource Management Journal*, 25(4) pp. 408–423.

13. The debateable leadership role of frontline managers

Keith Townsend, Ashlea Troth and Rebecca Loudoun

INTRODUCTION

Scholarship interest in leadership has grown to the point where the need for leadership is an assumed element of any role that involves managing people in the workplace (House and Aditya, 1997; Day et al., 2014). What remains under debate and discussion is the type of leadership behaviour most effective under different contextual circumstances and, in the workplace, the hierarchical level of the leader involved. Dinh et al. (2014) review the breadth of scholarly discussion and theoretical development in leadership, a total of 752 articles across ten journals between 2000 and 2012. They draw attention to the many well-established theories such as transformational leadership and leader–member exchange (LMX) and, additionally, point to emerging theories such as authentic and neurological perspectives on leadership. While most of the leadership research is focused on senior leaders or a more generic individual holding a position of seniority over others, there is often a presumption that the frontline manager (FLM) position embodies some aspects of leadership. Alvesson and Willmott (2012), though, point to the fact that there is rarely any evidence to support that presumption. In this chapter, we seek to better understand the leadership role and opportunities of FLMs.

For decades, FLMs have been neglected as a focus of research, returning to centre stage as a topic for investigation in the last 15 years. In leadership research, FLMs are typically overlooked, with the focus more on senior leaders. In human resource management (HRM) research, their leadership role is often disregarded in favour of a focus on HR policy implementation with the FLM viewed as a key player but one who is directed to implement policy rather than lead it. Consequently there remains limited consideration and knowledge of any leadership role that FLMs might play in the workplace. Developing theories that relate to this level of the organisational hierarchy is important, as it is well established within the broad people management literature (including HRM) that FLMs typically directly manage the greatest number of people in a workplace compared to any other leadership position. There is growing recognition of leadership as part of the FLM role, as modern organisations delayer and decentralise traditional human resources (HR) functions (Priestland and Hanig, 2005). Frontline managers play an important role between the senior managers and the HR office and generating performance from their subordinate employees; but is this leadership? We propose the conceptualisation of FLM leadership pillars as a means to understand, theoretically, this additional layer of leadership activity specific to FLMs.

This chapter proceeds as follows. First, we provide targeted reviews of three bodies of literature. We begin with the literature specific to the frontline manager, followed by literature on role theory and leadership respectively. This is followed by a description of the research design and methodology used in the present study. We then consider our FLMs' perceptions of their various managerial and leadership roles, as well as any challenges they perceive in reconciling these different responsibilities. Finally, we present a conceptual model of the pillars of FLM leadership.

THE FRONTLINE MANAGER

Developing the way we understand the role of FLMs, the way they perform their role, and how they might balance their place in the organization, has been slow compared with research on leaders (Hales, 2005). When the FLM is considered explicitly there is often a presumption that they are a leader without any evidence to support that presumption (Alvesson and Willmott, 2012). They hold a critical place in organisations, wedged between the longer-term strategic goals of senior managers and the immediate operational requirements of floor staff (Townsend and Russell, 2013). While this 'wedged' position is also the case for middle managers, there is an increased importance of the FLM for employees. The person in the FLM role is the first level of managerial personnel, and holds more general staff within their immediate purview and is thus more likely to oversee staff on a daily basis (Nehles et al., 2006).

Individuals have often been a technical or operational experts before being promoted to the managerial roles they hold (Hutchinson and Purcell, 2010; Townsend et al., 2012). Our interest lies in understanding if there is a difference between the management and leadership activities of the FLM, and if so, how they might co-exist. Leadership is about motivating and creating a common vision (Weathersby, 1999); while managers are typically assigned to organise, delegate and implement the vision that leaders have communicated to them. Based on this division, management appears to be a more structured and measurable activity, while leadership is fluid and about influence. If indeed the frontline manager is also a frontline leader, then they would inhabit, in hierarchical terms, the lowest-level leadership position within the organisation. So, if it is leadership, how might it differ from higher levels of leadership? In this chapter, we offer a theoretical contribution of the ways in which FLMs engage in leadership activities specific to their FLM role, built upon a base of operational and managerial responsibilities. This is important, because if organisations rely upon FLMs to be leaders then our expectations of what this requires must feed in to recruitment criteria, performance management processes and, indeed, rewards. Role theory has often been used in the past for FLM research (see, e.g., Evans, Chapter 4 in this book) and we use this as our framework to understand the roles of the FLM and the way people in these roles have the capacity, and willingness, to engage in leadership behaviours. We expand our knowledge in leadership theory by understanding what types of leadership behaviours frontline managers engage in throughout their workday.

There is a substantial body of organizational behavior literature that examines supervisors through social exchange theory (see Blau, 1964) and the norm of reciprocity (Gouldner, 1960). This research has been extensively used to explain the influence that leaders have on employee attitudes to their work and positive employee behaviors, or organizational citizenship behaviors. For example, under the umbrella of social exchange theory, LMX has been used to explain the quality of the exchange relationship between employees and their supervisors or line managers (Graen and Uhl-bien, 1995). Within this broad body of work, the general consensus is that positive relationships between employees and their supervisors can have a positive impact upon employees' job performance, job satisfaction, organizational commitment, organizational citizenship behaviors and safety (Penley et al., 1991; Gerstner and Day, 1997; Michael et al., 2006). Rosen et al. (2011: 822), perhaps rightly suggest that 'LMX theory has evolved into one of the more useful approaches for studying employee–supervisor relationships and how they affect employee outcomes'. However, while LMX has added value to our understanding of the leader–employee relationship in a very specific domain, it does not account for the full range of frontline leader behaviours, responsibilities and challenges. One reason is that while all FLMs are supervisors of employees, not all supervisors are FLMs; therefore the leader in LMX research is often narrower in span and scope than the FLM role.

With data collected over 15 years ago, Hales (2005: 502) provides a worthy contribution in a study of FLMs which demonstrates that rather than extensive changes in the role over the decades, there is a:

> stubborn persistence of hierarchy and external supervision as features of work organizations, a lingering absence of trust in the workplace, the winnowing of middle management and a crisis re-division of managerial labor. Rooted in supervision, staked to performance but here and there compelled to branch in to management, the FLM is the resilient, but put-upon, survivor of organizational change.

Lacking, though, is any reference or consideration of the FLM's leadership role, or indeed of whether their existing work responsibilities leave any space for a leadership role. More recently, Purcell and Hutchinson argue that the selection of FLMs must be considered with not only their technical FLM skills and knowledge but also their management skills and leadership capabilities as selection criteria (Purcell and Hutchinson, 2007; Hutchinson and Purcell, 2010). Evidence suggests that many organisations fall behind in their management of people because their internal systems and processes, beyond recruitment and appointment, fail. For many people within organisations there is often a lack of clear specifications of their role available; a phenomenon that may lead to conflict (Hutchinson and Purcell, 2010; Townsend et al., 2012). This conflict can be between the expectations of both superiors and subordinates clashing with the FLM, or indeed internal conflict as the FLM comes to terms with competing pressures in their role. For example, an FLM might be tasked with implementing a tight budget that necessitates the rationalisation of support staff, yet is also tasked with ensuring manageable workloads for their direct reports.

Recent research suggests that the role of FLM has always been crucial to organisational performance (Renwick, 2003, 2004; Jacoby, 2004; Martins, 2007; Townsend, 2013). This level of management is the 'lynchpin' that enacts intended human resource management policies (Wright and Kehoe, 2008) and translates 'paper plans into operational reality' (Child and Partridge, 1982). Wall and Wood (2007) argue that line managers are the crux of the HRM architecture, and Hutchinson and Purcell (2003) suggest that effective frontline management is a means by which HR strategies can 'come to life' in organisations. The leadership role of FLMs, however, remains underinvestigated.

ROLE THEORY, FLMs AND LEADERSHIP

Role theory, which holds at its centre the idea that everyday activities are the acting-out of socially defined categories (Sluss et al., 2011), can help to locate the leadership function of FLMs in perhaps the most poorly understood leadership role in organisations today. Within a workplace, employees are typically expected to perform their roles, and commonly this means engaging with other people. These other people are often managers, colleagues, and customers or clients. However, some employees are also asked to take on additional responsibilities in the form of the first tier of managerial work, that which is commonly referred to as the frontline manager. When employees are placed in a new role, a degree of uncertainty and ambiguity creeps into their work responsibilities (see, for examples, Kahn et al., 1964; Katz and Kahn, 1966; Patten, 1968).

According to Kahn et al. (1964), role ambiguity is a result of a lack of information, and hence the individual misses some clarity about the specific parts of their job. This lack of information could be attributed to a lack of individual skills, or lack of information provided from more senior managers about the role expectations. A situation where FLMs have a lack of information leads to uncertainty about their role, objectives, responsibilities and role stress. Increasingly, this role ambiguity seems to present itself around the leadership responsibilities of people within the frontline manager role.

While not using a role theory framework, some FLM research has shown how role ambiguity and conflict occurs when senior managers and line managers disagree on which HRM responsibilities are the obligation of which stakeholder (Wright et al., 2001). There is also evidence of FLM role overload (see Evans, Chapter 4 in this book). For example, FLMs are typically not provided with the training and development required for them to manage complex tasks such as the conflict management of staff (Teague and Roche, 2012). Additionally, the time to taken to perform their more routine operational tasks creates excess strain (Nehles et al., 2006). Previous evidence suggests that role expectations must be clear, and that role clarity is directly related to increases in job performance (Fried et al., 2003). Role clarity (as opposed to ambiguity) leads to proactivity, confidence and commitment (Saks and Ashforth, 1997), and the reduction of negative strain (Von Emster and Harrison, 1998). Conversely, role ambiguity is likely to stem from a number of different factors including the FLMs' experience and hence their expectations (e.g. Hutchinson and Purcell, 2010), as well as their preparation or training for the role (e.g. Townsend et al., 2012), in addition to the inherent ambiguity attached to roles that relate to managing people (Fried et al., 2003). While it is evident that role ambiguity has lower performance correlations than role clarity, any reduced performance of the FLMs is likely to have a direct, negative impact on the performance of their subordinates, and aggregated, on the organisation. Hence, if the FLMs are expected to play a leadership role, then their role and what it entails must be better understood.

As Dinh et al. (2014: 43) point out in their extensive review of theoretical trends and changing perspectives of leadership theories, scholars often explore the effects of leadership at the person, dyadic, group, and/or organisational levels. Yammarino and Dansereau (2011) suggest that there is an increasing trend towards complex theories of leadership at the expense of simple rules to explain complex behaviour. Dinh et al. (2014) further suggest that understanding leadership processes can help to illustrate the limitations of current theory, and can assist in developing a more comprehensive future agenda. In this chapter, we go back to the basics in theory development to understand what is involved in the FLM role and how leadership fits within that role.

For this research, we use Yukl's (1989: 253) definition that leadership is 'influencing task objectives, influencing commitment and compliance in task behaviour to achieve these objectives, influencing group maintenance and identification, and influencing the culture of an organisation'. We do note, though, that not all leadership is as positive as this definition might imply (see, for example, destructive/abusive/toxic leadership research; Einarsen et al., 2007).

As previously mentioned, there is a delineation in the literature about the differences between leadership and managerial roles; more recent research shows that rarely do employees occupying such positions move exclusively within one of these spaces (Lunenburg, 2011). Instead, many leaders perform managerial functions and vice versa (ibid.). What the optimal make-up is of leadership and managerial behaviours appears to be partly dependent upon the hierarchical level of their role; the number of direct reports, organisational structure and industry (Alvesson and Willmott, 2012) and, we would anticipate, very contextually sensitive. Very limited research has examined the relative leader and manager requirements of FLMs, the challenges they face in juggling these competing demands, or the strategies that they use to ensure the appropriate mix of leader and manager behaviours (Carroll and Levy, 2008). Our study will address some of these issues. This is important for the intersection between role theory and leadership theory, and the practical elements of organisational performance and employee experience, so that FLMs can be better supported to integrate what are often competing foci and demands of leader and manager roles. We currently know little about how FLMs are spending their time, so pushing the frontiers of theory requires, first, an understanding of FLMs roles and responsibilities.

In summary, there are parallel gaps within the relevant bodies of literature. Within the leadership literature there is a lack of focus and understanding of what FLMs do in leadership, and within the FLM-focused HRM literature there is a lack of attention on the leadership role of this level of manager. Role theory (Evans, Chapter 4 in this book) can assist with bridging the parallel gaps in knowledge. It is well accepted that FLMs play a distinctly different role in organisations from that of more senior-level managers and leaders. Hence, understanding the FLM overall role better is an important first stage of understanding the FLM's leadership role. Following pre-existing research on the FLM role (see, for examples, Hales, 2005; Townsend and Russell, 2013), our aim is to determine broad elements of FLM work, including a complex and context-specific mix of operational and managerial responsibilities. There is limited consideration of leadership responsibilities specific to the FLM role. This leads to our two research questions:

- RQ1: How do FLMs perceive differences between their management and leadership roles?
- RQ2: In what areas do FLMs have the capacity to exhibit leadership?

RESEARCH APPROACH

To align with the study aims of deeper understanding of the leadership responsibilities specific to the FLM role as identified by them, a qualitative research design was used. Interviews were deemed to be the most effective means of investigation, allowing an opportunity to explore not only how FLMs perceived their leadership role, but also how this differed from their operational and managerial tasks. Furthermore, this approach allowed us to understand the areas in which FLMs were succeeding or finding difficulties in their leadership, and what pressures influenced their leadership. Our goal was to impose limited structure on this phase of data collection, using open-ended questions and an opportunity to seek examples as a means to understand how and why the interviewee holds the perspective that they hold (King, 2012). This approach allowed us to develop themes from the data to provide a nuanced understanding of the FLM's leadership role in organisations.

The research team adopted a criterion sampling strategy to ensure that our participants were current frontline managers within their organisation. After gaining access through key

Table 13.1   *Interviewees and organisations*

Interview No.	Organisation	Sex	Interview No.	Organisation	Sex
1	Custodial	M	20	Insurance	F
2	Custodial	M	21	Insurance	F
3	Custodial	M	22	Insurance	M
4	Custodial	M	23	Leisure	F
5	Custodial	M	24	Leisure	F
6	Custodial	F	25	Leisure	M
7	Custodial	F	26	Hospital	F
8	Business Services	F	27	Hospital	F
9	Business Services	F	28	Hospital	F
10	Education	F	29	Business Services	F
11	Education	F	30	Business Services	F
12	Education	M	31	Police	F
13	Education	F	32	Police	M
14	Education	F	33	Police	M
15	Insurance	F	34	Hospitality	F
16	Insurance	F	35	Hospitality	F
17	Insurance	F	36	Hospitality	M
18	Insurance	F	37	Hospitality	M
19	Insurance	F	38	Hospitality	M

gatekeepers (typically HR managers), we managed to recruit a non-probability, convenience sample of 38 FLMs from five organisations (see Table 13.1). All organisations operated in the service sector. After collecting a range of demographic data, the interviews progressed through 12 key questions, including, for example: 'What tasks do you perform in your role and which of these tasks do you consider to be more management compared with the tasks that you consider more leadership?' And: 'Tell me about factors within your organisation that either assist you to show leadership or act as barriers to your leadership.' The interviews generally lasted around 45 minutes, although one interview lasted just 22 minutes, while another was 90 minutes in length. Two members of the research team completed all the interviews and had weekly meetings to discuss the ongoing findings throughout the 12-week data collection period.

For non-probability sampling techniques of interviewing, the question of 'how many interviews?' is ambiguous and, according to Saunders and Lewis (2012: 283), 'there are no rules'. For this project the research team continued to recruit and interview FLMs beyond the point that the researchers were confident that data saturation had been reached. Saturation was not achieved until around 32 interviews, and the data collection continued until 38 frontline manager interviews were complete. This number of interviews is within the range identified and recommended by Saunders and Townsend (2016) for multisite qualitative research.

DATA ANALYSIS

Interviews were electronically recorded in MP4 format and transcribed into Microsoft Word files. Following this, the interview transcriptions were loaded into NVivo and coded based on a priori codes including 'managerial responsibilities', 'operational responsibilities', 'percep-

Table 13.2   Summary of FLM responsibilities

Role	Description
Operational tasks	Those tasks that are the same as, or similar to, those of their team members. For example, a nursing ward manager is an FLM who would sometimes be required to interact with patients over medical matters and with patients' families. Indeed, most tasks that FLMs undertake have a very operational, or day-to-day, flavour to them. Smaller teams in most cases tend to have the FLM in a more 'hands-on' role, where they are performing the same duties as their subordinates; however, often at a higher level. That is to say, these FLMs might be responding to more complex customer problems that arise.
Short-term budget responsibilities	Where there are budget responsibilities they are commonly around implementing a budget that is provided, or meeting targets (sales). Often FLMs are expected to manage labour costs within their budgets and have minimal, if any, discretionary spending.
General paperwork/ administrative responsibilities	It is clear amongst FLMs interviewed that they have an increased level of responsibility in the administrative and bureaucratic functions within the organisation. These responsibilities can span a large number of areas.
Some recruiting and termination of employment	The extent to which FLMs are involved in this role varies, with some simply starting the process, some more actively involved in the process, and some having the final or only say in selection or termination.
Performance management	Very few managers were solely responsible for performance management, and indeed, many had no involvement in the formal process at all; but most frontline leaders recognised that their role contributed to daily performance management of staff in an informal way.
Daily communication	FLMs saw an integral part of their role to be one of communicating with and about their employees. Communication by FLMs was seen to contain two different elements: the easiest for many people is general and positive motivational communication, while the more difficult aspect was when there needed to be some form of communication over 'correcting' an employee's activities or, harder still, about the need for changes at a higher level to allow their employees to perform their roles.
External roles	Many FLMs were drawn to roles and responsibilities that allow for some external influence. This could be where FLMs are on development committees as a means to promote their team's role in the development of policy and strategy, or to protect their team's workload and position within the organisation.

tions of leadership role'. As coding and analysis progressed, more codes were incorporated, for example, 'internal barriers to leadership', 'communication', 'leadership activities'.

FLM Perceptions of the Difference between Management and Leadership

Our first research question is aimed at understanding how FLMs perceive the ambiguity between their managerial and leadership responsibilities. Given the preponderance of the term 'leadership' within the modern business lexicon and the focus on much leadership research at higher levels of management in organisations, it is important to understand whether FLMs see themselves as leaders, and if they do, how this might align or differ from their managerial responsibilities. The responses from our sample of FLMs makes it clear that the notion of leadership, and indeed, how leadership might be different from management, is a very subjective notion for FLMs that draws varied responses. Equally as important, FLMs reported performing a broad range of activities. We identified seven broad but commonly found roles, including 'operational tasks' which refer to those duties that are similar to those their team members are performing on a daily basis, and tasks which they are likely to have been performing before their ascension to an FLM role. These seven themes are summarised in Table 13.2.

This is not to say that these were the only roles for our sample of FLMs, but these were the seven most common themes and were found within all of our organisations. There was a consistent sense of clarity from our FLMs that activities which could be considered 'paperwork' or 'bureaucracy' are considered managerial duties by FLMs. Matters that relate to people, and more specifically to their team members, are those that are assigned by the FLMs to the category of leadership. The following response to our question asking about the difference between leadership and management captures this point: 'Leadership I think probably goes down to more personal qualities that you have and displaying probably a bit more emotional intelligence. Whereas the pure management I see as sort of the dollars and cents' (Int 15).

People operating in frontline manager roles tend to perceive the leadership component of their job as 'people management', related yet different from their managerial role containing bureaucratic responsibilities. While our FLMs explain that they are not given much role clarity from senior managers, they have determined and attributed different elements of their role to the leadership function, as we will discuss.

Related to this, we investigated whether FLMs see any role ambiguity between their managerial and leadership responsibilities. These ambiguities demonstrate the complexity of this role. When many frontline managers, and particularly those in professional employment, state that the people management roles are seen as time-wasters or issues that take them away from their 'real' job, we can see this tension. While many in our sample suggest that people management is leadership, it is also frustrating, and pulling them away from what is perceived as their key responsibilities. For example, when asked about the people management part of her role, one FLM noted:

> a lot of problems that people come to me with I'd like to deal in a management way, very unemotionally, coming to a solution and not worrying about the ripple effect on staff and morale and things like that. Whereas from a leadership perspective I have to take those things into account so as not to upset [team] because it's a small office people get upset fairly easily and that has a big ripple effect. (Int 12)

Another FLM noting the tensions between operational and managerial tasks suggests: 'When I'm having one of those days that I'd like to just be doing what I call my real job … and there is tension there, I do feel like it's a waste of time even though it's technically not' (Int 14).

One FLM explains the things that prevent her from more leadership behaviours are the bureaucratic responsibilities that she deems managerial work: 'over the years, I think that's added to costs in the [workplace], and complications. We have more rules and – it's called compliance isn't it? It's not just responsibility, it's compliance … it's protecting the individual as well as the organisation' (Int 26).

But these conflicts are not universal within our sample. Some of FLMs are very critical, perhaps even cynical, of the leadership aspect of their management position, as the following quotes demonstrate:

> Managers have to manage – leaders don't matter, it's senior managers just wanting people to follow orders and not ask questions. Look at the 'charge of the light brigade', typical army type mentality, where you go people will follow and you do as you're ordered. I don't want a leader to follow, I want someone to manage everything that's going on. (Int 1)

> I'm a big believer that leadership is for the weak – if you are a strong minded person then you know what you need to do, just get about and do it. But weak people need a leader, they need to be inspired.

If you're in this job and looking for a leader, then you'd be better off working somewhere else. Lead yourself, don't look to others to lead you. (Int 7)

As these examples from our analysis suggest, many FLMs do find ambiguity and conflict between the various elements of their role. Most of these seem to relate to the bureaucratic nature of their organisation, and the ambiguity that relates to managing people. However, there is a broader issue at play that deserves attention in further research, and that is the extent to which employees and FLMs are buying in to the rhetoric about the frontline manager playing a leadership role in organisations.

This brings us to RQ2: In what areas do FLMs have the capacity to exhibit leadership?

Role Capacity for Exhibiting Leadership

Our data suggest that there are four key ways that the FLM can show leadership: demonstrative actions, positive motivation communication, corrective communication and external influence. The first and most commonly present area is that of leadership through demonstrative actions. This behaviour is typically seen as pro-organisational actions, commonly associated with demonstrating to team members or subordinate employees. This is what would colloquially be termed, and is commonly referred to by our participants as, 'walking the talk'. As one of our FLMs states:

I see the administration as management – I either manage it or I don't and if I don't then we are all under more pressure. The leadership is more about the behaviours that I demonstrate to the guys. (Int 28)

And another:

Some days I just have to get out there and show them that this is how you clear tables, this is how you develop rapport with your customers, this is how you hustle, you know? I can tell them a thousand times but sometimes I just have to demonstrate it and show them what I expect. (Int 35)

This is an area where almost all FLMs reported engaging, and where they say they are most likely to revert when under pressure. In times of pressure, people are more likely to revert to the roles that they are familiar with; hence, FLMs are reverting to the roles that they mastered before their promotion to an FLM. This is, of course, the part of their job over which they have a great deal of role clarity. The other three areas of leadership are defined as positive motivational communication, corrective communication and external influence. Most participants discussed these four areas as potential leadership activities, but there were differences between the levels of involvement in these leadership activities. The differences seem to relate in some part to individual skills and agency, while others relate to the structure of the organisation.

The first of these remaining three areas relates to motivational communication, most notably by engaging in outward expressions of care. As one participant explained, upon her daily arrival she greets her employees with an upbeat 'Good morning, team' and attempts to maintain that positive tone and conversational style in her attempt to motivate the staff throughout the day. Another explains:

[That is] why people see me probably as a leader as well. We've had bad systems since last week. There was a group of girls not even in my team and I just went up to them the other day and how are you going today? Because I knew they'd had a tough week – because I came in to help out the other day. I said, 'how are you girls going after the weekend?' 'Oh, we're all a bit tired'. I said, 'right, what coffee do you want?' Off I went. 'Oh, no, we can get coffee from the kitchen'. I said, 'no, no, I'm going to go to the cafeteria. What coffee do you want?' Off [I] went. (Int 19)

Although many FLMs report engaging in positive motivational communication within teams, not all found it easy to do. For those who found it difficult, the next area of leadership potential was seen as particularly difficult. We have termed this area 'correctional communication', meaning conversations with employees where the FLM is required to engage in conversations where employee behaviour and organisational expectations are not in alignment.

Many participants in our study saw the notion of having 'difficult' conversations with employees to be much more complicated, and this is the task that they find most difficult to perform. Indeed, some FLMs preferred not to have to make the hard decisions, because they lacked confidence or they thought it interfered with their efforts to be 'one of the team'; hence, there was some degree of role conflict, and indeed, ambiguity. As one FLM expressed when asked if she would prefer to make decisions that affected the team, rather than communicate decisions made by others:

Because of the person I am, I'm glad I don't. That's being completely one hundred per cent honest. Because I am new to the role, so I've only been in the role since February I'm glad I'm not ... let's just say someone's employment does get terminated, I know that I could approach them face to face if need be and say, I really tried for you. I did try, you know that I put the effort in and it then fell out of my hands ... it does alleviate that pressure. (Int 14)

Another FLM explains:

I feel like I have to be the bad news guy – I have to listen to all the shit and whining that goes on, can't do anything about it operationally, but have to deliver the bad news to the guys when something has to change. It's funny though – good news comes from above, rare as it is, but bad news comes from me. (Int 22)

This is an important perception that many FLMs hold: that they are playing a role for the more senior managers in delivering the bad news to their staff, but it is the more senior managers who get to deliver the positive news. Consequently, the FLMs have an increased level of anxiety and frustration over the way they might be perceived by their team.

The final area of leadership activity or potential activity reported by FLMs was activities aimed at influencing events or people external to the group, but that have an impact on the group. We have termed this 'external influence activity'. When FLMs were engaged in external influence activities, they could be seen as more strategic activities as the FLM was genuinely involved in decision–making, not just being informed of decisions made by more senior managers and leaders. Some of FLMs we interviewed operated at this level, but most only operated in an internal team leadership role. One FLM explains:

There have been times ... where the team has been combative with other elements, and I've had to step in and go, no, this is what we're doing and this is why we're doing it, and show that leadership in terms of the right or – without getting moral about it, but the right thing to do. (Int 14)

Another from the same organisation suggests that they spend a lot of time in the realm of external influence, but that the time spent in meetings compared with tangible influence do not match:

> I do a lot of work around advising other … business areas … Lots of meetings. Lots of meetings that unfortunately, yes, feel very – because it's an advisory capacity – that I have little effect on … In a performance review recently … I reflected on the year and said, look, it feels like I spent a lot of time out and about talking to lots of people. But when it actually comes to actual output … you can't just be a meeting floater – it's like, 'I'm here for the sandwiches'. (Int 12)

This study provides a detailed picture of the leadership role of FLMs as perceived by them. Our study found that FLMs define leadership quite narrowly as only relating to person-to-person interaction; often, but not exclusively, with their team members. Equally, most FLMs do not see these activities as central to completing the role for which they were employed.

DISCUSSION

It is commonly accepted that there is a difference between leadership and management, and within scholarly research and 'pop-management' publications the debate continues to excite and sell. Conceptually, similarities between many of these publications can be drawn, including: management as a function compared with leadership as a relationship (Maccoby, 2000); managers organise, delegate and implement vision, while leaders communicate the vision, influence and motivate (Bohoris and Vorria, 2008); management is about controlling, leadership is about motivating and creating a common vision (Weathersby, 1999). So management appears to be a more structured and measurable activity, while leadership is fluid and about influence. This delineation sits comfortably with views of FLMs in this study. They explained the differences that they perceived between management and leadership, where management is seen as the bureaucratic elements of the role, while leadership is perceived to relate to people.

These results add to existing evidence that considers the broad range of activities that constituted the FLM role (see, for examples, Hales, 2005; Townsend and Russell, 2013). Our results show that frontline managers have a variety of duties, but are more likely to engage in operational rather than strategic activities. This is not surprising, as frontline managers have been considered critical for the effective daily management of employees for more than a century (Hutchinson and Purcell, 2003). While organisations can have multiple levels of managers, it is the frontline manager who is most likely to be situated within the same office or work area as the typical employee. At the top of the management ladder are the top executives and senior managers, whose tasks include strategic planning, liaising with external stakeholders, leading and setting organisational culture, monitoring the broader economic environment, allocating company resources, identifying trends and new opportunities, releasing information to the public (Kraut et al., 1989; Groysberg et al., 2006; Finkelstein et al., 2009). In contrast, frontline managers occupy the bottom rung on the management ladder and undertake tasks and practices that strongly centre around personnel supervision and people management (Kraut et al., 1989; Lowe, 1995; Purcell and Hutchinson, 2007).

This level of manager oversees day-to-day operations by planning and allocating work, while also performing health and safety requirements, attendance management, occasional recruitment, training, employee appraisals and team briefings (IRS, 2000; Purcell and

Hutchinson, 2007). FLMs also have a technical role in undertaking tasks such as quality and cost control, maintenance of plant and equipment (Lowe, 1995; Liu and McMurray, 2004; Brewer, 2005). This, in part, is related to the way that the work of FLMs is structured by more senior managers, but our findings suggest that it also relates to role clarity that FLMs have over their tasks.

Our results extend existing research by not just considering the activities performed by FLMs, and barriers and strains to performing leadership in the FLM role, but also identifying the key areas around which they saw potential within their role for displaying leadership. Our data suggest that there are four key ways that the FLM can show leadership, revolving around: (1) demonstrating required organisational behaviour to team members; (2) providing messages to motivate team members; (3) correcting actions that go against organisational demands; and (4) behaviour of external influence for the benefit of the team. These 'pillars' are presented in Figure 13.1; they relate to the leadership aspects of FLMs' roles, not the managerial functions that we would argue are precursors to the leadership pillars.

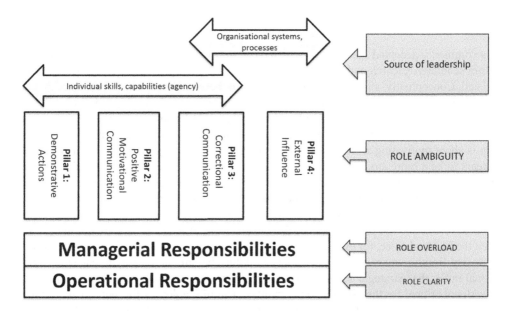

Figure 13.1   Pillars of frontline leadership

FLMs considered the first pillar of frontline leadership, demonstrative actions, to be a critical element of their leadership role. The ability to demonstrate to employees a high level of skill in their performance brings the credibility required for influential frontline leadership. When FLMs are under pressure, this is the area they are most likely to revert to, as it forms the core basis of their skill set; they have a great deal of role clarity here.

Data suggest that the second pillar of frontline leadership, motivational communication, can commonly include FLMs engaging in outward expressions of care. Many employees engage in positive motivational communication within teams; however, our data suggest that it becomes a core responsibility for FLMs. While not all FLMs reported finding it easy to do, it does appear to be the pillar of higher-order skills beyond demonstrative operational actions and the start of some role ambiguity for FLMs.

It is apparent from our data that FLMs find it difficult to move beyond the positive and begin to manage and lead their team in more sophisticated ways. Many FLMs reported finding the notion of having 'difficult' conversations (termed 'correctional communication' in Figure 13.1) to be difficult, and in conflict with other aspects of their role. Communicating with employees in a way that motivates and encourages the employees to conform to organisational expectations is a higher-order leadership skill, and it is clear from previous research that many FLMs who engage in this leadership role have limited support from HR departments (Townsend, 2013).

The fourth pillar of the frontline manager leadership is that of external influence. Very few FLMs work at this level, as most of them operate in a lower-level, supervisory capacity. When FLMs were engaged in external influence activities, they could be seen as more strategic activities. Actors were genuinely involved in decision-making, not just being informed of decisions made by superior managers and leaders. Some of FLMs we interviewed operate at this level, but most do not. Stepping outside the role ambiguity of the individual's perception of self, this demonstrates the ambiguity of roles that FLMs are performing. Clearly, FLMs are often constrained by organisational factors, including middle and senior managers' expectations of the FLM role, and the resources that are provided to the FLM.

Conceptually, we can identify that, in most cases, FLMs have operational responsibilities which are the same as those of their team members. Certainly, many have a lesser operational requirement than their team, but on top of that lies their managerial tasks (as our sample explains, paperwork and bureaucracy). Beyond these operational and managerial tasks are the pillars of leadership for FLMs. We would argue that a good frontline leader is effective in all four pillars, although our evidence suggests that each pillar is not additive. It is not unreasonable for a frontline leader to be effective in pillar 4, external influence, but this leader might not have the skills to successfully engage in the previous three pillars. When a leader engages in the activities of all pillars effectively, the positive influence over team performance is likely to be greater than if they only operate successfully on one or two pillars. This is an important area to be understood and quantified in future research. Here, Kilroy and Dundon (2015) have presented three different 'behavioural types' of FLMs that can help us to understand that individuals in this position do not all perform the same way; individual characteristics and context matter. Townsend et al. (2022) similarly present the notion that FLMs can find themselves in a conundrum where they can be a master of their work group or a leader of sorts, or alternatively, a victim of the policies of the HRM department.

Context and organisational design, along with the design and expectations for the FLM role, are important factors to consider in any study of the leadership role of FLMs. Not all organisations are structured similarly; nor indeed, are all teams within organisations. FLMs might, through organisational design or ineffective middle management, be restricted to the first two pillars, and simply not be required to engage in all pillars of frontline leadership. Equally, the FLM's response to their situation will have important implications for their own performance, their team, and aggregated organisational performance. Consequently, FLM responses to their context and organisational design is worthy of future research.

Aggregated, we can see the division between the various elements of the FLM's role, including leadership. However, the clarity is not as apparent for FLMs while they are in-role: there is confusion, frustration, ambiguity and overload. Furthermore, we identified not only a level of role ambiguity for the FLMs, but also a lack of role conflict between people within FLM roles. Child and Partridge (1982) explain that part of the difficulty in defining the FLM role is that the role is different between organisations, and also within organisations. Hence, FLMs can be asked to operate within different leadership pillars compared with their colleagues at a similar level. As we show in Figure 13.1, and as is considered by Townsend et al. (2022), individual agency and context-specific structure combine to be the source that either limits or enables FLMs to engage in leadership within their organisation. Clear planning and strategy to ensure that there is an alignment between the person, role and organisational expectations will assist FLMs in beginning to develop their leadership capabilities.

Similarly, most FLMs in our sample adopt an assumption that leadership is part of their job, despite the areas of leadership identified to be somewhat mundane, rather than the grandiose, hero leadership identified in the literature by Alvesson and Sveningsson (2003). We have not measured time spent in activities in this study; however, such measurement would allow a deeper understanding of differences between sectors and even within organisations. Hence, while leadership appears to be an exaggerated part of the FLM role, leadership for the FLMs is becoming increasing normalised. This suggests that the relationship between operational, managerial and leadership duties in the FLM role, and the variables that influence this relationship (for example public or private sector, organization size, team size and industry type), are worthy of further research investigation.

CONCLUSION

This study was designed to understand the leadership role requirements and capabilities of FLMs rather than to determine organisational or individual determinants of their performance with a view to generating new theory. This is the task of future research. However, our results do suggest that theories of leadership that are relevant to senior managers are not readily transferable to FLMs. Role theory does seem to offer insights into understanding the variability of the FLM role. It suggests that context is key to understanding FLM leadership, and that more research is needed to provide the nuances that context creates in order for it to be better understood in this important area of research.

REFERENCES

Alvesson, M. and Sveningsson, S. (2003). The great disappearing act: Difficulties in doing 'leadership'. *Leadership Quarterly*, 14: 359–381.
Alvesson, M. and Willmott, H. (2012) *Making Sense of Management: A Critical Introduction*. London: SAGE.
Blau, P. (1964). *Exchange and Power in Social Life*. New York: Wiley.
Bohoris, G.A. and Vorria, E.P. (2008). Leadership vs management: A business excellence/performance management view. In: *10th QMOD Conference. Quality Management and Organizational Development: Our Dreams of Excellence*, 18–20 June 2007, Helsingborg, Sweden (No. 026). Linköping University Electronic Press.
Brewer, G.A. (2005). In the eye of the storm: Frontline supervisors and federal agency performance. *Journal of Public Administration Research and Theory*, 15(4): 505–527.
Carroll, B. and Levy, L. (2008). Defaulting to management: Leadership defined by what it is not. *Organization*, 15(1): 75–96.

Child, J. and Partridge, B. (1982). *Lost Managers: Supervisors in Industry and Society*. Cambridge: Cambridge University Press.

Day, D.V., Fleenor, J.W., Atwater, L.E., Sturm, R.E. and McKee, R.A. (2014). Advances in leader and leadership development: A review of 25 years of research and theory. *Leadership Quarterly*, 25(1): 63–82.

Dinh, J.E., Lord, R.G., Gardner, W.L., Meuser, J.D., Liden, R.C. and Hu, J. (2014). Leadership theory and research in the new millennium: Current theoretical trends and changing perspectives. *Leadership Quarterly*, 25(1): 36–62.

Einarsen, S., Aasland, M.S. and Skogstad, A. (2007). Destructive leadership behaviour: A definition and conceptual model. *Leadership Quarterly*, *18*(3), 207–216.

Finkelstein, S., Hambrick, D.C. and Cannella, A. (2009). *Strategic Leadership: Theory and Research on Executives, Top Management Teams and Boards*. New York: Oxford University Press.

Fried, Y., Slowick, L., Shperling, Z., Franz, C., Ben-David, H., et al. (2003). The moderating effect of job security on the relation between role clarity and job performance: A longitudinal field study. *Human Relations*, 56: 787–805.

Gerstner, C.R. and Day, D.V. (1997). Meta-analytic review of leader–member exchange theory: Correlates and construct issues. *Journal of Applied Psychology*, 82: 827–844.

Gouldner, A.W. (1960). The norm of reciprocity. *American Sociological Review*, 25: 161–178.

Graen, G.B. and Uhlbien, M. (1995). Relationship based approach to leadership – Development of leader–member exchange (LMX) theory of leadership over 25 years: Applying a multilevel multidomain perspective. *Leadership Quarterly*, 6(2): 219–247.

Groysberg, B., McLean, A.N. and Nohria, N. (2006). Are leaders portable? *Harvard Business Review*, 84(5): 92–100.

Hales, C. (2005). Rooted in supervision, branching into management: Continuity and change in the role of the firstline manager. *Journal of Management Studies*, 42(3): 471–506.

House, R.J. and Aditya, R.N. (1997). The social scientific study of leadership: Quo vadis? *Journal of Management*, 23(3): 409–473.

Hutchinson, S. and Purcell, J. (2003). *Bringing Policies to Life: The Vital Role of Front Line Managers in People Management*. London: Chartered Institute of Personnel and Development.

Hutchinson, S. and Purcell, J. (2010). Managing ward managers for roles in HRM in the NHS: Overworked and under-resourced. *Human Resource Management Journal*, 20(4): 357–374.

IRS (2000). *IRS Employment Trends (2000)*. Industrial Relations Review and Report, No. 642, October.

Jacoby, S. (2004). *Employing Bureaucracies: Managers, Unions, and the Transformation of Work in the 20th Century*. Hillsdale, NJ: Lawrence Erlbaum.

Kahn, R.L., Wolfe, D.M., Quinn, R.P., Snoek, J.D. and Rosenthal, R.A. (1964). *Organizational Stress: Studies in Role Conflict and Ambiguity*. New York: Wiley.

Katz, D. and Kahn, Robert L. (1966). *The Social Psychology of Organizations*. New York: Wiley.

Kilroy, J. and Dundon, T. (2015). The multiple faces of the frontline managers: A preliminary examination of FLM styles and reciprocated employee outcomes. *Employee Relations*, 37(4): 410–427

King, N. (2012), Using interviews in qualitative research. In Cassell, C. and Symon, G. (eds), *Essential Guide to Qualitative Methods in Organizational Research*. London: SAGE, pp. 11–22.

Kraut, A.I., Pedigo, P.R., McKenna, D.D. and Dunnette, M.D. (1989). The role of the manager: What's really important in different management jobs. *Academy of Management Executive*, 3(4): 286–293.

Liu, L. and McMurray, A.J. (2004). Frontline leaders: The entry point for leadership development in the manufacturing industry. *Journal of European Industrial Training*, 28(2/3/4): 339–352.

Lowe, J. (1995). The supervisor in the automobile industry. Unpublished doctoral thesis, University of Wales, Cardiff.

Lunenburg, F.C. (2011). Leadership versus management: A key distinction – at least in theory. *International Journal of Management, Business, and Administration*, 14(1): 1–4.

Maccoby, M. (2000). Understanding the difference between management and leadership. *Research Technology Management*, 43(1): 57–59.

Martins, L. (2007). A holistic framework for the strategic management of first tier managers. *Management Decision*, 45(3): 616–641.

Michael, J.H., Guo, Z.G., Wiedenbeck, J.K. and Ray, C.D. (2006). Production supervisor impacts on subordinates' safety outcomes: An investigation of leader–member exchange and safety communication. *Journal of Safety Research*, 37: 469–477.

Nehles, A., Riemsdijk, M., Kok, I. and Looise, J.C. (2006). Implementing human resource management successfully: A first-line management challenge. *Management Revue*, 17(3): 256–273.

Patten, T.H. (1968). *The Foreman: Forgotten Man of Management*. New York: American Management Association.

Penley, L., Alexander, E., Jemigan, E. and Henwood, C. (1991). Communication abilities of managers: The relationship to performance. *Journal of Management*, 17(1): 57–76

Priestland, A., and Hanig, R. (2005). Developing first-level leaders. *Harvard Business Review*, 83(6): 112–120

Purcell, J. and Hutchinson, S. (2007). Front-line managers as agents in the HRM–performance causal chain: Theory, analysis and evidence. *Human Resource Management Journal*, 17(1): 3–20.

Renwick, D. (2003). Line manager involvement in HRM: An inside view. *Employee Relations*, 25(3): 262–280.

Renwick, D. (2004). Line managers and HR work. *Human Resources and Employment Review*, 2(3): 139–145.

Rosen, C.C., Harris, K.J. and Kacmar, K.M. (2011). LMX, context perceptions, and performance: An uncertainty management perspective. *Journal of Management*, 37(3): 819–838.

Saks, A. and Ashforth, B. (1997). Organizational socialization: Making sense of the past and present as a prologue for the future. *Journal of Vocational Behaviour*, 51: 234–279.

Saunders, M. and Lewis, P. (2012). *Doing Research in Business and Management: An Essential Guide to Planning Your Project*. Harlow: Financial Times Prentice Hall.

Saunders, M. and Townsend, K. (2016). Reporting and justifying the number of interview participants in organization and workplace research. *British Journal of Management*, 27(4): 836–852

Sluss, D., van Dick, R. and Thompson, B. (2011). Role theory in organizations: A relational perspective. In Zedeck, S. (ed.), *APA Handbook of Industrial and Organisational Psychology Vol 1*, Washington, CD: American Psychological Association, pp. 505–534.

Teague, P. and Roche, B. (2012). Line managers and the management of workplace conflict: Evidence from Ireland. *Human Resource Management Journal*, 22(3): 235–251.

Townsend, K. (2013). To what extent do line managers play a role in modern industrial relations? *Asia Pacific Journal of Human Resources*, 51(4): 421–436.

Townsend, K. and Russell, B. (2013). Investigating the nuances of change in frontline managers' work. *Labour and Industry*, 23(2): 168–181.

Townsend, K., Dundon, T., Cafferkey, K. and Kilroy, J. (2022). Victim or master of HRM implementation: The frontline manager conundrum. *Asia Pacific Journal of Human Resources*, 60(1): 79–96. https://doi.org/10.1111/1744-7941.12311.

Townsend, K., Wilkinson, A., Bamber, G. and Allan, C. (2012). Mixed signals in human resources management: The HRM role of hospital line managers. *Human Resource Management Journal*, 22(3): 267–282.

Von Emster, G. and Harrison, A. (1998). Toward a theory of organizational socialization. In Staw, B. (ed.), *Research in Organizational Behavior Vol 1*. Greenwich: JAI Press.

Wall, T. and Wood, S. (2007). The romance of human resource management and business performance, and the case for big science. *Human Relations*, 58(4): 429–462.

Weathersby, G. (1999). Leadership vs management. *Management Review*, 88(3): 5.

Wright, P.M. and Kehoe, R.R. (2008). Human resource practices and organizational commitment: A deeper examination. *Asia Pacific Journal of Human Resources*, 46(1): 6–20.

Wright, P.M., Gardner, T.M., Moynihan, L.M., Park, H.J., Gerhart, B. and Delery, J.E. (2001). Measurement error in research on human resources and firm performance: Additional data and suggestions for future research. *Personnel Psychology*, 54: 875–901.

Yammarino, F.J. and Dansereau, F. (2011). Multi-level issues in evolutionary theory, organization science, and leadership. *Leadership Quarterly*, 22(6), 1042–1057.

Yukl, G. (1989). Managerial leadership: A review of theory and research. *Journal of Management*, 15(2): 251–289.

14. Line managers' empowering leadership and employees' task i-deals: an explanation from self-determination theory

Elise Marescaux, Anja Van den Broeck and Sophie De Winne

INTRODUCTION

Throughout the past decade, increasing attention is being given to the pivotal role of line managers in the implementation of human resource management (HRM) practices as more and more HRM tasks are assigned to them by the HRM department (a process called "HRM devolution"; Bos-Nehles et al., 2013; Perry and Kulik, 2008). In parallel, we observe a movement towards the individualization of HRM practices (Bal and Dorenbosch, 2015). This is due to a decrease in collective agreements, a larger emphasis on employees' proactivity in shaping their jobs and careers, an increasingly diverse workforce characterized by a desire to feel individually treated, as well as increased competition for talent that is scarce, and more loyal to their career than to their organization (Liao et al., 2016; Marescaux et al., 2013a). To answer this trend towards individualization, line managers can grant tailor-made arrangements (Kehoe and Han, 2020; Knies et al., 2020). This implies that, rather than settling on standard working conditions, employees proactively negotiate with their line manager to secure unique working conditions that are tailored to their own preferences (so-called "i-deals"; Rousseau, 2005). These deals are intended to benefit both their recipients and the organization, as they are associated with increased employee well-being, attitudes and performance (Liao et al., 2016; Rosen et al., 2013). Hence, i-deals are a tool to attract, motivate and retain employees, and organizations therefore seek to understand how such i-deals (and their benefits) can be promoted.

Despite the key role of line managers in the negotiation and allocation of i-deals, we know surprisingly little about how they can foster them (Liao et al., 2016). Preliminary research has shown that a high-quality leader–member exchange (LMX) relationship fosters the negotiation of i-deals (Hornung et al., 2010, 2014; Rosen et al., 2013). This, however, tells us little about the specific leadership behaviors that line managers could use to stimulate the negotiation of i-deals (for an exception, see Hornung et al., 2011), while such leadership behaviors have a predominant impact on employees' (proactive) behaviors (Lee et al., 2018). This study aims to fill this void by focusing on the empowering leadership of line managers as a potential catalyst for i-deals. Empowering leadership refers to giving employees autonomy and freedom, consulting with them, motivating them to share their ideas, and coaching them to develop their skills and knowledge (Lee et al., 2018; Pearce and Sims, 2002). Importantly, it is distinct from LMX. Whereas LMX reflects the quality of an employee–line manager relationship, empowering leadership aims to transfer autonomy and control to employees to influence their proactive actions (Amundsen and Martinsen, 2014; Sharma and Kirkman,

2015). Considering its key ability to provide employees with the opportunity, relational basis and perceived ability to act proactively (Cheong et al., 2016; Kim et al., 2018), empowering leadership seems essential to foster the negotiation of i-deals. Therefore, we aim to study the role of line managers in fostering employees' successful negotiation of i-deals through their empowering leadership.

We specifically focus on task i-deals (Hornung et al., 2010; Rosen et al., 2013), which include arrangements to adapt work demands to one's preferences, capacities, or goals, make work more motivating, and/or increase the learning opportunities in one's job (Hornung et al., 2014). They represent a middle ground between top-down job design and bottom-up job crafting (Hornung et al., 2010). Moreover, research shows that task i-deals have the largest impact on employee attitudes and performance (Hornung et al., 2014; Rosen et al., 2013), yet are underresearched compared to, for example, developmental and flexibility i-deals. To explain why empowering line managers fosters task i-deals, we make use of self-determination theory (SDT) (Deci and Ryan, 2000). SDT proposes that employees' basic needs for autonomy, belongingness, and competence need to be satisfied in order to develop positive work attitudes and to perform (Gagné and Deci, 2005). We suggest that empowering line managers foster their employees' basic need satisfaction as they encourage them to take up responsibility and be autonomous, while at the same time showing care for them and trust in their competence (Amundsen and Martinsen, 2014; Kim et al., 2018). Employees' need satisfaction, in turn, helps them to take on the active role required in the negotiation of i-deals (Slemp and Vella-Brodrick, 2013). Rather than passively accepting their current situation, they are more likely to engage in interactions (for example, with their line manager) to improve their working environment (for example, through the negotiation of i-deals).

Through this study, we contribute in different ways. Firstly, we look into the role of empowering line managers as facilitators of i-deals, which are crucial yet often overlooked actors. More importantly, i-deals are a way for line managers to proactively enact their HRM responsibilities, implying that we also contribute to research on line managers' involvement in the implementation of HRM practices, which often considers line managers as "passive transmitters" of human resources (HR) practices (Kehoe and Han, 2020; Knies et al., 2020; Marescaux et al., 2021). Secondly, we theoretically and empirically expose the motivational process behind this by applying SDT. In doing so, we answer the call for more illuminating theories to uncover the dynamics of i-deals in the work environment beyond the current dominance of social exchange theory (Liao et al., 2016). Finally, we contribute to the empowering leadership literature by empirically testing the basic need satisfaction mechanism that has often been put forward (e.g., Amundsen and Martinsen, 2014; Kim et al., 2018) to explain its impact, yet has never been explicitly tested.

THEORY AND HYPOTHESES

I-Deals

Rousseau (2005) originally defined i-deals as unique working arrangements that are negotiated between the employer and a single employee (the recipient or i-dealer). While the i-dealer receives an arrangement tailored to their preferences, the employer benefits through increased motivation and retention of the i-dealer (Liao et al., 2016). Notably, the scope of the arrangement can go from one single feature (for example, an exceptional training, financial bonus, more challenging tasks or flexibility in work hours and location) in a rather standard employment package, to an entire set of idiosyncratic working conditions. Since the introduction of the concept, research has strongly focused on finding evidence for the benefits of i-deals, showing that they increase work engagement, commitment, job satisfaction, organizational citizenship behavior, and proactive behaviors (for an overview, see Liao et al., 2016). This is because they increase trust, foster employees' perceived value to the organization, and strengthen the social exchange relationship to which employees feel obliged to reciprocate.

Given the benefits of i-deals, research is increasingly looking into their antecedents, seeking to find the conditions in which organizations can foster such deals. Thus far, research has shown structural conditions to affect the degree to which employees can negotiate i-deals. For example, i-deal requests are more likely in groups with heterogeneous firm-specific skills and functional areas, as such groups are characterized by a wide range of different employee preferences (Lee et al., 2015). In contrast, when an organization already has well-developed practices (for example, promotion opportunities, on-the-job training), employees feel less of a need to bargain (Lee et al., 2015). Some type of jobs also provide more room for bargained flexibility, such as part-time and telecommuting jobs; while others constrain this room, such as jobs in large teams (which make i-deals less practically manageable) and jobs which require a lot of on-site presence (reducing the room for flexibility i-deals, for example) (Hornung et al., 2008, 2009). In addition to structural conditions, employee characteristics also matter, as some employees have more bargaining power or take more initiative to negotiate i-deals than others; for example, when they have strong firm-specific skills and knowledge, political skills, and emotional intelligence, or have a tendency to act proactively (Hornung et al., 2008, 2009; Lee et al., 2015; Rosen et al., 2013).

Despite i-deals being generally negotiated with line managers (Kehoe and Han, 2020; Knies et al., 2020), relatively little is known about how they foster (or hamper) the negotiation of i-deals. Most existing studies have focused on the quality of the relationship between line managers and employees reflected in the LMX relationship. The idea behind this is that if employees perceive themselves to be valuable members of the group (that is, part of the in-group of the line manager), they have more power to negotiate i-deals. Accordingly, employees who experience high leader–member exchange with their line manager negotiate more task, financial, career development, and flexibility i-deals (Hornung et al., 2010, 2014; Rosen et al., 2013).

However, the fact that LMX relates to i-deals does not necessarily provide much insight into which type of leadership behavior fosters or hampers the negotiation of i-deals (Liao et al., 2016), nor does it give us much theoretical and empirical insight into why and how line managers foster i-deals. Indeed, while LMX reflects the quality of the employee–line manager relationship, it does not reflect the specific behaviors that line managers exhibit and can be trained in. Accordingly, recent research has shown that LMX is clearly distinct from leadership behaviors such as empowering and transformational leadership, as employees who experience high LMX may very well report working for an authoritarian or transactional line manager (e.g., Amundsen and Martinsen, 2014; Kim et al., 2018: Lee et al., 2018; Sharma and Kirkman, 2015). Hornung et al. (2011) have taken a first step towards filling this gap by showing that leader consideration can foster the negotiation of developmental and flexibility i-deals. To further unravel the role of leadership behavior, our goal is to examine empowering leadership as an antecedent of task i-deals, using self-determination theory as an explanatory mechanism.

Empowering Leadership and Task I-Deals

Throughout the past decades, empowering leadership has been defined in different ways. Some scholars define empowering leadership as giving more autonomy and discretion to employees (e.g., Yukl et al., 2002). These definitions focus on the sharing of power with employees by providing them with more freedom, and consulting them when decisions need to be made (Chen et al., 2011). Others have taken a broader approach, emphasizing not only the importance of autonomy and employee consultation, but also the need to coach and develop employees to perform (autonomously) (e.g., Amundsen and Martinsen, 2014; Burke et al., 2006; Lee et al., 2018; Pearce and Sims, 2002). The logic behind this is that employees should not only be motivated to act autonomously and given the opportunity to do so, but should also be provided with relational support and (the encouragement to develop) the right skills and knowledge to do so. We adopt this latter, most comprehensive view, by considering empowering leadership as a collection of behaviors aimed at: (1) giving employees autonomy and freedom; (2) consulting them and motivating them to share their ideas; and (3) coaching them and developing their skills and knowledge (e.g., Amundsen and Martinsen, 2014; Pearce and Sims, 2002).

As i-deals result from an employee's proactive negotiation with their line manager, successfully negotiated i-deals emerge when employees perceive that they have the opportunity, the relational basis with their line manager, as well as the ability to negotiate them (Hornung et al., 2014; Lee et al., 2015; Rosen et al., 2013). Empowering leadership lays the groundwork for all three necessary determinants of i-deal negotiations. Firstly, empowering leadership implies that employees are given the autonomy and freedom to perform their tasks and responsibilities and to achieve their goals as they see fit (Pearce and Sims, 2002; Yukl et al., 2002). Moreover, they are encouraged to use their initiative related to the performance of their tasks, responsibilities, and goals, and to think and act independently, using their own judgment (Pearce and Sims, 2002; Yukl et al., 2002). This gives them the opportunity to take proactive actions specifically related to their tasks, responsibilities, and performance goals, such as the negotiation of task i-deals. Secondly, empowering leaders also signal employees that their opinions, needs, and interests matter by consulting them before decisions regarding their job are made, and act as coaches by helping them to develop the skills to act autonomously and proactively to perform their tasks and responsibilities and achieve their goals (Amundsen and Martinsen, 2014; Burke et al., 2006; Lee et al., 2018). As a result, they provide employees with the (perceived) ability to act proactively vis-à-vis certain job-related aspects (Cheong et al., 2016), for example by negotiating task i-deals. Thirdly, empowering leaders create a relational basis characterized by trust and reciprocity necessary for employees to feel comfortable and safe in taking proactive actions related to their job, such as the negotiation of task i-deals (Kim et al., 2018).

All of the above explains why empowering leadership is believed to unlock employees' potential to show initiative and improve their work roles. Accordingly, several studies have shown that empowering leadership creates room for employees to show initiative, for example in the form of creative, innovative, and proactive behavior (Chen et al., 2011; Martin et al., 2013; Thun and Bakker, 2018; Zhang and Bartol, 2010). As a result, we argue that empowering line managers can also foster employee initiative in the form of task i-deal negotiations, making task i-deals more likely to be successfully negotiated:

Hypothesis 1. Line managers' empowering leadership is positively related to employees' successful negotiation of task i-deals.

The Mediating Role of Basic Need Satisfaction

To unpack the above-mentioned relationship and study its underlying mediating psychological process, we rely on self-determination theory (Deci and Ryan, 2000), and its construct of basic need satisfaction in particular. The literature on task i-deals assumes that employees may take the initiative to actively interact with their work environment and negotiate to tailor and improve it in line with their preferences. Self-determination theory (Deci and Ryan, 2000; Gagné and Deci, 2005) fully aligns with this point of view, but argues that this proactive and growth-oriented approach does not surface automatically. Specifically, just like people need water, food, and shelter to function well on a physical level, SDT argues that people need to be satisfied in their basic psychological needs before they can start taking the initiative and realize their psychological potential (Deci and Ryan, 2000; Van den Broeck et al., 2016). Three essential needs have been identified: that is, the needs for autonomy, relatedness, and competence. The need for autonomy represents one's inclination to have an internal locus of control, that is, to feel the owner of one's own actions rather than to be pushed around like a pawn (DeCharms, 1968). The need for relatedness refers to building close relationships with others, to care for and be cared for (Baumeister and Leary, 1995). The need for competence involves feeling effective in one's tasks and looking for opportunities to further develop and grow (Deci and Ryan, 2000).

Satisfaction of the basic psychological needs requires a need-supportive environment (Gagné and Deci, 2005). Line managers play an important role in this because, through their specific behaviors towards their employees, they may satisfy or hinder the satisfaction of their employees' basic psychological needs. Meta-analytic evidence shows that leader autonomy and relatedness support as well as positive leader behaviors such as mentoring associates positively to the satisfaction of the three basic psychological needs (Van den Broeck et al., 2016). In terms of specific leadership styles, several studies have also shown that transformational leaders may support employees' basic needs for autonomy, competence, and relatedness (Hetland et al., 2011; Kovjanic et al., 2013). This is because such leaders have charisma, and communicate a clear and compelling vision, encouraging employees to see the value in the depicted future (that is, satisfying the need for autonomy) and supporting their competence in pursuing these goals (that is, satisfying the need for competence). They also show individualized consideration for followers (that is, satisfying the need for relatedness).

Within this study, we extend the potential of line managers to foster basic need satisfaction to an empowering style of leadership. Specifically, we would argue that empowering leaders are particularly supportive of employees' basic need satisfaction. As mentioned above, empowering leaders, firstly, focus on giving employees freedom and encouraging initiative (Pearce and Sims, 2002; Stogdill et al., 1962; Yukl et al., 2002). By doing so, they satisfy employees' need to feel they are the actors of their own actions, thereby likely satisfying their need for autonomy. In addition, empowering leadership is typically interpreted as a sign that the line manager likes and cares for the employees, can be trusted and is committed to a long-term relationship with them (Kim et al., 2018), which plays into their need for relatedness. Finally, by allowing employees to make their own choices, consulting them before decisions are made, and coaching them to develop the skills to act proactively and autonomously, empowering leaders nurture employees' need for competence (Amundsen and Martinsen, 2014; Burke et al., 2006; Lee et al., 2018). In short, based on the conceptual alignment between empowering leadership and need satisfaction detailed here, we argue that the characteristics and behaviors of empowering leaders make it likely for them to satisfy the basic needs of their employees.

Moreover, meta-analytic evidence shows that employees' basic need satisfaction guides them towards more proactive behavior to improve their environment (Van den Broeck et al., 2016). Indeed, when satisfied, the three basic needs reflect the necessary conditions for employees to negotiate i-deals proactively; that is, by giving them the opportunity and freedom to do so (autonomy satisfaction), the relational basis to do so (relatedness satisfaction), and the felt ability to do so (competence satisfaction) (Hornung et al., 2014; Lee et al., 2015; Rosen et al., 2013). As such, we argue that employees whose basic needs are satisfied will be able to actively interact with their work environment and negotiate i-deals, such that their tasks will become more aligned with their preferences and growth potential.

In short, based on theory development and the empirical research in the realm of empowering leadership and SDT, we argue that employees' basic need satisfaction will mediate the relationship between line managers' empowering leadership and employees' successful negotiation of i-deals (see Figure 14.1):

Hypothesis 2. The relationship between line managers' empowering leadership and employees' successful negotiation of task i-deals is mediated by employees' autonomy (H2a), relatedness (H2b), and competence (H2c) satisfaction.

Figure 14.1   Overview of hypotheses

METHODOLOGY

Sample and Procedure

Data was collected through an online survey, in cooperation with two national job magazines in Belgium. A total of 6100 employees started the questionnaire, of which 5747 completed it. As the survey was supported with a large advertisement campaign run by the job magazines we closely collaborated with, and a randomly drawn set of respondents were rewarded with prizes, the dropout rate throughout the survey was low (5.8 percent). Among those 5747 employees, we do have some missing values, as respondents could skip questions when they felt uncomfortable answering them. Yet, as a whole, there is very little missing data (for example, all employees reported on the task i-deals they negotiated, yet some left some of the questions on the empowering leadership of their line manager blank). The questionnaire measured employees' perceptions of their line manager's empowering leadership, their basic need satisfaction, and successfully negotiated task i-deals. Our sample mainly consisted of highly educated employees: 36 percent bachelor degrees, and 45 percent master degrees. Our sample was 56 percent male; and respondents were on average 34.63 years old (SD 8.60). On average, respondents had a tenure of 47.55 months (3.96 years) in their current job (SD 59.35). The sample covered a wide range of functional domains such as administration/central services (13 percent), sales (13 percent), information and communication tecxhnology (ICT)/ internet services (13 percent), general management (12 percent), and executive services (10 percent). Moreover, respondents were active at different hierarchical levels: administrative staff (10.1 percent), operational staff (27.2 percent), professional staff (30.3 percent), middle management (27.0 percent), and higher management (5.3 percent). This implies that the line managers evaluated in the survey were also active at different levels of the organization. Finally, and importantly, 54.9 percent of employees reported not having successfully negotiated a task i-deal. In contrast, 24.7 percent had negotiated one task i-deal, while 14.0 percent had negotiated two i-deals, and 6.4 percent had negotiated three.

Measures

Respondents were questioned on their successful negotiation of task i-deals, the empowering leadership of their line manager, and their basic need satisfaction.

Employees' successful negotiation of task i-deals

Task i-deals are arrangements negotiated by an employee that create a unique difference between the i-dealer's job content and that of their co-workers. Specifically, the unique nature of the arrangement may be related to the i-dealer's tasks, responsibilities, and performance goals (Hornung et al., 2010; Rosen et al., 2013). They are factual by nature, suggesting that employees have to have successfully negotiated them for the i-deal to be present (Liao et al., 2016). To capture these properties (that is, negotiated, unique compared to co-workers, related to job content, and factual), we asked respondents whether they had successfully negotiated for one or more of the following exceptional arrangements (yes or no): (1) specific tasks or assignments that none of their co-workers were assigned to; (2) more responsibilities within their jobs than their co-workers; and (3) other performance goals than their co-workers. We worked with a binary measure to reflect the factual nature of i-deals. Indeed, i-deals are formal arrangements, which means that an employee either successfully negotiated them or did not. In other words, it is not a matter of perceptual degree, but a fact. We realize that by measuring i-deals in such a way, we deviate from existing measures (Rosen et al., 2013), yet believe our measurement more accurately reflects what we intend to measure: that is, the factual and successful negotiation of task i-deals. Moreover, as task i-deals can be diverse in nature (that is, pertaining to specific tasks, responsibilities, or performance goals) and the negotiation of one task i-deal does not necessarily imply the negotiation of another one, we created a task i-deal index which reflected how many task i-deals respondents negotiated with their current employer in their current job.[1]

Line managers' empowering leadership

As explained above, empowering leaders show behaviors aimed at: (1) giving employees autonomy and freedom; (2) motivating them to share their ideas; and (3) developing their skills and knowledge. While there are many measures of empowering leadership (Amundsen and Martinsen, 2014; Arnold et al., 2000; Yukl et al., 2002), and no consensus on which is the best one to use, we included measures that capture these three dimensions separately and accurately. To capture the extent to which employees perceive their line manager as providing autonomy and freedom, we made use of six[2] items of the Leader Behavior Description Questionnaire (Stogdill et al., 1962) following Yukl et al.'s (2002) recommendation, as well as previous empirical research (e.g., Littrell, 2013). More specifically, we made use of the "tolerance of freedom" dimension, reflecting "to what extent the line manager allows followers' scope for initiative, decision and action" (Littrell, 2013: 576). A sample item includes: "my line manager is reluctant to allow me any freedom of action (reverse scored)" ($\alpha = 0.90$). To measure whether employees perceive their line manager to consult them before making decisions, we made use of the "participative decision-making" subscale of empowering leadership developed by Arnold et al. (2000). This consisted of six items (for example, "my line manager encourages me to express ideas/suggestions"; $\alpha = 0.89$). Finally, to measure line managers' engagement in the development of employees, we used Rafferty and Griffin's (2006) three-item measure (for example, "my line manager coaches me to help me improve my on-the-job performance"; $\alpha = 0.84$). All items had to be answered on a five-point scale going from 1 (totally disagree) to 5 (totally agree).

Employees' basic need satisfaction

This was captured using the Basic Need Satisfaction at Work Scale (Van den Broeck et al., 2010). For each need, six items were used to measure their satisfaction, which were to be answered on a five-point scale going from 1 (totally disagree) to 5 (totally agree). A sample item for autonomy is: "at work, I often feel like I have to do what others tell me to" (reverse coded) ($\alpha = 0.85$). Relatedness was measured through items such as "I feel part of a group at work" ($\alpha = 0.87$); and a sample item for competence includes "I don't feel very competent at work" (reverse coded) ($\alpha = 0.86$).

Control variables

As mentioned above, employee characteristics as well as structural conditions can affect the negotiation of i-deals. Hence, we control for employees' gender, tenure, age, and educational level, their tendency to act proactively, as well as the presence of HR practices, and the organization's size. Firstly, employee characteristics can increase the odds that they negotiate i-deals,

---

[1]   We adopted this method from the HRM research literature (e.g., Appelbaum et al., 2000; Macky and Boxall, 2007) which makes use of the same index method and logic: the existence of one HRM practice does not necessarily imply the existence of another, yet a higher score implies the existence of more HRM practices.

[2]   The original scale consisted of ten items. Yet, for parsimony's sake, and as some items overlapped very strongly in wording, we decided to use a focused subset of the items.

as i-deals require power and proactive behavior from the employee (Hornung et al., 2008). We measure this latter tendency through an employee's proactive and self-directed attitude (eight items) (Briscoe et al., 2006). Secondly, an organization's HRM practices can reduce the necessity for employees to negotiate i-deals, yet also create a strong employment relationship in which employees feel comfortable asking for additional support should they need it (for example, through i-deals) (Lee et al., 2015; Liao et al., 2016). We capture this by measuring HR practices which offer employees internal opportunities for development, advancement, and long-term employment (Lee et al., 2015); that is, career counseling, training, functional appraisals, and employee coaching (four items capturing the existence of these practices). Thirdly, as larger organizations are typically characterized by a stronger union presence, which emphasize collective, rather than individual, negotiations, size could be a hindering factor in the negotiation of i-deals. As such, we used different categories (number of employees: 1–9, 10–49, 50–199, 200–499, 500–999, 1000+) and subsequently transformed this categorical variable in five dummy variables (using the last group as a reference category) for all analyses.

RESULTS

Measurement Model

We specified a six-factor model: autonomy, relatedness, and competence satisfaction (that is, the aspects of need satisfaction), and giving autonomy, consulting, and developing employees (that is, the aspects of empowering leadership).[3] This model showed a satisfactory fit with the data (RMSEA = 0.06; CFI = 0.92; TLI = 0.91; SRMR = 0.05; $\chi^2(480)$ = 10089.11) (Bentler, 1990; Byrne, 2001). Yet, the modification indices showed that one item in the empowering leadership scale related to giving autonomy (that is, "my line manager encourages me to take initiative") strongly cross-loaded with the other two subdimensions of empowering leadership. This is probably due to the ambiguity in the item as it does not clearly specify what kind of initiative is expected (that is, initiative in autonomously performing one's job, giving one's opinion about work-related matters or in one's own self-development). As such, we removed this item to ensure that the three subdimensions of empowering leadership are sufficiently distinct. This resulted in a better fit to the data (RMSEA = 0.05, CFI = 0.94; TLI = 0.93; SRMR = 0.04; $\Delta\chi^2(31)$ = 2756.23; p < 0.05) and factor loadings ranging from 0.44 to 0.88.[4] We thus obtained a valid measurement model.

---

[3] We decided to keep the three dimensions of empowering leadership separate, rather than measuring it as one overarching construct, because the factor analyses indicate that this is the most valid fit to the data. Specifically, a CFA in which the three factors of leadership loaded onto a higher-order factor of "empowering leadership" produced a worse fit (root mean square error of approximation, RMSEA = 0.06; comparative fit index, CFI = 0.93; Tucker–Lewis index, TLI = 0.92; standardized root mean square residual, SRMR = 0.05; $\Delta\chi^2(6)$ = 1056.78; p < 0.05). Also a four-factor model in which all leadership items loaded together on one factor "empowering leadership" (next to the three other factors of autonomy, relatedness and competence satisfaction) rather than splitting them up into three different factors led to a comparatively poorer fit (RMSEA = 0.08; CFI = 0.86; TLI = 0.85; SRMR = 0.06; $\Delta\chi^2(9)$ = 8343.77; p < 0.05). All in all, our CFAs therefore support the choice to keep the dimensions separate.

[4] Detailed results are available upon request.

While we used validated measures for our variables (which are less susceptible to common method bias; Doty and Glick, 1998), we tested for common method bias in several ways. We performed a Harman's one-factor test to verify the presence of one general factor in the data. This implied first running an exploratory factor analysis. This resulted in six factors with eigenvalues of one or above, which were mapped on the six focal variables. Secondly, performing a one-factor confirmatory factor analysis (CFA) in which all items loaded on one and the same factor produced a bad fit compared to the six-factor model (RMSEA = 0.13; CFI = 0.58; TLI = 0.55; SRMR = 0.12; $\Delta\chi^2(15) = 38021.15$; $p < 0.05$), further attesting to the need to take into account several factors. Finally, we verified convergent and discriminant validity (Anderson and Gerbing, 1988). Convergent validity was achieved as a model in which all items loaded on their respected factor (cf. confirmatory factor analysis above) resulted in an acceptable fit to the data. To test the discriminant validity of our measures, on the other hand, we specified several factor models in which – in a pairwise manner – the correlation between two factors was set to 1. In all cases, these model restrictions significantly worsened the model fit ($\Delta\chi^2$ ranging between 1265.15 and 18 651.00; $p < 0.001$) suggesting that the factors are sufficiently distinct from one another to separate them in further analyses.

Analyses

Table 14.1 depicts the means, standard deviations of and correlations between our variables. Through pairwise deletion, this table is based on the full set of data (n = 5747). All three dimensions of empowering leadership were positively correlated with autonomy ($r = 0.50$ to 0.64; $p < 0.001$) and relatedness ($r = 0.31$ to 0.38; $p < 0.001$) satisfaction, yet only the dimensions of "giving autonomy" and "consulting" were related to competence satisfaction ($r = 0.19$ and 0.12; $p < 0.001$). Moreover, task i-deals showed to be positively correlated with all three dimensions of empowering leadership ($r = 0.15$ to 0.20; $p < 0.001$), as well as satisfaction of the needs for autonomy ($r = 0.19$; $p < 0.001$), relatedness ($r = 0.11$; $p < 0.001$), and competence ($r = 0.13$; $p < 0.001$). Considering the strong correlations between the different dimensions of empowering leadership, we checked for multicollinearity by verifying the variance inflation factors (VIF) values, which were well below the conservative cut-off of 5 (ranging between 2.08 and 3.37) (Sheather, 2009). As such, multicollinearity is not expected to affect our results. To test our hypotheses, we performed structural equation modeling in MPLUS. We estimated a model in which the three dimensions of empowering leadership relate to task i-deals through basic need satisfaction. The model, including a full mediation, resulted in an adequate fit (RMSEA = 0.04; CFI = 0.92; TLI = 0.92; SRMR = 0.04). Yet, the modification indices suggested that adding a direct path between the subdimension of "consulting" and task i-deals would improve the model significantly ($\Delta\chi^2(1) = 39.29$; $p < 0.001$), even though the overall fit indices remain unchanged (RMSEA = 0.04; CFI = 0.92; TLI = 0.92; SRMR = 0.04). The results of this model are depicted in Figure 14.2.

Firstly, we found two dimensions of empowering leadership to be positively related to autonomy satisfaction, that is, giving autonomy ($\beta = 0.53$; $p < 0.001$) and developing ($\beta = 0.15$; $p < 0.001$). Two dimensions were also significantly related to relatedness satisfaction, that is, developing ($\beta = 0.11$; $p < 0.05$) and consulting ($\beta = 0.24$; $p < 0.001$). Next, all three dimensions were significantly related to competence satisfaction, yet positively for giving autonomy ($\beta = 0.15$; $p < 0.001$) and consulting ($\beta = 0.17$; $p < 0.01$), while negatively for developing ($\beta = -0.22$; $p < 0.001$). Secondly, autonomy ($\beta = 0.07$; $p < 0.01$) and competence ($\beta = 0.09$;

Table 14.1   Descriptive statistics and correlations (n = 5747)

	Mean	SD	1	2	3	4	5	6	7	8	9	10	11	12	13	14	15	16	17	18
1. Autonomy satisfaction	3.32	0.84																		
2. Relatedness satisfaction	3.45	0.82	0.45																	
3. Competence satisfaction	4.20	0.61	0.25	0.17																
4. EL: Giving autonomy	3.76	0.88	0.64	0.31	0.19															
5. EL: Consulting	3.28	0.89	0.60	0.38	0.12	0.72														
6. EL: Developing	3.04	1.04	0.50	0.37	0.02	0.51	0.74													
7. Task i-deals	0.72	0.93	0.19	0.11	0.13	0.18	0.20	0.15												
8. Gender	0.44	0.50	0.02	0.03	-0.04	-0.00	-0.01	0.02	-0.08											
9. Age	34.63	8.60	0.05	-0.10	0.12	0.00	-0.06	-0.11	0.04	-0.10										
10. Tenure (months)	47.56	59.36	0.01	-0.03	0.12	-0.03	-0.10	-0.11	0.02	-0.04	0.46									
11. Education low	0.19	0.39	-0.01	-0.02	0.04	-0.07	-0.05	-0.02	0.01	-0.00	0.08	0.08								
12. Education medium	0.36	0.48	-0.01	0.02	0.02	-0.01	-0.04	-0.02	-0.02	0.02	0.02	0.08	-0.37							
13. Proactive attitude	4.03	0.54	0.12	0.03	0.22	0.14	0.11	0.06	0.06	-0.03	0.03	-0.04	0.01	-0.02						
14. HR practices	1.92	1.42	0.38	0.32	0.00	0.31	0.45	0.60	0.14	0.01	-0.10	-0.11	-0.04	-0.04	0.02					
15. Size: 1–9	0.09	0.28	-0.01	-0.04	-0.01	-0.03	-0.04	-0.05	-0.03	0.03	-0.01	-0.02	0.06	0.02	0.01	-0.16				
16. Size: 10–49	0.19	0.39	-0.01	-0.02	-0.05	-0.03	-0.04	-0.05	-0.02	0.02	-0.04	-0.04	0.05	0.01	0.01	-0.13	-0.15			
17. Size: 50–199	0.21	0.41	0.01	-0.02	0.06	0.01	-0.00	-0.04	0.01	0.01	0.04	0.02	-0.01	0.03	0.03	-0.05	-0.16	-0.25		
18. Size: 200–499	0.14	0.35	0.01	0.02	0.01	0.00	0.01	0.02	0.00	-0.01	-0.03	-0.03	-0.03	-0.00	-0.02	0.04	-0.13	-0.19	-0.21	
19. Size: 500–999	0.10	0.30	-0.01	0.01	-0.02	-0.00	0.00	0.03	0.00	0.02	-0.01	0.00	0.02	0.01	0.00	0.06	-0.10	-0.16	-0.17	-0.13

Notes: Correlations significant (p < 0.05) from 0.04 onwards; EL = empowering leadership.

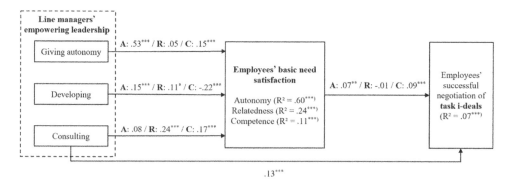

Notes: A = Autonomy satisfaction; R = Relatedness satisfaction; C = Competence satisfaction; * p < 0.05; ** p < 0.01; *** p < 0.001. When also including the control variables in the structural equation modelling (SEM) analyses, some observations were missing too much data on the independent variables for MPLUS to process them. As a result, the SEM analyses are based on 5635 respondents. Analyses under control of employee gender, tenure, age, educational level, proactive attitude; firm HR practices and size.

Figure 14.2   *Results of structural equation modelling analyses (n = 5635)*

p < 0.001) satisfaction related positively to the successful negotiation of task i-deals, whereas relatedness satisfaction was unrelated to the successful negotiation of task i-deals ($\beta = -0.01$; p > 0.05). These results largely confirm hypotheses 2a and 2c, but do not provide support for hypothesis 2b. Finally, a direct positive relationship was found between consulting leadership and the successful negotiation of task i-deals ($\beta = 0.13$; p < 0.001).

Next, we estimated the indirect effects between the different dimensions of empowering leadership and task i-deals through the satisfaction of the three basic needs and performed a delta test in MPLUS to test their significance (MacKinnon, 2008). Moreover, we performed a bootstrap analysis (k = 1000) to test the robustness of the mediation as it estimates a 95 percent confidence limit for indirect relationships (Preacher and Hayes, 2008). The results are summarized in Table 14.2. The empowering leadership dimension "giving autonomy" indirectly relates to task i-deals through autonomy and competence satisfaction, as the indirect paths are significant and zero does not fall within the 95 percent confidence interval. Consulting and developing, however, only indirectly relate to task i-deals through competence satisfaction, yet the former does so in a positive way, while the latter does so in a negative manner. Moreover, as mentioned earlier, we note that a strong direct relationship between consulting leadership and task i-deals was found, pointing towards a partial mediation. Finally, relatedness satisfaction does not mediate the relationship between any dimension of empowering leadership and task i-deals, as the indirect coefficients are all non-significant.

DISCUSSION

Exploring the role of line managers in the practice of task i-deals, this study sought to unpack the pathways through which line managers' empowering leadership relates to employees' successful negotiation of task i-deals. Specifically, we hypothesized that line managers' empowering leadership behavior is associated with proactive behavior among employees in the form

Table 14.2   *Indirect relationships between line managers' empowering leadership and task i-deals via basic need satisfaction (bootstrapping; k = 1000)*

	Via autonomy satisfaction			Via belongingness satisfaction			Via competence satisfaction		
	Lower 2.5%	Estimate	Upper 2.5%	Lower 2.5%	Estimate	Upper 2.5%	Lower 2.5%	Estimate	Upper 2.5%
Giving autonomy	0.01	0.04**	0.07	0.00	0.00	0.00	0.01	0.01***	0.02
Developing	0.00	0.01*	0.02	−0.01	−0.00	0.00	−0.03	−0.02***	−0.01
Consulting	−0.00	0.01	0.01	−0.01	−0.00	0.01	0.01	0.02**	0.03

Note: ** p < 0.01; *** p < 0.001

of task i-deal negotiations, by satisfying employees' basic needs for autonomy, relatedness, and competence. In testing our hypotheses, we distinguished between three subdimensions of empowering leadership, that is: (1) giving autonomy; (2) developing behavior; and (3) consulting behavior. In doing so, our analyses provide rich and nuanced insights that are valuable from both an academic and a practitioners' point of view.

Firstly, we found that the relationship between line managers' empowering leadership and employees' successful negotiation of task i-deals differs strongly between the different dimensions of empowering leadership. Line managers who are perceived to give autonomy, and to consult employees when decisions need to be made, seem to create more room for employees to successfully negotiate task i-deals. Importantly, our results suggest that this can – partly – be explained by employees' basic need satisfaction. On the one hand, line managers who give employees autonomy and freedom support employees' feelings of self-directedness, of being the owner of their own actions rather than being forced (for example, by their line manager), and their belief in their own competencies and effectiveness (Kim et al., 2018). This felt autonomy and competence subsequently relates positively to employees' proactive initiative to improve their own working conditions, reflected in their successful negotiation of task i-deals.

On the other hand, line managers' consulting behaviors relate positively to the successful negotiation of task i-deals through employees' competence satisfaction, yet not through autonomy satisfaction. Indeed, logically, when line managers consult their employees before decisions are made, they send a strong signal that they deem them competent to voice a valuable opinion (Cheong et al., 2016). As such, employees' sense of competence increases, which subsequently gives them more room to successfully negotiate task i-deals (Rosen et al., 2013). Yet, contrary to our predictions, we did not find autonomy satisfaction to play a role. We see a potential explanation for this that warrants future research. One could argue that it is not so much the line managers' consulting behaviors that fosters autonomy satisfaction, but the degree to which the line manager subsequently actually uses and values that opinion in making decisions. Yet, measures of consulting behavior (e.g., Arnold et al., 2000) mix both, which can downplay the relationships found.

Next, interestingly and contrary to our predictions, we found that line managers who are perceived to encourage employees' development are associated with less successfully negotiated task i-deals, because of lower competence satisfaction among their employees. Though counterintuitive, these findings point towards a potential "dark side" of developing line manager behavior, which is in line with previous research showing that organizations' investments in employee training and development can backfire by being interpreted as a sign of incompetence (Marescaux et al., 2013b). As a result, employees might lack the confidence in their own competence and value to successfully negotiate task i-deals. Alternatively, given that the Pearson correlation between managers' focus on development and satisfaction of the need for competence was non-significant, the unexpected result in our model could be explained statistically by a suppression effect and/or multicollinearity (Beckstead, 2012), which can affect both the direction and the strength of coefficients. Indeed, our three dimensions of empowering leadership are relatively highly correlated, though the variance inflation factor values do not raise concerns (ranging between 2.07 and 3.76). Future research might further examine the consequences of managers' encouragement of development and employees' experience of competence satisfaction, and explore the potential existence of a "dark side" to developing line manager behavior, preferably from a longitudinal perspective.

Research Implications

First and foremost, our results support the importance of line managers' leadership behavior towards employees in the context of task i-deals, as a means to individualize HRM practices. They suggest that empowering line managers may foster, but also counteract, the proactive behavior needed to successfully negotiate task i-deals, above and beyond employee characteristics and structural conditions. Hence, we add to previous research on the role of line managers (Hornung et al., 2010, 2014; Rosen et al., 2013) by showing that leadership style, in terms of empowering leadership, relates to the successful negotiation of task i-deals. Expanding the nomological net of the different leadership styles and behaviors which support the negotiation of task i-deals is important not only from an academic point of view, but also to foster the development of a broad range of interventions levering the negotiation of i-deals (and its related benefits).

Importantly, we also partly uncovered the underlying process by making use of SDT. Specifically, we showed that when employees perceive their line manager to be empowering (by giving autonomy and freedom and consulting them before decisions are made), employees perceive more room for initiative and/or feel more competence, creating the right circumstances for them to successfully negotiate task i-deals. We thus conclude that SDT provides a promising theoretical framework to explore the process through which the negotiation of (task) i-deals is fostered. As a result, we answered the call in i-deals research for more novel theoretical insights that can help to uncover the dynamics of i-deals in the work environment beyond the current dominance of social exchange theory (Liao et al., 2016).

Yet, we also need to stress its limits, as employees' relatedness satisfaction was not found to matter in the successful negotiation of task i-deals. While line managers who show developing and consulting behavior satisfy employees' need for relatedness, this is subsequently not related to a successful negotiation of task i-deals. In part, this could be explained by the measure of relatedness satisfaction, which focuses generally on relationships at work (that is, also with co-workers rather than with one's line manager alone). The feeling of being highly related to one's co-workers contradicts the individualized approach of i-deals in which employees negotiate a unique arrangement that others do not have. Employees might expect the negotiation of an i-deal to spark negative emotions and reactions among co-workers (for which there is indeed evidence; e.g., Marescaux et al., 2019b; Ng, 2017), which would subsequently harm their relationship with them. As a result, some highly related employees will negotiate task i-deals while others would not, to avoid negative side-effects, explaining our non-significant statistical relationship. Hence, we can conclude that SDT helps to explain when and how employees see the opportunity and freedom to negotiate i-deals (that is, through autonomy satisfaction) as well as feel able to do so (that is, through competence satisfaction). Yet, the relational base for them to successfully negotiate a task i-deal with their line manager would have to be created in another manner (for example, through LMX) (Hornung et al., 2010, 2014).

We also see the limits of SDT in a strong direct relationship between line managers' consulting behavior and the successful negotiation of task i-deals. It is possible that in discussing work with the line manager (which is the result of their consulting behavior), opportunities for task i-deals become very visible and are directly agreed upon between employee and line manager, without there even being a need for strong proactive behavior on the part of the employee. These discussions give employees a direct indication of what task i-deals the line manager would grant and support, and allow them to find a mutually satisfying solution straight away. So, irrespective of basic need satisfaction, consulting behavior would directly lead to agreements regarding task i-deals, potentially even initiated by the line manager in an effort to find a solution to a task-related issue (Rousseau, 2005).

A second major contribution is to the literature on empowering leadership. On the one hand, we empirically tested an often made, yet never tested, assumption that basic need satisfaction explains why empowering leaders foster more proactive behaviors among employees (e.g., Amundsen and Martinsen, 2014; Kim et al., 2018). On the other hand, and importantly, by distinguishing between the three subdimensions of giving autonomy, developing, and consulting behavior, we show that not all empowering leadership behaviors unequivocally foster employees' need satisfaction and, subsequently, the successful negotiation of task i-deals. Both the size and the direction of the relationships differed. Whereas giving autonomy and freedom most strongly related to task i-deals through autonomy satisfaction, consulting behaviors did so most strongly through competence satisfaction. Moreover, and in sharp contrast, developing behavior related negatively to task i-deals, because it reduced competence satisfaction. As such, we add to the scarce research showing a potential "dark side" to empowering leadership (Cheong et al., 2016), and thereby show that using a broad conceptualization of empowering leadership is both useful and highly relevant, as it can uncover which exact leadership behaviors are useful.

Finally, our study adds to the growing literature showing that need satisfaction allows employees to take on an active role and shape their environment. Previous research indicated that employees who experience basic need satisfaction may actively craft their job to make it more meaningful and easier to identify with (Slemp and Vella-Brodrick, 2013). We add to this by showing that employees also engage in negotiations with their line manager to customize their job content beyond what they can craft themselves. By looking at the needs separately, our research also answers the call to consider the needs as separate, non-compensatory entities (Van den Broeck et al., 2016). Although SDT conceptualizes each of the needs as distinct (Ryan and Deci, 2000), too often they have been combined in an overall index of need satisfaction, which implies that the needs are interchangeable and can compensate for each other. Our study, however, indicates that the need for relatedness cannot substitute for low autonomy or competence: while the latter two needs foster the negotiation of i-deals, a focus on relatedness satisfaction is rather unlikely to stimulate employees to engage in such negotiations. By showing differential results of the three basic needs, our research adds to the uncovering of their different nomological nets.

Practical Implications

Our results suggest that when organizations want to encourage the negotiation of task i-deals in order to benefit from their favorable outcomes (for example, increased work engagement, job satisfaction, organizational commitment, and job performance) (Liao et al., 2016), they should direct their focus towards the line managers of employees. Specifically, when line managers show empowering leadership behavior by giving autonomy to and consulting their employees, task i-deals are more likely to successfully be negotiated. As such, organizations can benefit from recruiting line managers who are able to show this behavior towards their subordinates, or training them in this style of leadership. Typical behaviors that can be trained are giving employees the freedom to do their job as they see fit, encouraging initiative and independent thinking and action, and allowing employees to use their own judgment in doing their job (Pearce and Sims, 2002; Stogdill et al., 1962; Yukl et al., 2002). Moreover, line managers can be actively trained and encouraged to make decisions more democratically by allowing their employees to voice their opinion in matters that affect them. Not only does this satisfy their needs for relatedness and competence, but because of the latter, it also stimulates them to negotiate task i-deals which can benefit both the employee and organization (Rosen et al., 2013). Moreover, it is an essential element of procedural justice, which in itself predicts a wide range of beneficial outcomes (Cohen-Charash and Spector, 2001).

In contrast, we would caution organizations in training their line managers to show developing leadership behavior in an effort to inspire employees to negotiate task i-deals. Indeed, overall, developing leadership actually related negatively to the successful negotiation of task i-deals, through employees' reduced competence satisfaction. Apart from less successfully negotiated task i-deals, this lowered sense of competence can subsequently have other negative outcomes (for example, less engagement, commitment, and retention) (e.g. Marescaux et al., 2013b). Yet, that being said, developing leadership can inspire a wide range of other beneficial outcomes such as positive work attitudes and behaviors (Marescaux et al., 2019a; Rafferty and Griffin, 2006). Moreover, to counter this negative relationship with competence satisfaction, line managers can be trained to inspire employees to develop their skills to grow further, rather than signaling a need for development because they have certain important shortcomings. In other words, developing leadership training can still be useful if line managers subsequently implement it without giving employees a sense of incompetence.

Limitations and Suggestions for Further Research

This study is not without its limitations. Firstly, the cross-sectional design of the study does not allow us to draw definitive causal conclusions. However, our hypotheses are grounded in a wide range of theoretical and empirical research on empowering leadership, self-determination theory, and i-deals. The literature on empowering leadership frames it as an external factor that – in a trickledown manner – affects employees' proactive behavior. Accordingly, many studies have theoretically argued that empowering leadership (as a factor external to the employee) precedes employees' (proactive) behavior (e.g., Arnold et al., 2000; Chen et al., 2011; Cheong et al., 2016; Martin et al., 2013; Thun and Bakker, 2018; Zhang and Bartol, 2010). Similarly, the literature on self-determination theory argues that (proactive) behaviors are fostered by basic need satisfaction, and not vice versa (Deci and Ryan, 2000; Gagné and Deci, 2005). Accordingly, several studies have empirically shown this (e.g., Leroy et al., 2015;

Van den Broeck et al., 2016). Nevertheless, we would encourage future research to make use of longitudinal designs or experimental research.

Secondly, we found no evidence that relatedness satisfaction explains why empowering leaders foster the negotiation of task i-deals. To address this, future studies could explore which relational base is needed for employees to successfully negotiate (task) i-deals. On the one hand, research suggests that a strong LMX relationship is needed for employees to negotiate i-deals with their line manager (e.g., Hornung et al., 2010, 2014; Rosen et al., 2013). Yet, the relational base that employees have with their co-workers might also matter, as employees might refrain from negotiating a unique deal with their line manager to avoid them being different from the group they perhaps so strongly identify with, and which cause harmful side-effects through co-worker reactions (Marescaux et al., 2019b). As such, future research could explore this tension and how it affects the negotiation of i-deals. Relatedly, given that previous research has shown that LMX affects the negotiation of i-deals (Hornung et al., 2010, 2014; Rosen et al., 2013), it would be particularly interesting for future research to study the combined effects of LMX and the leadership behaviors exhibited by the line manager. This would help to make firmer conclusions as to whether the effects are simply additive or, rather, synergetic. As we did not control for LMX in our study, we cannot draw any conclusions regarding this.

Thirdly, future research could explore the boundary conditions in the relationship between empowering leadership and (task) i-deals. Both job and organizational context can play a role here. In some jobs it might be more difficult for employees to negotiate (task) i-deals with their line manager; for example, because the job content is highly standardized and bound by job descriptions, procedures, and manuals (for example, in manufacturing or administrative environments), or because employees have relatively few opportunities to engage and communicate with their supervisors (for example, in the context of remote work) (Hornung et al., 2008, 2009). The latter has become all the more salient during the COVID-19 pandemic where many employees were forced to shift to telework, which reduced their interactions with their supervisors. Importantly, as we are starting to shift to a post-pandemic world of work, many organizations may consider continuing to allow employees to engage in telework, which would further reinforce the hurdle employees experience to negotiate i-deals. In any case, we would logically assume that the more restrictions the job or context puts on i-deal negotiations, the more important it becomes for line managers to display empowering leadership behaviors if they want employees to engage in the negotiation of (task) i-deals and benefit from them. In addition to the job context, the organizational context could also play a role. In organizations with a more secretive culture, employees might negotiate less visible i-deals (for example financial i-deals) as compared to organizations with a more transparent culture. As task i-deals are quite visible, they could be less common in organizations where secrecy prevails. As such, future research could explore this in more detail.

Finally, we only focused on the successful negotiation of task i-deals. However, employees may also attempt to negotiate i-deals which are rebuffed by their line manager. As such, future research could focus on disentangling the i-deal requests that employees make from their actual allocation, as line managers play a role in explaining both aspects of i-deal negotiation.

REFERENCES

Amundsen, S., and Martinsen, Ø.L. (2014). Empowering leadership: Construct clarification, conceptualization, and validation of a new scale. *Leadership Quarterly*, 25(3), 487–511.

Anderson, J.C., and Gerbing, D.W. (1988). Structural equation modeling in practice: A review and recommended two-step approach. *Psychological Bulletin*, 103(3), 411–423.

Appelbaum, E., Bailey, T., Berg, P.B., Kalleberg, A.L., and Bailey, T.A. (2000). *Manufacturing Advantage: Why High-Performance Work Systems Pay Off.* Ithaca, NY: Cornell University Press.

Arnold, J.A., Arad, S., Rhoades, J.A., and Drasgow, F. (2000). The empowering leadership questionnaire: The construction and validation of a new scale for measuring leader behaviors. *Journal of Organizational Behavior*, 21(3), 249–269.

Bal, P.M., and Dorenbosch, L. (2015). Age-related differences in the relations between individualised HRM and organisational performance: A large-scale employer survey. *Human Resource Management Journal*, 25(1), 41–61.

Baumeister, R.F., and Leary, M.R. (1995). The need to belong: Desire for interpersonal attachments as a fundamental human motivation. *Psychological Bulletin*, 117(3), 497–529.

Beckstead, J.W. (2012). Isolating and examining sources of suppression and multicollinearity in multiple linear regression. *Multivariate Behavioral Research*, 47(2), 224–246.

Bentler, P.M. (1990). Comparative fit indices in structural models. *Psychological Bulletin*, 107(2), 238–246.

Bos-Nehles, A.C., Van Riemsdijk, M.J., and Kees Looise, J. (2013). Employee perceptions of line management performance: Applying the AMO theory to explain the effectiveness of line managers' HRM implementation. *Human Resource Management*, 52(6), 861–877.

Briscoe, J.P., Hall, D.T., and DeMuth, R.L.F. (2006). Protean and boundaryless careers: An empirical exploration. *Journal of Vocational Behavior*, 69(1), 30–47.

Burke, C.S., Stagl, K.C., Klein, C., Goodwin, G.F., Salas, E., and Halpin, S.M. (2006). What type of leadership behaviors are functional in teams? A meta-analysis. *Leadership Quarterly*, 17(3), 288–307.

Byrne, B.M. (2001). *Structural Equation Modeling with Amos: Basic Concepts Application and Programming.* Mahwah, NJ: Lawrence Erlbaum Associates.

Chen, G., Sharma, P.N., Edinger, S.K., Shapiro, D.L., and Farh, J.L. (2011). Motivating and demotivating forces in teams: Cross-level influences of empowering leadership and relationship conflict. *Journal of Applied Psychology*, 96, 541–557.

Cheong, M., Spain, S.M., Yammarino, F.J., and Yun, S. (2016). Two faces of empowering leadership: Enabling and burdening. *Leadership Quarterly*, 27(4), 602–616.

Cohen-Charash, Y., and Spector, P.E. (2001). The role of justice in organizations: A meta-analysis. *Organizational Behavior and Human Decision Processes*, 86(2), 278–321.

DeCharms, R. (1968). *Personal Causation: The Internal Affective Determinants of Behavior.* New York: Academic Press.

Deci, E.L., and Ryan, M.R. (2000). The "what" and "why" of goal pursuits: Human needs and the self-determination of behavior. *Psychological Inquiry*, 11(4), 227–268.

Doty, D.H., and Glick, W.H. (1998). Common methods bias: Does common methods variance really bias results? *Organizational Research Methods*, 1(4), 374–406.

Gagné, M., and Deci, R.M. (2005). Self-determination theory and work motivation. *Journal of Organizational Behavior*, 26, 331–362.

Hetland, H., Hetland, J., Andreassen, C.S., Pallesen, S., and Notelaers, G. (2011). Leadership and fulfillment of the three basic psychological needs at work. *Career Development International*, 16(5), 507–523.

Hornung, S., Rousseau, D.M., and Glaser, J. (2008). Creating flexible work arrangements through idiosyncratic deals. *Journal of Applied Psychology*, 93(3), 655–664.

Hornung, S., Rousseau, D.M., and Glaser, J. (2009). Why supervisors make idiosyncratic deals: Antecedents and outcomes of i-deals from a managerial perspective. *Journal of Managerial Psychology*, 24(8), 738–764.

Hornung, S., Rousseau, D.M., Glaser, J., Angerer, P., and Weigl, M. (2010). Beyond top-down and bottom-up work redesign: Customizing job content through idiosyncratic deals. *Journal of Organizational Behavior*, 31, 187–215.

Hornung, S., Rousseau, D.M., Glaser, J., Angerer, P., and Weigl, M. (2011). Employee-oriented leadership and quality of working life: Mediating roles of idiosyncratic deals. *Psychological Reports*, 108(1), 59–74.

Hornung, S., Rousseau, D.M., Weigl, M., Müller, A. and Glaser, J. (2014). Redesigning work through idiosyncratic deals. *European Journal of Work and Organizational Psychology*, 34(4), 608–626.

Kehoe, R.R., and Han, J.H. (2020). An expanded conceptualization of line managers' involvement in human resource management. *Journal of Applied Psychology*, 105(2), 111–129.

Kim, M., Beehr, T.A., and Prewett, M.S. (2018). Employee responses to empowering leadership: A meta-analysis. *Journal of Leadership and Organizational Studies*, 25(3), 257–276.

Knies, E., Leisink, P., and van de Schoot, R. (2020). People management: Developing and testing a measurement scale. *International Journal of Human Resource Management*, 31(6), 705–737.

Kovjanic, S., Schuh, S.C., and Jonas, K. (2013). Transformational leadership and performance: An experimental investigation of the mediating effects of basic needs satisfaction and work engagement. *Journal of Occupational and Organizational Psychology*, 86, 543–555.

Lee, A., Willis, S., and Tian, A.W. (2018). Empowering leadership: A meta-analytic examination of incremental contribution, mediation, and moderation. *Journal of Organizational Behavior*, 39(3), 306–325.

Lee, J., Bachrach, D.G., and Rousseau, D.M. (2015). Internal labor markets, firm-specific human capital, and heterogeneity antecedents of employee idiosyncratic deal requests. *Organization Science*, 26(3), 794–810.

Leroy, H., Anseel, F., Gardner, W.L., and Sels, L. (2015). Authentic leadership, authentic followership, basic need satisfaction, and work role performance: A cross-level study. *Journal of Management*, 41(6), 1677–1697.

Liao, C., Wayne, S.J., and Rousseau, D.M. (2016). Idiosyncratic deals in contemporary organizations: A qualitative and meta-analytical review. *Journal of Organizational Behavior*, 37, S9–S29.

Littrell, R.F. (2013). Explicit leader behaviour: A review of literature, theory development, and research project results. *Journal of Management Development*, 32(6), 567–605.

Macky, K., and Boxall, P. (2007). The relationship between 'high-performance work practices' and employee attitudes: An investigation of additive and interaction effects. *International Journal of Human Resource Management*, 18(4), 537–567.

MacKinnon, D.P. (2008). *Introduction to Statistical Mediation Analysis*. Mahway, NJ: Erlbaum.

Marescaux E., De Winne S., and Brebels L. (2021). Putting the pieces together: A review of HR differentiation literature and a multilevel model. *Journal of Management*, 47(6), 1564–159.

Marescaux, E., De Winne, S., and Forrier, A. (2019a). Developmental HRM, employee well-being and performance: The moderating role of developing leadership. *European Management Review*, 16, 317–331.

Marescaux, E., De Winne, S., and Sels, L. (2013a). HR practices and affective organisational commitment: (When) does HR differentiation pay off? *Human Resource Management Journal*, 23(4), 329–345.

Marescaux, E., De Winne, S., and Sels, L. (2013b). HR practices and HRM outcomes: The role of basic need satisfaction. *Personnel Review*, 42(1), 4–27.

Marescaux, E., De Winne, S., and Sels, L. (2019b). Idiosyncratic deals from a distributive justice perspective: Examining co-workers' voice behavior. *Journal of Business Ethics*, 154(1), 263–281.

Martin, S.L., Liao, H., and Campbell, E.M. (2013). Directive versus empowering leadership: A field experiment comparing impacts on task proficiency and proactivity. *Academy of Management Journal*, 56(5), 1372–1395.

Ng, T.W. (2017). Can idiosyncratic deals promote perceptions of competitive climate, felt ostracism, and turnover? *Journal of Vocational Behavior*, 99, 118–131.

Pearce, C.L., and Sims, H.P. (2002). Vertical vs. shared leadership as predictors of the effectiveness of change management teams: An examination of aversive, directive, transaction, transformational and empowering behaviors. *Group Dynamics*, 6(2), 172–197.

Perry, E.L., and Kulik, C.T. (2008). The devolution of HR to the line: Implications for perceptions of people management effectiveness. *International Journal of Human Resource Management*, 19, 262–273.

Preacher, K.J., and Hayes, A.F. (2008). Asymptotic and resampling strategies for assessing and comparing indirect effects in multiple mediator models. *Behavior Research Methods*, 40(3), 879–891.

Rafferty, A.E., and Griffin, M.A. (2006). Refining individualized consideration: Distinguishing developmental leadership and supportive leadership. *Journal of Occupational and Organizational Psychology*, 79(1), 37–61.

Rosen, C.C., Slater, D.J., Chang, C.D., and Johnson, R.E. (2013). Let's make a deal: Development and validation of the ex-post i-deals scale. *Journal of Management*, 39(3), 709–742.

Rousseau, D.M. (2005). *I-deals: Idiosyncratic Deals Employees Bargain for Themselves*. Armonk, NY: M.E. Sharpe.

Ryan, R.M., and Deci, E. L. (2000). Self-determination theory and the facilitation of intrinsic motivation, social development, and well-being. *American Psychologist*, 55(1), 68–78.

Sharma, P.N., and Kirkman, B.L. (2015). Leveraging leaders: A literature review and future lines of inquiry for empowering leadership research. *Group and Organization Management*, 40(2), 193–237.

Sheather, S. (2009). *A Modern Approach to Regression with R*. New York: Springer Science and Business Media.

Slemp, G.R., and Vella-Brodrick, D.A. (2013). Optimising employee mental health: The relationship between intrinsic need satisfaction, job crafting, and employee well-being. *Journal of Happiness Studies*, 15(4), 957–977.

Stogdill, R.M., Goode, O.S. and Day, D.R. (1962). New leader behavior description subscales. *Journal of Psychology*, 54, 259–269.

Thun, S., and Bakker, A.B. (2018). Empowering leadership and job crafting: The role of employee optimism. *Stress and Health*, 34(4), 573–581.

Van den Broeck, A., Ferris, D.L., Chang, C.H., and Rosen, C.C. (2016). A review of self-determination theory's basic psychological needs at work. *Journal of Management*, 42(5), 1195–1229.

Van den Broeck, A., Vansteenkiste, M., De Witte, H., Soenens, B., and Lens, W. (2010). Capturing autonomy, competence, and relatedness at work: Construction and initial validation of the Work-related Basic Need Satisfaction scale. *Journal of Occupational and Organizational Psychology*, 83(4), 981–1002.

Yukl, G., Gordon, A., and Taber, T. (2002). A hierarchical taxonomy of leadership behavior: Integrating a half century of behavior research. *Journal of Leadership and Organizational Studies*, 9(1), 15–32.

Zhang, X., and Bartol, K.M. (2010). Linking empowering leadership and employee creativity: The influence of psychological empowerment, intrinsic motivation, and creative process engagement. *Academy of Management Journal*, 53(1), 107–128.

15. Global talent management: the central role of line managers throughout the organisation in shaping and implementing effective GTM

Karin A. King

INTRODUCTION

Global talent management (GTM) is widely recognised to be of central importance to organisations today as they seek to thrive and grow in the context of today's complex and dynamic global business environment, such that global talent management has become a central priority of chief executive officers and top management (Collings et al., 2017). Building the organisation's supply or pipeline of talent is recognised to be one of the most significant challenges faced by businesses globally (Al Ariss et al., 2014). With the recognised significance of talent to organisations globally (Collings et al., 2017), and more specifically, the challenge of creating and sustaining an effective future-looking pipeline of talent as one of utmost concern for global organisations (Cascio and Boudreau, 2016), it is important to understand how line managers contribute to the business imperative of GTM.

Strategic talent management is defined as:

> the systematic identification of key positions which differentially contribute to the organisation's sustainable competitive advantage, the development of a talent pool of high potential and high performing incumbents to fill these roles, and the development of a differentiated human resource architecture to facilitate filling these positions with competent incumbents and to ensure their continued commitment to the organisation. (Collings and Mellahi, 2009: 304)

Global talent management describes strategic talent management applied in the context of the multinational enterprise (MNE) to serve the priorities and stakeholders of the MNE (Tarique and Schuler, 2010). Managers at each level of the organisation have been identified as crucial contributors or central actors in the definition of talent strategy for their organisation, the design of the talent system of policies, programmes and practices, and the implementation of the talent system aligned with business priorities (King, 2015a).

Line managers today are not only business managers and supervisors of employees in their organisations but also, crucially, are managers of talent, and as such they play an important role in talent management in organisations today. The line manager is increasingly in focus and of interest in the strategic human resources management (HRM) literature as a central agent in the implementation of HRM practices (Purcell and Hutchinson, 2007), such as in performance management (Farndale and Kelliher, 2013) and in strategic talent management (King, 2015a). As with other components of human resource management implementation in organisations today in which line managers are increasingly involved (Cappelli, 2013), the implementation of GTM extends well beyond the mandate of senior management and includes middle and frontline managers as central actors in the implementation of GTM and its effectiveness. Collectively, managers at varying hierarchical levels in the organisation shape and implement talent management policy and practice, and in doing so, influence GTM effectiveness as a strategic people management practice, amongst the wider context of human resource management practices. Operationally, line managers are argued to be central actors in talent management (King, 2015a), and make an important contribution to global talent management through their influence on both shaping the design and implementation of the talent system as well as their influence on employee perceptions and response to GTM in their organisation. This chapter considers the active participation of line managers at varying levels of the organisational hierarchy in the implementation of global talent management.

In this chapter, we consider the role of managers at all levels in the organisation. 'Line manager', then, refers to any individual who manages other employees and is accountable for people management as part of their role. That is, the line manager is a people manager who works in the line of business. There may be several lines of business in the organisation, which all ultimately report to senior management and together form the overall organisational structure. Therefore these roles, which include accountability for management of people, whether frontline, middle or senior managers, are all managers of people embedded throughout the organisational structure and may exist at all levels. It is this structural people management accountability, embedded within the business structure, within each line of business, through which talent management is enacted in the business day to day. Each level of line management, whether frontline manager or senior management, plays a role in the execution of the organisation's talent management strategy, consistent with the scope and accountability of the line manager's role at a given level of authority.

This chapter considers what global talent management means for managers and their roles throughout the organisation. To do so, it draws on the extant talent management literature, to present a review of the varying activities and roles of management across the organisation in its practice of global talent management as recognised in the scholarly literature. Talent management has been introduced in the literature as an organisationally embedded system within which essential actors participate to collectively co-create talent management and its outcomes. The talent system, directly informed by business strategy, is comprised of the component parts of talent strategy, talent policies and practices, and the employee experience of talent management, all underpinned by communications, tools and processes to support talent management, which together facilitate the outcomes of talent management (King, 2015a). The central actors of the talent system are the talented employee and the organisation's line managers: the employee's supervising manager who manages performance and facilitates opportunities for in-role development of talent potential, the HR manager who facilitates talent management process and policy enactment, and the leadership and senior management of the firm who establish the talent strategy, communicate talent priorities and act as organisational sponsors of the many investments in talent (King, 2015a).

This first section has briefly introduced the topic of global talent management and the strategic talent system, and introduced line managers as central actors in the firm's talent management. The section which follows presents a review of the contribution of line managers to effective global talent management, and does so by specifying three levels in the organisational hierarchy: senior management, middle management, and frontline or first-line managers. The third section presents a critical discussion of the reviewed literature, and proposes areas of future research which emerge from the review as important to advancing our understanding of the role of line managers in global talent management, following which the final section concludes the chapter.

LINE MANAGERS AS CENTRAL ACTORS IN GLOBAL TALENT MANAGEMENT

At all levels in organisations today, line managers are identified as having some form of accountability for and making a contribution to the management of the organisation's talent or talent pools. The organisation's line management comprises managers of varying different levels in the organisation. In this section, three distinct levels of management will be considered in the review of the research literature, in regard to their varying respective roles in the effective management of talent in international organisations. Collectively, there is some identifiable shared effort and accountability in the implementation of talent management as a strategic human capital management practice, while there are also some discernible differences according to the hierarchical level of the line manager role. This section identifies examples of the activities of the line manager at each level in the organisational hierarchy which relate to the design or implementation of global talent management, and indicates the common areas of influence as well as the distinct activities which line managers undertake in managing the firm's talent and talent pools.

The literature is helpful in pointing to differing levels of authority in people management, and therefore the scope of accountability for management of the firm's people through the human resources (HR) architecture. Extending from the core HR architecture, a differentiated HR architecture exists for talent management (Collings and Mellahi, 2009). This differentiated HR architecture is based on the talent system, a strategic system which, extending beyond very good HR practice, enables the implementation of talent management in the organisation and includes talent-specific activities and processes such as talent identification, talent reviews and talent pool management (King, 2015a). As a strategic system, line managers at all levels play a strategic role as one of several central actors in the system and, as such, the roles of line managers can be delineated to specify the talent activities and processes in which they are involved at a given level of organisational authority (King, 2015a). This section introduces key activities in strategic talent management for line managers at various levels of organisational hierarchy and accountability in the implementation of talent strategy and all its related processes and practices.

Senior Management: Defining the Talent Strategy and Communicating GTM as a Strategic Priority

The senior management of an organisation comprises the cadre of individuals who are appointed to the most senior roles in the organisational hierarchy including the top management team (TMT). In keeping with the concept of the strategic apex introduced by Mintzberg (1979), whereby senior management are responsible for establishing the long-term strategic priorities and objectives of the organisation and the corresponding policies through which these objectives will be achieved, in regard to global talent management specifically, senior management hold the responsibility for talent strategy and the oversight of its implementation through policy and practice in the organisation. Senior management are one of the primary stakeholders of talent management who can be considered 'owners' of the talent agenda for the firm (King, 2015b). Forming the strategic apex of the organisation, senior management positions can be viewed as pivotal positions in the organisation, by virtue of the significant scope of senior management positions and the magnitude of influence such positions may have on business outcomes which are achieved (or undermined) through high (or low) performance in these roles. Pivotal positions are those specific roles within an organisation which disproportionately contribute to business performance (Boudreau and Ramstad, 2005b). As the organisation's most senior leadership, the activities of senior management have a significant influence over the organisation's approach to talent management, the design and implementation of global talent management strategy, talent management policy and practice, and therefore, ultimately, outcomes of the talent system. From a review of the literature, five main priorities emerge regarding the role of senior management in global talent management. These are presented briefly below.

Definition of talent strategy and business requirements for talent

Talent management is recognised to be one of the highest priorities of senior management today (Cappelli and Keller, 2014) and is expected to generate competitive value for the firm. As a strategic resource of the firm (Boudreau and Ramstad, 2005a), the strategic purpose of talent for the organisation is based on how talent creates advantage or value for the business. Talent is theorised to create value in four ways: value creation, value capture, value leverage and value protection (Sparrow and Makram, 2015). Managerial labour is seen as a significant talent pool for value creation, as senior management typically hold pivotal positions (Collings and Mellahi, 2009), which are positions in the organisation that have the opportunity to disproportionately create value for the business when compared with other roles (Becker et al., 2009). Management talent is also seen as one talent pool of utmost concern, in large part due to the scarcity of managerial talent (Mackey et al., 2013) which requires significant effort of management to select and retain. Seeking talent who have the ability to deliver high performance working in the global environment of international companies, organisations search for global competence, seen as fundamental to the management of international organisations (Cascio and Boudreau, 2016). The needs for talent may vary across the enterprise and a key principle in GTM effectiveness is to balance global and local needs for talent (Stahl et al., 2012), which senior management are well positioned to collectively determine as part of defining the firm's talent priorities and the strategy required to achieve them.

Establishment of talent pools and talent identification policies

One of the key principles in effective global talent management is the importance of aligning talent management with business strategy (Stahl et al., 2012), and it is the senior management who, informed by the scope and authority of their positions are responsible for setting talent strategy. Senior management use workforce planning (Cappelli, 2008) to identify their required supply for talent in one or more defined talent pools, which often include but extend well beyond the search for managerial labour as one defined talent pool. Through applying a workforce differentiation strategy (Becker et al., 2009) whereby segments of the workforce, individual talent and critical positions are identified, senior management can then refine talent strategy and associated policies, practices and investments to align to the priorities of the firm.

To implement talent management using a workforce differentiation strategy is known as the exclusive philosophy of talent management (Meyers and van Woerkom, 2014), whereby only a portion of the overall workforce is identified for active participation in talent programmes such as high-potential programmes, talent retention strategies and differentiated total rewards. However, in practice, most organisations employ a hybrid approach (Dries and De Gieter, 2014) whereby an inclusive philosophy of talent is applied such that all of the workforce is viewed as the organisation's talent (Meyers and van Woerkom, 2014) while, additionally, specific individuals are identified as high performers or those with high potential to contribute to the firm's priorities in future. To implement talent management which involves some degree of differentiation, the firm's leadership adopt a set of HR processes which are differentiated from the standard HR architecture (Collings and Mellahi, 2009). This differentiated talent architecture is employed to assess the talent potential of employees for the purposes of identifying employees with talent or talent potential of specific importance to the business. Talent-identified employees are then included in organisational talent programmes or talent pools. Talent pools are groups of individuals who the organisation identifies as having high performance and the potential to contribute differentiated performance in future through deployment to critical positions (Collings and Mellahi, 2009; Stahl et al., 2007). Critical positions are those roles in the organisation which disproportionately contribute to business outcomes (Becker et al., 2009). The main factor involved in the identification of employees to include in a talent pool is the observations arising from their performance appraisal (Mäkelä et al., 2010).

Talent reviews and talent decision-making
To effectively manage the differentially identified talent which exists within the wider workforce, and in recognition of the responsibility of management to allocate the inevitably limited resources of the firm, decision-making has become a central component of the role of senior management in effective GTM. Broadly speaking, talent management decisions are those management decisions which seek to optimize the human capital held within the firm (Khoreva and Vaiman, 2019). Management are urged to approach talent management with structure and meticulousness in decision-making, as they would for decisions about any other competitive resource or opportunity (Boudreau and Ramstad, 2005b). Senior management are in effect the 'sponsors' of the organisational talent strategy and, accordingly, make decisions on the range of investments the firm will make in talent as well. Talent investments may include the firm's use of high-potential development programmes (Dries and De Gieter, 2014; Dries and Pepermans, 2007), leadership development programmes (Dries and Pepermans, 2012), international assignments (McNulty and Cieri, 2016), and talent-specific rewards such as long-term incentives distributed on a highly selective basis for the dual purpose of differentiated reward and long-term retention.

Talent management decision-making by line managers at senior levels in the organisation may include a range of other decisions, such as remote working policies, career progression decisions, talent recruitment, and the setting up of recruitment and rewards programmes. Priorities for senior management decision-making in talent management include the individual talent identification process, and the collective organisational talent review in which senior management confirm the individual talent assessments undertaken by middle management. Having identified the firm's talent, talent investments are then directed towards these individuals and the critical roles in which they are deployed. However researchers argue that organisations overidentify talent in their workforce, owing to the lack of a disciplined decision science for talent assessment, thereby resulting in overinvestment in talent pools and underleveraged talent for business impact (Boudreau and Ramstad, 2005a, 2005b). Decision frameworks are needed to support key decisions regarding talent (Boudreau and Ramstad, 2007); however, decisions are often undertaken without sufficient data and the required analysis (Boudreau, 2010). Researchers also call for greater optimisation of talent allocation or deployment for increased value creation, as well as improved talent metrics for more effective senior management decision-making in the deployment of talent as the firm's strategic human capital (Boudreau and Ramstad, 2007).

Communication of talent priorities and fostering a climate for talent

Senior management are closely involved in ensuring that sufficient effort is given to attracting, selecting and retaining talent for leadership positions today and in future. As sensemakers, employees strive to make sense of their workplace environment and their relationship with their organisation. Leaders have been characterised as sense-givers (Nishii and Paluch, 2018), such that leaders help employees to interpret the meaning of HR practices relative to their individual roles. While this mechanism is theorised to be stronger for the direct manager or supervisor than for senior managers (Nishii and Paluch, 2018), senior management are directly involved in signalling the strategic priorities and rationale underlying the firm's approach to management of talent through their action choice of talent philosophy, at some point on the exclusive–inclusive continuum.

Signalling theory (Spence, 1973) explains that employees will perceive actions by senior management in the enactment of global talent management as signals of management's intended priorities for talent. Extending from signalling theory to attribution theory, researchers have argued that employees will form attributions of the meaning of, and rationale underlying, the use of HR practices and policies which they observe around them in the organisation (Nishii et al., 2008). HR attribution theory (HRA), then, could be applied to further consider how employees interpret the purpose of global talent management or the use of specific talent practices. While further empirical research is needed to understand the attributions which employees make regarding talent management (King, 2018) – that is, talent management attributions – it can be expected that the highly visible nature of management involvement in strategic talent management in organisations today will be instrumental in employee perceptions of the purpose of talent management in their organisations.

In keeping with signalling theory, leader communications have been shown to influence the establishment of culture in organisations. Leadership communications in directing talent management at their firms can then be an important factor in the effectiveness of GTM at the firm. The extent to which talent management is embedded in the culture of the firm has been shown to be a key principle in the effectiveness of the firm's GTM (Stahl et al., 2012). The strength of the talent system, including its embeddedness in the firm's culture, has been argued to be predictive of the effectiveness of talent outcomes for the organisation (King, 2016a).

Engagement with the external macro talent context

The activity of senior management and their structural decisions regarding the firm's investment in talent may also have tangible impact beyond the boundaries of the firm. For example, employer branding can be a competitive advantage for talent attraction, such as in the communication of CSR priorities valued by employees (Bhattacharya et al., 2008), and as such may help to attract external talent to the firm, through employer branding as a business which differentially invests in talent for the future. Talent inducements such as investments in high-potential development and new graduate programmes may be seen as positive invest-ments by employees. This may contribute to employer branding through differentiation of the firm from other firms, recognised to be a key principle of effective GTM (Stahl et al., 2012).

Recently, the concept of macro talent management has been introduced in the literature. Macro talent management is defined as 'the activities that are systematically developed by governmental and nongovernmental organizations expressly for the purpose of enhancing the quality and quantity of talent within and across countries and regions to facilitate innovation and competitiveness of their citizens and corporations' (Khilji et al., 2015: 237). Authors have argued that through greater investigation of the external macro talent-related factors which influence the organisation's ability to attract and retain a sustainable supply of talent, management have greater agency to influence the macro talent context (King and Vaiman, 2019). For example, management might interact with the other external actors in the talent system: senior management may engage in influential discussions with governmental bodies and decision-makers to argue the importance of greater access to foreign skilled talent through preferential immigration visa programmes, such as in Canada's efforts to increase skilled talent supply to enable economic growth (Government of Canada, 2017), or in the United Kingdom's (UK) efforts to mitigate the negative consequences of the UK's departure from the European Union, removing the previously free movement of skilled labour across borders (IOD, 2018).

Considering the role of senior management in setting talent strategy, defining talent policy and process, signalling talent priorities to the workforce, and the more focused activity of talent decision-making in active management of the organisation's pools of talent, it is evident that the involvement of senior managers as a central actor in global talent management requires further empirical consideration. Further, the current external context of the global Covid-19 pandemic crisis has presented a context of extreme uncertainty, which further high-lights the significance of senior management's crucial contribution to effective global talent management in alignment with possibly rapidly evolving conditions and strategic priorities. In summary, senior management involvement has been identified as a key principle in the effec-tiveness of GTM (Stahl et al., 2012). While this applies to senior management, it also applies to middle management, as core actors in GTM whose activities in managing talent span the full employee life cycle, from talent selection to talent retention.

Middle Management: Operationalising Global Talent Management Policy and Practice as Managers of Talent

The middle management of an organisation comprises the managerial positions which hold accountability for the day-to-day operation of the business. While middle managers have some direct oversight of the performance of individuals in their teams, these roles also include the mandate to manage other managers – frontline managers – who in turn are accountable for direct management of individuals within their own teams. As such, the activities of middle managers have a relatively significant span of influence on the organisational talent system and the employee perceptions of talent management. From a review of the literature, three main priorities emerge regarding the role of middle management in global talent management, and these are reviewed below.

Line managers are recognised to be agents of the organisation in their implementation of a range of HR practices today, such that line manager involvement in the implementation of

HR practices influences the causal link to performance outcomes (Purcell and Hutchinson, 2007). For example, in the implementation of high-performance work practices, the line manager has been shown to be significant in the link between HR practices and employee performance (Alfes et al., 2013). As with the distribution of many HR practices to the line manager (Cappelli, 2013, 2015), middle managers are also closely involved in the implementation of talent management practices. Line manager competence affects employee perceptions of the HRM practices (Sikora et al., 2015).

Fostering the employee–organisation relationship in the context of talent management
The employee relationship is one which is anchored in social exchange through which an employee-held psychological contract is formed. The psychological contract is the individual employee's beliefs regarding the reciprocal obligations which they believe they have undertaken with their employer (Rousseau, 1995). The psychological contract is recognised to regulate the employee–employer relationship over time (Rousseau, 1995). The employee–employee relationship is theorised to represent an intensified exchange-based relationship for talent, such that the relationship is transformed through the perceived significant event of talent identification and talent status in the organisation (King, 2016b). However, management are cautioned to avoid inadvertently establishing heightened expectations of exchange in the psychological contract (Coyle-Shapiro and Kessler, 2000). Psychological contract breach has been theorised to be a risk related to differentiated talent identification (Dries, 2013; King, 2016b). Clearer communication by organisational representatives, such as line managers, with their employees has been shown to be positively related with employee perceptions of fairer exchange and less frequent psychological contract breach (Guest and Conway, 2002).

Implementation of talent identification policy as practice
A central component of the implementation of talent management is the identification of talent identification of talented employees. Talent may be identified through performance appraisal observations (Mäkelä et al., 2010), or by the assessment of talent potential (Dries and Pepermans, 2012; Meyers et al., 2017), that is, the potential for ongoing development and advancement to increasingly senior or more influential positions in the company. As talent identification is central to the management of talent differentially, and also to the associated organisational investments which are afforded to talent segments of the workforce, validity of the talent appraisal process is paramount. However, in practice, the accurate assessment or measurement of talent still proves to be problematic (Nijs et al., 2014). As might be expected, research has measured the relationship between organisational identification and psychological commitments and found it to be greater for employees who believe they were formally identified as talent by their company than for the group who did not perceive that they were identified as talent (Björkman et al., 2013).

Talent identification is acknowledged to be an activity with some degree of subjectivity involved, as it is an outcome of interaction between assessor and assessee (Nijs et al., 2014). This underscores the importance of sufficient methods tools and frameworks underpinned by training of line managers, to avoid subjective errors and to increase the validity and reliability of the talent identification method. However, research has shown that even with the provision of HRM tools for selection and assessment decisions, line managers may persistently rely on their existing internally held views or their presumed natural ability when assessing others (Colarelli and Thompson, 2008). Such errors of judgement of one's own skill may limit the quality of line manager talent assessments, particularly where available methods and training are insufficiently established. These internally held views by line managers can be difficult to overcome during their implementation of HR practices (Highhouse, 2008). Organisations are encouraged to establish clear guidance for middle management who are centrally involved in talent identification, as to the nature of business talent requirements, and how to identify current talent performance or talent developmental potential in line with these business-specific priorities. To mitigate possible concerns with the fairness of talent differentiated identification and management, line managers can be instrumental in providing clear messaging as to how talent identification processes are implemented, and the rationale underlying the differentiated identification and management of talent for business priorities, in order to support employee perceptions of procedural fairness. Important to note here is that scholars have argued that employees in the workforce who have not been identified as 'high potential' are important supporting actors enabling the performance of others (DeLong and Vijayaraghavan, 2003). There is an important and noteworthy role here for line managers to actively support the performance and development of all employees.

A further consideration of talent identification or talent status is the extent to which the employee-held view differs from the organisationally held view as to whether or not the employee is seen as talent. This is referred to as talent status congruence (or incongruence). When incongruence exists, between the employee and employer (manager) perceptions of the employee's talent status, the employee's perceived fulfilment of their psychological contract may be negatively impacted (Sonnenberg et al., 2014). Ultimately, this incongruence may lead to breach of the implicit 'talent deal' (King, 2016b). Therefore, information asymmetry in the management and assessment of talent may be problematic (Dries and De Gieter, 2014), particularly where the organisation is not explicit about talent status, such that the employee must intercept indications from their manager. Indeed, researchers have found that employee responses to talent identification are not as straightforward as expected. Some incidence of a stress-based reaction to talent identification has been noted in the literature, such that being recognised as talent may not only be seen as positive, but may also be experienced as a significant demand on the employee to contribute greater effort based on the promise of future rewards, while those future rewards remain uncertain and may indeed not become tangible (Petriglieri and Petriglieri, 2017).

Management and development of talented employees in the business across the employee lifecycle

HR practices have been shown to act as signals perceivable by employees in the organisation as ways in which the firm communicates its priorities and preferred behaviours to its workforce (Farndale and Kelliher, 2013). HR attribution theory explains that employees will interpret these signals and attribute meaning to their organisation's use of HR practices (Nishii et al., 2008). By extension of HR attribution theory to talent management, researchers have theorised that employees will develop attributions of meaning to their organisation's use of global talent management (King, 2018). Without clear communications of the purpose of talent management, organisations risk unclear understanding of the priorities for talent in the business (King, 2018).

Leaders have been described as sense-givers in organisations (Nishii and Paluch, 2018), who can support effective HR implementation in part by interpreting the signals for employees, and shape the perceptions which employees develop regarding the observed signals.

To address these issues, middle management (and other line managers) can endeavour to clarify employee understanding and views of HR practices. This is also readily applicable to employee perceptions of talent management. Line managers can verbally clarify and articulate the intended meanings and expectations of talent management in order to help employees make sense of what talent management means in their organisation (Nishii and Paluch, 2018). By actively coaching employees in their teams to develop the key talent attributes and behaviours of priority interest to the company, line managers can support employees to develop their talent potential for greater person–organisation fit in both preferred performance contribution and future talent requirements. This collaboration between line manager and employee can enable career advancement opportunities, while also creating organisational value through talent management by aligning employee development of talent potential with organisational priorities for talent.

In summary, middle managers are central actors within the talent system who manage the firm's core talent pools and individuals day to day, thereby operationalising the firm's talent strategy, policy and programmes, as defined and set out by senior management. Internal consistency across the activities of middle managers then becomes an important consideration, and has been identified in research as a key principle in GTM effectiveness (Stahl et al., 2012). Scholars have pointed to the importance of line manager training for consistency in their implementation of global HR practices (Sparrow et al., 2013).

Frontline Managers: Fostering Employee Engagement in Talent Priorities and Development of Potential Through Effective Performance Management

Frontline managers, often described as first-level management, represent the level of management within an organisation which directs the work of individuals or teams of individuals who hold the positions in the organisation which comprise the wider, non-management workforce, and who do not hold people management mandates themselves. In the organisational hierarchy, frontline managers collectively directly manage the day-to-day performance of large portions of the workforce, and have a first-hand view of the performance contribution of large numbers of employees in the overall organisation. The frontline manager reports to middle management in the organisational hierarchy. The frontline manager role, as with other levels of line manager, is focused on the delivery of performance in alignment with the firm's priorities, and signalling of business talent requirements towards stated talent strategic priorities.

As representatives of the organisation, line managers are the organisational actor with whom the employee is most closely aligned, and it is through this primary role that resources are accessed by the employee in the course of their work and career advancement (Alfes et al., 2013). So significant is the relationship between the employee and their direct line manager, the supervisor, that the employee-held psychological contract is both developed and fulfilled (or not) by the supervisor (McDermott et al., 2013). To achieve this requires skilful management of the employee–organisation relationship in two ways: in-role performance and development of talent. Two priorities have been identified for frontline managers through review of the literature, as follows.

Fostering employee awareness of and engagement with organisational talent priorities through effective performance management

Through effective performance management of roles in the non-management levels of the organisation, employees in these positions make a core contribution to the overall business performance. Frontline managers, as with other line managers, are agents of the organisation and influence the extent to which HR practices lead to performance outcomes for the organisation (Purcell and Hutchinson, 2007). Frontline managers or supervisors can signal the HR priorities of the firm through their use of the regular performance management cycle of target setting, feedback and appraisal. Performance targets can be effectively aligned to support the business strategy. Goal setting theory (Locke, 2003; Locke and Latham, 2002) explains that where employees have participated in performance goal setting, they are more likely to be motivated by the goal. Using effective goal setting, frontline managers can support employees to find effective ways to contribute their talent to the organisation's priorities.

Development of talent potential through in-role performance feedback and coaching

Frontline managers, as with all other line managers in many organisations today, are accountable for the development of talented employees and their potential (Stahl et al., 2012). Frontline managers supervise the work of others, and in doing so they have the opportunity to identify employees with high performance levels, as well as the opportunity of individuals to develop and to progress in their careers to roles with greater responsibility (King, 2016b). Supervisors are 'talent-spotters' (Fernández-Aráoz, 2014), and line managers are involved in the process of talent identification (Dries and Pepermans, 2012) whereby organisations identify individuals to be included in the talent pool (Collings and Mellahi, 2009) to be developed for future roles of increasing responsibility in the organisation. Even in the context of today's employment relationship whereby many employees move between organisations and establish their career in many organisations rather than a single organisation, research has shown that employees skill expect career support (Sturges et al., 2005), which presents as important opportunity for frontline managers to offer career support, development and advice as a core activity within talent management for the workforce, whether talent or not.

Human Resources Managers: Facilitating Effective Talent Management and Optimising the Talent System

In addition to the three levels of line manager roles which have been considered above, a further category of manager role is worthy of more than brief mention. This is the functional manager role of human resources, in contrast to the business line manager role; and within that, a more specific role identified in some organisations as the 'head of talent' or talent manager. HR and talent manager roles also play an important role in the effective implementation of global talent management. Drawing on Ulrich's conceptualisation of the human resources organisation, HR managers, whether embedded in the business as dedicated HR or those HR manager roles within the corporate or functional HR team (Ulrich et al., 2008), HR managers provide expert functional knowledge and advise the business on policy and practice. In the implementation of talent management, HR and talent managers do so with a differentiated focus on the policy and practice specifically related to management, development and retention of talent and critical roles to which they are deployed. HR and talent managers support line manager talent decision-making through the provision of talent analytics. HR and talent managers have a distinct role in the organisational implementation of global talent management, as one of the multiple actors which, collectively, co-create the organisational talent management system and climate (King, 2014). HR managers facilitate the interactive involvement of other actors in the talent systems, applying a strong process orientation (Farndale et al., 2010) to the adoption of GTM as a business practice.

The corporate HR organisation is often seen as the 'champion of processes' (Evans et al., 2002), owing to its role in supporting horizontal alignment across the enterprise for the implementation of talent policy and practice (Farndale et al., 2010). Central to the processes managed by HR managers is their coordination of the annual talent review process, through which talent is identified and subsequently managed in talent pools (King, 2015a; Mäkelä et al., 2010). In global firms, the corporate HR manager may be involved in a diverse range of talent-focused activities, including leadership and management development, staffing for strategic positions, supporting executive rewards and facilitating global mobility for the cadre of managers who are deployed to international assignments, with the scope of the role depending on the degree of centralisation of the enterprise (Farndale et al., 2010). As with other actors in the talent system, the HR manager's involvement can foster value creation. For example, involvement in global staffing is one mechanism through which the HR manager helps to create value as a central actor in the talent system, as knowledge transfer in global staffing has been shown to support subsidiary performance (Mäkelä et al., 2010). The HR organisation also provides expertise in leadership and other talent development through the design and delivery of talent development programmes such as graduate programmes, emerging leader programmes, mentorship and coaching initiatives, and senior leadership development planning to support succession readiness for future senior appointments. Finally, the HR manager role also contributes to effective GTM through evaluating the effectiveness of talent policy and practice, and measuring and reporting outcomes of the talent system (King, 2015a).

In summary, this section has presented a review of the activities of three levels of line management with regard to global talent management, presenting examples of each from the extant literature, and has additionally considered the functional role of HR managers, which can be positioned at any of these three levels in the organisation. Line managers have been identified as central to a wide range of activities comprising the firm's management, ranging from the specification of business talent demand and the setting of talent strategy by senior management, to the operationalisation of talent strategy by middle management, and the management of frontline employees by frontline managers in alignment with business talent priorities, while development of talent is a priority at all levels of line manager activity. At each level in the organisational hierarchy, the role of the line manager in GTM varies in alignment with the nature of the management role, such that senior management lead talent strategy and define the priorities and policies of the organisation's approach to talent and are accountable for talent decision-making; middle management are the managers of talent, who are centrally involved in the management of the organisation's talent and talent pools and participate in talent identification and decision-making; frontline managers provide an essential people management function within which talent priorities are communicated and performance is actively managed such that individuals who demonstrate performance and potential of specific interest to talent priorities can be identified for participation in the organisation's talent-specific programmes and investments. Human resources and talent managers underpin the activities of the line organisation and line managers, in engaging, developing, deploying, retaining and rewarding talent across the business, applying differentiated talent-specific policies and practices to do so. Importantly, the HR manager reports talent analytics regularly as management information decision-making.

Table 15.1 presents a summary of the primary scope of activity and influence of line managers in the definition and implementation of global talent management for each of the three levels of line management roles, as well as the HR manager role, with accompanying examples from the literature.

While the review of the literature presented above presents a categorisation of the varying roles of each level of manager in the organisational hierarchy to the effort of talent management implementation, in practice these areas of influence necessarily overlap as co-creators of the talent system (King, 2015a). That is, it is reasonable to expect that each level of management role will not fully replace the mandate of another, but rather will complement, reinforce and extend it. For example, as managers progress in the hierarchical levels, their role mandates will still likely require them to manage performance of individuals in their teams while additionally taking on a wider responsibility for leading units of the organisation and higher levels of authority over the implementation of components of talent policy or practice, such as decision-making for discretionary compensation rewards for high-performing talent. The scope of influence on GTM for each level of manager is therefore shown to expand rather than narrow as the management role becomes increasingly senior in the hierarchy. The following section discusses limitations of the current literature and future research priorities.

DISCUSSION AND FUTURE RESEARCH

Limitations and Future Research Priorities

The review presented in this chapter highlights the significant involvement and notable effort of line managers at each level of the organisation in shaping and implementing the organisational talent system and its corresponding policies and practices. While the central role of line managers at multiple levels has been argued, a number of questions remain as to what is yet unknown regarding the influence of the manager in talent management, recognised as a dynamic, but often strategically ambiguous (Dries and De Gieter, 2014) activity. Given that the nature of organisational talent management activities may be highly visible, but just as often may be opaque, more needs to be understood regarding the line manager's role in talent management and the associated differentiated management of employees identified as talent.

The scholarly literature on the topic of global talent management has developed rapidly over the past ten years or more. However, the employee response to talent management, as the central character in talent management, has only recently been considered (Björkman et al., 2013; King, 2018). Similarly underexamined to date are the scope and boundaries of the role of the line manager, a further central actor in the talent system (King, 2015a), which continues to be largely unconsidered. Future research could examine a range of implications for the role of managers in the organisational hierarchy. For example, to what extent do line manager communications of talent policies and practices contribute to a climate for talent, and how may the implementation of talent management enable or foster a climate of inclusion? From a team perspective, how do manager selection practices influence overall team talent composition? How does manager distribution of discretionary talent-oriented rewards, such as the use of talent retention bonus programmes, influence team member perceptions of organ-

Table 15.1   *Global talent management and the important roles of line managers: senior, middle, frontline*

Organisational level of line management	Primary role in global talent management	Key activities related to this role	Selected examples presented in the extant literature
Senior managers	Talent strategy and the definition of the talent system of policies, programmes and practices	– Definition of talent strategy and business future demand and specified requirements for talent – Orient the firm's talent system to create value for the business – Establishment of talent pools and implementation of talent identification standards – Talent policy and oversight of annual talent reviews – Talent decision-making including: selection, deployment, retention, appointments to pivotal and leadership positions, talent-specific compensation and rewards, and performance incentives – Communication of talent priorities and fostering a climate for talent – Engagement with the external macro talent context – Sponsorship of and involvement in key talent development initiatives such as leadership development programmes – Involvement in decisions for pivotal talent and critical positions – Ownership of the firm's succession management	Stahl et al., 2012 King, 2015a Sparrow and Makram, 2015 Mäkelä et al., 2010 Boudreau and Ramstad, 2005a Khoreva and Vaiman, 2019
Middle managers	Implementation of talent management in the day-to-day business	– Operationalisation of the talent strategy through implementation of policy and practice – Articulating and translating firm-level talent strategy within the line of business. – In-role talent potential assessment and talent identification – Talent selection, deployment and reward decisions. – Active career management and progression of talent-identified employees – Managing the career deal and the talent deal – Talent coaching and development – Input to demand forecasting of talent supply in alignment with business planning	King, 2015a Björkman et al., 2013 Boudreau and Ramstad, 2005a Sturges et al., 2005 King, 2016b
Frontline or first-line managers	Performance management in the wider workforce in alignment with business strategic priorities for talent	– Managing employee performance in alignment with business strategic priorities including target setting, performance feedback, performance appraisal – Development of potential in-role	Sumelius et al., 2014 Farndale and Kelliher, 2013 Guest et al., 2012

Organisational level of line management	Primary role in global talent management	Key activities related to this role	Selected examples presented in the extant literature
HR and talent managers	Partnering with the management to establish talent policy, programmes and practices and their facilitation in the business	– Definition of policy and practice to enable senior management talent strategy – Alignment, integration and congruence of talent policy and practice across all people management priorities and systems (such as the integration of diversity and inclusion priorities into talent strategy, the link between talent strategy and performance management and the link between talent management and succession for pivotal positions) – The generation of talent analytics as a core management tool in evidence-based management decision-making regarding talent	Farndale et al., 2010 Evans et al., 2002
Shared responsibilities across management levels	Establishing effect talent communications and an inclusive talent culture	– Communication of talent strategy, priorities, purpose and policy – Fostering an inclusive climate for talent – Recognising potential and coaching the development of talent in the business – Fostering organisational justice perceptions in talent management practices and talent decision-making, including selection, talent investments, talent rewards – Talent retention across generational differences	Festing and Schäfer, 2014

isational justice in pay practices and the retention of talent long term? How effective are line managers in developing talent potential in-role? What methods for talent potential identification by the line manager are most valid and reliable? How have manager actions taken during the Covid-19 pandemic served to retain talent or leverage opportunities for development of talent potential? How does employee talent status awareness influence self-managed career progression and voluntary turnover? Which talent analytics are most valuable to managers for evidence-based talent decision-making?

Table 15.2 presents an illustrative overview of select future research directions in the continuing development of empirical literature regarding the role and contribution of line managers to effective global talent management.

Practical Implications for Management

This chapter has presented a detailed review of the role and contribution of line managers in the organisation's effective management of talent globally. In doing so, the role of management at three distinct hierarchical levels was presented – frontline managers, middle managers and senior management – resulting in the specification of talent management priorities for each of the three management roles as presented in Table 15.1. Of primary concern is the communication of talent strategy, policy and practice to employees, and the implementation of talent strategy fairly and consistently. The active involvement of line managers at all levels in the organisation, in line with the findings presented above, will be more likely to facilitate employee perceptions of fairness and organisational support in response to GTM. Using the mapping of talent priorities by management level, organisations can continue to refine their focus on the respective mandates of frontline, middle and senior management contributions to

Table 15.2   *The role of line managers in global talent management: future research directions (selected examples)*

Global talent management and line managers	Research themes	Future research questions	Senior	Middle	Frontline
Talent strategy	Definition of talent strategy in alignment with business requirements	How do senior managers assess business requirements for future talent supply?	✓		
		How do senior managers establish and define talent pools aligned to business strategic requirements?	✓		
		How do senior management contribute to employee-formed attributions of talent management purpose in their organisations?	✓		
Talent forecasting	Specification of talent demand and opportunities for development of talent supply	How do middle managers analyse and quantify forward-looking talent supply requirements?		✓	
		How do senior management challenge and stress-test the sufficiency of the business talent forecasting requirements?	✓		
Talent identification and potential assessment	Identification of talent and assessment of potential	What methods for talent potential identification and talent assessment are selected and defined by the organisation for use by the line manager? And to what extent are these assessments valid and reliable?	✓		
		How effectively, inclusively and consistently do people managers apply the defined set of talent identification and potential assessment standards?	✓	✓	✓
Talent development and sponsorship	Development of key talent in the workforce and sponsorship of talent programmes	How effective are line managers in developing talent potential in-role, at all levels of the organisation?	✓	✓	✓
		In what ways and to what extent are senior management visibly involved and engaged in the active sponsorship of the talent strategy and programmes for the firm?	✓		
Talent progression and career advancement	Decision-making for talent deployment, progression, advancement, succession	From a team perspective, how do manager selection practices influence overall team talent composition? To what extent are talent progression and succession management decisions aligned with the organisation's diversity and inclusion commitments and priorities?	✓	✓	✓

Global talent management and line managers	Research themes	Future research questions	Senior	Middle	Frontline
Talent reward and retention	Decision-making regarding talent rewards, their distribution and design	How does manager distribution of discretionary talent-oriented rewards, such as the use of talent retention bonus programmes, influence team member perceptions of organisational justice in pay practices and the retention of talent long term?	✓	✓	✓
		How have manager actions taken during the Covid-19 pandemic served to retain talent or leverage opportunities for development of talent potential?	✓	✓	✓
		How does employee talent status awareness influence self-managed career progression and voluntary turnover?	✓	✓	✓
		Which talent analytics are most valuable to managers for evidence-based talent decision-making?	✓		
Communication of talent strategy, priorities and policy	Performance management and the link to strategic talent priorities	How do organisations establish alignment across levels of management such that line manager signalling of talent priorities is not only consistent, but also perceived as relevant to employees' performance priorities at all levels?	✓		
		To what extent do line manager communications of talent policies and practices contribute to a climate for talent, and how may the implementation of talent management enable or foster a climate of inclusion?	✓	✓	✓

their organisation's strategic talent priorities. Ultimately, line managers at all levels throughout the organisation play an important role in developing and managing talent (Stahl et al., 2007), in service of identified business strategic priorities.

CONCLUSION

Global talent management is now an established priority of management in organisations today, as the search for global competence continues to present complex challenges (Cascio and Boudreau, 2016) and as global organisations continue to face a range of talent challenges (Cappelli and Keller, 2014; Schuler et al., 2011; Stahl et al., 2012). As the complexity of workforce and employment models continue to evolve in both domestic and multinational organisations, businesses will need to rely on increasingly skilled and competent line managers, at each level of the organisation, as managers of talent. As both the scholarly literature and management practice continue to increasingly consider the perspective of employees themselves with regards to talent management (largely overlooked until recently), line managers who can actively foster employee understanding of and engagement with the business priorities and requirements for talent will be essential to enabling the organisation's strategic advantage through talent.

REFERENCES

Al Ariss, A., Cascio, W.F., and Paauwe, J. (2014). Talent management: current theories and future research directions. *Journal of World Business, 49*(2), 173–179.

Alfes, K., Truss, C., Soane, E.C., Rees, C., and Gatenby, M. (2013). The relationship between line manager behavior, perceived HRM practices, and individual performance: examining the mediating role of engagement. *Human Resource Management, 52*(6), 839–859. doi:10.1002/hrm.21512.

Becker, B.E., Huselid, M.A., and Beatty, R.W. (2009). *The Differentiated Workforce: Transforming Talent into Strategic Impact.* Boston, MA: Harvard Business Press.

Bhattacharya, C.B., Sen, S., and Korschun, D. (2008). Using corporate social responsibility to win the war for talent. *MIT Sloan Management Review, 49*(2), 37–44.

Björkman, I., Ehrnrooth, M., Mäkelä, K., Smale, A., and Sumelius, J. (2013). Talent or not? Employee reactions to talent identification. *Human Resource Management, 52*(2), 195–214. doi:10.1002/hrm.21525.

Boudreau, J.W. (2010). *Retooling HR: Using Proven Business Tools to Make Better Decisions about Talent.* Boston, MA: Harvard Business Press.

Boudreau, J.W., and Ramstad, P.M. (2005a). Talentship, talent segmentation, and sustainability: a new HR decision science paradigm for a new strategy definition. *Human Resource Management, 44*(2), 129–136. doi:10.1002/hrm.20054.

Boudreau, J.W., and Ramstad, P.M. (2005b). Where's your pivotal talent? *Harvard Business Review, 83*(4), 23–24.

Boudreau, J.W., and Ramstad, P.M. (2007). *Beyond HR: The New Science of Human Capital.* Boston, MA: Harvard Business Press.

Canada, Government of (2017). International Experience Canada Program (IEC) – travel and work in Canada. Retrieved from http://www.cic.gc.ca/english/work/iec/index.asp.

Cappelli, P. (2008). *Talent on Demand: Managing Talent in an Age of Uncertainty.* Boston, MA: Harvard Business School Press Books.

Cappelli, P. (2013). HR for neophytes. *Harvard Business Review, 91*(10), 25–27.

Cappelli, P. (2015). Why we love to hate HR … and what HR can do about it. *Harvard Business Review, 93*(7/8), 54–61.

Cappelli, P., and Keller, J. (2014). Talent management: conceptual approaches and practical challenges. *Annual Review of Organizational Psychology and Organizational Behavior, 1*(1), 305–331. doi:doi: 10.1146/annurev-orgpsych-031413-091314.

Cascio, W.F., and Boudreau, J.W. (2016). The search for global competence: from international HR to talent management. *Journal of World Business, 51*(1), 103–114. doi:10.1016/j.jwb.2015.10.002

Colarelli, S.M., and Thompson, M. (2008). Stubborn reliance on human nature in employee selection: statistical decision aids are evolutionarily novel. *Industrial and Organizational Psychology, 1*(3), 347–351. doi:10.1111/j.1754-9434.2008.00060.x.

Collings, D.G., and Mellahi, K. (2009). Strategic talent management: a review and research agenda. *Human Resource Management Review, 19*(4), 304–313. doi:10.1016/j.hrmr.2009.04.001.

Collings, D.G., Mellahi, K., and Cascio, W.F. (2017). *The Oxford Handbook of Talent Management.* Oxford: Oxford University Press.

Coyle-Shapiro, J., and Kessler, I. (2000). Consequences of the psychological contract for the employment relationship: a large scale survey. *Journal of Management Studies, 37*(7), 903–930. doi:10.1111/1467-6486.00210.

DeLong, T.J., and Vijayaraghavan, V. (2003). Let's hear it for B players. *Harvard Business Review, 81*(6), 96–102.

Dries, N. (2013). The psychology of talent management: a review and research agenda. *Human Resource Management Review, 23*(4), 272–285. doi:https://doi.org/10.1016/j.hrmr.2013.05.001.

Dries, N., and De Gieter, S. (2014). Information asymmetry in high potential programs. *Personnel Review, 43*(1), 136–162. doi:doi:10.1108/PR-11-2011-0174.

Dries, N., and Pepermans, R. (2007). 'Real' high-potential careers: an empirical study into the perspectives of organisations and high potentials. *Personnel Review, 37*(1), 85–108. doi:doi:10.1108/00483480810839987.

Dries, N., and Pepermans, R. (2012). How to identify leadership potential: development and testing of a consensus model. *Human Resource Management, 51*(3), 361–385. doi:10.1002/hrm.21473.

Evans, P., Pucik, V., and Barsoux, J. (2002). *The Global Challenge: Framework for International Human Resource Management.* Irwin, NY: McGraw-Hill.

Farndale, E., and Kelliher, C. (2013). Implementing performance appraisal: exploring the employee experience. *Human Resource Management, 52*(6), 879–897. doi:10.1002/hrm.21575.

Farndale, E., Scullion, H., and Sparrow, P.R. (2010). The role of the corporate HR function in global talent management. *Journal of World Business, 45*(2), 161–168. doi:https://doi.org/10.1016/j.jwb .2009.09.012.

Festing, M., and Schäfer, L. (2014). Generational challenges to talent management: a framework for talent retention based on the psychological-contract perspective. *Journal of World Business, 49*(2), 262–271.

Fernández-Aráoz, C. (2014). 21st century talent spotting. *Harvard Business Review, 92*(6), 46–56.

Guest, D.E., and Conway, N. (2002). Communicating the psychological contract: an employer perspective. *Human Resource Management Journal, 12*(2), 22–38. doi:10.1111/j.1748-8583.2002.tb00062.x.

Guest, D.E., Paauwe, J., and Wright, P.M. (eds) (2012). *HRM and Performance: Achievements and Challenges.* Wiley.

Highhouse, S. (2008). Stubborn reliance on intuition and subjectivity in employee selection. *Industrial and Organizational Psychology, 1*(3), 333–342. doi:10.1111/j.1754-9434.2008.00058.x.

IOD (2018). Government immigration policy still needs work before it can help UK to compete on global stage. Press release. https://www.iod.com/news/news/articles/Government-immigration-policy-still -needs-work-before-it-can-help-UK-to-compete-on-global-stage-.

Khilji, S.E., Tarique, I., and Schuler, R.S. (2015). Incorporating the macro view in global talent management. *Human Resource Management Review, 25*(3), 236–248. doi:http://dx.doi.org/10.1016/j.hrmr .2015.04.001.

Khoreva, V., and Vaiman, V. (2019). Talent management: decision making in the global context. In I.E. Tarique (ed.), *Routledge Companion to Talent Management.* London: Routledge.

King, K.A. (2014). Talent management in the business: HR'S central role in a multiple actor's model. Paper presented at the EIASM. European Institue for Advanced Studies in Management. 3rd Workshop on Talent Management Berlin, Germany.

King, K.A. (2015a). Global talent management: introducing a strategic framework and multiple-actors model. *Journal of Global Mobility: The Home of Expatriate Management Research, 3*(3), 273–288. doi:doi:10.1108/JGM-02-2015-0002.

King, K.A. (2015b). Sustained value through talent management: a multi-stakeholder approach. Paper presented at the European Institute for Advanced Studies in Management (EIASM). 4th Workshop on Talent Management, Valencia, Spain.

King, K.A. (2016a). The talent climate: creating space for talent development through a strong talent system. Paper presented at the EIASM. European Institue for Advanced Studies in Management. 5th Workshop on Talent Management Copenhagen, Denmark.

King, K.A. (2016b). The talent deal and journey: understanding how employees respond to talent identification over time. *Employee Relations, 38*(1), 94–111. doi:doi:10.1108/ER-07-2015-0155.

King, K.A. (2018). Considering the talent in talent management: consequences of strategic talent management for the employee psychological contract and individual outcomes. PhD Thesis, London School of Economics and Political Science (LSE). http://etheses.lse.ac.uk/id/eprint/3831.

King, K.A., and Vaiman, V. (2019). Enabling effective talent management through a macro-contingent approach: a framework for research and practice. *BRQ Business Research Quarterly, 22*(3), 194–206. doi:https://doi.org/10.1016/j.brq.2019.04.005.

Locke, E. (2003). Motivation through conscious goal setting. In L. Porter, G. Bigley and R. Steers (eds), *Motivation and Work Behavior,* McGraw-Hill Series in Management (7th edn, pp. 113–125). Boston, MA: McGraw-Hill/Irwin.

Locke, E.A., and Latham, G.P. (2002). Building a practically useful theory of goal setting and task motivation: a 35-year odyssey. *American Psychologist, 57*(9), 705–717. doi:10.1037/0003-066X.57.9.705.

Mackey, A., Molloy, J.C., and Morris, S.S. (2013). Scarce human capital in managerial labor markets. *Journal of Management.* doi:10.1177/0149206313517265.

Mäkelä, K., Björkman, I., and Ehrnrooth, M. (2010). How do MNCs establish their talent pools? Influences on individuals' likelihood of being labeled as talent. *Journal of World Business*, *45*(2), 134–142. doi:https://doi.org/10.1016/j.jwb.2009.09.020.

McDermott, A.M., Conway, E., Rousseau, D.M., and Flood, P.C. (2013). Promoting effective psychological contracts through leadership: the missing link between HR strategy and performance. *Human Resource Management*, *52*(2), 289–310. doi:10.1002/hrm.21529.

McNulty, Y., and Cieri, H.D. (2016). Linking global mobility and global talent management: the role of ROI. *Employee Relations*, *38*(1), 8–30. doi:doi:10.1108/ER-08-2015-0157.

Meyers, M.C., and van Woerkom, M. (2014). The influence of underlying philosophies on talent management: Theory, implications for practice, and research agenda. *Journal of World Business*, *49*(2), 192–203. doi:http://dx.doi.org/10.1016/j.jwb.2013.11.003.

Meyers, M.C., De Boeck, G., and Dries, N. (2017). Talent or not. In D.G. Collings, K. Mellahi and W.F. Cascio (eds), *The Oxford Handbook of Talent Management* (pp. 169–192). Oxford: Oxford University Press.

Mintzberg, H. (1979). *The Structuring of Organizations*. Englewood Cliffs, NJ: Prentice-Hall.

Nijs, S., Gallardo-Gallardo, E., Dries, N., and Sels, L. (2014). A multidisciplinary review into the definition, operationalization, and measurement of talent. *Journal of World Business*, *49*(2), 180–191. doi: http://dx.doi.org/10.1016/j.jwb.2013.11.002.

Nishii, L.H., and Paluch, R.M. (2018). Leaders as HR sensegivers: four HR implementation behaviors that create strong HR systems. *Human Resource Management Review*, *28*(3), 319–323. doi:https://doi.org/10.1016/j.hrmr.2018.02.007.

Nishii, L.H., Lepak, D.P., and Schneider, B. (2008). Employee attributions of the 'why' of HR practices: their effects on employee attitudes and behaviors, and customer satisfaction. *Personnel Psychology*, *61*(3), 503–545. doi:10.1111/j.1744-6570.2008.00121.x.

Petriglieri, J., and Petriglieri, G. (2017). The talent curse: interaction. *Harvard Business Review*, *95*(4), 19–19.

Purcell, J., and Hutchinson, S. (2007). Front-line managers as agents in the HRM–performance causal chain: theory, analysis and evidence. *Human Resource Management Journal*, *17*(1), 3–20. doi:10.1111/j.1748-8583.2007.00022.x.

Rousseau, D.M. (1995). *Psychological Contracts in Organizations: Understanding Written and Unwritten Agreements*. Thousand Oaks, CA: SAGE Publications.

Schuler, R.S., Jackson, S.E., and Tarique, I. (2011). Global talent management and global talent challenges: strategic opportunities for IHRM. *Journal of World Business*, *46*(4), 506–516. doi:http://dx.doi.org/10.1016/j.jwb.2010.10.011.

Sikora, D.M., Ferris, G.R., and Van Iddekinge, C.H. (2015). Line manager implementation perceptions as a mediator of relations between high-performance work practices and employee outcomes. *Journal of Applied Psychology*, *100*(6), 1908–1918. doi:10.1037/apl0000024.

Sonnenberg, M., van Zijderveld, V., and Brinks, M. (2014). The role of talent–perception incongruence in effective talent management. *Journal of World Business*, *49*(2), 272–280. doi:http://dx.doi.org/10.1016/j.jwb.2013.11.011.

Sparrow, P.R., and Makram, H. (2015). What is the value of talent management? Building value-driven processes within a talent management architecture. *Human Resource Management Review*, *25*(3), 249–263. doi:http://dx.doi.org/10.1016/j.hrmr.2015.04.002.

Sparrow, P.R., Farndale, E., and Scullion, H. (2013). An empirical study of the role of the corporate HR function in global talent management in professional and financial service firms in the global financial crisis. *International Journal of Human Resource Management*, *24*, 1777–1798. doi:10.1080/09585192.2013.777541.

Spence, M. (1973). Job market signaling. *Quarterly Journal of Economics*, *87*(3), 355–374.

Stahl, G.K., Björkman, I., Farndale, E., Morris, S.S., Paauwe, J., and Stiles, P. (2012). Six principles of effective global talent management. *MIT Sloan Management Review*, *53*(2), 25–32.

Stahl, G.K., Björkman, I., Farndale, E., Morris, S.S., Paauwe, J., et al. (2007). Global talent management: how leading multinationals build and sustain their talent pipeline. http://720plan.ovh.net/~inseadpoq/knowledge2/stahl.pdf.

Sturges, J., Conway, N., Guest, D.E., and Liefooghe, A. (2005). Managing the career deal: the psychological contract as a framework for understanding career management, organizational commitment and work behavior. *Journal of Organizational Behavior*, *26*(7), 821–833. doi:10.1002/job.341.

Sumelius, J., Björkman, I., Ehrnrooth, M., Mäkelä, K., and Smale, A. (2014). What determines employee perceptions of HRM process features? The case of performance appraisal in MNC subsidiaries. *Human Resource Management*, *53*(4), 569–592.

Tarique, I., and Schuler, R.S. (2010). Global talent management: literature review, integrative framework, and suggestions for further research. *Journal of World Business*, *45*(2), 122–133. doi:http://dx.doi.org/10.1016/j.jwb.2009.09.019.

Ulrich, D., Younger, J., and Brockbank, W. (2008). The twenty-first-century HR organization. *Human Resource Management*, *47*(4), 829–850.

16. Line management and the resolution of workplace conflict in the UK

Richard Saundry, Virginia Fisher and Sue Kinsey

INTRODUCTION

Conflict is not only inherent within the employment relationship, but it is also an inevitable part of the working life of a line manager. Although there is relatively little robust data measuring the extent of workplace conflict, a recent representative survey from the United Kingdom (UK) found that almost one in three workers experience a conflict at work every 12 months (CIPD, 2020). In addition, a rather dated international estimate found that the average employee spends 2.1 hours a week dealing with conflict. This ranges from 0.9 hours in the Netherlands, to 2.8 in the United States of America, and 3.3 in Germany. In the UK, an average of 1.8 hours translates into an annual loss of 370 million days (OPP, 2008). Not only are workers in conflict more likely to seek the advice and guidance of their immediate boss, but also, in the majority of cases, the line manager is most likely to be the person who has triggered that conflict. Line managers are, therefore, at the same time, part of the solution and very much part of the problem.

Line managers have long been seen as playing a critical role in employee engagement (Dromey, 2014; MacLeod and Clarke, 2009; Purcell, 2010). However, their role has become even more important in many contexts due to the rapid erosion of representative structures of employee voice and the devolution of people management from human resources (HR) functions to the line. Moreover, there is growing international evidence of a link between management practices and strategic outcomes. Data gathered over the last 15 years through the World Management Survey, led by Nick Bloom, Raffaella Sadun and John Van Reenen, provides compelling evidence that poor management is one explanation for low productivity (Bloom and Van Reenen, 2007, 2011; Sadun et al., 2017). There is a strong argument that managerial quality fundamentally revolves around the management of people more generally and conflict in particular. Recent research by the UK's Advisory, Conciliation and Arbitration Service (ACAS) has found that conflict not only ties up managerial resources, but also leads to stress, anxiety and/or depression for 56 per cent of workers involved, with consequent impacts on absence and presenteeism (Urwin and Saundry, 2021). Furthermore, if managed poorly, conflict can have wider effects, undermining notions of organizational justice and eroding employee engagement (Saks, 2006; Purcell, 2012). Therefore, the ability of line managers to prevent, contain, manage and resolve conflict has significant consequences for organizations.

In this chapter, we explore the role played by line managers in workplace conflict. In doing so we draw on existing literature and two related research projects funded by ACAS. The first was conducted in 2016, comprising 22 focus groups of HR practitioners, trade union representatives and line managers, and explored the terrain of conflict management in the UK. The second was undertaken in 2018, and focused on the role of the HR function through 31 in-depth semi-structured interviews with HR practitioners. We first examine how the responsibilities of line managers in identifying and addressing conflict has developed over time. This leads into a discussion of the evolution of the relationship between HR and the line in relation to conflict management. We then assess the extent to which the conflict competence of line managers has been addressed by training and development. Finally, we explore the implications for the potential for early and informal resolution of workplace conflict and disputes.

THE CHANGING ROLE OF LINE MANAGERS: NATURALS, ROGUES, DODGERS AND DEPENDENTS

Line and operational managers have conventionally been assumed to have an aversion to conflict. In particular, it has been argued that managers dislike the bureaucracy and procedure associated with more formal, standardized disciplinary and grievance procedures, preferring more pragmatic and instinctual approaches (Cooke, 2006; Rollinson et al., 1996) grounded in their experience and personal relations with their subordinates. This points to the complex and contradictory position that line managers often find themselves in: on the one hand, encouraged to build good relationships with staff; while on the other, cast in the role of enforcer of organizational rules and standards.

In some respects, a preference for informality could be seen as a positive feature, with managers potentially more comfortable with having the 'difficult conversations' that are an inevitable aspect of managing conflict. Good personal relations may facilitate the early and informal resolution of workplace problems and pave the way for more creative and humane solutions. If a manager knows that poor timekeeping or a performance problem is due to difficulties in an employee's family life, they can provide support and guidance to try and help the individual improve (Cole, 2008). Similarly, line managers may want the flexibility to balance immediate operational imperatives against the demands of process and procedure. Importantly, our own research has found that this conflict competence and capability is often assumed to be closely linked with managerial 'experience'.

Line managers may also be reluctant to take disciplinary action against 'a good worker' because of the immediate disruption to production and the wider impact on team morale and motivation, if colleagues of the disciplined worker felt them to have been harshly or unfairly treated. As Edwards (2005: 384) argues, 'rules are thus interpreted in context. Any manager sticking to the letter of the rule book might well be surprised not merely by the workers' reactions but also by line managers, who have negotiated a form of workplace equilibrium that turns on rules in practice'.

However, flexible and pragmatic approaches can have negative ramifications in terms of fairness, equity and consistency. For example, managers may reward loyalty, long service and positive attitude with more lenient treatment in the event of a potential disciplinary issue (Rollinson, 2000). While long service may be something that managers should take into account, perceptions of loyalty and attitude are fundamentally subjective and risk the potential for nepotism and favouritism. Moreover, managers can reframe 'fairness', in order to embed their authority and shape the social and power relations within their work unit (Rollinson, 2000). This may also make it difficult for workers to raise concerns or challenge decision-making (Hook et al., 1996).

It can also be argued that a preference for informal approaches may simply become manifest in avoidance as managers lack the confidence to address capability and conduct issues,

Table 16.1   A typology of line managerial orientations to conflict management

Type	Characteristics
Naturals	Some managers are seen as 'naturals': they have good people skills and demonstrate high degrees of emotional intelligence. In most organizations, whether a manager is a 'natural' is by happenstance; however, some build people management competencies into recruitment processes.
Dodgers	A significant proportion of managers will seek to avoid managing conflict. Therefore, even if they see problems developing, they are unlikely to take any action. Unfortunately, by the time that conflict becomes manifest, the issue has escalated, attitudes are more entrenched, and resolution is more difficult.
Rogues	Respondents in our research often talked of 'rogue' managers who rely on their experience and 'gut feeling' and have a dislike of process and procedure. For HR practitioners, these are managers who need to be restrained and controlled. While managers in this group can be popular with some of their employees, they are often prone to negative behaviours.
Dependents	This represents most new managers, who lack confidence and training in people management issues but are aware that they need to address problems. They therefore lean heavily on HR for advice and guidance. Where there is sufficient HR support, they can develop the skills and abilities of 'naturals', but where that support is lacking, they are likely to 'dodge' and avoid difficult issues.

concerned about organizational criticism, or even litigation, if things go wrong (Harris et al., 2002). Our own research has also suggested that, if anything, these pressures have intensified over time and that new generations of line managers are more aware of these risks, possibly to an exaggerated level, and are therefore increasingly likely to hide behind the comfort blanket of process or HR advice. The following quote from an HR practitioner is typical:

> in my organization the managers are not confident of doing that early stage. A lot of what we're finding is it's a management skill that they're lacking … to have a difficult conversation is not easy face-to-face with staff … we tend to jump straight into a formal procedure because that's better as you get the support from HR, you get the support from the senior manager, rather than dealing with it locally first.

Overall, our research points to a variety of different managerial styles or types typically exhibited by line managers when handling conflict (see Table 16.1). In broad terms, while we might expect to see the proportion of 'rogues', 'dodgers' and 'dependents' reduce over time as organizations improve recruitment and development processes, our research has found relatively little evidence of this. While rogue behaviour may be less common through the influence of process, procedure and regulation, new generations of managers lack the confidence to address difficult issues and/or rely heavily on the on the support of HR.

One possible explanation for the lack of progress towards more independent and confident line managers is the absence of personal and organizational incentives. More specifically, it is highly questionable whether senior managers fully acknowledge the importance of conflict management activities when compared with more immediate operational imperatives (Hutchinson and Purcell, 2010; Teague and Roche, 2012). This means that managers rarely have the time and space needed to deal with these issues effectively (Hyde et al., 2013). The management of conflict is invariably quite an opaque activity: it is often carried out in private and behind closed doors, and its impacts are difficult to see and to measure. Therefore, for line managers who want to get noticed and to progress, spending time trying to prevent, contain and resolve conflict may not be very rational. An HR practitioner summed up this up very clearly as follows:

I think there are certain things in business that are easier to measure than others and those things therefore get given more importance … if they come in under-budget and they manage their projects on time, those are all very good measures … and those managers then tend to become more successful … being a good manager of people can manifest itself in improved productivity and it can manifest itself in maybe a more engaged workforce but those can also have other factors that affect them. It doesn't necessarily have a direct correlation to that manager.

DEVOLUTION? IT'S JUST A STORY …

The role played by line managers in conflict handling has become increasingly important as HR functions have attempted to devolve what are perceived as operational people management issues. This also relates to the widely held view among HR practitioners that conflict management is a transactional rather than a strategic activity (Jones and Saundry, 2012; Saundry and Wibberley, 2014). Our own recent research found that even those HR professionals who were actively in involved in advising managers on handling workplace conflict saw this as a 'day-to-day' activity, part of the 'bread and butter' of people management. The following quotation typifies practitioner perspectives of the division between the strategic work undertaken by HR business partners (HRBPs) and the 'day-to-day work' involving the conflict handling and resolution:

> The HRBPs are the strategic commissioning individuals in HR … so they act in that strategic space commissioning these operational services. Then there's the 'business as usual' which we all just get along with in our specialist teams. So, discipline cases, grievances, conflict, bullying and harassment and we'd deal with that as a matter of course as part of our day-to-day work.

This is problematic because it both devalues the importance of preventing, containing and resolving conflict, and also implies that the management of complex conflicts, such as bullying and harassment, is a straightforward and relatively simple task requiring basic skills. In this context it is hardly surprising, as we see below that it is an area of managerial development that has been largely overlooked and one which HR practitioners with strategic aspirations wish to leave behind.

Perhaps more importantly, the rhetoric of devolution and marginalisation of conflict management within HR stands in stark contrast to the reality of HR work. Researchers working in the late 1990s and early 2000s identified that, on the whole, issues such as grievance and discipline were still jointly regulated (Hales, 2005; Hall and Torrington, 1998; Kersley et al., 2006; Whittaker and Marchington, 2003). Decisions over such matters were generally only taken by managers, with HR playing an advisory or supporting role, although the extent of HR intervention would depend on the level of managerial capability. In addition, according to the Workplace Employment Relations Survey 2011, discipline and grievance was the issue on which more HR practitioners in the UK spent time than any other (92 per cent) (van Wanrooy et al., 2013).

While our (more recent) research confirmed that conflict management and resolution still takes up a significant amount of HR time, there is a continuing desire to leave this to the line, so that HR professionals can focus on what is often referred to as 'the strategic stuff'. HR practitioners who we interviewed repeatedly talked of trying to reduce dependence and 'hand-holding'. As this was seen as 'unhealthy' and disempowering, there was a fairly common view that line managers would only learn and take responsibility if they were left to fend for themselves:

> And I think we started to see a benefit that if actually the line manager took more responsibility for their people issues and the people that reported to them … it's really disempowering for a line manager if they're kind of only allowed to do half their job and then they're hauling in HR to do the other half. And then we get a bit of a bad press because we're seen as the police coming in.

At the same time, there is little evidence that HR practitioners have ceded control over the development, control and implementation of conflict management procedures. In the UK, Wood et al. (2017) found that despite the increased promotion of informal resolution, the extent of written disciplinary and grievance procedures and their application had increased in recent years. This arguably reflects a desire on the part of the HR profession to ensure consistency, fairness and legal compliance. Therefore, while HR practitioners may want to withdraw from playing a direct role in conflict management, they seem reluctant to dilute their identity as procedural specialists and legal experts.

Overall, while most HR practitioners recoil from being characterised as the HR 'police' (Renwick, 2003), the evidence suggests that in respect of conflict management at least, the regulation of line managerial behaviour remains as strong a preoccupation as ever. Most HR practitioners would appear to see themselves as reluctant 'police officers', with the need for close and continuing support rooted in the view that managers simply lack the skills and confidence they need to manage conflict effectively (Hunter and Renwick, 2009; Teague and Roche, 2012). However, a recurring feature of our research has been the suggestion that, irrespective of the rhetoric, there is a significant part of the profession that is reluctant to give up the authority and influence that arguably comes with procedural and legal expertise. The following quotation from a senior HR leader illustrates this in very stark terms: 'a lot of HR professionals like the policing role and they like that kind of authority and power that comes from that and it's awful and it's hard to break'.

CAPABILITY AND TRAINING: CLOSING THE COMPETENCE GAP?

The contradiction between the need for HR to ensure consistency and compliance, and the aversion of some managers to policy and procedure, could be expected to create an adversarial relationship between HR and the line. For HR practitioners, the responsibility for the limited progress towards genuine devolution and more strategic people management is put squarely at the door of line managers themselves (Caldwell, 2001; McCracken and Heaton, 2012; McCracken et al., 2017; Pritchard, 2010). Put simply, many HR practitioners have little faith in the abilities of the line managers they advise.

In particular, UK-based research has pointed to very negative assessments of the abilities of line managers to handle and resolve conflict. In 2007, a Chartered Institute of Personnel and Development (CIPD) survey of its members found that around two-thirds felt that line managers were either average or poor at resolving disputes informally (CIPD, 2007: 12). In 2008, the CIPD argued that line managers were neither 'willing' to nor 'capable' of taking on the challenge of early conflict resolution. Moreover, this problem is not limited to more junior managers. A survey of HR practitioners, conducted by the CIPD in 2016, reported that

83 per cent of respondents claimed that 'senior leaders' were 'very' or 'somewhat' effective in demonstrating technical skills. This fell to 50 per cent in respect of 'managing difficult conversations', and only 38 per cent in respect of 'conflict management', the lowest score of 15 competencies that the survey covered (CIPD, 2016).

The 'conflict competence' problem among line managers has three key features. First, organizations still tend to prioritise technical expertise within recruitment and promotion processes (Townsend, 2013). This was a recurring feature in our research:

> We promote people based on specialist knowledge, so we have people who are really brilliant at their specialist knowledge, they get promoted into a managerial role, and they don't really know how to manage. And they don't get the support in how to manage and they're expected to take on all this people stuff and they just don't know how to do it.

At the same time, first-line managers are often promoted and expected to manage difficult issues with their former teammates without any training at all (Townsend et al., 2012). One of our respondents explained this succinctly: 'They'll go home on Friday doing an operational role … come in on a Monday and you're a team leader and you know that but it's as though there's some kind of magic sprinkling of dust that somehow you're going to develop those skills'.

Second, skills deficits in relation to the ability of line managers to handle conflict arguably reflect a deeper problem, in that organizations have increasingly focused their development efforts on strategy and leadership to the exclusion of basic managerial competence (Sadun et al., 2017). The stereotype of conflict management as a transactional activity has meant that it has not been seen as priority for training investment. However, this contrasts with evidence suggesting that line managers face increasingly complex people management challenges. Even in the early days of devolution, the difficulties faced by line managers in balancing operational and people management responsibilities were noted (McGovern et al., 1997). This has been exacerbated by the contemporary emphasis on performance management (Newsome et al., 2013), which makes it increasingly likely that managers will find themselves having to have 'difficult conversations' with their subordinates.

Third, even when organizations recognise the importance of conflict management competence, it remains quite rare for these elements to be part of compulsory basic training. Instead, they are an added extra which, for reasons outlined earlier in this chapter, are unlikely to be a priority for busy managers. Consequently, training is often provided to those who are already interested and who have reasonable skills in these areas. The following quote from an HR practitioner in the third sector sums up this problem:

> We have a really good history of management development, the problem we have is when, as a charity with limited resources and people running around very busily, the training was not prioritised, so we'd put these things on and it was really hard to get people to come along and if they did come along it was hard to support them with the follow through.

This perhaps explains the disjuncture between continuing problems with managerial capability, at the same time as evidence that organizations are placing greater emphasis on training their managers to deal with 'difficult conversations' and conflict situations (Saundry et al., 2016). Our research found that where people management training for line managers was compulsory, HR practitioners had greater confidence in line managers:

> We have very few disciplinary and grievance cases in our organization. I think it's because we have a strong culture of openness and communication and we train our line managers. For the first six months we invite the line managers along to shadow other cases, so if there's absence or anything like that, so that they're confident and they're happy whenever they go into it. Then if there are any investigations, once they're a bit more comfortable they'll sit in with another manager and maybe take notes. Whenever we have any new managers we always ask them then to shadow our warehouse team and our logistics team because they're very well versed in handling conflict because they're doing it more regularly.

It is also widely assumed that HR practitioners themselves have the knowledge and confidence to manage conflict effectively. However, the same pressures that have sidelined employment relations as a core managerial competence have also been reflected in its marginalisation within the training and development of aspiring HR practitioners. In the UK, the CIPD (2015: 3) has argued that 'many HR managers lack confidence in developing informal approaches to managing conflict and continue to be nervous about departing from grievance procedures'. Interestingly, WERS 2011, the Workplace Employment Relations Survey 2011 (Van Wanrooy et al., 2013) found 'considerable evidence' of a greater reliance among workplace HR managers on external legal advice.

THE LIMITS ON INFORMALITY: THE TIES THAT BIND

It is important to note that the perceived desire of line managers to be freed of the 'HR police' appears to have little basis in contemporary evidence. Cunningham and Hyman (1999) found that line managers welcome HR advice and guidance, while other studies have suggested that managers welcome the cover and certainty provided by procedure (Cole, 2008; Cooke, 2006). Hunter and Renwick (2009: 407) have argued that procedure represents 'a form of codified HR knowledge for line managers'. In an environment in which the legal constraints on managers are perceived to be complex, and where managerial performance is increasingly scrutinised, it is perhaps not surprising that line managers can be risk-averse and welcome the safety of rigid procedural adherence (Saundry et al., 2016). This was also reflected in our own research by concerns from some line managers about the lack of HR support, particularly in larger organizations where HR was often located remotely:

> Employee relations sits with the line managers. You're expected to deal with everything that comes your way, and you're encouraged to deal with most things informally, which we do, and there are reams of guidance. If you phone the HR service centre for advice because you have a difficult multi-layered problem, the first thing they say to you is 'have you looked at the guidance?' Of course I have!! So, you're very much on your own I would say especially for the first part of it. Then if it got really out of hand, I think they do then start to worry in case of a tribunal, then they all jump in and say 'why didn't you contact us?' The level one HR people are no more experienced at conflict than me or my team, and it's all very, 'what do you think?' It's all very counselling! I don't really want a conversation about it, I want to know what legally can I do and can't do? Can I tell him to go home? Can I tell him to piss off, and never come back? What are the implications? But the answer is always, 'it's over to you'.

The tension between devolution and managerial capability has inevitably restricted the use of more informal approaches to conflict resolution. Indeed, our research points to the formalization of informal processes through the widespread use of management tools such as checklists, flowcharts and templates. In some respects, this reflected a view that managers who lacked confidence to resolve an issue informally, or to have a difficult conversation with a member of staff, felt more comfortable with some sort of process to follow. In some cases, organizations had even introduced written informal resolution procedures:

> we rewrote the grievance procedures, particularly focussed on the grievance procedure because we wanted to make it a requirement to be informal; within the procedure we've got a get out at any stage, so you can go into the formal ... but you can move out of the formal and you can have a discussion and try and solve it, even right through to an appeal point.

Ultimately, this reflects the HR profession's continuing lack of trust in line management: extending control into disciplinary and grievance processes, even if, in theory, authority and responsibility are devolved. For example, in one large organization with a remote HR function, HR was the 'keeper' of a range of forms, structured conversations and scripts for line managers to use in a variety of conflict situations. This was underpinned by the compulsory use of online technology, through which managers uploaded a range of information, such as fit notes, return-to-work interviews and the notes of informal disciplinary meetings. All personnel files were held electronically by HR, and line managers were explicitly told that they could not keep any records (including telephone contact numbers). Therefore, it could be argued that formal intervention had been replaced by informal control; enhanced by technology. Whether this helps managers to develop their skills, however, is questionable. Trade union representatives who we interviewed repeatedly argued that HR practitioners curtailed the discretion of managers, and that this in turn could hamper more creative resolutions:

> It's about HR taking the decision, not the manager anymore. The manager is frightened to say anything unless HR tells them what to say. They come in with sheets and they read off sheets. 'I've got to go through this process and ask this question'.

> It's out of the filing cabinet. Even in disciplinary, quite often it is drafted out of the room and brought in and they will read through it. Sometimes it's comical because they can't pronounce some of the things. They get halfway through and they say, 'I don't know what that word is'.

> what they do is they get a tick box sheet and a flow chart ... and every meeting the manager will sit there and go 'good afternoon', tick, 'are you fit to attend?', tick, 'is your representative here?', tick ... if the answer is X, look at your flow chart ... absence management policy is classic ... they are starved of making an independent decision and if that's how HR assists them by providing them the flow chart, that's devolving responsibility. No, they're just ticking boxes.

While HR practitioners, and especially HR business partners, have rejected their role in 'handholding', and what one respondent even referred to as 'arse-wiping', this has been replaced by longer 'reins', cementing control by providing managers with a bogus autonomy. While responsibility for decisions is left with line managers, the surrounding decision making framework is constructed and owned by HR. Those managers working outside procedure, or not in accordance with HR advice, are seen as 'rogue' managers who need to be controlled, monitored and regulated to rein them in from their natural tendencies and 'gut instinct'.

It could even be argued that true devolution is unachievable given the range of responsibilities expected of managers. In our research, HR practitioners working in high-pressure environments with scarce resources, such as healthcare, argued that many managers with high-level technical skills were simply not able to devote the time needed to unpick complex conflicts between staff. In one organization, what seemed like a progressive initiative through which managers were expected to conduct regular one-to-ones with their staff to manage performance and conflict was seen as unrealistic by HR practitioners, given existing workloads: 'I think the expectation of thinking that they'll be able to pick that up and really run with all that and they've got the time to do it is never going to work.'

Therefore, even with greater investment in training and development, it is arguably unrealistic to expect managers to find the time and space to manage conflict effectively. Accordingly, there is an argument, albeit a somewhat unfashionable one, that HR should maintain an active role in managing employment relations issues. Interestingly, our research suggested that this was more likely to be the case in smaller organizations in which the HR function had often been developed as a response to damaging workplace conflicts. In these contexts, line managers were expected to be able to communicate effectively with their teams and HR and address low-level conflicts. However, for more complex and difficult issues it was seen as important for HR to step in, to allow line managers time and space:

> I think in our industry we are really conscious that pushing too much to the line potentially has a consequential effect that you don't foresee, which is that the breadth of their role becomes too administrative ... that's not their forte and that's not what they're in situ for. To hamstring a creative, capable person with a procedural millstone is, I would say, is equally detrimental ... There will be stuff where we will just sometimes take control and take ownership ... when we have the skills and the experience and the expertise to deliver something, it makes zero sense to pass that responsibility over on to somebody else.

CONCLUSION

The problem of the conflict competence of line managers is not new. Over the past 20 to 30 years, researchers have regularly pointed to the priority given to technical skills in recruitment and promotion, and the lack of organizational support for the development of the 'softer' skills needed to negotiate and mediate effective solutions to difficult problems. More recently, robust data linking managerial capability and productivity has once again placed this important issue in the spotlight (Sadun et al., 2017). Our own research with HR practitioners and other key stakeholders in the UK has suggested that there is an awareness of this problem, and some evidence that organizations are trying to address this through new training programmes and skills interventions.

However, the discussion in this chapter suggests that there are more fundamental structural barriers, both to building the conflict competence of line managers, and in providing a framework in which they can use the skills that they have. The most significant challenge is created by the lack of support from senior managers, who prioritise short-term, operational imperatives and who fail to recognise conflict management as a strategic issue. This possibly reflects the fact that senior managers themselves often fail to have the skills needed to resolve conflict. Nonetheless, in this context there is little incentive for more junior managers to take the time needed to either contain and resolve conflict, or develop conflict management skills.

The view that the management of conflict is essentially a transactional rather than a strategic issue also extends to the HR profession. Consequently, conflict resolution has tended to be excluded from the developmental of agendas of senior HR practitioners preoccupied with concerns over talent management and leadership. This conceals a critical paradox in the orientation of HR to line managers. While HR practitioners pursue real devolution and bemoan the continuing dependence of many managers, they do not trust them sufficiently to release the reins of process and procedure. Instead, a range of arm's-length mechanisms are used to retain control while maintaining a kind of bogus autonomy. Resolving this paradox is critical not only to ensuring that organizations have the quality of management needed to maximise productivity and performance, but also to securing the role of the HR profession in improving working lives.

These issues have become increasingly salient as economies seek to 'build back' following the Covid-19 pandemic. For example, in the UK, labour shortages in key sectors have emphasised the need to boost productivity in order to avoid inflation being fuelled by rising wages. At the same time, mental health and well-being at work has become a focus for many organizations. Inevitably, line managers currently find themselves at the sharp end of these challenges. This creates a challenging agenda for employers, policy-makers and academics. Employers undoubtedly need to invest in developing managerial skills, and move away from their obsession with leadership. However, this is not straightforward in the context of critical constraints on time and financial resources. Therefore, creative approaches to skill development are necessary, alongside organizational commitment to view conflict management as a core strategic priority.

However, this is unlikely to happen in the absence of a policy framework that creates clear incentives for organizations. The policy emphasis in the UK in the last decade has been to reduce the costs of conflict for employers. Perhaps counterintuitively, making justice more accessible to workers and employees, while increasing the financial penalties associated with poor managerial practice, could increase the rates of return from investment in managerial capability. However, academic researchers also have a crucial role to play in building the case for conflict competence. There remains a dearth of high-quality research into workplace conflict, and particularly the experiences of workers and employees. In addition to studies gauging the impacts of conflict on those involved, we also lack robust evidence of the efficacy of managerial skills development, and particularly its relation to key outcomes in terms of engagement and productivity. Without high-quality empirical evidence, it is likely that the management of conflict and the critical role played by line managers will continue to be marginalized in both policy and practice.

REFERENCES

Bloom, N. and Van Reenen, J. (2007) 'Measuring and explaining management practices across firms and countries'. *Quarterly Journal of Economics*, 122(4): 1351–1408.
Bloom, N. and Van Reenen, J. (2011) 'Human resource management and productivity'. *Handbook of Labor Economics*, 4(Part B): 1697–1767.
Caldwell, R. (2001) 'Champions, adapters, consultants and synergists: the new change agents in HRM'. *Human Resource Management Journal*, 11(3): 39–52
CIPD (2007) 'Managing conflict at work'. London: CIPD.
CIPD (2015) 'HR Outlook: Winter 2014–15: views of our profession'. https://www.cipd.co.uk/Images/hr-outlook_2015-winter-2014-15-views-of-our-profession_tcm18-11010.pdf
CIPD (2016) 'HR Outlook – views of our profession, Winter 2016–17'. https://www.cipd.co.uk/Images/hr-outlook_2017_tcm18-17697.pdf.
CIPD (2020) 'Managing conflict in the modern workplace'. https://www.cipd.co.uk/knowledge/fundamentals/relations/disputes/managing-workplace-conflict-report.

Cole, N. (2008) 'Consistency in employee discipline: an empirical exploration'. *Personnel Review*, 37(5): 109–117.

Cooke, H. (2006) 'Examining the disciplinary process in nursing: a case study approach'. *Work, Employment and Society*, 20(4): 687–707.

Cunningham, I. and Hyman, J. (1999) 'Devolving human resource responsibilities to the line. Beginning of the end or a new beginning for personnel?' *Personnel Review*, 28(1/2): 9–27.

Dromey, J. (2014) 'Meeting the challenge: successful employee engagement in the NHS'. London: IPA.

Edwards, P. (2005) 'Discipline and attendance: a murky aspect of people management'. In Bach, S. (ed.), *Managing Human Resources. Personnel Management in Transition*, 4th edition. Oxford: Blackwell, pp. 376–397.

Hales, C. (2005) 'Rooted in supervision, branching into management: continuity and change in the role of first-line manager'. *Journal of Management Studies*, 42(3): 471–506.

Hall, L. and Torrington, D. (1998) 'Letting go or holding on – the devolution of operational personnel activities'. *Human Resource Management Journal*, 8(1): 41–55.

Harris, L., Doughty, D. and Kirk, S. (2002) 'The devolution of HR responsibilities – perspectives from the UK's public sector'. *Journal of European Industrial Training*, 26(5): 218–229.

Hook, C., Rollinson, D. and Foot, M. (1996). 'Supervisor and manager styles in handling discipline and grievance. Part one – comparing styles in handling discipline and grievance'. *Personnel Review*, 25(3): 20–34.

Hunter, W. and Renwick, D. (2009) 'Involving British line managers in HRM in a small non-profit organization'. *Employee Relations*, 31(4): 398–411.

Hutchinson, S. and Purcell, J. (2010) 'Managing ward managers for roles in HRM in the NHS: over-worked and under-resourced'. *Human Resource Management Journal*, 20(4): 357–374.

Hyde, P., Granter, E., Hassard, J., McCann, L. and Morris, J. (2013) 'Roles and behaviours of middle and junior managers: managing new organizational forms of healthcare. Final report'. NIHR Service Delivery and Organization programme.

Jones, C. and Saundry, R. (2012) 'The practice of discipline: evaluating the roles and relationship between managers and HR professionals'. *Human Resource Management Journal*, 22(3): 252–266.

Kersley, B., Alpin, C., Forth, J., Bryson, A., Bewley, H., et al. (2006) *Inside the Workplace: Findings from the 2004 Workplace Employment Relations Survey*. London: Routledge.

MacLeod, D. and Clarke, N. (2009) 'Engaging for success: enhancing performance through employee engagement. A report to government'. London: Department for Business, Innovation and Skills.

McCracken, M. and Heaton, N. (2012) 'From "tucked away" to "joined at the hip": understanding evolving relationships within the HRBP model in a regional energy company'. *Human Resource Management Journal*, 22(2): 182–198.

McCracken, M., O'Kane, P., Brown, T.C. and McCrory, M. (2017) 'Human resource business partner lifecycle model: exploring how the relationship between HRBPs and their line manager partners evolves'. *Human Resource Management Journal*, 27(1): 58–74.

McGovern, P., Gratton, L., Hope-Hailey, V., Stiles, P. and Truss, C. (1997) 'Human resource management on the line?' *Human Resource Management Journal*, 7(4): 12–29.

Newsome K., Thompson, P. and Commander, J. (2013) '"You monitor performance at every hour": labour and the management of performance in the supermarket supply chain'. *New Technology, Work and Employment*, 28(1): 1–15.

OPP (2008) 'Fight, flight or face it – celebrating the effective management of conflict at work'. Oxford: OPP.

Pritchard, K. (2010) 'Becoming an HR strategic partner: tales of transition'. *Human Resource Management Journal*, 20(2): 175–188.

Purcell, J. (2010) 'Building employee engagement'. Policy Discussion Paper, London: Acas.

Purcell, J. (2012) 'The management of employment rights'. In Dickens, L. (ed.), *Making Employment Rights Effective: Issues of Enforcement and Compliance*. Oxford: Hart Publishing, pp. 159–182.

Renwick, D. (2003) 'Line manager involvement in HRM: an inside view'. *Employee Relations*, 25(3): 262–280.

Rollinson, D. (2000) 'Supervisor and manager approaches to handling discipline and grievance: a follow-up study'. *Personnel Review*, 29(6): 743–768.

Rollinson, D., Hook, C. and Foot, M. (1996) 'Supervisor and manager styles in handling discipline and grievance. Part two – approaches to handling discipline and grievance'. *Personnel Review*, 25(4): 38–55.

Sadun, R., Bloom, N. and Van Reenen, J. (2017) 'Why do we undervalue competent management? Neither great leadership nor brilliant strategy matters without operational excellence'. *Harvard Business Review*, 95(5): 120–127.

Saks, A. (2006) 'Antecedents and consequences of engagement'. *Journal of Managerial Psychology*, 21(7): 600–619.

Saundry, R. and Wibberley, G. (2014) 'Workplace dispute resolution and the management of individual conflict – a thematic analysis of five case studies'. Acas Research Papers, 06/14.

Saundry, R., Adam, D., Ashman, I., Forde, C., Wibberley, G. and Wright, S. (2016) 'Managing individual conflict in the contemporary British workplace'. Acas Research Papers, 02/16.

Teague, P. and Roche, W. (2012) 'Line managers and the management of workplace conflict: evidence from Ireland'. *Human Resource Management Journal*, 22(3), 235–251.

Townsend, K. (2013) 'To what extent do line managers play a role in modern industrial relations?' *Asia Pacific Journal of Human Resources*, 51(4): 421–436.

Townsend, K., Wilkinson, A., Allan, C. and Bamber, G. (2012) 'Accidental, unprepared and unsupported: the ward manager's journey'. *International Journal of Human Resource Management*, 23(1): 204–220.

Urwin, P. and Saundry, R. (2021) 'Estimating the costs of workplace conflict'. London: Acas.

van Wanrooy, B., Bewley, H., Bryson, A., Forth, J., Freeth, S., et al. (2013) *Employment Relations in the Shadow of Recession – Findings from the 2011 Workplace Employment Relations Study*. London: Palgrave Macmillan.

Whittaker, S. and Marchington, M. (2003) 'Devolving HR responsibility to the line. Threat, opportunity or partnership?' *Employee Relations*, 25(3): 245–261.

Wood, S., Saundry, R. and Latreille, P. (2017) 'The management of discipline and grievances in British workplaces: the evidence from 2011 WERS'. *Industrial Relations Journal*, 48(1): 2–21.

17. Almost at the top, but not quite: senior management's sources of power and their influence on HRM

Atieh S. Mirfakhar, Jordi Trullen, and Mireia Valverde

The human resource management (HRM) process literature has paid increasing attention to the role played by managers (Steffensen et al., 2019) in the relationship between HRM content and HRM outcomes. For the most part, such interest has concentrated on frontline managers (Bos-Nehles et al., 2013), leaving knowledge about other line managers, more specifically senior managers (SMs)—understood as those at the apex of the organization in charge of strategic decisions (for example, chief executive officers, vice presidents)—in the dark (Boada-Cuerva et al., 2019). The term "line manager" covers a large spectrum of managers who are in charge of the products and services that a company delivers to its customers (Brewster et al., 2015), encompassing managers from different organizational levels including SMs, middle managers, and frontline managers (Farndale and Kelliher, 2013). Managers at each of these levels are charged with different responsibilities, have varying degrees of resources and power to accomplish them, and face different pressures in doing so. It is thus important to examine their realities separately to appreciate how their contribution to people management can be efficiently enacted.

While SMs have been extensively used as informants in HRM-related survey-based research when inquiring about HRM policies or the status of the HRM function, much less emphasis has been placed on understanding SMs' own people management responsibilities or how their actions affect HRM (both content and process-wise), with some exceptions (e.g. Arthur et al., 2016; Lopez-Cabrales et al., 2017; Stanton et al., 2010). Yet, SMs' influence in HRM processes cannot be denied. This point was already brought home by Hall and Torrington (1998: 43–44) more than 20 years ago when arguing that "to concentrate only on the progress of, and response to, devolution at the lower levels of manager/supervisor is to look at a tiny part of a big picture," and that "the way that these managers [frontline managers] are in turn managed by their own managers provides a role model, and demonstrates the commitment, or otherwise, of senior management to the changes which are being implemented." When lower-level or frontline managers look up, they see middle managers; and when the latter look up, they see SMs. Hence, SMs' importance is undeniable, and it is important to go beyond frontline managers to have a more comprehensive and holistic view of non-specialist managers in the HRM function.

While the expression "senior manager" is often employed in the HRM literature, its meaning is quite ambiguous. In reviewing the role of managers in the HRM literature, Steffensen et al. (2019) distinguish among the board of directors, chief executive officers (CEOs), the top management team, human resources (HR) managers, and lower to middle managers, without referring to senior line managers per se. Often, the expression "senior manager" is used for referring to the firm's general manager or CEO (e.g. Guest and Conway, 2011; Guthrie,

2001), hence the uppermost authority in the company. At other times, especially in the case of multinational companies, SMs are the general managers of subsidiaries (e.g. Björkman et al., 2011), therefore well above other managers, but still subject to the decisions of top managers at the headquarters.

We align with such views, and try to integrate them by considering SMs as those who are at the top of a business unit, that could be a fully independent company, but where an additional decision-making layer can make ultimate decisions over such managers, such as in the case of a general manager who is not the owner of a company, the CEO of a subsidiary of a holding group, and so on. In such cases, those who could be considered top managers should, in fact, be considered senior line managers. Hence the expression "at the top but not quite," meaning that these CEOs are the most senior employee within their firms, yet they still depend on someone else. The expression "at the top but not quite" also reflects an additional idea, as we will see, which is the fact that any management position, including the most senior ones, must be understood in a larger network of relationships and mutual dependencies. In other words, while CEOs in organizations are considered as the most powerful actors influencing middle and frontline managers, they themselves, as senior line managers, are also subject to dependencies. It is in this mutual network of dependencies, we argue, that HRM needs to be understood.

Therefore, the present chapter examines such dependencies by focusing on the concept of power. In particular, we address the following broad question: How can SMs affect HRM (both function-wise and power-wise) within the organization by means of different power sources? Specifically, we aim to understand how SMs are able to influence other actors in HRM, including frontline managers and HR professionals, and how these latter actors may react in turn (Sheehan et al., 2014), given the fact that the former represent the organization's almost (but not quite) ultimate decision-makers. On the basis of a comparative case study in an Iranian holding company, this chapter explores the power sources used by two managers sitting at the top of two of the firm's subsidiaries, as well as their effects on HRM processes. The study is novel inasmuch as it brings a power perspective to HRM processes and focuses on the role played by SMs, who are the highest authority in their business units, but not at the holding company.

Our analysis shows that SMs can act as a productive or a constraining force in advancing HRM within the firm, and that this is linked to the ways in which they yield their power. We start by reviewing previous work on SMs and their role in HRM, and introducing the power framework used in this study. This is followed by the description of the methodology used, and the findings of the comparative case study. The chapter concludes with insights based on the findings, managerial implications, and future research.

SENIOR MANAGERS AND HRM

Compared to the vast amount of research on frontline and middle managers, the fact is that little attention has been paid to SMs as HRM actors. Steffensen et al. (2019) found only 11 articles on the role of CEOs in HRM (articles that referred to CEOs only as targets or recipients of HRM policies—for example, compensation—were excluded), and 14 on top management teams (TMTs). Similarly, Boada-Cuerva et al. (2019) found only 30 papers that directly or indirectly addressed the role of SMs in HRM in the last 20 years. Much of this research has to do with SMs' views of the HRM function (e.g. Kelly and Gennard, 2007), SMs' values on HRM, or their support for strategic human resource management (SHRM) promoting commitment-based HR practices (Chadwick et al., 2015), SMs' leadership styles influencing the adoption of human capital-enhancing HRM (Zhu et al., 2005), and in some cases, the extent to which SMs' beliefs affect the HRM department status (e.g. Brandl and Pohler, 2010; Khatri and Budhwar, 2002; Stanton et al., 2010).

A much smaller number of studies focus on SMs' influence on the introduction and implementation of new HRM initiatives (e.g. Arthur et al., 2016). If we distinguish between studies that have focused on HRM content versus process, the fact is that research on TMTs and CEOs has for the most part concentrated on their impact on HRM content (Steffensen et al., 2019), showing that SMs' beliefs often have a direct impact on the type of HRM policies and initiatives that are adopted (Guest and Bos-Nehles, 2013). Some studies have also shown that HRM implementation is affected by factors such as SMs' value-based HRM beliefs (Arthur et al., 2016), their support (Kossek et al., 1994) and commitment (Kim and O'Connor, 2009), or trust in senior management (Farndale and Kelliher, 2013); but work on HRM process, broadly understood as "the manner and activities through which HRM content is enacted" (Steffensen et al., 2019: 2388), is less common.

Two main conclusions can be reached in reviewing previous work on SMs and HRM. First, little attention has been paid to these actors (in comparison to lower-level managers). Second, previous work has shown that despite being at the top of the organization and responsible for strategic (rather than operational) decisions, and influencing HRM systems through the values they hold (Chadwick et al., 2015) and the leadership styles they adopt (Zhu et al., 2005), SMs are also highly dependent on other actors. Strong HRM systems are only possible when SMs' messages are aligned with those of other actors, including middle and lower line managers as well as HR professionals (Bowen and Ostroff, 2004; Stanton et al., 2010; Stirpe et al., 2013). Such alignment is not always easy. Different organizational actors will have their own agendas and contextual pressures, which may or may not always align with those of SMs. For instance, HR managers may want to take bolder HRM initiatives, despite SMs not seeing them as a priority (Stanton et al., 2010); and vice versa, sometimes SMs may push for the introduction of new policies that can be resisted by lower-level managers or employees (Trullen et al., 2016). Establishing alignment among these actors, in such a situation where resistance can emerge easily, requires the use of power (Hardy, 1996).

A POWER PERSPECTIVE

While different conceptual approaches have been employed when studying SMs, such as upper echelons theory (Hambrick, 2007; Hambrick and Mason, 1984) or leadership (Kouzes and Posner, 1987; Zhu et al., 2005), both in general and when considering their role in people management (Boada-Cuerva et al., 2019), one concept that seems particularly relevant when thinking about SMs' impact on HRM is that of power (Sheehan et al., 2014). Indeed, a power perspective necessarily involves dependency (Emerson, 1962), and hence implicitly recognizes the fact that HRM strategies may be resisted or reshaped, hence distinguishing intended from actual HRM policies (Wright and Nishii, 2007), and thus could provide a more comprehensive understanding of the role of SMs in HRM. It follows that SMs need to use their power wisely if they want to succeed in setting a particular HRM strategy. Traditionally, power discussions in the HRM literature have analyzed the role played by the HRM function vis-à-vis other key actors in the organization (Ferris et al., 1995; Sheehan et al., 2014). But power-based frameworks can also be useful to analyze the ways in which SMs may affect HRM through their relationship with other organizational actors.

While there are various classifications for dimensions of power (e.g. Bass, 1960; French and Raven, 1959; Hardy, 1996; Hersey et al., 1979; Landells and Albrecht, 2013; Lukes, 1974), in this chapter Hardy's (1996) power dimensions are used. This approach is taken for two main reasons. First, Hardy's framework was developed in the context of strategy process research, clearly distinguishing intended from actual strategies in organizations. Second, Hardy's framework has also been used by other authors in HRM interested in the analysis of power (e.g. Sheehan et al., 2014).

In this regard, four dimensions of power are identified: systemic power, resource power, process power (Astley and Zajac, 1991; Hardy, 1996), and power of meaning (Hardy, 1996; Sheehan et al., 2014). Systemic power is similar to positional power—the power that comes from the position in the organizational structure (Bass, 1960)—and whether this position has higher or lower importance for the organization comes from how tasks are performed and how important these tasks are in the division of labor (Astley and Zajac, 1991), which could have historical, cultural (Hardy, 1996), or outcome-related (Astley and Zajac, 1991) bases. As a result, change in the structure of an organization might lead to change in the systemic power of different actors.

Resource power is related to the deployment of key resources on which other actors depend (Hardy, 1996). In the context of HRM, deployment of employees' skills can be considered as the resource power of HR departments (Sheehan et al., 2014). Expertise, access to information, relations, and networks as well as traditional resources such as financial and material, can be considered as resources that different actors and departments may possess, and which would provide them with a source of power.

The third dimension, process power, "refers to the procedures and political routines, both through formal and informal decision-making processes, that are invoked by dominant groups to influence outcomes" (Sheehan et al., 2014: 195). Where in the organizational hierarchy decisions are made is related to the structure of the organization; in other words, systemic power would influence process power. On the other hand, the exercise of process power might result in changes in the structure of the organization and hence the location of decision-making within the organization (Astley and Zajac, 1991), which means that process power can impact systemic power as well.

Last but not least is the power of meaning, also known as symbolic power, which "refers to the capacity to legitimize interests through the management of meaning, using symbols, rituals and language to make initiative appear legitimate, desirable, rational and inevitable" (Sheehan et al., 2014: 196). Symbolic power is one of the important power dimensions for HR departments, since they tend to have reduced power over resources due to outsourcing their responsibilities (Sheehan et al., 2014) and, depending on the industry, they may also hold low systemic power due to their position in the organizational structure (Farndale and Hope-Hailey, 2009).

Hardy's (1996) power dimensions will provide a conceptual background for this study's exploration of how SMs may influence HRM by deploying their different sources of power. Moreover, while the focus of the study is on SMs, the exertion of power is necessarily in relation to other actors and may, in turn, result in different reactions and even the emergence or disappearance of power in other actors. Thus, in this chapter, such changes in HRM and

HR departments' power, together with the reactions of different agents involved in HRM, will also be observed.

METHODOLOGY

The focus of this study is on the power dynamics between SMs and other actors who are involved in HRM processes. Given the broad nature of our research question we adopt an inductive qualitative approach (Graebner et al., 2012) by means of a comparative case study.

Research Setting

Our research setting is that of an Iranian holding company in an engineering field with multiple subsidiaries. A holding company setting is especially appropriate for this study because it provides a privileged standpoint to compare the role exerted by different senior line managers (CEOs of subsidiaries) in a similar organizational culture (that of the holding firm, which is very engineering-oriented), industry (anonymized), and for a similar set of HR practices. Among the subsidiaries of this Iranian holding company, two of them were specifically chosen because of their similar size in terms of number of employees (around 800 employees each) and the similar fields they work in among the subsidiaries of the holding company. Yet, both subsidiaries were different in terms of the position of their HR departments in the organizational architecture: Subsidiary A with an HR department where the HR manager and department are placed in a high structural position; and Subsidiary B with an HR unit located in the finance and administration department, where the HR manager is considered a middle manager with a lower structural position. One reason why such structural difference is taken into consideration is that organizational structure involves working processes, communication mechanisms, and power arrangements, and it influences organizational performance (Aryee et al., 2008; Xi et al., 2017). It is also important to highlight that their location in the organizational structure is decided by the SM of each subsidiary. Therefore, different organizational structures may involve different power arrangements. Another reason why this specific setting is chosen is to be able to compare the differences in the systemic power afforded to HR departments in a natural setting, a dimension of power that Sheehan et al. (2014) rightly pointed to as difficult to manipulate when carrying out research.

Within these two organizational settings, the unit of observation for the study focuses on the exercise of power by the two CEOs, and the network of reactions and corresponding exercise of power by the other actors who have an influence in the HR function of the two subsidiaries.

Data Collection

In this comparative case study, the main data collection method was the semi-structured in-depth interview, conducted with multiple actors involved in HR practices: vice presidents (VPs), frontline managers, employees, HR managers, and HR employees. The results of this study are based on 50 interviews (23 interviews from Subsidiary A, and 27 interviews from Subsidiary B; details are shown in Table 17.1). Moreover, a cascading interview procedure was applied, meaning that these semi-structured interviews were conducted with VPs, their middle/frontline managers, and the middle/frontline managers' subordinates further down the

Table 17.1   *Interviewees in each subsidiary*

Actors	Subsidiary A	Subsidiary B
VP	5	7
Middle/frontline manager	7	9
Employee	4	7
Member of HR department	7	4
Total	23	27

hierarchy, as well as the responsible HR employee. The two main targets of observation of the study—namely, the CEOs of each subsidiary—were not among the informants in data collection, as it could be expected that their accounts would be subject to social desirability bias. Although the same could be argued for any other informant to some extent, we only considered pieces of information as part of evidence for coding if the same facts, opinions, or arguments were made by at least two separate informants.

Prior to the interviews, interviewees were given consent letters to be signed, and participation was voluntary. The interviews were conducted in Farsi (Persian) and ranged from 35 minutes to two hours, with the average of one hour. Except for three interviews where the interviewees did not grant permission for recording, the rest of interviews were audio-recorded with the consent of the interviewees. During the three interviews which were not recorded, it was made sure that the information provided was written down carefully and as thoroughly as possible.

For our semi-structured interviews, we had three interview protocols: (1) for HR managers and HR employees; (2) for VPs and managers; and (3) for employees. The questions asked in these protocols were similar, with slight changes considering the roles they had. As the interviews were related to a larger project on HRM implementation, the main line of inquiry was related to implementation, and the questions about power were anchored on the answers to the questions dealing with the different agents involved in specific implementation processes. For instance, we asked questions such as: "Who or which departments were involved and who made the decision on which departments to be involved?", "Were there any occasions in implementation where you faced difficulties or problems? What were they and what did you do?", and "What factors have helped and which factors made it difficult to use the practice?"

There were also questions regarding the effectiveness of the practices and whether the practices were being used, for example: "Has the practice achieved what was expected?", "Do you use the practice?", "How often do you/others use the practice?", "How committed are you/others in using it?", "Do you/others know how to use it?" These questions guided us in determining which power sources had positive or negative effects on HR practices.

Data Analysis

For data analysis, after transcribing the interviews verbatim in the language they were conducted, Ritchie and Spencer's (1994) process was used. First, the data were coded based on the a priori topics related to the aim of the research. In other words, the purpose was to look for illustrations of dimensions of power in the actions of different actors. In addition, at this stage, relevant emergent issues that were raised by the interviewees unprompted were also coded. Then, analytical themes were generated by categorizing both sets of codes. Using this thematic framework, the indexing process was done by coding all the interviews. Atlas.ti was used for indexing since this program is compatible with right to left-reading languages. Finally, a charting process was carried out by rearranging the coded data according to the thematic framework, co-occurrences, and positive and negative outcomes, ultimately allowing us to generate the summary table of results shown and explained at the end of the "Findings" section.

At the early stages of data analysis, we realized that a more specific definition for process power should be adopted, since there were cases where it was hard to disentangle process power from systemic power. In order to distinguish between these two dimensions of power, we decided to identify as instances of process power those where actors exhibited decision-making roles based on a written procedure or policy. For example, there were occasions where CEOs and VPs were making decisions or having the final say on particular policies (for example, hiring), disregarding existing procedures or protocols. Those cases were coded as instances of SMs' systemic power overriding the process power of other actors.

FINDINGS

We start our description of findings by paying attention to the ways in which SMs (CEOs from subsidiaries) used their power sources to shape HRM and HR departments' power in the firms. Then we move on to describe the ways in which other actors (for example, VPs, line managers, HR professionals) used their own power sources to engage with the decisions made by SMs, affecting these in turn. These analyses are done comparatively for both subsidiaries, A and B.

How CEOs Affect Other Actors

One way in which CEOs impacted other actors in HR practices was through their process power. In each of the HR practices, there were decision-making roles assigned to various actors, CEOs included. For instance, recruitment and selection, as one of the HR practices, had a written procedure in both companies, assigning roles to different actors. In Subsidiary A, the HR department recruited the qualified candidates, and these candidates were then sent to the department with the open position for further interviews. After receiving the interested department's green light, the candidate was sent to the recruitment committee consisting of VPs. Finally, after the committee's confirmation, the CEO had to sign the recruitment form for the employee to be hired in the company. Similarly, performance management, and training and development, also had procedures providing process power for various actors, including the CEO.

Another way in which the CEO impacted HRM was by providing legitimacy to HR practices. In Subsidiary A, the CEO's insistence in following HRM policies closely increased the symbolic power of the HR department vis-à-vis VPs:

> To be fair, we had the support of the CEO. These changes were gradually added to the [recruitment] procedure, it was revised multiple times and the CEO approved it continuously. And in situations where the CEO was told by the VPs that the "HR [department] is resisting [the recruitment of a specific person], and I [the VP] can tell who is suitable for the job I need," the CEO would reply "if it is according to the procedure, I support it; if not, forget it." (Member of HR department from Subsidiary A)

Regarding performance management in Subsidiary A, the CEO himself was interested in having the practice in place, and supported the HR department to design and implement it. The CEO's and VPs' interest, belief, and support legitimized its adoption, resulting in frontline managers using the practice and finding it useful. Furthermore, the CEO, some VPs and frontline managers also acted as champions of this new practice by helping to facilitate it:

> We had a champion team consisting of some of our managers, VPs and middle managers ... they would comment on the practice as well as participate in different meetings sharing their experiences with other colleagues. (Member of HR department from Subsidiary A)

Subsidiary A's CEO also increased the symbolic power of the HR department through the appointment of an HR VP with HRM expertise, who was a member of HRM-related committees in prestigious universities. This, together with the HR VP's own decisiveness, his reasoning about the why and how of the implementation of the HR practices, and the presence of consultants and external experts in the field, all helped to boost the HR department's symbolic power and legitimize the introduction of HR policies:

> The HR manager is also very important, if you look at his position in the organization, how decisive he is, his position in the HR department and his relations with other VPs and the CEO, all these really impact [implementation]. (Member of HR department from Subsidiary A)

Being supported and provided with resources by the firm CEO meant that the HR department owned valuable resources, such as the HR VP's expertise, the tools and techniques provided by the consultants, and the HR VP's relation with the CEO and other VPs within the firm. This equipped the HR department with resource power.

These qualities were not observed nor mentioned in Subsidiary B. The HR manager appointed by the CEO of Subsidiary B as the head of the HR unit did not have relevant expertise in HRM:

> They [those in charge of HRM] are very distant from HRM knowledge, they have not studied management or industrial engineering to have such concepts in mind or they do not even feel the need to go after it now. (Member of HR department from Subsidiary B)

In Subsidiary B, the firm CEO seemed to devote little time or attention to HR issues. This meant that, differently from Subsidiary A, the existence of formal policies did not mean that they were followed as they should be. For example, despite the presence of a written policy for performance management, which followed the same procedures as in Subsidiary A, it was not carried out. Paradoxically, not following existing policies gave more power to the HR department vis-à-vis line managers and employees, as it reduced the process power of other actors, and made sure that, due to a lack of information on the performance of employees, the HR department management could make decisions subjectively based on their personal opinions of employees:

> This is because of its [HR department's] manager, its manager likes it this way ... that there exists no criterion, that everything be based on feelings, this feeling gives him power, because he is the only one that can manage that feeling, for example I cannot manage his feelings. He gathers all the feelings he has [towards everyone] and he creates a database and he makes decisions accordingly. (Employee from Subsidiary B)

Despite the ability to make arbitrary decisions providing the HR department with resource power, it also seriously harmed its reputation—and hence its symbolic power—internally, causing demotivation and dissatisfaction among employees.

To summarize, CEOs can impact HRM through their systemic, process, and resource power, and with their support they can in turn provide the HR departments with symbolic power. Overall, it seems that when CEOs use their systemic power to have HRM processes and procedures in place (the case of Subsidiary A), there will be positive outcomes in HRM. But when CEOs use their systemic power to override process-based decisions with person-based ones (the case of Subsidiary B), HRM's reputation can be harmed, and it can also result in negative outcomes overall.

How CEOs are Affected by Other Actors

Being a holding company, decisions made at the parent company need to be followed by the subsidiaries, and HRM-related decisions are no exception. Hence, the parent company holds systemic power over the subsidiaries. For example, based on a decision made by the parent company, recruitment and selection were halted in all subsidiaries for some time, with internal transfers being the only way to fill positions. Despite this mandatory freeze, Subsidiary A continued to recruit sporadically, as the CEO and the HR department persuaded headquarters that some positions needed experts who could not be found internally. In the case of Subsidiary B, the only new hires were either internal transfers from other subsidiaries, or candidates who were introduced by top managers from the parent company (using their systemic power) or other key external actors (for example, key customer or supplier firms). This forced the VPs or the CEO to recruit unqualified employees. These hirings, which were carried out in exchange for favors such as contracts or simply to maintain good relationships with key stakeholders, reflected the resource power that external actors held over SMs:

> We also have the employers [of the projects], we have the consultants [of the projects], each of them, based on their situation, have several [unemployed relatives]. Sometimes they [employers and consultants] impose them [the introduced unemployed ones] to us. We see that if we do not employ them, we cannot move forward in the project, see, this is what we are dealing with. (VP from Subsidiary B)

> There are people who have sat in positions which are not related to their educational background … there is an order [from the parent company] not to recruit, but a person with an unrelated educational background is recruited because he is the son of one of the board members of one of the companies. (Member of HR department from Subsidiary B)

Given the support they got from higher instances in headquarters, these hirings also held symbolic over their supervisors and co-workers. They became "untouchable" and their performance could not be questioned. Such imposed hirings were a source of demotivation for SMs and other employees alike, and resulted in decreased performance:

> Do you have the courage to do it [remove an incompetent employee]? It's impossible. [Imagine] he is related [to someone], would I say I don't want this employee? I won't even think about it because I have done something similar before. I say this because I have seen it. It won't result in anything but stress and ruining my image. So, I would say [to myself] let him stay and [let him] get his salary. What would happen next? This person is here and doesn't work, there are four other employees near him … this [the person not working] would have a negative impact on the others [the other four employees] … this would impact their performances. (VP from Subsidiary B)

Another factor influencing recruitment was internal lobbying. Sometimes managers from other departments tried to bypass the HR department by resolving their HRM issues through talking directly to the subsidiary CEO. In such cases, lobbying could happen due to the resource or symbolic power of such VPs, who tried to persuade the CEO to bypass due process:

> Sometimes there are political pressures on us, or there are requests made by them [VPs] coming to us through the CEO, or other VPs forcing the HR department to consider a person they have introduced for recruitment. These make the [recruiting] process difficult. (Member of HR department from Subsidiary A)

Summing up, despite their power, CEOs may have dependencies with other actors that may impact HR practices directly or indirectly. These actors could be external to the organization, providing key resources for the organization; or internal, such as VPs, whose own resources or symbolic power may be needed by the CEO. In addition, the CEOs of subsidiaries are dependent on executives in the parent company, whose power exceeds theirs. Despite this, as mentioned, subsidiary CEOs were sometimes able to circumvent headquarters decisions, such as the hiring freeze, by means of their symbolic power.

Table 17.2 summarizes our findings regarding the power held by different actors for each subsidiary, with an assessment of whether the use of such power had a positive or negative impact on HRM. The assessment of these positive and negative impacts was based on whether the HR practices were used in the subsidiaries, had reached the intended goals, and whether managers were skillful, committed, and consistent in using the HR practices. Rows and columns whose content is presented in italics and underlined highlight the power dependencies of subsidiary CEOs. Actors in the rows hold power over those in the columns. For example, in Subsidiary A, the CEO (the second row) had process power over the VPs (in the second column). This process power is marked with a positive sign as it had a positive effect on HRM.

To sum up, based on our findings, CEOs influence HR practices and HR departments' power using their different sources of power. With their systemic power, which came from their position in the organizational hierarchy, the CEO in Subsidiary A promoted HR practices and processes and acted based on the process power given to each actor—CEOs themselves included—to solidify the HR practices. Meanwhile, the CEO in Subsidiary B used his systemic power to disregard HR processes and disarm process-based decisions and the use of process power by other actors resulting in HR practices to be discarded. Moreover, the CEO at Subsidiary A, with his resource power, provided the HR department with resources and supported the HR department in the implementation of HR practices which provided the HR department with symbolic and resource powers. In contrast, the lack of support from the CEO in Subsidiary B reduced the symbolic power of the HR unit, which resulted in HR procedures not being practiced. Therefore, CEOs using their power and support could make HR departments either powerful and successful in executing their responsibilities, or powerless and weak in the execution of the simple tasks any HR department is created to fulfill. Our findings also show that CEOs were prone to dependencies, and they were also affected by the systemic power of the parent company in having to follow orders, by the resource power of external stakeholders, and by the symbolic and resource powers of internal VPs. Comparing the two subsidiaries, Subsidiary A's HR department was less affected by such powers in comparison to the HR unit of Subsidiary B, as it was more powerful in rejecting some of the imposed hirings.

Table 17.2   Matrix of actors' power sources

	CEO	VPs	HR department	Frontline managers	Employees
Subsidiary A					
Parent company	*‡ Systemic power (R&S)*	–	‡ Systemic power (R&S)	–	–
CEO	–	*+ Process power (R&S, PM)*	*+ Process power (R&S)*	*+ Process power (R&S)*	*+ Process power (R&S)*
VPs	*‡ Resource power*	–	+ Process power (R&S, T)	+ Process power (R&S, PM, T)	+ Process power (R&S, T)
HR department	–	+ Symbolic power (R&S, PM) + Process power (R&S, T) + Resource power (PM)	–	–	–
Employees	–	–	–	–	–
External actors	–	–	–	–	–
Consultants	*+ Resource power (PM)*	+ Resource power (PM)	–	–	–
Subsidiary B					
Parent company	*‡ Systemic power (R&S)*	–	‡ Systemic power (R&S)	–	–
CEO	–	–	*‡ Systemic power (R&S, PM)*	–	–
VPs	*‡ Resource power (PM)*	–	‡ Systemic power (R&S, PM) + Process power (T)	+ Process power (R&S, T)	+ Process power (R&S, T)
HR department	–	–	–	–	–
Employees	–	‡ Symbolic power (R&S)	–	–	–
External actors	*‡ Resource power (R&S)*	‡ Resource power (R&S)	–	–	–
Consultants	–	–	–	–	–

Notes: R&S: recruitment and selection; PM: Performance management; T: Training. +: Power source with positive effect on HRM; ‡: Power source with negative effect on HRM.

DISCUSSION

Steffensen et al. (2019) recently noted that HRM scholarship has largely advanced with a focus on HRM policies, practices, and systems, and their relative effectiveness, but with less emphasis on the managers who are responsible for their formulation and implementation. This statement seems especially true in the case of SMs, who have been largely absent from the HRM literature (Boada-Cuerva et al., 2019). In this chapter, we have explored the role they play in HRM processes by highlighting not only their large influence in HRM decisions, but also by describing how their influence may be constrained by other stakeholders on whom they depend. While different conceptual lenses (for example, leadership; Zhu et al., 2005) can be used to analyze the role of SMs in HRM, a power perspective seemed adequate given that HRM initiatives and the way they are implemented are inherently political (Trullen and Valverde, 2017). This is particularly relevant when taking into account that SMs are almost at the apex of the organizational hierarchy, and thus are both subject to the influence of those with the ultimate say, and also risk resistance from other actors below them if they try to force them to adopt particular policies.

Our findings show that when SMs (in this case subsidiary CEOs) support the HR function by and large, and the HR department in particular, this increases its symbolic, process, and resource power over frontline managers and employees, and facilitates the effective deployment of HRM policies. In the absence of such support, however, VPs and frontline managers may bypass the HR function, with person-based decisions eclipsing process-based ones, negating any efforts at establishing a formally designed HR system. SMs are thus key in any facet of HRM. They can prevent bypasses by using the power that comes with their higher position in the hierarchy, and they can also behave in ways that legitimize HR practices, providing HR departments with symbolic power. Hence, SMs' use of power has both direct and indirect impacts not only on the HR function, but also on how effectively this is going to be deployed.

On the other hand, while SMs' influence is potentially large, our findings also point at SMs' dependencies from other actors, whether internal or external to the organization. Internal actors include those higher up in the organizational chart (for example, top management at headquarters), but also those lower down the hierarchy (in our case, VPs), with their own interests and those of their business units. External actors include other individuals or organizations that have an influence through their bargaining power, such as suppliers and clients.

Based on our findings, SMs were consistently more effective when using their process power. It seems that, in general, when actors use their process power, positive HRM outcomes are achieved. Process power can be invoked when SMs do not want to interfere, yet they want to make sure that HRM policies are being applied. Therefore, having specific procedures for HR practices, where specific roles are assigned to actors, seems to regulate the use of power and result in positive HRM outcomes.

With regard to symbolic power, this is especially effective when introducing HRM initiatives that require the active participation of frontline managers, such as in the case of performance management. These cases seemed to require more than process power in order to make sure that involved actors were committed. This was the case for Subsidiary A, where the CEO's and the VPs' participation in performance management meetings sent a strong message to the rest of the organization.

In turn, systemic power was in this study a double-edged sword, as it could be used to avoid bypasses and result in positive HRM outcomes, or precisely to allow bypasses and result in HRM initiatives becoming useless, as happened in Subsidiary B where the weak status of the HR function combined with the strong position of the firm's CEO and VPs allowed the latter to disregard standard recruitment policy. The optimum situation would be to use systemic power to put procedures in place to regulate the power dynamics through process power. Finally, and in the same vein, although there were fewer examples of SMs' deployment of resource power, these could be directed at either highlighting or diminishing the importance of the HR function, thus subsequently operating in opposite directions towards its effectiveness.

Managerial Implications

In light of these results, a key contribution of this study highlights the need for CEOs and VPs to know how their own power influences HR practices both directly and indirectly through the empowerment they attribute to their HR departments. Indeed, whether by action or by omission, their influence is felt at all levels and in all processes involved in managing people. Thus, even if SMs' inclination or time availability to devote to HR are not high, they should still be aware of the crucial importance of the need to align their messages with those of the individuals and units charged with HRM responsibilities.

CEOs should also be mindful of the fact that they are susceptible to dependencies. Moreover, they should note the direct and indirect effects of such dependencies on HRM and consider their long-term impact when making HRM-related decisions.

In order to achieve the positive outcomes of HRM, we argue, first, that HR departments must be powerful, to make sure that such HR practices are implemented as intended. Therefore, HR departments need to have more systemic power, which can be improved by their position in the organizational hierarchy. CEOs can have a relevant role in making this possible. Second, the HR department needs to have more process power, which can be achieved by having HRM procedures in place that are acknowledged and acted upon by CEO and VPs. Moreover, the HR department needs symbolic power which can be achieved by CEO and VPs support. Third and last, the HR department needs more resource power. This can in part be supported by the CEO making sure that the HR department has sufficient resources to use, and the right people appointed as HR managers and other HR professionals. In addition, HR practitioners also need to empower themselves by equipping themselves with knowledge, tools, and techniques that can be beneficial to the organization.

Limitations and Future Research

This study is a comparative case study conducted in a holding company in Iran. Despite the fact that it is important not to limit such studies to American companies and Western cultures, the findings of this study could be specific to an Iranian context with an Iranian culture. Therefore, future research can explore the power dynamics among actors in the HR function in other countries and other cultures.

Another important limitation was that we could not interview the subsidiaries' CEOs, and hence our analysis of their actions is based on data collected from sources different from them. While CEOs' reports of their own actions would obviously be likely to have social desirability biases, not including their views could be a shortcoming, which we tried to overcome by bringing in the voices of many different actors who influenced and were influenced by the subsidiaries' CEOs, and noting only the facts and ideas that were shared by different individuals.

In this study, external actors were (unexpectedly) found to be influential in HRM. Although the role of unions as external actors has already been studied (Gill, 2009), almost no HRM research is devoted to examining the impact of other external actors such as consultants, suppliers, or customers. In this regard, future studies can explore further the role of such external actors. Overall, the study of SMs' role in HRM is still an underdeveloped line of research that could benefit from further insights from multiple theoretical and empirical angles.

REFERENCES

Arthur, J.B., Herdman, A.O., and Yang, J. (2016). How top management HR beliefs and values affect high-performance work system adoption and implementation effectiveness. *Human Resource Management*, 55(3), 413–435.

Aryee, S., Sun, L.Y., Chen, Z.X.G., and Debrah, Y.A. (2008). Abusive supervision and contextual performance: The mediating role of emotional exhaustion and the moderating role of work unit structure. *Management and Organization Review*, 4(3), 393–411.

Astley, W.G., and Zajac, E.J. (1991). Intraorganizational power and organizational design: Reconciling rational and coalitional models of organization. *Organization Science*, 2(4), 399–411.

Bass, B.M. (1960). *Leadership, Psychology, and Organization Behavior*. New York: Harper & Brothers.

Björkman, I., Ehrnrooth, M., Smale, A., and John, S. (2011). The determinants of line management internalisation of HRM practices in MNC subsidiaries. *International Journal of Human Resource Management*, 22(8), 1654–1671.

Boada-Cuerva, M., Trullen, J., and Valverde, M. (2019). Top management: The missing stakeholder in the HRM literature. *International Journal of Human Resource Management*, 30(1), 63–95.

Bos-Nehles, A.C., van Riemsdijk, M.J., and Looise, J.K. (2013). Employee perceptions of line management performance: Applying the AMO theory to explain the effectiveness of line managers' HRM implementation. *Human Resource Management*, 52(6), 861–877.

Bowen, D.E., and Ostroff, C. (2004). Understanding HRM–firm performance linkages: The role of the "strength" of the HRM system. *Academy of Management Review*, 29(2), 203–221.

Brandl, J., and Pohler, D. (2010). The human resource department's role and conditions that affect its development: Explanations from Austrian CEOs. *Human Resource Management*, 49(6), 1025–1046.

Brewster, C., Brookes, M., and Gollan, P.J. (2015). The institutional antecedents of the assignment of HRM responsibilities to line managers. *Human Resource Management*, 54(4), 577–597.

Chadwick, C., Super, J.F., and Kwon, K. (2015). Resource orchestration in practice: CEO emphasis on SHRM, commitment-based HR systems, and firm performance. *Strategic Management Journal*, 36, 360–376.

Emerson, R.E. (1962). Power–dependence relations. *American Sociological Review*, 27(1), 31–41.

Farndale, E., and Hope-Hailey, V. (2009). Personnel departmental power: Realities from the UK higher education sector. *Management Revue*, 20(4), 392–412.

Farndale, E., and Kelliher, C. (2013). Implementing performance appraisal: Exploring the employee experience. *Human Resource Management*, 52(6), 879–897.

Ferris, G.R., Galang, M.C., Thornton, M.L., and Wayne, S.J. (1995). A power and politics perspective on human resource management. In G.R. Ferris, S.D. Rosen, and D.T. Barnum (eds), *Handbook of Human Resource Management* (pp. 100–114). Oxford: Blackwell Publishing.

French, J.R.P.J., and Raven, B.H. (1959). The bases of social power. In D. Cartwright (ed.), *Studies in Social Power* (pp. 150–167). Ann Arbor, MI: Institute for Social Research.

Gill, C. (2009). Union impact on the effective adoption of high performance work practices. *Human Resource Management Review*, 19(1), 39–50.

Graebner, M.E., Martin, J.A., and Roundy, P.T. (2012). Qualitative data: Cooking without a recipe. *Strategic Organization*, 10(3), 276–284.

Guest, D.E., and Bos-Nehles, A.C. (2013). HRM and performance: The role of effective implementation. In J. Paauwe, D.E. Guest, and P.M. Wright (eds), *HRM and Performance: Achievements and Challenges* (1st edn, pp. 79–96). Chichester: Wiley.

Guest, D.E., and Conway, N. (2011). The impact of HR practices, HR effectiveness and a "strong HR system" on organisational outcomes: A stakeholder perspective. *International Journal of Human Resource Management*, 22(8), 1686–1702.

Guthrie, J.P. (2001). High-involvement work practices, turnover, and productivity: Evidence from New Zealand. *Academy of Management Journal*, 44(1), 180–190.

Hall, L., and Torrington, D. (1998). Letting go or holding on—The devolution of operational personnel activities. *Human Resource Management Journal*, 8(1), 41–55.

Hambrick, D.C. (2007). Upper echelons theory: An update. *Academy of Management Review*, 32(2), 334–343.

Hambrick, D.C., and Mason, P.A. (1984). Upper echelons: The organization as a reflection of its top managers. *Academy of Management Review*, 9(2), 193–206.

Hardy, C. (1996). Understanding power: Bringing about strategic change. *British Journal of Management*, 7(S1), S3–S16.

Hersey, P., Blanchard, K.H., and Natemeyer, W.E. (1979). Situational leadership, perception, and the impact of power. *Group and Organization Studies*, 4(4), 418–428.

Kelly, J., and Gennard, J. (2007). Business strategic decision making: The role and influence of directors. *Human Resource Management Journal, 17*(2), 99–117.

Khatri, N., and Budhwar, P.S. (2002). A study of strategic HR issues in an Asian context. *Personnel Review, 31*(1–2), 166–188.

Kim, S., and O'Connor, J.G. (2009). Assessing electronic recruitment in state governments: issues and challenges. *Public Personnel Management, 38*(1), 47–67.

Kossek, E.E., Young, W., Gash, D.C., and Nichol, V. (1994). Waiting for innovation in the human resources department: Godot implements a human resource information system. *Human Resource Management, 33*(1), 135–159.

Kouzes, J., and Posner, B. (1987). *The Leadership Challenge: How to Get Extraordinary Things Done in Organizations*. San Francisco, CA: Jossey-Bass Publishers.

Landells, E., and Albrecht, S.L. (2013). Organizational political climate: Shared perceptions about the building and use of power bases. *Human Resource Management Review, 23*(4), 357–365.

Lopez-Cabrales, A., Bornay-Barrachina, M., and Diaz-Fernandez, M. (2017). Leadership and dynamic capabilities: The role of HR systems. *Personnel Review, 46*(2), 255–276.

Lukes, S. (1974). *Power: A Radical View*. London and New York: Macmillan.

Ritchie, J., and Spencer, L. (1994). Qualitative data analysis for applied policy research. In A. Bryman and R.G. Burgess (eds), *Analyzing Qualitative Data* (pp. 173–194). London and New York: Routledge.

Sheehan, C., De Cieri, H., Cooper, B., and Brooks, R. (2014). Exploring the power dimensions of the human resource function. *Human Resource Management Journal, 24*(2), 193–210.

Stanton, P., Young, S., Bartram, T., and Leggat, S.G. (2010). Singing the same song: Translating HRM messages across management hierarchies in Australian hospitals. *International Journal of Human Resource Management, 21*(4), 567–581.

Steffensen, D.S., Ellen III, B.P., Wang, G., and Ferris, G.R. (2019). Putting the "management" back in human resource management: A review and agenda for future research. *Journal of Management, 45*(6), 2387–2418.

Stirpe, L., Trullen, J., and Bonache, J. (2013). Factors helping the HR function gain greater acceptance for its proposals and innovations: Evidence from Spain. *International Journal of Human Resource Management, 24*(20), 3794–3811.

Trullen, J., Stirpe, L., Bonache, J., and Valverde, M. (2016). The HR department's contribution to line managers' effective implementation of HR practices. *Human Resource Management Journal, 26*(4), 449–470.

Trullen, J., and Valverde, M. (2017). HR professionals' use of influence in the effective implementation of HR practices. *European Journal of International Management, 11*(5), 537–556.

Wright, P.M., and Nishii, L.H. (2007). Strategic HRM and organizational behavior: Integrating multiple levels of analysis. CAHRS Working Paper# 07-03. Ithaca, NY: Cornell University.

Xi, M., Zhao, S., and Xu, Q. (2017). The influence of CEO relationship-focused behaviors on firm performance: A chain-mediating role of employee relations climate and employees' attitudes. *Asia Pacific Journal of Management, 34*(1), 173–192.

Zhu, W., Chew, I.K.H., and Spangler, W.D. (2005). CEO transformational leadership and organizational outcomes: The mediating role of human-capital-enhancing human resource management. *Leadership Quarterly, 16*, 39–52.

18. The role of line managers in the implementation of work adjustment practices for chronically ill employees: a qualitative study

Silvia Profili, Alessia Sammarra, Laura Innocenti, and Anna Bos-Nehles

INTRODUCTION

The implementation of work adjustment practices (WAPs) does not always yield the desired outcomes. Such practices, including teleworking, flexible scheduling, and other arrangements intended to increase flexibility in the work domain (Shockley and Allen, 2010), are especially important for employees with unique and evolving needs, such as those with chronic health problems. Chronic conditions cover a wide range of health problems such as diabetes, coronary heart disease, cancer, and arthritis. These diseases are of long duration, generally progress slowly, and require "ongoing management over a period of years or decades" (Nolte and McKee, 2008). A quarter of the European Union working population can be classed as chronically ill employees (CIEs). The proportion increased by 8 percent between 2010 and 2017, and will rise further given the aging populations in many countries. Further, chronic conditions are not restricted to older employees, with 18 percent of young workers (aged 16–29) reporting chronic illness in 2017 (Eurofound, 2019).

Despite the widespread incidence of chronic disease in the workforce, little research has explored the specific implementation of work adjustment practices for this group of employees, and the role played by line managers in shaping this process. This is regrettable given that the effective implementation of WAPs will enable CIEs to manage job demands and perform effectively. WAPs have the potential to increase the possibility for these individuals to remain in work and have a positive work experience.

A consolidated stream of studies has explored accommodating jobs for people with disabilities, providing evidence of the complex nature of adopting work practices, with each implementation having its unique path and involving different actors with different roles (Baldridge and Swift, 2013; Colella, 2001; Stone and Colella, 1996). Although there is a strong connection between disability and chronic illness, they are distinct phenomena. Disability cannot be identified with illness, and not all chronically ill individuals develop a disability, or vice versa (Australian Institute of Health and Welfare, 2018). Further, a distinguishing feature of many chronic illnesses is their uneven and oscillatory progression, with peaks and periods of respite that may occur on a daily basis (Rolland, 1987). This places the "ill" employee in a "grey zone," being healthy and able at times, while having significant disabilities in other periods (Varva, 2015). By acknowledging these differences, one should recognize that CIEs can have needs and expectations that are different, although related, to those of workers with a disability. Consequently, we should question the implementation of WAPs for this specific group of employees who need work to accommodate their evolving needs. In doing so, we should move beyond the "what" of implementation (the content of practice) to explore the "how" and the "who" of implementation (the process), since these need to reflect the specific features of these workers. Hence, we here aim to explore the WAP implementation process for CIEs, and to identify conditions under which line managers in interaction with other stakeholders can implement WAPs in a way that meets the needs of this vulnerable group of workers. To this end, we conducted a qualitative study and adopted multiple perspectives, looking at the perceptions of all the actors directly or indirectly involved in the implementation of human resource management (HRM) practices.

Our study contributes to theory and practice in several ways. First, by drawing on HRM implementation studies and the literature on workplace accommodation, we take the first step towards building a theory of WAP implementation for CIEs. Although the field of HRM implementation is growing, current theorizing overlooks employees with chronic conditions, thereby ignoring specific features that affect HRM implementation for this significant group of employees. Specifically, we shed light on what happens during implementation (Trullen et al., 2020) by empirically examining how line managers and various internal actors on different levels interplay with contextual elements, what they do, and how they affect each other in shaping WAP implementation. Building on the studies of WAPs in the workplace and integrating some of the findings and insights from HRM implementation research, we gain a nuanced perspective of how line managers shape the way WAPs are implemented and experienced by CIEs and by the multiple actors who interact with them at work.

Our second contribution is to respond to growing calls for more attention to be given to context in HRM research (Cooke, 2018). Rather than treat context as a descriptive background, or as a set of antecedents that constrain implementation (Cooke, 2018; Paauwe, 2004), we put organizational context at the very heart of implementation, acknowledging that it interacts with multiple organizational actors to shape the paths of WAP implementation.

Third, this study contributes to the HRM stakeholder literature not only by acknowledging the active role of line managers and other actors in the process of HRM implementation (Bos-Nehles and Meijerink, 2018), but also by carrying this forward to look empirically at employees' agency (Meijerink and Bos-Nehles, 2017) and their influence on those who are generally considered to be the key players in the process.

Finally, by focusing on CIEs, the present study illuminates the experiences and perspectives of a significant category of vulnerable employees (Restubog et al., 2021) who, to date, have rarely been studied through HRM and organizational lenses.

THEORETICAL BACKGROUND

The HRM Implementation Process: From a Top-Down to a Dynamic and Recursive View

HRM implementation has recently attracted increasing research attention (Bondarouk et al., 2018; Bos-Nehles et al., 2013; Guest and Bos-Nehles, 2013; Trullen et al., 2020). Most studies have assumed a sequential approach that follows a single path regardless of the practices involved: from intended to actual, and from actual to perceived HRM practices, with distinct actors involved at each stage. In this assumed process, line managers and other HRM stake-holders play fixed roles that do not allow deviations from what is deemed to be the most effective way to implement intended HRM practices, thereby avoiding gaps between the developed, implemented, and perceived HRM practices (Makhecha et al., 2018; Wright and Nishii, 2013).

A criticism of the prevailing conceptualization of HRM implementation is the assumption of a linear sequential process. To overcome this limitation, some HRM authors conceptualize HRM implementation as a dynamic process (Bondarouk et al., 2018; Bos-Nehles et al., 2017; Van Mierlo et al., 2018) that starts with the decision to introduce a practice (initiation), continuing with adaptation, during which the practice is shaped by relevant actors to fit specific needs, until the practice becomes routinized (Trullen et al., 2020). Here, HRM practices do not follow a compliant route but may be shaped during usage, and line managers in interaction with other HRM actors may play a part during their implementation. As such, line managers and organizational actors on different hierarchical and functional levels are involved in HRM implementation, with other, less demarcated, responsibilities and tasks in the various stages of the process than are usually assumed (Budjanovcanin, 2018; Stirpe et al., 2015). In this respect, recent studies challenge the view that employees are mere passive recipients of HRM practices, suggesting that they actively shape their perceptions and interpretations of HRM (Janssens and Steyaert, 2009; Lepak and Boswell, 2012) and play an active role in co-creating and co-producing HRM practices (Meijerink and Bos-Nehles, 2017; Meijerink et al., 2016). As such, HRM implementation is seen as a complex and dynamic process with practices that evolve during implementation, and with line managers in interaction with other HRM stake-holders actively shaping the process.

The Implementation Challenge of Work Adjustment Practices

Such a complex and dynamic conceptualization of HRM implementation is especially needed when explaining work adjustment practices. WAPs include "alternative work options that allow work to be accomplished outside of the traditional temporal and/or spatial boundaries of a standard workday" (Rau, 2003). These adjustments allow employees some level of control over where work is completed (that is, telecommuting or "flexplace") and/or when work is completed (that is, "flextime" or scheduling flexibility) (Allen et al., 2013; Lambert et al., 2008; Rau and Hyland, 2002), and are often designed to promote "the integration of paid work with other important life roles such as family, education, or leisure" (Ryan and Kossek, 2008: 295), or to minimize the impact of employees' impairments and disability on performing their jobs (Cleveland et al., 1997).

These practices reflect a growing trend towards greater individualization and customization in the design of HRM systems to address personal needs (Kossek et al., 1999). Indeed, WAPs are often implemented in response to individual needs as part of the psychological contract, and require a negotiation process between individual employees and their employer (Hornung et al., 2008). Further, and distinct from most HRM practices (for example, performance management processes), employees themselves decide whether to participate in flexible work options. Consequently, these adjustments are often employee-initiated, and the availability of such practices says little about the extent to which they are effectively used (Ryan and Kossek, 2008).

Hence, WAPs pose unique implementation challenges. In their analysis of work–life policies, Ryan and Kossek (2008) suggest that although these policies are adopted with the specific intent of fostering inclusion, they often end up leading to exclusion because of the widespread belief that employees who use flexible work arrangements place a burden on co-workers and supervisors. Further, employees who opt to use an offered accommodation may be seen as signaling that they need assistance, thereby becoming vulnerable to stigmatization (Colella, 2001). Disability research (Stone and Colella, 1996) provides a broad view of accommodation processes, showing the critical role that building a flexible work environment plays in addressing the needs of people with disabilities and increasing their satisfaction at work (Baumgärtner et al., 2015). Several studies have focused on the specific features of accommodating such individuals, exploring the key barriers and opportunities in providing workplace accommodations (Moon and Baker, 2012), the way employers and employees negotiate accommodations (Gold et al., 2012), the factors affecting employees' decision to request an accommodation (Baldridge and Swift, 2013), and the key role played by co-workers in the implementation of these practices (Colella, 2001). Comparing the perspectives of employees, their co-workers, and their managers on accommodation costs and benefits, Schur et al. (2014) found that providing accommodations not only positively affected the attitudes of workers with disabilities but also those of co-workers, suggesting that flexible and supportive workplaces have broader benefits that foster overall workplace productivity.

Some research has specifically examined the provision of WAPs for CIEs. These studies suggest that chronic condition disclosure is an important predictor of WAPs (Pryce et al., 2007) and that group-based empowerment training programs for employees with chronic physical diseases who experience work-related problems increase self-efficacy and reduce fatigue complaints (Varekamp et al., 2011). Varekamp and van Dijk (2010) found that reduced work hours, working from home, a slower work pace, and greater autonomy in planning work tasks were some of the most desired accommodations by employees with a chronic disease. In their study of 203 working adults with chronic illnesses, McGonagle and Barnes-Farrell (2014) found that employees having greater work flexibility perceived a lower identity threat and that this, in turn, reduced strain and increased work ability. In a recent study, Boelhouwer et al. (2020) found that providing autonomy to employees with chronic diseases enhances their work ability and work engagement, and reduces burnout complaints, reinforcing the idea that flexibility at work is an important target for interventions aimed at enhancing occupational well-being of this population.

Despite these studies providing insights into the prevalence of WAPs for CIEs and the antecedents and consequences of their use, none have unraveled the specific role of line managers in interaction with other HRM actors and the nature of WAP implementation, or identified how the benefits of flexible working practices can be better realized for this group of employees.

In this study, we integrate theory and research on HRM implementation and accommodations to shed light on the role of line managers in the different stages of WAPs implementation, providing evidence on the way they affect this process and its outcomes as they interact with other HRM stakeholders.

Table 18.1   The Italian regulatory framework for CIEs

Provisions of the Italian civil code	In Italy, as in many other European countries, there is no specific body of law that protects CIEs. However, all employees have the right to take time off work to follow specific treatments, or to recover from a surgical procedure. During this absence, they are entitled to their salary and may not be dismissed (art. 2110, Italian Civil Code).
CIEs with recognized disability	If CIEs develop a disability and obtain a recognition of civil invalidity and/or disability by the National Social Security Institute, they can ask to shift from full-time to part-time employment for as long as necessary and can return full time when their health conditions improve (art.8, comma 3, Legislative Decree 81/2015). Additionally, they have the right to be assigned tasks appropriate to their working abilities. Moreover, if their health conditions worsen, with consequent further reduction or modification of work abilities, CIEs are entitled to be moved to a lower role/task while still enjoying, if more favorable, the privileges and economic treatment associated with their previous roles and tasks. CIEs suffering from a severe disability also have the right to work at the site closest to their home and may not be relocated without their consent (art.33, Law 104/92).
CIEs without a recognized disability	Where an illness does not cause a disability but has a severe impact on CIEs' abilities to perform their daily tasks, physicians and company doctors can demand the organization provides CIEs with appropriate work-adjusted solutions. Here, companies have to comply with medical prescriptions and provide, when requested, workplace accommodations such as accessible workstations or remote working solutions.

METHODOLOGY

Research Context and Sampling

To answer the research question posed in this study, we adopted a qualitative case study approach conducted in a global energy company headquartered in Italy. The company operates in more than 30 countries and employs around 30 000 workers in Italy and more than 68 000 workers worldwide. Table 18.1 illustrates the Italian regulatory framework for CIEs.

The WAPs analyzed in the study cover four practices: teleworking, smart working, job mobility, and job redesign. We focused on this set of practices because previous studies have suggested that they are the most desired accommodations by employees with a chronic disease (Varekamp and van Dijk, 2010). Table 18.2 displays the content of these practices as defined by the company.

We first asked the human resources (HR) department to introduce our research project to CIEs. Specifically, HR business partners (BPs) were invited to explain the study's aim and implications to CIEs under their responsibility, asking them whether they wanted to participate in the project. In order to ensure variety in the CIE sample, we provided the HR business partners with a list of criteria, such as type of chronic illness, gender, age, career stage, hierarchical level, and professional area, to ensure that we crossed functional boundaries, hierarchical layers, professional clusters, and demographic categorizations. The CIEs invited were made aware, on agreeing to take part to the project, that it would also involve their direct supervisor, their HR business partner, and their co-workers.

In total, 19 CIEs voluntarily participated in the study. They were permanent employees of the company, and a quarter had managerial roles. They were all affected by severe illnesses, ranging from cancer to neurodegenerative diseases, diabetes, and Crohn's disease (Table 18.3).

Table 18.2 Work adjustment practices included in our studies

WAP	Content of practice	Target of practice	Formal document
Teleworking	– The aim of teleworking is to promote the work–life balance and a culture of flexibility. Its adoption requires a formal written agreement between the employer and the employee that specifies conditions and duration of remote working. It is reversible and extendable. – The policy does not define a minimum or maximum number of days that remote workers have to work at the company site. The supervisor is supposed to decide, in each individual case, how many times a week the remote worker has to work in the office.	– All employees can apply for teleworking although a maximum of 4% of the workforce can adopt this practice. – Priority is given to employees who need care and support, who have to assist a relative with serious health problems such as drug addiction, alcoholism, AIDS, or disabilities, or maternity/paternity leave.	Company agreement with unions
Smart working	– This practice allows out-of-office working one day a week. The employee must program in advance (e.g., on a monthly basis) the "smart" working days in agreement with their supervisor. – It is a managerial approach that puts into practice the company's values of trust, proactivity, responsibility, and innovation. People working part-time or working remotely cannot use smart working.	– It does not have a specific focus on disability. It is not meant for single individuals but for business units. Once it is determined that the activity of a work team or organizational unit is compatible with smart working, then employees are free to make an individual written agreement with the company to use this arrangement.	Company agreement
Job redesign	Any kind of reorganization of job-related content, including tasks, duties, and responsibilities.	All employees.	None
Job mobility	Any movement of employees across positions within the organization. This can be proposed either by the employee or the supervisor and relies on the use of job posting.	All employees.	None

Table 18.3   CIEs' characteristics

	Age	Gender	Organizational function
1	44	F	Business Development: Europe and Middle East
2	34	F	Administration, Finance and Control
3	59	M	Planning
4	60	F	Geo-Resource Evaluation
5	61	M	Technical Support
6	52	M	Distribution Management
7	51	M	Technical Support
8	48	M	Back Office Sales Activities
9	44	F	Customer Care
10	55	M	Network Planning and Maintenance
11	54	M	Network Development
12	49	M	Network Development
13	56	F	Procurement
14	50	M	Quality Management
15	43	F	Administration: Finance and Control
16	44	F	HRM
17	52	M	Administration: Finance and Control
18	39	F	Customer Care
19	51	M	Technical Support

Note: CIEs were affected by the following illnesses (in alphabetical order): breast cancer (3), bone cancer (1), chronic kidney disease (2), Crohn's disease (2), colon cancer (1), chronical abdominal adhesions (1), coronary artery disease (2), deafness (1), diabetes (2), lung cancer (1), neurodegenerative disease (2), testicular cancer (1).

We then contacted the CIEs' line managers (19), HR BPs (10), and co-workers (22). This sampling strategy allowed us to study line mangers' role in their interdependency with all the relevant stakeholders involved in the process of WAP implementation by focusing not only on the line manager relationship with the individual CIE, but also with their HR BP and co-workers.

Data Collection

Qualitative data were collected through in-depth face-to-face interviews, focus groups, and company documents. The adoption of multiple sources of evidence enabled us to seek convergence and corroboration, and thus to reduce the potential biases that can occur in a single study. In total, the study involved 78 informants in a two-step process (Table 18.4).

We started by conducting eight semi-structured interviews with members of the HR department. The length of the interviews ranged from 40 to 110 minutes, amounting to 11 hours. During these interviews, informants were asked to describe the work adjustment practices adopted by the company and to explain the different phases of the implementation process. We recorded and transcribed these interviews and validated the transcripts with the respondents.

In the second stage, we conducted seven focus groups (FGs) involving a total of 70 informants. Participants were asked to illustrate the WAPs implementation process highlighting barriers and enabling factors at different stages of the process, and to describe the role of the stakeholders involved. We separated the FGs according to job role, covering the following categories: (1) employees with chronic diseases (2 FGs); (2) their supervisors (2 FGs); (3) their HR business partners (1 FG); and (4) their co-workers (2 FGs).

Table 18.4   Participants in the study

8 Semi-structured interviews	HR Development Director
(n = 8)	HR Development Vice-Director
	People Care and Diversity Manager
	Industrial Relations Manager
	HR Development specialist
	People Care and Diversity specialist
	People Care and Diversity specialist
	People Care and Diversity specialist
7 Focus groups	CIEs (n = 10)
(n = 70)	CIEs (n = 9)
	CIEs' supervisors (n = 10)
	CIEs' supervisors (n = 9)
	CIEs' co-workers (n = 11)
	CIEs' co-workers (n = 11)
	CIEs' HR BPs (n = 10)

We adapted the topics for the FG discussions to the different targets involved. Each FG lasted from 90 to 120 minutes, with one of the authors guiding the discussion and another taking notes. All data were recorded and transcribed while maintaining anonymity.

The collected data were complemented by internal documents that provided valuable information on the practices intended and designed by the company. The document analysis involved approximately 200 pages of internal documents (for example, agreements with unions, HRM policy manuals and guidelines).

Data Analysis

The data were analyzed using theoretical thematic analysis (Braun and Clarke, 2006). During the data collection process, three of the four authors who collected the data met regularly to discuss emerging patterns and recorded insights (Charmaz, 2006). Once we had completed our observations, face-to-face interviews, focus group interviews, and document analysis, we followed a three-stage data-coding process to build theory (Corbin and Strauss, 1990).

Concepts related to the WAPs implementation process were developed during the open-coding process by analytically breaking the data down in an interpretative process. In this, we followed Mirfakhar et al.'s (2018) review of HRM implementation antecedents, using a conceptual framework based on the work of Pettigrew (1987) on organizational change as the basis for our analysis. Hence, data were first separated into three groups according to which aspect of the implementation process the statements reflected: content (characteristics of the implemented practices), context (elements of the meso- and micro-organizational context), and process (actions, reactions, and interactions of the different actors involved) (Pettigrew, 1987: 657) (Table 18.5). Using an open coding logic, we relied heavily on *in vivo* codes or verbatim statements to categorize content, process, and context. The four authors met regularly during the coding process to discuss the codes with the aim of improving the quality of the coding process. To reveal second-order codes, our analytical strategy shifted to axial coding to understand how our first-order categories fitted together in more abstract, theoretical categories. Through a process of comparing and contrasting, we were able to connect concepts that emerged through open coding in the content–context–process framework. In the final stage, we aggregated the codes and themes into theoretical dimensions by iterating between data and theory to inform the patterns that were beginning to emerge in the data. As a result, we organized our findings according to three theoretical domains, which reflect different stages of WAPs implementation process (Trullen et al., 2020): WAP initiation, adaptation, and routinization.

RESULTS

WAP Initiation

The company explicitly devolved responsibility for implementing WAPs to its line managers in order to ensure effective responses to employees' specific needs and demands. Consistent with this, in many work teams, the line managers did take full responsibility for WAP implementation. Indeed, they played a primary role in initiating WAPs, often anticipating the evolving needs and motivation of CIEs. The following comment illustrates the impulse that some line managers gave to the WAPs: "On my side, I try to identify, day by day, the activities that he [the CIE] can carry out. For example, on the days following therapy I only ask him to do supervisory activities, so he does not get too tired" (Line manager C).

In other work units, however, line managers resisted the devolved responsibility. Some felt insufficiently trained to deal with CIEs' needs, felt ill-prepared to handle health problems and stressful working environments, or felt that they did not have time to devote to CIEs. Others argued that the support materials on WAP implementation provided by the HR department were inadequate for coping with the complexity of CIEs' requests: "The HR department did not provide me with any indications of how to manage this situation" (Line manager B).

In some work teams where line managers lacked motivation and/or abilities to make decisions related to WAP implementation, the HR BPs became key to enacting the WAPs. However, there were also other instances where HR BPs resisted devolving responsibilities for WAP implementation to line managers, and were perceived by CIEs as taking decisions on WAP initiation: "It really depends on the individual HR BP and on their sensitivity. A CIE can have an HR BP who proposes they opt for teleworking, while another CIE can have a HR BP that doesn't" (CIE A). We also observed work teams where the line manager and the HR BP collaborated closely in implementing WAPs, sharing the responsibility for making decisions and establishing effective communication with a CIE.

The overall picture that emerged is that the extent to which line managers and HR BPs take responsibility, and how they interpret their roles in WAP initiation, varies considerably across work teams. Moreover, we found evidence that CIEs themselves were often the initiators of WAPs, playing an agentic role in suggesting changes to the way tasks could be accomplished or to the content of the job itself: "I have redesigned my role to make it more consistent with my capabilities" (CIE D).

Interestingly, CIEs often exerted this agency-making aspect in alliance with their direct supervisor. Perhaps surprisingly, alliances often went beyond the CIE–supervisor relationship to also include co-workers. For instance, a co-worker played a key role in filling an information gap between a supervisor and his CIE, enabling the initiation of a new work arrangement: "I went to talk to my manager, and he was very surprised to discover that talking on the phone

Table 18.5 Example codes used to distinguish between elements of content, process, and context

Codes: Content	Codes: Process	Codes: Context
– Formalized/non-formalized practice	– CIE-initiated WAP	*Meso-level:*
– General/non-specific practice	– Line manager-initiated WAP	– Negative stereotype of WAPs
WAP target	– HR BP-initiated WAP	– Organizational culture of presenteeism
– Explicit devolution of WAP to line managers	– WAP initiated by multiple actors	– Work team climate
– WAP customization	– Line manager acts as WAP coach	– Lack of HR initiatives/tools to support line managers in
– WAP explicitly points to company values	– Co-workers take part in WAP implementation	implementing WAPs for CIEs
	– Ongoing adaptation in WAP implementation	*Micro-level:*
	– Emergence of informal rules of adoption	– Line manager's lack of ability in WAP implementation
	– Line manager/HR BP resists devolution of WAP	– Line manager's lack of motivation in WAP implementation
	– Line manager/HR BP takes responsibility for the devolution	– Line manager's leadership style
	of WAP	– CIE's individual proactivity
	– CIE resists WAP	– Supportive HR BP
	– CIE accepts WAP	– Supportive co-workers
	– WAP perceived as asset	
	– WAP perceived as burden	

was becoming very hard for my colleague after his illness. He immediately decided to change his tasks in order to reduce the number of phone calls he had to make" (Co-worker I).

Together, these results shed light on the micro-actions through which individuals and groups enacted WAPs, suggesting a considerably diffuse agentivity. Not only did we find that, as expected, CIEs have agentivity in enacting WAPs, but we also found that other actors such as supervisors and co-workers can take on this role. More importantly, partnerships between CIEs, co-workers, supervisors, and HR BPs resulted in an unexpected form of collegial WAP initiation that facilitated practice acceptance.

Our findings also suggest that individual or collective agency in initiating WAPs can be constrained by perceived ambiguity in messages to employees regarding who is eligible for WAPs. When it came to teleworking, the formalized policy was that this was open to all employees up to a maximum of 4 percent of the company workforce. Smart working was also not exclusively for ill or disabled employees, but intended for all workers. However, many supervisors and HR BPs only allowed employees with health-related impairments, or a need to manage a close relative with health problems, to telework or partake in smart working, even though the 4 percent limit was far from being breached in the company as a whole. As reported by an HR professional: "Even if teleworking does not have a specific connotation linked to particular forms of diversity and/or disability, it has mostly been implemented in situations of employee disability and/or health problems" (HR BP A).

In some work teams, this has led to a widespread belief that this arrangement is restricted to specific group of employees. For instance, a supervisor commented: "In my team, teleworking is used to manage employees with serious health impairments" (Line manager G). By doing so, supervisors signaled a different meaning of this practice to employees from the one originally intended by the HR department, thereby forging perceptions of teleworking as an exceptional option open only to employees with severe constraints and increasing ambiguity over criteria for WAP eligibility.

In another team, an employee stated: "In this work unit, employees with a health impairment can work one day a week from home. Good for them!" (Co-worker N). In this work team, the shared belief is that the option of smart working is ultimately restricted to employees with a chronic disease or other health impairments.

This might result in CIEs deliberately avoiding such accommodations because they are afraid of being stigmatized as "problematic" by their supervisor and colleagues. As one of them commented: "Even though it would be much easier for me to work from home given my health condition, I decided not to apply for teleworking because I do not want to feel like I'm diseased" (CIE F). This suggests the existence of a negative stereotype of teleworkers that has contributed to a negative attitude toward this work adjustment option, engendering resistance to teleworking even among some CIEs who would benefit from working from home.

WAP Adaptation

In formulating WAPs, by defining practices as open to all employees and flexible in terms of their use by considering individual needs, the company prioritized two main attributes: universality and flexibility. The decision to leave room for customized adaptation of practices is reflected in the low level of formalization in the WAPs. As a corporate HR manager explained: "The company decided not to be too specific in the definition of the work adjustment policy in order to allow for a flexible adoption" (HR Development Manager).

Consistent with the introduced practices, some line managers were key in putting WAPs into effect, adjusting the practices on a daily basis and acting as a coach on WAP adaptation. Moreover, several line managers described successful situations in which the CIE provided them with all the personal and contextual information needed to adopt the WAPs effectively: "We are trying to develop our own way ... She [the CIE] suggests to me the best way to manage each situation" (Line manager M).

This partnership between line managers and CIEs was a key success factor in the WAP adaptation process, positively affecting both employees' and line managers' satisfaction with their use.

However, although the organization formulated flexible WAPs to avoid a one-size-fits-all approach to implementation, the way that the practices were interpreted and applied in some work teams somewhat standardized them. In some instances, informal rules emerged and became part of the accepted way of implementing WAPs, regardless of what was prescribed (or not) at the corporate level. The emergence of informal contextual rules for implementation shaped the perceptions not only of employees but also of line managers and HR BPs, to such an extent that in some work units the boundary between formalized and informal/emergent rules disappeared. As a result, many individuals perceived WAPs as being highly regulated.

For instance, in terms of teleworking implementation, even though the general policy does not define a minimum or maximum number of days that teleworkers have to work at the company site, in some work teams an informal rule had emerged that teleworkers were not allowed to attend the office more than twice a week. We found evidence that this unwritten rule was often embedded at the work unit level, and drove employees' and other actors' behaviors, making the practice more rigid and less able to meet specific needs and situations, as the following comment illustrates: "To date, teleworking employees can work in the office twice a week maximum. There are employees who always work from home due to health problems. But other CIEs would definitely prefer to work in the office more than twice a week" (HR BP E).

The emergence of these informal rules not only altered the content of the policy by restricting the intended flexibility and adaptability, but it also contributed to a sense of unfairness in the negotiation process, as employees working in different work teams felt that the extent of WAP negotiability was unequal across the company, and that it depended on how supervisors or HR BPs interpreted the practice: "There is a formal policy. But, to tell the truth, it very much depends on the HR department or on your supervisor" (Co-worker E).

Summarizing, the customized implementation of WAPs was constrained by rules that emerged locally. Our data revealed that WAP content, defined on the corporate level, is interpreted in different ways on the local level, and that the local level meaning that emerges replaces what is intended by the central level. This local interpretation of the content of the practices resulted in an adapted implementation process and variations across different contexts. This finding suggests that universal practices might nevertheless have an individualistic implementation, and that WAPs that are intended and designed to be general and flexible might be standardized by local rules that emerge through the idiosyncratic understanding of those practices. Such an emerging process of WAP implementation is not always beneficial for CIEs because it may (albeit often involuntarily) constrain the adaptation of the practices to individual needs and increase stigmatization at work related to chronic illness.

WAP Routinization

Our study found that the actors involved in WAP implementation often reported contrasting experiences of the same practice. Overt policy paradoxes emerged in several circumstances where some CIEs referred to WAPs as undesirable options that they experienced as detrimental constraints. We observed that the negative perceptions were particularly evident in work teams where the leadership style and behaviors of line managers were least congruent with the declared principles of autonomy, trust, and responsibility, in so doing reinforcing the CIEs' perceptions of a company culture that values and rewards presenteeism: "There is a strong culture of presenteeism in this company. My supervisor thinks that if you are not present, you are not performing. This makes smart working very difficult" (CIE H).

As this quotation suggests, when line managers' behaviors are inconsistent with the WAPs' contents, the consequent misalignment generates a negative evaluation of these practices by both CIEs and the line managers. In some cases, line managers referred to WAPs as a burden, because of their perceived inexperience in dealing with employees having serious health impairments or their lack of managerial skills. As one line manager commented: "She [the CIE] forced me into a difficult position when asking to change her tasks. I've no clue what to do now. I should completely rethink my team organization" (Line manager R).

Conversely, in several other circumstances, CIEs referred to the perceived WAPs as an important asset that provided them with the opportunity to remain employable and to regain confidence in their abilities and competences despite health impairments. For instance, one HR BP commented: "After her illness, she was not able to perform the tasks assigned to her as she used to … We are a big company, I was confident I could find a job that fitted her new situation well. Now she is the best performer in her group" (HR BP S).

In some cases, co-workers played a key role in shaping a positive experience of the flexible arrangement. As one team supervisor commented:

> I assigned him [the CIE] to a different role to reduce business traveling because, after the illness, he is very limited in movement. Nevertheless, when we schedule an out-of-office meeting, his colleagues always arrange to connect him online so that he can contribute and be up to date. He is supported by the group on a daily basis." (Line manager A)

As this quotation illustrates, the work team members took the lead in ensuring the CIE's integration and minimizing the disruptive impact of physical and social distance, enabling an easier and more effective implementation of the accommodation, while also facilitating its acceptance by the line manager and the CIE.

To summarize, our results show that both positive and negative experiences with WAPs could be triggered by the interplay between actors' behaviors and contextual factors that together contribute to shaping how WAPs are routinized and experienced in the work teams. The implementation of WAPs frequently resulted in substantial changes to the work activities and behaviors of all the members of the work team, often resulting in a considerable threat to the status quo being perceived, not only by the CIEs themselves but also by line managers and co-workers. Most importantly, our findings show that the experiences and beliefs of all the actors involved are linked, and that they mutually influence one another.

DISCUSSION

In this study, we have focused on the WAP implementation process for CIEs to understand which factors are likely to enable or hinder the implementation of these practices for this specific target group, with a special attention on the key role that line mangers play together with other relevant stakeholders. The results that emerged from our qualitative study, displayed in Figure 18.1, provide a unique perspective on WAP implementation, showing that dualities and tensions emerge during the entire process of local WAP implementation, from initiation through adaptation to routinization.

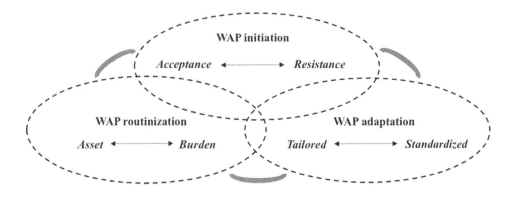

Figure 18.1   Facilitators and barriers of WAPs implementation for chronically ill employees

During their introduction, tensions between accepting and resisting WAPs were triggered by individual defensive mechanisms that actors enacted to avoid increased work demands and effort (for example, line managers feeling overwhelmed and unprepared to deal with CIE requests), to retain decision-making influence (for example, human resources BPs wanting to retain control over WAP implementation), or to reduce threats to belonging and self-identity (for example, CIEs' fear of stigmatization). During WAP adaptation, the company's choice for unarticulated policies made room for ambiguous interpretations of WAPs that, in some cases, favored a tailored implementation of WAPs; whereas in other cases they led to the emergence of local adoption rules that standardized WAPs, contradicting the policy aim. In the routinization stage, tensions emerged between opposing evaluations of WAPs, with some work teams considering them as assets with advantages for individual CIEs and their work teams, while others experienced them as detrimental constraints. The framework derived from our findings not only identified the main latent tensions that shaped WAP capacity to meet CIE needs, but also emphasized the interrelatedness of these tensions as WAP implementation unfolded.

Overall, this study contributes to the existing HRM literature in several ways. First, our study revealed that the balance between these opposing tensions differed across work teams, and that several individual and team level contextual factors shaped the prevailing outcome. This finding reinforces the influential role of contextual factors found in previous studies on HRM implementation (e.g., Bos-Nehles et al., 2013; Kuvaas et al., 2014; Sikora et al., 2015), and expands the set of elements found to affect both the content and the WAP implementation process. Among them, our data showed that line managers' HR-related competences and leadership style, as well as line managers' familiarity with chronic illness, were crucial to enable an effective initiation, adaptation, and routinization of WAPs.

Second, our results highlight the process that emerges, compared to the one that is planned, in HRM implementation. Most strategic HRM studies have focused on "planned consistency" (Bowen and Ostroff, 2004), although the recent literature on "differentiated HR architecture" has brought scholarly attention to the benefits and risks of "deliberate variance" in HRM systems (Kehoe and Han, 2020). We observed that the meaning that emerges locally often becomes part of the taken-for-granted way of implementing these practices, and replaces what was intended by the central level, leading to counterintuitive outcomes and contradictions. Our findings revealed that the routinization process of a practice could vary across work units. Moreover, this process does not always lead to effective implementation, as practices can be routinized in flawed ways (Trullen et al., 2020). As such, the perspective presented in this study implies the existence of contradictions in HRM, and the need to actively manage these contradictions (Keegan et al., 2018).

As a final contribution, this study adds to the HRM stakeholder perspective by showing that, as implementation unfolds, many organizational actors influence the content and process of HRM practices. While recent research has prominently focused on line managers as a source of variance in HRM implementation within organizations (Kehoe and Han, 2020; Vermeeren, 2014), our findings demonstrate that employees and even HR BPs themselves may understand WAPs, and how they should be implemented, in different ways from that intended in the design phase. This evidence provides empirical support for the view that all organizational actors interpret and enact HRM practices idiosyncratically (Van Mierlo et al., 2018), questioning the premise that discrepancies from intended practices only emerge when line managers become involved. Moreover, the perspective presented here sheds light on interactions between individuals and groups during the implementation process that cannot realistically be portrayed using fixed a priori defined roles. Not only did we find that CIEs or their co-workers were often the ones who gave an impetus to WAP implementation, contributing to co-constructing the practice (Meijerink and Bos-Nehles, 2017), but we also saw that the WAP implementation process seems to rely on a series of dyadic relationships (for example, HR BP–line manager) and, more importantly, a process of collective enactment where multiple stakeholders, both intentionally and unintentionally, shape WAP implementation.

IMPLICATIONS FOR PRACTICE

This study raises several important managerial implications to consider when implementing HRM practices. Our findings suggest that even if practices are appropriately designed, they cannot be considered in isolation from context and process if they are to be effectively implemented. Organizations should be aware that perceived fairness may increase if line managers are able to deliver idiosyncratic deals that do not contradict the overall HRM strategy, but recognize individual contributions (Kehoe and Han, 2020). Our results should encourage organizations to continuously look to balance flexibility and consistency in HRM implementation (Fu et al., 2018). To this end, HR BPs can play a key role as harmonizers across the different work teams. They are in a position to interact with multiple micro-contexts and to integrate the interests of different stakeholders, thereby promoting WAP customization while preventing the emergence of unintended forms of standardization. In addition, organizations that want to leave room for HRM practices to be adapted locally should set clear principles and values that underpin the HRM system, to ensure that all actors involved in the implementation process have a strong common reference point that allows them to enact their agentic roles effectively.

The results of this study also show that WAP implementation involves the active participation of a multiplicity of actors. Therefore, when evaluating the effectiveness of HRM systems, the views of actors other than the targeted employees should be included, because the way they experience a practice shapes the shared meaning attached to it. Furthermore, assuring consistency between messages sent by different HRM stakeholders is crucial to fostering consensus among employees and reducing the likelihood that they draw unintended interpretations from ambiguous situations (Bowen and Ostroff, 2004).

Our findings also highlight that line managers play a key role in WAP implementation, both alone and in collaboration with other stakeholders. This is consistent with findings in the HR attribution literature (Nishii and Paluch, 2018) suggesting that line managers are of crucial importance for the translation of HRPs to the work floor. Indeed, they provide important information regarding WAPs, hence contributing to shape the meaning that employees attach to these practices. In this study, we found that line managers' role is especially critical when HRPs are poorly formalized and require a bottom-up initiation, as in the case of WAPs that are intentionally designed in a very flexible way to leave room for customized adaptation, and that have a voluntarily nature as employees themselves decide whether to participate in flexible work options.

These results not only confirm the important role of line managers but also suggest some positive behaviors which they should adopt to reduce tensions that may emerge in the different stages of the implementation process. In the initiation stage, line managers should convey the right messages on the opportunities that WAPs offer to the team, and stimulate employees to suggest ways in which accommodations can improve work conditions and performance. In the adaptation stage, line managers should actively listen not only to CIEs' evolving needs, but also to other stakeholders' perspectives, to continuously reassess and adapt WAPs to CIEs' evolving expectations and motivations, and to the team's related requirements. In the routinization phase, line managers can contribute to WAPs acceptance by adopting behaviors that are consistent with values that sustain these practices, such as trust, autonomy, and responsibility.

Finally, this is the first study to explore the implementation of HRM practices that focuses on CIEs, and as such offers several practical implications. Our results suggest that organizations should put considerable effort into providing WAPs that increase CIEs' abilities to manage their work and to maintain employment. More importantly, organizations should respond to this challenge by offering universal practices, since our findings suggest that restricting specific arrangements to CIEs may unintentionally contribute to the emergence of negative stereotypes and illness-related stigma, eventually discouraging WAP acceptance. This study also shows that there is considerable heterogeneity in CIEs' needs and requests, that can only be met through WAPs which are flexible in terms of their use, and by supporting their customized implementation. The undesirable local standardization that we saw may stem from obstacles that the HR department could help to address. In this regard, our study suggests that an effective strategy is to create local conditions (for example, a trusting work team climate) that encourage CIEs' proactivity and constructive feedback, since they best know their evolving condition and support needs. Moreover, training and communication interventions that increase awareness of chronic illness conditions among all staff, in particular line management, can reduce negative attitudes and stigma and increase trust.

LIMITATIONS AND SUGGESTIONS FOR FURTHER RESEARCH

This study has a number of limitations, and the findings also suggest promising directions for future research. First, our study points towards time being an important factor in WAP implementation, and therefore we strongly recommend further qualitative research that includes the time dimension by collecting longitudinal data.

Second, as this study shows that tensions emerge along the entire implementation process, future studies could look into the mechanisms that can reduce these tensions at different stages of the process, exploring for example: which team's characteristics (dimension, diversity, goals) positively affect individual's and team's agentivity in the initiation stage; which line manager characteristics are the most relevant for the successful adaptation of WAPs; which leadership style and line manager behaviors make teams build a positive experience of WAPs in the routinization stage.

Third, we examined WAP implementation for CIEs, a process that is characterized by the considerable agentivity of employees, who often initiate the practice and actively contribute to its customized implementation. Here, an important direction for future research would be to examine whether our results can be extended to the implementation of other HRM practices that involve less individual agentivity.

Finally, the generalizability of our results is limited, as the participants all came from a single organization. However, when studying phenomena that are "context dependent and interdependent," as in HRM implementation, researchers should not be overly concerned about generalizability, but rather try to reveal the richness of the context (Cooke, 2018: 10) and the development of theory. Nevertheless, this limitation meant that we were unable to explore the impact of macro-contextual factors on the implementation process. Further research is therefore encouraged that empirically extends this study to other organizational contexts, industries, and countries.

ACKNOWLEDGMENTS

This study has been supported by grants from Lavoroperlapersona Foundation (Italy) and from the European Academy of Management (EURAM).

REFERENCES

Allen, T.D., Johnson, R.C., Kiburtz, K.M., and Schockley, K.M. (2013). Work–family conflict and flexible work arrangements: deconstructing flexibility. *Personnel Psychology*, 66, 345–376. https://doi.org/10.1111/peps.12012.

Australian Institute of Health and Welfare (2018). *Chronic Conditions and Disability 2015*. Cat. no. CDK 8. Canberra: AIHW.

Baldridge, D.C., and Swift, M.L. (2013). Withholding requests for disability accommodation: the role of individual differences and disability attributes. *Journal of Management*, 39, 743–762. https://doi.org/10.1177/0149206310396375.

Baumgärtner, M.K., Dwertmann, D.J.G., Boehm, S.A., and Bruch, H. (2015). Job satisfaction of employees with disabilities: the role of perceived structural flexibility. *Human Resource Management*, 54, 323–343. https://doi.org/10.1002/hrm.21673.

Boelhouwer, I.G., Vermeer, W., and van Vuuren, T. (2020) Work ability, burnout complaints, and work engagement among employees with chronic diseases: job resources as targets for intervention? *Frontiers in Psychology*, 11, 1805. https://doi.org/10.3389/fpsyg.2020.01805.

Bondarouk, T., Trullen, J., and Valverde, M. (2018). Special issue of *International Journal of Human Resource Management*: It's never a straight line: advancing knowledge on HRM implementation. *International Journal of Human Resource Management*, 29, 2995–3000. https://doi.org/10.1080/09585192.2018.1509535.

Bos-Nehles, A.C., Bondarouk, T., and Labrenz, S. (2017). HRM implementation in multinational companies: the dynamics of multifaceted scenarios. *European Journal of International Management*, 11, 515–536. https://doi.org/10.1504/EJIM.2017.086696.

Bos-Nehles, A.C., and Meijerink, J.G. (2018). HRM implementation by multiple HRM actors: a social exchange perspective. *International Journal of Human Resource Management*, 29, 3068–3092. https://doi.org/10.1080/09585192.2018.1443958.

Bos-Nehles, A.C., Van Riemsdijk, M.J., and Looise, J.K. (2013). Employee perceptions of line management performance: applying the AMO theory to explain the effectiveness of line managers' HRM implementation. *Human Resource Management*, 52, 861–877. DOI:10.1002/hrm.21578.

Bowen, D.E., and Ostroff, C. (2004). Understanding HRM–firm performance linkages: the role of the "strength" of the HRM system. *Academy of Management Review*, 29, 203–221. https://doi.org/10.2307/20159029.

Braun, V., and Clarke, V. (2006). Using thematic analysis in psychology. *Qualitative Research in Psychology*, 3, 77–101. https://doi.org/10.1191/1478088706qp063oa.

Budjanovcanin, A. (2018). Actions speak louder than words: how employees mind the implementation gap. *International Journal of Human Resource Management*, 29, 3136–3155. https://doi.org/10.1080/09585192.2018.1443959.

Charmaz, K. (2006). *Constructing Grounded Theory: A Practical Guide Through Qualitative Analysis*. Thousand Oaks, CA: SAGE.

Cleveland, J.N., Barnes-Farrell, J.L., and Ratz, J.M. (1997). Accommodation in the workplace. *Human Resource Management Review*, 7, 77–107. https://doi.org/10.1016/S1053-4822(97)90006-1.

Colella, A. (2001). Coworker distributive fairness judgments of the workplace accommodation of employees with disabilities. *Academy of Management Review*, 26, 100–116. https://doi.org/10.2307/259397.

Cooke, F.L. (2018). Concepts, contexts, and mindsets: putting human resource management research in perspectives. *Human Resource Management Journal*, 28, 1–13. https://doi.org/10.1111/1748-8583.12163.

Corbin, J.M., and Strauss, A. (1990). Grounded theory research: procedures, canons, and evaluative criteria. *Qualitative Sociology*, 13, 3–21. https://doi.org/10.1007/BF00988593.

Eurofound (2019). *How to Respond to Chronic Health Problems in the Workplace?* Luxembourg: Publications Office of the European Union.

Fu, N., Flood, P.C., Rousseau, D.M., and Morris, T. (2018). Line managers as paradox navigators in HRM implementation: balancing consistency and individual responsiveness. *Journal of Management*, 46, 203–233. https://doi.org/10.1177/0149206318785241.

Gold, P.B., Oire, S.N., Fabian, E.S., and Wewiorski, N.J. (2012). Negotiating reasonable workplace accommodations: perspectives of employers, employees with disabilities, and rehabilitation service providers. *Journal of Vocational Rehabilitation*, 37, 25–37. https://doi.org/10.1007/s10926-014-9548-z.

Guest, D.E., and Bos-Nehles, A.C. (2013). HRM and performance: the role of effective implementation. In Paauwe, J., Guest, D. and Wright, P.M. (eds), *HRM and Performance: Achievements and Challenges*. Chichester: Wiley, pp. 79–96.

Hornung, S., Rousseau, D.M., Glaser, J. (2008). Creating flexible work arrangements through idiosyncratic deals. *Journal of Applied Psychology*, 93, 655–664. https://doi.org/10.1037/0021-9010.93.3.655.

Janssens, M., and Steyaert, C. (2009). HRM and performance: a plea for reflexivity in HRM studies. *Journal of Management Studies*, 46, 143–155. https://doi.org/10.1111/j.1467-6486.2008.00812.x.

Keegan, A., Bitterling, I., Sylva, H., and Hoeksema, L. (2018). Organizing the HRM function: responses to paradoxes, variety, and dynamism. *Human Resource Management*, 57, 1111–1126. https://doi.org/10.1002/hrm.21893.

Kehoe, R.R., and Han, J.H. (2020). An expanded conceptualization of line managers' involvement in human resource management. *Journal of Applied Psychology*, 105, 111–129. https://doi.org/10.1037/apl0000426.

Kossek, E.E., Barber, A., and Winters, D. (1999). Using flexible schedules in the managerial world: the power of peers. *Human Resource Management Journal*, 38, 33–46. https://doi.org/10.1002/(SICI)1099-050X(199921)38:1<33::AID-HRM4>3.0.CO;2-H.

Kuvaas, B., Dysvik, A., and Buch, R. (2014). Antecedents and employee outcomes of line managers' perceptions of enabling HR practices. *Journal of Management Studies*, 51, 845–868. https://doi.org/10.1111/joms.12085.

Lambert A.D., Marler, J.H., and Gueutal, H.G. (2008). Individual differences: factors affecting employee utilization of flexible work arrangements. *Journal of Vocational Behavior*, 73, 107–117. http://dx.doi.org/10.1016/j.jvb.2008.02.004.

Lepak, D.P., and Boswell, W. (2012). Strategic HRM and employee organizational relationship (EOR). In L.M. Shore, J. Coyle-Shapiro, and L. Tetrick (eds), *The Employee–Organization Relationship: Applications for the 21st Century*. New York: Routledge, pp. 455–483.

Makhecha, U.P., Srinivasan, V., Prabhu, G.N., and Mukherji, S. (2018). Multi-level gaps: a study of intended, actual and experienced human resource practices in a hypermarket chain in India. *International Journal of Human Resource Management*, 29, 360–398. https://doi.org/10.1080/09585192.2015.1126336.

McGonagle, A.K., and Barnes-Farrell, J.L. (2014). Chronic illness in the workplace: stigma, identity threat and strain. *Stress Health*, 30, 310–321. https://doi.org/10.1002/smi.2518.

Meijerink, J., and Bos-Nehles, A. (2017). Toward a marketing perspective on how "active employees" create valuable human resource management outcomes: the role of HRM consumption and psychological ownership. In C. Olckers, L. van Zyl, and L. van der Vaart (eds), *Theoretical Orientations and Practical Applications of Psychological Ownership*. Springer: Cham, pp. 159–179.

Meijerink, J., Bondarouk, T., and Lepak, D.P. (2016). Employees as active consumers of HRM: linking employees' HRM competences with their perceptions of HRM service value. *Human Resource Management*, 55, 219–240. https://doi.org/10.1002/hrm.21719.

Mirfakhar, A.S., Trullen, J., and Valverde, M. (2018). Easier said than done: a review of antecedents influencing effective HR implementation. *International Journal of Human Resource Management*, 29, 3001–3025. https://doi.org/10.1080/09585192.2018.1443960.

Moon, N.W., and Baker, P.M.A. (2012). Assessing stakeholder perceptions of workplace accommodations barriers: results from a policy research instrument. *Journal of Disability Policy Studies*, 23, 94–109. https://doi.org/10.1177/1044207311425383.

Nishii, L.H., and Paluch, R.M. (2018). Leaders as HR sensegivers: four HR implementation behaviors that create strong HR systems. *Human Resource Management Review*, 28, 319–323. doi: 10.1016/j.hrmr.2018.02.007.

Nolte, E., and McKee, M. (eds) (2008). *Caring for People with Chronic Conditions. A Health System Perspective*. European Observatory on Health Systems and Policies series. New York: Open University Press.

Paauwe, J. (2004). *HRM and Performance: Achieving Long-Term Viability*. Oxford: Oxford University Press.

Pettigrew, A.M. (1987). Context and action in the transformation of the firm. *Journal of Management Studies*, 24, 649–670. https://doi.org/10.1111/j.1467-6486.1987.tb00467.x.

Pryce, J., Munir, F., and Haslam, C. (2007). Cancer survivorship and work: symptoms, supervisor response, co-worker disclosure and work adjustment. *Journal of Occupational Rehabilitation*, 17, 83–92. https://doi.org/10.1007/s10926-006-9040-5.

Rau, B.L. (2003). Flexible work arrangements. *Sloan Online Work and Family Encyclopedia*. Retrieved from: http://wfnetwork.bc.edu/encyclopedia_entry.php?id=240&area=All.

Rau, B.L., and Hyland, M.M. (2002). Role conflict and flexible work arrangements: the effects on applicant attraction. *Personnel Psychology*, 55, 111–136. https://doi.org/10.1111/j.1744-6570.2002 .tb00105.x.

Restubog, S.L.D., Midel Deen, C., Decoste, A., and He, Y. (2021). From vocational scholars to social justice advocates: challenges and opportunities for vocational psychology research on the vulnerable workforce. *Journal of Vocational Behavior*, 126. https://doi.org/10.1016/j.jvb.2021.103561.

Rolland, J.S. (1987). Chronic illness and the life cycle: a conceptual framework. *Family Process*, 26, 203–221. https://doi.org/10.1111/j.1545-5300.1987.00203.x.

Ryan, A.M., and Kossek, E.R. (2008). Work–life policy implementation: breaking down or creating barriers to inclusiveness? *Human Resource Management*, 47, 295–310. https://doi.org/10.1002/hrm .20213.

Schur, L., Nishii, L.H., Adya, M., and Kruse, D. (2014). Accommodating employees with and without disabilities. *Human Resource Management*, 53, 593–621. https://doi.org/10.1002/hrm.21607.

Shockley, K.M., and Allen, T.D. (2010). Investigating the missing link in flexible work arrangement utilization: an individual difference perspective, *Journal of Vocational Behavior*, 76, 131–142. https://doi.org/10.1016/j.jvb.2009.07.002.

Sikora, D.M., Ferris, G.R., and Van Iddekinge, C.H. (2015). Line manager implementation perceptions as a mediator of relations between high-performance work practices and employee outcomes. *Journal of Applied Psychology*, 100, 1908–1918. https://doi.org/10.1037/apl0000024.

Stirpe, L., Bonache, J., and Trullen, J. (2015). The acceptance of newly introduced HR practices: some evidence from Spain on the role of management behavior and organizational climate. *International Journal of Manpower*, 36, 334–353. http://doi.org/10.1108/IJM-10-2012-0155.

Stone, D.L., and Colella, A. (1996). A model of factors affecting the treatment of disabled individuals in organizations. *Academy of Management Review*, 21, 352–401. https://doi.org/10.2307/258666.

Trullen, J., Bos-Nehles, A., and Valverde, M. (2020). From intended to actual and beyond: a cross-disciplinary view of (human resource management) implementation. *International Journal of Management Reviews*, 22, 150–167. https://doi.org/10.1111/ijmr.12220.

Van Mierlo, J., Bondarouk, T., and Sanders, K. (2018). The dynamic nature of HRM implementation: a structuration perspective. *International Journal of Human Resource Management*, 29, 3026–3045. https://doi.org/10.1080/09585192.2018.1443957.

Varekamp, I., and van Dijk, F.J.H. (2010). Workplace problems and solutions for employees with chronic diseases. *Occupational Medicine*, 60, 287–293. https://doi.org/10.1093/occmed/kqq078.

Varekamp, I., Verbeek, J.H., de Boer, A., and Van Dijk, F.J.H. (2011). Effect of job maintenance training program for employees with chronic disease: a randomized controlled trial on self-efficacy, job satisfaction, and fatigue. *Scandinavian Journal of Work, Environment and Health*, 37, 288–297. doi: 10.5271/sjweh.3149.

Varva, S. (2015). *Malattie coroniche e lavoro*. Adapt Labour Studies, e-Book series n. 27. Adapt University Press, adapt.it.

Vermeeren, B. (2014) Variability in HRM implementation among line managers and its effect on performance: a 2-1-2 mediational multilevel approach. *International Journal of Human Resource Management*, 25, 3039–3059. https://doi.org/10.1080/09585192.2014.934891.

Wright, P.M., and Nishii, L.H. (2013). Strategic HRM and organizational behaviour: integrating multiple levels of analysis. In J. Paauwe, D.E. Guest, and P.M. Wright (eds), *HRM and Performance: Achievements and Challenges*. Chichester: John Wiley & Sons, pp. 97–110.

19. Mental disability disclosure in the workplace: the role of line managers
Rina Hastuti and Andrew R. Timming

INTRODUCTION

Research on occupational health and safety (OHS) has focused in large part on physical illnesses and accidents linked to unsafe workplaces (Fan et al., 2020). In recent years, however, the OHS literature has increasingly acknowledged the complex link between employment and mental illness (Quinlan, 2007; Van Eerd et al., 2021; Yoon et al., 2015). This renewed emphasis on mental illness at work has become even more pronounced in the light of the worldwide COVID-19 pandemic and its deleterious effects on flourishing and well-being more generally (French et al., 2020a, 2020b). Within the context of the growing literature on mental illness in the workplace, a key debate is slowly taking shape: whether or not job applicants and employees should disclose their mental illnesses to employers (Hastuti and Timming, 2021). This question is much more complex than just a simple cost–benefit calculation framed as a utility-maximizing "rational choice" (Coleman, 1994). Inherent in the choice to disclose, or to conceal, a mental illness is a complex tapestry of psychological, sociological, organizational, and legal factors that interact with one another, impacting the decision. To further complicate matters, those at the receiving end of many disclosures, that is, line managers, are often ill prepared and poorly trained to deal effectively with such profoundly personal revelations (Martin, 2010). To this end, the aim of this chapter is to outline the contours of the mental disability disclosure process, with a particular focus on the largely heretofore neglected role of line managers, or frontline supervisors.

Research on mental disability disclosure in the workplace is important because of the shocking prevalence of mental illness in most societies. Recent data from the United States demonstrate a striking increase in the number of adults with mental illness, from 17.7 percent in 2008, to 20.6 percent in 2019, estimated in absolute terms at around 51.5 million adults (SAMHSA, 2020). Likewise, the Australian National Health Survey reported that about one in five Australians, or 20 percent of the total population, have, or have had, mental health problems (AIHW, 2020). Although not all mental illnesses qualify as a disability, based on these alarming statistics it is clear that huge swathes of human populations across the globe suffer from psychological impairments that can negatively impact not only their employment status (Lo and Cheng, 2014), but also their ability to function effectively in the workplace (Baron and Salzer, 2002). In short, the topic discussed in this chapter is in dire need of greater scholarly attention.

This chapter makes an important contribution to the extant literature on mental illness disclosure in the workplace. Although much has been written on this topic (Elraz, 2018; Follmer and Jones, 2018; Martin, 2010), no one, to the best of our knowledge, has particularly emphasized the role of line managers within this process. The focus, instead, has been mostly on disclosers. But line managers often mediate the relationship between disclosers and the employer (Alfes et al., 2013), such that they play an essential role in a larger, indirect communication chain. Unfortunately, apart from those line managers employed in very large and well-resourced organizations, very few of them receive adequate training from human resources (HR) departments or from institutes of higher education on their obligations surrounding the disability disclosure event. This chapter aims to throw a much-needed conceptual light on the role of line managers in mental illness disclosure, thereby making an important contribution to the human resource management (HRM) literature.

The chapter is structured as follows. In the next section, we review and organize the previous work on mental disability disclosure in the workplace, drawing largely from a recent interdisciplinary review conducted by Hastuti and Timming (2021). After that, we detail the contours of the key processes surrounding the disclosure event and pose some questions about what makes an effective disclosure. Next, we draw out the key implications of our research for line managers, with a particular focus on the skills and competencies they require to effectively handle a mental disability disclosure in the workplace. Finally, we conclude the chapter with a brief discussion and recapitulation of our main arguments, and set out a few key directions for future research.

PREVIOUS WORK

The extant literature on the disclosure of mental illness in the workplace has been growing over the last several decades, mostly written by the scholars from psychiatry, psychology, and rehabilitation. Crucially, however, no previous work has examined specifically the role of line managers in mental illness disclosure. Overall, the extant studies center around two themes: firstly, the pre-disclosure event, consisting of the internal and external antecedents that contribute to the disclosure decision; and secondly, the post-disclosure event, containing the outcomes and consequences of a disclosure (Hastuti and Timming, 2021). Hence, the mental health disclosure process is best discussed in relation to the antecedents, decisions, and outcomes of the disclosure.

Disclosure Antecedents

The disclosure decision is driven by a set of internal factors that might foster or hinder the decision. Several studies have found that disclosure is related to the extent of one's symptoms and whether or not one has been involuntarily hospitalized while working (Ellison et al., 2003; Goldberg et al., 2005; Price, 2011; Yoshimura et al., 2018), as well as by the specific type of mental illness (Blais and Renshaw, 2014; Brown and Bruce, 2016). Occasionally, an individual is reluctant to disclose a mental illness at any management level, including frontline supervisors (line managers) and HR, as well as middle managers and senior managers, in order to mitigate negative perceptions (Burns and Green, 2019; Ridge et al., 2019) and to prevent employment prejudice and discrimination around the mental illness (Brohan et al., 2014; Peterson et al., 2011; Sayers et al., 2019). In addition to investigating stigma on the part of managers, the literature also points to self-stigma in respect to disclosure (Blais and Renshaw, 2014; Goldberg et al., 2005; Owen, 2004; Rüsch et al., 2017; Stratton et al., 2018; Toth and Dewa, 2014) such that employees internalize a type of self-prejudice against themselves.

Individuals' personalities and attitudes are also critical internal factors of the disclosure. Positive attitudes toward mental illness open a wider possibility of the individual to disclose at work (Adler et al., 2015; Brohan et al., 2014; Thomas et al., 2019) and, where relevant, facilitate a return to work and re-employment (Rüsch et al., 2018). Consistently, an individual's motives to secure health, financial support, emotional support, and moral worth were also associated with the disclosure decision (Banks et al., 2007; Cohen et al., 2016; King et al., 2011; Ridge et al., 2019). Sometimes the choice to conceal their mental illness can be seen as a way of securing their employment, as long as the illness can be self-managed. Self-management could prevent the individual from detrimental effects of the illness and keep work on track (Ridge et al., 2019).

An individual's environment also influences the disclosure decision, which at a certain point might affect their internal decision-making. To this end, management plays a key role in creating (or retarding) a disclosure climate (Henderson et al., 2013). Devonish (2017), for example, suggests that participation in a positive mental health promotion training program encourages a non-stigmatized and supportive workplace culture, and empirically, this training program can improve mental health awareness (Sage et al., 2016; Sayers et al., 2019). As such, improvements in a line manager's skills and confidence in dealing with mental health problems could be attained through training and educational programs. In addition to having the right policies and practices in place, the disclosure climate is also determined, or at least shaped, by the ability of the line manager to offer robust social support, since the right interpersonal context is central to an effective disclosure (Clair et al., 2005).

The disclosers are obviously influenced by social circumstances, such as organizational and public attitudes toward mental illness (Brohan et al., 2014), as well as empathy and support from immediate supervisors (Corbière et al., 2018; Peters and Brown, 2009; Ridge et al., 2019). A supervisor's ability to manage and create an inclusive work climate, based on the principle of individual care and development (Corbière et al., 2018; Kirsh et al., 2018), a high level of confidence and communication skills (Bryan et al., 2018), and outside working relationships with the mentally ill (Hand and Tryssenaar, 2006) could lead to a positive outcome of disclosure, such as long-term employment after a return to work (Negrini et al., 2018). However, the extent to which line managers possess these capabilities is not well understood in the extant literature.

The Disclosure Decision

The disclosure decision is a strategic action governed by a combination of structure and agency. The extant literature, unfortunately, looks at the disclosure event largely in binary terms—whether an individual chooses to disclose, or not—thus often neglecting wider contextual questions, such as to whom a disclosure is made. Within this oversimplified binary framework, several studies reveal that the percentage of those choosing to disclose is less than the percentage who choose non-disclosure (Burns and Green, 2019; Stuart, 2017). Other studies, however, have found that disclosure is more prevalent than non-disclosure (Banks et al., 2007; Cohen et al., 2016; Ellison et al., 2003). Hence, it is important for employment researchers to understand the unique management context underlying disclosure to resolve this inconsistency.

Ensuring that the disclosure is directed to the right recipients is essential to a successful disclosure event. Some studies reveal that line managers are preferable as disclosure recipients

(Granger, 2000; Ridge et al., 2019; Rollins et al., 2002). A targeted disclosure to an immediate supervisor, on the face of it, is reasonable since they are best positioned to provide the requisite accommodations and support. In addition, the timing of the disclosure is an important factor in its success. One study found that more than half of participants prefer to disclose at the beginning of the employment relationship (Cohen et al., 2016), while another study revealed that disclosure at a later stage of employment is preferable (Banks et al., 2007). In sum, the extant literature has been mostly silent, or at least inconsistent, on whether disclosure is best directed to a line manager, and if so, when such a disclosure is most effective.

Disclosure Outcomes

The disclosure outcome refers to the effectiveness (or lack thereof) of the disclosure event. Disclosure is obviously a prerequisite for accommodations and managerial support for mental illness (Stratton et al., 2018); thus, the opportunity to access such programs is predicated on an effective disclosure to management (Banks et al., 2007; Chow and Cichocki, 2016). A key outcome of effective disclosure is increased psychological well-being on the part of the discloser (Bergmans et al., 2009; Keith, 2013). The decision to disclose is also beneficial for nurturing an open and transparent climate regarding mental illness in the workplace: it may encourage other individuals to disclose and promote mental illness literacy at work (Elraz, 2018). The disclosure decision could also variously impact any number of employment outcomes. Several studies provide evidence that individuals with mental illnesses keep their jobs longer, maintain uninterrupted employment, and have better work performance after a successful disclosure (Allott et al., 2013; Corbière et al., 2014; DeTore et al., 2019; McGahey et al., 2016).

In contrast, however, unsuccessful disclosure to untrained or insensitive line managers can result in adverse discrimination when compared to non-disclosure, including failing to acquire or maintain a job (Banks et al., 2007; Dolce and Bates, 2019), negative career consequences (Mendel et al., 2015; Rüsch et al., 2017), and even job loss (Stratton et al., 2018). Stigma on the part of line managers is oftentimes grounded in a form of negative labelling (Rüsch et al., 2017). Thus, Corbière et al. (2018) explained that disclosers are at times labelled by management and co-workers as weak and less competent, and thus experience prejudice at work. Discrimination and stigma might, unfortunately, manifest in the form of work dismissal and termination, differential treatment, negative attitudes, task or job exclusion, and avoidance (Gladman and Waghorn, 2016). In practice, such kinds of discrimination might be mitigated against by line managers through appropriate job crafting and flexible work.

In short, this review of the literature on mental illness disclosure in the workplace shows that while much has been written on this topic, key questions remain to be answered. Crucially, for the purposes of this chapter, we still do not properly understand the role of line managers in the disclosure process. In order to better understand their role, we now turn to a series of key questions that they can and should consider as part of their training and development. These questions are posed from the point of view of potential disclosers and therefore can provide line managers with a unique perspective or point of view.

KEY QUESTIONS SURROUNDING MENTAL ILLNESS DISCLOSURE

At first glance, the decision to disclose or conceal a mental illness in the workplace may seem like a simple, rational choice (Hechter and Kanazawa, 1997) based on expected returns, positive or negative. If an agent perceives a net positive benefit of disclosure, then they are more likely to disclose than not; alternatively, if an agent perceives a net loss associated with disclosure, then they are more likely to conceal than not. There are, however, several problems with this utility-maximizing model, not least of which is the "bounded" nature of rationality (Selten, 1990; Simon, 1990) and the limits of rational choice. Alternatively stated, agents do not make purportedly rational choices in a non-social vacuum (Timming, 2009), hence, any analysis of the decision to disclose a mental disability in the workplace must be couched in wider psychological, sociological, organizational, and legal frameworks. In real-world organizational decision-making, agents must always contend with imperfect information (Phlips, 1988) and are therefore prone to the possibility of human error when it comes to estimating net positive gains or net negative losses associated with a particular behavior.

The key questions surrounding the disclosure decision that line managers should ponder include: What do employees (or job applicants) disclose? When do employees (or job applicants) disclose? How do mental illness disclosures take place? What are the advantages and disadvantages of disclosure from the point of view of the employee (or job applicant)? And crucially, for the purposes of this chapter, to whom should a disclosure be made? We will now examine each of these questions in turn.

What Do Employees (or Job Applicants) Disclose?

Disclosure of a mental disability obviously requires a formal diagnosis that must be verified by the employer. Not all mental illnesses qualify as a disability, the definition of which is stipulated and regulated by law in those countries that explicitly outlaw disability discrimination (for example, the United States, the United Kingdom, and Australia). In order to trigger the legal obligation for organizations to provide what are commonly referred to as reasonable adjustments (Granger, 2000; MacDonald-Wilson et al., 2002), or reasonable accommodations (Fabian et al., 1993; MacDonald-Wilson et al., 2002), an individual job applicant or employee is typically expected to have a mental impairment that significantly negatively affects their ability to function in the workplace. This definition is simultaneously legal and medical in nature. Thus, a self-diagnosis of a mental disability would be a dubious foundation for adjustments, and it is typically only through assessment and evaluation by a physician, psychiatrist, psychologist, or occupational health professional referral that a mental disability is confirmed, and recommended adjustments and/or accommodations are made.

Although not all people with mental illness are disabled, the following conditions are, or at least can be, sufficiently pathological to one's day-to-day functioning that they qualify a sufferer as disabled: severe depression and anxiety (Gorman, 1996; Tiller, 2013), schizophrenia and schizoaffective disorder (Smith et al., 2000), bipolar disorder (Paykel et al., 2006), obsessive-compulsive disorder (Thomsen, 2013), borderline personality disorder (Oldham, 2006), and post-traumatic stress disorder (Helzer et al., 1987), are among many other impairments that place a significant burden on an individual's daily functioning. Line managers, as will be discussed later in this chapter, should be trained in the symptomatology of these primary disorders.

The unique characteristics of a mental illness and its symptoms are reflected in one's behavior, which can be misunderstood by others who have no knowledge about the illness. Haslam et al. (2005) has addressed that disclosure is often driven in the wrong direction when the disclosers feel that their supervisor fails to respond. Therefore, line managers should understand the physical and psychological characteristics of the symptoms. This knowledge can help to guide how line managers should behave with the disclosers.

When Do Employees (or Job Applicants) Disclose?

The timing of disclosure will vary for each individual according to their unique circumstances and needs. Of course, disclosure is not an obligation, but rather a matter of choice for any employee. For some job applicants, disclosure precedes the interview so that reasonable adjustments and support can be put in place to enable participation. Other job applicants prefer to conceal their disability during the interview so as to obviate potential discrimination on that basis (Allen and Carlson, 2003; Wheat et al., 2010). Still others choose to disclose at the start of employment or during its course. Regardless of the precise timing of a disclosure, it is worth noting that no job applicant or employee can secure access to their legal rights (where afforded) to adjustments and/or accommodations in the workplace unless they first disclose their disability to management. In other words, should a disabled individual choose to conceal their mental disability, they are not normally entitled to reasonable adjustments under the law. For this reason, many disclosers who require adjustments to continue work choose to disclose sooner rather than later. Therefore, line managers should be prepared for disclosures across all phases of employment, including pre-employment.

How Do Mental Illness Disclosures Take Place?

There are two broad forms of mental disability disclosure: informal and formal. The latter is, in our view, eminently preferable in the event of a legal dispute surrounding discrimination or failure to make reasonable adjustments on the part of the employer (Nardodkar et al., 2016). An informal disclosure includes, for example, a verbal conversation between an individual and their line manager and/or HR manager in which a disability is discussed briefly, but not properly evaluated, documented, or assessed. An informal disclosure also can happen unintentionally, such as when an employee is hospitalized or experiences visible workplace distress, or when HR or line managers are aware of the symptoms or hear about a mental illness from other employees. The key problem with verbal disclosures is that there is often no documentation of the disclosure, thus enabling disreputable organizations to claim *post hoc* that no disclosure was ever made. A formal disclosure is best done in writing for the avoidance of doubt. Formal disclosures should either be accompanied by medical evidence to corroborate the nature and extent of the disability or, in the absence of such evidence, a formal disclosure should trigger the supervisor or HR (to whom the disclosure is directed) to organize a consultation with a physician or occupational health professional. Job applicants and employees should be as forthcoming as they feel comfortable with when disclosing a mental illness, and should seek legal and/or medical help, especially if requested by their supervisor.

What are the Advantages and Disadvantages of Disclosure from the Point of View of the Employee or Job Applicant?

Disclosure of a mental disability in the workplace can have positive or negative outcomes for the discloser. Whether or not the outcomes are positive or negative depends on a number of factors, including the organizational culture, quality of leadership, and managers' and supervisors' commitment to the principles of diversity, equality, and inclusion (DEI). The key advantages of disclosure are, in our view, three. Firstly, a successful disclosure can result in the provision of additional support and reasonable adjustments, without which the job applicant or employee could not sustain continued employment. The logic underlying reasonable adjustments is that they enable an individual with a disability to participate fully in work tasks on an equal footing vis-à-vis non-disabled employees. Secondly, a successful disclosure can have a positive cultural "spillover effect," such that the initial disclosure serves to encourage other persons with disability within the organization to similarly disclose to management. This cascading effect can strengthen the DEI organizational culture. Thirdly, a successful disclosure can be empowering for the individual with a disability, especially insofar as it bolsters self-confidence and generates a strong sense of inclusion and belonging, two traits that supervisors should seek to foster.

These advantages notwithstanding, disclosure of one's mental disability at work also comes with serious risks to the job applicant or employee. For job applicants, although a disclosure might trigger reasonable adjustments needed to participate in a job interview process, at the same time it can explicitly flag to interviewers that the individual in question suffers from a mental illness. The associated stigma (Stuart, 2004) can potentially result in negative evaluations on the part of the hirer, thus resulting in the job applicant's failure to attain employment. In a similar vein, employees choosing to disclose can equally be subjected to discrimination, recrimination, and victimization. Because a disclosure clearly triggers legal obligations that can result in claims of disability discrimination, disreputable organizations often bully and dismiss mentally disabled employees in order to free themselves of the responsibility of making reasonable adjustments (Stratton et al., 2018) and to prevent future lawsuits. In this light, disclosure can be a double-edged sword: on the one hand, it can enable continued employment; but on the other, it can also precipitate exclusion from employment, resulting in a "Catch-22" for potential disclosers and a tightrope for line managers to walk.

To Whom Should a Disclosure be Made?

Given that the focus of this book is on line managers, we now turn to the crucial question of who should be at the receiving end of a mental disability disclosure. Job applicants requiring reasonable adjustments typically disclose to the HR manager in charge of organizing the job interview process. Employees, however, have a number of avenues through which they can disclose their mental disability, including a trade union or co-workers (either can mediate the disclosure between the employee and management), HR managers, or perhaps most commonly, line managers, as we examine in this chapter. Because of the day-to-day relationship between the employee and line managers, many disclosures, both formal and informal, are made to the immediate supervisor, at least in the first instance. In the next section of this chapter, we focus on the crucial role of line managers in the disability disclosure process.

THE ROLE OF LINE MANAGERS IN MENTAL ILLNESS DISCLOSURE

Throughout the disclosure process, support from the immediate supervisor has a significant influence on the outcome, positive or negative. Employees with mental illness can receive support via two different processes. Firstly, support can be secured through indirect communication with the line manager, which takes place in the pre-disclosure phase of the process. In this phase, the individuals informally evaluate the line manager's attitude and behavior toward mental illness through casual social interaction (Farina and Ring, 1965; Farina et al., 1966). Because an individual's disclosure decision is based on this experience, line managers must develop their competencies, as discussed below, regarding mental illness awareness. Secondly, the individual with mental illness can also receive support through direct, formal communication, which is usually built into the organization's policies and procedures. The quality of both the relationship and communication between the discloser and the line manager will determine the disclosure outcome. Positive outcomes, such as an improvement in well-being, increased accessibility to support, and long-term career opportunities, are achieved when the line manager can build robust communication and engagement with the mentally ill employee. However, when the disclosure falls on unsympathetic ears, the outcomes may dramatically harm the discloser. Hence, understanding the key managerial responsibilities and mastering the requisite competencies around the process are crucial to the success (or failure) of a disclosure.

Line Manager Responsibilities

Line managers have two key responsibilities when it comes to a mental illness disclosure. Firstly, the line manager is responsible for being an agent of diversity and inclusivity, and is charged with creating a friendly organizational ecosystem for people with mental illness. Secondly, the line manager is the communication mediator between the discloser and senior management. The line manager's job is to ensure that the disclosure results in positive outcomes for both parties. As a diversity agent, the manager needs to embrace and share the message to end the stigma surrounding mental health problems, which is known as a central impediment to disclosure (Hastuti and Timming, 2021). The role of the line manager is thus not as a passive receiver, but as an active player in seeking to encourage the decision to disclose. Given that social support is a key antecedent of disclosure (Chaudoir and Fisher, 2010), the line manager has responsibilities in nurturing an inclusive and diverse climate within the workplace. The task of line managers therefore lies between, on the one hand, encouraging subordinates to disclose through proper signalling, and on the other, ensuring that the disclosure is handled properly and effectively by the organization.

Another role of the line manager is to provide accommodations or adjustments to the discloser to achieve a positive outcome and a continuation of employment. As such, the line manager plays a central role in moderating the communication between the discloser and senior management, including human resources. As the first port of call for most disclosures, the line manager should proactively manage and promote an inclusive social climate; support the individual at work or, where relevant, in their return to the workplace; and encourage individual's self-care and personal and professional development (Kirsh et al., 2018). It is essential for the line manager to understand the discloser's feelings, challenges, and necessities, such as how the symptoms may potentially worsen their psychological and physical condition, and how to accommodate and advocate their interests to match the organization's support and its policies and procedures.

Because line managers work directly and intimately with the individual employee, they they can most effectively manage the reasonable adjustments, including time management and workloads. Line managers should monitor at the practical level, whether or not the benefits of disclosure, such as workload and schedule adjustment, the employee assistance program, and other health program benefits, could effectively help the disclosers to manage their employment and reduce mental illness symptoms at work.

Guidelines to Increase Line Manager Competencies

To perform effectively in relation to the mental illness disclosure process, the line manager should accumulate a toolkit of knowledge and skills around mental illnesses. Although larger organizations usually have mental health specialists and professionals at their disposal, line managers should also acquire such competencies to deal effectively with mental health problems at work. Such a toolkit can be used to offer guidlines to increase line manager competencies in regard to the effective disclosure of mental health problems. One of the most important competencies that a line manager must acquire is a working knowledge surrounding the symptomology of mental illnesses. This basic knowledge can help the line manager to communicate with, and advocate for, employees who have disclosed their illness. In addition, the manager should master vital communication skills that enable them to interact smoothly with subordinates. More formal training in these areas could be a good strategy to increase these competencies. Indeed, participation in such training programs has been found to increase the likelihood of a supportive climate and a stigma-free workplace culture (Sage et al., 2016; Sayers et al., 2019). Beyond formal training, line managers could also initially acquire these literacies from other sources such as books and the internet. Another strategy includes periodic meetings with mental health specialists and professionals to keep up to date with current information, and to discuss recent experiences. A two-way communication strategy is effective since line managers would not only receive information, but also bring their real practical problems into a facilitated discussion.

Some basic knowledge is recommended for the manager, such as information about illness types and symptomatology, stigma and prejudice related to mental illness, adjustments and rehabilitation programs, organizational policies and procedures, and, of course, legal obligations. Several types of mental illnesses (for example, anxiety, depression, schizophrenia, bipolar disorder, borderline personality disorder, obsessive-compulsive disorder, and many others) have different symptoms that variously impact on individuals' performance and social lives, as well as different treatments and recommended reasonable adjustments and accommodations. This knowledge might help the line manager to identify whether the employee has a potential mental health problem, initiate a respectful and confidential conversation with the individual, and assist the employee who has decided to disclose. Another competency that line managers need to develop pertains to understanding of the social stigma surrounding mental illnesses, especially insofar as said stigma serves as an obstacle to a disclosure. By understanding the stigma associated with mental illness, the line manager can make a strategic plan to reduce stigma at the level of the organizational culture, at least in their department. Highly developed knowledge regarding reasonable adjustments and accommodations is also essential for the line manager to effectively manage mental illness at work. This knowledge will help the line manager to meet the needs of the discloser and to access the organization's particular support structures. Lastly, knowledge of organizational policies and procedures and, of course, the legal context, are essential for the line manager to effectively carry out their role in protecting the discloser from disadvantage and advocating in favor of support.

Beyond simple knowledge acquisition around mental health issues, communication is arguably the most fundamental skill associated with disclosure success. Good communication is necessary to understand the discloser's condition and increase engagement within the workplace, or prior to returning to work. Effective communication between the discloser and the immediate supervisor can reduce worries and anxieties before and after the disclosure (Hatchard, 2008), and maintain the discloser's long-term career prospects (Negrini et al., 2018). In order to build communication skills, a line manager should have a strong, compassionate, confident personality, and a low level of stigmatization toward mental illness in general. The line manager's confidence in discussing mental health problems, and their attitude toward mental health, shape their ability to communicate effectively (Bryan et al., 2018). Therefore, the line manager should seek to increase their capabilities and competencies by participating in some designated training programs aimed at bolstering knowledge and traits that are needed to facilitate a successful disclosure. Furthermore, having relationships outside of the workplace with mentally ill individuals is another factor associated with successful communication with mentally ill employees (Hand and Tryssenaar, 2006).

CONCLUSIONS

Disclosure is a means by which people with mental illness can communicate with an employer regarding their mental health condition. The line manager plays an important, albeit poorly understood, connecting or mediating role between employees and employers in helping to bridge the communication. Line managers can therefore make or break the success of the disclosure. This chapter contributes substantively to the literature on mental illness disclosure in the workplace, especially pertaining to the unique role of the line manager as the mediator of the disclosure.

Disclosure is not merely a simple decision to disclose or not to disclose. It is a complex event surrounded by a set of risks and potential benefits. Individuals with mental illness should calculate the obstacles and enablers of the disclosure. This pre-disclosure step is essential in determining whether or not the event will take place. Disclosure is based on a cost–benefit calculation of the advantages of the action compared to how it might disrupt their employment and career. The role of the line manager spans from nurturing a positive disclosure climate, to serving as an unsupportive obstacle to disclosure. To achieve the former, line managers should possess several cognitive and behavioral assets that can be improved or honed through training and education programs, and a commitment to self-improvement. One cognitive asset includes mental health literacy, such as knowledge about mental illness symptoms and treatments, social stigma around mental illness, support programs, organizational policies and procedures, and a thorough understanding of the legal obligations surrounding disclosure. Behavioral assets include communication skills around mental illness and the ability to connect with sufferers.

Although this chapter has sought to set out the contours of the role of line managers in the disclosure process, it has only scratched the surface of this area of research. At a minimum, future studies should measure empirically the efficacy of line managers' roles in disclosure. For example, evaluation studies are needed to assess how training and education programs can influence the ability of line managers to facilitate an employee disclosure. Another example of a direction for future research is to look at how confidence and communication can enable a successful disclosure. Further research that focuses on line managers' perceptions of disclosure of mental illness and the discloser's perceptions of the line manager's role is warranted. Lastly, future research is needed that focuses on the rich qualitative and contextual aspects surrounding disclosure.

REFERENCES

Adler, A.B., Britt, T.W., Riviere, L.A., Kim, P.Y., and Thomas, J.L. (2015). Longitudinal determinants of mental health treatment-seeking by US soldiers. *British Journal of Psychiatry*, *207*(4), 346–350. https://doi.org/10.1192/bjp.bp.114.146506.

AIHW (2020). Mental health services in Australia. https://www.aihw.gov.au/reports/mental-health -services/mental-health-services-in-australia.

Alfes, K., Truss, C., Soane, E.C., Rees, C., and Gatenby, M. (2013). The relationship between line manager behavior, perceived HRM practices, and individual performance: examining the mediating role of engagement. *Human Resource Management*, *52*(6), 839–859. https://doi.org/10.1002/hrm .21512.

Allen, S., and Carlson, G. (2003). To conceal or disclose a disabling condition? A dilemma of employment transition. *Journal of Vocational Rehabilitation*, *19*(1), 19–30.

Allott, K.A., Turner, L.R., Chinnery, G.L., Killackey, E.J., and Nuechterlein, K.H. (2013). Managing disclosure following recent-onset psychosis: utilizing the individual placement and support model. *Early Intervention in Psychiatry*, *7*(3), 338–344. https://doi.org/10.1111/eip.12030.

Banks, B.R., Novak, J., Mank, D., and Grossi, T. (2007). Disclosure of a psychiatric disability in supported employment: an exploratory study. *International Journal of Psychosocial Rehabilitation*, *11*, 69–84.

Baron, R.C., and Salzer, M.S. (2002). Accounting for unemployment among people with mental illness. *Behavioral Sciences and the Law*, *20*(6), 585–599. https://doi.org/10.1002/bsl.513.

Bergmans, Y., Carruthers, A., Ewanchuk, E., James, J., Wren, K., and Yager, C. (2009). Moving from full-time healing work to paid employment: challenges and celebrations. *Work*, *33*(4), 389–394. https://doi.org/10.3233/WOR-2009-0887.

Blais, R.K., and Renshaw, K.D. (2014). Self-stigma fully mediates the association of anticipated enacted stigma and help-seeking intentions in National Guard service members. *Military Psychology*, *26*(2), 114–119.

Brohan, E., Evans-Lacko, S., Henderson, C., Murray, J., Slade, M., and Thornicroft, G. (2014). Disclosure of a mental health problem in the employment context: qualitative study of beliefs and experiences. *Epidemiology and Psychiatric Sciences*, *23*(3), 289–300.

Brown, N.B., and Bruce, S.E. (2016). Stigma, career worry, and mental illness symptomatology: Factors influencing treatment-seeking for Operation Enduring Freedom and Operation Iraqi Freedom soldiers and veterans. *Psychological Trauma: Theory, Research, Practice, and Policy*, *8*(3), 276–283.

Bryan, B., Gayed, A., Milligan-Saville, J., Madan, I., Calvo, R., et al. (2018). Managers' response to mental health issues among their staff. *Occupational Medicine*, *68*(7), 464–468.

Burns, E., and Green, K.E. (2019). Academic librarians' experiences and perceptions on mental illness stigma and the workplace. *College and Research Libraries*, *80*(5), 638–657.

Chaudoir, S., and Fisher, J. (2010). The disclosure processes model: understanding disclosure decision making and postdisclosure outcomes among people living with a concealable stigmatized identity. *Psychological Bulletin*, *136*(2), 236–256.

Chow, C.M., and Cichocki, B. (2016). Predictors of job accommodations for individuals with psychiatric disabilities. *Rehabilitation Counseling Bulletin, 59*(3), 172–184. https://doi.org/10.1177/0034355215583057.

Clair, J.A., Beatty, J.E., and MacLean, T.L. (2005). Out of sight but not out of mind: managing invisible social identities in the workplace. *Academy of Management Review, 30*(1), 78–95. https://doi.org/10.2307/20159096.

Cohen, D., Winstanley, S., and Greene, G. (2016). Understanding doctors' attitudes towards self-disclosure of mental ill health. *Occupational Medicine, 66*(5), 383–389.

Coleman, J.S. (1994). *Foundations of Social Theory.* Harvard University Press.

Corbière, M., Bergeron, G., Negrini, A., Coutu, M.-F., Samson, E., et al. (2018). Employee perceptions about factors influencing their return to work after a sick-leave due to depression. *Journal of Rehabilitation, 84*(3), 3–13.

Corbière, M., Villotti, P., Lecomte, T., Bond, G.R., Lesage, A., and Goldner, E.M. (2014). Work accommodations and natural supports for maintaining employment. *Psychiatric Rehabilitation Journal, 37*(2), 90–98.

DeTore, N.R., Hintz, K., Khare, C., and Mueser, K.T. (2019). Disclosure of mental illness to prospective employers: clinical, psychosocial, and work correlates in persons receiving supported employment. *Psychiatry Research, 273*, 312–317.

Devonish, D. (2017). Managers' perceptions of mental illness in Barbadian workplaces: an exploratory study. *Journal of Mental Health Training, Education and Practice, 12*(3), 161–172.

Dolce, J.N., and Bates, F.M. (2019). Hiring and employing individuals with psychiatric disabilities: focus groups with human resource professionals. *Journal of Vocational Rehabilitation, 50*(1), 85–93.

Ellison, M.L., Russinova, Z., MacDonald-Wilson, K.L., and Lyass, A. (2003). Patterns and correlates of workplace disclosure among professionals and managers with psychiatric conditions. *Journal of Vocational Rehabilitation, 18*(1), 3–13.

Elraz, H. (2018). Identity, mental health and work: how employees with mental health conditions recount stigma and the pejorative discourse of mental illness. *Human Relations, 71*(5), 722–741. https://doi.org/10.1177/0018726717716752.

Fabian, E.S., Waterworth, A., and Ripke, B. (1993). Reasonable accommodations for workers with serious mental illness: type, frequency, and associated outcomes. *Psychosocial Rehabilitation Journal, 17*(2), 163–172.

Fan, D., Zhu, C.J., Timming, A.R., Su, Y., Huang, X., and Lu, Y. (2020). Using the past to map out the future of occupational health and safety research: where do we go from here? *International Journal of Human Resource Management, 31*(1), 90–127.

Farina, A., and Ring, K. (1965). The influence of perceived mental illness on interpersonal relations. *Journal of Abnormal Psychology, 70*(1), 47–51.

Farina, A., Holland, C.H., and Ring, K. (1966). Role of stigma and set in interpersonal interaction. *Journal of Abnormal Psychology, 71*(6), 421–428.

Follmer, K.B., and Jones, K.S. (2018). Mental illness in the workplace: an interdisciplinary review and organizational research agenda. *Journal of Management, 44*(1), 325–351.

French, M.T., Mortensen, K., and Timming, A.R. (2020a). Changes in self-reported health, alcohol consumption, and sleep quality during the COVID-19 pandemic in the United States. *Applied Economics Letters, 29*(3), 219–225.

French, M.T., Mortensen, K., and Timming, A.R. (2020b). Psychological distress and coronavirus fears during the initial phase of the COVID-19 pandemic in the United States. *Journal of Mental Health Policy and Economics, 23*(3), 93–100.

Gladman, B., and Waghorn, G. (2016). Personal experiences of people with serious mental illness when seeking, obtaining and maintaining competitive employment in Queensland, Australia. *Work, 53*(4), 835–843.

Goldberg, S.G., Killeen, M.B., and O'Day, B. (2005). The disclosure conundrum: how people with psychiatric disabilities navigate employment. *Psychology, Public Policy, and Law, 11*(3), 463–500.

Gorman, J.M. (1996). Comorbid depression and anxiety spectrum disorders. *Depression and Anxiety, 4*(4), 160–168. https://doi.org/10.1002/(SICI)1520-6394(1996)4:4<160::AID-DA2>3.0.CO;2-J.

Granger, B. (2000). The role of psychiatric rehabilitation practitioners in assisting people in understanding how to best assert their ADA rights and arrange job accommodations. *Psychiatric Rehabilitation Journal, 23*(3), 215–223.

Hand, C., and Tryssenaar, J. (2006). Small business employers' views on hiring individuals with mental illness. *Psychiatric Rehabilitation Journal, 29*(3), 166–173.

Haslam, C., Atkinson, S., Brown, S., and Haslam, R. (2005). Anxiety and depression in the workplace: effects on the individual and organisation (a focus group investigation). *Journal of Affective Disorders, 88*(2), 209–215.

Hastuti, R., and Timming, A.R. (2021). An inter-disciplinary review of the literature on mental illness disclosure in the workplace: implications for human resource management. *International Journal of Human Resource Management, 32*(15), 3302–3338. https://doi.org/10.1080/09585192.2021.1875494.

Hatchard, K. (2008). Disclosure of mental health. *Work, 30*(3), 311–316.

Hechter, M., and Kanazawa, S. (1997). Sociological rational choice theory. *Annual Review of Sociology, 23*(1), 191–214.

Helzer, J.E., Robins, L.N., and McEvoy, L. (1987). Post-traumatic stress disorder in the general population. *New England Journal of Medicine, 317*(26), 1630–1634. https://doi.org/10.1056/nejm198712243172604.

Henderson, C., Williams, P., Little, K., and Thornicroft, G. (2013). Mental health problems in the workplace: changes in employers' knowledge, attitudes and practices in England 2006-2010. *British Journal of Psychiatry, 202*(s55), s70–s76.

Keith, L.C. (2013). A phenomenological study of women and mental illness: stigma and disclosure in the workplace. Thesis, Alliant International University. (Order No. 3605910). Available from ProQuest Central; ProQuest Dissertations and Theses Global. (1491380981). https://www.proquest.com/dissertations-theses/phenomenological-study-women-mental-illness/docview/1491380981/se-2?accountid=14681.

King, J., Cleary, C., Harris, M.G., Lloyd, C., and Waghorn, G. (2011). Employment-related information for clients receiving mental health services and clinicians. *Work, 39*(3), 291–303. https://doi.org/10.3233/WOR-2011-1177.

Kirsh, B., Krupa, T., and Luong, D. (2018). How do supervisors perceive and manage employee mental health issues in their workplaces? *Work, 59*(4), 547–555.

Lo, C.C., and Cheng, T.C. (2014). Race, unemployment rate, and chronic mental illness: a 15-year trend analysis. *Social Psychiatry and Psychiatric Epidemiology, 49*(7), 1119–1128.

MacDonald-Wilson, K.L., Rogers, E.S., Massaro, J.M., Lyass, A., and Crean, T. (2002). An investigation of reasonable workplace accommodations for people with psychiatric disabilities: quantitative findings from a multi-site study. *Community Mental Health Journal, 38*(1), 35–50.

Martin, A. (2010). Individual and contextual correlates of managers' attitudes toward depressed employees. *Human Resource Management, 49*(4), 647–668.

McGahey, E., Waghorn, G., Lloyd, C., Morrissey, S., and Williams, P.L. (2016). Formal plan for self-disclosure enhances supported employment outcomes among young people with severe mental illness. *Early Intervention in Psychiatry, 10*(2), 178–185. https://doi.org/10.1111/eip.12196.

Mendel, R., Kissling, W., Reichhart, T., Bühner, M., and Hamann, J. (2015). Managers' reactions towards employees' disclosure of psychiatric or somatic diagnoses. *Epidemiology and Psychiatric Sciences, 24*(2), 146–149.

Nardodkar, R., Pathare, S., Ventriglio, A., Castaldelli-Maia, J., Javate, K.R., et al. (2016). Legal protection of the right to work and employment for persons with mental health problems: a review of legislation across the world. *International Review of Psychiatry (Abingdon, England), 28*(4), 375–384. https://doi.org/10.1080/09540261.2016.1210575.

Negrini, A., Corbière, M., Lecomte, T., Coutu, M.-F., Nieuwenhuijsen, K., et al. (2018). How can supervisors contribute to the return to work of employees who have experienced depression? *Journal of Occupational Rehabilitation, 28*(2), 279–288.

Oldham, J.M. (2006). Borderline personality disorder and suicidality. *American Journal of Psychiatry, 163*(1), 20–26.

Owen, C.L. (2004). To tell or not to tell: disclosure of a psychiatric condition in the workplace. Thesis, Boston University. (Order No. 3124867). Available from ProQuest Dissertations and Theses

Global. (305217271). https://www.proquest.com/dissertations-theses/tell-not-disclosure-psychiatric-condition/docview/305217271/se-2?accountid=14681.

Paykel, E.S., Abbott, R., Morriss, R., Hayhurst, H., and Scott, J. (2006). Sub-syndromal and syndromal symptoms in the longitudinal course of bipolar disorder. *British Journal of Psychiatry*, *189*(2), 118–123.

Peters, H., and Brown, T.C. (2009). Mental illness at work: an assessment of co-worker reactions. *Canadian Journal of Administrative Sciences / Revue Canadienne Des Sciences de l'Administration*, *26*(1), 38–53. https://doi.org/10.1002/cjas.87.

Peterson, D., Currey, N., and Collings, S. (2011). "You don't look like one of them": disclosure of mental illness in the workplace as an ongoing dilemma. *Psychiatric Rehabilitation Journal*, *35*(2), 145–147.

Phlips, L. (1988). *The Economics of Imperfect Information*. Cambridge University Press.

Price, T.A. (2011). Stigma threat and psychological help-seeking attitudes in military personnel. (Order No. 3471666). Available from ProQuest Central; ProQuest Dissertations and Theses Global. (886783104). https://www.proquest.com/dissertations-theses/stigma-threat-psychological-help-seeking/docview/886783104/se-2?accountid=14681.

Quinlan, M. (2007). Organisational restructuring/downsizing, OHS regulation and worker health and wellbeing. *Special Issue: Work and Mental Health*, *30*(4), 385–399. https://doi.org/10.1016/j.ijlp.2007.06.010.

Ridge, D., Broom, A., Kokanović, R., Ziebland, S., and Hill, N. (2019). Depression at work, authenticity in question: experiencing, concealing and revealing. *Health*, *23*(3), 344–361.

Rollins, A.L., Mueser, K.T., Bond, G.R., and Becker, D.R. (2002). Social relationships at work: does the employment model make a difference? *Psychiatric Rehabilitation Journal*, *26*(1), 51–61.

Rüsch, N., Corrigan, P.W., Waldmann, T., Staiger, T., Bahemann, A., et al. (2018). Attitudes toward disclosing a mental health problem and reemployment: a longitudinal study. *Journal of Nervous and Mental Disease*, *206*(5), 383–385.

Rüsch, N., Rose, C., Holzhausen, F., Mulfinger, N., Krumm, S., et al. (2017). Attitudes towards disclosing a mental illness among German soldiers and their comrades. *Psychiatry Research*, *258*, 200–206.

Sage, C., Brooks, S., Jones, N., and Greenberg, N. (2016). Attitudes towards mental health and help-seeking in railway workers. *Occupational Medicine*, *66*(2), 118–121.

SAMHSA (2020). Key substance use and mental health indicators in the United States: result from the 2019 National Survey on Drug Use and Health (HHS Publication No. PEP20-07-01-001, NSDUH Series H-55). Rockville, MD: Center for Behavioral Health Statistics and Quality, Substance Abuse and Mental Health Administration. https://www.samhsa.gov/data/.

Sayers, E., Rich, J., Rahman, M.M., Kelly, B., and James, C. (2019). Does help seeking behavior change over time following a workplace mental health intervention in the coal mining industry? *Journal of Occupational and Environmental Medicine*, *61*(6), e282–e290.

Selten, R. (1990). Bounded rationality. *Journal of Institutional and Theoretical Economics (JITE) / Zeitschrift Für Die Gesamte Staatswissenschaft*, *146*(4), 649–658.

Simon, H.A. (1990). Bounded rationality. In J. Eatwell, M. Milgate, and P. Newman (eds), *Utility and Probability* (pp. 15–18). Palgrave Macmillan UK. https://doi.org/10.1007/978-1-349-20568-4_5.

Smith, T.E., Hull, J.W., Israel, L.M., and Willson, D.F. (2000). Insight, symptoms, and neurocognition in schizophrenia and schizoaffective disorder. *Schizophrenia Bulletin*, *26*(1), 193–200. https://doi.org/10.1093/oxfordjournals.schbul.a033439.

Stratton, E., Einboden, R., Ryan, R., Choi, I., Harvey, S.B., and Glozier, N. (2018). Deciding to disclose a mental health condition in male dominated workplaces; a focus-group study. *Frontiers in Psychiatry*, *9*, 684. https://doi.org/10.3389/fpsyt.2018.00684.

Stuart, H. (2004). Stigma and work. *Healthcare Papers*, *5*(2), 100–111.

Stuart, H. (2017). Mental illness stigma expressed by police to police. *Israel Journal of Psychiatry and Related Sciences*, *54*(1), 18–23.

Thomas, T.L., Muliyala, K.P., Jayarajan, D., Angothu, H., and Thirthalli, J. (2019). Vocational challenges in severe mental illness: a qualitative study in persons with professional degrees. *Asian Journal of Psychiatry*, *42*, 48–54.

Thomsen, P.H. (2013). Obsessive-compulsive disorders. *European Child and Adolescent Psychiatry*, *22*, 23–28.

Tiller, J.W. (2013). Depression and anxiety. *Medical Journal of Australia*, *199*(6), S28–S31.

Timming, A.R. (2009). Trust in cross-national labour relations: a case study of an Anglo-Dutch European works council. *European Sociological Review*, *25*(4), 505–516.

Toth, K.E., and Dewa, C.S. (2014). Employee decision-making about disclosure of a mental disorder at work. *Journal of Occupational Rehabilitation*, *24*(4), 732–746.

Van Eerd, D., Cullen, K., Irvin, E., Le Pouésard, M., and Gignac, M. (2021). Support for depression in the workplace: perspectives of employees, managers, and OHS personnel. *Occupational Health Science*. https://doi.org/10.1007/s41542-021-00090-9.

Wheat, K., Brohan, E., Henderson, C., and Thornicroft, G. (2010). Mental illness and the workplace: conceal or reveal? *Journal of the Royal Society of Medicine*, *103*(3), 83–86. https://doi.org/10.1258/jrsm.2009.090317.

Yoon, C.-G., Bae, K.-J., Kang, M.-Y., and Yoon, J.-H. (2015). Is suicidal ideation linked to working hours and shift work in Korea? *Journal of Occupational Health*, *57*(3), 222–229.

Yoshimura, Y., Bakolis, I., and Henderson, C. (2018). Psychiatric diagnosis and other predictors of experienced and anticipated workplace discrimination and concealment of mental illness among mental health service users in England. *Social Psychiatry and Psychiatric Epidemiology*, *53*(10), 1099–1109. https://doi.org/10.1007/s00127-018-1561-7.

20. Line management in emergency services occupations: exploring personal challenges and organizational change in a uniformed culture

Joanne Mildenhall and Leo McCann

INTRODUCTION

Certain features of line management are common to any context. But it is also true that the nature, experiences, and processes of line management are always deeply influenced by the organizational, cultural, and occupational settings in which it takes place. This chapter explores line management in the context of emergency services organizations, a field where specific social and cultural features place particularly powerful imprints on the nature and structure of work and employment relations. This chapter provides an overview of the complex and distinct nature of emergency services settings, alongside an individual personal reflection from one of the authors about her own experiences of operating as a line manager in this environment. While one person's experiences and viewpoints can never fully capture the broad and diverse nature of any specific occupation, the chapter links individual experiences into a more general overview of the employment context of uniformed occupations. In doing so, we show that the emergency services world has many of its own unique challenges, but that some of the experiences, behaviours and coping tactics of line managers in those settings also have resonance with line management in any workplace setting.

'Emergency services' encompasses a range of settings and occupations, from the largest organizations involved in policing, fire and rescue, and paramedic and ambulance services, through to smaller organizations such as lifeboats and coastguards, mountain rescue and cave rescue. These organizations differ in their governance and structure, with many of them employing thousands of public sector workers, and others being smaller, often staffed by volunteers (Desmond, 2006; Lois, 2003; O'Toole and Calvard, 2020). All tend to have a 'uniformed' culture, that is, staff on duty wear a uniform not unlike police or military garb: heavy-duty combat-style trousers, protective steel-capped boots, and shirts with epaulettes and rank insignia. The uniform brings with it certain connotations about the status, duties and expected behaviour of the wearer (Joseph and Alex, 1972). The uniform itself is a useful metaphor for understanding the relatively distinct employment culture of emergency services occupations and organisations.

Line management in emergency-focused organisations has a distinctly hierarchical legacy. The military, fire and policing style and roots of the occupations endow them with certain enduring traits. They tend to have a 'command and control' mentality, which is deeply embedded into their rank structures (McCann and Granter, 2019). The operational style, habitus, everyday language and aesthetic of emergency organizations reflects a traditionally masculine, activist language of 'response' and 'operations' (Desmond, 2006). These occupations have historically recruited and retained significantly higher numbers of men than women.

They tend not to be diverse, and have struggled to recruit and retain persons from ethnicity minority backgrounds (Chetkovitch, 1997; Perrott, 2016). The repeated use of 'command' as a form of leadership tends to leave long-lasting effects on the management style of the organization (Grint, 2010, 2020). Many uniformed emergency occupations struggle with a low-trust culture, a blame culture, fear of management reprisal, a lack of open speaking, and poor management–staff relations. The work conditions faced by emergency responders are often challenging, involving regular exposure to stress, illness and injury (Granter et al., 2019; Henckes and Nurok, 2015; Kellner et al., 2019; Maguire et al., 2014; Mildenhall, 2012), emotionally challenging situations (Boyle, 2005; Boyle and Healy, 2003; Filstad, 2010; Shay, 2014), plus exhausting and disruptive shift patterns (Kuhn, 2001). On top of this, emergency services organizations are often characterized by troublesome employment relations and dated, authoritarian management styles (Hyde et al., 2016; Lewis, 2017).

Nevertheless, emergency occupations and organizations are changing. Although they have a history as blue-collar work with training 'on the job', they are arguably becoming more and more important in societies where their specialist skills and abilities are becoming ever more in demand and valued. Shortages and breakdowns elsewhere in society (for example, the overload of provision by hospitals and family doctors, lack of in-hospital or in-community psychiatric care, lack of adequate public housing) create a dynamic whereby 'everyday' needs morph into 'emergency' needs. Complex events such as pandemics, acts of terrorism, and floods and wildfires are growing priorities that require expert responses. 'Wicked problems' with no obvious solution (drug abuse, domestic violence) call for interagency working. All of these developments have increased the demand for and complexity of emergency services work. Emergency occupations are moving beyond their blue-collar roots and are starting to become more widely recognized as professions in which staff are educated to higher levels and expected to conform to increasingly demanding intellectual, operational and practical expectations (McCann and Granter, 2019). These developments are creating significant impulses which are changing the nature of employment and line management in emergency services occupations and organizations.

This chapter provides socio-cultural insights into management practice and organizational culture that is relevant not only within the extreme setting of emergency response organizations (Granter et al., 2015), but also to those in more general occupations. Through personal reflection upon lived experience, we highlight the various challenges and tensions of line management associated with the intensity of working within an environment that is complex and demanding. Broader analysis emphasizes the developments and struggles of a changing organizational climate characterized by high strain, conflict, and demand pressures which are posing new problems of their own. Furthermore, we discuss how, in a high-stakes environment, a heightened workplace intensity places considerable risk, strain, exhaustion and stress on all staff, and perhaps especially on the shoulders of line managers, whose support is undoubtedly critical to the well-being of employees and the success of the organization.

BACKGROUND

Emergency services occupations often developed out of statutory government provision of core or essential services to the public. The roots of their operational doctrine are often derived from formal or legal concepts relating to public order, safety and national security.

For example, part of the United Kingdom's (UK) ambulance training grew out of civil defence doctrine (Fellows and Harris, 2019; Kilner, 2004). At heart, their organizational design and everyday bearing circulates around the notion of responding to emergencies: dangerous events or incidents that appear suddenly and require urgent and effective attention from expert practitioners. The centrality of 'emergency' to these services has tended to shape their culture. The traditional traits of emergency occupations are similar to many of those famously described as central to police culture, a hierarchical command structure, a bias for action, intergroup solidarity, suspicion of outsiders, and machismo (Herbert, 1998; Loftus, 2010; Reiner, 2010).

These traits are unattractive from many points of view, especially from those associated with progressive and open employment cultures. Uniformed cultures are traditionally low-trust, exclusionary and lacking in workplace democracy. Police and military staff usually cannot join unions and are barred from taking industrial action. Indeed, uniformed workplaces are often characterized by a great deal of conflict and disagreement, and are notorious settings for bullying and harassment. Operators out on the road are often not closely scrutinized, meaning there is often a degree of conflict and misunderstanding over the degree of autonomy and discretion they ought to have (Bacon, 2019; Corman and Melon, 2014). Senior management, under pressure of their own to hit performance targets and to project an aura of credibility, tend to want to establish control wherever they can. Management will extensively utilize new technologies to make mobile work visible, tractable, and amenable to metric-based analysis (Corman, 2017).

In the UK ambulance service, the management hierarchy (deeply influenced by uniformed notions of rank) has several layers, from frontline supervision, to middle management at station level, then perhaps one or two layers of upper-middle management such as area managers, then up to senior managers such as directors of operations, clinical directors and chief executives. As the grades go up, the work becomes more abstract, and becomes ever more related to the imperatives to perform and deliver in an audit culture. As providers of public services they face a battery of standards and indicators to meet; quality enhancement targets, response times and a range of other key performance indicators (Bevan and Hood, 2006; Brodkin, 2011; Power, 1997; Strathern, 1996). Senior management have usually worked their way up from the frontline level over many years. There is an unspoken assumption among the ranks that people who come into emergency services leadership from direct entry are somehow unsuited to the role: senior police leaders should be cops who understand the culture and realities of policing, fire officers should have experience of handling major incidents. There are significant moves to change this mindset and to make the leadership of emergency organizations more general and more diverse, partly to reassert civilian authority over these organizations, given a history of failures, scandals and a lack of accountability, and partly because of evidence in some areas that the best frontline practitioners do not always make the best managers and leaders. The old mindset of ranks and rank insignia ('pips on the shoulder' and time served as automatic indicators of authority) is coming under pressure both from external sources trying to modernize and change the services, and from internal sources in the form of a new breed of emergency services professional opposed to the limitations of authoritarian management styles. This is increasingly the case where new entrants to a profession are university-educated rather than trained in-house.

Emergency services occupations have often worked the assumption that good technicians and operators with years of hard-won experience and trusted by colleagues at frontline levels are the obvious candidates to move into line management roles, and then further up the ranks.

While this is an understandable viewpoint, insufficient attention has been paid to the dynamics and complexities of the transition from frontline responder to manager, with many line managers historically receiving little or no official leadership training or development. As a result, many feel badly unprepared for the different nature and demands of managerial roles. This is also a widespread issue in other healthcare occupations (Townsend et al., 2012). What little management education exists is often generic and not always valuable (Kellerman, 2018).

Lack of adequate managerial training is often the result of the intensity of demand pressures on emergency services organizations. It can be very difficult to take staff off the operational roster to allow time for training, education and professional reflection. Many managers are themselves still operational clinicians in a dual, hybrid role (Burgess et al., 2015; Hyde et al., 2016). Yet in a setting often marred by a low-trust climate, a blame culture and a bullying culture, managers and leaders might benefit from extensive training and education, rather than the minimal provision traditionally on offer. Under such conditions, line managers are left to figure out how to develop their own managerial style and will often seek out trusted role models, who are typically in short supply and face stressful conditions of their own (Kellner et al., 2019).

All of the above demonstrates the intense difficulties facing line managers in the emergency services world. But the managerial cultures of emergency occupations are starting to change. All of them are increasingly exposed to interagency working, which broadens their horizons. All have been affected by scandals and failure, which has increased the influence of external scrutiny and has challenged the orthodoxies of rank privilege and command-and-control managerial styles. Audit cultures create new imperatives to change behaviour, as does the rise of commercial-type organizational transformation (outsourcing, contracting-out, cost control, employment restructuring). These organizational dynamics are accompanied by occupational change towards professionalization, whereby rank-and-file members of emergency occupations are increasingly trained in external, higher education institutions, and are (at least theoretically) encouraged to be more autonomous and to question established practice. In what follows, we provide a personal reflection from one of the authors about the direct experience of managing in a changing UK ambulance service, highlighting the distinct challenges of becoming a line manager in such a demanding setting; a setting which is undergoing significant change yet also features powerful entrenched norms, behaviours and culture.

PERSONAL REFLECTION

It is ironic that in writing this reflection, I have recently come to the end of the chapter in my direct management and operational leadership of ambulance personnel. It is a journey that started more than a decade ago, when I had just over 12 years' emergency response service as a paramedic and mentor under my belt.

Traditionally, the ideology of the ambulance service was that of transportation of the sick and injured for treatment by doctors within a hospital setting. However, alignment within the National Health Service (NHS), the development of paramedicine towards clinical, specialist and advanced practice, as well as organisational transformative change, has reflected a paradigm shift in progressing the organisational identity of the NHS ambulance services away from this primitive model, and towards that of professionalised emergency and urgent mobile clinical healthcare providers (Givati et al., 2018; McCann and Granter, 2019). Slower to follow suit, however, has been a shift in organizational culture and in performance management regimes (McCann, 2022).

Of Carrots and Sticks: The Traditional Operator Culture

As I reflect on the beginnings of my leadership journey, the rank and structure of the ambulance service at that time tended to facilitate a masculinist, patriarchal culture, whereby organisational position signified power. This dominant philosophy of hierarchy favoured a unitary day-to-day, top-down, command-and-control management style, often colloquially referred to by the staff with a 'carrot and stick' analogy. In addition, the transactional notion of ambulance officers (managers) as authoritative 'parental' figures in contrast to the staff as submissive 'children' was frequently surmised by those on the ground to illustrate the hierarchical power imbalance and almost tribal separation between the two working groups.

Looking back, this style of management was seemingly a legacy of the deeply rooted, intergenerational culture of the ambulance service when it had quasi-military associations and was wholly reliant on organizational symbolism in the form of a uniform, discipline, rank and structure. Learned behaviours, cultural norms and assumed management practices were passed down from one to another, especially in a context where formal mechanisms for management selection, education and mentoring training were limited or absent.

Expectations and behaviours were heavily gendered, especially in the earlier years of my employment. At that time, being female in a very male-dominated occupation could be challenging. I had entered into an existing paradigm that valued managers with a strong masculinist sense of self; people who held, projected and normalized a particular ambulance version of 'hegemonic masculinity' (Boyle, 2002; Connell and Messerschmidt, 2005). This created a narrative valuing extroversion, strength and success, where adversity could be confronted by an ethos of 'man-up and get on with it'. At its worst, the culture would border on one of 'toxic masculinity'.

Being a female with a quiet nature challenged the traditional hegemonic view of what management and a manager looked like in the service. Questions were raised as to whether I would be assertive (or perhaps aggressive) and loud enough to lead. In such an environment it was extremely challenging to be afforded a secondment to the role of operational supervisor: the first-line manager responsible for the day-to-day running of an ambulance station, and the person at the interface between senior officers and the staff. Needless to say, my first opportunity acting into this position was tough, and brought with it challenges and frustrations in terms of gender assumptions and role expectations which were overtly masculinist.

Critically, I recall reflecting upon and rejecting the masculine norms with a determination of presenting diversity and inclusivity within the leadership team. I did not realize it at the time, but in contemplating these early experiences, my internalized feelings of suppression motivated me to challenge traditional models of leadership. I (and others) perceived that the prevailing social discourse may be hindering both inclusion and productivity and was not conducive to supportive and healthy working relationships or practices.

Moving into the Unknown: Learning to Become a Line Manager in a Changing Environment

Following organizational change which modernized and brought in more progressive notions of team working, I was eventually successful in gaining a substantive first-line manager position, where I was responsible for around 20 clinical and non-clinical staff based in one geographical location.

In a time of uncertainty when the organization was evolving in its structures, strategic processes and leadership dynamics, it was exciting to be starting this newly created role. But it also brought many new challenges. Adapting to a shifting culture with a more progressive management system was a change that brought personal and professional reflection upon the meanings and values of what this new position should achieve, and how to adapt practices to meet the organization's evolving vision and overarching goals. These organizational aspects were undergoing significant change, as the clinical scope of the ambulance service was being broadened, and its operational focus was shifting increasingly away from traditional life-threatening calls and towards unplanned primary care, social care and psychiatric-related calls. Moving into the unknown required dynamic ways of thinking and a new collective approach to managing staff.

Communicating with colleagues as to the changes was paramount. But, for a considerable time, there was great unease locally, and in the service more generally, as to the decisions and changes being made. There was a sense of people feeling unsettled, and this was very much present within me, too. Having achieved promotion into the role, there was an expectation from some that in 'gaining the pips' one should somehow instantly know how to be and how to perform as a good leader; at that point, with no additional training. As a new leader, I felt an overwhelming responsibility that I should immediately hold all the answers. To show a lack of knowledge was, indeed, to appear incompetent; a label I wished to avoid at all costs.

Over time, however, I realized that there is actually great merit in admitting that it is impossible to know everything. No matter how experienced a person is, there will always be some things a person does not know. Any manager or supervisor will inevitably find themselves grappling with various grey areas that require reflection, consultation, discretion and experiential thinking through, rather than snap, absolute answers. This is particularly true in public service work, where the use of discretion and the 'muddling through' of complexity are unavoidable (Brodkin, 2011; Evans and Harris, 2004). The key, I found, was to be authentic and genuine in dealing with the situation. While the emergency services world will often generate incidents which require direct leadership, it also features broad opportunities where supervisors and managers can empower others in a problem-solving approach, facilitating an inclusive and engaging day-to-day work culture.

Co-existing alongside the formal management structures, informal hierarchies (Oedzes et al., 2018) were socially constructed within small groups of workers, such as those based at an ambulance station. This natural differentiation was seemingly ordered amongst the staff via rites of passage associated with length of service, roles held, levels of influence and, often, popularity amongst other members of the group. The subtle omnipresence of an informal social hierarchy within the subculture of our workplace appeared to serve as a socialization process to distinguish identities, power and status amongst peers. Importantly, formal organizational change can challenge these social networks and relationships, and thus, in response to tension, informal hierarchies can undermine organizational change efforts.

One of my earliest challenges was managing some of the effects of organizational change on these subcultures. A small number of colleagues who were core to the authoritarian masculinist culture found the restructure particularly challenging and threatening to their identity and perceived position within the informal hierarchy. A few felt disenchanted with the organization and seemed to feel bitterness towards me, a younger female who represented change to assumed positions within the informal hierarchy of the operational team. It was a difficult situation for me, and for a small number of others who felt betrayed and frustrated. For my part, I felt guilty to have succeeded into a role that perhaps others felt should have been theirs.

I questioned myself on how I was going to find a solution to resolve these issues into a more meaningful, collegial and manageable situation. I decided on a compassionate approach by addressing 'the elephant in the room'. Sitting down individually with a small number of troubled colleagues in turn, I encouraged them to share their experiences and feelings about the situation. My role at that stage was simply to listen, to really listen, so that their voices could be heard. Thoughts were vocalized in private meetings about struggling to come to terms with the situation. Emotions were expressed such as anger, frustration, fear, sadness and loss: of identity, of hopes for the role, of control and of respect.

The experience was a powerful one in terms of providing bounded, confidential spaces in which staff could express their feelings, and me my own. As we reflected and shared our thoughts, we built rapport. I was able to authentically share how challenging I had found the situation to be, allowing me to communicate my understanding, empathy and respect for others and the difficult situation we were collectively experiencing, albeit from differing perspectives. 'Talking it out' defused some of the powerful emotions that hitherto characterized the situation, so that they became more manageable for them and for me. From then, there was a noticeable change in the persona of some individuals; the location was calmer, their behaviour more reasonable, and interactions with myself and others became more positive.

From this early experience (and others similar in nature), I learned that leading people is a multidimensional process, particularly in periods of significant organizational change. It will naturally encompass conflicts and challenges to social relationships and working practices, but will also bring moments of true inspiration, innovation and positivity. Conflict and unhappiness were far from continuous, however, and overall, the staff were mutually supportive and approachable at that local setting. While emergency services are distinct occupations with their own unique cultures and stressors, there are general experiences of the challenges and rewards of line management that also apply.

Developed predominantly through experiential learning, my own leadership philosophy rests on the fundamental need to know ourselves, as individuals and as leaders, and how our way of being influences those around us; including that which is often subtly and barely within the periphery of consciousness. I came to learn that effective line management is probably impossible without the development of managers' own sense of self-awareness, emotional intelligence, and self-knowledge as leaders. This is indispensable to establishing insight into our own psychology and that of others. My experience, such as the situation illustrated above, highlighted the vital importance of knowing yourself and your own responses, and to know your staff. This meant developing a managerial version of what emergency service practitioners often call 'situational awareness': knowing my team personally as well as professionally, knowing what was happening in their lives (within reason) particularly around things which may be impacting upon their work, and what was important to them. Even within the same profession, individual team members' personal situations, motivations and makeup can differ widely. An effective supervisor will try to understand that, and will soon notice that various persons under their supervision will respond differently to different stimuli. Some staff are highly independent in nature and will rarely, if ever, approach management for anything. Others need near continual contact, communication, engagement, feedback and encouragement. Some staff will never raise contentious issues about the organization or their work duties. Others will complain incessantly. Similar features can also apply to subgroups, subcultures, or even specific locations or individual ambulance stations that seem to take on certain collective identities and reputations.

Support the Needs of Others, but Do Not Neglect Your Own

With all of this in mind, I learned to develop and project a managerial persona of authenticity and being genuine. These are not easy concepts to define. But my aim was to elicit trust, lead with competence and professionalism, and gain credibility with staff members. This required congruence in my behaviour: between what I thought and what I felt, and in the verbal inter-actions and written correspondence I had with all of my staff.

Sometimes this was challenging, because my thoughts and beliefs did not always align with those of the senior management and the tasks, rules and procedures that we were required to implement and abide by as line managers and at street level. Whilst some of these impositions could be challenged, there was often an imperative to deliver on others. For me – and I am sure for a middle manager in any organization – this sometimes generated uncomfortable emotional dissonance, where I had to act in accordance with aspects of the role that I did not agree with, but had no choice but to follow. It was at moments like this that the acute confusions and entanglements around management and leadership (Kellerman, 2018; Martin and Learmonth, 2010) often left me questioning whether I was a manager, a leader, or both. This identity narrative was often ambiguous and paradoxical, reflecting organizational and professional confusion as to the expectations of the line management role in its contemporary guise as team leader. The managerial aspects of the work comprised productivity, performance man-agement, efficiency and scrutiny; whereas the leadership elements were less tangible: being a role model, inspiring and motivating staff to be their best selves at work, while also being somehow wrapped up in what it means to be a clinical professional answerable to patients and to the occupation's professional standards. My experience raised existential questions around management, leadership and professionalism, and provoked much reflexivity in exploring these organizational role discourses within the context of the NHS, itself a complex giant made up of many distinct occupations and professions with their own codes of conduct, and hundreds of distinct organizations with their own cultures and subcultures. Each manager has to work this out for themselves, always coming to terms with the reality that there are huge areas of activity that are simply beyond their own scope of influence.

Having a fundamental and thorough understanding of the work and organizational processes was essential to managing daily operations and completing associated business administra-tion (Hyde et al., 2016). Also necessary was the ability to number-crunch performance data extrapolated around call volumes and clinical demands; a particular focus within ambulance services, which are monitored, scrutinized and held to account by extra-organizational stake-holders such as government departments, over their timely ability to respond to those who request services for emergency and urgent healthcare needs. The audit culture was inescapable (Power, 1997; Strathern, 1996).

With this came the challenges of achieving targets as mandated by senior managers within the local NHS Trust who set the organization's strategic direction and guidance. While the deep controversies around performance targets will not be discussed here (Bevan and Hood, 2006; Power, 1997; Strathern, 1996), the institutionalized performance regime necessitated particular focus on operational productivity. It required looking at the figures and checking on a regular basis that each individual was meeting national and local objectives, such as how quickly they log-on to an ambulance, or whether they 'go mobile' to an incident within 30 seconds of receiving the call. Every aspect of the call cycle (from the time the emergency call is received until closure of the incident) was examined. It was my role to manage individuals who were not meeting the expected levels of performance, and to follow employment practices set within policies by, for example, providing support, or addressing any issues of conduct or capability. As the organization became established into these new ways of working, management training was offered which covered sickness absence, appraisals, disciplinary practices and an NHS leadership development programme.

Having clinical experience was also essential to the line manager role as there was still the requirement to respond to emergency calls, albeit to only the most serious or complex of cases, to provide clinical skills or scene management. Adapting from being a clinical practitioner to a clinical leader was an interesting dynamic which required a significant shift in thinking, away from that of providing immediate care, to that of taking overall account of the scene, including crew and patient safety, strategic deployment of resources in the event of a multi-casualty incident, hazards management, interagency collaborative working and hospital liaison. It is not an easy thing to take that step back when all your professional experience and learning to that point has directed you to step in and provide care. For me, this initially presented internal conflict, and it took much effort to hold back and not become involved as a clinical practitioner. Now, many years later, it has become second nature to provide scene management and to undertake clinical care only as required. However, it is interesting to reflect upon the clinical versus leadership role dispensation and conflicts that those new to and transitioning into the role also experience. Again, while the emergency services context can make this tension especially acute, anxieties about not wanting to step back and delegate are a common challenge for any manager.

Importantly, after an involved incident, or indeed any event that has had a distressing emotional impact upon a member of staff, there is a need to provide effective psychosocial support, defusing and, where appropriate, crisis management. It was standard procedure that after such a call, defusing (referred to in-house as 'debriefing') was provided by a team leader who had not attended the scene. Held shortly after the call, this enables those involved to talk through the incident from start to finish, to discuss any positives that can be drawn upon and any learning that can be considered. Whilst this type of support is provided after a difficult incident, a significant part of the team leader's role is to provide occupational welfare support to their staff at any time, as required. What really helped here was knowing my team, so that I was aware of when they were having an off-day or were just 'not themselves'. Having an open-door work culture, whereby staff know that you are approachable and will make time for them, helps further. This can be hard to do where smaller ambulance stations are closing and being agglomerated into larger, out-of-town facilities where staff will see each other less often, and where managerial spans of control get ever wider.

The scale, intensity and importance of operations means that one of the hardest things to do is to take time for self-care. This is true in any environment where the demands and pace of work are non-stop. Reflecting upon my time as a leader, there was a powerful emphasis placed upon always being there for your team, and for some colleagues this extended into their days off and annual leave. It can be difficult for managers and professionals to guard against the build-up of unreasonable expectations, excessive or extreme work demands, and to avoid work addiction (Burke, 2006; Granter et al., 2015; Hassard et al., 2009; Hewlett and Luce, 2006). However, taking care of a team starts with taking care of oneself. A manager in any organization needs to place boundaries between home and work, to acknowledge that there are distinct limits to what a person can reasonably achieve within a period of time. This is crucial. Exhaustion and burnout are inevitable if this is not achieved. Leaders set a tone. A leader who actively develops as a role model for enacting work–life balance then psychologically permits their team members to do the same. In essence, as much as leadership is about physical presence, it is also a state of mind and well-being.

Personally, I feel I have been very fortunate in my line management journey to have had the privilege of leading an amazing team of people over the years. I have enjoyed the richness of diversity that individuals have brought. I have loved seeing individuals flourish and develop. Through my experiences, I have come to see leadership as a continuum; a complex and contested process that ebbs and flows through human interactions within organizations, their processes, structures and culture. In any setting, working out quite how to succeed as a line manager is no straightforward task. It requires continual reflection, practice and reappraisal.

DISCUSSION

Line management in an emergency services or healthcare profession is a difficult endeavour. The challenges associated with the round-the-clock clinical and operational demands can be extreme. Sometimes they are unsustainable, with line managers struggling with a range of well-being problems, including anxiety, chronic stress, burnout and depression. However, it is encouraging to see times and attitudes changing and the traditional narrative of command-and-control being slowly chipped away to allow the development of new narratives of diversity, discretion, professionalism, autonomy and compassion.

Whilst acknowledging the inherent limits of generalizing from one experiential account of line management, personal accounts can be useful in providing broad and contextual insights which may be valuable to those studying and performing line management in various settings. From this reflection, three points for discussion can be drawn for further consideration.

Firstly, the narrative provides socio-cultural recognition of deeply embedded tensions that can arise in various guises, not only within organizational relationships and culture, but also within oneself, experienced as internal conflict. This was particularly apparent in the author's experiences of the selection and promotion processes associated with applying for a line management position. Joanne's narrative briefly explores underlying gender assumptions and traditional discourse within the emergency services, whereby informal judgements and inherent, gendered beliefs held by others were influential in determining one's perceived suitability to align with the expected values and behaviours modelled by others within the peer group. While unspoken norms and tight identities may provide powerful and functional elements of uniformity within management structures, there are inherent dangers that a person whose 'face does not fit' will likely be rejected and excluded from supervision and leadership positions. This places organizations at a distinct disadvantage, providing a narrow, non-diverse corridor of possible selection of managers and leaders which does not recognize alternative viewpoints, perspectives and experiences. Deeply held, taken-for-granted assumptions associating the reputation of being a good frontline practitioner with being a good manager can be risky, and can lead to the promotion of individuals who are not always best suited to the role.

The narrative also describes internalized tensions that may be felt in terms of transitioning between the roles of clinical practitioner and manager. Ambulance services first-line managers are in a hybrid role, encompassing elements of both clinical practice and general management. Whilst much of the managerial work undertaken within uniformed settings takes place backstage within office and operational station settings, they may, at a moment's notice, have to attend some of the more complex emergency scenes. This requires the individual to quickly transition between roles, both of which may be demanding and intense in very different ways.

Secondly, the style of management and conduct in the role is an important consideration.

While emergency services traditions have favoured robust and direct forms of interpersonal behaviour, such approaches are becoming rapidly outdated, just as they have in other, less intense organizational settings. It is now much more widely accepted that the most effective forms of day-to-day management and supervision involve compassion, consultation and understanding, rather than directing, commanding and judging. Indeed, the research literature across many different occupational settings highlights the positive well-being and organizational benefits associated with supportive, engaging and non-judgemental management (Kowalski and Loretto, 2017). Furthermore, seemingly simple communications with staff – noticing and recognizing the efforts of direct reports and appreciating their input – is associated with increased morale (White, 2014). Developing a manager's self-awareness of personal behavioural and emotional responses is highly advantageous in facilitating a basic understanding of and empathy with those who they are managing. Whilst this may be achieved in part by personal reflection, a manager may also greatly benefit from seeking the feedback of others to gain insight into their persona and how they are perceived.

Finally, the narrative highlighted the considerable importance of taking stock of one's own well-being whilst managing that of others. By its very nature, line management can be challenging, overwhelming and sometimes thankless. This is even more true in high-pressure environments such as emergency services work where operational pressure is intense and high stakes are commonplace. An individual who is experiencing burnout, stress and/or exhaustion is unable to function effectively. For managers who are feeling this way, it is likely that they will have limited personal resources to offer support, advice and compassion to their direct reports and colleagues. Whilst seeking help and personal support may challenge traditional self-beliefs and identity associated with being a manager, in fact it not only provides good role-modelling behaviour to junior staff and peers, but can also facilitate an important space to decompress and offload. It is vital for managers to show humanity. To connect with and show compassion in managing others is imperative and conducive to a healthy working environment. To recognize boundaries – between work and home life, and limits to knowledge, and personal and professional capacity – is fundamental to one's well-being and optimal functioning. Challenging deeply held beliefs and organizational ways of doing things that are not facilitative of personal development and sustainability in the workplace is essential in promoting inclusive, equitable and professional work cultures.

CONCLUSION

Public servants face robust challenges in dealing with complex and never-ending caseloads. They confront potentially severe consequences for failure. Working with the public often means incessant grey areas and few unambiguously right or wrong approaches (Brodkin, 2011; Dallyn and Marinetto, 2022; Evans and Harris, 2004; Zacka, 2017). This is also true as regards line managers' interactions with subordinates in an employment relationship. As Joanne's narrative demonstrates, a line manager is well advised to be self-reflective, thoughtful and sensitive to their contexts and surroundings. Even when the stakes are high – in fact, especially so – the emphasis should always be on compassion, honesty, trust, and mutual support and learning.

Sadly, some employment contexts simply are not conducive to this kind of progressive and humanistic approach. If the overall organizational culture – from above and below – does not allow the cultivation of that kind of management style, then hard choices need to be made about whether that environment is really the right one to work in at all. Ambulance services in the UK have slowly adapted away from their traditions embedded in a masculinist, action-oriented culture. Whilst at present the paradigm shift towards more progressive and inclusive leadership models is incomplete, it is a journey of transitional change that is positively under way.

Different economic sectors, professions and employing organizations, and the specific sub-cultures within them, will always feature a complex range of operating styles, traditions and behaviours. Learning how to navigate the various currents of workplace cultures – sometimes supportive, sometimes restrictive – is an ongoing challenge that all persons moving into line management roles are likely to confront at various times in their career. Though the roles may sometimes feel thankless and unsung, personnel in mid-level and line manager positions are key to encouraging and inspiring the development of future generations and are critical in supporting the well-being of those who they work with, and alongside. The overall effectiveness of any organization is attributable to those who work and manage within the operational system. However, individuals can only fulfil these roles well when the climate is supportive, and where genuine opportunities exist for them to develop as reflexive and compassionate professionals.

REFERENCES

Bacon, C. (2019) 'Beyond the scope of managerialism: exploring the organisational invisibility of police work', in Wankhade, P., McCann, L. and Murphy, P. (eds), *Critical Perspectives on the Management and Organization of Emergency Services*. Abingdon: Routledge, pp. 107–121.

Bevan, G. and Hood, C. (2006) 'What's measured is what matters: targets and gaming in the English public health system', *Public Administration*, 84(3): 517–538.

Boyle, M.V. (2002) '"Sailing twixt Scylla and Charybdis": negotiating multiple organisational masculinities', *Women in Management Review*, 17(3/4): 131–141.

Boyle, M.V. (2005) '"You wait until you get home": emotional regions, emotional process work and the role of onstage and offstage support', in Härtel, C.E.J., Zerbe, W.J. and Ashkanasy, N.M. (eds), *Emotions in Organizational Behavior*. London: Routledge, pp. 45–65.

Boyle, M.V. and Healy, J. (2003) 'Balancing Mysterium and Onus: doing spiritual work within an emotion-laden context', *Organization*, 10(2): 351–373.

Brodkin, E.Z. (2011) 'Policy work: street-level organizations under new managerialism', *Journal of Public Administration Research and Theory*, 21(2): i253–i277.

Burgess, N., Strauss, K., Currie, G. and Wood, G. (2015) 'Organizational ambidexterity and the hybrid middle manager: the case of patient safety in UK hospitals', *Human Resource Management*, 54(S1): s87–s109.

Burke, R.J. (2006) 'Work hours and work addiction', in Burke, R.J. (ed.), *Research Companion to Working Time and Work Addiction*. Cheltenham, UK and Northampton, MA, USA: Edward Elgar Publishing, pp. 3–35.

Chetkovich, C. (1997) *Real Heat: Gender and Race in the Urban Fire Service*. New Brunswick, NJ: Rutgers University Press.

Connell, R.W. and Messerschmidt, J.W. (2005) 'Hegemonic masculinity: rethinking the concept', *Gender and Society*, 19(6): 829–859.

Corman, M.K. (2017) *Paramedics On and Off the Streets: Emergency Medical Services in the Age of Technological Governance*. Toronto: University of Toronto Press.

Corman, M.K. and Melon, K. (2014) 'What counts? Managing professionals on the front line of emergency services', in Griffith, A.I. and Smith, D.E. (eds), *Under New Public Management: Institutional Ethnographies of Changing Front-Line Work*. Toronto: University of Toronto Press, pp. 148–176.

Dallyn, S. and Marinetto, M. (2022) 'From resistance and control to normative orders: *The Wire*'s Cedric Daniels as an ethical bureaucrat', *Human Relations*, 75(3): 560–582.

Desmond, M. (2006) 'Becoming a firefighter', *Ethnography*, 7(4): 387–421.

Evans, T., and Harris, J. (2004) 'Street-level bureaucracy, social work and the (exaggerated) death of discretion', *British Journal of Social Work*, 34(6): 871–895.

Fellows, B. and Harris, G. (2019) 'History of the UK paramedic profession', in Wankhade, P., McCann, L. and Murphy, P. (eds), *Critical Perspectives on the Management and Organization of Emergency Services*. Abingdon: Routledge, pp. 30–51.

Filstad, C. (2010) 'Learning to be a competent paramedic: emotional management in emotional work', *International Journal of Work, Organisation and Emotion*, 3(4): 368–383.

Givati, A., Marckham, C. and Street, K. (2018) 'The bargaining of professionalism in emergency care practice: NHS paramedics and higher education', *Advanced Health Science: Education, Theory and Practice*, 23(2): 353–369.

Granter, E., McCann, L. and Boyle, M. (2015) 'Extreme work/normal work: intensification, storytelling and hypermediation in the (re)construction of "the New Normal"', *Organization*, 22(4): 443–456.

Granter, E., Wankhede, P., McCann, L., Hassard, J. and Hyde, P. (2019) 'Multiple dimensions of work intensity: ambulance work as edgework', *Work, Employment and Society*, 33(2): 280–297.

Grint, K. (2010) 'The cuckoo clock syndrome: addicted to command, allergic to leadership', *European Management Journal*, 28(4): 306–313.

Grint, K. (2020) 'Leadership, management and command in the time of the coronavirus', *Leadership*, 16(3): 314–319.

Hassard, J., McCann, L. and Morris, J. (2009) *Managing in the Modern Corporation: The Intensification of Managerial Work in the USA, UK and Japan*. Cambridge: Cambridge University Press.

Henckes, N. and Nurok, M. (2015) '"The first pulse you take is your own – but don't forget your colleagues": emotion teamwork in pre-hospital emergency medical services', *Sociology of Health and Illness*, 37(7): 1023–1038.

Herbert, S. (1998) 'Police culture reconsidered', *Criminology*, 36(2): 343–369.

Hewlett, S.A. and Luce, C.B. (2006) 'Extreme jobs: the dangerous allure of the 70-hour workweek', *Harvard Business Review*, 84(12): 49–59.

Hyde, P., Granter, E., Hassard, J. and McCann, L. (2016) *Deconstructing the Welfare State: Managing Healthcare in the Age of Reform*. Abingdon: Routledge.

Joseph, N. and Alex, N. (1972) 'The uniform: a sociological perspective'. *American Journal of Sociology*, 77(4): 719–730.

Kellerman, B. (2018) *Professionalizing Leadership*. Oxford: Oxford University Press.

Kellner, A., Townsend, K., Loudoun, R., Dao-Tran, T.-H. and Wilkinson, A. (2019) 'Balancing formal and informal support for psychological health in emergency services: creating multiple pathways for ambulance staff', in Wankhade, P., McCann, L. and Murphy, P. (eds), *Critical Perspectives on the Management and Organization of Emergency Services*, Abingdon: Routledge, pp. 270–287.

Kilner, T. (2004) 'Educating the ambulance technician, paramedic and clinical supervisor: using factor analysis to inform the curriculum', *Emergency Medicine Journal*, 21: 379–385.

Kowalski, T.H.P. and Loretto, W. (2017) 'Well-being and HRM in the changing workplace', *International Journal of Human Resource Management*, 28(16): 2229–2255.

Kuhn, G. (2001) 'Circadian rhythm, shift work and emergency medicine', *Annals of Emergency Medicine*, 37(1): 88–98.

Lewis, D. (2017) *Bullying and Harassment at South East Coast Ambulance Service.* Independent report commissioned by South East Coast Ambulance Service. http://www.secamb.nhs.uk/about_us/news/2017/bullying__harassment_report.aspx.

Loftus, B. (2010) 'Police occupational culture: classic themes, altered times', *Policing and Society*, 20(1): 1–20.

Lois, J., (2003) *Heroic Efforts: The Emotional Culture of Search and Rescue.* New York: New York University Press.

Maguire, B.J., O'Meara, P.F., Brightwell, R.F., O'Neill, B.J. and Fitzgerald, G.J. (2014) 'Occupational injury risk among Australian paramedics: an analysis of national data', *Medical Journal of Australia*, 200(8): 477–480.

Martin, G.P. and Learmonth, M. (2010) 'A critical account of the rise and spread of "leadership": the case of UK healthcare', *Social Science and Medicine*, 74: 281–288.

McCann, L. (2022) *The Paramedic at Work: A Sociology of a New Profession.* Oxford: Oxford University Press.

McCann, L. and Granter, E. (2019) 'Beyond "blue-collar professionalism": continuity and change in the professionalization of uniformed emergency services work', *Journal of Professions and Organization,* 6(2): 213–232.

Mildenhall, J. (2012) 'Occupational stress, paramedic informal coping strategies: a review of the literature', *Journal of Paramedic Practice*, 4(6): 318–328.

Oedzes, J.J., Van der Vegt, G.S., Rink, F.A. and Walter, F. (2018) 'On the origins of informal hierarchy: the interactive role of formal leadership and task complexity,' *Journal of Organisational Behaviour*, 40: 311 – 324.

O'Toole, M. and Calvard, T. (2020) 'I've got your back: volunteering and solidarity in lifeboat crews', *Work, Employment and Society*, 34(1): 73–90.

Perrott, T. (2016) 'Beyond "token" firefighters: exploring women's experiences of gender and identity at work', *Sociological Research Online*, 21(1): 51–64.

Power, M. (1997) *The Audit Society: Rituals of Verification.* Oxford: Oxford University Press.

Reiner, R. (2010) *The Politics of the Police.* Oxford: Oxford University Press.

Shay, J. (2014) 'Moral injury', *Psychoanalytic Psychology*, 31(2): 182–191.

Strathern, M. (1996) 'From improvement to enhancement: an anthropological comment on the audit culture', *Cambridge Anthropology*, 19(3): 1–21.

Townsend, K., Wilkinson, A., Bamber, G. and Allan, C. (2012) 'Accidental, unprepared and unsupported: clinical nurses becoming managers', *International Journal of Human Resource Management*, 21(1): 204–220.

White, P. (2014) 'Improving staff morale through authentic appreciation', *Development and Learning in Organizations*, 28(5): 17–20.

Zacka, B. (2017) *When the State Meets the Street: Public Service and Moral Agency.* Harvard, MA: Harvard University Press.

PART III

FUTURE DIRECTIONS IN LINE MANAGEMENT RESEARCH

21. The future of work: implications for the frontline manager's role in HR implementation

Kathy Monks and Edel Conway

INTRODUCTION

The future of work is a topic that has long been of interest to researchers in an array of disciplines. These researchers have often focused on trying to predict the impact that new technologies may have on the design and nature of work, and the consequent ramifications for the work and non-work lives of individuals. This chapter started life in a similar vein. Its original aim was to explore the impact of new 21st century technologies on the ways in which line managers implement human resources (HR) practices. These new technologies, underpinned by artificial intelligence (AI), have led to the introduction of performance initiatives such as electronic monitoring and surveillance (EMS) and gamification which have the potential to disrupt fundamentally the nature of the social arrangements that have traditionally characterized work (Kaplan, 2015; Spencer, 2018). However, our plans for this chapter were overtaken in March 2020 by the Covid-19 pandemic that has fundamentally disrupted life throughout the world. At the time of writing in 2021, huge job losses have been recorded, and many organizations and industries are under threats that are far greater than those predicted to occur because of technological change. For those who still have jobs, the nature of their work and where it is undertaken has in many cases altered dramatically.

This chapter draws on both the academic and grey literatures to consider how both new technologies and Covid-19 are changing the nature of work, and how these changes then impact the ways in which frontline managers implement HR policies and practices. To contextualize these changes, the chapter first draws on Morgan's (1997) work on organizational metaphors, in particular the notion of organizations as organisms and its attention to socio-technical and open systems theories. We then examine some of the new technologies of the 21st century and the ways in which they shape working arrangements. The implications for the role of frontline managers in managing the interaction between the technical, the social and the environmental consequences of both technological change and Covid-19 are then discussed, with particular emphasis on various aspects of HR implementation, including the design of work and the management of employee performance. Consideration is also given to the ways in which the very nature of management itself is changing as a result of technological advances.

CONTEXTUALIZING THE FUTURE OF WORK: ORGANIZATIONS AS ORGANISMS

Gareth Morgan (1997) proposed a range of metaphors for understanding the nature of organizations. One metaphor, that of organizations as organisms, views them as 'living systems, existing in a wider environment on which they depend for the satisfaction of various needs'

(Morgan, 1997: 33). These various needs encompass both the human and technical aspects of work, a duality captured in socio-technical systems theory. This theory originated from the work of the Tavistock Institute in the United Kingdom during the 1950s, in particular from research conducted in the coal mines (Trist and Bamforth, 1951). From a socio-technical systems perspective, the work system is viewed as comprising both social and technical elements that need to work together to produce both physical products and social/psychological outcomes. It proposes that higher performance can be achieved by leveraging workers' intimate knowledge about how the technology operates, and their ability to deal with technological uncertainty, challenging workers to have greater input into how their work is designed and giving them greater control over the work process (Pasmore et al., 2019). The aim is to design work so that the outcomes for both the technical and the social elements of the system are positive (for example, increasing job variety, goal-directed behaviour, teamwork and taking responsibility for performance), while considering that the socio-technical system operates within the larger organizational and environmental system. In this regard, Morgan points to the role of open systems theory as a way of recognizing the interdependence of social, technical and environmental requirements and how organizations, in common with organisms, can be viewed as sets of interacting subsystems. Thus, it is not just technologies that can impact upon working arrangements: a major environmental shift such as Covid-19 can alter fundamentally the ways in which individuals interact with technology and with each other. Such changes have implications for both HR policies and practices, and for the ways in which frontline managers implement them.

NEW TECHNOLOGIES AND THE FUTURE OF WORK

Speculation about the future of work is not new; in fact, debates on the impact that new technologies will have on the nature of jobs have raged throughout history. Core to these debates has been the question of whether the introduction of new technologies will lead to job losses, thus substituting for workers, or whether they will create new openings, thereby creating new complementarities between individuals and machines (Autor, 2015: Petterson, 2019). The predictions as to which outcome will prevail are underpinned by two opposing theories, of continuity and discontinuity (Shestakofsky, 2017). Continuity theories argue that the dynamic interaction between humans and machines will continue, and that while some existing jobs may disappear, new types of jobs will be created through enhanced complementarities between humans and machines (Autor, 2015; Mokyr et al., 2015). In contrast, discontinuity theorists suggest that innovations such as machine learning and AI signal a major break in the link between technological innovation and job creation (Jaharri, 2018). At the same time, there is also the possibility of discontinuity in continuity (Shestakofsky, 2017). Thus, technology may rationalize work and decrease the dependence on human knowledge, skills and abilities; it may also increase the information content of tasks, to reconfigure work and social relationships, including the management of workers.

The technologies that are at the heart of contemporary debates on the future of work encompass *inter alia* AI, data analytics including HR analytics, robotics, social media, blockchain and digital platforms. Lupushor and Fradera (2017: 481) propose three classifications for these future changes: (1) datafication, 'the conversion into bits and bytes of activities, interactions and relationships between entities participating in the world of work, making it easier to understand the workflow and work dynamics'; (2) digitization, 'the transformation of work, knowledge distribution, and workplace itself through the use of tools and apps, devices, sensors, robotics, artificial intelligence etc.'; and (3) disintermediation, 'the decomposition of the value chain of work and removal of intermediaries driven by disruptions introduced by cross-chain players, reshaping how work gets done and reconfiguring the work ecosystem around the consumer's experience versus the traditional value chain'. These shifts are dramatically changing the ways in which work is both organized and experienced (European Group on Ethics in Science and New Technologies, 2018; Global Commission on the Future of Work, 2019; OECD, 2019; Servoz, 2019). Emerging technologies are becoming increasingly intelligent, with capabilities for learning and decision-making and at the same time for storing and analysing vast quantities of information that enable employers to track and monitor the behaviour and performance of their employees. The claims for what this might mean for managers range from predictions about the demise of their administration and coordination roles (Kolbjørnsrud et al., 2016), to the emergence of robots as leaders (Samani et al., 2012). Before examining some of these developments in more detail, we first consider evidence on the role of the frontline manager in implementing HR policies and practices.

FRONTLINE MANAGERS AND THE IMPLEMENTATION OF HR PRACTICES

There is now an extensive literature on the role that frontline managers play in enacting the HR practices that are critical to organizational performance (e.g., Guest and Bos-Nehles, 2013; Kehoe and Han, 2019; Kuvaas et al., 2014; Trullen et al., 2020). This enactment can encompass many responsibilities, that include interviewing prospective employees, engaging in performance management, and delivering and supporting training and development (Wright and Nishi, 2013). The process of enactment is not straightforward. Differences between intended and implemented HR practices can emerge as the HR policies designed by an HR department are translated (and sometimes reinterpreted) by frontline managers into practices which are first implemented and then experienced by employees. One recent study suggests that frontline managers engage with HR policies and procedures in three ways: 'they can decide and propose a decision within the remit of their formal role, they can ask and negotiate an outcome outside of formal policies and procedures, and they can avoid and circumvent policies and procedures' (López-Cotarelo, 2018: 266). Most research suggests that HR managers should be involved in HR policy formation and then retain a quality assurance role, remaining distanced from the actual implementation of HR practices (Guest and Bos-Nehles, 2013). However, the study undertaken by López-Cotarelo (2018) suggests that HR managers cannot simply design HR processes and then hand over their implementation to frontline managers, but may need to engage in day-to-day HR decision-making to foster, shape and control the discretion of frontline managers.

While the skills of the frontline manager in the implementation process are crucial to the success of initiatives, they may not always possess the necessary implementation abilities (Bos-Nehles et al., 2013). For example, there is evidence that managers are more likely to plan work for others that is poorly rather than well designed, and to blame the worker, rather than the design of the job, for poor performance (Parker et al., 2019). This finding resonates with the earlier Tavistock Institute research, which found that coal mines in which management believed that poor performance was due to workers' failure to follow direction had lower productivity and higher accident rates, compared to coal mines where management trusted workers and respected their advice and input regarding how new technology should work (Pasmore et al., 2019; Trist and Bamforth, 1951). This brings to the fore the central role of frontline managers in the design of work and the management of employee performance.

The original studies of line manager implementation of HR practices were conducted within organizations where most employees were located together. However, a combination of political, cultural and institutional forces, as well as technological advances, together with the necessities of social distancing created by Covid-19, have created a situation where work is no longer bound by time or place. In tandem, the widespread use of personal laptops and mobile phones, and the availability of high-speed broadband connections, have created the technical capacity to underpin a work culture of ever-increasing connectivity and instantaneity (Aroles et al., 2019). These changes have led to the emergence of a wide variety of alternative work arrangements, with increasing flexibility in the employment relationship, in the scheduling of work, and in where work is accomplished (Spreitzer et al., 2017). The next section examines the implications for frontline managers of one aspect of these alternative working arrangements: the shift to remote work.

THE MANAGEMENT OF REMOTE WORK

The literature distinguishes between telecommuters who work at home or another location between one and three days each working week, and remote or virtual workers who rarely or never work within an organizational setting (Eddleston and Mulki, 2017). Virtual work has been viewed as 'any work interaction with others that is not conducted in person (face-to-face) and that uses technology tools to transfer thoughts and ideas' (Makarius and Larson, 2017: 160). A further distinction has also been made between workers who work in the same country as their employer and those who work in another country: the notion of geographic flexibility (Choudhury et al., 2019). While there are a variety of terms to describe this type of work, the distinction between them is one of degree rather than substance. For the sake of clarity, in this chapter we use the term 'remote work' as a hypernym to constitute those who work away from a traditional workplace setting either some or all of the time.

While the notion of remote working is not new, it is important to take account of the large numbers of employees and their managers across the globe who were transformed – willingly or otherwise – into remote workers because of the lockdowns associated with Covid-19. A recent European survey estimates that almost 40 per cent of employees started working remotely in March 2020, with around 60 per cent of employees working from home in Finland, followed by over 50 per cent in Denmark, Belgium and the Netherlands (Eurofound, 2020). However, many of these employees now worked at kitchen tables, rather than office desks, and given the suddenness of lockdown restrictions, there was little time to prepare either employees or their managers to adapt to this mode of working.

In traditional working arrangements, communication is face-to-face and there are opportunities for both the sharing of information and informal interaction between work colleagues and between managers and their staff. While the implementation of HR practices by frontline managers is already complex, even when employees and managers are co-located, this implementation becomes much more complicated where managers and employees interact remotely.

These difficulties are compounded by the fact that managers are dealing with employees not just as virtual workers, but frequently also as members of virtual teams.

Some research suggests that the separation of manager and subordinate decreases the quality of their relationship due to poorer communication (Cummings and Haas, 2012), and in the social and informal interactions that enable the building of rapport and trust (Hinds and Cramton, 2014). For example, problems with trust among workers emerged as an issue for supervisors in a survey of federal employees in the United States (US) (United States Office of Personnel Management, 2019). This rapport and trust seem to be particularly important in regard to the line manager's ability to engage with their subordinates in relation to issues such as performance management and skill development, crucial aspects of the remote implementation of HR practices. Research in the software maintenance centre of a global consulting and technology firm (Bonet and Salvador, 2017) suggests that the potentially negative impact on performance that results from the separation of managers and workers depends on factors such as task complexity, co-location of workers with experienced peers, and manager experience. In some cases, remote supervision was found to lead to superior worker performance, suggesting that a manager's physical presence can exert unnecessary interference on work processes, thereby inhibiting employees from experimenting with new ways of working. This was particularly so when managers were less experienced and therefore less willing to trust employees to undertake responsibility for their own performance. Other research on remote workers points to the fact that perceived supervisor support is positively related to job satisfaction, and negatively related to psychological strain (Bentley et al., 2016). There is also evidence that remote workers are more likely to perform better, to experience less work–family conflict, and to help their colleagues where managers stay in close contact by sharing information, rather than tightly monitoring work schedules (Lautsch et al., 2009).

A review of the literature on remote work (Makarius and Larson, 2017) suggests that there is a range of managerial processes that can support remote workers. These include creating predictable patterns of communication to facilitate interpersonal interactions; clarifying the performance management process; and setting and enforcing the ground rules for using technology, while at the same time allowing for some degree of flexibility. The same review also identified key elements in work design, such as empowering employees and building their psychological control through greater autonomy, as some of the factors that enable successful remote working. The importance of these areas of human resource management (HRM) are also relevant in the management of remote teams. For example, a recent evidence-based analysis of the processes required to build effective remote teams (CIPD, 2020) identified the encouragement of rich media, such as video conferencing, to enhance communication; the synchronizing of work schedules for team members to ensure the overlapping of working hours, leading to communication enhancement; and the sharing of information about issues relevant to specific locations or teams, rather than the wider organization. Most of these activities can be considered as part of the frontline manager's HR portfolio, which is broadly encapsulated under the themes of communications, performance management and the design of work. This suggests that the people management responsibilities of frontline managers are no different in the virtual or physical workplace; however, it is thought that management processes and interactions are required to be much more explicit and deliberate in virtual or remote settings (Geister et al., 2006; Kasper-Fuehrer and Ashkanasy, 2001).

One of the problems that may arise in regard to remote work is the blurring of work and non-work boundaries. The rapid increase in remote working following Covid-19 led to reports of employees increasingly working in their free time, due to problems in balancing caring and housework responsibilities (CIPD, 2020; Eurofound, 2020). Earlier research also identified issues with maintaining work–life balance while working remotely (Felstead and Henseke, 2017). Problems with the intensification of work and with the propensity for remote workers to overwork have also been noted (Eddleston and Mulki, 2017; Felstead and Henseke, 2017; Kelliher and Anderson, 2010). The term 'autonomy paradox' (Mazmanian et al., 2013) has been coined to describe the dilemma of professionals' remote working lives where reliance on mobile devices both increases and diminishes their autonomy. Thus, professionals who manage their work through such devices find that while they provide flexibility and control in the short term, simultaneously they intensify their availability to management, thereby reducing their ability to disconnect from work. Support by frontline managers for employees regarding the management of both work schedules and work/non-work boundaries seems to be particularly critical elements in HR implementation where remote working takes place. There is also evidence to suggest that frontline managers who are more involved in the development of work–life balance policies are more likely to engage with such policies; at the same time, frontline managers can be inconsistent in their enactment of these policies (McCarthy et al., 2010).

For managers who themselves work remotely, evidence from one US study suggests that the work experiences of subordinates regarding feedback, professional development, empowerment and workload are less positive than in traditional working arrangements, which can lead to lower job satisfaction and higher turnover intentions (Golden and Fromen, 2011). There are also deficits reported in the training provided to frontline managers in the management of remote employees, including line managers' ability to manage and assess employees' performance (United States Office of Personnel Management, 2019). The need for frontline managers to develop management styles that both empower employees in self-management and are at the same time supportive, as well as the practicalities of managing virtual teams, appears particularly crucial (Eurofound, 2020). There is also the need for line managers to identify the training required to develop the types of skills that employees need in order to engage in remote work. Table 21.1 provides a summary of the key features of the frontline manager's HR portfolio to support remote working.

THE MANAGEMENT OF EMPLOYEE PERFORMANCE IN THE DIGITAL AGE

The management of employee performance is a long-established, if somewhat flawed, practice in organizations. However, in addition to changes in the location of work, technological advances, particularly the use of algorithms to enable increased electronic monitoring and surveillance (EMS) of employees, can have a major impact on how frontline managers manage employee performance (Bales and Stone, 2020; Holland and Tham, 2020; Leonardi, 2020; Wood et al., 2019). EMS currently takes many forms that include, but are not limited to, the following: video recordings of staff, smart cards, computer logins and activity, email checks, use of company smartphones, Global Positioning System (GPS) tracking of employees in company-owned vehicles, fingerprint and facial scans, and recording of telephone calls and idle time. Recent developments have seen the expansion of EMS to encompass non-performance data that includes health and safety information. This capability has been

Table 21.1　　*The frontline manager's HR portfolio to support remote working*

Elements of HR portfolio	Employee needs	Manager behaviours
Communications	– Predictable/regular patterns of communications to facilitate interaction and information sharing. – Rich media sources for communications. – Sharing of information relevant to their teams.	– Setting and reinforcing the ground rules for new technology, while allowing for some flexibility. – Communicating to workers the importance of managing their work schedules and the boundaries between home and work.
Performance management	– Clear performance management processes, especially for new employees. – Skills development to work remotely (e.g., conflict management skills, self-management skills).	– Empowering leadership styles. – Avoidance of tight performance monitoring, allowing for flexibility and the development of trust.
Work design	– Empowerment through greater autonomy. – Synchronized work schedules.	– Awareness of the pressures inherent in remote work and the need for flexibility to promote employee work–life balance and well-being. – Monitoring of work schedules for employee well-being.

enhanced by the advent of sensor technology embedded in smartphones and what have been described as 'smart wearables' (Bernstein, 2017; European Commission, 2017), which enable the tracking of individuals in real time. EMS can also be used to block employee access to social networking platforms or certain websites, and may be extended to surveillance outside the organization with the accessing of postings on social media sites such as Twitter and Facebook, as well as the monitoring of personal blogs.

The growth in the monitoring and surveillance of employees raises all sorts of ethical issues about how digital data is owned and governed (European Group on Ethics in Science and New Technologies, 2018). Such practices may also be at odds with HR practices that emphasize empowerment, involvement and relationship-building (Jensen and Raver, 2012) and which, with their underpinnings of trust, are at the heart of the frontline manager–employee relationship. There is also the added complexity of the reshaping of public–private boundaries (McDonald and Thompson, 2016) that is incurred as a result of the extension of EMS to the private domain. There is a good deal of research that indicates the negative impact of EMS and how this may affect different types of employees. For example, research based on the Australian workplace survey (Holland and Cooper, 2015) found that in the case of employees engaged in manual work, EMS was negatively related to overall trust in management, and that as the number of EMS practices increased, employees perceived that they had less trust in managers to make competent decisions, and they were more likely to report them as deceptive. However, trust did not emerge as an issue in regard to non-manual employees. This difference was linked to factors such as the number and greater use of EMS practices such as video cameras and electronic tracking in manual work, which are much more overt than the potentially more insidious EMS practices that may be used to monitor clerical work (for example, time and attendance). A study based on a factorial survey that required individuals to react to hypothetical descriptions of situations (Abraham et al., 2019) found that respondents were more likely to accept monitoring if it increased work efficiency and if the coordination of tasks gave rise to greater productivity. However, respondents were more likely to reject these technologies if they were used to monitor health and performance. The focus on metrics that is associated with the growth in EMS also means that line managers' assessment of performance will shift towards a primarily quantitative analysis, and so elements of the manager–employee relationship that are qualitative, such as helping others or informal sharing of knowledge, are eroded from performance evaluation. Indeed, experiments have found that in jobs that require frequent monitoring, leaders prefer to engage with their subordinates via avatars because they feel socially threatened (Raveendhran et al., 2020). Thus, the use of avatars might provide a psychological safety net for managers when interacting with employees, because it reduces their social presence, and this distance protects them against negative evaluation. This could possibly give rise to the increased use of avatars in the management of employees in the future.

In their efforts to create fun working experiences and to enhance employee engagement and well-being, many frontline managers are increasingly engaging in work design principles based on advanced gamified technologies (Mitchell et al., 2020; Robson et al., 2016). Gamification can be described as 'a process of enhancing a service with affordances for gameful experience to support users' overall value creation' (Huotari and Hamari, 2017: 25). Gaming initiatives can include electronic leaderboards, escape rooms, or awarding points for exceeding work targets. While increasingly popular across a range of sectors, relatively little research has considered how gamification has altered the frontline employment experience (Hammedi et al., 2021). It is suggested, for example, that where employees feel coerced by frontline managers to participate, the influence on engagement and well-being can be derailed (e.g., Oppong-Tawiah et al., 2020; Vesa et al., 2017). Recent research by Hammedi et al. (2021) highlights the potential negative impacts of gamified work on employee engagement and well-being, although their findings also suggest that these negative impacts may be reduced when employees are willing to participate. These findings therefore suggest that frontline managers need to consider the implementation of gamified technologies in work designs. In particular, they need to strike a balance between enhancing engagement levels and placing additional pressures on employees. At the same time, frontline managers must ensure that such gamified technologies will fit with the climate of the organization; since their use is intended to create fun and playfulness, established rules will need to be abandoned, and employees will need to be completely willing to participate.

THE AUTOMATION OF LEADERSHIP

The discussion has so far concentrated on the role of frontline managers in managing the interaction between technology, work, structures and people. However, one final scenario requires consideration: the automation of the leadership embedded in the frontline manager role. While such a scenario might once have been dismissed as both impossible and undesirable, advancements in human–computer interaction (HCI) have made this a reality. HCI was originally confined to situations in which computers performed tasks decided by humans. But technological advances have seen computers move from initially subordinate positions as tools, to having more equal roles as partners or teammates and, more recently, to leadership relationships (Chamorro-Premuxic and Ahmetoglu, 2016; de Winter and Hancock, 2015; Höddinghaus et al., 2021; Parry et al., 2016; Wesche and Sonderegger, 2019). Wesche and Sonderegger (2019) label this as computer–human (CH) leadership, defining it as: 'a process whereby purposeful influence is exerted by a computer agent over human agents to guide, structure, and facilitate activities and relationships in a group or organization' (ibid.: 9). The basis for this leadership is algorithmic management: 'a system of control where self-learning algorithms are given the responsibility for making and executing decisions affecting labour, thereby limiting human involvement and ownership of the labour process' (Duggan et al., 2020: 119). The notion of self-learning is particularly crucial: algorithms do not require human intervention. As a result, algorithms increasingly make decisions that have until now been made by line managers or HR specialists. Algorithmic management is at the heart of what is described as 'app-work', a variant of gig work 'wherein the offering of traditional work activities in local markets is conducted through apps, managed by intermediary digital platform organizations, that intervene in setting minimum quality standards of service and in the selection and management of individuals who perform the work' (Duggan et al., 2020: 116). Wesche and Sonderegger (2019) give an example of how Uber Technologies automates leadership functions such as task allocation, shift planning, performance feedback and compensation, and makes decisions that were previously the remit of frontline and middle managers. With further advances in technology expected, Wesche and Sonderegger conceptualize computers taking over many of the leadership functions one hierarchy level higher. Thus, the possibility of computers leading humans without the intervention of human leaders becomes increasingly possible (Ferràs-Hernández, 2018). In addition, it is likely that algorithmic management will extend well beyond app-work. The existence of CH leadership therefore raises questions regarding its advantages and disadvantages, and particularly regarding how different leadership functions might be assigned between human and computer leaders, and the likelihood of acceptance by employees. This assignment of leadership functions regarding HR practices is particularly complex as HR implementation requires an underpinning of trust. All these factors have significant implications for frontline managers as well as their subordinates, in addition to ethical implications (European Group on Ethics in Science and New Technologies, 2018).

THE FUTURE OF WORK FOR FRONTLINE MANAGERS

The issues identified above indicate the possibility for several tensions between employee performance and well-being regarding the management of work and workers in the future. At a strategic level, there is a growing body of research signalling the important role that employee attributions about management's strategic intentions can have in shaping employee and organizational outcomes. These attributions reflect what employees think the organization's motives are for particular practices (Nishii et al., 2008). For example, employees may consider external attributions (for example, the organization is adopting a practice to comply with legislation), or internal attributions (for example, the practice is in place to protect employee well-being). These attributions have been associated with important outcomes such as organizational citizenship behaviour (OCB) (Nishii et al., 2008), commitment, job strain and emotional exhaustion (Shantz et al., 2016; Van de Voorde and Beijer, 2015), turnover intentions and task performance (Chen and Wang, 2014). These studies show that 'employee-centred' attributions are associated with desirable outcomes, while performance- or control-centred attributions are generally related to undesirable outcomes (Hewett et al., 2018). Recent research by Beijer et al. (2019) highlights the key role that frontline managers can play in shaping employees' attributions, and the role that employees play in reinforcing those attributions among each other. This highlights a need for clarity about both the intentions of HR practices and the types of behaviours that are valued and rewarded to be clearly communicated from the senior-level managers to the frontline managers to ensure that there are no implementation gaps.

One of the fallouts of Covid-19 may be an increase in disengagement among employees who become more detached from their organizations. Frontline managers will therefore need to be more 'hands-on' in managing the employment relationship, possibly placing additional pressures on their own time. This may give rise to some of the tensions that were apparent with the growth of strategic HRM in the 1980s, where there was resistance from frontline managers to taking on greater management responsibilities (McGovern et al., 1997). Given recent reports of the negative impacts of remote working on employee well-being (CIPD, 2020; Eurofound, 2020), a renewed focus on work–life balance will be crucial in maintaining a healthy employment relationship. This will require redoubling efforts to maximize supports available to employees; that is, those from the organization, from frontline managers and from colleagues. These forms of 'social' support, in addition to practical supports, will therefore be critical in engaging workers in the future. Recent research points to the increased use of social media platforms by employees to voice dissatisfaction with aspects of their working lives (Conway et al., 2019). This study noted the high incidence of individuals tweeting about the behaviour of their immediate managers, which raises issues about their ability to voice this dissatisfaction directly with their line manager within the confines of the organization, rather than feeling that the only forum available to them is the public domain. At a practical level, while remote working is a completely new phenomenon for many organizations, there is already an established body of knowledge on the topic which can help organizations to navigate this new terrain. There are also lessons to be learned from the many organizations already 'ahead of the curve' regarding remote working, particularly in the global tech sector (for example, Microsoft, Twitter and Facebook).

Finally, an important question regarding the future of work concerns the types of competencies that frontline managers will need in the future. One study of managers (Kolbjørnsrud et al., 2016) noted that skills regarded as particularly important were focused on digital and technology, creative thinking and experimentation, data analysis and interpretation, strategy development and planning, and administration. This was followed by a focus on people management skills including social networking, people development and coaching, and collaborating. This primary focus on technical and strategic capabilities rather than on people management skills resonates with some of the tensions inherent in models of strategic HRM regarding whether the focus should be on the pursuit of strategic goals or on becoming an 'employee champion' (Ulrich and Brockbank, 2005). Other research by Kane et al. (2019) suggests that the most important requirements for managers in the future will be to have a transformative vision, a forward-looking perspective (that is, knowledge of how technology is transforming the business), and to be change-oriented. While frontline managers will not need to engage in high-level data analytics, they will play a key role in providing data about people management initiatives and activities that demonstrate their value to the organization. They will also play an important role in supporting employees to engage with new technology in their work.

CONCLUSIONS

This chapter has considered some of the changes that are taking place in the world of work, and their implications for the role of the line manager in HR implementation. We situated our analysis within the notion of organizations as organisms (Morgan, 1997), focusing on the relationship between the social and the technical, in examining the impact of new technologies, as well as considering the environmental impact of Covid-19 from a systems persepective. The analysis suggests that HR functions may need to rebalance their HR activities and to rethink the ways in which frontline managers might be enabled to enact HR policies and practices to support employees engaged in the new working arrangements that have emerged. Training and development appear key in this regard. For example, work design, traditionally a neglected aspect of HRM, is a critical feature of new working arrangements, but there is evidence that frontline managers lack skills in work planning and design (Parker et al., 2019). Similarly, the management of employee performance is frequently difficult even in face-to face situations, but these difficulties become exacerbated in virtual environments. It is also evident that there are options for organizations and line managers in how technologies might be used. Underpinning their use will be the competencies of frontline managers themselves, and their ability to adapt to these technologies. However, even greater challenges may by posed by the ongoing impact of Covid-19, as frontline managers grapple with not just new working arrangements, but possibly also an economic recession and a reduced workforce that may bedevil their organizations for the foreseeable future.

REFERENCES

Abraham, M., Neissen, C., Schnabel, C., Lorek, K., Grimm, V., et al. (2019). Electronic monitoring at work: the role of attitudes, functions and perceived control for the acceptance of tracking technologies. *Human Resource Management Journal*, 29: 657–675.

Aroles, J., Mitev, N. and de Vaujany, F-X. (2019). Mapping themes in the study of new work practices. *New Technology, Work and Employment*, 34(3): 285–299.

Autor, D.H. (2015). Why are there still so many jobs? The history and future of workplace automation. *Journal of Economic Perspectives*, 29(3): 3–30.

Bales, R. and Stone, K. (2020). The invisible web at work: artificial intelligence and electronic surveillance in the workplace. *Berkley Journal of Employment and Labor Law*, 41(1): 1–62.

Beijer, S., Van De Voorde, K. and Tims, M. (2019). An interpersonal perspective on HR attributions: examining the role of line managers, coworkers, and similarity in work-related matters. *Frontiers in Psychology*, 10: 1–10.

Bentley, T.A., McLeod, L., Tan, F., Bosua, R. and Gloet, M. (2016). The role of organizational support in teleworker wellbeing: a socio-technical systems approach. *Applied Ergonomics*, 52: 207–215.

Bernstein, E.S. (2017). Making transparency transparent. The evolution of observation in management theory. *Academy of Management Annals*, 11: 217–266.

Bonet, R. and Salvador, F. (2017). When the boss is away: manager–worker separation and worker performance in a multisite software maintenance operation. *Organization Science*, 28(2): 244–261.

Bos-Nehles, A.C., Van Riemsdijk, M.J. and Kees Looise, J. (2013). Employee perceptions of line management performance: applying the AMO theory to explain the effectiveness of line managers' HRM implementation. *Human Resource Management*, 52(6): 861–877.

Chamorro-Premuzic, T. and Ahmetoglu, G. (2016). The pros and cons of robot managers. *Harvard Business Review*, December 12.

Chen, D. and Wang, Z. (2014). The effects of human resource attributions on employee outcomes during organizational change. *Social Behavior and Personality,* 42(9): 1431–1444.

Choudhury, P., Foroughi, C. and Larson, B. (2019). Work-from-anywhere. The productivity effects of geographic flexibility. Working Paper 19-054, Harvard Business School.

CIPD (2020). *Developing Effective Virtual Teams: Lessons from Research*. London: CIPD.

Conway, E., Rosati, P., Monks, K. and Lynn, T. (2019). Voicing job satisfaction and dissatisfaction through Twitter: employees' use of cyberspace. *New Technology, Work and Employment*, 34(2), 139–156.

Cummings, J.N. and Haas, M.R. (2012). So many teams, so little time: time allocation matters in geographically dispersed teams. *Journal of Organizational Behavior*, 33(3): 316–341.

de Winter, J.C.F. and Hancock, P.A. (2015). Reflections on the 1951 Fitts lists: do humans believe now that machines surpass them? *Procedia Manufacturing*, 3: 5334–5341.

Duggan, J., Sherman, U., Carbery, R. and McDonnell, A. (2020). Algorithmic management and app-work in the gig economy: a research agenda for employment relations and HRM. *Human Resource Management Journal*, 30: 114–132.

Eddleston, K. and Mulki, J. (2017). Towards understanding remote workers' management of work–family arrangements: the complexity of work embeddedness. *Group and Organization Management*, 42(3): 346–387.

Eurofound (2020). *Telework and ICT-Based Mobile Work: Flexible Working in the Digital Age*. New Forms of Employment Series. Luxembourg: Publications Office of the European Union.

European Commission (2017). *Smart Wearables: Reflection and Orientation Paper*. European Commission, Directorate-General for Communications Networks, Content and Technology. Luxembourg: Publications Office of the European Union.

European Group on Ethics in Science and New Technologies (2018). *Future of Work, Future of Society*. Luxembourg: Publications Office of the European Union.

Felstead, A. and Henseke, G. (2017). Assessing the growth of remote work and its consequences for effort, well-being and work–life balance. *New Technology, Work and Employment*, 32(3): 195–212.

Ferràs-Hernández, X. (2018). The future of management in a world of electronic brains. *Journal of Management Inquiry*, 27: 260–263.

Geister, A., Konradt, U. and Hertel, G. (2006). Effects of process feedback on motivation, satisfaction, and performance in virtual teams. *Small Group Research*, 37(5): 459–489.

Global Commission on the Future of Work (2019). *Work for a Brighter Future*. Geneva: International Labour Office.

Golden, T. and Fromen, A. (2011). Does it matter where your manager works? Comparing managerial work mode (traditional, telework and virtual) across subordinate work experiences and outcomes. *Human Relations*, 64(11): 1451–1475.

Guest, D.E. and Bos-Nehles, A.C. (2013). HRM and performance: the role of effective implementation. In D.E. Guest, J. Paauwe and P. Wright (eds), *HRM and Performance: Achievements and Challenges* (pp. 79–96). Chichester: Wiley-Blackwell.

Hammedi, W., Leclercqb, T., Poncind, I. and Alkire, L. (2021). Uncovering the dark side of gamification at work: Impacts on engagement and well-being. *Journal of Business Research*, 122: 252–269.

Hewett, B., Shantz, A., Mundy, J. and Alfes, K. (2018). Attribution theories in human resource management research: a review and research agenda. *International Journal of Human Resource Management*, 29(1): 87–126.

Hinds, P.J. and Cramton, C.D. (2014). Situated co-worker familiarity: how site visits transform relationships among distributed workers. *Organization Science*, 25(3): 794–814.

Höddinghaus, M., Sondern, D. and Hertel, G. (2021). The automation of leadership functions: would people trust decision algorithms? *Computers in Human Behavior*. https://doi.org/10.1016/j.chb.2020.106635

Holland, P. and Cooper, B. (2015). Electronic monitoring and surveillance in the workplace. *Personnel Review*, 44(1): 161–175.

Holland, P. and Tham, T. (2020). Total surveillance: electric monitoring and surveillance in the 21st century. In P. Holland and C. Brewster (eds), *Contemporary work and the Future of Employment in Developed Countries* (pp. 135–150). London: Routledge.

Huotari, K. and Hamari, J. (2017). A definition for gamification: anchoring gamification in the service marketing literature. *Electronic Markets*, 27: 21–31.

Jaharri, H.H. (2018). Artificial intelligence and the future of work: human: AI symbiosis in organizational decision-making. *Business Horizons*, 61(4): 577–586.

Jensen, J. and Raver, J. (2012). When self-management and surveillance collide: consequences for employees' organizational citizenship and counterproductive work behaviors, *Group and Organization Management*, 37: 308–346.

Kane, G.C., Palmer, D., Phillips, A.N., Kiron, D. and Buckley, N. (2019). Accelerating digital innovation inside and out: agile teams, ecosystems, and ethics: findings from the 2019 digital business global executive study and research project. *MIT Sloan Management Review*, 4 June.

Kaplan, J. (2015). *Humans Need Not Apply: A Guide to Wealth and Work in the Age of Artificial Intelligence*. New Haven, CT: Yale University Press.

Kasper-Fuehrer, E. and Ashkanasy, N.M. (2006). Communicating trustworthiness and building trust in interorganizational virtual organizations. *Journal of Management*, 27(3): 235–254.

Kehoe, R.R. and Han, J.H. (2019). An expanded conceptualization of the line manager's involvement in human resource management. *Journal of Applied Psychology*, 105(2): 111–129.

Kelliher, C. and Anderson, D. (2010). Doing more with less? Flexible working practices and the intensification of work. *Human Relations*, 63(1): 83–106.

Kolbjørnsrud, V., Amico, R. and Thomas, R.J. (2016). How artificial intelligence will redefine management. *Harvard Business Review*, 2 November: 1–6.

Kuvaas, B., Dysvik, A. and Buch, R. (2014). Antecedents and employee outcomes of line managers' perceptions of enabling HR practices. *Journal of Management Studies*, 51: 845–868.

Lautsch, B., Kossek, E. and Eaton, S. (2009). Supervisory approaches and paradoxes in managing telecommuting implementation. *Human Relations*, 62(6): 795–827.

Leonardi, P. (2020). Covid-19 and the new technologies of organizing: digital exhaust, digital footprints and artificial intelligence in the wake or remote work. *Journal of Management Studies*. doi:10.1111/joms.12648.

López-Cotarelo, J. (2018). Line managers and HRM: a managerial discretion perspective. *Human Resource Management Journal*, 28: 255–271.

Lupushor, S. and Fradera, A. (2017). The future of work. In G. Herrel, D. Stone, R. Johnson and J. Passmore (eds), *The Wiley Blackwell Handbook of the Psychology of the Internet at Work* (pp. 481–506). Chichester: John Wiley & Sons.

Makarius, E. and Larson, B. (2017). Changing the perspective of virtual work: building virtual intelligence at the individual level. *Academy of Management Perspectives*, 31(2): 159–178.

Mazmanian, M., Orlikowski, W. and Yates, J. (2013). The autonomy paradox: the implications of mobile email devices for knowledge professionals. *Organization Science*, 24(5): 1337–1357.

McCarthy, A., Darcy, C. and Grady, G. (2010). Work–life balance policy and practice: understanding line manager attitudes and behaviours. *Human Resource Management Review*, 20: 158–167.

McDonald, P. and Thompson, P. (2016). Social media(tion) and the reshaping of public/private boundaries in employment relations. *International Journal of Management Reviews*, 18: 69–84.

McGovern, P., Gratton, L., Hope-Hailey, V., Stiles, P. and Truss, C. (1997). Human resource management on the line? *Human Resource Management Journal*, 7(4): 12–29.

Mitchell, R., Schuster, L. and Jin, H.S. (2020). Gamification and the impact of extrinsic motivation on needs satisfaction: making work fun? *Journal of Business Research*, 106: 323–330.

Mokyr, J., Vickers, C. and Ziebarth, N.L. (2015). The history of technological anxiety and the future of economic growth: is this time different? *Journal of Economic Perspectives*, 29(3): 31–50.

Morgan, G. (1997). *Images of Organization*, 2nd edition. London: SAGE Publications.

Nishii, L.H., Lepak, D.P. and Schneider, B. (2008). Employee attributions of the 'why' of HR practices: their effects on employee attitudes and behaviors, and customer satisfaction. *Personnel Psychology*, 61(3): 503–545.

OECD (2019). *OECD Employment Outlook 2019: The Future of Work*. Paris: OECD Publishing. https://doi.org/10.1787/9ee00155-en. Accessed 15 May 2020.

Oppong-Tawiah, D., Webster, J., Staples, S., Cameron, A.F., Ortiz de Guinea, A. and Hung, T.Y. (2020). Developing a gamified mobile application to encourage sustainable energy use in the office. *Journal of Business Research*, 106: 388–405.

Parker, S.K., Andrei, D.M. and Van den Broeck, A. (2019). Poor work design begets poor work design: capacity and willingness antecedents of individual work design behavior. *Journal of Applied Psychology*, 104(7): 907–928.

Parry, K., Cohen, M. and Bhattarcharya, S. (2016). Rise of the machines: a critical consideration of automated decision making in organizations. *Group and Organization Management*, 42: 571–594.

Pasmore, W., Winby, S., Albers Mohrman, S. and Vanasse, R. (2019). Reflections: sociotechnical systems design and organization change. *Journal of Change Management*, 19(2): 67–85.

Petterson, L. (2019). Why artificial intelligence will not outsmart complex knowledge work. *Work, Employment and Society*, 33(6): 1058–1067.

Raveendhran R., Fast, N.J. and Carnevale, P.J. (2020). Virtual (freedom from) reality: evaluation apprehension and leaders' preference for communicating through avatars. *Computers in Human Behavior*. doi: https://doi.org/10.1016/j.chb.2020.106415.

Robson, K., Plangger, K., Kietzmann, J.H., McCarthy, I. and Pitt, L. (2016). *Business Horizons*, 59(1): 29–36.

Samani, H.A., Koh, J.T., Saadatian, E. and Polydorou, D. (2012). Towards robotics leadership: an analysis of leadership characteristics and the roles robots will inherit in future human society. In J.S. Pan, S.M. Chen and N.T. Nguyen (eds), *ACIIDS 2012 Part II, LNAI 7197* (pp. 158–165). Berlin: Springer-Verlag.

Servoz, M. (2019). *AI The Future of Work? The Work of the Future!* EU Commission. https://ec.europa.eu/digital-single-market/en/news/future-work-work-future. Accessed 15 May 2020.

Shantz, A., Arevshatian, L., Alfes, K. and Bailey, C. (2016). The effect of HRM attributions on emotional exhaustion and the mediating roles of job involvement and work overload. *Human Resource Management Journal*, 26(2): 172–191.

Shestakofsky, B. (2017). Working algorithms: software automation and the future of work. *Work and Occupations*, 44(4): 376–423.

Spencer, D. (2018). Fear and hope in an age of mass automation: debating the future of work. *New Technology, Work and Employment*, 33(1): 1–12.

Spreitzer, G., Cameron, L. and Garrett, L. (2017). Alternative work arrangements: two images of the world of work. *Annual Review of Organizational Psychology and Organizational Behavior*, 4: 473–499.

Trist, E.L., and Bamforth, K.W. (1951). Some social and psychological consequences of the longwall method of coal-getting. *Human Relations* 4(1): 3–38.

Trullen, J., Bos-Nehles, A. and Valverde, M. (2020). From intended to actual and beyond: a cross-disciplinary view of human resource management implementation. *International Journal of Management Reviews*, 1–27. DOI: 10.1111/ijmr.12220.

United States Office of Personnel Management (2019). Status of telework in the federal government. Report to Congress. https://www.telework.gov/reports-studies/reports-to-congress/2018-report-to-congress.pdf. Accessed 22 May 2020.

Van de Voorde, K. and Beijer, S. (2015). The role of employee HR attributions in the relationship between high-performance work systems and employee outcomes. *Human Resource Management Journal*, 25(1): 62–78.

Vesa, M., Hamari, J., Harviainen, J.T. and Warmelink, H.J.G. (2017). Computer games and organization studies. *Organization Studies*, 38(2): 273–284.

Ulrich, D. and Brockbank, W. (2005). *The HR Value Proposition*. Boston, MA: Harvard Business School Press.

Wesche, J. and Sonderegger, A. (2019). When computers take the lead: the automation of leadership. *Computers in Human Behavior*, 101: 197–209.

Wood, A., Graham, M. and Lehdonvirta, V. (2019). Good gig, bad gig: autonomy and algorithmic control in the gig economy. *Work, Employment and Society*, 33(1): 56–75.

Wright, P.M. and Nishii, L.H. (2013). Strategic HRM and organizational behaviour: integrating multiple levels of analysis. In J. Paauwe, D. Guest and P. Wright (eds), *HRM and Performance: Achievements and Challenges* (pp. 97–110). Chichester: Wiley.

22. The role of line managers in the implementation of digitalization

Violetta Khoreva, Anna Bos-Nehles and Sari Salojärvi

INTRODUCTION

Digitalization has been identified as one of the major trends influencing businesses due to the changes associated with the application of digital technologies (Faraj et al., 2018; Raisch and Krakowski, 2021; Ross et al., 2019; Zuboff, 2019). Countries that are at an advanced stage of digitalization gain 20 per cent more economic growth compared to countries that are in the initial stage of implementation (Sabbagh et al., 2012). This is because digitalization allows organizations to operate more efficiently (Parviainen et al., 2017; Raisch and Krakowski, 2021; Ross et al., 2019). Referring to the adoption of digital technologies by organizations, digitalization evidently impacts upon every industry and organization (World Economic Forum, 2019). At the same time, digitalization is considered as a disruptive process that generates uncertainty and difficulties for many organizational members, since it changes the way of working and organizational members' roles (Bondarouk et al., 2019).

Digitalization can be understood as a socio-technical phenomenon. It is a process of adopting and using the technologies in a broader individual, organizational and societal context (Legner et al., 2017). The implementation of digitalization has implications for the entire organization, especially the users of technology who need to change their habits and ways of working to be more collaborative and interactive (Henriette et al., 2015). Many implementation processes of digitalization fail at this hurdle since organizations are reluctant to change mindsets and processes or to build a culture that fosters change.

The implementation process of digitalization is not a 'one-time' exercise as organizational members perceive and interpret digital technologies, and make sense of it (Parviainen et al., 2017). During the implementation process, organizational members respond to the constraints of the technology and, thus, socially construct it through usage (Klein and Kleinman, 2002; Leonardi and Barley, 2010). Hence, the implementation process requires continuous adaptation and reorganization to meet the changing demands of the business and its users (Parviainen et al., 2017). These ongoing adjustments may extend well beyond the initial implementation strategy (Robertson et al., 2012).

In this study, we thus take a process approach, often applied in innovation processes (Klein and Sorra, 1996; Real and Poole, 2005), in which the implementation of digitalization is perceived as a process that starts with the adoption and ends with routinization (Trullen et al., 2020). In line with the process approach, the implementation of digitalization begins when organizational decision-makers have started to digitalize the business, and ends only when digital usage has become the new routine and is no longer novel.

Although the decision to implement digitalization is commonly reached by senior organizational members, we know from various literature streams that the responsibility for implementation of any kind lies in the hands of line managers, that is, the people representing the level of management to whom non-managerial employees report (Bos-Nehles et al., 2020; Hales, 2005). This is because line managers need to implement the changes at the operational level by translating policy into daily practice (Bos-Nehles et al., 2013; Hasson et al., 2014; Townsend and Dundon, 2015). Thus, it is line managers who are largely responsible for the process in day-to-day business (Bondarouk et al., 2019; Bondarouk and Brewster, 2016).

We also know that failed implementation of any kind is often associated with failed management of the implementation, and that line managers are often regarded as incompetent, ill-prepared and unwilling to implement changes in the organization (Bos-Nehles et al., 2013; Govindarajan and Immelt, 2019). Ultimately, it is the line managers who need to change their habits and ways of working for greater collaboration and more interaction (Bondarouk et al., 2019; Henriette et al., 2015).

Against this backdrop, the overall objective of the study is to explore the implementation process of digitalization in organizations and distinguish the role of line managers in the process. In other words, we investigate what happens in between digitalization implementation and social construction (Klein and Kleinman, 2002; Leonardi and Barley, 2010). Our study contributes to the existing research in the fields of organizational studies, human resources management (HRM), and technology in two ways. First, by socially constructing the implementation process of digitalization and breaking it down into phases, we thoroughly elucidate every phase of the implementation process, and define what modifications and adaptations are needed to implement the process effectively. Second, by emphasizing line managers' roles in each phase of the implementation process, we advance scholarly discovery of their function in the process.

In line with these contributions, our study also delivers several managerial implications. First, by portraying different phases of the process, we recommend what organizations need to do in order to proceed to the next stage. Second, by outlining the line managers' role in every phase, we recommend to organizations what line managers need to do to implement the process successfully, and what is needed from line managers to encourage others to accept the process and execute it in daily operations.

THEORETICAL BACKGROUND

The Implementation Process of Digitalization

The implementation process of digitalization in organizations is 'the process of gaining targeted employees' appropriate, committed, and skillful use' of digital tools (Klein and Sorra, 1996: 1057). It is the process by which organizations adopt new digital technologies and streamline processes, improve existing services, dismantle useless practices, and offer new services (Parviainen et al., 2017). This process causes changing organizational roles and impacts upon the type of work offered to the entire workforce (Parviainen et al., 2017).

Many organizations face immense challenges in implementing digitalization (Sjödin et al., 2018), and underestimate its impact on organizations and people dynamics (Kohnke, 2017). The implementation process requires ongoing adjustments; it may extend well beyond the initial implementation of specific digital technologies (Robertson et al., 2012; Hasson et al., 2014; Trullen et al., 2020). It involves implementing digital capabilities that influence the entire organization, including operational processes, resources, as well as internal and external users (Henriette et al., 2015; Rogers, 2016). It also incorporates a major change in habits and ways of working based on collaboration and intensive interactions.

Social Construction of the Implementation Process of Digitalization

Applying social constructivism lenses, we see the implementation process of digitalization as an ongoing process with no clear beginning or end, or time and place boundaries, emerging and in the course of becoming rather than already achieved. The process is an open and dynamic concept that mirrors an ongoing course, where organizational members socially construct the implementation process of digitalization by continuously adopting and streamlining it to meet the changing demands of the business environment. Social construction of the process is about implementing and validating the actions defined in the roadmap. During the process, organizational members respond to the constraints of the technology and thus socially construct it through usage (Klein and Kleinman, 2002; Leonardi and Barley, 2010). Consequentially, organizational members make sense of the process by treating it as a course of shaping, reshaping, modifying and adapting digital technologies.

The Role of Line Managers in the Implementation Process of Digitalization

In the implementation process of digitalization, data are being centralized in one place instead of spreading throughout the organization. Data centralization makes it easier for employees to work on information-intensive projects and improves cost-efficiency (Parviainen et al., 2017). Furthermore, data centralization provides line managers with more information on the course of the organization, and illustrates which employees are doing well (Parviainen et al., 2017). Data are more accessible and line managers can employ more standardized models in managing their subordinates (Markovitch and Wilmott, 2014). Hence, line managers can address problems before they become critical (Markovitch and Willmott, 2014).

Digitalization generates a less hierarchical structure, as employees do not need to contact their managers for specific information. The growth in data accessibility and internal networks results in employees having to take fewer steps up the hierarchical ladder to acquire the necessary information. So, digitalization flattens organizational structure, which in turn enhances organizational flexibility and operational excellence (Ross et al., 2019; Schwarzmüller et al., 2018).

The digitalization literature posits that the implementation process of digitalization requires a strong leadership role, especially from senior and top managers, since these actors need to develop a vision and strategy on digitalization and a roadmap for digital transformation (Fitzgerald et al., 2014; Petry, 2018; Westerman et al., 2014). However, we argue that developing a vision and roadmap is not sufficient for implementing digitalization in an organization. To accept digitalization at the operational level and to change working behaviours and attitudes in a way that leads to the routinization of digitalization, organizations need the full support of line managers. Indeed, it is the line managers who are responsible for, for example, recruiting and empowering employees with digital competences, providing autonomy and flexibility for members of their teams, and developing capabilities to manage the implementation process (Sjödin et al., 2018). We also know from other research streams that line managers play a crucial role in the implementation of new policies or practices, since they are responsible for executing digital practices at the operational level, managing and developing the digital abilities, and motivating employees for whom they are responsible (Bos-Nehles et al., 2013, 2020; Trullen et al., 2020).

Notwithstanding the importance of line managers, to the best of our knowledge none of the studies have explored the role of line managers in the implementation process of digitalization. We believe that this is a serious omission, since as Hales (2006: 34) noted, line managers' duties are often 'undertaken in circumstances of considerable ambiguity: being accountable for operational effectiveness but having limited authority or influence over the "system" decisions that could determine effectiveness'. We thus anticipate that the role of line managers in the process entails their ability to create a clear and meaningful implementation vision for employees, and their capability to execute actualization strategies. Furthermore, we expect that line managers' role in the implementation process involves their ability to engage all organizational members in the course of action. However, we have no clear prescription here. Hence, the next step is to explore empirically the implementation process in organizations, and to distinguish the role of line managers in it.

METHODS

Given that the study explores an emerging field of practice, an explorative, inductive, qualitative research design was adopted for its flexibility and ability to capture in-depth and nuanced data on context, meanings, processes and effects (Langley, 1999). The data collection method was in-depth semi-structured interviews to capture both the opinions and the experiences of participants (Zalan and Lewis, 2004), and thereby gain a broader understanding of the implementation process of digitalization in organizations and the role of line managers in it through the meanings adopted and generic themes involved.

Research Setting

In inductive exploration, the research setting is selected for its ability to reveal observable phenomena that generate novel theoretical insights (Eisenhardt and Graebner, 2007). The context and sample facilitate the generation of new theoretical insights and causal mechanisms (Corley and Gioia, 2011; Langley, 1999). Since our aim was to examine the role of line managers in the implementation process of digitalization, we used a process approach to develop theory on the implementation process and line managers' role therein. Consequently, we sought a context that would allow us to reveal observable phenomena that generate novel theoretical insights.

We considered the Finnish context suitable for our study, since its line managers are likely to be among the first to face the influence of digitalization. Finland ranks second out of the 27 EU Member States in the European Commission's 2021 edition of the Digital Economy and Society Index (DESI, 2021). Finland continues to lead in human capital, integration of digital technology and digital public services, improving its scores in several DESI dimensions (DESI, 2021). Furthermore, according to the latest Digibarometer (2020), Finland ranks second in international comparison of the use of digitalization. Finally, a world-class cluster of machinery companies, such as Kone, Metso, Valmet and Wärtsilä, combined with a high concentration of information and communication technoloy (ICT) professionals, has enabled Finland to become a pioneer in digitalization. Hence, we collected our data in Finland among Nordic multinational enterprises (MNEs) with diverse characteristics in terms of sector, size and number of countries of operation. Our sample organizations included 32 Finnish MNEs, two Swedish, one Danish, and one Norwegian (see Table 22.1). All organizations were in the process of digitalizing business processes. Since we wanted to understand the implementation process of digitalization, we did not select organizations with specific types or advancement levels of digitalization, but included all organizations who were in the process of digitalizing.

Data Collection and Sample

In total, we conducted 36 interviews with leadership professionals who had many years of experience in human resources (HR), each of whom was responsible for human resources in their organizations. The anonymity of the interviewees and their organizations was guaranteed, and the interviews were conducted using a semi-structured interview guideline, which included the following topics: digitalization and the process of its implementation (understanding what digitalization meant for the interviewees, and understanding at what phase of the implementation process of digitalization the organization was), and line management and digitalization (understanding the role of line managers in the process).

Following Welch and Piekkari (2006), the interviews were matched to the respondents' preferred language. Hence, 30 interviews were conducted in Finnish, four in Swedish, and two in English. This yielded richer and more accurate data than if we had used only English, and helped to build even better rapport and maximize authenticity. In order to make the data readily accessible to the whole research team, the Finnish and Swedish interviews were translated into English by the interviewer, an academically highly qualified native speaker of the respective languages using English as her working language (see Harzing et al., 2011 for a similar procedure).

The interviews lasted from 50 to 70 minutes and were all conducted in person in 32 headquarters and four subsidiaries of Nordic MNEs, producing 38 hours of conversation in total. We made certain that the respondents were aware of the study's organizational focus, otherwise personal views could permeate (and bias) the interviews.

Data Analysis

Following the ideas of the process approach, we developed an integrated set of concepts that provides a thorough theoretical explanation of the social phenomena in this study. Since the process approach emphasizes the process of change, it suggests breaking a phenomenon down into stages. As such, our data analysis was divided into stages that overlapped and intertwined with each other in a recursive process. During the open coding process, we developed concepts of the implementation process of digitalization by analytically breaking down the data in the interpretative process. These concepts were given conceptual labels. In the first stage, we explored what the sample organizations did when faced with digitalization for the first time, when a disruption (that is, digitalization) was first noticed and enacted as an issue. In the second stage, we investigated the process that the sample organizations adopted to make sense of and transform their actions in line with the implementation of digitalization. Here, we followed Langley's (1999) inductive theorizing methods to analyse the data, and gradually identified distinctive features of every phase of the process. Coding at this stage was based on the respondents' own words and descriptions, used where possible to code distinctive features of every implementation phase. In the final stage, codes and themes were further examined,

Table 22.1   Overview of sample organizations and respondents

Sector	Origin	Number of employees	Number of countries of operation	Position/title	Phase of the implementation process of digitalization
Construction	Swedish	16 000	11	Senior Vice President, HR and Communications	Resistance
Financial Services	Finnish	249	4	Head of HR and Legal Affairs	Resistance
Manufacturing and Engineering	Finnish	24 455	35	Talent Lead	Resistance
Manufacturing and Engineering	Finnish	11 552	4	Vice President, HR	Resistance
Retail and Consumer Goods	Finnish	4 790	60	Head of People and Culture	Resistance
Information Technology (IT), Electronics and Telecommunications	Finnish	24 000	20	Executive Vice President, HR	Experimentation
Manufacturing and Engineering	Finnish	55 075	60	Head of Competence Management	Experimentation
Manufacturing and Engineering	Finnish	13 600	30	Senior Vice President, HR	Experimentation
Manufacturing and Engineering	Finnish	15 000	100	Vice President, Talent and Management	Experimentation
Pharmaceuticals	Finnish	3 446	12	Vice President, HR	Experimentation
Business Services	Finnish	2 100	6	Senior Vice President, HR	Conviction
Construction	Finnish	2 583	45	Senior Vice President, HR	Conviction
Construction	Swedish	33 585	17	Executive Vice President, HR	Conviction
Extractive	Finnish	4 400	14	Director, HR Development	Conviction
Manufacturing and Engineering	Finnish	18 700	12	Vice President, HR	Conviction
Manufacturing and Engineering	Finnish	17 076	30	Senior Vice President, HR	Conviction
Retail and Consumer Goods	Finnish	9 734	5	Talent Lead	Conviction
Retail and Consumer Goods	Finnish	24 000	5	TM Lead	Conviction
Retail and Consumer Goods	Finnish	7 304	30	Director, People, Processes and Culture	Conviction
Transport	Finnish	6 788	127	Senior Vice President, HR	Conviction
Business Services	Finnish	2 250	4	People and Culture Manager	Reorganization
Extractive	Finnish	8 191	15	Senior Vice President, HR	Reorganization
Financial Services	Finnish	12 269	16	Leadership Development Manager	Reorganization
Infrastructure and Utilities	Finnish	7 500	4	Talent Lead	Reorganization
IT, Electronics and Telecommunications	Finnish	750	20	Senior Vice President, HR	Reorganization

Sector	Origin	Number of employees	Number of countries of operation	Position/title	Phase of the implementation process of digitalization
Manufacturing and Engineering	Finnish	4 018	26	Head of Talent Management	Reorganization
Retail and Consumer Goods	Finnish	2 473	11	Senior Vice President, HR Development	Reorganization
Financial Services	Danish	20 683	16	Leadership Development Director	Routinization
IT, Electronics and Telecommunications	Finnish	5 097	4	Executive Vice President, HR	Routinization
Manufacturing and Engineering	Finnish	18 000	70	Executive Vice President, HR	Routinization
Manufacturing and Engineering	Finnish	3 380	4	Senior Vice President, HR and Communication	Routinization
Manufacturing and Engineering	Finnish	4 881	45	Vice President, HR	Routinization
Retail and Consumer Goods	Finnish	22 476	8	Director, Talent and Organizational Development	Routinization
Retail and Consumer Goods	Finnish	13 242	9	Head of People Development and Wellbeing	Routinization
Retail and Consumer Goods	Norwegian	12 883	50	Vice President, HR	Routinization
Retail and Consumer Goods	Finnish	3 491	24	Senior Vice President, HR	Routinization

and we sought to infer from our data the distinctive roles of line managers in each phase of the process. This stage involved an iterative process of comparing and contradicting the codes and themes, relating them back to the interview transcripts and the study's conceptualization of the process and line managers' role therein.

RESULTS

In line with our analysis, we were able to identify five phases of the digital implementation process: resistance (five organizations), experimentation (five organizations), conviction (ten organizations), reorganization (seven organizations) and routinization (nine organizations) (Figure 22.1). As presented in Table 22.1, we could not identify sectors or industries that were more advanced in the implementation process, and thus need to conclude that the implementation process of digitalization does not depend on the sector or industry of an organization. However, we distinguished particular roles of line managers for each of these phases: outside observer, playmate, ambassador, inspirator and conductor. Line managers play a different role in each of these phases, and thus are in a position to help or hinder the digitalization process. The further organizations move along the implementation process, the more supporting and involved line managers are in the digitalization. In the following section, we unpack these phases and roles. The examples of interviewees' expressions related to the phases and roles are reflected in Table 22.2.

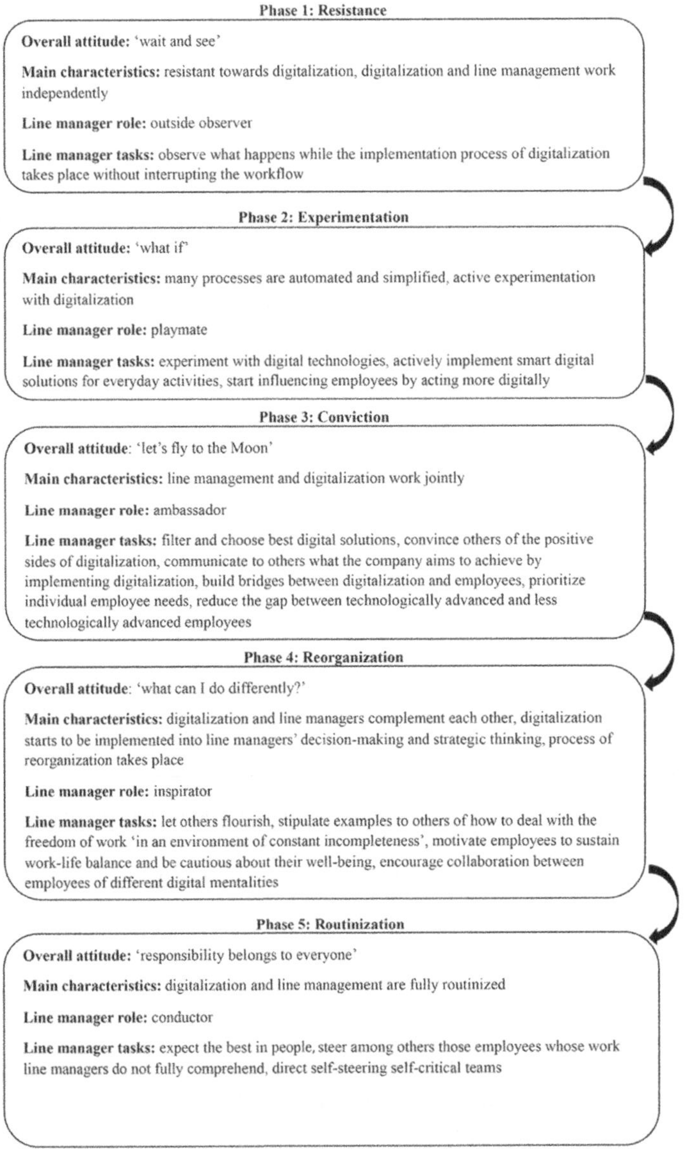

Phase 1: Resistance

Overall attitude: 'wait and see'

Main characteristics: resistant towards digitalization, digitalization and line management work independently

Line manager role: outside observer

Line manager tasks: observe what happens while the implementation process of digitalization takes place without interrupting the workflow

Phase 2: Experimentation

Overall attitude: 'what if'

Main characteristics: many processes are automated and simplified, active experimentation with digitalization

Line manager role: playmate

Line manager tasks: experiment with digital technologies, actively implement smart digital solutions for everyday activities, start influencing employees by acting more digitally

Phase 3: Conviction

Overall attitude: 'let's fly to the Moon'

Main characteristics: line management and digitalization work jointly

Line manager role: ambassador

Line manager tasks: filter and choose best digital solutions, convince others of the positive sides of digitalization, communicate to others what the company aims to achieve by implementing digitalization, build bridges between digitalization and employees, prioritize individual employee needs, reduce the gap between technologically advanced and less technologically advanced employees

Phase 4: Reorganization

Overall attitude: 'what can I do differently?'

Main characteristics: digitalization and line managers complement each other, digitalization starts to be implemented into line managers' decision-making and strategic thinking, process of reorganization takes place

Line manager role: inspirator

Line manager tasks: let others flourish, stipulate examples to others of how to deal with the freedom of work 'in an environment of constant incompleteness', motivate employees to sustain work-life balance and be cautious about their well-being, encourage collaboration between employees of different digital mentalities

Phase 5: Routinization

Overall attitude: 'responsibility belongs to everyone'

Main characteristics: digitalization and line management are fully routinized

Line manager role: conductor

Line manager tasks: expect the best in people, steer among others those employees whose work line managers do not fully comprehend, direct self-steering self-critical teams

Figure 22.1   The implementation process of digitalization: the role of line managers

First Phase: Resistance

At this phase, organizations consider that digitalization restricts them rather than provides new opportunities. They possess a relatively hostile, 'wait and see', attitude towards digitalization. As the respondents from the sample organizations at this phase clarified, line managers are afraid of losing control and authority due to the rapid implementation of advanced digital tech-

Table 22.2   *Examples of interviewees' expressions related to the phases of the implementation process of digitalization and the roles of line managers*

Phase of resistance	
Interview excerpt	'so far, we've not noticed the existence of such [digital] tools that would enable real wow experiences' (Manufacturing and Engineering 6)
Interpretation	According to the interviewee, their organization is in the resistance phase
Coded as	Evidence that the organization is in the resistance phase
Interview excerpt	'our [line] managers are not using many digital elements, they mainly observe how others get acquainted with them' (Manufacturing and Engineering 6)
Interpretation	Interviewee describes line manager as outside observer
Coded as	Evidence that the line managers' role is to be an outside observer
Phase of experimentation	
Interview excerpt	'we do not take this too seriously, we play and experiment with digital technologies ... if we see there something interesting, we then develop these things [digital technologies] slowly further' (Manufacturing and Engineering 7)
Interpretation	According to the interviewee, their organization is in the experimentation phase
Coded as	Evidence that the organization is in the experimentation phase
Interview excerpt	'[line] managers experiment with new digital technologies and apply them to their daily work and practices' (Manufacturing and Engineering 8)
Interpretation	Interviewee describes line manager as playmate
Coded as	Evidence that the line manager's role is to be a playmate
Phase of conviction	
Interview excerpt	'digitalization makes co-operation a lot easier in our company, it helps with knowledge sharing and brings new opportunities ... now the question is how to convince others to use digital technologies more broadly, and how to filter it, too' (Retail and Consumer Goods 7)
Interpretation	According to the interviewee, their organization is in the conviction phase
Coded as	Evidence that the company is in the conviction phase
Interview excerpt	'to be able to lead others, [line] managers share their own positive experiences of working with digital tools' (Construction 2); '[line] managers convince others that digitalization makes work easier and simplifies our processes instead of complicating them' (Construction 3); '[line] managers capture digital opportunities externally and internally, and convince others of their value' (Retail and Consumer Goods 7); 'they [line managers] inspire and awaken people to the limitless opportunities of digitalization' (Retail and Consumer Goods 7)
Interpretation	Interviewee describes line manager as ambassador
Coded as	Evidence that the line manager's role is to be an ambassador
Phase of reorganization	
Interview excerpt	'a lot more self-initiative and intelligence is needed to go through this restructuring process' (Extractive 2); 'digitalization changes management ... we have now a lot less rules, control and hierarchies, instead we have an open enabling culture. We invest currently in lean leadership, self-steering teams and experts, and strategic renewal. The time calls for change in thinking' (Infrastructure and Utilities); 'we are in the process of restructuring' (Financial Services 1); 'the old hierarchies disappear ... the modern ways of working are included...there are more individual solutions, wide scope of alternatives ... it [digitalization] changes the whole organizational structure' (Retail and Consumer Goods 6)
Interpretation	According to the interviewee, their company is in the reorganization phase
Coded as	Evidence that the company is in the reorganization phase

Interview excerpt	'[line] manager is like a "Northern Star" who guides the inspiring light so that we can jointly go through this process of [digital] transformation' (Infrastructure and Utilities); '[line] managers inspire people to become more digitally savvy' (IT, Electronics and Telecommunications 3); 'they [line managers] deal with constant uncertainty … they [line managers] challenge themselves and inflate around "what can I do differently" attitude' (Financial Services 1)
Interpretation	Interviewee describes line manager as inspirator
Coded as	Evidence that the line manager's role is to be an inspirator
Phase of routinization	
Interview excerpt	'complex worlds of digitalization and decision-making have been integrated' (Financial Services 2); 'we have established partnering relationships between us and digitalization' (Manufacturing and Engineering 11)
Interpretation	According to the interviewee, their company is in the routinization phase
Coded as	Evidence that the company is in the routinization phase
Interview excerpt	'[line] managers understand how digitalization has changed our behavior, communication and organization … they [line managers] lead without physical presence … their visionary skills where they [line managers] relate digitalization to strategy and competitive edge are important' (Retail and Consumer Goods 2)
Interpretation	Interviewee describes line manager as conductor
Coded as	Evidence that the line manager's role is to be a conductor

nologies. Organizations see no major influential benefits for line managers which could come with the implementation of digitalization in the workforce at this phase. Hence, digitalization runs independently of the line managers' work, and their role in the process is to act as outside observers who monitor how the implementation takes place, without workflow interruption. Line managers themselves are not particularly active in using various digital technologies.

Second Phase: Experimentation

At this phase, organizations believe that digitalization eases interaction between workforce members, facilitates idea and knowledge sharing through virtual communities of sharing, and boosts active experimentation among users. In this phase, many organizational processes are automated and simplified. Digitalization influences the workforce, but not its organizational structure. Line managers actively experiment with digital technologies and implement smart digital solutions in their everyday activities. According to the respondents from the organizations affiliated with this phase, the prevalent attitude among line managers is 'what if': they step out of their comfort zones, experiment with 'out-of-the-box' thinking, and start exposing examples of how to use digital technologies to others. Hence, line managers take on the role of playmate. Particularly, they start influencing other employees by acting more digitally themselves, and demonstrating to others that digitalization makes work easier and more efficient.

Third Phase: Conviction

At this phase, organizations perceive digitalization as a new method of operation, as it intertwines with the workforce. Management becomes more dialogue-based and less authoritarian, and the employees' perception that a manager should be physically present changes: 'you have a good boss even if you see him only twice a year'. However, this does not replace the need for human communication and interaction. Physical instances become less frequent but more meaningful, deep and personal, avoiding the creation of two separate workplace realities: digital and real.

Line managers now act as the ambassadors of digitalization. First, as the respondents from the organizations at this phase recall, line managers take a helicopter perspective on the interplay between digital technologies and the current workforce. They do not use the whole technological pallet. Instead, they have a wide understanding of what is most relevant and thus filter and choose the best digital solutions. Line managers 'capture' new opportunities both internally and externally. They also pass 'driving licences' on how to implement digital technologies delivering 'the same slang which digi-natives use' to the rest of the personnel, lessening the gap between technologically advanced and less technologically advanced employees. Next in this phase, line managers dynamically convince others of the positive aspects of digitalization, prioritize what is more important, keep employees in line with digital developments, and show direction. In addition, line managers communicate to employees what the organization is aiming to achieve by implementing digitalization to its various operations. As the respondents from the organizations affiliated with this phase mentioned, at this stage, line managers build bridges between digitalization and personnel, and transform the mindset of employees from 'new is scary' to 'ta-daa' moments. Since some employees are 'like kids in a candy store', line managers communicate (or, as the respondents themselves called it, 'translate') the impact of digitalization for them. They build dialogues with employees in order to define together how to apply the new opportunities of digitalization to the work obligations of employees, and how to 'fly to the Moon'. To do so, they seek to distinguish what drives each employee and prioritize individual employee needs. It is the responsibility of line managers to make sure that employees 'do not become lonely the in digital environment'.

Fourth Phase: Reorganization

The major difference between this and the previous phase is that here the business landscape is changing, the external environment is in flux. According to the interviewees from the organizations in this phase, their organizations operate 'in the environment of constant incompleteness', where 'everything happens at accelerated speed'. Digitalization and management complement each other. Collaboration between employees with different digital mentalities (that is, digi-natives and non-natives) becomes smoother. Digitalization starts to be implemented into decision-making. Yet, the idea that people change more slowly than technologies is recognized and taken into consideration. Hence, this phase marks the process of reorganization.

At this phase, digitalization endorses self-management, where 'leadership belongs to everyone'. Employees are themselves responsible for steering their careers. They become less dependent on line managers. They are provided with more authority, and frequently ask themselves 'What can I do differently?' to make their work more productive and meaningful. They are inspired by 'learn it yourself' and 'learning by doing' standpoints. Line managers act as inspirators. They stipulate examples to others of how to deal with the freedom of work. Furthermore, they ensure that employees 'do not hide behind technology' and cultivate among employees the capacity to 'adapt quickly to new circumstances'. Line managers stay in the shadows, let others flourish, and dare to become 'disliked'. At this phase, line managers also pay a lot of attention to employee well-being. According to the respondents from the organizations at this phase, line managers remind employees of 'the importance of silent moments in the middle of all the hustle', and motivate employees to sustain a work–life balance and attend to their well-being. They deliver the message that 'there is life apart from work, too' and encourage employees to maintain strict borders between work and private life instead of 'being always available'.

Fifth Phase: Routinization

Digitalization is now integrated with organizational strategy, strategic positioning, and decision-making processes. A collaborative arrangement between humans and machines where businesses achieve the greatest performance improvements is accomplished in this phase. At this stage, companies can make faster, more efficient and more effective decisions. Self-leadership becomes standard. Similarly, self-management and self-renewal with features such as authenticity, curiosity and empathy are strongly underlined. The start-up culture where 'responsibility belongs to everyone' and 'collective emotional intelligence is exercised' is seen as a norm. A 'pull model' with joint problem-solving and experiment-sharing is emphasized. Positive psychology and positive expectations also become standard.

Line managers act as conductors. In particular, the line managers' role is to steer for those employees whose work they do not necessarily fully comprehend. Furthermore, according to the respondents from the relevant organizations, the line managers' role is also to expect the best in people. Line managers and other workforce members 'do not want to be digital for the sake of being digital'. In this phase, self-steering self-critical teams are assembled, since technology and people work as a team. These teams are driven by continuous learning, rapid experimentation and the 'fail fast' approach.

DISCUSSION

In the 36 sample organizations we studied, the implementation process of digitalization follows a clear course comprising five phases: starting with resistance, moving to experimentation, conviction and reorganization, and ending with routinization. Since the decision to implement digitalization in the organization is usually undertaken by top managers, organizational members' initial response to the change in working is often resistance (Fitzgerald et al., 2014). The implementation process of digitalization requires quite a few deviations from the status quo, and thus the common response in some companies is 'wait and see' instead of launching enthusiastically on the digital transformation journey (first stage: resistance). The next stage of that journey, and second phase of the implementation process, is organizational members' experimentation with digital technologies. By playing with the technologies, organizational members consider the options for engaging in the process. In the next phase, conviction, organizational actors are convinced of the opportunities offered by digitalization, and essentially engage in the process. To continue the implementation process, organizations need to reorganize operations to become less hierarchical and control-oriented. In fact, organizational members need more self-initiative and self-management to master the digitalization journey. The final phase, routinization, is where digital technologies and decision-making functions are fully integrated in the organization. It is suggested that this phase routinizes and ends the implementation process.

Line managers play a role in each of the five implementation phases. Although they act as 'outside observers' in the resistance phase, they can extend and prolong that phase by actively resisting the implementation process (Bos-Nehles et al., 2013; Fitzgerald et al., 2014;

Townsend and Dundon, 2015). Due to their influence on employees in the organization, their behaviour also mirrors the behaviour of employees (Bos-Nehles et al., 2020; Trullen et al., 2020). In the experimentation phase, line managers can act as 'playmates' by allowing and providing organizational members space and time to experiment or play with digital technologies. In this phase, line managers can also heavily influence the general attitude towards digitalization through their initial reactions, feedback and encouragement concerning the implementation process. Once line managers are convinced of the digital opportunities in the conviction phase, they can act as ambassadors by communicating, filtering information, and convincing others of digital benefits and successes in the reorganization phase to come. There, line managers undertake the role of inspirator, by acting as a digital role model, motivating colleagues to engage in digitalization, and encouraging digital collaborations. In the last phase, routinization, line managers become the 'conductors' towards digital routinization, coaching employees to work digitally, and leading digitalization.

In the implementation process of digitalization, the line management function becomes more people-oriented and conscious of people's feelings (Huang et al., 2019). The implementation process of digitalization is not so much a technical process, as a matter of communicating its relevance to employees, empowering those employees by allowing them to explore and learn, and helping them to anticipate the obsolescence of a part of their current skill set. A line manager's main role is to encourage this almost organic skill improvement by identifying learning opportunities based on strategic corporate goals. Line managers support and encourage learning and unlearning so that employees continually train and acquire new know-how. Finally, they need to guide employees in their understanding of multiple viewpoints, and communicate the company's overall mission, so that the personnel fully recognize the company's total ecosystem instead of seeing only part of it. Ultimately, it is line managers' role to translate digital transformation into individual objectives.

Theoretical Relevance

The implementation of digitalization is a process, not a one-time 'push-button' event. It is a time-consuming process of becoming, where organizations and organizational members make sense of it by adopting digital technologies and streamlining them to meet the demands of the business. As such, organizations follow a five-phase path until digitalization is routinized. However, not all organizations reach the last phase, or will ever be able to do so. Indeed, some organizations might choose not to move to the next stage, as they are satisfied with their current position. And some may not steer a sequential route through the phases, adopting different time paths in moving from phase to phase, omitting a phase, or moving back to a phase they have already undertaken. The speed and process of implementing digitalization are dependent, for example, on the resources available to facilitate digitalization and the strategic goals of the organization. This illustrates that the implementation process of digitalization is a dynamic course that does not follow a one-way street (Trullen et al., 2020). This is true because this process is a social construction in which digitalization emerges through its implementation in the organization.

Our findings have highlighted that line managers play a vital role in the implementation process of digitalization, since they socially construct digitalization through using it themselves and by sharing the interpretation of digitalization with their departments and teams. They play a different role in each of the five implementation phases. The implementation of digitalization advances also because line managers change their attitude towards digitalization and become more active in the digitalization process. Through engaging in 'interpretive flexibility' (Klein and Kleinman, 2002: 29), line managers implement digitalization in such a way that multiple designs are created through intergroup negotiations. Through experimenting with digital technologies, the outcome of the process becomes unpredictable and results in adopted business solutions. By implementing digital solutions in the business, line managers become digitalization agents whose actions manifest the meaning they impart to digitalization. As such, they are able to develop a shared cognitive digitalization frame among their team members (Bijker, 1995). They do so by translating digital solutions for their teams as well as coaching, steering and directing employees to the new digital reality, resulting in a general conviction that digitalization offers opportunities for employees and the business. Once this phase has been reached, line managers steer their teams to reorganize the business and themselves by becoming less dependent on the manager and popularizing self-management. When all digitalization conflicts are solved, the implementation process of digitalization can be closed by stabilizing the business through routinization. The social construction process ends here, since digitalization becomes an integrated part of the business. However, once the digital opportunities change and organizations decide to modify the digital tools or processes, or internal or external developments alter the status quo, the implementation process may need to start all over again, or move back a couple of steps to reform.

Managerial Relevance

The main message of this study for practitioners is that the continuous assurance of line management involvement in the implementation process of digitalization is a priority for its success. Organizations need to change the mindset of line managers rather than worrying about whether technology is someday going to obviate their work. It is more constructive for line managers to learn how to work with digital technologies and think of technology as a team member whose skills must be utilised (Ross et al., 2019). Although most line managers will not be technology experts, they need to have solid knowledge of technology strengths and weaknesses. They also need to be able to communicate the benefits of digitalization to employees.

Limitations and Future Research Outlook

Our study has certain limitations, and we hope these can open up avenues for future investigation. First, there may be a limitation to the transferability of the results beyond the study's Finnish context. At the same time, our theoretical background was not bound to a company geographical location. Yet, further exploration is needed to see how our findings transfer to other settings. To do this, researchers may want to consider differences between digital transformations of various intensities. We could imagine that the implementation process may proceed faster and steps may be skipped in digitalization projects of lower intensities, such as the implementation of digital tools that are only used a couple of times a year, for example, digital performance appraisal tools; or that are only used by a part of the organization, for example, digital enterprise resource planning (ERP) systems in manufacturing. We may also need to distinguish between digital transformations of high-tech digitalization such as cyber-physical systems or robotization, and low-tech digitalization such as developing existing paper-based systems into digital systems. Also, the experience of organizational stakeholders with previous digitalization efforts does influence the implementation process of digitalization (e.g. Gjellebæk et al., 2020). We know that employees can suffer from innovation or technology fatigue (e.g. Fitzgerald et al., 2014), and thus imagine that they can also get tired of digitalization. Companies suffer from 'digitalization paradoxes' (Gebauer et al., 2020), because their investment in digitalization does not pay off. All this may influence their experiences with digitalization and thus alter the implementation process.

Furthermore, our study is based on interviews with leadership professionals, and we acknowledge that it may have focused more on the intentional side of the implementation process of digitalization, as well as on the intentional role of line managers in the process. Thus, future research projects should focus on the differences between intended digitalization, implemented or enacted digitalization, and actual digitalization as perceived by employees in the organization (Nishii and Wright, 2008), and could focus on the gaps between what was intended, implemented and perceived (Makhecha et al., 2018), as well as the differences in perceptions between different stakeholders in the implementation process. To understand the realized transformation of digitalization, future research could benefit from drawing on the experiences of the following key stakeholders: HR managers, IT managers, top managers, middle and frontline managers, and employees, and how they influence the implementation process. However, instead of taking a top-down implementation process in which line managers need to implement digitalization as intended, research could focus on the agency of line managers in the implementation process (Kehoe and Han, 2020) to deviate from intended courses or develop new practices (Bos-Nehles et al., 2017), or bottom-up digital implementation processes, in which the need for digitalization comes from the line and is then implemented in the entire organization (Thomann et al., 2018).

Future researchers could analyse the implementation process on the basis of different theoretical lenses. One suitable option would be the understanding of the sensegiving and sensemaking process of various stakeholders in the organization (Weick, 1995), and how sensegiving of higher managers influences the sensemaking of digitalization of lower-level managers and employees. Studying the sensemaking process of key stakeholders in the implementation process of digitalization could help us to understand why some organizations resist digitalization, while others reorganize or routinize digitalization in their business processes. Another option, also in combination with the sensemaking theory, is to analyse the attributions of digitalization, and why different organizational stakeholders think the organization adopted digitalization (Kelley and Michela, 1980; Nishii et al., 2008). We know that employee attributions influence individuals' attitudes and behaviours, and thus negative attributions about digitalization could result in negative attitudes and behaviours of employees or resistance to digitalization. Recent research has also shown that line managers' attributions influence the effective implementation of HRM policies and practices (Bos-Nehles et al., 2020), and thus they may influence the effective implementation of digitalization. Another theoretical lense which would be interesting to explore in the implementation of digitalization would be institutional theory and the analysis of institutional logics. The implementation process of digitalization may be dependent on the institutional environment of organizations and the process of isomorphism influencing the legitimacy of the digitalization. Bunduchi et al. (2019), for example, have shown that institutional logics, and especially competing institutional logics, influence the coping process of organizational stakeholders with digitalization. Line managers could help employees in coping with or making sense of digitalization, or may be the source of employee disapproval or rejections of digitalization. Studying the external and internal influences on the implementation process, and the coping mechanisms of users of digitalization, may be relevant approaches to understand the implementation of digitalization and the role of line managers in this.

REFERENCES

Bijker, W. (1995). *Of Bicycles, Bakelites, and Bulbs: Toward a Theory of Sociotechnical Change.* Cambridge, MA: MIT Press.

Bondarouk, T., and Brewster, C. (2016). Conceptualising the future of HRM and technology research. *International Journal of Human Resource Management,* 27(21), 2652–2671.

Bondarouk, T., Ruel, H., and Roeleveld, B. (2019). Exploring electronic HRM: management fashion or fad? In Wilkinson, A., Bacon, N., Redman, T., and Snell, S. (eds), *The SAGE Handbook of Human Resource Management,* 2nd edition. London: SAGE Publications, pp. 271–291.

Bos-Nehles, A., Bondarouk, T., and Labrenz, S. (2017). HRM implementation in multinational companies: the dynamics of multifaceted scenarios. *European Journal of International Management,* 11(5), 515–536.

Bos-Nehles, A., Van der Heijden, B., Van Riemsdijk, M., and Looise, J.K. (2020). Line management attributions for effective HRM implementation. *Employee Relations: The International Journal,* 42(3), 735–760.

Bos-Nehles, A.C., Van Riemsdijk, M.J., and Looise, J.K. (2013). Employee perceptions of line management performance: applying the AMO theory to explain the effectiveness of line managers' HRM implementation. *Human Resource Management,* 52(6), 861–877.

Bunduchi, R., Tursunbayeva, A., and Pagliari, C. (2019). Coping with institutional complexity. *Information Technology and People,* 33(1), 311–339.

Corley, K.G., and Gioia D.A. (2011). Building theory about theory building: what constitutes a theoretical contribution? *Academy of Management Review* 36(1), 12–32.

DESI (2021). The Digital Economy and Society Index. Available at: https://digital-strategy.ec.europa.eu/en/policies/desi.

Digibarometer (2020). Digibarometer. Available at: https://www.etla.fi/julkaisut/digibarometri-2020-kyberturvan-tilannekuva-suomessa/.

Eisenhardt, K.M., and Graebner, M.E. (2007). Theory building from cases: opportunities and challenges. *Academy of Management Journal,* 50(1), 25–32.

Faraj, S., Pachidi, S., and Sayegh, K. (2018). Working and organizing in the age of the learning algorithm. *Information Organization,* 28(1), 62–70.

Fitzgerald, M., Kruschwitz, N., Bonnet, D., and Welch, M. (2014). Embracing digital technology: a new strategic imperative. *Sloan Management Review,* 55(2), 1–13.

Gebauer, H., Fleisch, E., Lamprecht, C., and Wortmann, F. (2020). Growth paths for overcoming the digitalization paradox. *Business Horizons,* 63(3), 313–323.

Gjellebæk, C., Svensson, A., Bjørkquist, C., Fladeby, N., and Grundén, K. (2020). Management challenges for future digitalization of healthcare services. *Futures,* 124, 102636.

Govindarajan V., and Immelt, J. (2019). The only way manufacturers can survive. *MIT Sloan Management Review,* 60(3), 24–33.

Hales, C. (2005). Rooted in supervision, branching into management: continuity and change in the role of first-line manager. *Journal of Management Studies,* 42(3), 471–506.

Hales, C. (2006). Moving down the line? The shifting boundary between middle and first-line management. *Journal of General Management,* 32(2), 31–55.

Harzing, A., W., Köster, K., and Magner, U. (2011). Babel in business: the language barrier and its solutions in the HQ–subsidiary relationship. *Journal of World Business,* 46(3), 279–287.

Hasson, H., Villaume, K., von Thiele Schwarz, U., and Palm, K. (2014). Managing implementation: roles of line managers, senior managers, and human resource professionals in an occupational health intervention. *Journal of Occupational and Environmental Medicine,* 56(1), 58–65.

Henriette, E., Feki, M., and Boughzala, I. (2015). The shape of digital transformation: a systematic literature review. *MCIS 2015 Proceedings*, 431–443.

Huang, M.-H., Rust, R., and Maksimovic, V. (2019). The Feeling Economy: managing in the next generation of artificial intelligence. *California Management Review*, 61(4), 43–65.

Kehoe, R.R., and Han, J.H. (2020). An expanded conceptualization of line managers' involvement in human resource management. *Journal of Applied Psychology*, 105(2), 111.

Kelley, H.H., and Michela, J.L. (1980). Attribution theory and research. *Annual Review of Psychology*, 31(1), 457–501.

Klein, K.H., and Kleinman, D.L. (2002). The social construction of technology: structural considerations. *Science, Technology, and Human Values*, 27(1), 28–52.

Klein, K.J., and Sorra, J.S. (1996). The challenge of innovation implementation. *Academy of Management Review*, 21(4), 1055–1080.

Kohnke, O. (2017). It's not just about technology: the people side of digitization. In Oswald, G., and Kleinemeier, G. (eds), *Shaping the Digital Enterprise: Trends and Use Cases in Digital Innovation and Transformation*. Heidelberg: Springer, pp. 69–92.

Langley, A. (1999) Strategies for theorizing from process data. *Academy of Management Review*, 24(4), 691–710.

Legner, C., Eymann, T., Hess, T., Matt, C., Böhmann, T., et al. (2017). Digitalization: opportunity and challenge for the business and information systems engineering community. *Business and Information Systems Engineering*, 59(4), 301–308.

Leonardi, P.M., and Barley, S.R. (2010). What's under construction here? Social action, materiality, and power in constructivist studies of technology and organizing. *Academy of Management Annals*, 4(1), 1–51.

Makhecha, U.P., Srinivasan, V., Prabhu, G.N., and Mukherji, S. (2018). Multi-level gaps: a study of intended, actual and experienced human resource practices in a hypermarket chain in India. *International Journal of Human Resource Management*, 29(2), 360–398.

Markovitch, S., and Willmott, P. (2014). Accelerating the digitization of business processes. *McKinsey – Corporate Finance Business Practise*, May, 1–4.

Nishii, L.H., and Wright, P. (2008). Variability at multiple levels of analysis: implications for strategic human resource management. In Smith, D.B. (ed.), *The People Make the Place*. Mahwah, NJ: Lawrence Erlbaum Associates, pp. 225–248.

Nishii, L.H., Lepak, D.P., and Schneider, B. (2008). Employee attributions of the 'why' of HR practices: their effects on employee attitudes and behaviors, and customer satisfaction. *Personnel Psychology*, 61(3), 503–545.

Parviainen, P., Tihinen, M., Kääriäinen, J., and Teppola, S. (2017). Tackling the digitalization challenge: how to benefit from digitalization in practice. *International Journal of Information Systems and Project Management*, 5(1), 63–77.

Petry, T. (2018). Digital leadership. In North, K., Maier, R. and Haas, O. (eds), *Knowledge Management in Digital Change*. Cham: Springer, pp. 209–218.

Raisch, S., and Krakowski, S. (2021). Artificial intelligence and management: the automation–augmentation paradox. *Academy of Management Review*, 46(1), 192–210.

Real, K., and Poole, M.S. (2005). Innovation implementation: conceptualization and measurement in organizational research. *Research in Organizational Change and Development*, 15, 63–134.

Robertson, P.L., Casali, G.L., and Jacobson, D. (2012). Managing open incremental process innovation: Absorptive Capacity and distributed learning. *Research Policy*, 41(5), 822–832.

Rogers, D.L. (2016). *The Digital Transformation Playbook: Rethink Your Business for the Digital Age*. New York: Columbia University Press.

Ross, J.W., Beath, C.M., and Mocker, M. (2019). *Designed for Digital: How to Architect your Business for Sustained Success*. Cambridge, MA: MIT Press.

Sabbagh, K., Friedrich, R., El-Darwiche, L., Singh, M., and Ganediwalla, S. (2012). Maximizing the impact of digitization in the Global Information Technology Report. Edited by the World Economic Forum.

Schwarzmüller, T., Brosi, P., Duman, D., and Welpe, I.M. (2018). How does the digital transformation affect organizations? Key themes of change in work design and leadership. *Management Review*, 29, 114–138.

Sjödin, D.R., Parida, V., Leksell, M., and Petrovic, A. (2018). Smart factory implementation and process innovation. *Research Technology Management*, 61(5), 22–31.

Thomann, E., van Engen, N., and Tummers, L. (2018). The necessity of discretion: a behavioral evaluation of bottom-up implementation theory. *Journal of Public Administration Research and Theory*, 28(4), 583–601.

Townsend, K., and Dundon, T. (2015). Understanding the role of line managers in employment relations in the modern organisation. *Employee Relations*, 37(4), 1–10.

Trullen, J., Bos-Nehles, A., and Valverde, M. (2020). From intended to actual and beyond: a cross-disciplinary view of (human resource management) implementation. *International Journal of Management Reviews*, 22, 150–167.

Weick, K.E. (1995). *Sensemaking in Organizations* (Vol. 3). Thousand Oaks, CA: SAGE Publications.

Welch, C., and Piekkari, R. (2006). Crossing language boundaries: qualitative interviewing in international business. *Management International Review*, 46(4), 417–437.

Westerman, G., Bonnet, D. and McAfee, A. (2014). The nine elements of digital transformation. *MIT Sloan Management Review*, 55(3), 1–8.

World Economic Forum (2019). Shaping the future of digital economy and new value creation. https://www.weforum.org/system-initiatives/shaping-the-future-of-digital-economy-and-society/articles. Accessed 5 June 2020.

Zalan, T., and Lewis, G. (2004). Writing about methods in qualitative research: towards a more transparent approach. In Marschan-Piekkari, R. and Welch, C. (eds), *Handbook of Qualitative Research Methods for International Business*. Cheltenham, UK and Northampton, MA, USA: Edward Elgar Publishing, pp. 507–528.

Zuboff, S. (2019). *The Age of Surveillance Capitalism: The Fight for a Human Future at the New Frontier of Power*. New York: Public Affairs.

23. Reconceptualizing the HRM role of the line manager in the age of artificial intelligence

Ewold Drent, Maarten Renkema and Anna Bos-Nehles

INTRODUCTION

Technical Developments and AI Opportunities

We are witnessing an abundant stream of articles, books, blogs, videos, and other publications about artificial intelligence (AI) in the workplace. Technology in general, and AI specifically, increasingly influence the way we work, communicate, and manage our organizations (Cascio and Montealegre, 2016). This is reflected in the predicted doubling of global spending on AI between 2020 and 2024 (IDC, 2020). AI focuses on developing computer programs to complete tasks that would otherwise require human intelligence, and is commonly defined as "a system's ability to interpret external data correctly, to learn from such data, and to use those learnings to achieve specific goals and tasks through flexible adaptation" (Haenlein and Kaplan, 2019: 5). Most often AI is implemented for specific processes in which AI techniques such as algorithms are used to analyze data. Organizations increasingly use AI in information technology (IT) systems that aid managers in their daily operations and decision-making (Kolbjørnsrud et al., 2016).

The developments in AI present opportunities and challenges for human resource management (HRM) research. Not only do scholars attempt to grasp in what ways AI changes our work and how we collaborate, but they are also interested in how AI changes management practices. AI offers potentially valuable applications, especially in HRM; for example, in recruitment and selection, assessments, performance, and service delivery (Charlier and Kloppenburg, 2017; Fountaine et al., 2019; Kazuo, 2017). These applications can be helpful to aid decision-making of managers and HRM professionals. With the rapid advancement of AI, it is expected that the role of the line manager will be impacted in several ways. AI can replace activities normally done by line managers, such as interpreting information and employee data analysis. In this chapter we focus on first-line managers (line managers) who are regarded as those managers "representing the first level of management to whom non-managerial employees report" (Hales, 2005: 473).

AI and the Impact on Work and Management

AI is adopted in different HR practices and processes (Jia et al., 2018), and different AI techniques are used (Strohmeier and Piazza, 2015). We find the application of AI in various HR software systems that line managers use on a day-to-day basis. For example, developments are seen in the area of recruitment, in which AI is used to crawl internet profiles for potential candidates, assess and pre-select job candidates, and analyze job interviews and assessments (Upadhyay and Khandelwal, 2018). The current applications of AI in HRM are based on so-called weak or narrow AI systems (Strohmeier, forthcoming). Whereas "strong" or "general" AI describes systems that could be seen as generally intelligent and as being able to perform multiple tasks, "weak" AI is related to smart technologies that can perform specific tasks that resemble human intelligence (Russell and Norvig, 2021). In this chapter we only consider "weak" or "narrow" AI systems used for HRM activities by line managers.

The increasing presence of AI in HRM processes and software systems affects employees' perceptions of these technologies and their view of management. Several surveys that inquired into people's opinions about robots and AI show that employees are not necessarily opposed to being managed or supported by AI. For example, in a survey of Oracle and Future-Workspace (He et al., 2019), 64 percent of people indicated that they would trust a robot more than their manager, and half turned to a robot for advice instead of their manager. The same study shows that 82 percent of people think that robots can do things better than managers. These results indicate that in work-related settings people seem to rely more on technology, and they perceive it as more reliable or trustworthy. For instance, Van Esch et al. (2019) show that AI in recruitment increases the chance of completing a job application. However, there are others who report that some people experience negative feelings toward AI, such as cynicism and depression (Brougham and Haar, 2018).

AI can take over and support many parts of the current HRM tasks that were normally only accessible for HRM professionals to execute; for example, complex strategic workforce planning tasks, or analysis. However, the same can be said for employees: more and more HRM tasks are organized in a "straight-through" way in which line managers and HRM professionals no longer have a role, as all checks and balances are done by technology and AI. To put this another way, AI may extend the tasks of line managers, but may also decrease the number of HRM tasks in which line managers are involved. The latter usually happens in combination with organizational design developments in which flexible self-managing working teams are the norm.

It seems that the introduction of AI in HRM tasks could make the role of line managers in HRM obsolete. If tasks that were normally the responsibility of the line manager are automated by AI, or if AI tools help employees and teams to manage themselves, this may significantly change the role of the line manager or make line managers redundant. After the devolution of HRM responsibilities from HRM professionals to line managers (Hall and Torrington, 1998; Whittaker and Marchington, 2003), and to employees in self-managing teams (Bondarouk et al., 2018; Renkema et al., 2020), we could witness further devolution of responsibilities to AI, resulting in a possible dissolution of the role of line managers in HRM.

However, there are also other developments. There are predictions about a shift in the necessary skills, such as empathy (Bughin et al., 2018), which indicate that employees and teams still require some form of management. This would imply that the line manager's role is changing to a focus toward more "soft" people management skills and competences, such as coaching. In addition, from an employee well-being perspective, line managers may develop the role of acting as a guardian of an ethical, healthy, and human approach to work and working teams. From this perspective, the line manager's role may change completely: from a focus on operational effectiveness, and performance based on interests of the organization and its shareholders, toward a focus on development, and well-being of employees based on the interests of the employee and society as a whole.

Contribution of this Chapter

The main contribution of this chapter is the in-depth analysis of the use and impact of AI on the role of line managers in performing HRM activities. Most of the work on AI and HRM has focused on the human resources (HR) department and HRM policies and practices. In this chapter we specifically focus on the role of line managers, since they have a crucial role in, for example, the implementation of HR policies (Nehles et al., 2006). This adds a new perspective to the impact of AI on organizations and HRM practices. First, building on the managerial responsibilities of Hales (2005), we explore in what way the responsibilities of line managers change due to the introduction of AI in work processes. Moreover, we contribute to the HRM devolution literature by conceptually and empirically exploring the next phase of HRM devolution: passing over HRM responsibilities to AI systems. Finally, we aim to combine perspectives from theory and practice on the adoption of AI, and illuminate this process in which developments are moving fast, although practical adoption may be slower than expected.

To our knowledge, there have been no studies focusing on the impact of AI on line managers yet. We base our arguments on literature about AI and its influence on line management. Although a topic of much attention, our literature search showed little to no results in scientific and non-scientific literature where the role of line managers in the implementation and use of AI is considered. Results that we did find highlighted a general impact of AI in business or HRM processes, and on people in general. We found many non-scientific publications about this topic. In these publications, the attention to the line manager, similarly to the scientific literature, is minimal and refers to the effects of AI in general terms. To understand how AI may influence the role of the line manager, we also rely on some practical examples of how AI can be used, and how it may change the work of line managers.

To do that, we undertook semi-structured interviews with three leading HRM software vendors. These organizations sell AI-based HRM applications to companies, and thus know what the technical opportunities of these technologies are and how they change HRM in practice. The HRM software vendors we included were: Infor, an international enterprise software provider; Workday, an international enterprise software provider for finance, HR, and planning; and Visma-Raet, a European HR and payroll software provider. Since there are not many organizations that already use AI applications in HRM, we could not include interviews with line managers about their use of AI in the organizations. A number of the organizations we contacted were in the process of deciding whether AI would benefit their HRM processes, or were in the process of adopting AI in existing HRM processes. However, line managers were usually not involved in this process. This is why we asked the HRM software vendors about the opportunities and challenges of AI software for different HRM activities, the role of line managers in this, and the qualities and skills that line managers have, and need, to implement HRM activities effectively with the help of AI technologies. We use the insights of these interviews mainly to explain the responsibilities of line managers with AI applications.

Hence, this chapter consists of different building blocks to provide insights. First, we look at the widely accepted general responsibilities of the line manager and illustrate how AI affects these responsibilities and related HRM processes. We then look at the stages of devolutions of HRM responsibilities, and answer the question of whether we can speak of a third "round" of HRM devolution toward AI. We conclude this chapter with a discussion about what HR scholars and practitioners can do to bridge the gap between the current role of line managers and the predicted role in the future, followed by interesting directions for further research.

RESPONSIBILITIES OF LINE MANAGERS AND AI

The introduction of AI in the workplace will lead to profound changes in the work and in the management of work (see, e.g., Brynjolfsson and McAfee, 2014; Manyika and Sneader, 2018). These changes will inevitably have effects on the responsibilities and roles of the line manager. Line managers are commonly responsible for the management of employees at the operational level (Nehles et al., 2006). To show how these technological changes affect their role, we categorize the overarching responsibility of the line manager into six overlapping groups of responsibilities developed by Hales (2005): performance-oriented supervision, monitoring quality, looking after people and the work area, translating strategy into operations, financial responsibility, and business management responsibility. We suggest that Hales's responsibilities are useful to review to what extent and how the responsibilities and related HR practices are susceptible to change caused by the use of AI. To understand and explain these developments, we present the opportunities and challenges that are related to each responsibility.

Performance-Oriented Supervision

According to Hales (2005), the performance-oriented supervision responsibility encompasses tasks such as day-to-day direction and control, monitoring reporting and improving work performance, allocating work and planning, and scheduling and coordinating the team. In this role, line managers oversee work by providing direction and control regarding operational work tasks and the quality of work. This requires line managers to engage in various formal and informal activities with their employees, such as performance appraisals or coaching interactions (Van Waeyenberg and Decramer, 2018). Line managers need data and information to fulfill this responsibility. For them it is often a task that demands a lot of time spent acquiring the necessary information, processing this information, discussing the outcomes with their employees, and entering these outcomes back into a system. Hence, line managers have an important role in performance management, which is influenced by AI in three main ways.

First, AI can take over several administrative tasks, such as collecting performance data and transforming the data into a performance dashboard (Buck and Morrow, 2018; Euchner, 2019). These data help line managers to analyze how employees perform and where improvements are needed. Eventually, this may improve the performance management process, as illustrated by one interviewee:

> If you think about it, if we start using data whether or not someone is performing well in their job and add a little bit of human intuition and subjectivity at the end of that process, we will have a much more accurate picture of how that person is performing.

Second, the continuous and real-time availability of data leads to more insights and is input for more complex analytical models (Ewenstein et al., 2016). This creates the possibility of forward-looking feedback (instead of backward-looking); for example, suggestions for specific training to improve future performance based on earlier performance and other employees' performances related to that specific training. Line managers can make use of historical data to make predictions about the future performance of their employees:

You see, an analysis has taken place, certain trends are visible, certain risks have been identified by the system … And from that point of view you can spend your time more on "what will be our strategy, given these data?" And then it will be much less a "wild guess".

Third, in cases where the performance data is available not only for the line manager, but also for the individual employee, this creates the situation in which the system can analyze performance for each specific individual and can support them in increasing their performance, by making suggestions for improvement or learning from high-performing peers. For example, digital assistants can be deployed to help employees with recurring questions about policies, thereby facilitating employee self-service (Maedche et al., 2019).

These three changes have an impact on the line manager's role. If AI takes over many administrative tasks, line managers can spend more time on coaching and motivating their employees: tasks that usually require human effort:

> Motivating people, creating an authentic and genuine relationship with people and then also recognize that your viewpoint over time is going to change … part of the role of the manager is to understand where you are today, and what do you want to do next year and the year after that. You cannot let technology do that.

The line manager remains responsible for the performance review. Nevertheless, in the AI-supported process and the eventual outcome, they are not, or may not feel, responsible for the outcome that is generated by AI systems. In this case, it is possible that employees have no one to appeal to for empathy (Kellogg et al., 2020). It seems that there is a need for a human review of AI outcomes before decisions are made permanent (see the example in Box 23.1). Line managers become responsible for connecting all quantitative and qualitative performance indicators, combining them with observations and contextual information to aid the process of improving individual and team performance. The line manager will become responsible for feeding the AI system with data, and will be an important source to train the AI system and verify its outcomes. Eventually, the emphasis is laid on adding contextual knowledge about an individual employee to AI system performance outcomes to review performance in an ethical and honest way.

BOX 23.1 FIRED BY AN AI SYSTEM

The AI system of Amazon, a company that is a front runner in using AI for all kinds of business processes, almost fired an employee who performed badly. However, it turned out that the worker was actually performing particularly well, since he was helping many of his colleagues to meet their performance targets, although this unfortunately meant that his own performance was low compared to these others and the AI decided that he should be fired (Lecher, 2019). A concerned, people-centred, and sincere line manager would immediately "ring the bell" if this kind of malpractice occurred. Other companies, such as Uber, also seem to use AI to determine whether drivers are fired (Lomas, 2020).

Monitoring Quality

The monitoring quality responsibility involves the tasks related to dealing with problems concerning customers, the work process, equipment and staffing, and implementing changes and improvements (Hales, 2005). It covers planning, reviewing, and reporting the performance of employees, but is also concerned with dealing with problems relating to customers and work processes. It is therefore strongly related to the performance-oriented supervision responsibility.

We will focus on the availability of data in relation to quality of work outcomes that is strongly related with employee performance. With increasing digitalization of processes and products, customers are also more accustomed to using digital means to buy products and services. Many organizations choose to frequently monitor quality and perceived quality (and customer satisfaction) through digital means. Consequently, more and more data is gathered, independently of the line manager. In manufacturing, automatic quality checks are implemented that make use of sensors. Even in the service industry, algorithms are used to automatically assess customer service quality by analyzing phone call records (Prentice and Nguyen, 2020). Using algorithms, these quality assessments can be processed and combined with individual, team, and department information, providing up-to-date and specific quality reports that not only highlight quality issues in the past, but can also predict quality issues in the future (for example, when client demands are high, but employee capacity low). Based on the information and suggestions, the specific individual or team is responsible for selecting the interventions needed to improve or maintain quality standards.

Similar to the performance-oriented responsibility, it is expected that the line manager is not relieved from this responsibility, but that there is a shift in focus. The responsibility to monitor quality by observing, gathering, and analyzing data is needed less since it is automated and no longer done by line managers. However, line managers may indeed be capable of assessing and analyzing data coming from AI-enabled quality assessments. Or, as the following quote highlights, managers need to search for the "why" behind the data:

> You can't read the why of the data. And that's why we need humans. To understand why someone is performing well or why are they not performing well. And then how do we take and emulate to somewhere else. AI cannot necessarily do that for you. We need to perform interpretations and extrapolations of how we apply this new knowledge in another part of the organization that will then be helpful.

If these quality data assessments are integrated with individual employee performance data, then it would become possible for AI to suggest improvements in teams, training, or recruitment. These kinds of analyses were also originally a line manager's task:

> When I look at my own team of project managers, the project data I have are the financial data, the data of the implementation, the system's data and the data that I have from client evaluations. And if you bring that all together, you can have a more objective image about how an employee really performs. And then some employees that are more on the "background" will come more forward. I think that really helps.

The change in responsibility of the line manager lies in the area of employee coaching and development. If a lack of quality or a need to improve quality is proposed and this has a relationship with the availability, competences, well-being, or skills of employees, the line manager needs to take action to support individuals and teams to improve these aspects.

Looking After People

The responsibility of looking after people is achieved through maintaining equipment, tidiness, and cleanliness, as well as looking after people through counseling and making recommendations for promotion (Hales, 2005). In this definition this responsibility refers to looking after people on the work floor; however, in the past decade the workplace is less physical than it used to be. The context of the work environment is increasingly shifting from a physical workplace to a digital or hybrid workplace in which physical and digital contact is supported. Manufacturing plants are robotized, logistic organization automized, and many other services are offered online, with people increasingly collaborating digitally in virtual environments (Zahidi et al., 2020). As well as the shift in workplace context, line managers are responsible for hiring the right people and taking care of their development and career opportunities, which we will focus on in the following section.

An important component of looking after people is ensuring that competent employees with a good fit for the job and organization are hired. Recruitment and selection are some of the HRM practices that line managers carry out, together with developing the right working conditions and overseeing possible career opportunities for their subordinates. Nevertheless, AI can also influence the ways in which line managers are involved in hiring. Hiring processes can be (partly) automated by adopting AI systems. AI can potentially take over and automate several tasks in the recruitment and selection process, such as the pre-selection and screening of candidates, conducting and analyzing job interviews, engaging candidates through chatbots, and ranking of prospective candidates (Johnson et al., 2021; Upadhyay and Khandelwal, 2018). When these processes are automated, the responsibilities of line managers to perform recruitment and selection tasks decrease. These changes could lead to a more effective hiring process, as one interviewee indicated:

> One of the big opportunities AI presents is to simplify recruiters' life by not requiring that they truly look at every single one of those people. So, AI can help weed out those candidates that are unquestionably not qualified. And then it can rank order those individuals based on information in their resume or LinkedIn profiles. Other publicly available data that can be scraped and aggregated and scored ... and now a recruiter can have a top 20 list instead of having to screen 300 candidates.

In this scenario, the line manager is still involved in the hiring decision-making process but is presented with a shortlist based on what the AI system suggests. Furthermore, the use of AI can augment line managers by taking away administrative tasks in the recruitment and selection process. By automating these repetitive tasks, AI can help line managers to focus on human interaction instead of bureaucratic activities. Multiple interviewees signaled that this was one of the most important benefits of AI:

> Doing the administrative and transactional functions of a [line manager's] role ... and augmenting human intelligence ... to help us make better decisions.

> Simplifying [administrative] tasks for the HR back-office, resulting in more streamlined processes.

> Bringing a lot of information together ... that [the line manager] can focus much more on human interaction.

Despite the automation of specific tasks, the interviewees did not think that humans can be entirely replaced in the recruitment process. Instead, AI can help to make better-informed decisions and enable line managers to focus on human interaction and coaching:

> you will never be able to fully quantify human behavior, you just won't. We are very complex ... So, I think there is always going to be a need for some human intuition, in discerning between candidates. Again, it should not be the only thing. But it will always be a necessity.

To date, AI can be considered less capable of achieving a high level of rapport or empathy with people. People's emotions cannot be digitized and recognized by programming, although some would claim they can (Jiang et al., 2019). In addition, a hybrid workplace creates many new questions regarding the responsibility of "looking after people." How do you take care of people who you do not bump into spontaneously anymore, because they work at home, in another office or abroad? How do you develop a team? How do you consider everyone's well-being and happiness? Technology and AI are fundamentally changing this aspect of a line manager's responsibility. Line managers are no longer the kind of "supervisor" who walks around the work floor and sees how everyone is doing, or is available in their office when a problem occurs; instead, line managers need to be more proactive in approaching their employees and asking about their situation and well-being. Line managers become facilitators of online work environments, taking care of the "tooling, tidiness, and cleanness" of this virtual environment (Bosua et al., 2013).

In summary, the line manager continues to have a responsibility for creating fundamental healthy work conditions. This will increasingly involve creating a tidy and clean virtual working environment. In this scenario the line manager becomes a sort of "technology champion" of the team, connecting team needs and issues of a technological nature, within a virtual environment, with individuals or teams that are able to help. This means that the line manager should possess more knowledge and skills in understanding the technology and articulating business questions (Kolbjørnsrud et al., 2016). Technological developments will be much more business-driven, focusing on "agile" ways of working that incrementally improve how technology supports employees.

Translating Strategy into Operations

In the "translating strategy into operations" responsibility, line managers communicate organizational objectives, substituting for staff, allocating equipment to jobs, and dealing with materials and supplier problems (Hales, 2005). To translate strategy into operations requires employees to be responsible for achieving desired outcomes for the organization, and contributing to organizational strategic goals. Job design choices are important to realize organizational strategies, and are generally related to the "the content and organization of one's work tasks, activities, relationships, and responsibilities" (Parker, 2014: 662). We will elaborate in more detail on this HRM aspect of translating strategy into operations in the next paragraphs.

The line manager has an important responsibility in terms of job design by composing and distributing tasks and activities among subordinates. At the same time, AI may influence job design and the role of the line manager, because AI potentially automates certain (routine) tasks and responsibilities of employees (Parker and Grote, 2020), forcing line managers to make decisions about how the remaining tasks and activities are organized and distributed among employees. In addition, the automation of tasks through AI may require reskilling of employees, which necessitates coaching by line managers. Two quotes from interviews illustrate that some tasks will be automated, and new tasks may arise: "The idea is to automate manual processes, that were repetitive and sensitive to errors," and "You still need skills like creativity and solving complex problems."

Line managers could be helpful in facilitating this transition toward new tasks that require novel capabilities. This also involves identifying the right abilities, the motivation of individuals, and the circumstances in which changes are proposed. AI can contribute to helping line managers to focus on developing their employees by taking away administrative tasks. At the same time, this means that line managers also require new skills, and that their organizations should help them in gaining these. This way, line managers need to be facilitated to help their employees in making the necessary changes. These developments are described by the following interviewees:

> If a line manager does not have to do that [administrative tasks] anymore, my contention is: you know what they can do? They can develop a meaningful, authentic relationship with their people and understand them in a more intimate way. So that they are helping that person to reach their full potential.

> Train managers a lot more on skill coaching and skill collaboration.

The challenge for line managers will be how to foster employees' willingness and commitment to these strategic choices and changes. This may lead to a development in which the line manager become a change manager. The responsibility would shift from translating strategy toward implementing strategy from a more change management perspective. Line managers will play an important role in helping and explaining how employees can best perform in their jobs and align their personal goals with organizational goals. Line managers could help each employee in crafting their job in such a way that it remains meaningful and satisfying for the individual. This can also lead to specific attention for individuals in, for example, developing idiosyncratic deals.

Financial Responsibilities and Managing Budgets

The financial responsibility includes the management of budgets and stock levels, as well as the responsibility for people management, such as conducting appraisals, training, and development, giving verbal warnings, and allocating staff to shifts (Hales, 2005). According to the definition of Hales, this concept consists of roughly two elements: first, it is about managing budgets from a financial management perspective; and second, it involves training and development of employees and giving them (financial) appraisals or warnings if necessary. It is the HRM process of training and development which is the subject of our following elaboration.

Regarding this responsibility, one of the major HRM practices where AI is being rapidly developed is in training and development practice (George and Thomas, 2019). Training and development policies can be supported by AI tools. These tools can be used to identify which training and development sessions are appropriate for certain stages of an employee's career, based on statistics of current and former employees (Cheng and Hackett, 2021). For example, IBM uses algorithms to advise employees which training to take, based on current abilities and future career paths (Tambe et al., 2019). This way, AI can contribute to employee development and career planning. This is also something our interviewees foresee for the future:

> AI has to make your life easier. One of the things we do is looking at career opportunities. We look at what others have done in a similar role, but also at what skills you should gain to make the next steps. And we consider what education you need. So which training options are relevant to enroll in and which skills to gain to make new steps?

Development in technology and AI may help line managers to be better informed about financial performance indicators and financial information. Predictive models help to aid decision-making in the areas of investments, procurement, and stock levels; for example, the Deep Brew AI systems that Starbucks uses for different business processes (Warnick, 2020). Therefore, this responsibility may not completely dissolve, but may be devolved to the broader team. However, financial choices in hiring, firing, and promoting people should remain a final responsibility of the line manager.

Business Management Responsibility

Hales (2005) mentions the business management responsibility as an exceptional responsibility that line managers have. This responsibility covers the coordination of various teams, keeping personnel records, and disciplining staff. It often occurs in small businesses, when there is no clear middle management, or where this middle management is not effective, leaving broader responsibilities to the line manager. One could argue that, with the current technological developments, line managers are increasingly aided by data, information, and intelligence to make decisions over a larger group of people and beyond the borders of a single team. It enables line managers to take responsibilities for more teams and more tasks. In this sense, AI increases the opportunities, or necessity, for line managers to take on more business management responsibilities (Wamba-Taguimdje et al., 2020).

To conclude, our in-depth exploration of the various areas of line manager responsibilities shows that the groups of responsibilities (Hales, 2005) are indeed changing in the light of technological developments. Some of these responsibilities require an updated definition and description. Also, Hales (2005) categorizes the responsibilities in order of importance, and the order seems to be different in the current context.

The most profound change is that the role of line managers seems to shift from operational performance and control, toward coach and people manager. AI and technology will be used for decision-making based on data and algorithms. These technical and rational processes can be automated. In addition, workers will also rely on, and are steered, much more by technology. Hence, a line manager who plans, makes certain decisions, and tells people what to do, is obsolete. Either the technology takes over this role, or employees and teams are capable of making the right choices themselves.

However, in this context it seems to be increasingly important that there is enough attention for employees. This is partly incorporated in Hales's "looking after people"; however, this definition is too narrowly formulated. For example, line managers need to pay special attention to employees' personal situations, their struggles and development, their well-being, and how they collaborate to counteract the objective and rational AI. This is a specific responsibility that becomes the main responsibility of the line manager, in addition to the ability to explain and contextualize AI-generated decisions when employees request information about decisions that were made (Kellogg et al., 2020).

AI AND THE DEVOLUTION OR DISSOLUTION OF LINE MANAGERS' HRM TASKS

We have highlighted that the use of AI affects the role of line managers in performing HRM practices in various ways. Specific developments that have already been set in motion are enabled and accelerated by AI. As such, in this section we identify and describe the devolution of HRM responsibilities away from the line manager. HRM tasks and responsibilities may either further devolve or disappear as a line management responsibility. To do so, we will briefly recapitulate the notion of HRM devolution.

HRM practices are implemented and enacted with substantial variation within organizations, which can largely be attributed to the involvement of line managers (Kehoe and Han, 2020). The variation can be explained by the delegation of HRM responsibilities to line managers, which is also termed HRM devolution, and the HRM implementation behaviors of line managers (Intindola et al., 2017). Devolution refers to the transfer of HRM responsibilities from HR managers to the line managers (see Brewster and Larsen, 2000). It is a decentralization move to redistribute HRM tasks and responsibilities closer to the operational level.

Bondarouk et al. (2018) distinguished between two phases of HRM devolution. Phase one characterizes the redistribution of HRM responsibilities from the HR department to line managers, and describes the increase in HRM responsibilities of line managers. The second phase considers a further redistribution of HRM responsibilities down the line toward employees. In the first devolution phase, line managers gained responsibility for the implementation of HRM policies and practices in their business units. As a result, line managers became responsible for the selection, motivation, development, training, performance management, and compensation of employees in their teams. To make use of this new responsibility, they also needed more autonomy and authority to become key decision-makers in people management issues (Harris et al., 2002; Larsen and Brewster, 2003).

The second phase in the devolution of HRM responsibilities describes the transfer of tasks and responsibilities to work-floor employees in self-managing teams (Renkema et al., 2020). Self-managing teams become empowered to make operational decisions independently, and thus gain more autonomy for how they want to implement HRM responsibilities in their teams. As such, they become responsible for the execution and implementation of HRM practices in their teams. Although line managers may still be involved as a coach for self-managing employees, it is employees themselves who perform HRM activities such as selection, development, performance management scheduling, or operational work tasks (Renkema et al., 2020). Variation in HRM practices can be explained by variations in experiences of individual employees, and because employees themselves are engaged in co-creating and implementing HRM practices.

With the advancements in AI technologies, a third phase in the devolution of HRM responsibilities may take shape, with AI systems being used for performing HRM activities such as hiring, performance management, and scheduling. This so-called algorithmic management automates HRM activities that line managers traditionally performed (Duggan et al., 2020), devolving HRM responsibility away from line managers and employees to AI technologies.

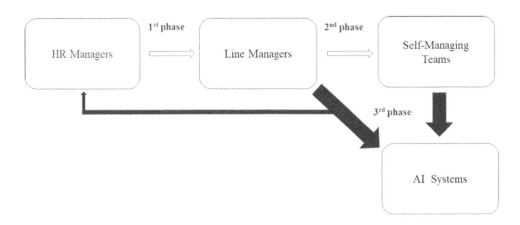

Figure 23.1   The three phases of devolution of HRM responsibilities

In doing so, the use of AI in HRM could lead to decision support for line managers (augmentation) by providing AI-supported suggestions. Alternatively, the devolution of HRM responsibilities could lead to a disintermediation of managers (Kellogg et al., 2020), which would mean that line managers were cut out of the HRM delivery process or supply chain. The three phases of devolution of HRM responsibilities are illustrated in Figure 23.1.

As we highlighted earlier, tasks are in some cases fully automated, meaning that the line manager's responsibility and role is completely taken over by AI. This is currently the case in repetitive, standard, and simple tasks. In addition, AI may be used to enable managers and employees to make better decisions in a shorter period of time. This refers to augmented decision-making, in which processes may be supported instead of replaced. AI may take over certain tasks within this process, such as information gathering and analysis, but eventually line managers make the final decision and act upon the provided information.

In the previous section we have shown how line managers' responsibilities change due to the introduction of AI. At the same time, organizations still use hiring, performance management, and training practices, and therefore we could state that the HRM policy areas remain largely unchanged. Nevertheless, we argue that the actors involved, and the level of responsibility, will change. To compare the three different phases of devolution, we explore current developments in AI based on recent publications, reports, and interviews, and compare them with the two earlier phases of devolution as described in Bondarouk et al. (2018). We present an overview of the devolution dimensions and the third phase of HR devolution to provide a better understanding of how responsibilities for HRM policies and practices change. We follow the work of Cascón-Pereira and Valverde (2014), who argued that devolution of HRM is a multidimensional phenomenon that consists of four dimensions: task implementation, decision-making power, financial power, and knowledge.

Task Implementation

This dimension involves the transfer of HR-related tasks and the execution of HRM practices. Whereas the first wave of devolution meant that line managers became increasingly responsible for task implementation, in the second wave these responsibilities are devolved to teams and employees. Still, many of the HRM tasks that line manager perform are administrative and repetitive in nature (for example, holiday leave, entering performance appraisals, managing sickness, or processing contractual agreements).

In the third wave of devolution, algorithms will take over many of those repetitive tasks, and will do most of the preparation, pre-selection, and probability calculations. However, the trigger for all of these tasks lies within the context of the line manager and employees. Therefore, the responsibility for the implementation of the HRM tasks lies either with employees who become more empowered by AI systems to implement HR-related tasks, or with line managers who decide how to act upon the suggestions and advice of the AI technology. Hence, parts of the tasks will be transferred to AI (such as checks and controls, or analysis); however, final responsibility will likely remain with managers or employees.

Decision-Making Power

The decision-making power entails the ability to decide on the material and human resources that are managed. Task implementation was an important aspect of HRM devolution in the first phase, as line managers became responsible for implementing and performing HRM practices. Nevertheless, they did not necessarily have the power to make decisions on HRM policies and practices. These decisions usually stayed with HR or higher management, whereas the execution of policies and practices at the operational level was the responsibility of line managers. Also, in the second phase, self-managing employees become responsible for executing (some) HRM policies but do not always have the decision-making power to decide which practices to implement and how to implement them. Bondarouk et al. (2018) explain that often line managers still have the sole authority to sign, order, or make important decisions, although they are officially no longer responsible for the management of a team of employees. Decision-making responsibilities are thus slower to be devolved to the operational levels, and often line managers retain an important role in decision-making.

Based on the literature and interviews, we suggest that the third phase of devolution will not change the line manager's decision-making power for HRM. At least two basic scenarios for the decision-making power in the third phase of devolution can be identified. The first scenario entails that decision-making power for HRM will not change: AI will support the actions to be taken by line managers, but the decision-making power will not be devolved to AI-supported systems. The second scenario involves automated decision-making, in which algorithms make decisions and line managers are disintermediated.

In this chapter we have argued that line managers have a responsibility in how the AI system will work with the right data to make better automated decisions. First, line managers should be involved in the policies detailing how AI is deployed, and what the consequences of its usage might be. What are its goals, and why do we use it? This also involves an ethical discussion about automated decision-making. Second, line managers need to provide insights into the dimensions and criteria on which the AI system's decisions are based. Third, the AI system needs to be fed data of the current situation based on line managers' experience to create a foundation for the design of the algorithm decision-making process. And fourth, after its deployment, line managers need to give feedback to the AI system (and its designers) in which they connect the AI's outcomes with line managers' own perception of these outcomes.

However, whether these four moments of involvement of line managers will become common practice will greatly depend on the organizational culture, structure, and power/

politics dynamics. The outcome of the third wave of devolution will depend on which types of software systems organizations adopt, and how they are implemented and used.

Financial Power

Financial power is related to the budgets that are available to manage human and material resources. According to Bondarouk et al. (2018), financial power was not devolved to line managers in the first phase of devolution. Since top management often needed to decide how to distribute budgets, line managers lacked the budgetary decision-making authority to finance their own areas of responsibility. In the second devolution wave, financial power is partly devolved to self-managing teams, which results in these teams being able to independently decide on how they want to spend their education, service, or purchasing budgets. However, they are limited in financial independence regarding the employment of new people.

In the third wave of devolution, we see that top management is gaining importance in terms of financial power, as they make decisions about which AI systems the organization purchases and, therefore, can also influence the characteristics of those systems. These AI systems require large datasets and can be expected to perform best when they are fed with data from the whole organization. Furthermore, when HRM systems are implemented throughout the whole organization, they are strategically important. Top management are involved in such strategic considerations and have the financial resources to make decisions. Line managers do not have the budgets to make decisions about implementing AI systems.

Knowledge

To make decisions about HRM policies and implement them requires specific knowledge and instruction, such as information about the nature of policies, and training about how to carry out the (new) responsibilities. In the first devolution phase, line managers often perceived a lack of knowledge transfer. Much of the HR-related knowledge that line managers developed was gained through their own initiatives and proactive behaviors. Although in some cases training and information budget was available, line managers lacked time to increase their knowledge base. Knowledge acquisition remains an issue in the second phase of devolution. Although many self-managing teams have their own training budget, they also perceive a lack of knowledge transfer and additional training to carry the new HRM responsibilities.

Although this is not crystalized yet, we expect knowledge to become an important issue in the third phase of devolution. Specifically, line managers may lack the knowledge about how the AI system works, and how suggestions and decisions are being made by AI. The lack of knowledge comes in at least two areas of expertise: HRM knowledge (policies, regulation, way of working) and knowledge about algorithms (knowing how the technology works, and interpreting the results in the right context). This explainability element is related to whether line managers understand the criteria and data used for AI-based HR decisions (Tambe et al., 2019). As these systems are black boxes, line managers may not feel competent and confident to make decisions based on the suggested solutions (Cheng and Hackett, 2021), or could make decisions that may even be harmful. Since the knowledge gap was widened during the first phase of devolution, this increases the chance of further stretching of the knowledge gap. The risk is that line managers are not capable of making the right decision, based on their own knowledge and understanding. This is an important factor in the execution of the changing responsibilities of the line manager, as reported in the earlier section.

To conclude, we see that tasks are usually relatively easily and quickly devolved to the operational level, but that decision-making power, financial power, and knowledge devolve more slowly and with more difficulty. Lessons learned about the effectiveness of HRM devolution in the previous two phases should be considered for the third phase as well. It does not matter to whom or what HRM responsibilities are devolved, HRM should always play an important role in supporting the devolution (e.g. Bos-Nehles, 2010; Gilbert et al., 2015; Op de Beeck et al., 2018). It should not be expected that the devolution of tasks will automatically lead to effective implementation of HRM policies and practices.

THE LINE MANAGER AS GUARDIAN OF HUMANITY?

In this chapter we have shown that with the introduction of AI the role of the line manager is indeed susceptible to change. Several responsibilities that were generally considered to be the line manager's obligations are automated or augmented, and in some cases dissolved, which results in the line manager changing toward a more people-centered, technological mastering, change manager. Future research should establish how the role of line managers shifts, what skills and behaviors are required from them, how line managers perceive their novel tasks and responsibilities, and how they can be supported in performing in such an environment. In doing so, future research can be directed toward predictions for the future that we have distilled in this chapter. These predictions reflect a movement from previous and current elements of the line manager's role, toward future elements. We will present these predictions next, followed by our discussion about how this third phase of HRM devolution should be supported by HRM, resulting in scenarios for the future.

Predictions for the Development of the Line Manager's Role and Future Research Outlook

We have argued that the growing use of AI in all kinds of organizational IT systems seems to have a profound impact on the line manager's HRM role. We also argue that scholars and practitioners need to be aware of neglecting the line manager in this development. In general, we suggest that scholars can focus their empirical research specifically on the role of the line manager in the implementation, use, and improvement of AI-supported systems. Since we expect the line manager's role to change in several areas, we also suggest that future research needs to focus on this changing role, what it entails, the pace of it, and how it should be guided by top management and the HR department. In addition, scholars could take a different focus of analysis and look specifically at the technological form of AI that is used, and whether this form influences how the line manager's role is developing. Finally, as we only considered the currently dominant application of narrow AI, future research should also consider the (potential) ways in which super-intelligent systems can fulfill line manager roles in multiple areas.

We foresee the following five developments for the role of line managers and believe that they provide opportunities for line managers regarding how to become and remain engaged in people management. These developments offer more areas for future research.

From compliancy officers toward people manager
Line managers may currently be acting mainly as managers who make sure that the work that is done is compliant with organizational plans, rules, and regulations. They need to take responsibility for meeting deadlines, budgets, and targets. Many of the administrative and analytical tasks that are related to this are devolved to AI. Therefore, it is predicted that in the future this role will mainly concern facilitating and coaching employees. Line managers are expected to focus on the development of social skills, such as people development, coaching, and collaboration (Kolbjørnsrud et al., 2016). Compliance issues are moved to another level in the organization; either higher into management teams, or lower into self-managing teams and employees. This offers opportunities for future researchers to study the competences and define the talents that line managers need to have in order to foster people management with AI. Research could explore the skills and attitudes needed to become a good coach for employees.

From directly managing operations toward data analytics and tech enabler
Line managers are, in most cases, working directly in operations and are concerned with operational planning and managing employees. It is predicted that in the future these tasks will be executed by AI systems, for example, by generating detailed working schedules and planning (Serengil and Ozpinar, 2017). However, line managers need to understand how these tasks work, including why and how certain output is created. Line managers need to be increasingly concerned with data analytics, and are asked to use their process data to improve algorithms. The shift is from directly making operational decisions, toward a more indirect role to support, fine-tune, and improve AI to decide how their people work.

The line manager will be the link between their team and actors that are involved in technology development. This means that line managers will require basic knowledge and skills regarding AI, data analytics, and technology (Fountaine et al., 2019). Here we also see opportunities for future research in the understanding of line management skills. However, the focus in research should be on the technical skills needed to co-design, manage, feed, execute, and review AI systems for HRM practices. Ideally, researchers could explore the complete line management skillset and develop a new function profile for line managers working with AI systems. Optimally, this would contain the development of technical and analytical skills to develop, improve, and understand the AI system and the social skills needed to coach employees on the basis of AI inputs.

From direct communication and actions on the work floor toward proactive digital team-building and guardian of employee well-being
It is expected that work will be much more decentralized and flexible. When line managers and their teams were mostly in the same physical space it was easy to see each other and notice things. In a new way of working, the work floor is transferred to a digital work environment. The responsibility of looking after people and their well-being is placed in a totally different perspective. Jobs need to be redesigned when tasks are taken over by technology (Parker and Grote, 2020), AI needs to be fair toward all employees (Robert et al., 2020), and line managers have an important role to support employees in a digital environment (Bentley et al., 2016).

These changes require different ways to approach team-building and other ways to involve employees. Therefore, they place a different emphasis on the line manager's responsibility. This development offers opportunities to study what line managers could do to protect employees who are selected, managed, and appraised by AI systems, and to secure their well-being and satisfaction. Future researchers may explore how job-crafting techniques may be applied to keep jobs challenging and interesting, or how to apply tailored working conditions (i-deals) to develop employees and keep them committed and engaged. These approaches may counteract the suggestions made by AI systems for efficiency and productivity but may be needed to safeguard the well-being of employees.

From subject of change toward managing change
When line managers are no longer responsible for results, but are for the team process and coaching, this also lays an emphasis on their role as change agent. The implementation and use of AI require a different approach toward change management. Line managers are an important link between business goals, technology, and employee development and well-being. In the new situation they will be more involved in supporting change processes in the team. In that sense, they will not promote change, but will look for ways to help employees in coping with change.

Although researchers know about the role of line managers in organizational change (Hartley et al., 1997; Mcguire et al., 2008), future researchers should explore the role of line managers in managing the change to AI. Chapter 22 in this book has looked at the role of line managers in digital transformation processes and the implementation of digitalization. However, in the implementation of AI systems the role of line managers may be different. Future research projects may therefore also focus on the attributions of line managers regarding the use of AI, and how they influence the attributions employees give to the use of AI by their manager or organization (Nishii et al., 2008).

From pragmatic decision-maker toward nuancing decisions by involving context and the human touch
It is expected that AI will take over tasks from the line manager. It is also predicted that AI will never be able to reach the level of understanding and empathy that humans have (Bolander, 2019; Tambe et al., 2019). Therefore, line managers will represent the human conscience in processes that are supported, or even completely regulated, by AI. A line manager is the person who checks that the AI output does not do things that are unethical, unfair, or harmful in any way. In this sense, the line manager becomes a guardian of humanity. Future researchers are invited to explore this role of guardian of humanity by investigating the ways in which line managers can protect ethical procedures, the mechanisms needed to steer the AI system in an ethical way, and conditions and boundary factors needed to build ethical AI systems.

How HRM Should Support the Third Phase of HRM Devolution

We have revealed that the HRM processes in which line managers are actors, in themselves do not change, in the sense that they become obsolete in some way in the future. However, the role of the line manager and how that role is enabled by AI is indeed changing, as illustrated in the predictions presented earlier. AI takes over dull, repetitive, and simple tasks, leaving (in theory) more time for new responsibilities, people management, managing technology, and change. AI is indeed enabling better and faster decision-making by line managers in these HRM practices, which is called augmented decision-making. We proposed looking at these changes as a third phase in the devolution of HRM in which, for many organizations, quite radical change seems to occur concerning the line manager's role. Labeling this development as a third phase in the devolution of HRM is a claim not to be taken lightly and is indeed our goal.

From previous devolution research we know that every change that occurs in HRM devolution requires specific and extensive support from the organization (e.g. Bondarouk et al., 2018). Line managers do not simply adapt to new roles overnight, and some that currently hold the position may no longer be suited for the role, for reasons of competences, skills, or simply personal interest. In devolution research, the line manager is involved as one of the major forces for successful HRM policies, implementations, and organizational success. Therefore, we are surprised and concerned to find so few researchers and practitioners who seem to appreciate the value of the line manager and pay attention to this role in their publications.

From the previous phases of devolution, we have learned that devolutions can go terribly wrong and can be potentially harmful for individual and organizational performance (Conway and Monks, 2010; Renwick, 2003); for example, by trying to force a consistent and "equal" treatment of employees by creating highly structured, technocratic procedures in which the procedure becomes a goal in itself (Harris et al., 2002). One of the conclusions drawn in previous phases of devolution was the structural lack of effective support, or systems of support, toward the subjects of devolution (Intindola et al., 2017). Line managers need this kind of support with these developments; for example, through training programs to understand how AI systems work and how they can be designed. We conclude that lack of attention to this specific role creates the risk of personal and organizational issues when making use of AI. Since technology is involved, and we leave parts of our tasks, processes, and thinking to AI, it is more important than ever to educate, train, and support line managers in the field. However, this also requires a strong digital mindset of HR professionals to be part of digital transformation (Isari et al., 2019). If HR and line managers are not able to engage in AI developments, they are at risk that other forces in the business, such as computer science and data analysis, will take over the decision-making (Tambe et al., 2019).

However, how this third phase of devolution will eventuate remains difficult to predict, and needs to be explored in future research. Based on our discussion, we see three main scenarios. In the first scenario, AI enables more tasks and decision-making power toward employees and self-managing teams, and less to HR and line managers. Central to this scenario is the idea that organizations might take an approach in which more decisions are devolved toward employees or self-managing teams, and that these individuals and teams are supported by AI systems.

The second scenario entails that the third phase of devolution will be a reverse: most responsibilities for HR will go back to the HR department. In other words, HR departments gain a more important role because the software is designed and maintained by HR, leaving less responsibilities and autonomy for line managers. This is supported by the idea that AI systems and supporting data enable the HR department to centralize certain HRM tasks; for example, by creating tailor-made employment arrangements that do not need the approval of the line manager (Isari et al., 2019).

In the third scenario, a third phase of devolution may be similar to the first phase of devolution in which more HRM-related responsibilities are transferred to the line manager. Especially when line managers increasingly take on a people management role and become a link between deployment of AI systems and employees, they will step into the gap that may be left by less innovative and progressive HR departments. Each of these scenarios is subject to contingency factors that may direct certain choices (Intindola et al., 2017). Nevertheless, since we are on the brink of broader implementation of AI, the time to lay a well-grounded foundation of knowledge about the effects of AI and the line manager's role is now.

REFERENCES

Bentley, T.A., Teo, S.T.T., McLeod, L., Tan, F., Bosua, R., and Gloet, M. 2016. The role of organisational support in teleworker wellbeing: a socio-technical systems approach. *Applied Ergonomics*, 52: 207–215.

Bolander, T. 2019. What do we lose when machines take the decisions? *Journal of Management and Governance*, 23(4): 849–867.

Bondarouk, T., Bos-Nehles, A., Renkema, M., Meijerink, J., and De Leede, J. 2018. *Organisational Roadmap Towards Teal Organisations*. Emerald Group Publishing.

Bos-Nehles, A. 2010. The line makes the difference: line managers as effective HR partners. Unpublished doctoral thesis, University of Twente, Netherlands.

Bosua, R., Gloet, M., Kurnia, S., Mendoza, A., and Yong, J. 2013. Telework, productivity and wellbeing: an Australian perspective. *Telecommunications Journal of Australia*, 63(1): 11.1–11.12.

Brewster, C., and Larsen, H.H. 2000. The Northern European dimension: a distinctive environment for HRM. In C. Brewster and H. Holt Larsen (eds), *Human Resource Management in Northern Europe: Trends, Dilemmas and Strategy* (pp. 24–38). Blackwell Publishing.

Brougham, D., and Haar, J. 2018. Smart Technology, Artificial Intelligence, Robotics, and Algorithms (STARA): employees' perceptions of our future workplace. *Journal of Management and Organization*, 24(2): 239–257.

Brynjolfsson, E., and McAfee, A. 2014. *The Second Machine Age: Work, Progress, and Prosperity in a Time of Brilliant Technologies*. W.W. Norton & Company.

Buck, B., and Morrow, J. 2018. AI, performance management and engagement: keeping your best their best. *Strategic HR Review*, 17(5): 261–262.

Bughin, J., Hazan, E., Lund, P.S., Dahlström, P., Wiesinger, A., and Subramaniam, A. 2018. Skills shift—automation and the future of the workplace. McKinsey Global Institute.

Cascio, W.F., and Montealegre, R. 2016. How technology is changing work and organizations. *Annual Review of Organizational Psychology and Organizational Behavior*, 3(1): 349–375.

Cascón-Pereira, R., and Valverde, M. 2014. HRM devolution to middle managers: dimension identification. *BRQ Business Research Quarterly*, 17(3): 149–160.

Charlier, R., and Kloppenburg, S. 2017. Artificial intelligence in HR: a no brainer. PWC white paper. https://www.pwc.nl/nl/assets/documents/artificial-intelligence-in-hr-a-no-brainer.pdf.

Cheng, M.M., and Hackett, R.D. 2021. A critical review of algorithms in HRM: definition, theory, and practice. *Human Resource Management Review*, 31(1): 100698.

Conway, E., and Monks, K. 2010. The devolution of HRM to middle managers in the Irish health service. *Personnel Review*, 39(3): 361–364.

Duggan, J., Sherman, U., Carbery, R., and McDonnell, A. 2020. Algorithmic management and appwork in the gig economy: a research agenda for employment relations and HRM. *Human Resource Management Journal*, 30(1): 114–132.

Euchner, J. 2019. Little ai, big AI—good AI, bad AI. *Research-Technology Management*, 62(3): 10–12.

Ewenstein, B., Hancock, B., and Komm, A. 2016. Ahead of the curve: the future of performance management. *McKinsey Quarterly*, 2: 64–73.

Fountaine, T., McCarthy, B., and Saleh, T. 2019. Building the AI powered organization. *Harvard Business Review*, July–August: 62–73.

George, G., and Thomas, M.R. 2019. Integration of artificial intelligence in human resource. *International Journal of Innovative Technology and Exploring Engineering (IJITEE)*, 9(2): 5069–5073.

Gilbert, C., De Winne, S., and Sels, L. 2015. Strong HRM processes and line managers' effective HRM implementation: a balanced view. *Human Resource Management Journal*, 25(4): 600–616.

Haenlein, M., and Kaplan, A. 2019. A brief history of artificial intelligence: on the past, present, and future of artificial intelligence. *California Management Review*, 61(4): 5–14.

Hales, C. 2005. Rooted in supervision, branching into management: continuity and change in the role of first-line manager. *Journal of Management Studies*, 42(3): 471–506.

Hall, L., and Torrington, D. 1998. Letting go or holding on—the devolution of operational personnel activities. *Human Resource Management Journal*, 8(1): 41–55.

Harris, L., Doughty, D., and Kirk, S. 2002. The devolution of HR responsibilities—perspectives from the UK's public sector. *Journal of European Industrial Training*, 26(5): 218–229.

Hartley, J., Benington, J., and Binns, P. 1997. Researching the roles of internal-change agents in the management of organizational change. *British Journal of Management*, 8(1): 61–73.

He, E., Bertallee, E., Jones, S., Lyle, L., Meister, J., and Schawbel, D. 2019. AI@Work Global Study Online report. Oracle and Future-Workspace LLC. https://www.oracle.com/webfolder/s/assets/ebook/ai-work/index.html.

IDC. 2020. Worldwide spending on artificial intelligence is expected to double in four years, reaching $110 billion in 2024, according to new IDC spending guide. www.idc.com.

Intindola, M., Weisinger, J.Y., Benson, P., and Pittz, T. 2017. The evolution of devolution in HR. *Personnel Review*, 46(8): 1796–1815.

Isari, D., Bissola, R., and Imperatori, B. 2019. HR devolution in the digital era: what should we expect? In R. Bissola and B. Imperatori (eds), *HRM 4.0 For Human-Centered Organizations*, Advanced Series in Management, Vol. 23 (pp. 41–61). Emerald Publishing.

Jia, Q., Guo, Y., Li, R., Li, Y., and Chen, Y. 2018. A conceptual artificial intelligence application framework in human resource management. In: *Proceedings of the 18th International Conference on Electronic Business* (pp. 106–114). ICEB, Guilin, China, December 2–6.

Jiang, F., Du, C., Fu, T., and Xiao, R. 2019. Research on the application of artificial intelligence in human resource management. *Journal of Social Sciences Studies*, 4: 258–262.

Johnson, R.D., Stone, D.L., and Lukaszewski, K.M. 2021. The benefits of eHRM and AI for talent acquisition. *Journal of Tourism Futures*, 7(1): 40–52.

Kazuo, Y. 2017. How artificial intelligence will change HR. *People and Strategy*, 40(3): 42–46.

Kehoe, R.R., and Han, J.H. 2020. An expanded conceptualization of line managers' involvement in human resource management. *Journal of Applied Psychology*, 105(2): 111–129.

Kellogg, K.C., Valentine, M.A., and Christin, A. 2020. Algorithms at work: the new contested terrain of control. *Academy of Management Annals*, 14(1): 366–410.

Kolbjørnsrud, V., Amico, R., and Thomas, R.J. 2016. How artificial intelligence will redefine management. *Harvard Business Review*, 2: 1–6.

Larsen, H.H., and Brewster, C. 2003. Line management responsibility for HRM: what is happening in Europe? *Employee Relations*, 25(3): 228–244.

Lecher, C. 2019. How Amazon automatically tracks and fires warehouse workers for "productivity". The Verge, www.theverge.com.

Lomas, N. 2020. Uber's "robo-firing" of drivers targeted in latest European lawsuit. Tech Crunch. https://techcrunch.com/2020/10/27/ubers-robo-firing-of-drivers-targeted-in-latest-european-lawsuit.

Maedche, A., Legner, C., Benlian, A., Berger, B., Gimpel, H., et al. 2019. AI-based digital assistants. *Business and Information Systems Engineering*, 61(4): 535–544.

Manyika, J.S., and Sneader, K. 2018. AI, automation, and the future of work: ten things to solve for. McKinsey & Company.

Mcguire, D., Stoner, L., and Mylona, S. 2008. The role of line managers as human resource agents in fostering organizational change in public services. *Journal of Change Management*, 8(1): 73–84.

Nehles, A.C., Van Riemsdijk, M., Kok, I., and Looise, J.K. 2006. Implementing human resource management successfully: a first-line management challenge. *Management Revue*, 17(3): 256–273.

Nishii, L.H., Lepak, D.P., and Schneider, B. 2008. Employee attributions of the "why" of HR practices: their effects on employee attitudes and behaviors, and customer satisfaction. *Personnel Psychology*, 61(3): 503–545.

Op de Beeck, S., Wynen, J., and Hondeghem, A. 2018. Explaining effective HRM implementation: a middle versus first-line management perspective. *Public Personnel Management*, 47(2): 144–174.

Parker, S.K. 2014. Beyond motivation: job and work design for development, health, ambidexterity, and more. *Annual Review of Psychology*, 65(1): 661–691.

Parker, S.K., and Grote, G. 2020. Automation, algorithms, and beyond: why work design matters more than ever in a digital world. *Applied Psychology: An International Review*: 1–45. https://doi.org/10.1111/apps.12241.

Prentice, C., and Nguyen, M. 2020. Engaging and retaining customers with AI and employee service. *Journal of Retailing and Consumer Services*, 56: 102186.

Renkema, M., Bos-Nehles, A., and Meijerink, J. 2020. Implications of self-managing teams for the HRM function. *Baltic Journal of Management*, 15(4): 533–550.

Renwick, D. 2003. Line manager involvement in HRM: an inside view. *Employee Relations*, 25(3): 262–280.

Robert, L.P., Pierce, C., Marquis, L., Kim, S., and Alahmad, R. 2020. Designing fair AI for managing employees in organizations: a review, critique, and design agenda. *Human–Computer Interaction*, 35(5–6): 545–575.

Russell, S., and Norvig, P. 2021. *Artificial Intelligence: A Modern Approach* (4th global edition). Pearson Education.

Serengil, S.I., and Ozpinar, A. 2017. Workforce optimization for bank operation centers: a machine learning approach. *International Journal of Interactive Multimedia and Artificial Intelligence*, 4(6): 81–87.

Strohmeier, S. (forthcoming). Artificial intelligence in human resource management—an introduction. In S. Strohmeier (ed.), *Handbook of Research on Human Resource Management and Artificial Intelligence.*

Strohmeier, S., and Piazza, F. 2015. Artificial intelligence techniques in human resource management—a conceptual exploration, *Intelligent Systems Reference Library*, 87: 149–172.

Tambe, P., Cappelli, P., and Yakubovich, V. 2019. Artificial intelligence in human resources management: challenges and a path forward. *California Management Review*, 61(4): 15–42.

Upadhyay, A.K., and Khandelwal, K. 2018. Applying artificial intelligence: implications for recruitment. *Strategic HR Review*, 17(5): 255–258.

Van Esch, P., Black, J.S., and Ferolie, J. 2019. Marketing AI recruitment: the next phase in job application and selection. *Computers in Human Behavior*, 90: 215–222.

Van Waeyenberg, T., and Decramer, A. 2018. Line managers' AMO to manage employees' performance: the route to effective and satisfying performance management. *International Journal of Human Resource Management*, 29(22): 3093–3114.

Wamba-Taguimdje, S.-L., Fosso Wamba, S., Kala Kamdjoug, J.R., and Tchatchouang Wanko, C.E. 2020. Influence of artificial intelligence (AI) on firm performance: the business value of AI-based transformation projects. *Business Process Management Journal*, 26(7): 1893–1924.

Warnick, J. 2020. AI for humanity: how Starbucks plans to use technology to nurture the human spirit, *Starbucks Stories and News*. https://stories.starbucks.com/stories/2020/how-starbucks-plans-to-use-technology-to-nurture-the-human-spirit/.

Whittaker, S., and Marchington, M. 2003. Devolving HR responsibility to the line: threat, opportunity or partnership? *Employee Relations*, 25(3): 245–261.

Zahidi, S., Ratcheva, V.S., Hingel, G., and Brown, S. 2020. *The Future of Jobs Report 2020*. World Economic Forum.

24. Line managers and the gig economy: an oxymoron? Paradox navigation in online labor platform contexts

Jeroen Meijerink, Philip Rogiers and Anne Keegan

INTRODUCTION

This chapter discusses the implications of platform-enabled gig work for line managers and asks the question of whether online labor platforms (OLPs) diminish the role and status of line managers, or in fact render them more important than ever. Platform-enabled gig work is defined as short-term work (or "gig") assignments, where supply and demand for labor is matched by an online labor platform (Meijerink and Keegan, 2019). Intrinsic to this definition are two key terms—gig work and online labor platforms (OLPs)—that require further explanation. Gig work, as defined by Caza et al. (2021: 7), is "externalized paid work organized around 'gigs' (that is, projects or tasks) that workers engage in on a term-limited basis without a formal appointment within a particular organization." It is an inclusive term that covers several forms of contingent labor (Cappelli and Keller, 2013; Fischer and Connelly, 2017), such as e-lancing (Aguinis and Lawal, 2013), app work (Duggan et al., 2020), crowd work (Boons et al., 2015), on-demand work (Aloisi, 2016; van Doorn, 2017), micro entrepreneurship (Kuhn and Maleki, 2017), and dependent contracting (Connelly and Gallagher, 2006). Each of these gig activities differs in duration, ranging from work that lasts a few seconds or minutes, such as tagging a photo or delivering a meal (Boons et al., 2015; Gegenhuber et al., 2021; Meijerink et al., 2021b; Newlands, 2021; Veen et al., 2019), to project work that continues for months (Rogiers et al., 2021). Irrespective of duration, platform-enabled gig labor is organized by OLPs, which are organizations that use information technology to create an online marketplace to mediate supply and demand for contingent labor (Kuhn and Maleki, 2017; Meijerink and Keegan, 2019). Well-known OLPs are those that operate in the "gig economy" (McKinsey, 2016) where freelance workers offer on-demand services to consumers and organizations in industries such as transportation (for example, Uber, Lyft), meal delivery (Deliveroo, Uber Eats), cleaning (for example, Helpling), micro work (for example, Amazon Mechanical Turk, Clickworker), programming (for example, Fiverr, Upwork), and consultancy (for example, GigNow, Toptal).

In an opinion piece for the *New York Times* in 2018, Alex Rosenblat asks us to consider the implications of "when your boss is an algorithm" (Rosenblat, 2018b), referring to the many individuals today who work in an OLP and are managed not by a traditional line manager, but instead by an algorithm. Here, an algorithm refers to a computational formula that autonomously makes decisions based on statistical models or decision rules without explicit intervention by a human manager (Duggan et al., 2020; Newlands, 2021), which is a common management technique applied by OLPs. One striking issue arising from Rosenblat's (2018a) in-depth ethnographic study of Uber and Lyft platforms is how fundamentally different it is for workers to be managed by algorithms in OLPs rather than human managers, as well as how technology is being used to replace, or displace, human managers in various ways. In line with these observations, subsequent research has shown that OLPs may diminish the role of line managers in the labor processes in at least three fundamental ways. First, gig work—such as e-lancing and crowd work—takes place outside the confines of the standard employment relationship (Kuhn et al., 2021). As labor market intermediaries, many OLPs rely on a workforce of independent contractors who they match with consumers or organizations that request freelance services (Koutsimpogiorgos et al., 2020). Freelance gig workers neither have an employment relationship with the OLP, nor with the organizations that contract with them via an OLP (Meijerink and Keegan, 2019; Stanford, 2017). In platform-enabled gig work, line managers are therefore no longer responsible for the kinds of activities that are associated with maintaining the employment relationship, including communicating with and offering support to employees (Bos-Nehles et al., 2013; Den Hartog et al., 2013). Second, OLPs automate human resource management (HRM) activities traditionally performed by (first-) line managers, including organizing, allocating, and coordinating work (Bondarouk et al., 2009; Purcell and Hutchinson, 2007; Sikora et al., 2015). Their reliance on "algorithmic management" (Duggan et al., 2020; Lee et al., 2015; Leicht-Deobald et al., 2019; Meijerink et al., 2021a) to control worker behaviors (Möhlmann et al., 2021; Veen et al., 2019) and automate the execution of HRM activities in areas such as staffing (for example, granting workers access to the online marketplace), compensation (for example, surge pricing and algorithm-based pay rates), performance management (for example, algorithmic deactivation/dismissal), and workforce planning (for example, allocating workers to tasks), replaces frontline managers with algorithms (Meijerink and Bondarouk, 2021). By replacing managers as key HRM actors, and delegating HRM responsibilities to machines, the very role of line managers is called into question. Finally, HRM activities traditionally performed by line managers are also devolved to other (non-HRM) actors (Kuhn et al., 2021; Meijerink and Keegan, 2019). OLPs devolve performance appraisal to consumers by means of online rating schemes (Rosenblat et al., 2017), involve project managers in posting and organizing projects that gig workers can join (Rogiers et al., 2021), and work with procurement managers as clients to facilitate the contracting of freelance workers, similar to long-standing practices in project-based organizations (Keegan and Den Hartog, 2019). Taken together, this implies that OLPs diminish and displace the role of line managers in coordinating the labor processes and implementing HRM activities.

Despite the seemingly stark implications of OLPs for line managers, we contend that the (HRM) role of line managers is still worthy of academic inquiry and far from irrelevant in the context of platform-enabled gig work. The gig economy gives rise to new managerial responsibilities and challenges, and raises questions about the management of workers and execution of HRM activities (Kuhn et al., 2021). Current labor management practices deployed by OLPs are increasingly under pressure, and even seen as exploitative or illegitimate by societal stakeholders (Frenken et al., 2020), suggesting that OLPs need managers who are able to navigate societal pressures (Meijerink et al., 2021b). Moreover, freelance platform workers may strongly influence internal employment in contracting organizations by collaborating with employees and joining projects that are supervised by line managers. Incumbent organizations are also increasingly experimenting with establishing OLPs themselves to give line managers and employees the possibility to join projects in other organizational units (Rogiers et al., 2021), as well as to attract scarce talent to (internal) projects. In line with the idea that technology replaces tasks, but also causes new tasks to emerge (Frey and Osborne, 2017), we see an urgent need for more research into the consequences of OLPs for line managers. The aim of this chapter is therefore to outline the ways in which managerial responsibilities take shape in the gig economy, and to consider the implications for line managers. In doing so, we show the complexity that platform-enabled gig work presents to line managers, and call for research into how line managers navigate paradoxical tensions in the context of OLPs.

THE DEFINING CHARACTERISTICS OF PLATFORM-ENABLED GIG WORK

Platform-enabled gig work is organized by OLPs that match supply and demand for contingent labor. Three key features that characterize platform-enabled gig work merit particular attention—the organization of online marketplaces, short-term contingent labor, and the use of information technology—which are critical to understand the implications of this type of work for line managers (as discussed further in this chapter).

The Organization of Online Marketplaces

OLPs are (for-profit) organizations that assume the role of a labor market intermediary. The core value proposition of OLPs is the optimal matching of workers to those who are in need of short-term labor. These services rely on information technologies (such as smartphone applications, software algorithms, online databases, and review systems) that enable an online marketplace where labor supply and demand meet, and where liquidity of transactions is optimized (Frenken et al., 2020) between 'requesters (organizations and/or consumers) that post work assignments online, and gig workers who react to, accept, and work on these assignments. OLPs take an active role in brokering the transactions between requester and workers in several ways: (1) they may break down work assignments into smaller tasks, assign workers to tasks, and coordinate the overall delivery to the requestor; (2) they may recommend to organizations/consumers which worker(s) to hire; and (3) they may deploy reward and/or control systems that incentivize in various ways responsiveness of workers to the (time-pressured) requests of customers. OLPs rely on economic control systems to organize their online marketplace (Frenken et al., 2020; Gegenhuber et al., 2021; Meijerink et al., 2021b; Veen et al., 2019). They decide which requesters and workers are provided access to the online marketplace, set terms and conditions, and sanction those who do not comply. They decide on (minimum levels of) worker pay, set performance criteria, and exert (partial) control over the allocation of work. Accordingly, OLPs can be seen as corporations that organize markets (Frenken et al., 2020). Accordingly, we need to differentiate between platforms as organizations versus platforms as marketplaces. When we write about an OLP, we refer to the organization that organizes a market for contingent labor, while a platform marketplace refers to the transactions between workers and requesters as orchestrated by an OLP.

Short-Term Labor

The transactions that workers and requesters engage in, and that OLPs orchestrate, are fixed-term in nature (Duggan et al., 2020; Kuhn and Maleki, 2017). Although OLP workers and requesters may repeatedly engage in transactions, they can, in principle, decide to disengage at any time. Moreover, gig workers are nominally free not to use the OLP to access work assignments, and can decide to discontinue using the OLP's intermediation service and work for a requester just once. Given the episodic nature of platform-enabled gig work, most gigs are relatively short in duration. Depending on the tasks performed, gigs may last a few seconds (for example, tagging a photo via the Amazon Mechanical Turk platform), several minutes (for example, delivering a meal via Deliveroo or performing a taxi ride via Uber), a few hours (for example, cleaning via the Helpling platform), a day (for example, a freelance chef/cook who works via Temper), or several weeks or months (for example, joining a project via the GigNow platform).

Use of Information Technology for On-Demand Intermediation and Control

OLPs are heavily reliant on the use of information technology to automate matching processes. This makes them different from labor market intermediaries such as temp agencies (Meijerink and Arets, 2021; Meijerink and Keegan, 2019). Temp agencies employ human matchmakers to assign contingent workers to hiring organizations, while OLPs automate the assignment of workers to gigs by means of software algorithms (Meijerink and Arets, 2021). For example, Uber deploys algorithms that match passengers to freelance taxi drivers without involvement by a human (Rosenblat, 2018a), while Deliveroo relies on an algorithmic system that automates the dispatching of orders to meal deliverers (Meijerink et al., 2021b; Newlands, 2021; Veen et al., 2019). In contrast to temp agencies, OLPs hire very few (or no) employees who meet with hiring organizations and/or search for job candidates (Meijerink and Arets, 2021). Accordingly, the matching activities of OLPs are less labor-intensive—and thus involve lower operating costs—than those of temp agencies. While temp agencies have a financial incentive to intermediate work assignments that are longer-term in nature, to compensate for their operating costs, OLPs broker short-term and on-demand activities against lower costs achieved by delegating the matching of workers and requesters to technology. The system works as follows. Requesters can turn to a website or smartphone app that is designed by the OLP to post a work assignment. Via similar interfaces, gig workers in turn can react to these posts, (sometimes) negotiate terms and conditions, and accept the work offer made by a requester; all with no or little involvement by the platform organization. This self-service matching not only lowers costs to the OLP, but also offers flexibility to workers and requesters, who themselves can initiate transactions on-demand (Meijerink and Arets, 2021).

Although offering freedom and flexibility to workers and requesters as discussed already, OLPs nevertheless also control labor processes (Möhlmann et al., 2021; Newlands, 2021; Veen et al., 2019; Wood et al., 2019). This makes OLPs different from other labor market intermediaries such as job boards, search firms, or headhunters, that withdraw from the triadic relationship with workers and requesters once labor supply and demand are matched (Bonet et al., 2013; Meijerink and Keegan, 2019). In contrast, OLPs remain involved throughout transactions between workers and requesters. Specifically, OLPs operate algorithmic management systems to control worker–requester interactions at scale (Duggan et al., 2020; Newlands, 2021), and use a business model that involves skimming a fee from each transaction in their online marketplace to capture surplus value from labor power (Gandini, 2019; Kellogg et al., 2020; Veen et al., 2019).

VARIETIES OF ONLINE LABOR PLATFORMS

OLPs also come in different forms, and thereby impact line managers differently. For the purpose of this chapter, we differentiate between three types of OLPs. Although each type meets the defining characteristics of OLPs that we outlined earlier (that is, online marketplaces for short-term labor that is orchestrated and controlled by means of information technology), they differ in terms of corporate governance, business model, and employment relationships. In line with the work by Kuhn et al. (2021) and Rogiers et al. (2021), we distinguish three types of OLPs: standalone freelance platforms, spin-off freelance platforms of incumbent organizations, and intraorganizational gig platforms. We then detail the ways in which line managers confront and navigate the paradoxes posed by these platform types.

Stand-Alone Freelance Platforms

Standalone freelance platforms are OLPs that match independent contractors to those that request freelance services in industries such as transportation (for example, Uber, Lyft), meal delivery (Deliveroo, Uber Eats), cleaning (for example, Helpling), micro work (for example, Clickworker), programming (for example, Fiverr, Upwork), leisure (for example, Temper and YoungOnes), and consultancy (for example, Toptal). Rather than instituting an employment relationship with workers, standalone freelance platforms work with solo self-employed workers who offer freelance services to consumers (for example, Uber and Helpling) or organizations and businesses (for example, Temper). The standalone nature of these freelance platforms follows from their governance structure, where one (or a small group of) individual entrepreneur(s) sees a business opportunity for an online marketplace, establishes an OLP and attracts venture capital (in return for stock options) to grow the online marketplace (van Doorn and Badger, 2021). Many iconic platforms in the gig economy such as Uber (founded by Travis Kalanick and Garrett Camp) and Deliveroo (founded by Will Shu) are new business ventures, or start-ups, that recently launched an initial public offering (IPO). A standalone platform attempts to become a "winner takes all" that outcompetes rival platforms by attracting a growing number of platform users (Cennamo and Santalo, 2013), and leveraging network effects which Katz and Shapiro (1994: 94) explain as "the value of membership to one user is positively affected when another user joins and enlarges the network." These competitive processes are costly, as evidenced by standalone platforms' continued loss-making and alleged "burning" of venture capital on discounts to attract workers and requesters to their online markets (van Doorn and Badger, 2021). In the expectation of making future profits (Birch et al., 2021), standalone platforms attempt to control labor processes to ensure workers and requesters remain transacting via the OLP, increase the number of platform-generated transactions, and ultimately extract value from transactions once they are the "last platform standing" in a particular market space.

Spin-Off Freelance Platforms

Spin-off freelance platforms are similar to their standalone counterparts in that they work with freelancers and, in most cases, are recently founded. Instead of being founded by an individual (or small group of) entrepreneur(s), however, spin-off platforms are established by incumbent organizations seeking to augment their current business activities by using a platform model to attract clients and freelance workers (Kuhn et al., 2021). There are broadly two reasons why incumbent organizations work with freelancers, based on which we distinguish two types of spin-off platforms. First, spin-off platforms allow temp agencies to offer novel labor market intermediation services and enter new markets for on-demand labor offered by independent contractors (Meijerink and Arets, 2021). An example is the YoungOnes freelance platform, which is a spin-off of the YoungCapital temp agency. YoungCapital engages with temp workers who are co-employed at both the temp agency and the hiring organization. Additionally, targeting an extra market for intermediation services, YoungOnes also augments its incumbent-owner by attracting workers (for example, when freelance workers move from the spin-off platform to YoungCapital) and requesters (for example, offering a one-stop shop for organizations looking for different types of contingent labor).

A second type of spin-off platform helps incumbent-owners with the possibility to augment their permanent workforce with on-demand freelance labor. An example is the GigNow platform, which is a spin-off of the consultancy company Ernst & Young (EY). GigNow enables EY to recruit freelance workers who work alongside the permanent workforce of consultants on projects that EY executes for its clients, or performs for itself. EY attempts to leverage its brand image to organize contingent labor itself, rather than outsourcing the hiring of project contractors to temp agencies of standalone freelance platforms, which is the traditional way in which these organizations procure additional resources to manage peak workloads on projects (Keegan and Den Hartog, 2019).

Intraorganizational Gig Platforms

Intraorganizational gig platforms (IGPs) differ from standalone and spin-off freelance platforms because their workforce consists of a pool of regular, salaried workforce employees. In fact, as IGPs operate within the bounds of a single organization, both workers and requesters of IGPs are employees to the same employer or organization. Inspired by the success of freelance platforms, and driven by the need to reskill the workforce and encourage labour mobility (Schrage et al., 2020), IGPs orchestrate an intraorganizational marketplace, enabling project leaders to recruit colleagues from other organizational units that want to join a project on a temporary and/or part-time basis (Rogiers et al., 2021). This means that workers who join a project via an IGP do so in addition to their main job roles. Although working within organizational boundaries, project workers do not work under the authority of the IGP. Rather, the CLIP is an intraorganizational intermediary to employees who continue to report to their line manager while simultaneously working on a part-time project that is organized by (an employee supervised) by another line manager (Rogiers et al., 2021).

Paradoxical Tensions in The Three Types of OLPs

The three types of OLPs outlined above have their unique features in terms of governance structure and platform–worker relationships. OLPs are established for different reasons and may therefore engage with workers as freelancers or employees. These differences mean that OLPs impact on the role of line managers in different ways, and have different implications for them. To better understand the implications of OLPs for line managers in their different roles, we adopt a paradox theoretical lens (Smith and Lewis, 2011). As outlined next, each OLP type is characterized by paradoxical tensions that line managers need to address. Line managers engage with the gig economy in different ways: as an executive of a standalone freelance platform; as a supervisor that sources contingent labor through a stand-along or spin-off platform; or as a direct report to employees who temporarily engage in another project via an IGP. In what follows, we outline the impact of platform-enabled work on line managers in several of their roles, and discuss how this is characterized by paradox navigation (Chapter 6 in this book; Fu et al., 2020; Keegan et al., 2018).

PARADOX NAVIGATION BY LINE MANAGERS IN THE GIG ECONOMY

Poole and Van de Ven (1989: 565) define paradoxes as contradictory "well-founded, well-reasoned, and well-supported alternative explanations of the same phenomenon" which "are in some sense incompatible or hard to reconcile." In management and organization studies, paradoxes are defined as "contradictory yet interrelated elements that exist simultaneously and persist over time" (Smith and Lewis, 2011: 382). As noted by Jarzabkowski and Lê (2017), core to most definitions of paradox is the juxtaposition of contradictory interrelated elements that must be handled simultaneously, often causing far-reaching tensions for actors who must navigate "interrelated elements that seem consistent in isolation but incompatible or contradictory in conjunction" (ibid.: 434). Examples of organizational paradoxes include the complex and persistent interrelationships between exploration and exploitation (O'Reilly and Tushman, 2013), standardization and localization (Ghoshal and Bartlett, 1990), or automation and augmentation (Raisch and Krakowski, 2021).

In HRM scholarship, numerous paradoxes have been identified and studied (see Aust et al., 2015; Keegan et al., 2019). For example, paradoxes relating to the distribution of HRM responsibilities among different actors (Keegan et al., 2018), and the demands on HR policies to meet the contradictory needs of different audiences (Brandl and Bullinger, 2017), have all been studied. To date, there has been less attention paid to paradoxical tensions linked specifically with the roles of line managers, although this is slowly changing (Chapter 6 in this book). If not well managed, paradoxes manifest as tensions which can be debilitating for actors due to clashes between interests, ideas, principles, or actions. Paradoxical HRM tensions must therefore be viewed as complex and co-evolving dynamically over time (Keegan et al., 2018), and require active and reflexive engagement by actors (Fu et al., 2020). Research suggests that business models pursued by OLPs can cause tensions with organizational and societal actors both in the case of (standalone) freelance platforms (Meijerink et al., 2021b) as well as for internal labor platforms (Rogiers et al., 2021). Although line managers are unlikely to be sheltered from platform-generated paradoxes, and experience different tensions depending on the type of OLP considered, there has been almost no research on this issue to date. We therefore examine the implications for line managers of the further spread of OLP models to engage workers.

Managers Employed by Standalone Freelance Platforms

The organization of gig work by standalone freelance platforms involves balancing tensions between autonomy and control, which has implications for line managers who are employed by these platforms. One the one hand, freelance platforms favor working with freelancers to avoid paying for social security benefits (which freelancers are not entitled to) and offering financial compensation when gig workers are waiting for tasks to be completed. Legally, OLPs need to provide worker autonomy to affirm the freelance status of their contingent workforce. This involves the freedom for gig workers to decide on when, how, and for who they want to work. Moreover, as independent contractors, gig workers are nominally free to decide on the fee they charge to requesters. On the other hand, freelance platforms need to control gig worker behavior, which contradicts the autonomy that freelancers ought to enjoy. As corporations that organize online markets (Frenken et al., 2020), OLPs need to exercise control to balance supply and demand for labor, ensure that gig workers meet the needs of requesters, and avoid situations where requesters go against gig worker interests (Meijerink and Keegan, 2019; Veen et al., 2019). Ultimately, this ensures liquidity in transactions in the online marketplace from which the standalone freelance platform can capture economic rent.

Such autonomy–control paradoxes (Wood et al., 2019) pervade platform-enabled gig work and draw scrutiny from stakeholders which can challenge the legitimacy of OLPs (Frenken et al., 2020; Meijerink et al., 2021b). Tensions between these contradictory yet simultaneous elements are well documented, as are their implications for the very existence of platform-based organizing. Legal scholars describe how autonomy–control paradoxes manifest as false self-employment by freelance platforms, which have led to labor unions around the globe initiating reclassification lawsuits (Aloisi, 2016; Meijerink et al., 2021b; Zekić, 2019). To understand the source of these paradoxical tensions, Frenken et al. (2020) conceptually show how freelance platforms create institutional complexity. In the case of freelance platforms, institutional complexity manifests as incompatibilities between the market logic and corporation logic (Frenken et al., 2020; Meijerink et al., 2021b). The market logic propagates freedom and autonomy to ensure that freelancers—as the smallest of small businesses—can engage in free, unregulated competition. The corporation logic, on the other hand, legitimizes the exercise of control over employees who receive a salary in return for helping their employer to gain market share. As (pre-IPO) start-up ventures, freelance platforms control their freelance workforce to grow their marketplace to outcompete rivals and become the "winner takes all" of the market for intermediation services (that is, corporation logic), which contradicts the freelance status that these OLPs also propagate (that is, market logic), which is consistent with freelancer autonomy rather than control. Ultimately, the institutional complexity created by this dynamic threatens freelance platforms' legitimacy, as evidenced by numerous reclassification court cases on the employment status of gig workers (Frenken et al., 2020; Meijerink et al., 2021b).

The managers of freelance platforms are responsible for addressing the institutional complexity associated with the autonomy–control paradox (Meijerink et al., 2021b). OLPs employ a workforce of marketing, operations, programmers, and legal specialists who are responsible for orchestrating the platform firms' online marketplaces (Kuhn et al., 2021). These specialists can exercise control over freelance gig workers in both direct way (for example, giving instructions) and indirect ways (for example, designing software algorithms that delegate authority over gig workers to clients) (Gandini, 2019; Meijerink et al., 2021b; Veen et al., 2019). This creates tensions when platform-directed control (that is, corporation logic) negates the autonomy and freelance status of gig workers (that is, market logic). As shown by Meijerink et al. (2021b), the managers of freelance platforms are responsible for balancing these tensions. These managers—and the employees they supervise—do so through response strategies to institutional complexity such as "playing with discourse" (for example, the platforms suggests "tips and tricks" to freelancers, rather than giving instructions), covert HRM implementation (for example, increasing the opaqueness of algorithmic management to mask platform-directed control), HRM outsourcing (for example, offering training to gig workers via a third party), and HRM devolution (for example, asking requesters to leave customer reviews) (Meijerink et al., 2021b). As such, the management of freelance platforms can be seen as an attempt to navigate paradoxes in terms of balancing between gig worker autonomy (that is, market logic) and control (that is, corporation logic). However, the tensions arising also attract critical scrutiny from institutional actors observing these tensions as indications of institutionally illegitimate or questionable practices.

Managers Who Source Labor using a Freelance Platform

Line managers of contracting organizations face paradoxical tensions in terms of managing interactions between freelance workers. Contracting organizations are those that rely on freelance platforms to augment their permanent workforces (Kuhn et al., 2021). Although contracting organizations outsource work via freelance platforms that "core" employees typically do not perform (for example, cleaning), there are cases where freelance gig workers work alongside the permanent workforce of a contracting organization, as for example in project-based organizations that augment project teams with contractors (Keegan et al., 2012). In such cases, line managers (or project managers) supervise teams where permanent employees and freelance gig workers are interdependent in completing work assignments. Examples include freelance cooks who a restaurant contracts with via the Temper platform and who work alongside the chef who is employed by that restaurant; or hospitals that hire freelance nurses and medical specialists via the Jellow platform. Paradoxical tensions occur when freelance workers—with scarce or unique skills—are able to negotiate terms and conditions that are more favorable than those of permanent workers.

As noted by McKeown and Pichault (2021), these challenges can be understood using the HR architecture model of Lepak and Snell (1999) that classifies workers via a two-by-two matrix depending on the strategic value and uniqueness of their human capital. The HR architecture proposes that organizations internalize human capital that is unique and of high strategic value. Human capital that is non-core to the organization and widely available in the labor market is outsourced and managed by means of arm's-length relationships. Workers who possess unique or scarce competence may decide, however, to work as a freelancers and offer their services to the highest bidders via a freelance platform. This creates tensions for line managers of contracting organizations: the value and uniqueness of a freelancer's human capital creates push-and-pull tensions between internalizing the worker (as desired by the contracting organization) and externalizing the worker (as desired by the freelancer). As shown by McKeown and Pichault (2021), line mangers therefore need to navigate paradoxical tensions between treating freelancers as a resource that needs to be committed to the organization and strategically managed, while simultaneously upholding their freelance status and establishing an arm's-length relationships in terms of making them comply with contractual terms.

Even in cases where contracting organizations and their line managers wish to outsource work to individuals with non-strategic and non-unique human capital via a freelance platform, paradoxes may occur. Theory predicts that managers rely on freelance platforms to source contingent labor in order to lower transaction costs (Lepak and Snell, 1999). The online marketplace of freelance platforms lowers barriers to transactions and allows workers and requesters to be matched without much human involvement (Rosenblat, 2018a). Moreover, when human capital is widely available in the labor market and of little strategic value to the firm, there is little need to incur governance costs (that is, organizational control over workers). Instead, market dynamics are considered a more efficient way of controlling the individuals that an organization contracts with. As said before, however, freelance platforms need to delegate (organizational) control over gig workers to requesters, to limit institutional complexity and avoid reclassification lawsuits (Meijerink et al., 2021b). In doing so, requesters spend time on managerial activities such as the selection and/or appraisal of gig workers that nominally are enacted by a labor market intermediary such as temp agencies (Cappelli and Keller, 2013). Put differently, while turning to freelance platforms to lower (transaction) costs (Fisher and Connelly, 2017), managers of contracting organizations simultaneously incur (governance) costs that freelance platforms put onto them. For instance, Rahman and Valentine (2021) show that the use of platform-provided control tools (for example, review systems) by "client managers"—those using freelance platforms to hire and manage workers—resulted in higher costs to these managers in terms of uncompleted project outcomes by a freelancer. Similarly, Claussen et al. (2020) showed that organizational control mechanisms that platforms delegate to client managers were negatively related with perceived project success, as rated by both the manager of the contracting organization and the freelancer (Claussen et al., 2020). As these examples show, managers who contract with freelance gig workers need to navigate between paradoxical tensions related to cost reduction and market mechanisms, on the one hand, and the freelance platform requiring them to deploy organizational control mechanisms that drive up governance costs to the hiring organization, on the other.

Managers Employed by Organizations with a Spin-Off Freelance Platform

Spin-off platform such as the GigNow platform are set up by an incumbent organization to contract with freelancers that join projects to be coordinated by the incumbent. Paradoxical tensions in project work that is organized by spin-off platforms become manifest when organizational line managers or project managers are asked to evaluate freelance contractors, even though there is no formal employment relationship with these workers, and at the same time these workers remain dependent on such evaluations for their further career development and employability in ways that may influence their commitment to projects and loyalty to project managers (Keegan and Den Hartog, 2019). Likewise, from an organizational perspective, even though meeting core psychological needs of project workers for competence development is likely to contribute to project success and other outcomes including the health and well-being of project workers (Gagné and Deci, 2005), platform-enabled hiring of project contractors places line (and project) managers in a tension-filled position of having to both support workers (to ensure their commitment to projects and competence to perform), while maintaining boundaries with them consistent with their freelancer status. These dynamics create paradoxical situations and place organizational line and project managers in a bind of being "damned if they do, and damned if they don't." Such dilemmas are not entirely new for project-based organizations (Bredin and Söderlund, 2011; Keegan et al., 2012), but the increased spread of OLP-type constructions for hiring project workers might expose such tensions between the need to support, and the need to maintain distance from, project workers hired through platforms.

Managers Who Organize Intraorganizational Gig Platforms

Intraorganizational gig platforms, or IGPs, are run by line managers who face the critical challenge of balancing the platform's supply and demand of labor. This problem consists of two related challenges: (1) drawing sufficient users to the platform; and (2) maintaining user activity. While freelance OLPs especially struggle with the first challenge, IGPs mostly wrestle with the latter, for two reasons (Rogiers et al., 2020b). First, IGPs are less exposed to competition from other platforms, as they operate inside an organization and can tap into a continuous potential source of labor supply and demand, corresponding to the collective of workforce employees in an organization. Second, IGPs rely on employees' voluntary participation in part-time and fixed-term projects (for example, for a maximum of 20 percent of their weekly work time) without the lure of additional remuneration (Rogiers et al., 2021). These platform characteristics require IGP managers to be particularly considerate of platform users' goals when designing and managing user interactions.

Nevertheless, reconciling platform users' goals can be a daunting task, especially when the goals of users misalign in paradoxical ways. On one side are the employees who decide to take on projects in the IGP (that is, project workers). These individuals are motivated to learn new things and expand their horizons; but often also feel limited in their ability to pursue these goals in their regular jobs (Stengård et al., 2017; Verbruggen and De Vos, 2020). While side-hustles or freelance activities can offer a resolution (Sessions et al., 2021), working outside the organization's bounds can be a step too far for many. To these people, the IGP offers a space where they can pursue their developmental goals within their broader organization, but outside of their regular work environment (Rogiers et al., 2021; Schrage et al., 2020). On the other side, then, are the employees who post projects in the online marketplace of the IGP, to whom we refer as project posters. These people often come to the IGP with a specific project requiring an extra pair of hands. To them, the IGP embodies a convenient tool to source a volunteer from the platform's intraorganizational pool of workers without the administrative and HR-related burdens associated with bringing in temporary workers from outside the organization.

While workers' and posters' goals (that is, development versus labor outsourcing) are not contradictory in and of themselves, either side can pursue them in ways that are in tension with their counterparts' goals in the platform (Rogiers et al., 2020b), potentially creating paradoxes. For instance, our ongoing study of the United States (US) government's Open Opps platform suggests that project workers may want to venture outside of their comfort zone by taking on projects that lie beyond their expertise, yet they may sometimes do so without considering the output or competence expectations of project posters. As a result, workers may oversell their ability to deliver on a project, or leave a project prematurely when their interest wanes. Such behavior, in turn, can be experienced as a significant burden by project posters, who hoped to source a reliable and competent worker to help them get their project done. These interactions can leave users disillusioned and create tensions in the IGP's online marketplace. We also find that the reverse can be true, as some project posters may not care about creating a long-term reciprocal relation with project workers. If project posters enact their role this way, they may negate workers' expectations of practicing new skills and receiving mentorship and support from project posters. In short, tensions are likely to arise when project posters or project workers set off to realize their goals without considering the goals of others, and their mutual dependence in the realization of each other's goals, which can generate paradoxical tensions that IGP managers need to navigate (Rogiers et al., 2020b; Schrage et al., 2020).

As IGP managers navigate these emerging tensions, they face a paradoxical question: whose preferences and needs do they prioritize when posters and workers' goals misalign? That is to say, if they adopt an either/or approach, and do not simultaneously cater to both users, this will leave the IGP managers ineffective as matchmakers of labor supply and demand, and risk creating imbalances in the platform (Weller et al., 2019). As IGP managers address tensions between project workers and posters, arising from users' interdependence combined with contradictory goals (Smith and Lewis, 2011), IGP managers' actions must carefully consider the goals of both sides, and aim to achieve both/and outcomes rather than siding with one or the other. The context of Open Opps in the US government illustrates this balancing act. In response to emerging tensions between project workers and project posters, for instance, IGP managers introduced a new platform feature that allowed project sponsors to reopen the project to new applicants when a project worker had dropped out. This feature reduced the impact on project posters when workers could not follow through on their promises of delivering on a project, yet without punishing project workers in such a situation. Another example is IGP managers' introduction of a positive performance evaluation system in Open Opps that accommodates posters' desire to vet their prospective project workers, as well as workers' aversion to negative performance feedback (which would cause them to refrain from taking risks and stepping outside of their comfort zone). In the newly introduced performance evaluation system, workers can earn badges that signal positive achievements, while avoiding negative feedback on their profiles. These examples illustrate how IGP managers can develop both/and solutions (Smith and Lewis, 2011) to the tensions that emerge between project posters and workers in the IGP (Rogiers et al., 2020b). These examples also highlight that IGP managers' responses to paradoxes must be seen as dynamically co-evolving with previous solutions to tensions which generate new paradoxes over time and which resist one-off solutions (Jarzabkowski et al., 2013). While these solutions to IGP tensions need not be complex, they must cater to both project posters and project workers simultaneously, as to accommodate both sides as well as acknowledging their interdependencies (Smith and Lewis, 2011) that characterize these platforms (Weller et al., 2019). It is further critical for IGP managers to realize that working dynamically through tensions (Keegan et al., 2018) between workers and posters is a continuous occupation, and inherent to IGP managers' role as paradox navigators. Paradoxical tensions are by their nature unavoidable, and they require both/and responses based on constant monitoring and, at times, preventive actions, to avoid escalations that can offset the matching equilibrium in an IGP.

Managers of Workers that Perform Work via an Intraorganizational Gig Platform

Seen from a line managerial perspective, IGPs further create several opportunities for organizations and their line managers to fill critical skills gaps, identify untapped potential, and match employees to work where they can add the most value (Bidwell, 2017; Boudreau et al., 2015; O'Shea and Puente, 2017). As line managers allow (and encourage) employees' practicing of new skills in the IGP beyond their usual work environment and job responsibilities, employees' internal employability can also be expected to increase (van der Heijden and Bakker, 2011), thereby shaping a new source of workforce flexibility (Fuller et al., 2019). These benefits primarily stem from IGPs' ability to identify and mitigate skills gaps that formerly remained hidden in the organization. For instance, as employees sign up to work in the platform, they start by creating an online profile where they list their current skillsets and the areas in which they would like to develop themselves further. Worker profiles in IGPs also offer a view into people's achievements and platform work history, affording them an outlet to unveil their hidden talents and give voice to their developmental aspirations (Rogiers et al., 2020a). Extrapolated, the data provided and created by workers in the platform then shape the potential for line managers to better identify and utilize available skills in the workforce (Gantcheva et al., 2020; Schrage et al., 2020), and share internal talent across departmental boundaries (Bidwell, 2017; O'Shea and Puente, 2017; Weller et al., 2019). Through this function, IGPs can be a critical aid to line managers, who often do not sufficiently tap into employees' skills and full potential (De Boeck et al., 2019) and often do not possess the insights or tools to do so effectively (Fuller et al., 2019; Gantcheva et al., 2020; Schrage et al., 2020).

Nonetheless, employees' participation in IGPs involves a paradox from the standpoint of individual line managers, which can keep them from realizing the IGP's benefits. Through the IGP, personal knowledge becomes public, such as employees' untapped skills or willingness to try different tasks, jobs, and locations (Schrage et al., 2020). While rendering this information public yields several benefits for organizations and their line managers, as discussed above, line managers may simultaneously have reservations. In particular, they may fear that letting employees work beyond their purview would negatively affect their power and status in the organization. For instance, while line managers formerly could use private knowledge to reward high-performing employees and tie them to their team through the promise of promotions (Weller et al., 2019), IGPs start to take this discretion out of the manager's hands (Schrage et al., 2020), reducing their sense of control and authority. Additionally, the work of Rogiers et al. (2021) shows that image concerns may also arise among line managers whose employees request to participate in an IGP. Managers were especially concerned with what signal would be sent to the broader organization as employees took on part-time projects outside of their formal responsibilities and beyond their assigned work units. Would it signal to colleagues and superiors that their employees are not satisfied, sufficiently challenged, and optimally deployed by the line manager? Altogether, these dynamics constitute important explanations for the line managers' resistance to IGPs.

While it is easy to critique line managers for putting their needs above those of their employees, it should be acknowledged that their position as paradox navigator is not an easy one. As IGPs are a new phenomenon in most workplaces where they appear, these platforms are often not yet explicitly endorsed by senior (line) management (Rogiers et al., 2020a). This lack of leadership endorsement then puts all the weight on individual line managers' shoulders to decide whether or not to endorse employees' participation in the platform (Rogiers et al., 2021). This is especially true in large organizations consisting of multiple business units and/ or departments and multiple layers of leadership, such as large multinational enterprises or governmental organizations that have started to experiment with IGPs (Gantcheva et al., 2020; Schrage et al., 2020). There, line managers often fear repercussions for letting their employees take on projects that do not directly contribute to the targets or performance indicators of the units for which they are accountable. In environments where the pressure to perform is high and resources are limited (Rogiers et al., 2021), IGPs risk being perceived as a threat by individual line managers rather than as an opportunity (Gardner et al., 2010), resulting in managers' steadying—instead of easing—of their (perceived) grip over organizational rules and conventions (Langfred and Rockmann, 2016).

Despite these power struggles, ample opportunities exist for line managers to rethink their role vis-à-vis IGPs' entrance into today's organizations. Evidence from a pioneering IGP suggests that managers who participate in IGPs can benefit in several ways. For instance, as managers encourage their employees to gain new experience by taking on part-time projects with new people in new places, these employees are ideally positioned to identify new practices and build new networks that can further their original business units' goals (Rogiers et al., 2021). Moreover, by fostering initiative and becoming ambassadors for this new working style (for example, by posting projects and hiring workers from other departments), line managers can further take the IGP as an opportunity to brush up their image and reputation within their respective organizations. In short, ample opportunities exist for line managers who dare to rethink their stance toward new phenomena such as IGPs. Creating a managerial culture that supports managers in navigating emerging paradoxes associated with IGPS is critical, for these managers are key gatekeepers to the successful adoption and operation of these new work platforms that challenge existing assumptions and generate new, and possibly fruitful, tensions.

CONCLUSION

At a first glance, line managers seem to play a minor role in platform-enabled gig work. Traditionally, line managers are responsible for managing employment relationships and executing HRM activities; these organizational artifacts are diminished by online labor platforms that erode the standard employment relationship and operate software algorithms to automate people management. Moreover, online labor platforms devolve responsibilities to non-managerial actors such as consumers and workers themselves, thereby putting line managers on the sidelines of labor processes.

At the same time, and if we look beyond the obvious, we see that online labor platforms bring about opportunities for line mangers, and may even change line managerial roles. Throughout this chapter, we have discussed how the role of line managers in a gig economy context can be seen as that of a paradox navigator. Specifically, and depending on what type of platform-enabled labor is concerned, line managers need to address different paradoxical tensions. For instance, line managers within freelance platforms such as Uber and Deliveroo need to strike a balance between controlling and granting autonomy to gig workers, while line mangers who source labor from online labor platforms need to strike a balance in terms of integrating freelance platform workers within their teams of standard workers. Where intraorganizational gig platforms are concerned, line managers need to align the conflicting goals of different platform users (for example, project workers who want to learn, while project posters are in need of on-demand, short-term labor) as well as manage tensions between the regular work activities of workers and the project work they engage in via an internal gig platform.

Rather than diminishing the role of line managers, our analysis shows that the gig economy changes and challenges the conventional work of line managers. A paradox-theoretical lens is valuable and useful as it allows us to see which challenges (and opportunities) online labor platforms bring to managers, together with the strategies that line managers can rely on to address and handle tensions. We hope that this chapter offers fertile ground for future studies at the intersection between line management, gig work, and online labor platforms.

REFERENCES

Aguinis, H., and Lawal, S.O. 2013. eLancing: A review and research agenda for bridging the science–practice gap. *Human Resource Management Review*, 23(1): 6–17.

Aloisi, A. 2016. Commoditized workers: Case study research on labor law issues arising from a set of on-demand/gig economy platforms. *Comparative Labor Law and Policy Journal*, 37(3): 653–690.

Aust, I., Brandl, J., and Keegan, A. 2015. State-of-the-art and future directions for HRM from a paradox perspective: Introduction to the Special Issue. *German Journal of Human Resource Management*, 29(3–4): 194–213.

Bidwell, M. 2017. Managing talent flows through internal and external labor markets. In D.G. Collings, K. Mellahi, and W. Cascio (eds), *The Oxford Handbook of Talent Management* (pp. 283–300). Oxford: Oxford University Press.

Birch, K., Cochrane, D., and Ward, C. 2021. Data as asset? The measurement, governance, and valuation of digital personal data by Big Tech. *Big Data and Society*, 8(1): 20539517211017308.

Bondarouk, T., Looise, J.K., and Lempsink, B. 2009. Framing the implementation of HRM innovation: HR professionals vs line managers in a construction company. *Personnel Review*, 38(5): 472–491.

Bonet, R., Cappelli, P., and Hamori, M. 2013. Labor market intermediaries and the new paradigm for human resources. *Academy of Management Annals*, 7(1): 341–392.

Boons, M., Stam, D., and Barkema, H.G. 2015. Feelings of pride and respect as drivers of ongoing member activity on crowdsourcing platforms. *Journal of Management Studies*, 52(6): 717–741.

Bos-Nehles, A.C., Van Riemsdijk, M.J., and Looise, J.K. 2013. Employee perceptions of line management performance: Applying the AMO theory to explain the effectiveness of line managers' HRM implementation. *Human Resource Management*, 52(6): 861–877.

Boudreau, J.W., Jesuthasan, R., and Creelman, D. 2015. *Lead the Work: Navigating a World Beyond Employment*. Hoboken, NJ: John Wiley & Sons.

Brandl, J., and Bullinger, B. 2017. Individuals' considerations when responding to competing logics: Insights from identity control theory. *Journal of Management Inquiry*, 26(2): 181–192.

Bredin, K., and Söderlund, J. 2011. The HR quadriad: A framework for the analysis of HRM in project-based organizations. *International Journal of Human Resource Management*, 22(10): 2202–2221.

Cappelli, P., and Keller, J.R., 2013. Classifying work in the new economy. *Academy of Management Review*, 38(4): 575–596.

Caza, B.B., Reid, E.M., Ashford, S., and Granger, S. 2021. Working on my own: Measuring the challenges of gig work. *Human Relations*, p.00187267211030098.

Cennamo, C., and Santalo, J. 2013. Platform competition: Strategic trade-offs in platform markets. *Strategic Management Journal*, 34(11): 1331–1350.

Claussen, J., Kretschmer, T., Khashabi, P., and Seifried, M. 2020. Two to tango? Psychological contract breach in online labor markets. Paper presented at the Academy of Management Annual Meeting.

Connelly, C.E., and Gallagher, D.G. 2006. Independent and dependent contracting: Meaning and implications. *Human Resource Management Review*, 16(2): 95–106.

De Boeck, G., Dries, N., and Tierens, H. 2019. The experience of untapped potential: Towards a subjective temporal understanding of work meaningfulness. *Journal of Management Studies*, 56(3): 529–557.

Den Hartog, D.N., Boon, C., Verburg, R.M., and Croon, M.A. 2013. HRM, communication, satisfaction, and perceived performance a cross-level test. *Journal of Management*, 39(6): 1637–1665.

Duggan, J., Sherman, U., Carbery, R., and McDonnell, A. 2020. Algorithmic management and app-work in the gig economy: A research agenda for employment relations and HRM. *Human Resource Management Journal*, 30(1): 114–132.

Fischer, S.L. and Connelly, C.E. 2017. Lower cost or just lower value: Modeling the organizational costs and benefits of contingent work. *Academy of Management Discovery*, 3: 165–186.

Frenken, K., Vaskelainen, T., Fünfschilling, L., and Piscicelli, L. 2020. An institutional logics perspective on the gig economy. In I. Maurer, J. Mair, and A. Oberg (eds), *Theorizing the Sharing Economy: Variety and Trajectories of New Forms of Organizing* (Vol. 66, pp. 83–105). Bingley: Emerald Publishing.

Frey, C.B., and Osborne, M.A. 2017. The future of employment: How susceptible are jobs to computerisation? *Technological Forecasting and Social Change*, 114(1): 254–280.

Fu, N., Flood, P.C., Rousseau, D.M., and Morris, T. 2020. Line managers as paradox navigators in HRM implementation: Balancing consistency and individual responsiveness. *Journal of Management*, 46(2): 203–233.

Fuller, J.B., Raman, M., Wallenstein, J., and de Chalendar, A. 2019. Your workforce is more adaptable than you think. *Harvard Business Review*, 97(3): 118–126.

Gagné, M., and Deci, E.L. 2005. Self-determination theory and work motivation. *Journal of Organizational Behavior*, 26(4): 331–362.

Gandini, A. 2019. Labour process theory and the gig economy. *Human Relations*, 72(6): 1039–1056.

Gantcheva, I., Jones, R., Kearns-Manolatos, D., Schwartz, J., Lee, L., and Rawat, M. 2020. Activating the internal talent marketplace: Accelerate workforce resilience, agility and capability, and impact the future of work. Deloitte Workforce Transformation Practice.

Gardner, W.L., Lowe, K.B., Moss, T.W., Mahoney, K.T., and Cogliser, C.C. 2010. Scholarly leadership of the study of leadership: A review of *The Leadership Quarterly*'s second decade, 2000–2009. *Leadership Quarterly*, 21(6): 922–958.

Gegenhuber, T., Ellmer, M., and Schüßler, E. 2021. Microphones, not megaphones: Functional crowdworker voice regimes on digital work platforms. *Human Relations*, 74(9): 1473–1503.

Ghoshal, S., and Bartlett, C.A. 1990. The multinational corporation as an interorganizational network. *Academy of Management Review*, 15(4): 603–626.

Jarzabkowski, P.A., and Lê, J.K. 2017. We have to do this and that? You must be joking: Constructing and responding to paradox through humor. *Organization Studies*, 38(3–4): 433–462.

Jarzabkowski, P., Lê, J.K., and Van de Ven, A.H. 2013. Responding to competing strategic demands: How organizing, belonging, and performing paradoxes coevolve. *Strategic Organization*, 11(3): 245–280.

Katz, M.L., and Shapiro, C. 1994. Systems competition and network effects. *Journal of Economic Perspectives*, 8(2): 93–115.

Keegan, A., and Den Hartog, D. 2019. Doing it for themselves? Performance appraisal in project-based organisations, the role of employees, and challenges to theory. *Human Resource Management Journal*, 29(2): 217–237.

Keegan, A., Bitterling, I., Sylva, H., and Hoeksema, L. 2018. Organizing the HRM function: Responses to paradoxes, variety, and dynamism. *Human Resource Management*, 57(5): 1111–1126.

Keegan, A., Brandl, J., and Aust, I. 2019. Human resource management and paradox theory. In K. Townsend, K. Cafferkey, A. McDermott, and T. Dundon (eds), *Elgar Introduction to Theories of Human Resources and Employment Relations* (pp. 199–216). Cheltenham, UK and Northampton, MA, USA: Edward Elgar Publishing.

Keegan, A., Huemann, M., and Turner, J.R. 2012. Beyond the line: Exploring the HRM responsibilities of line managers, project managers and the HRM department in four project-oriented companies in the Netherlands, Austria, the UK and the USA. *International Journal of Human Resource Management*, 23(15): 3085–3104.

Kellogg, K.C., Valentine, M.A., and Christin, A. 2020. Algorithms at work: The new contested terrain of control. *Academy of Management Annals*, 14(1): 366–410.

Koutsimpogiorgos, N., van Slageren, J., Herrmann, A.M., and Frenken, K. 2020. Conceptualizing the gig economy and its regulatory problems. *Policy and Internet*, 12(4): 525–545.

Kuhn, K.M., and Maleki, A. 2017. Micro-entrepreneurs, dependent contractors, and instaserfs: Understanding online labor platform workforces. *Academy of Management Perspectives*, 31(3): 183–200.

Kuhn, K.M., Meijerink, J., and Keegan, A. 2021. Human resource management and the gig economy: Challenges and opportunities at the intersection between organizational HR decision-makers and digital labor platforms. In M. Buckley, A.R. Wheeler, J.E. Baur, and J.R. Halbesleben (eds), *Research in Personnel and Human Resources Management* (pp. 1–46). Bingley: Emerald Publishing.

Langfred, C.W., and Rockmann, K.W. 2016. The push and pull of autonomy: The tension between individual autonomy and organizational control in knowledge work. *Group and Organization Management*, 41(5): 629–657.

Lee, M.K., Kusbit, D., Metsky, E., and Dabbish, L. 2015. Working with machines: The impact of algorithmic and data-driven management on human workers. Paper presented at the Proceedings of the 33rd Annual ACM Conference on Human Factors in Computing Systems, New York.

Leicht-Deobald, U., Busch, T., Schank, C., Weibel, A., Schafheitle, S., et al. 2019. The challenges of algorithm-based HR decision-making for personal integrity. *Journal of Business Ethics*, 160(2): 377–392.

Lepak, D.P., and Snell, S.A. 1999. The human resource architecture: Toward a theory of human capital allocation and development. *Academy of Management Review*, 24(1): 31–48.

McKeown, T., and Pichault, F. 2021. Independent professionals as talent: Evidence from individual views of working as a contractor. *Human Resource Management*, 60(2): 313–328.

McKinsey. 2016. *Independent Work: Choice, Necessity, and the Gig Economy*. New York: McKinsey Global Institute.

Meijerink, J.G., and Arets, M. 2021. Online labor platforms versus temp agencies: What are the differences? *Strategic HR Review*, 20(4): 119–124.

Meijerink, J., and Bondarouk, T. 2021. The duality of algorithmic management: Toward a research agenda on HRM algorithms, autonomy and value creation. *Human Resource Management Review*, 100876.

Meijerink, J.G., and Keegan, A. 2019. Conceptualizing human resource management in the gig economy: Toward a platform ecosystem perspective. *Journal of Managerial Psychology*, 34(4): 214–232.

Meijerink, J., Boons, M., Keegan, A., and Marler, J. 2021a. Algorithmic human resource management: Synthesizing developments and cross-disciplinary insights on digital HRM. *International Journal of Human Resource Management*, 32(23): 2545–2562.

Meijerink, J.G., Keegan, A., and Bondarouk, T. 2021b. Having their cake and eating it too? Online labor platforms and human resource mangement as a case of institutional complexity. *International Journal of Human Resource Management*, 32(19): 4016–4052.

Möhlmann, M., Zalmanson, L., Henfridsson, O., and Gregory, R. 2021. Algorithmic management of work on online labor platforms: When matching meets control. *MIS Quarterly*, 45(4): 1999–2022.

Newlands, G. 2021. Algorithmic surveillance in the gig economy: The organisation of work through Lefebvrian conceived space. *Organization Studies*, 42(5): 719–737.

O'Reilly III, C.A., and Tushman, M.L. 2013. Organizational ambidexterity: Past, present, and future. *Academy of Management Perspectives*, 27(4): 324–338.

O'Shea, P.G., and Puente, K.E. 2017. How is technology changing talent management? In D.G. Collings, K. Mellahi, and W. Cascio (eds), *The Oxford Handbook of Talent Management* (pp. 537–556). Oxford: Oxford University Press.

Poole, M.S., and Van de Ven, A.H. 1989. Using paradox to build management and organization theories. *Academy of Management Review*, 14(4): 562–578.

Purcell, J., and Hutchinson, S. 2007. Front-line managers as agents in the HRM–performance causal chain: Theory, analysis and evidence. *Human Resource Management Journal*, 17(1): 3–20.

Rahman, H.A., and Valentine, M.A. 2021. How managers maintain control through collaborative repair: Evidence from platform-mediated "gigs." *Organization Science*, 32(5): 1300–1326.

Raisch, S., and Krakowski, S. 2021. Artificial intelligence and management: The automation–augmentation paradox. *Academy of Management Review*, 46(1): 192–210.

Rogiers, P., De Stobbeleir, K., and Viaene, S. 2021. Stretch yourself: Benefits and burdens of job crafting that goes beyond the job. *Academy of Management Discoveries*, 7(3): 367–380.

Rogiers, P., Viaene, S., and Leysen, J. 2020a. The digital future of internal staffing: A vision for transformational electronic human resource management. *Intelligent Systems in Accounting, Finance and Management*, 27(4): 182–196.

Rogiers, P., Viaene, S., and Meijerink, J.G. 2020b. When online labor platforms and bureaucracy meet: An analysis of platform affordances and their tensions inside the organizational workplace. Paper presented at the 9th Annual EIASM Workshop on Talent Management 2020.

Rosenblat, A. 2018a. *Uberland: How Algorithms Are Rewriting the Rules of Work*. Oakland, CA: University of California Press.

Rosenblat, A. 2018b. When your boss is an algorithm. *New York Times*, 12 October.

Rosenblat, A., Levy, K.E., Barocas, S., and Hwang, T. 2017. Discriminating tastes: Uber's customer ratings as vehicles for workplace discrimination. *Policy and Internet*, 9(3): 256–279.

Schrage, M., Schwartz, J., Kiron, D., Jones, R., and Buckley, N. 2020. Opportunity marketplaces: Aligning workforce investment and value creation in the digital enterprise. *MIT Sloan Management Review*, April: 1–35.

Sessions, H., Nahrgang, J.D., Vaulont, M.J., Williams, R., and Bartels, A.L. 2021. Do the hustle! Empowerment from side-hustles and its effects on full-time work performance. *Academy of Management Journal*, 64(1): 235–264.

Sikora, D.M., Ferris, G.R., and Van Iddekinge, C.H. 2015. Line manager implementation perceptions as a mediator of relations between high-performance work practices and employee outcomes. *Journal of Applied Psychology*, 100(6): 1908–1918.

Smith, W.K., and Lewis, M.W. 2011. Toward a theory of paradox: A dynamic equilibrium model of organizing. *Academy of Management Review*, 36(2): 381–403.

Stanford, J. 2017. The resurgence of gig work: Historical and theoretical perspectives. *Economic and Labour Relations Review*, 28(3): 382–401.

Stengård, J., Bernhard-Oettel, C., Berntson, E., and Leineweber, C. 2017. Stuck in the job: Does helplessness precede being locked-in at the workplace or vice versa? An analysis of cross-lagged effects. *Journal of Vocational Behavior*, 102: 15–27.

van der Heijden, B.I., and Bakker, A.B. 2011. Toward a mediation model of employability enhancement: A study of employee–supervisor pairs in the building sector. *Career Development Quarterly*, 59(3): 232–248.

van Doorn, N. 2017. Platform labor: on the gendered and racialized exploitation of low-income service work in the "on-demand" economy. *Information, Communication and Society*, 20(6): 898–914.

van Doorn, N., and Badger, A. 2021. Dual value production as key to the gig economy puzzle. In J. Meijerink, G. Jansen, and V. Daskalova (eds), *Platform Economy Puzzles* (pp. 123–139). Cheltenham, UK and Northampton, MA, USA: Edward Elgar Publishing.

Veen, A., Barratt, T., and Goods, C. 2019. Platform-capital's "app-etite" for control: A labour process analysis of food-delivery work in Australia. *Work, Employment and Society*, 34(3): 388–406.

Verbruggen, M., and De Vos, A. 2020. When people don't realize their career desires: Toward a theory of career inaction. *Academy of Management Review*, 45(2): 376–394.

Weller, I., Hymer, C.B., Nyberg, A.J., and Ebert, J. 2019. How matching creates value: Cogs and wheels for human capital resources research. *Academy of Management Annals*, 13(1): 188–214.

Wood, A.J., Graham, M., Lehdonvirta, V., and Hjorth, I. 2019. Good gig, bad gig: Autonomy and algorithmic control in the global gig economy. *Work, Employment and Society*, 33(1): 56–75.

Zekić, N. 2019. Contradictory court rulings on the status of Deliveroo workers in the Netherlands. *Dispatch for Comparative Labor Law and Policy Journal*, Dispatch 17, 2019: 1–5.

Index

Printed and bound by CPI Group (UK) Ltd, Croydon, CR0 4YY

16/04/2025

14658392-0002